THE MAHABHARATA

D1871039

THE MAHABHARATA

OF

KRISHNA-DWAIPAYANA VYASA

Translated into English Prose from the Original Sanskrit Text.

Translator

KISARI MOHAN GANGULI

VOL X

SANTI PARVA (Part III)

and

ANUSASANA PARVA (Part I)

GYAN

Published by

Gyan Publishing House
5, Ansari Road
Daryaganj, New Delhi-110002
Phone: 011-47034999, 9811692060
E-mail: books@gyanbooks.com

Distribution Network
gyanbooks.com
India, USA, Canada, UK, Australia, France

© Publisher

All rights reserved. No part of this work may be reproduced, stored, adapted, or transmitted in any form or by any means, electronic, mechanical, photocopying, micro-filming, recording or otherwise, or translated in any language, without the prior written permission of the copyright owner and the publisher.

ISBN : 978-81-212-6117-3 (Set)
ISBN : 978-81-212-6107-4 (PB)
First Published, 1884

2nd Impression 2022

Printed at: Gyan Press, Delhi.

The book is sold subject to the condition that it shall not, by way of trade or otherwise, be lent, resold, hired out, or otherwise circulated without the prior publisher's written consent.

The Mahabharata, Vol. X
Translator Kisari Mohan Ganguli

THE MAHABHARATA

OF

KRISHNA-DWAIPAYANA VYASA

Translated into English prose from the original Sanskrit Text.

BY

Kisari Mohan Ganguli

VOL X

SANTI PARVA (Part III)

and

ANUSASANA PARVA (Part I)

SANTI PARVA

SECTION CCCII

"Yudhishthira said,—'O king, thou hast duly propounded unto me, in the way in which it should be, the path of Yoga which is approved by the wise, after the manner of a loving preceptor unto his pupil. I ask now about the principles of the Sankhya philosophy. Do thou discourse to me on those principles in their entirety. Whatever knowledge exists in the three worlds is known to thee!'

"Bhishma said,—'Listen now to what the subtile principles are of the followers of the Sankhya doctrine have been established by all the great and puissant Yatis having Kapila their first. In that doctrine O chief of men, no errors are discoverable. Many, indeed, are its merits. In fact, there is no fault in it. Comprehending with the aid of knowledge that all objects exist with faults, indeed, understanding that the objects—so difficult to cast off—with which human beings and Pisachas and Rakshasas and Yakshas and snakes and Gandharvas and pitris and those that are wandering in the intermediate orders of being (such as birds and animals) and great birds (such as Garuda and others) and the Maruts and royal sages and regenerate sages and Asuras and Viswedevas and the celestial Rishis and Yogins invested with supreme puissance and the Prajapatis and Brahman himself are engaged, and understanding truly what the highest limit is of one's period of existence in this world, and apprehending also the great truth, O foremost of eloquent men, about what is called felicity here, having a clear knowledge of what the sorrows are that overtake when the hour comes all those that are concerned with (transitory) objects, and knowing full well the sorrows of those that have fallen into the intermediate orders of being and of those that have sunk into hell, perceiving all the merits and all the faults of heaven, O Bharata, and all the demerits that attach to the declarations of the Vedas and all the excellencies that are connected with them recognising the faults and merits of the Yoga and the Sankhya systems of philosophy, realizing also that the quality of Sattwa has ten properties, that of Rajas has nine, and that of Tamas has eight, that the Understanding has seven properties, the Mind has six, and Space has five, and once more conceiving that the Understanding has four properties and Tamas has three, and Rajas has two and Sattwa as. one, and truly apprehending the path that is followed by all objects when destruction overtakes them and what the course is of self knowledge, the Sankhyas, possessed of knowledge and experience and exalted by their perceptions of causes, and acquiring thorough auspiciousness, attain to the felicity of Emancipation like the rays of the Sun, or the Wind taking refuge in Space.[1] Vision is attached to from; the sense of scent to smell; the ear to sound; the tongue to juices; and the skin (or body) to touch. The wind has for its refuge Space. Stupefaction has Tamas (Darkness) for its refuge. Cupidity has the objects of the senses for its refuge. Vishnu is attached to (the organs of) motion. Sakra is attached to (the organs of) strength. The deity of fire is attached to the stomach. Earth is attached to the Waters. The Waters have Heat (or fire) for their refuge. Heat attaches itself to the Wind; and the wind has Space for its refuge; and Space has Mahat for its refuge, and Mahat has the Understanding for its foundation. The Understanding has its refuge in Tamas; Tamas has Rajas for its refuge; Rajas is founded upon Sattwa; and Sattwa is attached to the Soul. The soul has the glorious and puissant Narayana for its refuge. That glorious deity has Emancipation for his refuge. Emancipation is independent of all refuge. Knowing that this hody, that is endued with six and ten possessions, is the result of the quality of Sattwa, understanding fully the nature of the physical organism and the character of the Chetana that dwells within it, recognising the one existent Being that live in the body viz., the Soul, which stands aloof from every concern of the body and in which no sin can attach, realising the nature of that second object, viz.; the acts of persons attached to the objects of the senses, understanding also the character of the senses and the sensual objects which have their refuge in the Soul, appreciating the difficulty of Emancipation and the scriptures that bear upon it knowing fully the nature of the vital breaths called Prana, Apana, Samana, Vyana, and Udana, as also the two other breaths, viz., the one going downward and the other moving upward indeed, knowing those seven breaths ordained to accomplish seven different functions, ascertaining the nature of the Prajapatis and the Rishis and the high paths, many in number, of virtue or righteous-

1 The ten properties included in Sattwa or Goodness are gladness, cheerfulness, enthusiasm, fame righteousness, contentment, faith, sincerity, liberality, and lordship. The nine properties included in Rajas or Passion are belief in the deities, (ostentatious) charity, enjoyment and endurance of happiness and sorrow, disunion, exhibition of manliness, lust and wrath, intoxication, pride, malice, and disposition to revile. The eight qualities included in Tamas or Darkness are unconsciousness, stupefaction, excess of stupefaction. muddiness of the understanding, blindness (of results), sleep, heedlessness, and procrastination The seven incidents of Buddhi or the Understanding are Mahat, consciousness, and the five subtile essences. The six incidents of Mind are Mind and the five senses. The five incidents appertaining to Space are space, water, wind, light, and earth According to a different school of philosophy, Buddhi or the Understanding is said to have four incidents appertaining to it, Viz., doubt, ascertainment, pride, and memory. Tamas (Darkness) also is otherwise regarded to have only three incidents, Viz, inability of comprehension, partial comprehension, and totally erroneous comprehension, Rajas (Passion) is (according to this school) regarded as having only the two incidents of inclination (to act) and sorrow. Sattwa has but one incident Viz., Enlightenment.—T.

ness, and the seven Rishis and the innumerable royal Rishis. O scorcher of foes, and the great celestial Rishis and the other regenerate Rishis endued with the effulgence of the Sun, beholding all these falling away from their puissance in course of many long ages, O monarch, hearing of the destruction of even of all the mighty beings in the universe, understanding also the inauspicious end that is attained, O king, by creatures of sinful acts, and the miseries endured by those that fall into the river Vaitarani in the realms of Yama, and the inauspicious wanderings of creatures through diverse wombs, and the character of their residence in the unholy uterus in the midst of blood and water and phlegm and urine and fæces, all of foul smell, and then in bodies that result from the union of blood and the vital seed, of marrow and sinews, abounding with hundreds of nerves and arteries and forming an impure mansion of nine doors, comprehending also what is for his own good what those divers combinations are which are productive of good beholding the abominable conduct of creatures whose natures are characterised by Darkness or Passion or Goodness, O chief of Bharata's race,—conduct that is reprehended, in view of its incapacity to acquire Emancipation, by the followers of the Sankhya doctrine who are fully conversant with the Soul, beholding the swallowing up of the Moon and the Sun by Rahu, the falling of stars from their fixed positions and the diversions of constellations from their orbits, knowing the sad separation of all united objects and the diabolical behaviour of creatures in devouring one another, seeing the absence of all intelligence in the infancy of human beings and the deterioration and destruction of the body, marking the little attachment creatures have to the quality of Sattwa in consequence of their being overwhelmed by wrath and stupefaction, beholding also only one among thousands of human beings resolved to struggle after the acquisition of Emancipation, understanding the difficulty of attaining to Emancipation according to what is stated in the scriptures, seeing the marked solicitude that creatures manifest for all unattained objects and their comparative indifference to all objects that have been attained, marking the wickedness that results from all objects of the senses O king and the repulsive bodies, O son of Kunti, of persons reft of life, and the residence, always fraught with grief, of human beings, O Bharata, in houses (in the midst of spouses and children), knowing the end of those terrible and fallen men who become guilty of slaying Brahmanas, and of those wicked Brahmanas that are addicted to the drinking of alcoholic stimulants, and the equally sad end of those that become criminally attached to the spouses of their preceptors, and of those men, O Yudhishthira, that do not properly reverence their mothers, as also of those that have no reverence and worship to offer to the deities, understanding also, with the help of that knowledge (which their philosophy imparts), the end that of all perpetrators of wicked acts, and the diverse ends that overtake those who have taken birth among the intermediate orders, ascertaining the diverse declarations of the Vedas, the courses of seasons, the fading of years, of months, of fortnights, and of days, beholding directly the waxing and the waning of the Moon, seeing the rising and the ebbing of the seas, and the diminution of wealth and its increase once more, and the separation of united objects, the lapse of Yugas, the destruction of mountains, the drying up of rivers, the deterioration of (the purity of) the several orders and the end also of that deterioration occurring repeatedly, beholding the birth, decrepitude, death, and sorrows of creatures, knowing truly the faults attaching to the body and the sorrows to which human beings are subject, and the vicissitudes to which the bodies of creatures are subject, and understanding all the faults that attach to their own souls, and also all the inauspicious faults that attach to their own bodies (the followers of the Sankhya philosophy succeed in attaining to Emancipation).

"Yudhishthira said,—'O thou of immeasurable energy, what are those faults that thou seest attaching to one's body ? It behoveth thee to expound this doubt to me fully and truly !'

"Bhishma said,—'Listen, O slayer of foes! The Sankhyas or followers of Kapila, who are conversant with all paths and endued with wisdom, say that there are in all five faults, O puissant one, in the human body. They are Desire and Wrath and Fear and Sleep and Breath. These faults are seen in the bodies of all embodied creatures. Those that are endued with wisdom cut the root of wrath with the aid of Forgiveness. Desire is cut off by casting off all purposes. By cultivation of the quality of Goodness (Sattwa) sleep is conquered, and Fear is conquered by cultivating Heedfulness. Breath is conquered by abstemiousness of diet O king. Truly understanding *gunas* by the aid of hundreds of *gunas*, hundreds of faults, and diverse causes by hundreds of causes, ascertaining that the world is like the froth of water, enveloped by hundreds of illusions flowing from Vishnu, like a painted edifice, and as unsubstantial as a reed, beholding it to be (as terrible as) a dark pit, or as unreal as bubbles of water, for the years that compose its age are as shortlived (compared to the duration of eternity) as bubbles, seeing it exposed to immediate destruction, bereft of happiness, having certain ruin for its end and from which it can never escape, sunk in Rajas and Tamas, and utterly helpless like an elephant sunk in mire,—noting all this—the Sankayas, O king, endued with great wisdom, casting off all affection arising from one's relation towards one's children, by the aid, O king, of that extensive and all-embracing knowledge which their system advocates and cutting off quickly, with the weapon of knowledge and the bludgeon of penances, O Bharata, all inauspicious scents born of Rajas and all scents of a like nature arising from Tamas and all auspicious scents arising from Sattwa and all pleasures of the touch (and of the other senses) born of the same three qualities and inhering to the body,—indeed, O Bharata, aided by the Yoga of knowledge, these Yatis crowned with success,—cross the Ocean of life. That Ocean, so terrible has sorrow for its waters. Anxiety and grief constitute its deep lakes. Disease and death are its gigantic alligators. The great fears that strike the heart at every step are its huge snakes. The deeds inspired by Tamas are its tortoises. Those inspired by Rajas are its fishes. Wisdom constitutes the raft for crossing it. The affections entertained for objects of the senses are its mire. Decrepitude constitutes its region of grief and trouble.[1] Knowledge, O chastiser of foes, is its island. Acts constitute its great depth. Truth is its shores. Pious observances constitute the verdant weeds floating on its bosom.[2] Envy constitutes its rapid and mighty current. The diverse sentiments of the heart constitute its mines. The diverse kinds of gratification are its valuable gems. Grief and fever are its winds. Misery and thirst are its mighty eddies. Painful and fatal diseases are its huge elephants. The assemblage of bones are its flights of steps, and phlegm is its froth. Gifts are its pearl-banks. The lakes of blood are its corals. Loud laughter constitutes its roars. Diverse sciences are its impassability. Tears are its brine. Renunciation of company constitutes the high refuge (of those that seek to cross it). Children and spouses are its unnumbered leeches. Friends and kinsmen are the cities and towns on its shores. Abstention from injury, and Truth, are its boundary line. Death is its storm-wave. The knowledge of Vedanta is its island (capable of affording refuge to those that are tossed upon its waters). Acts of compassion towards all creatures constitute its life-buoys,[3] and Emancipation is the priceless commodity offered to those voyaging on its waters in search of merchandise. Like its substantive prototype with its equine head disgorging flames of fire, this ocean too has its fiery terrors. Having transcended the liability, that is so difficult to transcend, of dwelling within the gross body, the Sankhyas enter into pure space.[4] Surya then bears, with his rays, those righteous men that

---

1 'Durga' is an inaccessible region such as a forest or wilderness which cannot be passed through except with great pain and danger.—T.

2 The correct reading seems to be 'sthita-vratati-samkulam'—T.

3 'Udadhi' is, literally, a water-jar. In this country most people, while swimming, use water-jars as buoys. The mouth of jar being dipped into the water the air confined within it serve to support heavy weights. I have heard that the most rapid currents are crossed by milkmaids in this way, all the while bearing milk pails on their heads—T.

4 In the second line of 72, 'dustaram janma' means janma-yuktam dustaram.'—T.

are practicers of the Sankhya doctrines. Like the fibres of the lotus-stalk conveying water to the flower into which they all converge, Surya, drinking all things from the universe, conveys them unto those good and wise men.[1] Their attachments all destoyed, possessed of energy, endued with wealth of penances, and crowned with success, these Yatis, O Bharata, are borne by that wind which is subtile, cooling, fragrant, and delicious to the touch, O Bharata! In fact, that wind which is the best of the seven winds, and which blows in regions of great felicity, conveys them, O son of Kunti, to that which is the highest end in space.[2] Then space into which they are carried, O monarch, conveys them to the highest end of Rajas.[3] Rajas then bear them to the highest end of Sattwa. Sattwa then bears them, O thou of pure soul, to the Supreme and puissant Narayana. The puissant and pure-sould Narayana at last, through himself, bears them to the Supreme Soul. Having reached the Supreme Soul, those stainless persons who have (by that time) become the body of (what is called), That[4] attain to immortality, and they have never afterwards to return from that position. O King! That is the highest end, O son of Pritha, which is attained by those high-souled men who have transcended the influence of all pairs of opposites.'"

"Yudhishthira said,—'O sinless one, have those persons of firm vows after they have attained to that excellent position which is fraught with puissance and felicity, any recollection of their lives including birth and death? It behoveth thee to tell me properly what the truth is in respect, O thou of Kuru's race. I do not think it proper to question any one else than thee! Observing the scriptures bearing upon Emancipation, I find this great fault in the subject (for certain scriptures on the topic declare that consiousness disappears in the emancipate state, while other scriptures declare the very reverse of this). If, having attained to this high state, the Yatis continue to live in consciousness, it would seem, O king, that the religion of Pravritti is superior. If, again, consciousness disappears from the emancipate state

1 The sense seems to be that by practising the Sankhya doctrines men cease to have any regard for even their gross bodies. They succeed in realising their existence as independent of all earthly or heavenly objects. What is meant by the Sun bearing them in his rays and conveying to them all things from every part of the universe is that these men acquire great puissance. This is not the pusissance of Yoga but of knowledge. Everything being regarded as unsubstantial and transitory, the position of Indra himself, or of Brahman, is looked upon as desirable and unworthy of acquisition. Sincere conviction of this kind and the course of conduct that is confirmable to it is literally puissance of the highest kind, for all the purposes of puissance are capable of being served by it.—T.

2 This is taken as meaning that the Sankhyas are conveyed to the firmament of the heart. Perhaps, what is intended by it is that they become withdrawn from external objects and even the impressions of all external things.—T.

3 Perhaps, this means the pleasures of heaven.—T.

4 I. e., they who have identified themselves with Brahma.—T.

and one who has become emancipate only resembles a person sunk in dreamless slumber, then nothing can be more improper than to say that there is really no consciousness in Emancipation (for of all that happens in dreamless slumber is that one's consciousness is temporarily overshadowed and suspended, but never lost, for it returns when one awakes from that slumber)[1]'

"Bhishma said,—'However difficult it may be to answer it, the question which thou hast asked, O son, is proper. Verily, the question is of such a kind that even they that are possessed of great learning become stupefied in answering it, O chief of Bharata's race. For all that, hear what the truth is as expounded by me. The high-souled followers of Kapila have set their high understandings on this point. The senses of knowledge, O King, planted in the bodies of embodied creatures, are employed in their respective functions of perception. They are the instruments of the Soul, for it is through them that subtile Being perceives.[2] Disunited with the Soul, the senses are like lumps of wood, and are without doubt, destroyed (in respect of the functions they serve) like the froth that is seen on the bosom of the ocean.[3] When the embodied creature, O scorcher of foes, sinks into sleep along with his senses, the subtile Soul then roves among all subjects like the wind through space.[4] The subtile Soul, during slumber, continues to see (all forms) and touch all objects of touch, O king, and taken in other perceptions, as well as when it is awake. In consequence of their inability to act without their director, the senses, during sleep, all become extinguished in their respective places (and lose their powers) like snakes deprived of poison.[5] At such times, the subtile Soul, repairing into the respective place of all the senses, without dout, discharges all their functions.[1] All the

1 Yudhisthira's question seems to be this. Is there or is there not consciousness in the emancipate state? Different scriptures answer this question differently. If it be said that there is consciousness in that state, then why discard heaven and its pleasures, or the religion of Pravritti or acts which lead to those pleasures? Where is the necessity then of Sannyasa or the religion of Nivritti or abstention from all acts? On the supposition of there being consciousness in the emancipate state, the Religion of Pravritti should be taken as superior. If, on the other hand, the existence of consciousness be denied, that would be an error. 'Dukshataram' is 'ayuktaram'—T.

2 Although I make use of the word 'perceive' yet remembering that the mind is included among the senses and regarded as the sixth sense, the functions of recollection, representation, &c, are also implied by the word 'pasyati.' The Burdwan translator gives a ridiculously erroneous version of this Verse—T.

3 The Commentator explains that the simile of the froth is introduced in consequence of its disappearance with the disappearance of water. K. P. Singha is incorrect in taking the instance of froth as illustrative of the quickness of the destuction —T.

4 'Sarvatra' does not mean 'through every part of the sleeper's body' as. P. Singha takes it, but 'sarvavishaye' as the Commentator correctly explains it.—T.

5 'Iha' is 'sapne' 'Anisah' is 'nasti isah or pravartaah yasya.'—T.

6 For the Soul, in dreams, sees and hears and touches and smells &c, precisely as it does while awake—T.

qualities of Sattwa, all the attributes of the Understanding, O Bharata, as also those of Mind, and Space, and Wind, O thou of righteous soul, and all the attributes of liquid substances, of Water, O Partha, and of Earth,—these senses with these qualities,—O Yudhishthira, which inhere to Jiva-souls, are along with the Jiva-soul itself, overwhelmed by the Supreme Soul or Brahma. Acts also, good and bad, overwhelm that Jiva-soul. Like disciples waiting upon their preceptor with reverence, the senses too wait upon the Jiva-soul transcends Prakriti' it attains to Brahma that is without change, that is highest, that is Narayana, that is beyond all pairs of opposites, and that transcends Prakriti. Freed from both merit and demerit, the Jiva-soul entering the Supreme Soul which is divested of all attributes, and which is the home of all auspiciousness, does not return thence, O Bharata. What remains, O son, is the mind with the senses, O Bharata. These have to come back once more at the appointed season for doing the bidding of their great Master.[1] Soon after, O son of Kunti, (when this body is cast off) the Yati striving after Emancipation, endued as he is with knowledge and desirous as he is of Guna, succeeds in attaining to that Peace of Emancipation which is his who becomes bodiless.[2] The Sankhyas, O king, are endued with great wisdom. They succeed in attaining to the highest end by means of this kind of knowledge. There is no knowledge that is equal to this. Do not yield to any kind of doubt. The Knowledge which is described in the system of the Sankhyas is regarded as the highest. That knowledge is immutable and is eternally fixed. It is eternal Brahma in fulness. It has no beginning, middle and end. It transcends all pairs of opposites. It is the cause of the creation of the universe. It stands in fulness. It is without deterioration of any kind. It is uniform, and everlasting. Thus are its praises sung by the wise. From it flow creation and destruction and all modifications. The great Rishis speak of it and applaud it in the sciptures. All learned Brahmanas and all righteous men regard it as flowing from Brahma, Supreme, Divine, Infinite, Immutable, and Undeteriorating. All Brahmanas again that are attached to objects of the senses adore and applaud it by ascribing to it attributes that belong to illusion.[4] The same is the view of Yogins well observant of penances and meditation and of Sankhyas of

1 The sense seems to be that a person who becomes emancipate in this life becomes so in Samadhi. When the state of Samadhi is over, his mind and senses return; and returning they do the bidding of the Supreme, i e. bring about both happiness and misery, which, of course, are the consequences of the acts of past lives though that happiness and misery are not feft. In the next Verse is said that these men very soon leave their bodies and become freed frcm rebirth.—T.

2 There are two kinds of Emancipation; one is attainable here, in this body. It is 'Jivan-mukti' the other is 'Videha-kaivalya' or that which becomes one's when one is bodiless. In 98, Jivan-mukti has been spoken of. In this Verse, the observations apply to 'Videhakaivalya.'—T.

3 'Vadanti' is 'stuvanti.' Such men hymn its praises by regarding it as Supreme Deity possessed of attributes. Those attibutes. of course, are the result of illusion, for in its real nature there can be no attributes in Brahma.—T.

immeasureble insight. The Srutis declare, O son of Kunti, that the Sankhya form of philosophy is the form of that Formless one. The cognitions (according to that philosophy) have, O chief of Bharata's race, been said to be the knowledge of Brahma.[1]

"'There are two kinds of creatures on Earth, O lord of Earth, *viz.*, mobile and immobile. Of these that are mobile are superior, That high knowledge, O king, which exists in perons conversant with Brahma, and that which occurs in the Vedas, and that which is found in other scriptures, and that in Yoga, and that which may be seen in the diverse Puranas, are all, O monarch, to be found in Sankhya philosophy.[2] Whatever knowledge is seen to exist in high histories whatever knowledge occurs. O king, in the sciences appertaining to the acquisition of wealth as approved by the wise, whatever other knowledge exists in this world,—all these,—flow, O high-souled monarch, from the high knowledge that occurs among the Sankhays. Tranquillity of soul high puissance all subtile knowledge of which the scriptures speak, penances of subtile force, and all kinds of felicity. O king, have all been duly ordained in the Sankhya system. Failing to acquire, O son of Pritha, that compelete knowledge which is recommended by their system, the Sankhays attain to the status of deities and pass many years in felicity. Lording it over the celestials as they will, they fall, upon the expiration of the allotted period, among learned Brahmanas and Yotis.[3] Casting off this body, those regenerate ones that follow the Sankhya system enter into the superior state of Brahma like the celestials entering into the firmament by devoting themselves wholly to that adorable system which is theirs and which is worshipped by all wise men. Those regenerate persons that are devoted to the acquisition of that knowledge which is recommended in the Sankhya system, even if they fail to attain to eminence, are never seen to fall among intermediate creatures, or to sink into the status of sinful men. That high-souled person who is fully conversant with the vast, high, ancient, ocean-like, and immeasurable Sankhya system that is pure and liberal and agreeable, becomes, O king, equal to Narayna. I have now told thee, O god among men, the truth about the Sankhya system. It is the embodiment of Narayana, of the universe as it exists

---

1 Brahma is knowledge without duality' *i. e.*, knowledge without the consciousess of knower and known. The knowledge or cognition of an object, when object is arnihilated, assumes the form of that knowledge which is called Brahma.—T.

2 The Commentator explains that the object of this Verse is to show that among mobile creatures those endued with knowledge are superior, and among all kinds of knowledge, the knowledge occuring in the Sankhya system is the highest.—T.

3 *I. e.*, if in consequence of any defect of practice or *Sadhana*, the Sankhyas foil to attain to Emancipation, they at least become translated into gods.—T.

from the remotest time.[1] When the time of Creation comes, He causes the Creation to start into life, and when the time comes for destruction, He swallows up everything. Having withdrawn everything into his own body he goes to sleep,—that inner Soul of the universe."[2]

SECTION CCCIII

"Yudhishthira said,—'What is that which is called Undeteriorating and by attaining to which no one has to come back ? What, again, is that which is called Deteriorating, and by attaining to which one has to rerurn once more ? O slayer of foes, I ask thee the distinction that exists, O thou of mighty arms, between the Deteriorating and the Undeteriorating ones for understanding them both truly, O delighter of the Kurus, Brahmanas conversant which the Vedas speak of thee as an Ocean of knowledge. Highly-blessed Rishis and Yatis of high souls do the same. Thou hast very few days to live. When the Sun turns from the southern path for entering into the northern, thou shalt attain to thy high end. When thou shalt leave us, from whom shall we hear of all that is beneficial for us ? Thou art the lamp of Kuru's race. Indeed thou art always blazing with the light of knowledge. O perpetuator of Kuru's race, I desire, therefore to hear all this from thee. Listening to thy discourses that are always sweet like nectar, my curiosity, without being satiated is always increasing !'

"Bhishma said—'I shall, in this connection, relate to thee the old narrative of the discourse that took place between Vasishtha and king Karala of Janaka's race. Once on a time when that foremost of Rishis. *Viz.*, Vasishtha, endued with the effulgence of the Sun, was seated at his ease, king Janaka asked him about that highest knowledge which is for our supreme good. Highly proficient in that department of knowledge which is concerned with the Soul and possessed of certain conclusions in respect of all branches of that science,[3] as Maitravaruni, that foremost of Rishis, was seated the king approaching him with joined hands, asked him in humble words, well pronounced and sweet and destitute of all controversial spirit, the question,—O holy one, I desire to hear, of Supreme and Eternal Brahma by attaining to which men of wisdom have not to come back. I desire also to know that which is called Destructible and That into which this universe enters when destroyed. Indeed, what is That which is said to be indestructible, suspicious, beneficial and free from evil of every kind ?—'

---

1 *I. e.*, it is everything.—T.

2 That Narayana who does all this is the embodiment of the Sankhya system.—T.

3 The Commentator explains the compound 'Adhyatmagatinischayam, differently.—*T.*

"Vasishtha said,—Hear, O lord of Earth, as to how this universe is destroyed, and, of That which was never destroyed and which will never be destroyed at any time. Twelve thousand years, (according to the measure of the celestials), make a Yuga, four such Yugas taken a thousand times, make a Kalpa which measures one day of Brahman.[1] Brahman's night also, O king, is of the same measure. When Brahman himself is destroyed.[2] Sambhu of formless soul and to whom the Yuga attributes of Anima, Laghima, &c, naturally inhere, awakes, and once more creates that First or Eldest of all creatures, possessed of vast proportions of infinite deeds, endued with form, and identifiable with the universe. That Sambhu is otherwise called Isana (the lord of everything). He is pure Effulgence, and transcends all deterioration, having his hands and feet stretching in all directions, with eyes and head and mouth everywhere, and with ears also in every place. That Being exists, overwhelming the entire universe. The eldest-born Being is called Hiranyagarbha. This holy one has (in the Vedanta) been called the Understanding. In the Yuga scriptures He called the Great, and Virinchi, and the Unborn. In the Sankhya scriptures, He is indicated by diverse name, and regarded as having Infinity for his Soul. Of diverse forms and constituting the soul of the universe. He is regarded as One and Indestructible. The three worlds of infinite ingredients have been created by Him without assistance from any source and have been overwhelmed by him. In consequence of His manifold forms, He is said to be of universal form. Undergoing modifications He creates Himself by Himself. Endued with mighty energy, He first creates Consciousness and that Great Being called Prajapati endued with Consciousness. The Manifest (or Hiranyagarbha) is created form the Unmanifest. This is called by the learned the Creation of Knowledge. The creation of Mahan (or Virat) and Consciousness, by Hiranyagarbha, is the Creation of Ignorance.[3] Ascription of attributes (worthy of worship) and the destruction thereof, called respectively by the names of Ignorance and Knowledge by persons learned by the interpretation of the Srutis, then arose, referring to this, that, or the other of the three (*viz.*, Akshara, Hiranyagarbha, or Virat).[4] Know, O king, that the creation of the

1 Both the Vernacular translators render this Verse wrongly.—T.

2 'Vasyante' is explained by the Commentator as implying Brahmanah ante,' and not 'at the end of that night'. The line occurs in Manu (Chap 1. 74) where 'ante' refers to Brahmana's day and night. Vasishtha here refers to Mohapralaya, and not any intermediate Pralaya.—T

3 In the creation of Mahan or Prajapati or Virat, and of Consciousness, the element of Tamas or Ignorance predominates.—T.

4 This is a very abstruse Verse. I am not sure that I have understood it correctly. What is said here seems to be this: from Akshara arose Hiranyagarbha: from Hiranyagarbha arose Virat. This, that or the other is worshipped by ordinary men, while persons possessed of real insight do not invest any of them with attributes worthy of

(subtile) elements from consciousness is the third.[1] In all kinds of consciousness is the fourth creation which flows modification of the third. This fourth creation comprises Wind and Light and Space and Water and Earth, with their properties of sound, touch, form, taste and scent. This aggregate of ten arose, without doubt, at the same time. The fifth creation, O monarch, is that which has arisen from combination of the primal elements (named above). This comprises the ear, the skin, the eyes, the tongue, and the nose forming the fifth, and speech, and the two hands, and the two legs, and the lower duct, and the organs of generation. The first five of these constitute the organs of knowledge, and the last five the organs of action. All these, with mind, arose simultaneously O king. These constitute the four and twenty topics that exist in the forms of all living creatures. By understanding these properly, Brahmanas possessed of insight into the truth have never to yield to sorrow. In the three worlds a combination of these, called body, is possessed by all embodied creatures. Indeed, O king a combination of those is known as such in deities and men and Danavas, and Yakshas and spirits and Gandharvas and Kinnaras and great snakes, and Charanas and Pisachas, in celestial Rishis and Rakshasas, in biting flies, and worms, and gnats, and vermin born of filth and rats, and dogs and Swapakas and Chaineyas and Chandalas and Pukkasas in elephants and steeds and asses and tigers, and trees and kine. Whatever other creatures exist in water or space or on earth, for there is no other place in which creatures exist as we have heard, have this combination. All these, O sire, included within the class called Manifest, are seen to be destroyed day after day. Hence, all creatures produced by union of these four and twenty are said to be destructible.

"This then is the Indestructible. And since the universe, which is made up of Manifest and Unmanifest, meet with destruction, therefore, it is said to be Destructible. The very Being called Mahan who is the eldest-born is always spoken of as an instance of the Destructible. I have now told thee, O monarch, all that thou hadst asked me. Transcending the four and twenty topics already adverted to is the twenty-fifth called Vishnu. That Vishnu in consequence of the absence of all attributes, is not a topic (of knowledge) though as then which pervades

---

worship. The speaker says that the ascription of attributes, called Ignorance, and the non-ascription for destruction of that ascriptions called Knowledge, (with respect to Virat or Hiranyagarbha or Akshara), then arose. It might be asked that when there were no men as yet to worship or to condemn such worship, how could the two arise? The answer is that the two, in their subtile forms, came into existence and were afterwards availed of by men when men come into being.—T.

1 From Akshara or the Indestructible is Hiranyagarbha. From Hiranyagarbha is Mahan or Virat and Consciousness. From the last are the subtile elements.—T.

all the topics, he has been called so by the wise. Since that which is destructible has caused all this that is Manifest, therefore, all this is endued with form. The twenty-fourth, which is Prakriti, is said to preside over all this (which has sprung from her modifications). The twenty-fifth, which is Vishnu, is formless and, therefore, cannot be said to preside over the universe.[1] It is that Unmanifest (Prakriti), which, when endued with body (in consequence of union with Chit) dwells in the hearts of all creatures endued with body. As regards eternal Chetana (the Indestructible), although he is without attributes and without form, yet he (in consequence of a union with Prakriti) assumes all forms. Uniting with Prakriti which has the attributes of birth and death, he also assumes the attributes of birth and death. And in consequence of such union he becomes an object of perception and though in reality divested of all attributes yet he comes to be invested therewith. It is in this way that the Mahan-Soul (Hiranyagarbha), becoming united with Prakriti and invested with Ignorance, undergoes modifications and becomes conscious of Self. Uniting with the attributes of Sattwa and Rajas and Tamas, he becomes identified with diverse creatures belonging to diverse orders of Being, in consequence of his forgetfulness and his waiting upon Ignorance. In consequence of his birth and destruction arising from the fact of his dwelling in upon with Prakriti, he thinks himself to be no other than what he apparently is. Regarding himself as this or that, he follows the attributes of Sattwa, Rajas, and Tamas. Under the influence of Tamas, he attains to diverse kinds of conditions that are affected by Tamas. Under the influence of Rajas and Sattwa, he attains similarly to conditions that are affected by Rajas and Sattwa. There are three colours in all, *viz.*, White, Red, and Dark. All those colours appertain to Prakriti (so that He it is who becomes White or Red or Dark according as the nature of the Prakriti with which is He becomes identified for the time being). Through Tamas one goes to hell. Through Rajas one attains to and remains in the status of humanity. Through Sattwa, people ascend to the regions of the deities and become sharers of great felicity. By adhering to sin continuously one sinks into the intermediate order of beings. By acting both righteously and sinfully one attains to the status of the deities. In this way the twenty-fifth, *viz.*, Akshara (the Indestructible), the wise say, by union with the unmanifest (Prakriti), becomes transformed into Kshara (destructible). By means of knowledge however, the Indestructible becomes displayed in His true nature—"

1 The meanings of such Verses depend upon the grammatical significations of certain words that are used. They can scarcely be rendered accurately into any other language not derived from Sanskrit. What is said here is that it is Prakriti which must be said to be the *Adhishthatri* of the universe. Vishnu is not so. Vishnu Brahma, Akshara, or the Indestuctible, however, is said to *cover* or *pervade* the universe (vyapnoti). Vishnu is *Vyapka* but no *Adhishthatri*.—T.

SECTION CCCIV

"'Vasishtha said,—Thus in consequence of his forgetfulness the Soul follows ignorance and obtains thousands of bodies one after another. He attains to thousands of births among the intermediate orders and sometimes among the very gods in consequence of his union with (particular) attributes and the puissance of attributes.[1] From the status of humanity, he goes to heaven and from heaven he comes back to humanity, and from humanity he sinks into hell for many long years. As the worm that fabricates the cocoon shuts itself, completely on every side by means of the threads it weaves itself, even so the Soul, though in reality transcending all attributes, invests himself on every side with attributes (and deprives himself of liberty).[2] Though transcending (in his real nature) both happiness and misery, it is thus that he subjects himself to happiness and misery. It is thus also that, though transcending all diseases, the Soul regards himself to be afflicted by headache and opthalmia and toothache and affections of the throat and abdominal dropsy, and burning thirst, and enlargement of glands, and cholera, and vitiligo, and leprosy, and burns, and asthma and phthisis, and epilepsy, and whatever other diseases of diverse kinds are seen in the bodies of embodied creatures. Regarding himself, through error, as born among thousands of creatures in the intermediate orders of being, and sometimes among the gods, he endures misery and enjoys the fruits of his good deeds. Invested with Ignorance he regards himself as robed sometimes in white cloth and sometimes in full dress consisting of four pieces or as lying on floors (instead of on beds on bedsteads) or with hands and feet contracted like those of forgs or as seated upright in the attitude of ascetic contemplation, or as clad in rags or as lying or sitting under the canopy of heaven or within mansions built of bricks and stone or on rugged stones or on ashes or bare stones or on the bare earth or on beds or on battlefields or in water or in mire or on wooden planks or on diverse kinds of beds; or impelled by desire of fruits, he regards himself as clad in a scant piece of cloth made of grass or as totally nude or as robed in silk or in skin of the black antelope or in cloth made of flax or in sheep-skin or in tiger-skin or in lion-skin or in fabric of hemp, or in barks of birch or in cloths made of the produce of prickly plants, or in vestures made of threads woven by worms or of torn rags or in diverse other kinds of cloth too numerous to mention. The soul regards

---

1 In the previous Section it has been said that through Tamas he takes birth among the intermediate orders, through Rajas among human beings, and through Sattwa among gods. The root "kshi" in 'Gunakshayat' means 'aisaryya or puissance —T.

2 The soul weaves a cocoon with attributes (or, acts which result from attributes), and though free deprives himself of freedom.—T.

himself also as wearing diverse kinds of ornaments and gems, or as eating diverse kinds of food. He regards himself as sometimes eating at intervals of one night, or once at the same hour every day, or as at the fourth, the sixth, and the eighth hour every day, or as once in six or seven or eight nights, or as once in ten or twelve day, or as once in a month, or as eating only roots, or fruits, or as subsisting upon air or water alone, or on cakes of sesame husk, or curds or cowdung, or the urine of the cow or potherbs or flowers or moss or raw food, or as subsisting on fallen leaves of trees or fruits that have fallen down and lay scattered on the ground, or diverse other kinds of food, impelled by the desire of winning (ascetic) success. The Soul regards himself as adopting the observance of Chandrayana according to the rites ordained in the scriptures, or diverse other vows and observance, and the courses of duty prescribed for the four modes of life, and even direlictions of duty, and the duties of other subsidiary modes of life included in the four principal ones, and even diverse kinds of practices that distinguish the wicked and sinful. The Soul regards himself as enjoying retired spots and delightful shades of mountains and the cool vicinity of spring and fountains, and solitary river banks and secluded forests, and sacred spots dedicated to the deities, and lakes and waters withdrawn from the busy hunts of men, and lone mountain caves affording the accomodation that houses and mansions afford. The Soul regards himself as employed in the recitation of different kinds of hidden *Mantras* or as observing different vows and rules and diverse kinds of penances, and sacrifices of many kinds, and rites of diverse sorts. The Soul regards himself as adoptiug sometimes the way of traders and merchants and the practices of Brahmanas and Kshatriyas and Vaisyas and Sudras, and gifts of diverse kinds unto those that are destitute or blind or helpless. In consequence of his being invested with Ignorance, the Soul adopts different attributes of Sattwa and Rajas and Tamas, and Righteousness and Wealth and pleasure. Under the influence of Prakriti the Soul, undergoing modification himself, observes and adopts and practises all these and regards himself as such. Indeed, the Soul regards himself as employed in the utterance of the sacred *mantras* Swaha and Swadha and Vashat, and in bowing unto those he regards as his Superiors; in officiating in the sacrifices of others, in teaching pupils, making gifts and accepting them ; in performing sacrifices and studying, the scriptures, and doing all other acts and rites of this kind. The Soul regards himself as concerned with birth and death and disputes and slaughter. All these, the learned say, constitute the path of acts good and bad. It is the goddess Prakriti who cause birth and death. When the time approaches for universal Destruction, all existent objects and attributes are withdrawn by the Supreme Soul which then exists alone like the Sun withdrawing at evening all his rays ; and when the time comes for Creation He once more creates and spreads them out like the Sun shedding and spreading out his rays when morning comes. Even thus the Soul, for the sake of sport, repeatedly regards himself invested with all these conditions, which are his own forms and attributes, infinite in number, and agreeable to himself. It is this way that the Soul, though really transcending the three attributes, becomes attached to the path of acts and creates by modification Prakriti invested with the attributes of birth and death and indentical with all acts and conditions which are characterised by the three attributes of Sattwa, Rajas, and Tamas. Arrived at the path of action, the Soul regards particular acts to be endued with particular characteristics and productive of particular ends. O monarch, the whole of this universe has been blinded by Prakriti and all things have been diversely overwhelmed (through Prakriti) by the attributes of Rajas and Tamas. It is in consequence of the Soul being invested by Prakriti that these pairs of opposites productive of happiness and woe, repeatedly come. It is in consequence of this Ignorance that Jiva regards these sorrows to be his and imagines them as pursuing him. Indeed, O monarch, through that Ignorance it is that Jiva imagines he should anyhow cross those sorrows, and that he should, going into the regions of the gods, enjoy the felicity that awaits all his good acts. It is through Ignorance that he thinks he should enjoy and endure these delights and these woes here in this world. Through Ignorance Jiva thinks,—I should secure my happiness. By continually doing good acts, I may have happiness in this life till its close and I shall be happy in all my future lives. Though, again the (evil) acts I do in this life unending sorrow may become mine. The status of humanity is fraught with great misery, for from it one sinks into hell. From hell, it will take many long years before I can come back to the status of humanity. From humanity I shall attain to the status of the gods. From that superior status I shall have to come back again to humanity and thence to sink into hell once more !—One who always regards this combination of the primal elements and the senses. with the Chit's reflection in it, to be thus invested with the characteristics of the Soul, has repeatedly to wander among gods and human beings and to sink into hell. Being always invested with the idea of meum, Jiva has to make a round of such births. Millions upon millions of birth have to be gone through by Jiva in the successive forms he assumes, all of which are liable to death. He who does acts in this way, which are all fraught with good and bad fruits, has in the three worlds to assume successive form and to enjoy and endure fruits corresponding therewith. It is Prakriti that cause acts fraught with good and bad acts ; and it is Prakriti that enjoys and endures the fruits thereof in the three worlds. Indeed, Prakriti follows the course of acts. The status of the intermediate beings, of humanity, and of the gods as well,—these three fields,—should be known as originating in Prakriti and has been said to be destitute of all attributes. Her existence is affirmed only in consequence of her acts (beginning with Mahat). After the same manner, Purusha (or Soul), though without attributes himself, has his existence affirmed in consequence of the acts which the body does when it receives his reflection. Although the Soul is not subject to modifications of any kind and is the active principle that sets Prakriti in motion, yet entering a body that is united with the senses of knowledge and action, he regards all the acts of those senses as his own. The five senses of knowledge beginning with the ear, and those of action beginning with speech, uniting with the attributes of Sattwa and Rajas and Tamas, become engaged in numerous object. Jiva imagines that it is he who does the acts of his life and that the senses of knowledge and acts belong to him, although in reality he has no senses. Indeed, though unequipt with body, he imagines that he has a body. Though destitute of attributes, he regards himself as endued therewith, and though transcending Time, imagines himself to be under Time's control. Though destitute of understanding, he still regards himself as endued therewith, and though transcending the (four and twenty) topics, regards himself as one included among them. Though deathless, he still regards himself as liable to death, and though motionless regards himself to be endued with motion. Though not possessed of a material case, he still regards himself as possessed of one; and though unborn, he still regards himself as invested with birth. Though transcending penances, he still regards as engaged in penances, and though he has no end (after which to strive), he still regards himself as liable to attain to ends (of diverse kinds). Though not endued with motion and birth, he still regards himself as endued with both, and though transcending fear, still regards himself as liable to fear. Though Indestructible, he still regards himself Destructible. Invested with Ignorance, the Soul thus thinks of himself.—"

SECTION CCCV

" 'Vasishtha said,—It is thus, in consequence of his Ignorance and his association with others that are invested with Ignorance, that Jiva has recourse to millions and millions of births every one of which has dissolution in the end. In consequence of his transformation into Chit invested with Ignorance, Jiva betakes himself to millions of abodes one of which is liable to end in destruction, among intermediate beings and men and the deities. In consequence of Ignorance, Jiva, like Chandramas, has to wax and wane thousands and thousands of times. This is truly the nature of Jiva when invested with Ignorance. Know that Chandramas has in reality full sixteen portions. Only fifteen of these are subject to increase and decrease. The sixteenth (*i.e.*, that portion which remains invisible and which appears on the night of the New-moon) remains constant. After the manner of Chandramas, Jiva too has full sixteen portions. Only fifteen of these, (*viz.*, Prakriti with Chit's reflection, the ten senses of knowledge and action, and the four inner faculties) appear and disappear. The sixteenth (*viz.*, Chit in its purity) is subject to no modification. Invested with Ignorance, Jiva repeatedly and continually takes birth in the fifteen portions named above. With the eternal and immutable portion on Jiva primal essence become united and this union takes place repeatedly. That sixteenth portion is subtile. It should be known as Soma (eternal and immutable). It is never upheld by the senses. On the other hand, the senses are upheld by it. Since those sixteen portions are the cause of the birth of creatures, creatures can never, O monarch, take birth without their aid. They are called Prakriti. The destruction of Jiva's liability to be united with Prakriti is called Emancipation. The Mahat-Soul, which is the twenty-fifth, if it regards that body of sixteen portions called the Unmanifest,[1] has to assume it repeatedly. In consequence of not knowing That which is stainless and pure, and for its devotion to what is the result of a combination of both Pure and Impure, the Soul, which is in reality pure, becomes, O king Impure. Indeed, in consequence of its devotion to Ignorance, Jiva, though characterised by Knowledge becomes repeatedly associated with Ignorance. Though, O monarch, free from error of every kind, yet in consequence of its devotion to the three attributes of Prakriti, it becomes endued with those attributes.—' "

SECTION CCCVI

' "Janaka said,—O holy one, it has been said that the relation between male and female is like that which subsists between the Indestructible and the Destructible (or Purusha and Prakriti). Without a male, a female can never conceive. Without a female a male also can never create form. In consequence of their union with each other, and each depending upon the attributes of the other, forms (of living creatures) are seen to flow. This is the case with all orders of being. Through each other's union for purposes of (sexual) congress, and through each depending upon the attributes of the other, forms (of living

1 Made of Chit and Not-Chit combined.—T.

creatures) flow in menstrual seasons. I shall tell to thee the indications thereof. Hear what the attributes are that belong to the sire and what those are that belong to the mother. Bones, sinews and marrow, O regenerate one, we know, are derived from the sire. Skin, flesh, and blood, we hear are derived from the mother. Even this, O foremost of regenerate persons, is what may be read of in the Vedas and other scriptures. Whatever is read as declared in the Vedas and in other scriptures is regarded as authority. The authority, again, of the Vedas and other scriptures (not inconsistent with the Vedas), is eternal. If Prakriti and Purusha be always united together in this way by each opposing and each depending on the other's attributes, I see, O holy one, that Emancipation cannot exist. Thou, O holy one, art possessed of spiritual vision so that thou seest all things as if they are present before thy eyes. If, therefore, there be any direct evidence of the existence of Emancipation, do thou, speak of it to me. We are desirous of attaining to Emancipation. Indeed, we wish to attain to That which is auspicious, bodiless, not subject to decrepitude, eternal beyond the ken of the senses, and having nothing superior to it!—

'"Vasishtha said,—What thou sayest about the indications of the Vedas and the other scriptures (in respect of the matter) is even so. Thou takest those indications in the way in which they should be taken. Thou bearest, however, in thy understanding, only the texts of the Vedas and the other scriptures. Thou art not, O monarch, truly conversant with the real meaning of those texts. That person who bears in his understanding merely the texts of the Vedas and the other scriptures without being conversant with the true sense or meaning of those texts, bears them fruitlessly. Indeed, one who holds the contents of a work in memory without comprehending their meaning is said to bear an useless burden. He, however, who is conversant with the true meaning of a treatise, is said to have studied that treatise to purpose. Questioned regarding the meaning of a text, it behoveth one to communicate that meaning which he has comprehended by a careful study. That person of dull intelligence who refuses to expound the meanings of texts in the midst of a conclave of the learned, that person of foolish understanding, never succeeds in expounding the meaning correctly.[1] An ignorant person, going to expound the true meaning of treatises, incurs ridicule. Even those possessed of a knowledge of the Soul have to incur ridicule on such occasions (if what they go to explain has not been acquired by study). Listen now to me, O monarch, as to how the subject of

1 The sense seems to the that the obligation to explain a treatise in the midst of a conclave always stimulates the best faculties, and if it is a conclave of the learned the friction of intellects is sure to bring out the correct sense.—T.

Emancipation has been explained (by preceptors to disciple from days of old) among high-souled persons conversant with the Sankhya and the Yoga systems of philosophy. That which the Yogin, behold is precisely that which the Sankhayas arrive after to attain. He who sees the Sankhya and the Yoga systems to be one and the same is said to be endued with intelligence. Skin, flesh, blood, fat, bile, marrow, and sinews, and these senses (of both knowledge and action), about which thou wert speaking unto me, exist Objects flow from objects ; the senses from the senses. From body one obtains a body, as a seed is obtained from seed. When the Supreme Being is without senses, without seed, without matter, without body, He must be divested of all attributes ! and in consequence of His being so, how, indeed, can He have attributes of any kind ? Space and other attributes arise from the attributes of Sattwa and Rajas and Tamas, and disappear ultimately in them. Thus the attributes arise from Prakriti. Skin, flesh, blood, fat, bile, marrow, bones, and sinews,—these eight that are made of Prakriti, know, O king, may sometimes be produced by the vital seed alone (of the male). The Jiva-soul and the universe are said to both partake of Prakriti characterised by the three attributes of Swatta, Rajas, and Tamas. The Supreme Soul is different from both the Jiva-soul and the universe. As the seasons though unendued with forms, are nevertheless inferred from the appearance of particular fruits and flowers, after the same manner, Prakriti, though formless, is inferred from the attributes of Mahat and the rest that spring from it. In this way from the existence of Chaitanya in the body, the Supreme Soul, divested of all attributes whatever and perfectly stainless, is inferred. Without beginning and destruction, without end, the overseer of all things, and auspicious, that Soul, only in consequence of its identifying itself with the body and other attributes, comes to be taken as invested with attributes. Those persons that are truly conversant with attributes know that only objects endued with attributes can have attributes but that That which transcends all attributes can have none. When the Jiva-soul conquers all attributes born of Prakriti and which it assumes under error, only then does it behold the Supreme Soul. Only the highest Rishis conversant with the Sankhya and the Yoga systems know that Supreme Soul which Sankhya and Yogins and believers in all other systems say is beyond the Understanding, which is regarded as Knower and endued with the highest wisdom in consequence of its casting off all consciousness of identification with Prakriti, which transcends the attribute of Ignorance or Error, which is Unmanifest, which is beyond all attributes, which is called the Supreme, which is dissociated from all attributes, which ordains all things, which is Eternal and Immutable, which overrules Prakriti and all the attributes born of Prakriti, and which, transcending the four and twenty topics of enquiry, forms the twenty-fifth. When men of knowledge, who stand in fear of birth, of the several conditions of living consciousness, and of death, succeed in knowing the Unmanifest, they succeed in understanding the Supreme Soul at the same time. An intelligent man regards the unity of the Jiva-soul with the Supreme Soul as consistent with the scriptures and as perfectly correct; while the man destitute of intelligence looks upon the two as different from each other. This forms the distinction between the man of intelligence and man that is destitute of it. The indications of both Kshara and Akshara (destructible and indestructible) have now been said unto thee. Akshara is Oneness or Unity, while multiplicity or variety is said to be Kshara. When one begins to study and understands properly the five and twenty topics of enquiry, one then comperhends that the Oneness of the Soul is consistent with the scriptures and its multiplicity is what is opposed to them. These are the several indications of what is included in the tale of topics or principles created and what transcends that tale. The wise have said that the tale of topics numbers only five and twenty. That which transcends the topics is beyond that number and forms the twenty-sixth. The study or comprehension of created things (numbered five and twenty) according to their aggregates (of five) is the study and comprehension of topics. Transcending these is That which is eternal.—' "

SECTION CCCVII

" 'Janaka said,—Thou hast, O foremost of Rishis, said that Unity is the attribute of that which is Akshara (Indestructible) and variety or multiplicity is the attribute of what is known as Kshara (Destructible). I have not, however, clearly understood the nature of these two. Doubts are still lurking in my mind. Ignorant men look upon the Soul as endued with the incident of multiplicity. They, however that are possessed of knowledge and wisdom regard the Soul to be one and the same. I, however, have a very dull understanding. I am, therefore, unable to comprehend how all this can happen. The causes also that thou hast assigned for the unity and the multiplicity of Akshara and Kshara I have almost forgotten in consequence of the restlessness of my understanding. I therefore, desire to hear thee once more discourse to me on those same incidents of unity and multiplicity, on him who is knowing, on what is destitute of knowledge, on Jiva-soul, Knowledge, Ignorance. Akshara, Kshara, and on the Sankhya and the Yoga systems, in detail and separately and agreeable to the truth—

" 'Vasishtha said,—I shall tell thee what thou askest! Listen how ever, to me, O monarch, as I expound to thee the practices of Yoga separately. Contemplation, which constitutes an obligatory practices with Yogins, is their highest puissance.[1] Those conversant with Yoga say that Contemplation is of two kinds. One is the concentration of the mind, and the other is called *Pranayama* (regulation of breath). Pranayama is said to be endued with substance ; while concentration of mind is unendued with it.[2] Excepting the three times when a man passes urine and stools and eats, one should devote the whole of his time to contemplation. Withdrawing the senses from their objects by the aid of the mind, one possessed of intelligence, having made oneself pure, should agreeably to the two and twenty modes of transmitting the Prana breath, unite the Jiva-soul with That which transcends the four and twentieth topic (called Ignorance or Prakriti)[3] which is regarded by the wise as dwelling in every part of the body and as transcending decay and destruction. It is by means of those two and twenty methods that the Soul may always be known, as heard by us. It is certain that this practice of Yoga is his whose mind is never affected by evil passions. It is not any other person's. Dissociated from all attachments, abstemious in diet, and subduing all the senses, one should fix one's mind on the Soul, during the first and the last part of the night, after having, O king of Mithila, suspended the functions of the senses, quieted the mind by the understanding, and assumed a posture as motionless as that of a block of stone. When men of knowledge, conversant with the rules of Yoga, become as fixed as a stake of wood, and as immovable as a mountain, then are they said to be in Yoga. When one does not hear, and smell, and taste, and see ; when one is not conscious of any touch ; when one's mind becomes perfectly free from every purpose ; when one is not conscious of any thing, when one cherishes no thought ; when one becomes like a piece of wood, then is one called by the wise to be in perfect Yoga. At such a time one shines like a lamp that burns in a place where there is no wind ; at such a time one becomes freed even from one's subtile form, and perfectly united with Brahma. When one attains to such progress, one has no longer to ascend or to fall among intermediate beings. When persons like ourselves say that there has been a complete identification of the Knower, the Known, and Knowledge, then is the Yogin said to behold the Supreme Soul.[4] While in

1 For enables them to conquer Ignorance.—T.

2 When Pranayama is performed with the aid of *mantras* or *yapa*, it is said to be *saguna* or *sagarbha* or endued with substance. Concentration of mind, however, is made without the aid of such *yapa*.—T.

3 The two and twenty 'sanchodans' of 'Preranas are the two and twenty modes of transmitting the Prana breath from the toe of the foot to the crown of the head. That which transcends Prakriti is the Supreme Soul.—T.

4 The reading I adopt is 'na-kathyate.'—T.

Yoga, the Supreme Soul displays itself in the Yogin's heart like a blazing fire, or like the bright Sun, or like the lightning's flame in the sky. That Supreme Soul which is Unborn and which is the essence of nectar, that is seed by high-souled Brahmanas endued with intelligence and wisdom and conversant with the Vedas, is subtiler than what is subtile and greater than what is great. That Soul, though dwelling in all creatures, is not seen by them. The creator of the worlds, He is seen only by a person endued with wealth of intelligence when aided by the lamp of the mind. He dwells on the other share of thick Darkness and transcends him called Iswara.[1] Persons conversant with the Vedas and endued with omniscience call Him the dispeller of Darkness, stainless, transcending Darkness, without attributes and endued therewith.

" 'This is what is called the Yoga of Yogins. What else is the indication of Yoga? By such practices do Yogins succeeded in beholding the Supreme Soul that transcends destruction and decay. This much that I have told thee in detail concerns about the science of Yoga. I shall now discourse to thee of that Sankhva philosophy by which the Supreme Soul is seen through the gradual destruction of errors.[2] The Sankhyas, whose system is built on Prakriti, say that Prakriti, which is Unmanifest, is the foremost. From Prakriti, they say, O monarch, the second principle called Mahat, is produced. It is heard by us that from Mahat flows the third principle called Consciousness. The Sankhyas blessed with sight of the Soul say that from Consciousness flow the five subtile essence of sound, form, touch, taste, and scent. All these eight they call by the name of Prakriti. The modifications of these eight are sixteen in number. They are the five gross essence of space, light, earth, water, and wind, and the ten senses of action and of knowledge including the mind. Men of wisdom devoted to the Sankhya path and conversant with all its ordinances and dispensations regard these four and twenty topics as embracing the whole range of Sankhya enquiry. That which is produced becomes merged in the producing. Created by the Supreme Soul one after another, these principles are destroyed in a reverse order. At every new Creation, the Gunas start into existence in the lateral order (as stated above), and (when Destruction comes) they merge, (each into its progenitor) in a reverse order, like the waves of the ocean disappearing in the ocean that gives them birth. O best of kings, this is the manner in which the Creation and the Destruction of Prakriti takes place. The Supreme Being is all that remains when Universal Destruction takes place, and it is He that assumes multifarious

1 Atmạnah is 'Iswarat parah.'—T.

2 'Parisankhyadarsanam' is explained by the Commentator thus: 'Parisankhyanam,' is 'parivarianam,' *i.e.*, the gradual 'pravilapam' of errors; 'tena darsanam or sakshatkaram.'—T.

forms when Creation starts into life. This is even so, O king, as ascertained by men of knowledge. It is Prakriti that causes the Over-presiding Purusha to thus assume diversity and revert back to unity. Prakriti also herself has the same indications. Only fully conversant with the nature of the topics of enquiry knows that Prakriti also assumes the same kind of diversity and unity, for when Destruction comes she reverts into unity and when Creation flows she assumes diversity of form. The Soul makes Prakriti, which contains the principles of production or growth, to assume manifold forms. Prakriti is called Kshetra (or soil). Transcending the four and twenty topics or principles is the Soul which is great. It presides over that Prakriti or Kshetra. Hence, O great king, the foremost of Yatis say that the Soul is the Presider. Indeed, it has been heard by us that in consequence of the Soul's presiding over all Kshetras. He is called the Presider. And because He knows that Unmanifest Kshetra, He is, therefore, also called Kshetrajna (Knower of Kshetra). And because also the Soul enters into Unmanifest Kshetra (*viz.*, the body), therefore he is called Purusha. Kshetra is something quite different from Kshetrajna. Kshetra is Unmanifest. The Soul, which transcends the four and twenty principles, is called the Knower. Knowledge and the object known are different from each other. Knowledge, again, has been said to be Unmanifest, while the object of knowledge is the Soul which transcends the four and twenty principles. The Unmanifest is called Kshetra. Sattwa (understanding), and also Iswara (the supreme Lord), while Purusha, which is the twenty-fifth principle has nothing superior to it and is not a principle (for it transcends all principles and is only called a principle conventionally). This much O king, is an account of the Sankhya philosophy. The Sankhayas called the cause of rhe universe, and merging all the grosser principles into the Chit behold the Supreme Soul. Rightly studying the four and twenty topics along with Prakriti, and ascertaining their true nature, the Sankhyas succeed in beholding That which transcends the four and twenty topics or principles,[1] Jiva in reality is that very Soul which transcends Prakriti and is beyond the four and twenty topics. When he succeeds in knowing that Supreme Soul by dissociating himself from Prakriti, he then becomes indentifiable with the Supreme Soul. I have now told thee everything about the Sankhya System truly. Those who are conversant with this philosophy succeed in attaining to tranquility. Indeed, as men whose understandings are subject to error have direct cognisance of Brahma. They that succeed in attaining to that state have never to come back to this world after the dissolution of

1 The Commentator explains that 'nistattwah' means nirgatam tattwam aparoksham yasmat ;—T.

their bodies; while as regards those that are said to be emancipate in this life, puissance, and that indescribable felicity which attaches itself to Samadhi, and immutability, become theirs, in consequence of their having attained to the nature of the Indestructible.[1] They who behold this universe as many (instead of seeing it as one and uniform) are said to see incorrectly. These men are blind to Brahma. O chastiser of foes, such persons have repeatedly to come back into the world and assume bodies (in diverse orders of Being). They, who are conversant with all that has been said above become possessed of omniscience, and accordingly when they pass from this body no longer become subject to the control of any more physical frames. All things, (or the entire universe), have been said to be the result of the Unmanifest. The Soul, which is the twenty fifth, transcends all things. They who know the Soul have no fear of returning to the world.' "

SECTION CCCVIII

" 'Vasishtha said,—I have thus far discoursed to thee on the Sankhya philosophy. Listen now to me as I tell thee what is *Vidya* (knowledge) and what is *Avidya* (Ignorance), one after the other. The learned say that that *Prakriti*, which is fraught with the attributes of Creation and Destruction, is called Avidya; while *Purusha*, who is freed from the attributes of Creation and Destruction and who transcends the four and twenty topics or principles, is called Vidya. Listen to me first as I tell thee what is Vidya among successive sets of other things, as expounded in the Sankhya philosophy. Among the senses of knowledge and those of action, the senses of knowledge are said to constitute what is known as Vidya. Of the senses of knowledge and their object, the former constitute Vidya as has been heard by us. Of objects of the senses and the mind, the wise have said that the mind constitutes Vidya. Of mind and the five subtile essences, the five subtile essences constitute Vidya. Of the five subtile essences and Consciousness, Consciousness constitutes Vidya. Of Consciousness and Mahat, Mahat, O king, is Vidya. Of all the topics or principles beginning with Mahat, and Prakriti, it is Prakriti, which is unmanifest and supreme, that is called Vidya. Of Prakriti, and that called *Vidhi* which is Supreme, the latter should be known as Vidya. Transcending Prakriti is the twenty-fifth (called

1 'Param,' 'Apatam,' and 'Avyayam' are theirs in consequence of 'Akshara-bhavatwa.' 'Aparam' means satyakamatwa, satyasamkalpatwa, &c. i.e., puissance. 'Param' is the indescribable felicity of Samadhi. The Srutis declare that knower of Brahma becomes Brahma.—T.

Purusha) who should be known as Vidya. Of all Knowledge that which is the Object of Knowledge has been said to be the Unmanifest, O king.[1] Again, Knowledge has been said to be Unmanifest and the Object of knowledge to be that which transcends the four and twenty. Once more, Knowledge has been said to be Unmanifest, and the Knower is that which transcends the four and twenty. I have now told thee what is truly the import of Vidya and Avidya. Listen now to me as I tell thee all that has been said about the Indestructible and the Destructible. Both Jiva and Prakriti have been said to be Indestructible, and both of them have been said to be Destructible. I shall tell thee the reason of this correctly as I have understood it. Both Prakriti and Jiva are without beginning and without end or destruction. Both of them are regarded as supreme (in the matter of Creation). Those that are possessed of knowledge say that both are to be called topics or principles. In consequence of its attributes of (repeated) Creation and Destruction), the Unmanifest (or Prakriti) is called Indestructible. That Unmanifest becomes repeatedly modified for the purpose of creating the principle. And because the principles beginning with Mahat are produced by Purusha as well, and because also Purusha and the Unmanifest are mutually dependant upon each other, therefore is Purusha also, the twenty-fifth, called Kshetra (and hence Akshara or Indestructible).[2] When the Yogin withdraws and merges all the principles into the Unmanifest Soul (or Brahma) then the twenty-fifth (*viz.*, Jiva or Purusha) also, with all those principles disappears into it. When the principles become merged each into its progenitor, then the one that remains is Prakriti. When Kshetrajna too,[3] O son, becomes merged into his own producing cause then (all that remains is Brahma and, therefore) Prakriti with all the principles in it becomes Kshara (or meets with destruction), and attains also to the condition of being without attributes in consequence of her dissociation from all the principles. Thus it is that Kshetrajna, when his knowledge of Kshetra disappears, becomes, by his nature, destitute of attributes, as it has been heard by us. When he becomes Kshara he then assumes attributes. When, however, he attains to his

---

1 Hence, as the commentator explains, by knowing what is called the Unmanifest one is capable of attaining to omniscience.—T.

2 What is stated here is this; the Unmanifest or Prakriti, by modification, produces Mahat and the other principles. But the agency of Purusha also is necessary for such production, for Prakriti can do nothing without Purusha, and Purusha also can do nothing without Prakriti. The principles of Mahat and the rest, therefore, may be said to have their origin as much in Purusha as in Prakriti. Beside, the two being naturally dependent on each other, if Prakriti be called Kshara, Purusha also may be so called.—T.

3 *I.e.*, Jiva or Purusha.—T.

own real nature, he then succeeds in understanding his own condition of being really destitute of attributes. By casting off Prakriti and beginning to realise that he is different from her, the intelligent Kshetrajna then comes to be regarded as pure and stainless. When Jiva ceases to exist in a state of union with Prakriti, then does he become identifiable with Brahma. When, however, he exists united with Prakriti, he then, O king, seems to be different from Brahma. Indeed, when Jiva shows no affection for Prakriti and her principles, he then succeeds in beholding the Supreme and having once beheld Him wishes not to fall away from that felicity. When the Knowledge of truth dawns upon him, Jiva begins to lament in this strain :—Alas, how foolishly have I acted by falling through ignorance into this frame composed of Prakriti like a fish entangled in a net! Alas, through ignorance, I have migrated from body to body like a fish from water to water thinking that water is the element in which alone it can live. Indeed, like a fish that does not know anything else than water to be its element, I also have never known anything else than children and spouses to be my own! Fie on me that through ignorance, I have been repeatedly migrating from body to body in forgetfulness (of the Supreme Sou) ! The Supreme Soul alone is my friend. I have capacity for friendship with Him. Whatever be my nature and whoever I may be, I am competent to be like Him and to attain an identity with Him. I see my similarity with Him. I am, indeed, like Him. He is stainless. It is evident that I am of the same nature. Through Ignorance and stupefaction, I have become associated with Inanimate Prakriti. Though really without attachments, I have passed this long time in a state of attachment with Prakriti. Alas, by her was I so long subdued without having been able to know it. Various are the forms—high, middling, and low,—that Prakriti assume. Oh, how shall I dwell in those forms ?[1] How shall I live conjointly with her ? In consequence only of my ignorance I repair to her companionship. I shall now be fixed (in Sankhya or Yoga). I shall no longer keep her companionship. For having passed so long a time with her, I should think that I was so long deceived by her, for myself being really exempt from modification, how could I keep company with one that is subject to modification ? She cannot be held to be responsible for this. The responsibility is mine, since turning away from the Supreme Soul I become of my own accord attached to her. In consequence of that attachment, myself, though formless in reality, had to abide in multifarious forms. Indeed, though formless by nature I become endued with forms in consequence of my sense of *meum*, and thereby insulted

1 High, such as gods, middling, such as human beings and low, such as animals.—T.

and distressed. In consequence of my sense of *meum*, concerning the result of Prakriti, I am forced to take birth in diverse orders of Being. Alas, though really destitute of any sense of *meum*, yet in consequence of affecting it, what diverse acts of an evil nature have been committed by me in those orders in which I took birth while I remained in them with a soul that had lost all knowledge ! I have no longer anything to do with him who, with essence made up of consciousness, divides herself into many fragments and who seeks to unite me with them. It is only now that I have been awakened and have understood that I am by nature without any sense of *meum* and without that consciousness which creates the forms of Prakriti that invest me all around. Casting off that sense of *meum* which I always have with respect to her and whose essence is made up of consciousness, and casting off Prakriti herself, I shall take refuge in Him who is auspicious. I shall be united with Him, and not with Prakriti which is inanimate. If I unite with Him, it will be productive of my benefit. I have no similarity of nature with Prakriti !—The twenty-fifth, (*viz.*, Jiva), when he thus succeeds in understanding the Supreme, becomes able to cast off the Destructible and attain to identity with that which is Indestructible and which is the essence of all that is auspicious. Destitute of attributes in his true nature and in reality Unmanifest, Jiva becomes invested with what is Manifest and assumes attributes. When he succeeds in beholding that which is without attributes and which is the origin of the Unmanifest, he attains, O ruler of Mithila, to identify the same.

" 'I have now told thee what the indications are of what is Indestructible and what is Destructible, according to the best of my knowledge and according to what has been expounded in the scriptures. I shall now tell thee, according to what I have heard, as to how Knowledge that is subtile, stainless, and certain, arises. Do thou listen to me. I have already discoursed to thee what the Sankhya and the Yoga systems are according to their respective indications as expounded in their respective scriptures. Verily, the science that has been expounded in Sankhya treatises is identical with what has been laid down in the Yoga scriptures. The knowledge, O monarch, which the Sankhya preach, is capable of awakening every one. In the Sankhya scriptures, that Knowledge has been inculcated very clearly for the benefit of disciples. The learned say that this Sankhya system is very extensive. Yogin have great regard for that system as also for the Vedas. In the Sankhya system no topic or principle transcending the twenty-fifth is addmitted. That which the Sankhyas regard as their highest topic or principles has been duly described (by me). In the Yoga philosophy, it is said that Brahma, which is the essence of knowledge without duality, becomes Jiva only when invested with Ignorance. In the Yoga scriptures, therefore, both Brahma and Jiva are spoken of,—' "

SECTION CCCIX

" 'Vasishtha said,—Listen now to me as I discourse to thee on *Buddhas* (Supreme Soul) and *Abuddha* (Jiva) which is the dispensation of attributes (of Sattwa, Rajas, and Tamas). Assuming many forms (under the influence of illusion) the Supreme Soul, becoming Jiva, regards all those forms as real.[1] In consequence of (his regarding himself identical with) such transformations, Jiva fails to understand the Supreme Soul, for he bears the attributes (of Sattwa and Rajas and Tamas) and creates and withdraws into himself what he creates. Ceaselessly for his sport, O monarch, does Jiva undergo modifications, and because he is capable of understanding the action of the Unmanifest, therefore is he called *Budhyamana* (the Comprehender).[2] The Unmanifest or Prakriti can at no time comprehend Brahma which is really without attributes even when it manifests itself with attributes. Hence is Prakriti called Unintelligent. There is a declaration of the Srutis to the effect that if ever Prakriti does succeed in knowing the twenty-fifth (*i.e.* Jiva) Prakriti then (instead of being something differentiated from Jiva) becomes identified with Jiva who is united with her. (As regards, however, the Supreme Soul, which is ever disunited and dissociated, and which transcends the twenty-fifth Prakriti can never comprehend it). In consequence of this (*viz.*, his attachment to or union with Prakriti), Jiva or Purusha, who is not manifest and which in his real nature is not subject to modifications, comes to be called as the Unawakened or Ignorant. Indeed because the twenty-fifth can comprehend the Unmanifest, he is therefore, called Budhymana (or Comprehender). He cannot, however, readily comprehend the twenty-sixth, which is stainless, which is Knowledge without duality, which is immeasurable, and which is eternal. The twenty-sixth, however, can know both Jiva and Prakriti, numbering the twenty-fifth and the twenty-fourth respectively. O thou of great effulgence, only men of wisdom succeed in knowing that Brahma which is Unmanifest, which inheres in its real nature to all that is seen and unseen, and which, O son is the one independent essence in

---

1 'Budha' is 'Bodha' or pure Knowledge. 'Abudha' is the reverse of 'Buddha.' The Supreme Soul is Knowledge, while Jiva is Ignorance.—

2 In consequence of Jiva's union with or attachment to Prakriti, Jiva takes this object for a vessel, that for a mountain, and that other for a third. When knowledge comes, Jiva succeeds in understanding that all his impressions are erroneous and that the external world is only a modification of Self. In consequence of Jiva's capacity to comprehend this, he is called Budhyamana or Comprehender.—T.

the universe.[1] When Jiva considers himself different from what he trully is, (i. e., when he regards himself as far or lean, fair or dark a Brahmana or a Sudra), it is only then that he fails to know the Supreme Soul and himself and Prakriti with which he is united. When Jiva succeeds in understanding Prakriti (and knowing that she is something different from him) then he is said to be restored to his true nature and then does he attain to that high understanding which is pure and stainless (and which is concerned with Brahma). When Jiva succeeds, O tiger among kings, in attaining to that excellent understanding, he then attains to that Pure Knowledge (without duality) which is called the twenty-sixth (or Brahma). He then casts off the Unmanifest or Prakriti which is fraught with the attributes of Creation and Destruction. When Jiva succeeds in knowing Prakriti which is unintelligent and subject to the action of the three attributes of Sattwa, and Rajas and Tamas, he then becomes destitute of attributes himself. In consequence of his thus understanding the Unmanifest (to be something different from him), he succeeds in acquiring the nature of the Supreme Soul. The learned say that when he is freed from the attributes (of Sattwa and Rajas and Tamas) and united in the nature with the Supreme Soul then does Jiva become identified with that Soul. The Supreme Soul is called Tattwa as well as Not-Tattwa, and transcends decay and destruction.[2] O giver of honours, the Soul, though it has the manifest principles (*viz.* the body) for its resting place, yet it cannot be said to have acquired the nature of those principles. The wise say that (including the Jiva-soul) there are five and twenty principles in all. Indeed, O son, the Soul is not to be regarded as possessed of any of the principles (Mahat and the rest). Endued with Intelligence, it transcends the principles. It casts off quickly even that principle which is the indication of the Knowing (or awakened) one.[3] When Jiva comes to regard himself as the twenty-sixth which is divested of decay and destruction, it is then that, without doubt, he succeeds by his own force in attaining to similarity with the twenty-sixth. Though awakened by the twenty-sixth

1 'Drisya' and 'Adrisya,' are the Seen and the Unseen, that is the gross and the subtile, or effects and causes. 'Swabhavena anugatam' is 'inhering (unto all of them, in its own nature, that is, Brahma prevades all things and unites with them without itself being changed as regards its own nature. Vudhyate has 'manishibhih' understood after it.—T.

2 'Tattwa' is explained by the Commentator as 'anaropitarupam' i. e., uninvested with any form in consequence of Ignorance; 'Not-Tattwa' is 'nityaparoksham,' i.e., always within the ken of the understanding.—T.

3 That indication is 'I am Brahma.' Such conviction or knowledge even, which characterises those that are awakened or Buddha, is cast off by the twenty-sixth.—T.

which is Pure Intelligence, Jiva still becomes subject to Ignorance. This is the cause of Jiva, multifariousness (in respect of forms) as explained in the Srutis and the Sankhya scriptures, When Jiva, who is endued with *Chetana* (and Unintelligent Prakriti), loses all Consciousness of a distinct or individual Self, then does he, losing his multifariousness, resume his Oneness. O ruler of Mithila, when Jiva, who is found to be in union with happiness and misery and who is seldom free from the consciousness of Self, succeeds in attaining to a similarity with the Supreme Soul which is beyond the reach of the understanding, then does he become freed from virtue and vice. Indeed, when Jiva, attaining to the twenty-sixth which is Unborn and Puissant and which is dissociated from all attachments, succeeds in comprehending it thoroughly, he himself becomes possessed of puissance and entirely casts off the Unmanifest or Prakriti. In consequence of understanding the twenty-sixth, the four and twenty principles seem to Jiva to be unsubstantial or of no value. I have thus told thee, O sinless one, according to the indications of the Srutis, the nature of the Unintelligent (or Prakriti), and of Jiva, as also of that which is Pure Knowledge (*viz.*, the Supreme Soul), agreeably to the truth. Guided by the scriptures, variety and oneness are thus to be understood. The difference between the gnat and the Udumvara, or that between the fish and water, illustrates the difference between the Jiva-soul and the Supreme Soul.[1] The Multiplicity and Oneness of these two are then understood in this way. This is called Emancipation, viz., this comprehension or knowledge of oneself as something distinct from Unintelligent or Unmanifest Prakriti. The twenty-fifth, which resides in the bodies of living creatures, should be emancipated by making him know the Unmanifest or the Supreme Soul which transcends the understanding. Indeed, that twenty-fifth is capable of attaining to Emancipation in this way only and not through any other means, it is certain. Though really different from the Kshetra in which he resides for the time being, he partakes of the nature of that Kshetra in consequence of his union wlth it.[2] Uniting with what is Pure, he becoces Pure. Uniting with the Intelligent, he becomes Intelligent. By uniting, O foremost of men, with one that is

---

1 These examples are often used to explain the difference between the Jiva-soul and the Supreme Soul. The Udumvara is the fruit of the Ficus glomerata. When ripe and broken, the hollow centre is seen to contain many full-grown gnats. The gnat lives in the frurt but is not the fruit, just as the fish though living in the water is not the water that is its home. Jiva, after the same way, though living in the Supreme Soul, is not the Supreme Soul.—T.

2 'Parah' is 'Anyah' or 'Chidatman.' 'Paradharma' means 'partaking' of the nature of Kshetra in which he resides. 'Sametya' is kshetrena iva ekibhuya.'—T.

Emancipate, he becomes Emancipated. By uniting with one that has been freed from attachments of every kind, he becomes freed from all attachments. By uniting with one striving after Emancipation, he himself, partaking of the nature of his companion, strives after Emancipation. By uniting with one of pure deeds he becomes pure and of pure deeds and endued with blazing effulgence. By uniting with one of unstained soul, he becomes of unstained soul himself. By uniting with the One independent Soul, he becomes One and Independent. Uniting with One that is dependent on One's own Self, he becomes of the same nature and attains to Independence.—

"'—O monarch, I have duly told thee all this that is perfectly true. Candidly have I discoursed to thee on this subject, *viz.*, the Eternal and Stainless and Primeval Brahma. Thou mayst impart this high knowledge, capable of awakening the soul, unto that person, O king, who though not conversant with the Vedas is nevertheless, humble and has a keen desire for acquiring the knowledge of Brahma. It should never be imparted unto one that is wedded to falsehood, or one that is cunning or roguish, or one that is without any strength of mind or one that is of crooked understanding, or one that is jealous of men of knowledge, or one that gives pain to others. Listen to me as I say who they are unto whom this knowledge may safely be communicated. It should be given to one that is endued with faith, or one that is possessed of merit, or one that always abstains from speaking ill of others, or one that is devoted to penances from the purest of motives, or one that is endued with knowledge and wisdom, or one that is conversant of the sacrifices and other rites laid down in the Vedas, or one that is possessed of a forgiving disposition, or one that is inclined to take compassion on and do good to all creatures; or one that is fond of dwelling in privacy and solitude, or one that is fond of discharging all acts laid down in the scriptures, or one that is averse to quarrels and disputes, or one that is possessed of great learning or one endued with wisdom or one possessed of forgiveness and self-restraint and tranquillity or soul. This high knowledge of Brahma should never be communicated to one that is not possessed of such qualifications. It has been said that by imparting this knowledge to one that cannot be regarded as fit receptacle for holding it no advantage or good fruit can arise. Unto one that is not observant of any vows and restraints, this high knowledge should never be communicated even if he gives in exchange the whole Earth full of gems and wealth of every kind. Without doubt, however, O king, this knowledge should be given to one that has conquered one's senses. O Karala, let no fear be thine any longer, since thou hast heard all this regarding high Brahma from me today! I have discoursed to thee duly about high and holy Brahma that is without beginning and middle (and end) and that is capable of dispelling all kinds of grief. Beholding Brahma whose sight is capable of dispelling both birth and death, O king which is full of auspiciousness, which removes all fear, and which benefit, and having acquired this essence of all knowledge, cast off all error and stupefaction today! I had acquired this knowledge from the eternal Hiranyagarbha himself, O king, who communicated it to me for my having carefully gratified that great Being of every superior Soul. Asked by thee today, I have, O monarch, communicated the knowledge of eternal Brahma to the just as I had myself acquired it from my teacher. Indeed, this high knowledge that is the refuge of all persons conversant with Emancipation has been imparted to thee exactly as I had it from Brahman himself!—'

"Bhishma continued,—'I have thus told thee of high Brahma agreeably to what the great Rishi (Vasishtha) had said (unto king Karala of Janaka's race), by attaining to which the Twenty-fifth (or Jiva) has never to return. Jiva, in consequence of his not knowing truly the Supreme Soul which is not subject to decay and death, is obliged to frequently come back into the world. When, however, Jiva succeeds in acquiring that high knowledge, he has no longer to come back. Having heard it, O king from the celestial Rishi, I have, O son, communicated to thee high knowledge productive of the highest good. This knowledge was obtained from Hiranyagarbha by the high-souled Rishi Vasishtha. From that foremost of Rishis, viz, Vasishtha, it was acquired by Narada. From Narada I have acquired that knowledge which is truly identifiable with the eternal Brahma. Having heard this discourse of high import, fraught with excellent words, do not, O foremost of the Kurus, yield any longer to grief. That man who knows Kshara and Akshara becomes freed from fear. He, indeed, O king, is obliged to cherish fear who is destitute of this knowledge. In consequence of Ignorace (of Brahma), the man of foolish soul hath repeatedly to come back into this world. Indeed, departing from this life, he has to be born in thousands and thousands of orders of Being every one of which hath death in the end. Now in the world of the deities, now among men, and now among intermediate orders of Being, he has to appear again and again. If in course of time he succeeds in crossing that Ocean of Ignorance in which he is sunk, he then succeeds in avoiding rebirth altogether and attaining to identity with the Supreme Soul. The Ocean of Ignorance is terrible. It is bottomless and called the Unmanifest. O Bharata, day after day, creatures are seen to fall and sink in that Ocean. Since thou, O king, hast been freed from that eternal and limitless Ocean of Ignorance, thou, hast, therefore become freed from Rajas and also Tamas.' "

SECTION CCCX

"Bhishma said,—'Once on a time a king of Janaka's race, while ranging the uninhabited forests in pursuit of deer, saw a superior Brahmana or Rishi of Bhrigu's race. Bowing with his head unto the Rishi who was seated at his ease, king Vasuman took his seat near him and obtaining his permission put to him this question :—O holy one, what is productive of the highest benefit, both here and hereafter, to man who is endued with an unstable body and who is the slave of his desires? Properly honoured by the king, and thus questioned, that high-souled Rishi possessed of ascetic merit then said these words unto him that were highly beneficial.

"The Rishi said,—If thou desirest both here and hereafter what is agreeable to thy mind, do thou then, with restrained senses, abstained from doing what is disagreeable to all creatures. Righteousness is beneficial unto them that are good. Righteousness is the refuge of those that are good. From Righteousness have flowed the three worlds with their mobile and immobile creatures. O thou that art eagerly desirous of enjoying all agreeable objects, how is it that thou art not yet satiated with objects of desire? Thou seest the honey, O thou of little understanding, but art blind to the fall.[1] As one desirous of earning the fruits of knowledge should set oneself to the acquisition of knowledge, even so one desirous of earning the fruits of Righteousness should set oneself to the acquisition of Righteousness. If a wicked man from desire of virtue, strives to accomplish an act that is pure and stainless, the fulfilment of his desire becomes impossible. If, on the other hand, a good man, impelled by the desire of earning virtue, strives to accomplish an act that is even difficult, its accomplishment becomes easy for him. If, while residing in the woods, one acts in such a way as to enjoy all the pleasures of a residence amidst men in towns, one comes to be looked upon not as a forest recluse but as a denizen of towns. Similarly, if one, while residing in towns, acts in such a way as to enjoy the felicity that attaches to the life of a forest recluse, one comes to be looked upon not as a denizen of towns but as a forest recluse. Ascertaining the merits of the religion of Acts and that of Abstention from acts, do thou, with concentrated senses, be devoted to the practices of righteousness that appertain to thought, word, and deed. Judging of the propriety of time and place, purified by the observance of vows and other cleansing rites, and solicited (by them), do thou, without

1 This is a simile very often used for illustrating the danger of pursuing objects of the senses. Collectors of honey used to rove over mountains, guided by the sight of flying bees. These men frequently met with death from falls from precipices.—T.

malice, make large gifts unto them that are good.[1] Acquiring wealth by righteous means, one should give it away unto those that are deserving. One should make gifts, casting off anger ; and having made gifts one should never give way to sorrow nor proclaim those gifts with one's own mouth. The Brahmana who is full of compassion, who is observant of candour, and whose birth is pure, has been regarded as a person deserving of gifts. A person is said to be pure in birth when he is born of mother that has only one husband and that belongs to the same order to which her husband belongs. Indeed, such a Brahmana, conversant with the three Vedas, viz., Rich, Yajush, and Saman, possessed of learning, duly observant of the six duties (of sacrificing on his own account, officiating at the sacrifices of others, learning, teaching, making gifts, and receiving gifts), has been regarded as deserving of gifts. Righteousness becomes unrighteousness, and unrighteousness becomes righteousness, according to the character of the doer, of time, and of place.[2] Sin is cast off like the filth on one's body,—a little with a little exertion and a greater quantity when the exertion is greater. A person, after purging his bowels, should take *ghee*, which operates most beneficially on his system (as a healthy tonic). After the same manner, when one has cleansed oneself of all faults and sets oneself to the acquisition of righteousness, that righteousness, in the next world, proves to be productive of the highest happiness. Good and evil thoughts exist in the minds of all creatures. Withdrawing the mind from evil thoughts, it should always be directed towards good thoughts. One should always reverence the practices of one's own order. Do thou strive, therefore, to act in such a way that thou mayst have faith in the practices of thy own order. O thou that art endued with an impatient soul, betake thyself to the practice of patience. O thou that art of a foolish understanding, seek thou to be possessed of intelligence ! Destitute of tranquillity, seek thou to be tranquil, and bereft of wisdom as thou art, do thou seek to act wisely ! He who moves in the companionship of the righteous succeeds, by his own energy, in acquiring the means of accomplishing what is beneficial for him both in this and the next world. Verily, the root of that benefit (which thus becomes his here and hereafter) is unwavering firmness. The royal sage Mahabhisha, through want of this

1 The Burdwan translator renders this Verse incorrectly.—T

2 This has been repeatedly laid down in the Hindu scriptures. Gifts produce no merit unless made to deserving persons. If made to the undeserving, instead of ceasing to produce any merit, they become positively sinful. The considerations of time and place also are to be attended to. By failing to attend to them, sin is incurred where merit is expected. Truth becomes as sinful as a lie, under particular circumstances ; and a falsehood becomes as meritorious as truth under circumstances. The Hindu scriptures make circumstances the test of acts.—T.

firmness, fell from heaven. Yayati, also, though his merits had become exhausted (in consequence of his boastfulness and though whe as hurled down from heaven) succeeded in regaining regions of felicity through his firmness. Thou art sure to attain to great intelligence, as also to what is for thy highest good, by paying court to virtuous and learned persons possessed of ascetic merit.—'

"Bhishma continued,—'Hearing these words of the sage, king Vasuman, possessed of a good disposition, withdrawing his mind from the pursuits of desire, set it upon the acquisition of Righteousness.' "

SECTION CCCXI

"Yudhishthira said,—'It behoveth thee, O grandsire, to discourse to me on that which is freed from duty and its reverse, which is freed from every doubt, which transcends birth and death, as also virtue and sin, which is auspiciousness, which is eternal fearlessness, which is Eternal and Indestructible, and Immutable, which is always Pure, and which is ever free from the toil of exertion.'

"Bhishma said,—'I shall in this connection recite to thee the old narrative, O Bharata, of the discourse between Yajnavalkya and Janaka. Once on a time the famous king Daivarati of Janaka's race, fully conversant with the import of all questions, addressed this question to Yajnavalkya, that foremost of Rishis.

" 'Janaka said,—O regenerate Rishi, how many kinds of senses are there? How many kinds also are there of Prakriti? What is the Unmanifest and highest Brahma? What is higher than Brahma? What is birth and what is death? What are the limits of Age? It behoveth thee, O foremost of Brahmanas, to discourse on all these topics unto me that am solicitous of obtaining thy grace; I am ignorant while thou art an Ocean of knowledge. Hence, I ask thee! Verily, I desire to hear thee discourse on all these subjects!—

" 'Yajnavalkya said,—Hear, O monarch, what I say in answer to these questions of thine. I shall impart to thee the high knowledge which Yogins value, and especially that which is possessed by the Sankhyas. Nothing is unknown to thee. Still thou askest me. One however, that is questioned should answer. This is the eternal practice. Eight principles have been called by the name of Prakriti, while sixteen have been called modifications. Of Manifest, there are seven. These are the views of those persons who are conversant with the science of Adhyatma. The Unmanifest (or original Prakriti), Mahat, Consciousness, and the five subtile elements of Earth, Wind, Space, Water, and

Light,—these eight are known by the name of Prakriti. Listen now to the enumeration of those called modifications. They are the ear, the skin, the tongue, and the nose; and sound, touch, form, taste, and scent, as also speech, the two arms, the two feet, the lower duct (within the body), and the organs of pleasure.[1] Amongst these, the ten beginning with sound, and having their origin in the five great principles,[2] are called *Visesha.* The five senses of knowledge are called *Savisesha* O, ruller of Mithila. Persons conversant with the science of Adhyatma regard the mind as the sixteenth. This is conformable to thy own views as also to those of other learned men well acquainted with the truths about principles. From the Unmanifest, O king, springs the Mahat-soul. The learned say this to be the first creation relating to Pradhana (or Prakriti): From Mahat, O king of men, is produced Consciousness. This has been called the second creation having the Understanding for its essence.[3] From Consciousness hath sprung the Mind which is the essence of sound and the others that are the attributes of space and the rest. This is the third creation, said to relate to Consciousness. From mind have sprung the great elements, (numbering five). O king! Know that this is the fourth creation called mental, as I say. Persons conversant with the primal elements say that Sound and Touch and Form and Taste and Scent are the fifth creation, relating to the Great (primal) elements. The creation of the Ear, the Skin, the Tongue, and the Scent, forms the sixth and is regarded as having for its essence multiplicity of thought. The senses that come after the Ear and the others (*i.e.*, the senses of action) then arise, O monarch. This is called seventh creation and relates to the senses of Knowledge. Then, O monarch, come the breath that rises upward (*viz.*, Prana) and those that have a transverse motion (*viz.*, Saman, Udana, and Vyana). This is the eighth creation and is called Arjjava.[4] Then come those breaths that course transversely in the lower parts of the body (*viz.*, Samana, Udana and Vyana) and also that called Apana coursing downwards. This, ninth creation, is also called Arjjava, O king. These nine kinds of creation, and these principles, O monarch, which latter number four

1 These, including Mind, form the tale of sixteen called Vikriti or modifications of Prakriti.—T.

2 These are the subtile principles or Tanmatras and not the gross elements.—T.

3 'Mahat' is sometimes called 'Buddhi' hence the creation of Consciousness from Mahat must be creation relating to Buddhi.—T.

4 'Arjjava' mean 'relating to straight paths or courses,' so called from the straight course of these winds or breaths. By reference to these breaths is intended the other limbs of the physical system besides those already indicated.—T.

and twenty, are declared to thee according to what has been laid down in the scriptures. After this, O king, listen to me as I tell thee durations of time as indicated by the learned in respect of these principles or attribute.—' "

SECTION CCCXII

"Yajnavalkya said,—Listen to me, O foremost of men, as I tell thee what the duration of time is in respect to the Unmanifest (or the Supreme Purusha). Ten thousand Kalpas are said to constitute a single day of his. The duration of his night is equal. When his night expires, he awakes, O monarch, and first creates herbs and plants which constitute the sustenance of all embodied creatures. He then creates Brahman who springs from a golden egg. That Brahman is the form of all created things, as has been heard by us. Having dwelt for one whole year within that egg, the great ascetic Brahman, called also Prajapati (Lord of all creatures), came out of it and created the whole Earth, and the Heaven above. The Lord then, it is read in the Vedas, O king, placed the sky between Heaven and Earth separated from each other. Seven thousand and five hundred Kalpas measure the day of Brahman. Persons conversant with the science of Adhyatma say that his night also is of an equal duration. Brahmana, called Mahan, then creates Consciousness called Bhuta and endued with excellent essence.[1] Before creating any physical bodies out of the ingredients called the Great elements, Mahan or Brahma, endued with penances, created four others called his sons. They are the sires of the original sires, O Best of kings, as heard by us.[2] It hath been also heard by us, O monarch that the senses (of knowledge) along with the four inner faculties, have sprung from the (five Great elements called) Pitris, and that the entire universe of mobile and immobile Beings has been filled with those Great elements.[3] The puissant Consciousness created the five Bhutas. These

---

1 'Rishi' here means 'Mahan' or Great. Consciousness is said to have an excellent essence, and is also a Bhuta because of its capacity to produce the Great Bhutas, five in number.—T.

2 These, the Commentator explains, are Mind, Buddhi or Understanding Consciousness, and Chitwa, considered as Vyashti instead of as Samashthi. These are the sires of the primeval sires, *i.e.*, from these sprung the Mahabhutas or Great creatues (*vis.*, the five primal Elements).—T.

3 'Devah' is explained by the Commentator as meaning the Senses and the four inner faculties. 'Devaih' he thinks, refers to the Bhutas or Great elements. Literally rendered, the Verse would read as 'the Devas are the Children of the Pitris; with the Devas, all the worlds of Mobile Being have been covered.' It is not safe to reject the learned Commentator.

are Earth, Wind, Space, Water, and Light numbering the fifth. This Consciousness (who is a Great Being and) from whom springs the third creating, has five thousand Kalpas for his night, and his day is of equal duration. Sound, Touch, Form, Taste, and Scent,—these five are called *Visesha.* They inhere into the five great Bhutas. All creatures, O king, incessantly pervaded by these five, desire one another's companionship, become subservient to one another; and challenging one another, transcend one another; and led by those immutable and seductive principles, creatures kill one another and wander in this world entering into numerous orders of Being.[1] Three thousands of Kalpas represent the duration of their day. The measure of their night also is the same.[2] The Mind roveth over all things, O king, led on by the Senses. The Senses do not perceive anything. It is the Mind that perceives through them. The Eye sees forms when aided by the Mind but never by itself. When the Mind is distracted, the Eye fails to perceive with even the objects fully before it. It is commonly said that the Senses perceive. This is not true, for it is the Mind that perceives through the Senses. When the cessation takes place of the activity of the Mind, the cessation of the activity of the Senses follows. That is the cessation of the activity of the Senses which is the cessation of the activity of the Mind. One should thus regard the Senses to be under the domination of the Mind. Indeed, the Mind is said to be the Lord of all the Senses. O thou of great fame, these are all the twenty Bhutas in the Universe.—' "

SECTION CCCXIII

"Yajnavalkya said,—I have, one after another, told thee the order of the creation, with their total number, of the various principles, as also the extent of the duration of each. Listen now to me as I tell thee of their destruction. Listen to me how Brahman, who is eternal and undecaying, and who is without beginning and without end, repeatedly creates and destroys all created objects. When his day expires and night comes, he becomes desirous of sleep. At such a time the unmanifest and holy one urges the Being called Maharudra, who is conscious of his great powers, (for destroying the world). Urged by the unmanifest,

1 These two Verses refer to the power of the attributes of sound &c., over Jiva Loves and hates, and all kinds of relationship of Jiva are due to the action of the attributes named.—T.

2 The duration here given has reference to the day and the night of the Mahabhutas.—T.

that Being assuming the form of Surya of hundreds of thousands of rays, divides himself into a dozen portions each resembling a blazing fire. He then consumes with his energy, O monarch, without any loss of time, the four kinds of created beings, *Viz.*, viviparous, oviparous, fifth-born, and vegetable. Within the twinkling of the eye all mobile and immobile creatures being thus destroyed, the Earth becomes on every side as bare as a totoise shell. Having burnt everything on the face of the Earth, Rudra, of immeasurable might, then quickly fills the bare Earth with Water possessed of great force He then creates the Yuga-fire which dries up that Water (into which the bare Earth has been dissolved). The Water disappearing, the great element of Fire continues to blaze fiercely. Then comes the mighty Wind of immeasurable force, in his eight forms, who swallows up quickly that blazing fire of transcendant force, possessed of seven flames, and identifiable with the heat existing every creature. Having swallowed up that fire, the Wind courses in every direction, upwards, downwards, and transversely. Then space of immeasurable existent swallowed up that Wind of transcendant energy. Then Mind cheerfully swallows up that immeasurable Space. Then that Lord of all creatures, *viz.*, Consciousness, who is the Soul of everything, swallows up the Mind. Consciousness, in his turn, is swallowed up by the Mahat-soul who is conversant with the Past, the Present, and the Future. The incomparable Mahat-soul or Universe is then swallowed up by Sambhu, that Lord of all things, to whom the Yoga attributes of Anima, Laghima, Prapti, &c., naturally inhere, who is regarded as the Supreme and pure Effulgence that is Immutable. His hands and feet extend over every part; his eyes and head and face are everywhere, his ears reach every place, and he exists overwhelming all things. He is the heart of all creatures; His measure is of a digit of the thumb. That Infinite and supreme Soul, that Lord of all, thus swallows up the Universe. After this, what remains is the Undecaying and the Immutable. One who is without defect of any kind, who is the Creator of the Past, the Present, and the Future; and who is perfectly faultless, I have thus, O monarch, duly told thee of Destruction. I shall now discourse to thee on the subjects of Adhyatma, Adhibhuta, and Adhidaivata.—'"

SECTION CCCXIV

"'Yajnavalkya said,—Brahmanas conversant with the topics of enquiry speak of the two feet as Adhyatma, the act of walking as Adhibhuta, and Vishnu as Adhidaivatam (of those two limbs). The lower duct (anal canal) is Adhyatma; its function of throwing out the excreta is Adhibhuta, and Mitra (Surya) is the Adhidaivata (of that organ). The organ of generation is called Adhyatma. Its agreeable function is called Adhibhuta, and Prajapati is its Adhidaivata. The hands are Adhyatma; their function as represented by acts is Adhibhuta; and Indra is the Adhidaivata of those limbs. The organs of speech are Adhyatma; the words uttered by them are Adhibhuta; and Agni is their Adhidaivata. The eye is Adhyatma; vision or form is its Adhibhuta; and Surya is the Adhidaivata of that organ. The ear is Adhyatma; sound is Adhibhuta; and the points of the horizon are its Adhidaivata. The tongue is Adhyatma, taste is its Adhibhuta; and Water is its Adhidaivata. The sense of scent is Adhyatma; odour is its Adhibhuta; and Earth is its Adhidaivata. The skin is Adhyatma; touch is its Adhibhuta; and Wind is its Adhidaivata. Mind has been called Adhyatma; that with which the Mind is employed is Adhibhuta; and Chandramas is its Adhidaivata. Consciousness is Adhyatma; conviction in one's identity with Prakriti is its Adhibhuta; and Mahat or Buddhi is its Adhidaivata. Buddhi is Adhyatma; that which is to be understood is its Adhibhuta; and Kshetrajna is its Adhidaivata. I have thus truly expounded to thee, O king, with its details taken individually, the puissance of the Supreme (in manifesting Himself in different forms) in the beginning, the middle, and the end. O thou that art fully conversant with the nature of the original topics or principles, Prakriti, cheerfully and of her own accord, as if for sport, O monarch, produces, by undergoing modifications herself, thousands and thousands of combinations of her original transformations called Gunahs. As men can light thousands of lamps from but a single lamp, after the same manner Prakriti, by modification, multiplies into thousands of existent objects the (three) attributes (of Sattwa and Rajas and Tamas) of Purusha. Patience, joy, prosperity, satisfaction, brightness of all faculties, happiness, purity, health, contentment, faith, liberality, compassion, forgiveness, firmness, benevolence, equanimity, truth, acquittance of obligations, mildness, modesty, calmness, external purity, simplicity, observance of obligatory practices, dispassionateness, fearlessness of heart, disregard for the appearance or otherwise of good and evil as also for past acts,—appropriation of objects only when obtained by gift, the absence of cupidity, regard for the interests of others, compassion for all creatures,—these have been said to be the qualities that attach to the attribute of Sattwa. The tale of qualities attaching to the attribute of Rajas consists of pride of personal beauty, assertion of lordship, war, disclination to give, absence of compassion, enjoyment and enduring of happiness and misery, pleasure in speaking ill of others, indulgence in quarrels and disputes of every kind, arrogance, discourtesy, anxiety, indulgence in hostilities, sorrow, appropriation of what belongs to others, shamelessness, crookedness, disunions, roughness, lust, wrath, pride, assertion of superiority, malice, and calumny. These are said to spring from the attributes of Rajas. I shall now tell thee of that assemblage of qualities which springs from Tamas. They are stupefaction of judgment, obscuration of every faculty, darkness, blind darkness. By darkness is implied death, and by blind darkness is meant wrath. Besides these, the other indications of Tamas are greediness in respect of all kinds of food, ceaseless appetite for both food and drink, taking pleasure in scents and robes and sports and beds and seats and sleep during the day and calumny and all kinds of acts proceeding from heedlessness, taking pleasure, from ignorance (of purer sources of joy) in dancing and instrumental and vocal music, and aversion for every kind of religion. These, indeed, are the indications of Tamas—' "

SECTION CCCXV

" 'Yajanvalkya said,—These three, O foremost of men, (*viz.*, Sattwa, Rajas, and Tamas), are the attributes of Prakriti. These attach to all things of the universe and always inhere to them. The Unmanifest Purusha endued with the six Yoga attributes transforms himself by himself into hundreds and thousands and millions and millions of forms (by embracing these three attributes). Those that are conversant with the science of Adhyatma, say that unto the attribute of Sattwa is assigned a high, unto Rajas a middling, and unto Tamas, a low place in the universe. By the aid of unmixed righteousness one attains to a high end (viz., that of the deities or other celestial beings). Through righteousness mixed with sin one attains to the status of humanity. While through unmixed sin one sinks into a vile end (by becoming an animal or a vegetable &c.). Listen now to me, O king, as I speak to thee of the intermixture or compounds of the three attributes of Sattwa, Rajas, and Tamas. Sometimes Rajas is seen existing, with Sattwa. Tamas also exists with Rajas. With Tamas may also be seen Sattwa. Then also may Sattwa and Rajas and Tamas be seen existing together and in equal proportions. They constitute the Unmanifest or Prakriti. When the Unmanifest (Purusha) becomes endued with only Sattwa, he attains to the regions of the deities. Endued with both Sattwa and Rajas, he takes birth among human beings. Endued with Rajas and Tamas, he takes birth among the intermediate order of Being. Endued with all three, viz., Sattwa and Rajas and Tamas, he attains to the status of humanity. Those high souled persons that transcend both righteousness and sin, attain, it is said, to that place which is eternal, immutable, undecaying, and immortal. Men of knowledge attain to births that are very superior, and their place is faultless and undecaying, transcending the ken of the senses, free from ignorance, above birth and death, and full of light that dispels all kinds of darkness. Thou hadst asked me about the nature of the Supreme residing in the Unmanifest, (viz., Purusha). I shall tell thee. Listen to me, O king. Even when residing in Prakriti, He is said to reside in His own nature without partaking of the nature of Prakriti.[1] Prakriti, O king, is inanimate unintelligent. When presided over Purusha, then only can she create and destroy,—

" 'Janaka said,—Both Prakriti and Purusha, O thou of great intelligence, are without beginning and without end. Both of them are without form. Both of them are undecaying. Both of them, again, incomprehensible. How then, O foremost of Rishis, can it be said that one of them is inanimate and unintelligent ? How, again, is the other said to be animate and intelligent ? And why is the latter called Kshetrajna ? Thou, O foremost of Brahmanas, art fully conversant with the entire religion of Emancipation. I desire to hear in detail of the religion of Emancipation in its entirety. Do thou discourse to me then of the existence and Oneness of Purusha, of his separateness from Prakriti, of the deities which attach to the body of the place to which embodied creatures repair when they die, and that place to which they may ultimately, in course of time, be able to go. Tell me also of the Knowledge described in the Sankhya system, and of the Yoga system separately. It behoveth thee also to speak of the premonitory symptoms of death, O best of men. All these topics are well known to thee even as an (emblic) myrobalan in thy hand !—' "

---

1 'Prakritisthah' means 'in his own Prakriti or nature.' The sense of the line is that Purusha, even when residing in the case that Prakriti provides him with, does not partake of the nature of Prakriti but continues to be undefiled by her.—T.

SECTION CCCXVI

"'Yajnavalkya said,—That which is without attributes, O son, can never be explained by ascribing attributes to it. Listen, however, to me as I expound to thee what is possessed of attributes and what is devoid of them. High-souled Munis conversant with the truth regarding all the topics or principles say that when Purusha seizes attributes like a crystal catching the reflection of a red flower, he comes to be called as possessed of attributes; but when freed from attributes like the crystal freed from reflection, he comes to be viewed in his real nature, that is, as beyond all attributes.[1] Unmanifest Prakriti is by her nature endued with attributes. She cannot transcend them. Destitute of intelligence by nature, she becomes attached to attributes. Unmanifest Prakriti cannot know anything, while Purusha, by his nature, is possessed of knowledge.—There is nothing higher than myself,—even this is what Purusha is always conscious of. For this reason the unmanifest (or Prakriti), although naturally inanimate and unintelligent, still becomes animate and intelligent in consequence of her union with Purusha who is Eternal and Indestructible instead of remaining in her own nature due to her destructibility.[2] When Purusha, through ignorance, repeatedly becomes associated with attributes, he fails to understand his own real nature and therefore he fails to attain to Emancipation. In consequence Purusha's lordship over the principles that flow from Prakriti, he is said to partake of the nature of those principles. In consequence also of his agency in the matter of creation, he is said to possess the attribute of creation. In consequence of his agency in the matter of Yoga, he is said to possess the attribute of Yoga. For his lordship over those particular principles known by the name of Prakriti, he is said to possess the nature of Prakriti.[3] For his agency in the matter of creating the seeds (of all immobile objects), he is said to partake of the nature of those seeds. And because he causes the several principles or attributes to start into life, he is, therefore, said to be

1 I expand this Verse for bringing out the meaning. A verbal rendering will become unintelligible.—T.

2 This is a difficult Verse. I am not sure that I have understood it correctly. The sense to be that Prakriti, which is really unintelligent and incapable of enjoyment or endurance, becomes intelligent and capable of enjoyment or endurance in consequence of being united with Purusha who is intelligent. Thus when pleasurable or painful sensations are felt, it is the body that seems to feel it only in consequence of the Soul that presides over it —T.

3 The first line of 7 is the same in sense as the second line of 8. In the Bombay text, only the second line of 8 occurs, while the first line of 7 has been justly omitted. In fact, Tattwa and the Prakriti are the same thing.—T.

subject to decay and destruction (for those principles themselves are subject thereto). In consequence, again, of his being the witness of everything, and in consequence also of there being nothing else than he, as also for his consciousness of identity with Prakriti, Yatis crowned with ascetic success, conversant with Adhyatma, and freed from fever of every kind, regard him as existing by himself without a second, immutable, unmanifest (in the form of Cause), unstable, and manifest (in the form of effects). This is what has been heard by us. Those Sankhyas, however, that depend upon Knowledge only (for their Emancipation) and the practice of compassion for all creatures, say that it is Prakriti which is One but Purushas are many.[1] As a matter of fact, Purusha is different from Prakriti which though unstable, still appears as stable. As a blade of reed is different from its outer cover, even so is Purusha different from Prakriti. Indeed, the worm that is ensconced within the Udumvara should be known as different from the Udumvara. Though existing with the Udumvara, the worm is not to be regarded as forming a portion of the Udumvara. The fish is distinct from the water in which it lives, and the water is distinct from the fish that lives in it. Though the fish and water exist together, yet it is never drenched by water. The fire that is contained in an earthen sauce-pan is distinct from the earthen sauce-pan, and the sauce-pan is distinct from the fire it contains. Although the fire exists in and with the sauce-pan, yet it is not to be regarded as forming any part of it. The lotus-leaf that floats on a piece of water is distinct from the piece of water on which it floats. Its co-existence with water does not make it a portion of the water. The perennial existence of those objects in and with those mentioned, is never correctly understood by ordinary people. They who behold Prakriti and Purusha in any other light are said to possess a vision that is incorrect. It is certain that they have repeatedly to sink into terrible hell. I have thus told thee the philosophy of the Sankhyas that excellent science by which all things have been correctly ascertained. Ascertaining the nature of Purusha and Prakriti in this way, the Sankhyas attain to Emancipation. I have also told thee of the systems of those others that are conversant with the great principles of the universe. I shall now discourse to thee on the science of the Yogins.—' "

SECTION CCCXVII

"Yajnavalkya said,—I have already spoken to thee of the science of the Sankhyas. Listen now to me as I truly discourse on the science

1 This refers to the opinion of the atheistic Sankhyas.—T.

of the Yogins as heard and seen by me, O best of kings! There is no knowledge that can compare with that of the Sankhyas. There is no puissance that compares with that of Yoga. These two ordain the same practices, and both are regarded as capable of leading to Emancipation. Those men that are not blest with intelligence regard the Sankhya and the Yoga systems to be different from each other. We, however, O king, look upon them as one and the same, according to the conclusion to which we have arrived (after study and reflection). That which the Yogins have in view is the very same which the Sankhyas also have in view. He who sees both the Sankhya and the Yoga systems to be one and the same is to be regarded as truly conversant with the topics or principles that ordain the universe. Know, O king, that the vital breaths and the senses are the chief means for practising Yoga. By only regulating those breaths and the senses, Yogins wander everywhere at their will.[1] When the gross body is destroyed, Yogins, endued with subtile bodies possessed of the eight Yoga attributes (of Anima, Laghima Prapti, &c.,) wander over the universe, enjoying (in that body) all kinds of felicities, O sinless one. The wise have, in the scriptures, spoken of Yoga as conferring eight kinds of puissance. They have spoken of Yoga as possessed of eight limbs.[2] Indeed, O king, they have not spoken of any other kind of Yoga. It has been said that the practices of Yogins excellent as these are (for their results), are of two kinds. Those two kinds, according to the indications occurring in the scriptures, are practices endued with attributes and these freed from attributes. The concentration of the mind (on the sixteen objects named), with simultaneous regulation of the breath, O king, (is one kind). The concentration of the mind (in such a way as to destroy all difference between the contemplater, the object contemplated, and the act of contemplation) along with subjugation of the senses, (is of another kind). The first kind of Yoga is said to be that possessed of attributes; the second kind is said to be that freed from attributes.[3] Then, again, Regulation of

1 By the word 'Rudra' is meant *Prana* and the other breaths. The Commentator explains that the etymolgy is utkramana kale dehinam rodayanti iti Rudrah Pranah. By regulating the vital breaths and the Senses, Yogins attain to Yoga-puissance and succeed in roving wherever they please in their *linga-sarira* or subtile bodies.—T.

2 The Eight limbs of Yoga are Pranayma Pratyahara, Dhyana, Dharana, Tarka, Samadhi, with the two additional ones of Yama and Niyama,—T.

3 In the first line of 9 the word 'Pranayma' is used to mean regulation of the vital breaths. In the second line, the same word implies the 'ayamah or nigrahah' of the senses with the mind. By 'Dharana' is meant the fixing of the mind, one after another, on the sixteen things named in treatises on Yoga. By 'ekagrata' of the mind is meant that concentration in which there is no longer any consciousness of difference between, Dhyatri, Dheya, and Dhyana.'—T.

the breath is Yoga with attributes. In Yoga without attributes, the mind, freed from its functions, should be fixed. Only the regulation of the breath which is said to be endued with attributes should, in the first instance, be practised, for, O ruler of Mithila, if the breath (that is inhaled and suspended) be exhaled without mentally reflecting the while upon a definite image (furnished by a limited *mantra*), the wind in the neophyte's system will increase to his great injury.[1] In the first Yama of the night, twelve ways of holding the breath are recommended. After sleep, in the last Yama of the night, other twelve ways of doing the same have been laid down. Without doubt, one endued with tranquillity, of subdued senses, living in retirement, rejoicing in one's own self, and fully conversant with the import of the scriptures, should (regulating one's breath in these four and twenty ways) fix one's Soul (on the Supreme Soul).[2] Dispelling the five faults of the five senses, *viz.*, (withdrawing them from their objects of) sound, form, touch, taste, and scent, and dispelling those conditions called Pratibha and Apavanga, O ruler of the Mithilas, all the senses should be fixed upon the mind. The mind should then be fixed on Consciousness, O king; Consciousness should next be fixed on intelligence or Buddhi, and Buddhi, should then be fixed on Prakriti. Thus merging these one after another, Yogins contemplate the Supreme Soul which is One, which is freed from Rajas, which is stainless, which is Immutable and Infinite and Pure and without defect, who is Eternal Purusha, who is unchangeable, who is Indivisible, who is without decay and death, who is everlasting, who transcends diminution, and which is Immutable Brahma. Listen now, O monarch, to the indications of one that is in Yoga. All the indications of cheerful contentment that are his who is slumbering in contentment are seen in the person, that is in Samadhi. The person in Samadhi, the wise say, looks like the fixed and upward flame of a lamp that is full of oil and that burns in a breezeless spot. He is like a rock which is incapable of being moved in the slightest degree by ever a heavy downpour from the clouds. He is incapable of being moved by the din of conches and drums, or by songs or the sound of hundreds of musical

1 It is difficult for those who do not practise Pranayama to understand this fully. The fact is, Saguna Pranayama, when the breath is inhaled, the inhalation is measured by the time taken up in mentally reciting a well-known mantra. So when inhaled breath is suspended, the suspension is measured by the time taken in mentally reciting a particular mantra. When, therefore, the suspended breath should be exhaled, it should be done by similarly measuring the time of exhaling For beginners, this Saguna Pranayama is recommended. Of course only exhalation has been spoken of but it applies equally to inhalation and suspension. These three processes, in Yoga language, are Puraka, Kumbhaka, and Rechaka.—T.

2 'Ekantasilin' means a 'Sannyasin'; 'atmarama' is one who takes pleasure in one's soul instead of in spouses and children.—T.

instruments beat or blown together. Even this is the indication of one in Samadhi. As a man of cool courage and determination, while ascending a flight of steps with a vessel full of oil in his hands, does not spill even a drop of the liquid if frightened and threatened by persons armed with weapons even so the Yogin, when his mind has been concentrated and when he beholds the Supreme Soul in Samadhi, does not, in consequence of the entire stoppage of the functions of his senses at such a time, move in the slightest degree. Even these should be known to be the indication of the Yogin while he is in Samadhi. While in Samadhi, the Yogin beholds Brahma which is Supreme and Immutable, and which is situated like a blazing Effulgence in the midst of thick Darkness. It is by this means that he attains, after many years, to Emancipation after casting off this inanimate body. Even this is what the eternal Sruti declares. This is called the Yoga of the Yogins. What else is it? Knowing it, they that are endued with wisdom regard themselves as crowned with success,—

SECTION CCCXVIII

'Yajnavalkya said,—Listen now to me, with attention, O king, as to what the places are to which those who die have to go. If the Jiva-soul escapes through the feet, it is said that the man goes to the region of the Vishnu. If through the calves, it has been heard by us, that the man repairs to the regions of the Vasus. If through the knees, he attains to the companionship of those deities that are called Sadhyas. If through the lower duct, the man attains to the regions of Mitra. If through the posteriors, the man returns to the Earth, and if through the thighs to the region of Prajapati. If through the flanks, the man attains to the regions of the Maruts, and if through the nostrils, to the region of Chandramas. If through the arms, the man goes to the region of Indra, and if through the chest, to that of Rudra. If through the neck, the man repairs to the excellent region of that foremost of asceties known by the name of Nara. If through the mouth, the man attains to the region of the Viswadevas and if through the ears, to the region of the deities of the several points of the horizon. If through the nose, the man attains to the region of the Windgod; and if through the eyes, to the region of Agni. If through the brows, the man goes to the region of the Aswins; and if through the forehead, to that of Pitris. If through the crown of the head, the man attains to the region of the puissant Brahman, that foremost of the gods. I have thus told thee, O ruler of Mithila, the several places to which men repair according to the manner in which their Jiva-souls escape from their bodies. I shall now tell thee the premonitory indication, as laid down by the wise of those who have but one year to live. One who, having previously seen the fixed star called Arandhati, fails to see it, or that other star called Dhruva,[1] or one that sees the full Moon or the flame of a burning lamp to be broken towards the south, has but one year to live. Those men, O king, who can no longer see images of themselves reflected in the eyes of others, have but one year to live. One who being endued with lustre loses it, or being endued with wisdom loses it,—indeed, one whose inward and outward nature is thus changed,—has but six months more to live. He who disregards the deities, or quarrels with the Brahmanas, or one who being naturally of a dark complexion becomes pale of hue, has but six months more to live. One who, sees the lunar disc to have many holes like a spider's web or one who sees the solar disc to have similar holes, has but one weak more to live. One who, when smelling fragrant scents in place of worship, perceives them to be as offensive as the scent of corpses, has but one week more to live. The depression of the nose or of the ears, the discolour of the teeth or of the eye, the loss of all consciousness, and the loss also of all animal heat, are symptoms indicating death that very day. If, without any perceptible cause a stream of tears suddenly flows from one's left eye, and if vapours be seen to issue from one's head, that is a sure indication that the man will die before that day expires. Knowing all these premonitory symptoms, the man of cleansed soul should day and night unite his soul with the Supreme Soul (in Samadhi). Thus should he go on till the day comes for his dissolution. If, however, instead of wishing to die he desires to live in this world, he casts off all enjoyments,—all scents and tastes,—O king, and lives on in abstinence. He thus conquers death by fixing his soul on the Supreme Soul. Indeed, the man who is blessed with knowledge of the Soul, O monarch, practises the course of life recommended by the Sankhyas and conquers death by uniting his soul with the Supreme Soul. At last, he attains to what is entirely indestructible, which is without birth, which is auspicious, and immutable, and eternal, and stable, and which is incapable of being attained to by men of uncleansed souls.—

1 The pole-star.—T.

SECTION CCCXIX

"'Yajnavalkya said,—Thou hast asked me, O monarch, of that Supreme Brahma which resides in the Unmanifest. Thy question relates to a deep mystery. Listen to me with close attention, O king! Having conducted myself with humility according to the ordinances laid down by the Rishis I obtained the Yajushes, O king, from Surya. Without the austerest penances I formerly adored the heat-giving deity. The puissant Surya, O sinless one, gratified with me, saying,—Solicit thou, O regenerate Rishi, the boon upon which thou hast set thy heart, however difficult it may be of acquisition. I shall, with cheerful Soul, grant it to thee. It is very difficult to incline me to grace!—Bowing unto him with a bend of my head, that foremost of heat-giving luminaries was addressed by me in these words,—I have no knowledge of the Yajushes. I desire to know them without loss of time!—The holy one, thus solicited, told me,—I shall impart the Yajushes unto thee. Made up of the essence of speech, the goddess Saraswati will enter into thy body.—The deity then commanded me to open my mouth. I did as I was commanded. The goddess Saraswati then entered into my body, O sinless one. At this, I began to burn. Unable to endure the pain I plunged into a stream. Not understanding that what the high-souled Surya had done for me was for my good, I became even angry with him. While I was burning with the energy of the goddess, the holy Surya told me,—Do thou endure this burning sensation for only a little while. That will soon cease and thou wilt be cool. Indeed I became cool. Seeing me restored to ease, the Maker of light said unto me,—The whole Vedas, with even those parts that are regarded as its appendix, together with the Upanishads, will appear in thee by inward light, O regenerate one! The entire Satapathas also thou wilt edit, O foremost of regenerate ones. After that, thy understanding will turn to the path of Emancipation. Thou wilt also attain to that end which is desirable and which is coveted by both Sankhyas and Yogins!—Having said these words unto me, the divine Surya proceeded to the Asta hills. Hearing his last words, and after he had departed from the spot where I was, I came home in joy and then remembered the goddess Saraswati. Thought of by me, the auspicious Saraswati appeared instantly before my eyes, adorned with all the vowels and the consonants and having placed the syllable Om in the van. I then, according to the ordinance, offered unto the goddess the usual Arghya, and dedicated another to Surya, that foremost of all heat-giving deities. Discharging this duty I took my seat, devoted to both those deities. Thereupon the entire Satapatha Brahmanas, with all their mysteries and with all their abstracts as also their appendices, appeared of themselves before my mental vision, at which I became filled with great joy.[1] I then taught them to a hundred good disciples and thereby did what was disagreeable to my high-souled maternal uncle (Vaisampayana) with the disciples gathered round him.[2] Then shining in the midst of my disciples like the Sun himself with his rays, I took the management of the Sacrifice of thy high-souled sire, O king. In that Sacrifice a dispute arose between me and my maternal uncle as to who should be permitted to appropriate the Dakshina that was paid for the recitation of the Vedas. In the very presence of Devala, I took half of that Dakshina, (the other half going to my maternal uncle). Thy sire and Sumanta and Paila and Jaimini and other articles all acquiesced in that arrangement.[3]

"'I had thus got from Surya the five times ten Yajushes, O monarch. I then studied the Puranas with Romaharshan. Keeping before me those (original) Mantras and the goddess Saraswati, I then, O king, aided by the inspiration of Surya, set myself to compile the excellent Satapatha Brahmanas, and succeeded in achieving the task never before undertaken by any one else. That path which I had desired to take has been taken by me and I have also taught it to my disciples. Indeed, the whole of those Vedas with their abstracts have been imparted by me to those disciples of mine. Pure in mind and body, all those disciples have, in consequence of my instructions, become filled with joy. Having established (for the use of others) this knowledge consisting of fifty branches which I had obtained from Surya, I now meditate on the great object of that knowledge *viz.*, (Brahma). The Gandharva Viswavasu, well conversant with the Vedanta scriptures, desirous, O king, of ascertaining what is beneficial for the Brahmanas in this knowledge and what truth occurs in it, and what is the excellent object of this knowledge, once questioned me. He put

---

1 'Chakre' literally means 'I made.' The Commentator explains it as equivalent to 'swayam avirabhut.'—T.

2 'Vipriya' evidently means 'what is not agreeable.' There was evidently a dispute between Yajnavalkya and his maternal uncle Vaisampayana, the celebrated disciple of Vyasa. This dispute is particularly referred to in the next Verse. Vaisampayana had been a recognised teacher of the Vedas and had collected a large number of disciples around him. When, therefore, the nephew Yajnavalkya, having obtained the Vedas from Surya, began to teach them, he was naturally looked upon with a jealousy, which culminated (as referred to in the next Verse) into an open dispute about the Dakshina to be appropriated in the Sacrifice of Janaka. The Burdwan translator incorrectly renders the word 'vipriya' which he takes to mean as 'very agreeable.' In the Vishnu Purana it is mentioned that a dispute took place between Yajnavalkya and Paila. The latter's preceptor, Vyasa, came, and taking his side, asked Yajnavalkya to return him the Vedas which he had obtained from him. Yajnavalkya vomitted forth the Vedas. These were instantly devoured by two other Rishis in the form of Tittiri birds. These afterwards promulgated the Taittiriya Upanishads.—T.

3 This shows that I was then regarded as the equal of Vaisampayana himself in the matter of Vedic knowledge. Sumanta and Paila and Jaimini, with Vaisampayana, were the rishis that assisted the great Vyasa in the task of arranging the Vedas.—T.

to me altogether four and twenty questions, O king, relating to the Vedas. Finally, he asked me a question, numbered twenty-fifth which relates to that branch of knowledge which is concerned with the inferences of ratioscination. Those questions are as follow :—What is universe and what is not-universe ? What is Aswa and what Aswa ? What is Mitra ? What is Varuna ? What is Knowledge ? What is Object of knowledge ? What is Unintelligent ? What is Intelligent ? Who is Kah ? Who is possessed of the principle of change ? Who is not possessed of the same ? What is he that devours the Sun and what is the Sun ? What is Vidya and what is Avidya ? What is Immobile and what Mobile ? What is without beginning, what is Indestructible, and what is Destructible ? These were the excellent questions put to me by that foremost of Gandharvas. After king Viswavasu, that foremost of Gandharvas, had asked me these questions one after another, I answered them properly. At first, however, I told him,—Wait for a brief space of time, till I reflect on thy questions !—So be it, Gandharva said, and sat in silence. I then thought once again of the goddess Saraswati in my mind. The replies then to those questions naturally arose in my mind like butter from curds. Keeping in view the high science of inferential ratioscination, I churned with my mind, O monarch, the Upanishads and the supplementary scriptures relating to the Vedas. The fourth science then that treats of Emancipation, O foremost of kings, and on which I have already discoursed to thee, and which is based upon the twenty-fifth, *viz.*, Jiva, I then expounded to him.[1] Having said all this, O monarch, to king Viswavasu, I then addressed him, saying,—Listen now to the answers that I give unto the several questions that thou hast put to me. I now turn to the question which, O Gandharva, thou askest, *viz.*,—What is Uuniverse and what is not-universe ?—The Universe is Unmanifest and original Prakriti endued with the principles of birth and death which are terrible (to those that are desirous of Emancipation). It is, besides, possessed of the three attributes (of Sattwa, Rajas, and Tamas), in consequence of its producing principles all of which are fraught with those attributes.[2] That which is Not-universe is Purusha divested of all attributes. By Aswa and Aswa are meant the female and the male, *i.e.*, the former is Prakriti and the latter is Purusha. Similarly, Mitra is Purusha,

---

1 This is called the Fourth Science, the three others being the three Vedas, Agriculture, and the Science of Morality and Chastisement.—T.

2 Prakriti is regarded as something in which Sattwa, Rajas, and Tamas reside in exactly equal proportion. All the principles of Mahat, &c., which flow from Prakriti, are characterised by these three attributes in diverse measure.—T.

and Varuna is Prakriti[1] Knowledge, again, is said to be Prakriti, while the object to be known is called Purusha. The Ignorant (Jiva), and the Knowing or Intelligent are both Purusha without attributes (for it is Purusha that becomes Jiva when invested with Ignorance). Thou hast asked what is Kah, who is endued with change and who is unendued therewith. I answer, Kah is Purusha.[2] That which is endued with change is Prakriti. He that is not endued therewith is Purusha. Similarly, that which is called Avidya (the unknowable) is Prakriti; and that which is called Vidya is Purusha. Thou hast asked me about the Mobile and the Immobile. Listen to what my answer is. That which is mobile is Prakriti, which undergoing modification, constitutes the cause of Creation and Destruction. The Immobile is Purusha, for without himself undergoing modifications he assists at Creation and Destruction. (According to a different system of philosophy) that which is Vedya is Prakriti; while that which is Avedya is Purusha. Both Prakriti and Purusha are said to be unintelligent, stable, indestructible, unborn, and eternal, according to the conclusions arrived at by philosophers conversant, with the topics included in the name of Adhyatma. In consequence of the indestructibility of Prakriti in the matter of Creation. Prakriti, which is unborn, is regarded as not subject to decay or destruction. Purusha, again, is indestructible and unchangeable, for change it has none. The attributes that reside in Prakriti are destructible, but not Prakriti herself. The learned, therefore, call Prakriti indestructible. Prakriti also, by undergoing modifications, operates as the cause of Creation. The created results appear and disappear, but not original Prakriti. Hence also is Prakriti called indestructible. Thus have I told thee conclusions of the fourth Science based on the principles of ratiocinative inference and having Emancipation for its end. Having acquired by the science of ratiocinative inference and by waiting upon preceptors, the Rich, the Samans, and the Yajushes, all the obligatory practices should be observed and all the Vedas studied with reverence. O Viswavasu! O foremost of Gandharvas, they who study the Vedas with all their branches but who do not know the Supreme Soul from which all things take their birth and into which all things merge when destruction comes, and which is the one object whose knowledge the Vedas seek to inculcate,—indeed, they who have no acquaintance with that which the Vedas seek to establish,—study the Vedas to no purpose and bear their burthen of such study in vain. If a person desirous of butter churns

1 By Mitra is meant here the deity giving light and heat. By Varuna is meant the waters that compose the universe.—T.

2 'Kah', the commentator explained, is 'anandah' or felicity.—T.

the milk of the she-ass, without finding what he seeks he simply meets with a substance that is as foul of smell as ordure. After the same manner, if one, having studied the Vedas, fails to comprehend what is Prakriti and what is Purusha, one only proves one's own foolishness of understanding and bears a useless burthen (in the form of Vedic lore).[1] One should, with devoted attention, reflect on both Prakriti and Purusha, so that one may avoid repeated birth and death. Reflection upon the fact of one's repeated births and deaths and avoiding the religion of acts that is productive at best of destructible results, one should betake oneself to the indestructible religion of Yoga. O Kasyapa, if one continuously on the nature of the Jiva-soul and its connection with the Supreme Soul, one then succeeds in divesting oneself on all attributes and in beholding the Supreme soul. The Eternal and Unmanifest Supreme Soul is regarded by men of foolish understandings to be different from the twenty-fifth or the Jiva-soul. They are endued with wisdom that behold both these as truly one and the same. Frightened at repeated births and deaths, the Sankhyas and Yogins regard the Jiva-soul and the Supreme Soul to be one and the same.—

" 'Viswavasu then said,—Thou hast, O foremost of Brahmanas, said that Jiva-soul is indestructible and truly undistinguished from the Supreme Soul. This, however, is difficult to understand. It behoveth thee to once more discourse on this topic to me. I have heard discourses on this subject from Jaigishavya. Aista, Devala, the regenerate sage Parasara, the intelligent Varshaganya, Bhrigu, Panchasikha, Kapila, Suka, Gautama, Arshtisena, the high-souled Garga, Narada, Asuri, the intelligent Paulastya, Sanatkumara, the high-souled Sukra, and my sire Kasyapa. Subsequently I heard the discourses of Rudra and the intelligent Viswarupa, of several of the deities, of the Pitris, and the Daiteyas. I have acquired all that they say, for they generally discourse that eternal object of all knowledge. I desire, however, to hear what thou mayst say on those topics with the aid of thy intelligence. Thou art the foremost of all persons, and a learned lecturer on the scriptures, and endued with great intelligence. There is nothing that is unknown to thee. Thou art an ocean of the Srutis, as described, O Brahmana, in the world of both the deities and Pitris. The great Rishis residing in the region of Brahma say that Aditya himself, the eternal lord of all luminaries, is thy preceptor (in the matter of this branch of knowledge). O Yajnavalkya, thou hast obtained the entire science, O Brahmana, of the Sankhyas, as also the scriptures of the Yogins in

1 The comparison lies in the folly of the two persons indicated. One churning ass's milk for butter is only a fool. Similarly, one failing to understand the nature of Prakriti and Purusha from the Vedas is only a fool.—T.

particular. Without doubt, thou art enlightened, fully conversant with the mobile and immobile universe. I desire to hear thee discourse on that knowledge, which may be likened to clarified butter endued with solid grains.

" 'Yajnavalkya said,—thou art, O foremost of Gandharvas, competent to comprehend every knowledge. As, however, thou askest me do thou hear me then discourse to thee according as I myself have obtained it from my preceptor. Prakriti, which is unintelligent, is apprehended by Jiva. Jiva, however, cannot be apprehended by Prakriti, O Gandharva. In consequence of Jiva being reflected in Prakriti, the latter is called Pradhana by Sankhyas and Yogins conversant with the original principles as indicated in the Srutis. O sinless one, the other, beholding, beholds the twenty-fourth (Prakriti) and the twenty-fifth (Soul); not beholding, it beholds the twenty-sixth.[1] The twenty-fifth thinks that there is nothing higher than itself. In reality, however, though beholding, it does not behold that (*viz.*, the Twenty-sixth) which beholds it.[2] Men possessed of wisdom should never accept the Twenty-fourth (*viz.*, Prakriti, which is unintelligent or inert) as identifiable with the Twenty-fifth or the Soul which has a real and independent existence. The fish live in water. It goes thither impelled by its own nature. As the fish, though living in the water, is to be regarded as separate from it, after the same manner is the Twenty-fifth to be apprehended, (*i.e.*, though the Twenty-fifth exists in a state of contact with the Twenty-fourth or Prakriti, it is, however, in its real nature, separate from and independent of Prakriti. When overwhelmed with the consciousness of *meum* or Self, and when unable to understand its identity with the Twenty-sixth, in fact, in consequence of the illusion that invests it, of its co-existence with Prakriti, and of its own manner of thinking, the Jiva-soul always

1 I give a literal rendering of this Verse for showing how difficult it is to understand the meaning. The Commentator correctly explains the sense which is as follows: 'anyah' or the other is the Soul as distinguished from its reflection upon Prakriti, that is the Soul in its real character as independent of Prakriti. What is said here is that when the Soul, in its real character beholds, or acts as a witness of everything (i.e., as exists in the states of wakefulness and dream), becomes conscious of both itself (the Twenty-fifth) and Prakriti (the Twenty fourth) when, however, it ceases to behold or act as such witness (i.e., in the state of dreamless slumber of Yoga-samadhi), it succeeds in beholding the Supreme Soul or the Twenty-sixth. In simple language what is said here is that the Soul becomes conscious of both itself and Prakriti in the state of wakefulness and dream. In Samadhi alone, it beholds the Supreme Soul.—T.

2 What is said here is that the Twenty-sixth or the Supreme Soul always beholds the Twenty-fifth or the Jiva-soul. The latter, however, filled with vanity, regards that there is nothing higher than it. It can easily, in Yoga-samadhi, behold the Twenty-sixth. Though thus competent to behold the Supreme Soul, it fails ordinarily to behold it. The Commentator sees in this Verse a reputation of the doctrine of the Charvakas and the Saugatas who deny that there is a Twenty sixth Tattwa or even a Twenty fifth which they identify with the Twenty fourth.—T.

skins down, but when freed from such consciousness it goes upwards. When the Jiva-soul succeeds in apprehending that it is one, and Prakriti with which resides is another, then only does it, O regenerate one, succeed in beholding the Supreme Soul and attaining to the condition of Oneness with the universe. The Supreme is one, O king, and the Twenty-fifth (or Jiva-soul) is another. In consequence, however, of the Supreme overlying the Jiva-soul the wise regard both to be one and the same[1] For these reasons, Yogins, and followers of the Sankhya system of philosophy, terrified by birth and death, blessed with sight of the Twenty-sixth, pure in body and mind, and devoted to the Supreme Soul, and do not welcome the Jiva-soul as indestructible.[2] When one beholds the Supreme Soul and losing all consciousness of individuality becomes identified with the Supreme, one then becomes omniscient, and possessed of such omniscience one becomes freed from the obligation of rebirth. I have thus discoursed to thee truly, sinless one, about Prakriti which is unintelligent, and Jiva-soul which is possessed of intelligence, and the Supreme Soul which is endued with omniscience, according to the indications occurring in the Srutis. That man who beholds not any difference between the knower of the known, is both Kevala and not Kevala, is the original cause of the universe, is both Jiva-soul and the Supreme Soul.[3]—

"'Viswavasu said,—O puissant one, thou hast duly and adequately discoursed on that which is the origin of all the deities and which is productive of Emancipation. Thou hast said what is true and excellent. May inexhaustible blessings always attend thee, and may thy mind be ever united with intelligence!—

"'Yajnavalkya continued,—Having said those words, the prince of Gandharvas proceeded towards heaven, shining in resplendence of beauty. Before leaving me, the high-souled one duly honoured me

---

1 'Tatsthanat' is explained by the Commentator as 'Varasya avaradhisthanat, i.e., in consequence of 'vara' overlying the 'avara.' The instance of the string and the snake is cited. At first the string is erroneously taken for the snake. When the error is dispelled, the string appears as the string. Thus the Supreme and the Jiva soul come to be taken as one when true knowledge comes.—T.

2 The ordinary doctrine is that the Jiva soul is indestructible, for it is both unborn and deathless, its so called births and deaths being only changes of the forms which Prakriti undergoes in course of her association with it, an association that continues as long as the Jiva-soul does not succeed in effecting its emancipation. In this Verse the ordinary doctrine is abandoned. What is said here is that the Jiva-soul is not deathless, for when it becomes identified with the Supreme Soul, that alteration may be taken as its death.—T.

3 This is a very difficult Verse. 'Pasya' and 'apasya' are 'drashtri' and 'drisya', *i.e*; knower and known (or Soul and Prakriti) 'Kshemaya' and 'Tattwa are 'drik' and 'drisya' *i.e.*, knowledge and known. One that sees no difference between these that is, one that regards all things as one and the same, is both 'Kevala' and 'not-Kevale,' &c., meaning that such a person, though still appearing as a Jiva (to others) is in reality identifiable with the Supreme Soul.—T.

me by taking the accustomed turns round my person, and I looked upon him, highly pleased. He inculcated the science he had obtained from me unto those celestials that dwell in the regions of Brahman and other deities, unto those that dwell on Earth, unto also the denizens of the nether regions, and unto them that had adopted the path of Emancipation, O king. The Sankhyas are devoted to the practices of their system. The Yogins are devoted to the practices inculcated by their system. Others there are that are desirous of achieving their Emancipation. Unto these latter this science is productive of visible fruits, O lion among king. Emancipation flows from Knowledge. Without Knowledge it can never be attained. The wise have said it, O monarch. Hence, one should strive one's best for acquiring true Knowledge in all its details, by which one may succeed in freeing oneself from birth and death. Obtaining knowledge from a Brahmana or a Kshatriya or Vaisya or even a Sudra who is of low birth, one endued with faith should always show reverence for such knowledge. Birth and death cannot assail one that is endued with faith. All orders of men are Brahmanas. All are sprung from Brahma. All men utter Brahma.[1] Aided by an understanding that is derived from and directed to Brahma. I inculcated this science treating of Prakriti and Purusha. Indeed, this whole universe is Brahma. From the mouth of Brahma sprung the Brahmanas; from his arms, sprung the Kshatriyas; from his navel, the Vaisya; and from his feet, the Sudras. All the orders, (having sprung in this way) should not be regarded as pilfering from one another. Impelled by Ignorance, all men meet with death and attain, O king, to birth that is the cause of acts.[2] Divested of Knowledge, all orders of men, dragged by terrible Ignorance, fall into varied orders of being due to the principles that flow from Prakriti. For this reason, all should, by every means, seek to acquire Knowledge. I have told thee that every person is entitled to strive for its acquisition. One that is possessed of Knowledge is a Brahmana. Others, (*viz.*, Kshatriyas and Vaisyas and Sudras) are possessed of knowledge. Hence, this science of Emancipation is always open to them all. This, O king has been said by the Wise. The questions thou hadst asked me have all been answered by me agreeably to the truth. Do thou, therefore, cast off all grief. Go thou to the other end of this enquiry. Thy questions were good. Blessings on thy head for ever!—

1 This may mean that as men speak, and as speech is Brahma, all men must be regarded as utterers of Brahma. It, again, Brahma be taken to mean the Vedas in special, it may imply that all men utter the Vedas or are competent to study the Vedas. Such an exceedingly liberal sentiment from the mouth of Yajnavalkya is compatible only with the religion of Emancipation which he taught.—T.

2 The doctrine is that unless acts are destroyed, there can be no Emancipation.—T.

"Bhishma continued—Thus instructed by the intelligent Yajnavalkya the king of Mithila became filled with joy. The king honoured that foremost of ascetics by walking round his person. Dismissed by the monarch, he departed from his court. King Daivarati, having obtained the knowledge of the religion of Emancipation, took his seat, and touching a million of kine and a quantity of gold and a measure of gems and jewels, gave them away unto a number of Brahmanas. Installing his son in the sovereignty of the Videhas, the old king began to live, adopting the practices of the Yatis. Thinking mainly of all ordinary duties and their derelictions (as laid down in the scriptures), the king began to study the science of the Sankhyas and the Yogins in their entirety. Regarding himself to be Infinite, he began to reflect on only the Eternal and Independent One. He cast off all ordinary duties and their derelictions, Virtue and Vice, Truth and Falsehood, Birth and Death, and all other things appertaining to the principles produced by Prakriti. Both Sankhyas and Yogins, agreeably to the teachings of their sciences, regard this universe to be due to the action of the Manifest and the Unmanifest. The learned say that Brahma is freed from good and evil, is self-dependent, the highest of the high, Eternal, and Pure. Do thou, therefore, O monarch, become Pure! The giver, the receiver of the gift, the gift itself, and that which is ordered to be given away, are all to be deemed as the unmanifest Soul. The Soul is the Soul's one possession. Who, therefore, can be a stranger to one? Do thou think always in this way. Never think otherwise. He who does not know what is Prakriti possessed of attributes and what is Purusha transcending attributes, only he, not possessed as he is of knowledge, repairs to sacred waters and performs sacrifices. Not by study of the Vedas, not by penances, not by sacrifices O son of Kuru, can one attain to the status of Brahma. Only when one succeeds in apprehending the Supreme or Unmanifest, one comes to be regarded with reverence. They who wait upon Mahat attain to the regions of Mahat. They who wait upon Consciousness, attain to the spot that belongs to Consciousness. They who wait upon what is higher attain to places that are higher than these. Those persons, learned in the scriptures, who succeed in apprehending Eternal Brahma who is higher than Unmanifest Prakriti, succeed in obtaining that which transcends birth and death, which is free from attributes, and which is both existent and nonexistent I got all this knowledge from Janaka. The latter had obtained it from Yajnavalkya. Knowledge is very superior. Sacrifices cannot compare with it. With the aid of Knowledge one succeeds in crossing the world's ocean which is full of difficulties and dangers. One can never cross that ocean by means of sacrifices. Birth and death, and other impediments, O king, men of knowledge say, one cannot pass over by ordinary exertion.[1] Men attain to heaven through sacrifices, penances, vows, and observances. But they have again to fall down therefrom on the Earth. Do thou, therefore, adore with reverence that which is Supreme, most pure, blessed, stainless, and sacred, and which transcends all states (being Emancipation itself). By apprehending Kshetra, O king, and by performing the Sacrifice that consists in the acquisition of Knowledge, thou wilt really be wise. In former time, Yajnavalkya did that good to king Janaka which is derivable from a study of the Upanishads. The Eternal and Immutable Supreme was the topic about which the great Rishi had discoursed to the king of Mithila. It enabled him to attain to that Brahma which is auspicious, and immortal, and which transcends all kinds of sorrow."

SECTION CCCXX

"Yudhishthira said,—'Having acquired great power and great wealth, and having obtained a long period of life how may one succeed in avoiding death? By which of these means, *viz.*, penances, or the accomplishment of the diverse acts (laid down in the Vedas), or by knowledge of the Srutis, or the application of medicines, can one succeed in avoiding decrepitude and death?'

"Bhishma said,—'In this connection is cited the old narrative of Panchasikha who was a Bhikshu in his practices and Janaka. Once on a time Janaka, the ruler of the Videhas, questioned the great Rishi Panchasikha, who was the foremost of all persons conversant with the Vedas and who had all his doubts removed in respect of the purpose and import of all duties. The King said,—By what conduct, O holy one may one transcend Decrepitude and death? It is by penances, or by the understanding, or by religious acts (like sacrifices and vows), or by study and knowledge of the scriptures?—Thus addressed by the ruler of the Vedas the learned Panchasikha, conversant with all invisible things, answered, saying,—There is no prevention of these two (*viz.*, decrepitude and death); nor is it true that cannot be prevented under any circumstances. Neither days, nor nights, nor months, cease to go on. Only that man, who, though transitory, betakes himself to the eternal path (of the religion of Nivritti or abstention from all acts) succeeds in avoiding birth and death. Destruction overtakes, all creatures. All creatures seem to be ceaselessly borne along the infinite current of time. Those that are borne along the infinite current of time which is without a raft (to rescue) and which is infested by those two mighty alligators, viz., decrepitude and death, sink down without anybody coming to their assistance.

---

1 Literally, 'these are not obstacles by external nature,' and are therefore irremovable by personal exertion of the ordinary kind.—T.

As one is swept along that current, one fails to find any friend for help and one fails to be inspired with interest for any one else. One meets with spouses and other friends only on one's road. One had never before enjoyed this kind of companionship with any one for any length of time. Creatures, as they are borne along the current of time, become repeatedly attracted towards one another like masses of clouds moved by the wind meeting one another with loud sound. Decrepitude and death are devourers of all creatures, like wolves. Indeed, they devour the strong and the weak, the short and the tall. Among creatures, therefore, which are all so transitory, only the Soul exists eternally. Why should he, then, rejoice when creatures are born and why should he grieve when they die? Whence have I come. Who am I? Whither shall I go? Whose am I? Before what do I rest? What Shall I be? For what reason then dost thou grieve for what? Who else then thou wilt behold heaven or hell (for what thou doest)? Hence, without throwing aside the scriptures, one should make gifts and perform sacrifices!—"

SECTION CCCXXI

"Yudhishthira said,—'Without abandoning the domestic mode of life, O royal sage of Kuru's race, who ever attained to Emancipation which is the annihilation of the Understanding (and the other faculties)? Do tell me this! How may the gross and the subtile form be cast off? Do thou also, O grandsire, tell me what the supreme excellence of Emancipation is.'

"Bhishma said,—'In this connection is cited the old narrative of the discourse between Janaka and Sulabha, O Bharata! In days of yore there was a king of Mithila, of the name of Dharmadhyaja, of Janaka's race. He was devoted to the practices of the religion of Renunciation. He was well conversant with the Veda, with the scriptures on Emancipation, and with the scriptures bearing on his own duty as a king. Subjugating his senses, he ruled this Earth. Hearing of his good behaviour in the world, many men of wisdom, well-conversant with wisdom, O foremost of men, desired to imitate him. In the same *Satya* Yuga, a woman of the name of Sulabha, belonging to the mendicant order, practised the duties of Yoga and wandered over the whole Earth. In course of her wanderings over the Earth, Sulabha heard from many *Dandis* of different places that the ruler of Mithila was devoted to the religion of Emancipation. Hearing this report about king Janaka and desirous of ascertaining whether it was true or not, Sulabha became desirous of having a personal interview with Janaka. Abandoning, by her Yoga powers, her former form and features, Sulabha assumed the most faultless features and unrivalled beauty. In the twinkling of an eye and with the speed of the quickest shaft, the fair-browed lady of eyes like lotus-petals repaired to the capital of the Videhas. Arrived at the chief city of Mithila teeming with a large population, she adopted the guise of a mendicant and presented herself before the king. The monarch, beholding, her delicate form, became filled with wonder and enquired who she was, whose she was, and whence she came. Welcoming her, he assigned her an excellent seat, honoured her by offering water to wash her feet, and gratified her with excellent refreshments. Refreshed duly and gratified with the rites of hospitality offered unto her, Sulabha, the female mendicant, urged the king, who was surrounded by his ministers and seated in the midst of learned scholars, (to declare himself in respect of his adherence to the religion of Emancipation). Doubting whether Janaka had succeeded in attaining to Emancipation, by following the religion of Nivritti, Sulabha, endued with Yoga-power, entered the understanding of the king by her own understanding. Restraining, by means of the rays of light that emanated from her own eyes, the rays issuing from the eyes of the king, the lady, desirous of ascertaining the truth, bound up king Janaka with Yoga bonds.[1] That best of monarch, priding himself upon his own invincibleness and defeating the intentions of Sulabha seized her resolution with his own resolution.[2] The king, in his subtile form, was without the royal umbrella and sceptre. The lady Sulabha, in hers, was without the triple stick. Both staying then in the same (gross) form, thus conversed with each other. Listen to that conversation as it happened between the monarch and Sulabha.

"Janaka said,—O holy lady, to what course of conduct art thou devoted? Whose art thou? Whence hast thou come? After finishing thy business here, whither wilt thou go? No one can, without questioning, ascertain another's acquaintance with the scriptures, or age, or order of birth. Thou shouldst, therefore, answer these questions of mine, when thou has come to me. Know that I am truly freed from all vanity in respect of my royal umbrella and sceptre. I wish to know thee thoroughly. Thou art deserving, I hold, of my respect.[3] Do thou listen to me as I speak to thee on Emancipation for there is none else (in this world) that can discourse to thee on that topic. Hear me also I tell thee who that person is from whom in days of old I acquired this

---

1 'Sanchodayishyanti' implies 'questioned.' Here it means questioning the king internally or by Yoga power.—T.

2 'Utsmayan' is explained by the Commentators as 'priding himself upon his own invincibleness.' 'Ayaya bhavam' implies 'her determination to make the king dumb' 'Viseshayan' is abhibhavan.—

3 'Sammantum' is explained by the Commentator as equivalent to 'samyak jnatum.'—T.

distinguishing knowledge.[1] I am the beloved disciple of the high-souled and venerable Panchasikha, belonging to the mendicant order, of Parasara's race. My doubts have been dispelled and am fully conversant with the Sankhya and the Yoga systems, and the ordinances as in respect of sacrifices and other rites, which constitutes the three well-known paths of Emancipation.[2] Wandering over the earth and pursuing the while the path that is pointed out by the scriptures, the learned Panchasikha formerly dwelt in happiness in my abode for a period of four months in the rainy season. That foremost of Sankhyas discoursed to me, agreeably to the truth, and in an intelligible manner suited to my comprehension, on the several kinds of means for attaining to Emancipation. He did not, however, command me to give up my kingdom. Freed from attachments, and fixing my Soul on supreme Brahma, and unmoved by companionship, I lived, practising in its entirety that triple conduct which is laid down in treatiseson Emancipation. Renunciation (of all kinds of attachments) is the highest means prescribed for Emancipation. It is from Knowledge that Renunciation, by which one becomes freed is said to flow. From Knowledge arises the endeavour after Yoga, and through that endeavour one attains to knowledge of Self or Soul. Through knowledge of Self one transcends joy and grief. That enables one to transcend death and attain to high success. That high intelligence (knowledge of Self) has been acquired by me, and accordingly I have transcended all pairs of opposites. Even in this life have I been freed from stupefaction and have transcended all attachments. As a soil, saturated with water and softened theryby, causes the (sown) seed to sprout forth, after the same manner, the acts of men cause rebirth. As a seed, fried on a pan or otherwise, becomes unable to sprout forth although the capacity for sprouting was there, after the same manner my understanding having been freed from the productive principle constituted by desire, by the instruction of the holy Panchasikha of the mendicant order, it no longer produces its fruit in the form of attachment to the object of the senses. I never experience love for my spouse or hate for my foes. Indeed, I keep aloof from both, behold-

---

1 It is difficult to say in what sense the word 'vaiseshikam' is used here. There is a particular system of philosophy called Vaiseshika or Kanada the system believed to have been originally promulgated by a Rishi of the name of Kanada. That system has close resemblance to the atomic theory of European philosophers. It has many points of striking resemblance with Kapila's system or Sankhya. Then, again, some of the original principles, as enunciated in the Sanakhya system, are called by the name of Visesha.—T.

2 The mention of 'Vidhi' indicated, as the Commentator explains, 'Karmakanda.' The value of 'Karma' in the path of Emancipation' is to purify the Soul.—T.

ing the fruitlessness of attachment and wrath. I regard both persons equally, *viz.*, him that smears my right hand with sandal-paste and him that wounds my left. Having attained my (true) object, I am happy, and look equally upon a clod of earth, a piece of stone, and a lump of gold. I am freed from attachments of every kind, though am engaged in ruling a kingdom. In consequence of all this I am distinguished over all bearers of triple sticks. Some foremost of men that are conversant with the topic of Emancipation say that Emancipation has a triple path. (These are knowledge, Yoga, and sacrifices and rites). Some regard Knowledge having all things of the world for its object as the means of Emancipation. Some hold that the total renunciation of acts (both external and internal) is the means thereof. Another class of persons conversant with the scriptures on Emancipation say that Knowledge is the single means. Other, *viz.* Yatis, endued with subtile vision, hold that acts constitute the means. The high-souled Panchasikha, discarding both the opinion about knowledge and acts, regarded the third as the only means or path of Emancipation. If men leading the domestic mode of life be endued with Yama and Niyama, they become the equals of Sannyasins. If, on the other hand, Sannyasins be endued with desire and aversion and spouses and honour and pride and affection, they become the equals of men leading domestic modes of life.[1] If one can attain to Emancipation by means of knowledge, then may Emancipation exist in triple sticks (for there is nothing to prevent the bearers of such stick from acquiring the needful knowledge). Why then may Emancipation not exist in the umbrella and the sceptre as well, especially when there is equal reason in taking up the triple stick and the sceptre ?[2] One becomes attached to all those things and acts with which one has need for the sake of one's own self for particular reasons.[3] If a person, beholding the faults of the domestic mode of life, casts it off for adopting another mode (which he considers to be fraught with great merit), he cannot, for such rejection and adoption, be regarded as one that is a once freed from all attachments, (for all that he has done has been to

---

1 K. P. Singha wrongly translates this Verse.—T.

2 'There is equal reason in taking up &c.,' implies that the bearing of the sceptre is only a mode of life like that of holders of the triple stick. Both the king and the Sannyasin are free to acquire knowledge and both, therefore, may attain to Emancipation notwithstanding their respective emblems. In the emblems themselves there is no efficacy or disqualification.—T.

3 The object of this Verse is to show that all persons, led by interest, become attached to particular things. The littleness or greatness of those things cannot aid or bar people's way to Emancipation. 'I may be a king, says Janaka, and thou mayst be a mendicant. Neither thy mendicancy nor my royalty can aid or obstruct our Emancipation. Both of us, by Knowledge, can achieve what we wish, notwithstanding our outward surroundings.—T.

attach himself to a new mode after having freed himself from a previous one).[1] Sovereignty is fraught with the rewarding and the chastising of others. The life of a mendicant is equally fraught with the same (for mendicants also reward and chastise those they can). When, therefore, mendicants are similar to kings in this respect, why would mendicants only attain to Emancipation, and not kings? Notwithstanding the possession of sovereignty, therefore, one becomes cleansed of all sins by means of knowledge alone, living the while in Supreme Brahma. The wearing of brown cloths, shaving of the head, bearing of the triple stick, and the Kamandalu,—these are the outward signs of one's mode of life. These have no value in aiding one to the attainment of Emancipation. When, notwithstanding the adoption of these emblems of a particular mode of life, knowledge alone becomes the cause of one's Emancipation from sorrow, it would appear that the adoption of mere emblems is perfectly useless. Or, if, beholding the mitigation of sorrow in it, thou hast betaken thyself to these emblems of Sannyasi, why then should not the mitigation of sorrow be beheld in the umbrella and the sceptre to which I have betaken myself? Emancipation does not exist in proverty; nor is bondage to be found in affluence. One attains to Emancipation through Knowledge alone, whether one is indigent or affluent. For these reasons, know that I am living in a condition of freedom, though ostensibly engaged in the enjoyments of religion, wealth, and pleasure, in the form of kingdom and spouses, which constitute a field of bondage (for the generality of men). The bonds constituted by kingdom and affluence, and the bondage to attachments, I have cut off with the sword of Renunciation whetted on the stone of the scriptures bearing upon Emancipation. As regards myself then, I tell thee that I have become freed in this way. O lady of the mendicant order, I cherish an affection for thee. But that should not prevent me from telling thee that thy behaviour does not correspond with the practices of the mode of life to which thou hast betaken thyself! Thou hast great delicacy of formation. Thou hast an exceedingly shapely form. The age is young. Thou hast all these, and thou hast Niyama (subjugation of the senses). I doubt it verily. Thou hast stopped up my body (by entering into me with the aid of the Yoga power) for ascertaining as to whether I am really emancipated or not. This act of thine ill corresponds with that mode of life whose emblems thou bearest. For Yogin that is endued with desire, the triple stick is unfit. As regards thyself, thou dost not adhere to thy stick. As regards those that are freed, it behoves even

---

1 Hence, by changing my royal life for that of a bearer of the triple stick I can gain nothing.—T.

them to protect themselves from fall.[1] Listen now to me as to what thy transgression has been in consequence of thy contact with me and thy having entered into my gross body with the aid of thy understanding. To what reason is thy entrance to be ascribed into my kingdom or my palace ? At whose sign hast thou entered into my heart ?[2] Thou belongest to the foremost of all the orders, being, as thou art, a Brahmana woman. As regards myself, however, I am a Kshatriya. There is no union for us two. Do not help to cause an intermixture of colours. Thou livest in the practice of those duties that lead to Emancipation. I live in the domestic mode of life. This act of thine, therefore, is another evil thou hast done, for it produces an unnatural union of two opposite modes of life. I do not know whether thou belongest to my own *gotra* or dost not belong to it. As regards thyself also, thou dost not know who I am (viz., to what *gotra* I belong). If thou art of my own *gotra*, thou hast, by entering into my person, produced another evil,—the evil, viz., of unnatural union. If, again, thy husband be alive and dwelling in a distant place, thy union with me has produced the fourth evil of sinfulness, for thou art not one with whom I may be lawfully united. Dost thou perpetrate all these sinful acts, impelled by the motive of accomplishing a particular object ? Dost thou do these from ignorance or from perverted intelligence ? If, again, in consequence of thy evil nature thou hast thus become thoroughly independent or unrestrained in thy behaviour, I tell thee that if thou hast any knowledge of the scriptures, thou wilt understand that everything thou hast done has been productive of evil. A third fault attaches to thee in consequence of these acts of thine, a fault that is destructive of peace of mind. By endeavouring to display thy superiority, the indication of a wicked woman is seen in thee. Desirous of asserting thy victory as thou art, it is not myself alone whom thou wishest to defeat, for it is plain that thou wishest to obtain a victory over even the whole of my court (consisting of these learned and very superior Brahmanas), by casting thy eyes in this way towards all these meritorious Brahmanas, it is evident that thou desirest to humiliate them all and glorify thyself (at their expense). Stupefied by thy pride of Yoga-puissance that has been born of thy jealousy (at sight of my power,) thou hast caused a union of thy understanding with mine and thereby hast really mingled together nectar with poison. That union, again, of man and woman, when each

---

1 'Yukte' in the first line means 'in the Yogin.' The Bombay reading 'Tridandanke' is a mistake for 'Tridandakam.' The Bombay text reads 'na muktasyasti gopana,' meaning that 'there is no relief for one that has fallen down after having arisen in Yoga.' The Bengal text reads 'vimuktasya' I adopt the Bengal reading.—T.

2 What the king says is that he, the king, had made no assignation with the lady in consequence of which she could be justified in entering his body. The word 'Sannikarsha' here means 'sanketa.' Both the Vernacular translators render this word wrongly.—T.

covets the other, is sweet as nectar. That association, however, of man and woman when the latter, herself coveting, fails to obtain an individual of the opposite sex that does not covet her, is, instead of being a merit, only a fault that is as noxious as poison. Do not continue to touch me. Know that I am righteous. Do thou act according to thy own scriptures. The enquiry thou hadst wished to make, viz., whether I am or I am not emancipated, has been finished. It behoves thee not to conceal from me all thy secret motives. It behoves thee not, that thus disguisest thyself, to conceal from me what thy object is, that is whether this call of thine has been prompted by the desire of accomplishing some object of thy own or whether thou hast come for accomplishing the object of some other king (that is hostile to me). One should never appear deceitfully before a king; nor before a Brahmana; nor before one's wife when that wife is possessed of every wifely virtue. Those who appear in deceitful guise before these three very soon meet with destruction. The power of kings consists in their sovereignty. The power of Brahmanas conversant with the Vedas is in the Vedas. Women wield a high power in consequence of their beauty and youth and blessedness. These then are powerful in the possession of these powers. He, therefore, that is desirous of accomplishing his own object should always approach these three with sincerity and candour. Insincerity and deceit fail to produce success (in these three quarters). It behoveth thee, therefore, to apprise me of the order to which thou belongest by birth, of thy learning and conduct and disposition and nature, as also of the object thou hast in view in coming to this place!—"

"Bhishma continued,—'Though rebuked by the king in these unpleasant, improper, and ill-applied words, the lady Sulabha was not at all abashed. After the king had said these words, the beautiful Sulabha then addressed herself for saying the following words in reply that were more handsome than her person.

" 'Sulabha said,—O king, speech ought always to be free from the nine verbal faults and the nine faults of judgment. It should also, while setting forth the meaning with perspicuity, be possessed of the eighteen well-known merits.[1] Ambiguity, ascertainment of the faults and merits of premises and conclusions, weighing the relative strength or weakness of those faults and merits, establishment of the conclusion, and the element of persuasiveness or otherwise that attaches to the conclusion thus arrived at,—these five characteristics appertaining to the sense—constitute the authoritativeness of what is said. Listen now to the characteristics of these requirements beginning with ambiguity, one after another, as I expound them according to the combinations. When

1 These faults and merits are set forth in the Verses that follow.—T.

knowledge rests on distinction in consequence of the object to be known being different from one another, and when (as regards the comprehension of the subject) the understanding rests upon many points one after another, the combination of words (in whose case this occurs) is said to be vitiated by ambiguity.[1] By ascertainment (of faults and merits), called Sankhya, is meant the establishment, by elimination, of faults or merits (in premises and conclusions), adopting tentative meanings.[2] *Krama* or weighing the relative strength or weakness of the faults or merits (ascertained by the above process), consists in settling the propriety of the priority or subsequence of the words employed in a sentence. This is the meaning attached to the word *Krama* by persons conversant with the interpretation of sentences or texts. By Conclusion is meant the final determination, after this examination of what has been said on the subjects of religion, pleasure, wealth, and Emancipation, in respect of what it particularly is that has been said in the text.[3] The sorrow born of wish or aversion increases to a great measure. The conduct, O king, that one pursues in such a matter (for dispelling the sorrow experienced) is called Prayojanam.[4] Take it for certain, O king, at my word, that these characteristics of Ambiguity and the other (numbering five in all), when occurring together, constitute a complete and intelligible sentence.[5] The words I shall utter will be fraught with

---

1 'Saukshmyam,' is literally 'minuteness,' It means ambiguity here. I have rendered Verse 81 very closely to give the reader an idea of the extreme terseness of these Verses. For bringing out the meaning of the Verse, the following illustration may serve. A sentence is composed containing some words each of which is employed in diverse senses, as the well-known Verse of Parasara which has been interpreted to sanction the remarriage of Hindu widows. Here, the object indicated by the words used are varied. Definite knowledge of the meaning of each word is arrived at by means of distinctions, *i.e.*, by distinguishing each meaning from every other. In such cases, the understanding before arriving at the definite meaning, rests in succession upon diverse points, now upon one, now upon another. Indeed, the true meaning is to be arrived at in such cases by a process of elimination. When such processes become necessary for seizing the sense of any sentence, the fault is said to be the fault of minuteness or ambiguity.—T.

2 To take the same example : first take the well-known words of Parasara as really sanctioning the remarriage of widows. Several words in the Verse would point to this meaning, several others would not. Weighing probabilities and reasons, let the meaning be tentatively adopted that second husbands are sanctioned by the Rishi for the Hindu widow. This is Sankhya.—T.

3 Having tentatively adopted the meaning the second husbands are sanctioned by the Verse referred to, the conclusion should be either its acceptance or rejection. By seeing the incompatibilty of the tentative meaning with other settled conclusions in respect of other texts other writers, the tentative meaning is capable of being rejected, and the final conclusion arrived at, to the effect, that the second husband is to be taken only according to the Niyoga-vidhi and not by marriage.—T.

4 By 'prayojanam' is meant the conduct one pursues for gratifying one's wish to acquire or avoid any object. Wish, in respect of either acquisition or avoidance, if ungratified, becomes a source of pain. The action or conduct that one adopts for removing that pain is called 'Prayojanam.' In the Gautama-sutras it is said that 'yamarthamadhikritya pravartate, tat prayojanam.' The two definitions are identical.—T.

5 By occurrence of these five characteristics together is meant that when these are properly attended to by a speaker or writer, only then can his sentence be said to be

sense, free from ambiguity (in consequence of each of them not being symbols of many things), logical, free from pleonasm or tautology, smooth, certain, free from bombast, agreeable or sweet, truthful, not inconsistent with the aggregate of three, (*viz*., Righteousness, Wealth and Pleasure), refined (*i.e*., free from Prakriti), not elliptical or imperfect, destitute of harshness or difficulty of comprehension, characterised by due order, not far-fetched in respect of sense, corrected with one another as cause and effect and each having a specific object.[1] I shall not tell thee anything, prompted by desire or wrath or fear or cupidity or abjectness or deceipt or shame or compassion or pride. (I answer thee because it is proper for me to answer what thou hast said). When the speaker, the hearer, and the words said, thoroughly agree with one another in course of a speech, then does the sense or meaning come out very clearly. When, in the matter of what is to be said, the speaker shows disregard for the understanding of the hearer by uttering words whose meaning is understood by himself, then, however good those words may be, they become incapable of being seized by the hearer.[2] That speaker, again, who, abandoning all regard for his own meaning, uses words that are of excellent sound and sense, awakens only erroneous impressions in the mind of the hearer. Such words in such connection become certainly faulty. That speaker, however, who employs words that are, while expressing his own meaning, intelligible to the hearer, as well, truly deserves to be called a speaker. No other man deserves the name. It behoveth thee, therefore, O king, to hear with concentrated attention these words of mine, fraught with meaning and endued with wealth of vocables. Thou hast asked me who I am, whose I am, whence I am coming, &c. Listen to me, O king, with undivided mind, as I answer these questions of thine. As lac and wood, as grains of dust and drops of water, exist commingled when brought together, even so are the existences of all creatures.[3] Sound, touch, taste, form, and scent, these and the senses, though diverse in respect of their essences, exist yet in a state of commingling like lac and wood. It is again well known that nobody asks any of these, saying, who art thou ? Each of them also has

---

complete and intelligible. In Nyaya philosophy, the five requisites are 'Pratijna,' 'Hetu,' 'Udaharana' 'Upanaya,' and 'Nigamana.' In the Mimansa philosophy, the five requisites have been named differently. 'Vishaya,' 'Samsaya,' 'Purvapaksha,' 'Uttara,' and 'Nirnaya.'—T.

1 These characteristics, the Commentator points out, though numbering sixteen, include the four and twenty mentioned by Bhojadeva in his Rhetoric called 'Saraswati-kanthabharana.'—T.

2 'Parartham' means, as the Commentator explains, 'of excellent sense.' It does not mean 'Paraprayojanam' as wrongly rendered by the Burdwan Translator. The latter's version of the text is thoroughly unmeaning.—T.

3 What Sulabha says here is this: the great primal elements are the same whether they make up this body or that other body; and then it is the same Chit that pervades

no knowledge either of itself or of the others. The eye cannot see itself. The ear cannot hear itself. The eye, again, cannot discharge the functions of any of the other senses, nor can any of the senses discharge the functions of any sense save its own. If all of them even combine together, even they fail to know their own selves as dust and water mingled together cannot know each other though existing in a state of union. In order to discharge their respective functions, they await the contact of objects that are external to them. The eye, form, and light, constitute the three requisites of the operation called seeing. The same, as in this case, happens in respect of the operations of the other senses and the ideas which is their result. Then, again, between the functions of the senses (called vision, hearing, &c.,) and the ideas which are their result (viz., form, sound, &c.), the mind is an entity other than the senses and is regarded to have an action of its own. With its help one distinguishes what is existent from what is non-existent for arriving at certainty (in the matter of all ideas derived from the senses). With the five senses of knowledge and five senses of action, the mind makes a total of eleven. The twelfth is the Understanding. When doubt arises in respect of what is to be known, the Understanding comes forward and settles all doubts (for aiding correct apprehension). After the twelfth, Sattwa is another principle numbering the thirteenth. With its help creatures are distinguished as possessing more of it or less of it in their constitutions.[1] After this, Consciousness (of self) is another principle (numbering the fourteenth). It helps one to an apprehension of self as distinguished from what is not self. Desire is the fifteenth principle, O king. Unto it inheres the whole universe.[2] The sixteenth principle is Avidya. Unto it inhere the seventeenth and the eighteenth principles called Prakriti and Vyakti (*i.e.*, Maya and Prakasa). Happiness and sorrow, decrepitude and death, acquisition and loss, the aggreable end the disagreeable,—these constitute the nineteenth principle and are called couples of opposites. Beyond the nineteenth principle is another, viz., Time called the twentieth. Know that the births and death of all creatures are due to the action of this twentieth principle. These twenty exist together. Besides these, the five Great primal elements, and existence and non-existence, bring up the tale to seven and twenty. Beyond

---

every combination of the great elements. The object of this observation is to show that Janaka should not have asked these questions about Sulabha, he and she being essentially the same person. To regard the two as different would indicate obscuration of vision.—T.

1 What is meant by this is that when creatures are said to possess more of sattwa and less of sattwa, sattwa seems to be a principle that is existent in the constitutions of creatures.—T.

2 By the word 'Kala' is meant the 16 principles beginning with Prana. What is intended to be said is that as long as the principle of Desire exists, rebirth becomes possible. The universe, therefore, rests on the principle of Desire or Vasana. The senses, &c., all arise from this principle of Vasana.—T.

these, are three others, named Vidhi, Sukra, and Vala, that make the tale reach thirty.[1] That in which these ten and twenty principles occur is said to be body. Some persons regard unmanifest Prakriti to be the source or cause of these thirty principles. (This is the view of the atheistic Sankhya school). The Kanadas of gross vision regard the Manifest (or atoms) to be their cause. Whether the Unmanifest or the Manifest be their cause, or whether the two (viz., the Supreme or Purusha and the Manifest or atoms) be regarded as their cause, or fourthly, whether the four together (viz., the Supreme or Purusha and his Maya and Jiva and Avidya or Ignorance) be the cause, they that are conversant with Adhyatma behold Prakriti as the cause of all creatures. That Prakriti which is Unmanifest, becomes manifest in the form of these principles. Myself, thyself, O monarch, and all others that are endued with body are the result of that Prakriti (so far as our bodies are concerned). Insemination and other (embryonic) conditions are due to the mixture of the vital seed and blood. In consequence of insemination the result which first appears is called by the name of 'Kalala.' From 'Kalala' arises what is called Vudvuda (bubble). From the stage called 'Vudvuda' springs what is called 'Pesi'. From the condition called 'Pesi' that stage arises in which the various limbs become manifested. From this last condition appear nails and hair. Upon the expiration of the ninth month, O king of Mithila, the creature takes its birth so that, its sex being known, it comes to be called a boy or girl. When the creature issues out of the womb, the form it presents is such that its nails and fingers seem to be of the hue of burnished copper. The next stage is said to be infancy, when the form that was seen at the time of birth becomes changed. From infancy youth is reached, and from youth, old age. As the creature advances from one stage into another, the form presented in the previous stage becomes changed. The constituent elements of the body, which serve diverse functions in the general economy, undergo change every moment in every creature. Those changes, however, are so minute that they cannot be noticed.[2] The birth of particles, and their death, in each successive condition, can not be marked, O king, even as one cannot mark the changes in the flame of a burning lamp.[3] When such is the state of the bodies of all creatures,

1 By 'Vidhi' is meant that righteousness and its reverse which constitute the seed of Desire. By 'sukra' is meant that which helps that seed to grow or put forth its rudiments. By 'Vala' is meant the exertion that one makes for 'gratifying one's desire.'—T.

2 The fact then of continual change of particles in the body was wellknown to the Hindu sages. This discovery is not new of modern physiology. Elsewhere it has been shown that Harvey's great discovery about the circulation of the blood was not unknown to the Rishis.—T.

3 The instance mentioned for illustrating the change of corporal particles is certainly a very happy one. The flame of a burning lamp, though perfectly steady (as

—that is when that which is called the body is changing incessantly even like the rapid locomotion of a steed of good mettle,—who then has come whence or not whence, or whose is it or whose is it not, or whence does it not arise ? What connection does there exist between creatures and their own bodies ?[1] As from the contact of flint with iron, or from two sticks of wood when rubbed against each other, fire is generated, even so are creatures generated from the combination of the (thirty) principles already named. Indeed, as thou thyself seest thy own body in thy body and as thou thyself seest thy soul in thy own soul, why is it that thou dost not see thy own body and thy own soul in the bodies and souls of others ? If it is true that thou seest an identity with thyself and others, why then didst thou ask me who I am and whose ? If it is true that hast, O king been freed from the knowledge of duality that (erroneously) says—this is mine and this other is not mine,—then what use is there with such questions as Who art thou, whose art thou and whence dost thou come ? What indications of Emancipation can be said to occur in that king who acts as others act towards enemies and allies and neutrals and in victory and truce and war ? What indications of Emancipation occur in him who does not know the true nature of the aggregate of three as manifested in seven ways in all acts and who, on that account, is attached to that aggregate of three ?[2] What indications of Emancipation exist in him who fails to cast an equal eye on the agreeable, on the weak, and the strong ? Unworthy as thou art of it, thy pretence to Emancipation should be put down by thy counsellers ! This thy endeavour to attain to Emancipation (when thou hast so many faults) is like the use of medicine by a patient who indulges in all kinds of forbidden food and practices. O chastiser of foes, reflecting upon spouses and other sources of attachment, one should behold these in one's own soul. What else can be looked upon as the indication of Emancipation ? Listen now to me as I speak in detail of these and certain other minute sources of attachment appertaining to the four well

---

in a breezeless spot), is really the result of the succesive combustion of particles of oil and the successive extinguishment of such combustion. Both this and the previous Verse have been rendered inaccurately by K. P. Singha.—T.

1 Hence the questions of Janaka, asking as to who the lady was or whose, were futile.—T.

2 The seven ways are as follow Righteousness and Wealth and Pleasure independently and distinct from one another count three, then the first and second, the first and third, and second and third, count three and lastly, all three existing together. In all acts, one or other of these seven may be found. The first and second exist in all acts whose result is the righteous acquisition of wealth ; the first and third exist in the procreation of children in lawful wedlock ; the second and third in ordinary acts of worldly men. Of acts in which all three combine, the rearing of children may be noticed, for it is at once a duty, a source of wealth, and a pleasure. K. P. Singha omits all reference to these seven ways, while the Burdwan translator, misunderstanding the gloss, makes utter nonsense of it.—T.

known acts (of lying down for slumber, enjoyment, eating, and dressing) to which thou art still bound though thou professest thyself to have adopted the religion of Emancipation. That man who has to rule the whole world must, indeed, be a single king without a second. He is obliged to live in only a single palace. In that palace he has again only one sleeping chamber. In that chamber he has, again, only one bed on which at night he is to lie down. Half that bed again he is obliged to give to his Queen-consort. This may serve as an example of how little the king's share is of all he is said to own. This is the case with his objects of enjoyment, with the food he eats, and with the robes he wears. He is thus attached to a very limited share of all things. He is, again, attached to the duties of rewarding and punishing. The king is always dependent on others. He enjoys a very small share of all he is supposed to own, and to that small share he is forced to be attached (as well as others are attached to their respective possessions). In the matter also of peace and war, the king cannot be said to be independent. In the matter of women, of sports and other kinds of enjoyment, the king's inclinations are exceedingly circumscribed. In the matter of taking counsel and in the assembly of; his councillors what independence can the king be said to have ? When, indeed, he sets his orders on other men, he is said to be thoroughly independent. But then the moment after, in the several matters of his orders, his independence is barred by the very men whom he has ordered.[1] If the king desires to sleep, he cannot gratify his desire, resisted by those who have business to transact with him. He must sleep when permitted, and while sleeping he is obliged to wake up for attending to those that have urgent business with him—Bathe, touch, drink, eat, pour libations on the fire, perform sacrifices, speak, hear,—these are the words which kings have to hear from others and hearing them have to slave to those that utter them. Men come in batches to the king and solicit him for gifts. Being, however, the protector of the general treasury, he cannot make gifts unto even the most deserving. If he makes gifts, the treasury becomes exhausted. If he does not, disappointed solicitors look upon him with hostile eyes. He becomes vexed and as the result of this, misanthropical feelings soon invade his mind. If many wise and heroic and wealthy men reside together, the king's mind begins to be filled with distrust in consequence. Even when there is no cause of fear, the king entertains fear of those that always wait upon and worship him. Those I have mentioned O king, also find fault with him. Behold, in what way the king's fears may arise from even them ! Then again all men are kings

1 The king may order some men to do somethings. These men, after obeying those orders, return to him to report the fact of what they have accomplished. The king is obliged to grant them interviews for listening to them.—T.

in their own houses. All men, again, in their own houses are householders. Like kings, O Janaka, all men in their own houses chastise and reward. Like kings others also have sons and spouses and their own selves and treasuries and friends and stores. In these respects the king is not different from other men.—The country is ruined,—the city is consumed by fire,—the foremost of elephants is dead,—at all this the king yields to grief like others, little regarding that these impressions are all due to ignorance and error. The king is seldom freed from mental griefs caused by desire and aversion and fear. He is generally afflicted also by headaches and diverse diseases of the kind. The king is afflicted (like others) by all couples of opposites (as pleasure and pain, &c). He is alarmed at everything. Indeed, full of foes and impediments as kingdom is, the king, while he enjoys it, passes nights of sleeplessness. Sovereignty, therefore, is blessed with an exceedingly small share of happiness. The misery with which it is endued is very great. It is as unsubstantial as burning flames fled by straw or the bubbles of froth seen on the surface of water. Who is there that would like to obtain sovereignty, or having acquired sovereignty can hope to win tranquillity? Thou regardest this kingdom and this palace to be thine. Thou thinkest also this army, this treasury, and these counsellers to belong to thee. Whose, however, in reality are they, and whose are they not? Allies, ministers, capital, provinces, punishment, treasury, and the king,—these seven which constitute the limbs of a kingdom exist, depending upon one another, like three sticks standing with one another's support. The merits of each are set off by the merits of the others. Which of them can be said to be superior to the rest? At those times those particular ones are regarded as distinguished above the rest when some important end is served through their agency. Superiority, for the time being, is said to attach to that one whose efficacy is thus seen. The seven limbs already mentioned, O best of kings, and the three others, forming an aggregate of ten, supporting one another, are said to enjoy the kingdom like the king himself.[1] That king who is endued with great energy and who is firmly attached to Kshatriya practices, should be satisfied with only a tenth part of the produce of the subject's field. Other kings are seen to be satisfied with less than a tenth part of such produce. There is no one who owns the kingly office without some one else owing it in the world, and there is no kingdom without a king.[2] If there be no kingdom, there can be no righteousness,

---

1 The Commentator explains that the three others are Vriddhi, Kshaya, and Sthana, all of which arise from policy. Some of the seven limbs are inanimate, such as the Treasury. But it is said that the Treasury supports the ministers, and the ministers support the Treasury.—T.

2 Hence, when every kingdom has a king, and kings too are many, no one should indulge in pride at the thought of his being a king.—T.

and if there be no righteousness, whence can Emancipation arise? Whatever merit is most sacred and the highest, belongs to kings and kingdoms.[1] By ruling a kingdom well, a king earns the merit that attaches to a Horse-sacrifice with the whole Earth given away as Dakshina. (But how many kings are there that rule their kingdoms well?) O ruler of Mithila, I can mention hundreds and thousands of faults like these that attach to kings and kingdoms. Then, again, when I have no real connection with even my body, how then can I be said to have any contact with the bodies of others? Thou canst not charge me with having endeavoured to bring about an intermixture of castes. Hast thou heard the religion of Emancipation in its entirety from the lips of Panchasikha together with its means, its methods, its practices, and its conclusion?[2] If thou hast prevailed over all thy bonds and freed thyself from all attachments, may I ask thee, O king, who thou preservest thy connections still with this umbrella and these other appendages of royalty? I think that thou hast not listened to the scriptures, or, thou hast listened to them without any advantage, or, perhaps, thou hast listened to some other treatises looking like the scriptures. It seems that thou art possessed only of worldly knowledge, and that like an ordinary man of the world thou art bound by the bonds of touch and spouses and mansions and the like. If it be true that thou hast been emancipated from all bonds, what harm have I done thee by entering thy person with only my Intellect? With Yatis, among all orders of men, the custom is to dwell in uninhabited or deserted abodes. What harm then have I done to whom by entering thy understanding which is truly of real knowledge? I have not touched thee, O king, with my hands, or arms, or feet, or thighs, O sinless one, or with any other part of the body. Thou art born in a high race. Thou hast modesty. Thou hast foresight. Whether the act has been good or bad, my entrance into thy body has been a private one, concerning us two only. Was it not improper for thee to publish that private act before all thy court? These Brahmanas are all worthy of respect. They are foremost of preceptors. Thou also art entitled to their respect, being their king. Doing them reverenee, thou art entitled to receive reverence from them. Reflecting on all this, it was not proper for thee to proclaim before these foremost of men the fact of this congress between

1 The object of this Verse is to show that as Janaka rules his kingdom without being attached to it, he cannot lay claim to the merit that belongs to kings.—.

2 'Upaya' or 'means' implies here the attitude of sitting (as in Yoga). 'Upanishad' or 'method' implies 'sravana and manana, i.e., listening and thinking. 'Upasanga' or 'practices' imply the several limbs of 'Dhyana,' &c. 'Nischaya' or 'conclusion' has reference to Brahma.—T.

two persons of opposite sexes, if, indeed, thou art really acquainted with the rules of propriety in respect of speech. O king of Mithila, I am staying in thee without touching thee at all even like a drop of water on a lotus leaf that stays on it without drenching it in the least. If, notwithstanding instructions of Panchasikha of the mendicant order, thy knowledge has become abstracted from the sensual objects to which it relates? Thou hast, it is plain, fallen off from the domestic mode of life but thou hast not yet attained to Emancipation that is so difficult to arrive at. Thou stayest between the two, pretending that thou hast reached the goal of Emancipation. The contact of one that is emancipated with another that has been so, or Purusha with Prakriti, cannot lead to an intermingling of the kind thou dreadest. Only those that regard the soul to be identical with the body, and that think the several orders and modes of life to be really different from one another, are open to the error of supposing an intermingling to be possible. My body is different from thine. But my soul is not different from thy soul. When I am able to realise this, I have not the slightest doubt that my understanding is really not staying in thine though I have entered into thee by Yoga.[1] A pot is borne in the hand. In the pot is milk. On the milk is a fly. Though the hand and pot, the pot and milk, and the milk and the fly, exist together, yet are they all distinct from each other. The pot does not partake the nature of the milk. Nor does the milk partake the nature of the fly. The condition of each is dependent on itself, and can never be altered by the condition of that other with which it may temporarily exist. After this manner, colour and practices, though they may exist together with and in a person that is emancipate, do not really attach to him. How then can an intermingling of orders be possible in consequence of this union of myself with thee? Then, again, I am not superior to thee in colour. Nor am I a Vaisya, nor a Sudra. I am, O king, of the same order with thee, born of a pure race. There was a royal sage of the name of Pradhana. It is evident that thou hast heard of him. I am born in his race, and my name is Sulabha. In the sacrifices performed by my ancestors, the foremost of the gods, *viz.*, Indra, used to come, accompanied by Drona and Satasringa, and Chakradwara (and other presiding geniuses of the great mountains). Born in such a race, it was found that no husband could be obtained for me that would be fit for me. Instructed then in the religion of Emancipation, I wander over the Earth alone, observant of the practices of asceticism. I practise no hypocrisy in the matter of the life of Renunciation. I am not a thief that appropriates what belongs to others. I am not a confuser of the practices belonging to the

1 I expand this Verse fully.—T.

different orders. I am firm in the practices that belong to that mode of life to which I properly belong. I am firm and steady in my vows. I never utter any word without reflecting on its propriety. I did not come to thee, without having deliberated properly, O monarch! Having heard that thy understanding has been purified by the religion of Emancipation, I came here from desire of some benefit. Indeed, it was for enquiring of thee about Emancipation that I had come. I do not say it for glorifying myself and humiliating my opponents. But I say it, impelled by sincerity only. What I say is he that is emancipated never indulges in that intellectual gladiatorship which is implied by a dialectical disputation for the sake of victory. He, on the other hand, is really emancipate who devotes himself to Brahma, that sole seat of tranquillity.[1] As a person of the mendicant order resides for only one night in an empty house (and leaves it the next morning), even after the same manner I shall reside for this one night in thy person (which, as I have already said, is like an empty chamber, being destitute of knowledge). Thou hast honoured me with both speech and other offers that are due from a host to a guest. Having slept this one night in thy person, O ruler of Mithila, which is as it were my own chamber now, tomorrow I shall depart.—

"Bhishma continued,—'Hearing these words fraught with excellent sense and with reason, king Janaka failed to return any answer thereto.[2]' "

SECTION CCCXXII

"Yudhishthira said,—'How was Suka, the son of Vyasa, in days of old, won over to Renunciation? I desire to hear thee recite the story. My curiosity in this respect is irrepressible. It behoveth thee, O thou of Kuru's race, to discourse to me on the conclusions in respect of the Unmanifest (Cause), the Manifest (Effects), and of the Truth (or Brahma) that is in, but unattached to, them, as also of the acts of the self-born Narayana, as they are known to thy understanding.

---

1 The 'na' in the second line is connected with 'Vyayachchate.'—T.

2 The object of this Verse is to show that the words uttered by Sulabha were unanswerable. To attain to Emancipation one must practice a life of Renunciation instead of continuing in the domestic mode.—T.

"Bhishma said,—'Beholding his son Suka living fearlessly as ordinary men do in practices that are considered harmless by them, Vyasa taught him the entire Vedas and then discoursed to him one day in these words.

" 'Vyasa said,—O son, becoming the master of the senses, do thou subdue extreme cold and extreme heat, hunger and thirst, and the wind also, and having subdued them (as Yogins do), do thou practise righteousness. Do thou duly observe truth and sincerity, and freedom from wrath and malice, and self-restraint and penances, and the duties of benevolence and compassion. Rest thou on truth, firmly devoted to righteousness, abandoning all sort of insincerity and deceit. Do thou support thy life on what remains of food after feeding gods and guests. Thy body is as transitory as the froth on the surface of water. The Jiva-soul is sitting unattached in it as a bird on a tree. The companionship of all agreeable object is exceedingly short-lived. Why then, O son, dost thou sleep in such forgetfulness? Thy foes are heedful and awake and ever ready (to spring on thee) and always watchful of their opportunity. Why art thou so foolish as not to know this?[1] As the days are going one after another, the period of thy life is being lessened. Indeed when thy life is being incessantly shortened, why dost thou not run to preceptors (for learning the means of rescue)? Only they that are destitute of faith (in the existence of next life) set their hearts on things of this world that have the only effect of increasing flesh and blood. They are totally unmindful of all that is concerned with the next world. Those men that are stupefied by erroneous understandings display a hatred for righteousness. The man who walks after those misguided persons that have betaken themselves to devious and wrong paths is afflicted equally with them. They however, that are contented, devoted to the scriptures, endued with high souls, and possessed of great might, betake themselves to the part of righteousness. Do thou wait upon them with reverence and seek instruction from them. Do thou act according to the instructions received from those wise men whose eyes are set upon righteousness. With understanding cleansed by such lessons and rendered superior, do thou then restrain thy heart which is ever ready to deviate from the right course. They whose understandings are always concerned with the present, who fearlessly regard the tomorrow as something quite remote,—they who do not observe any restrictions in the matter of food,—are really senseless persons that fail to understand that this world is only a field of probation.[2] Repairing

---

1 These foes are, of course, the passions,—T.

2 Literally, 'the world is only a field of action,' implying that creatures, coming here, have to act: these actions lead to rewards and punishments, both here and hereafter. The way to Emancipation is, as has been

to the flight of steps constituted by Righteousness, do thou ascend those steps one after another. At present thou art like a worm that is employed in weaving its cocoon round itself and thereby depriving itself of all means of escape. Do thou keep to thy left, without any scruple, the atheist who transgresses all restraints, who is situated like a house by the side of a fierce and encroaching current, (for the destruction he courts), and who (to others) seems to stand like a bamboo with its tall head erected in pride.[1] Do thou with the raft of Yoga, cross the ocean of the world whose waters are constituted by thy five senses. Having Desire and Wrath and Death for its fierce monsters, and owning birth for its vortex. Do thou cross, with the raft of Righteousness, the world that is affected by Death and afflicted by Decrepitude, and upon which the thunder-bolts constituted by days and nights are falling incessantly. When Death is seeking thee at all moments, *viz.*, when thou art sitting or lying down, it is certain that Death may get thee for his victim at any time. Whence art thou to obtain thy rescue ! Like the she-wolf snatching away a lamb, Death snatches away one that is still engaged in earning wealth and still unsatisfied in the indulgence of his pleasures. When thou art destined to enter into the dark, do thou hold up the blazing lamp made of righteous understanding and whose flame has been well-husbanded out. Falling into various forms one after another in the world of men, a creature obtains the status of Brahmanhood with great difficulty. Thou hast obtained that status. Do thou then, O son endeavour to maintain it (properly).[2] A Brahmana hath not been born for the gratification of desire. On the other hand, his body is intended to be subjected to mortification and penances in this world so that incomparable happiness may be his in the next world. The status of Brahmanhood is acquired with the aid of long-continued and austere penances. Having acquired that status, one should never waste one's time in the indulgence of one's senses. Always engaged in penances and self-restraint and desirous of what is for thy good, do thou live and act, devoted to peace and tranquillity. The period of life, of every man, is like a steed. The nature of that steed is unmanifest. The (sixteen) elements (mentioned before) constitute its body. Its nature is

---

often shown before, by exhausting the consequences of acts by enjoyment or sufferance and by abstaining, from further acts by adopting the religion of Nivritti.—T.

1 'Kulapatam' is explained by the Commentator as 'Mahanadipuram,' In Naram' &c, 'venumivodahritam' (as in the Bombay text) or 'venumivoddhhatam' (as in the Bengal text) is rather unintelligible unless it be taken in the sense in which I have taken it. K. P. Singha mistranslates 'Kulapatam,' and the Burdwan translator misunderstands both 'Kulaparam' and venumivoddhatam.'—T.

2 I. e., to uphold it by doing the duties of a Brahmana.—T.

exceedingly subtile. Kshanas, and Trutis, and Nimeshas are the hair on its body. The twilights constitute its shoulder-joints. The lighted and the dark fortnights are its two eyes of equal power. Months are its other limbs. That steed is running incessantly. If thy eyes be not blind, beholding then that steed incessantly moving forward in its invisible course, do thou set thy heart on righteousness, after hearing what thy preceptors have to say on the question of the next world. They that fall away from righteousness and that conduct themselves recklessly, that always display malice towards others and betake themselves to evil ways are obliged to assume (physical) bodies in the regions of Yama and suffer diverse afflictions, in consequence of their unrighteous acts of diverse kind.[1] That king who is devoted to righteousness and who protects and chastises the good and the wicked with discrimination, attains to those regions that belong to man of righteous deeds. By doing diverse kinds of good acts, he attains to such felicity as is faultless and as is incapable of being attained to by undergoing even thousands of births.[2] Furious dogs of frightful mien, crows of iron beaks, flocks of ravens and vultures and other birds, and blood-sucking worms, assail the man who transgresses the commands of his parents and preceptors when he goes to hell after death.[3] That sinful wretch who, in consequence of his recklessness, transgresses the ten boundaries that have been fixed by the Self-born himself, is obliged to pass his time in great affliction in the wild wastes that occur in the dominions of the king of Pitris.[4] That man who is tainted with cupidity, who is in love with untruth, who always takes a delight in deception and cheating, and who does injuries to others by practising hypocrisy and deception, has to go to deep hell and suffer great woe and affliction for his acts of wickedness. Such a man is forced to bathe in the broad river called Vaitarani whose waters are scalding, to enter into a forest of trees whose leaves are as sharp as swords, and then to lie down on a bed of

1 'Prachalita-dharma &c., implies those that have fallen away from righteousness. The Burdwan translator misunderstands the Verse. 'Karanabhih' is 'kriabhih.'—T.

2 The Commentator explains that this Verse is for assuring Yudhishthira that kings are competent to obtain felicity in the next world. 'Anupagatam' is explained by the Commentator as 'not attainable in even thousands of births.'—T.

3 'Rudhirapah' is blood-sucking worms. 'Uparatam' is dead.—T.

4 The ten boundaries or commandments, as mentioned by the Commentator, are the five positive ones, viz,, Purity, Contentment, Penances, Study of the Vedas, Meditation on God, and the five negative ones, viz., abstention from cruelty, from untruth, from theft, from non-observance of vows, and from acquisition of wealth.—T.

battle-axes. He has thus to pass his days in frightful hell in great affliction. Thou beholdest only the regions of Brahman and other deities, but thou art blind to that which is the highest (viz., Emancipation). Alas, thou art ever blind also to that which brings Death on its train (viz., decrepitude and old age).[1] Go (along the path of Emancipation)! Why tarriest thou? A frightful terror, destructive of thy happiness, is before thee! Do thou take prompt steps for achieving thy Emancipation! Soon after death thou art sure to be taken before Yama at his command. For obtaining felicity in the next world, strive to attain to righteousness through the practice of difficult and austere vows. The puissant Yama, regardless of the sufferings of others, very soon takes the lives of all persons, that is of thyself and thy friends. There is none capable of resisting him. Very soon the wind of Yama will blow before thee (and drive thee to his presence). Very soon wilt thou be taken to that dread presence all alone. Do thou achieve what will be for thy good there. Where now is that Death-wind which will blow before thee very soon? (Art thou mindful of it?) Very soon will the points of the compass, when that moment arrives, begin to whirl before thy eyes. (Art thou mindful of that?) O son, soon (when that mement comes) will thy Vedas disappear from thy sight as thou goest helplessly into that dread presence. Do thou, therefore, set thy heart on Yoga abstraction which is possessed of great excellence.[2] Do thou seek to attain that one only treasure so that thou mayst not have to grieve at the recollection (after Death) of thy former deeds good and bad all of which are characterised by error.[3] Decrepitude very soon weakens thy body and robs thee of thy strength and limbs and beauty. Do thou, therefore, seek that one only treasure. Very soon the Destroyer, with Disease for his charioteer, will with a strong hand, for taking thy life, pierce and break thy body. Do thou, therefore, practise austere penance. Very soon will, those terrible wolves that reside within thy body, assail thee from every side. Do thou endeavour, therefore, to achieve acts of righteousness.[4] Very soon

---

1 'Chirasya' is grammatically connected with 'na vudhyase,' meaning that 'thou art always blind &c.' The Burdwan translator misunderstands it completely and takes it as equivalent to 'achirena.' K. P. Singha skips over it.—T.

2 The Burdwan translator gives a ridiculous version of the Verse.—T.

3 'Kevalam nidhim' is literally, 'one only treasure'. It may imply either Samadhi or Brahma. Acts, whether good or bad, all arise from error. Abstention from acts is the true way to Emancipation.—T.

4 The passions are spoken of as wolves.—T.

wilt thou, all alone, behold a thick darkness, and very soon wilt thou behold golden trees on the top of the hill. Do thou, therefore, hasten to achieve acts of righteousness.[1] Very soon will those evil campanions and foes of thine, (*viz.*, the senses), dressed in the guise of friends, swerve thee from correct vision. Do thou, then, O son, strive to achieve that which is of the highest good. Do thou earn that wealth which has no fear from either kings or thieves, and which one has not to abandon even at Death. Earned by one's own acts, that wealth has never to be divided among co-owners. Each enjoys that wealth (in the other world) which each has earned for himself. O son, give that to others by which they may be able to live in the next world. Do thou also set thyself to the acquisition of that wealth which is indestructible and durable. Do not think that thou shouldst first enjoy all kinds of pleasures and then turn thy heart on Emancipation, for before thou art satiated with enjoyment thou mayst be overtaken by Death. Do thou, in view of this, hasten to do acts of goodness.[2] Neither mother, nor son, nor relatives, nor dear friends even when solicited with honours, accompany the man that dies. To the regions of Yama one has to go oneself, unaccompanied by any one. Only those deeds, good and bad, that one did before death accompany the man that goes to the other world. The gold and gems that one has earned by good and bad means do not become productive of any benefit to one when one's body meets with dissolution. Of men that have gone to the other world, there is no witness, better than the soul, of all act done and undone in life. That when the acting-Chaitanya (Jiva-soul) enters into the witness-Chaitanya the destruction of the body takes place, is seen by Yoga-intelligence when Yogins enter the firmament of their hearts.[3] Even here, the god of Fire, the Sun, and the Wind,—these three reside in the body. These, beholding as they do all the practices of one's life become one's witnesses. Days and Nights,—the former characterised by the virtue of displaying all things and the latter characterised by the virtue of concealing all things,—are running incessantly and touching all things (and thereby lessening their allotted periods of existence). Do thou, therefore, be

---

1 The sight of golden trees is a premonitory sign of Death.—T.

2 Literally rendered, the Verse would run thus : 'Before the cooking is complete of the Yavaka of a rich man, in fact, while it is still uncooked, thou mayst meet with death.' Do thou, therefore, hasten.' By 'Yavaka' is meant a particular kind of food made of ghee and flour or barley.—T.

3 In Verse 53 it is said that the Soul is the witness in the other world of all acts and omission in this life. In Verse 54, what is said is that the existence of the Soul when the body is not, is possible, for Yogins, in Yoga, live in their Soul, unconscious the while of their bodies. The entrance of the acting-Chaitanya into that Chaitanya which survives as the witness means the death of the body.—T.

observant of the duties of thy own order.[1] The road in the other world (that leads to the regions of Yama), is infested by many foes (in the form of iron-beaked birds and wolves) and by many repulsive and terrible insects and worms. Do thou take care of thy own acts, for only acts will accompany you along that road. There one has not to share one's acts with others, but every one enjoys or endures the fruits of those acts which every one has himself performed. As Apsaras and great Rishis attain to fruits of great felicity, after the same manner, men of righteous deeds, as the fruits of their respective righteous acts, obtain in the other world cars of transcendent brightness that move everywhere at the will of the riders. Men of stainless deeds and cleansed souls and pure birth obtain in the next world fruits that correspond with their own righteous acts in this life. By walking along the high road constituted by the duties of domesticity, men acquire happy ends by attaining to the region of Prajapati or Vrihaspati or of him of a hundred sacrifices. I can give thee thousands and thousands of instructions. Know, however, that the puissant cleanser (*viz.*, Righteousness), keeps all foolish persons in the Dark.[2] Thou hast passed four and twenty years. Thou art now full five and twenty years of age. Thy years are passing away. Do thou be in to lay thy store of righteousness. The Destroyer that dwells within error and heedlessness will very soon deprive thy senses of their respective powers. Do thou before that consummation is brought about, hasten to observe thy duties, relying on thy body alone.[3] When it is thy duty to go along that road in which thyself only shalt be in front and thyself only in the rear, what need then hast thou with either thy body or thy spouse and children?[4] When men have to go individually and without companions to the region of Yama, it is plain that in view of such a situation of terror, thou shouldst seek to acquire that one only treasure (*viz.*, Righteousness or Yoga-samadhi). The puissant Yama, regardless of the afflictions of others, snatches, away the friends and relatives of one's race by the very roots.

---

1 The Burdwan translator gives an erroneous version of this Verse.—T.

2 I think the sense is that only righteousness can bring a man to the path that leads to happiness and not mere instructions howsoever repeated—T.

3 The Commentator explains that 'Pramadagah' is equivalent to Pramadagrihavasin and refers to 'Antakah.' Chamum' is 'Indriyasenam 'Grahitam' is body. 'Yathagrahitam' is 'dehamanatikramya.' In this Verse 'pura' may mean either 'in the near future' or 'soon,' or 'pura' may mean 'before,' *i.e.*, 'before the Destroyer makes thy senses so, &c.'—T.

4 The road in which thyself shalt be in front and thyself in the rear' is the road of Self-knowledge. The Burdwan translator does not understand how the first line comes to mean 'Knowledge of Self! accordingly, though he uses the word 'atmajnana' (following the Commentator), yet he erroneously repeats some of the words used in the line.—T.

There is no one that can resist him. Do thou, therefore, seek to acquire a stock of righteousness I impart to thee these lessons, O son, that are all agreeable with the scriptures I follow. Do thou observe them by acting according to their import. He who supports his body by following the duties laid down for his own order, and who makes gifts for earning whatever fruits may attach to such acts, becomes freed from the consequences that are born of ignorance and error.[1] The knowledge which a man of righteous deeds acquires from Vedic declarations leads to omniscience. That omniscience is identical with the science of the highest object of human acquisition (*viz.*, Emancipation). Instruction, imparated to the grateful, became beneficial (in consequence of their leading to the attainment of that highest object of human acquisition).[2] The pleasure that one takes in living amidst the habitations of men is truly a fast-binding cord. Breaking that cord, men of righteous deeds repair to regions of great felicity. Wicked men, however, fail to break that bond. What use hast thou of wealth, O son, or with relatives, or with children, since thou hast to die: Do thou employ thyself in seeking for thy soul which is hidden in a cave. Where have all thy grandsires gone? Do that today which thou wouldst keep for tomorrow. Do that in the forenoon which thou wouldst keep for the afternoon. Death does not wait for any one, to see whether one has or has not accomplished one's task. Following the body after one's death (to the crematorium), one's relatives and kinsmen and friends come back, throwing it on the funeral pyre. Without a scruple do thou avoid those men that are sceptics, that are destitute of compassion, and that are devoted to wicked ways, and do thou endeavour to seek, without listlessness or apathy, that which is for thy highest good. When, therefore, the world is thus afflicted by Death, do thou, with thy whole heart, achieve righteousness, aided all the while by unswerving patience. That man who is well conversant with the means of attaining to Emancipation and who duly discharges the duties of his order, certainly attains to great felicity in the other world. For thee that dost not recognise death in the attainment of a different body and that dost not deviate from the path trod by the righteous, there is no destruction. He that increases the stock of righteousness is truly wise. He, on the other hand, that falls away

---

1 The last word of the second line is 'muchyate' and not yujyate.' If yujyate' be adhered to, meaning would be 'freed the consequences of ignorance and error, he would succeed in attaining to Brahma.—T.

2 This is a very abstruse Verse. I have rendered it, following the lead of the Commentator, 'Srutam,' he explains is 'the knowledge, born of vedic declarations like *Tattwamasi* &c. 'Sarvamasnute' is equivalent to 'samastam Brahmandam vyapnoti,' meaning 'such knowledge leads to *sarvatmyam*, *i.e.*, omniscience' 'Tadetat-&c.,' is 'that omniscience is the *darsanam*, of param-purushartha or Mokhsa.' Kritajna upadishtam artham' is 'sambitam.'—T.

from righteousness is said to be a fool. One that is engaged in the accomplishment of good deeds attains to heaven and other rewards as the fruits of those deeds ; but he that is devoted to wicked deeds has to sink in hell. Having acquired the status of humanity, so difficult of acquisition, that is the stepping-stone to heaven, one should fix one's soul on Brahma so that one may not fall away once more. That man whose understanding, directed to the path of heaven, does not deviate therefrom, is regarded by the wise as truly a man of righteousness and when he dies his friends should indulge in grief. That man whose understanding is not restless and which is directed to Brahma and who has attained to heaven, becomes freed from a great terror (*viz.*, hell). They that are born in retreats of ascetics and that die there, do not earn much merit by abstaining all their life from enjoyments and the indulgence of desire. He, however, who though possessed of objects of enjoyment casts them off and engages himself in the practice of penances, succeeds in acquiring everything. The fruits of the penances of such a man are, I think, much higher. Mothers and sires and sons and spouses, by hundreds and thousands, every one had and will have in this world. Who, however, were they and whose are we ?[1] I am quite alone. I have no one whom I may call mine. Nor do I belong to any one else. I do not see that person whose I am, nor do I see him whom I may call mine. They have nothing to do with thee. Thou hast nothing to do with them. All creatures take birth agreeably to their acts of past lives. Thou also shalt have to go hence (for taking birth in a new order) determined by thy own acts. In this world it is seen that the friends and followers of only those that are rich behave towards the rich with devotion. The friends and followers of those, however, that are poor fall away during even the life-time of the poor. Man commits numerous evil acts for the sake of his wife (and children). From those evil acts he derives much distress both here and hereafter. The wise man beholds the world of life devastated by the acts performed by every living being. Do thou, therefore, O son, act according to all the instructions I have given thee ! The man possessed of true vision, beholding this world to be only a field of action, should, from desire of felicity in the next world, do acts that are good. Time, exerting his irresistible strength, cooks all creatures (in his own cauldron), with the aid of his ladle constituted by months and seasons, the sun for his fire, and days and nights for his fuel,—days and nights, that is that are the witnesses of the fruits of every act

1 The sense is that in course of our repeated rebirths we have got these relations repeatedly and will get them as repeatedly. But we are, in reality, quite unconnected with them. Their union with us like the union of pieces of wood floating in a river, now joined together temporarily, now separated—T.

done by every creature. For what purpose is that wealth which is not given away and which is not enjoyed ? For what purpose is that strength which is not employed in resisting or subjugating one's foes ? For what purpose is that knowledge of the scriptures which does not impel one to deeds of righteousness ? And for what purpose is that soul which does not subjugate the senses and abstain from evil acts ?—

"Bhishma continued,—'Having heard these beneficial words spoken by the Island-born (Vyasa), Suka, leaving his sire, proceeded to seek a preceptor that could teach him the religion of Emancipation.' "[1]

SECTION CCCXXIII

"Yudhishthira said,—'If there is any efficacy in gifts, in sacrifices, in penances well-performed, and in dutiful services rendered to preceptors and other reverend seniors, do thou, O grandsire, speak of the same to me !'

"Bhishma said,—'An understanding associated with evil causes the mind to fall into sin. In this state one stains one's acts, and then falls into great distress. Those that are of sinful acts have to take birth as persons of very indigent circumstances. From famine to famine, from pain to pain, from fear to fear, is their change. They are more dead than those that are dead. Possessed of affluence, from joy to joy, from heaven to heaven, from happiness to happiness, proceed they that are possessed of faith, that are self-restrained, and that are devoted to righteous deeds. They that are unbelievers have to pass, with groping hands, through regions infested by beasts of prey and elephants and pathless tracts teeming with snakes and robbers and other causes of fear. What more need be said of these ? They, on the other hand, that are endued with reverence for gods and guests, that are liberal, that have proper regard for persons that are good, and that make gifts in sacrifices, have for theirs the path (of felicity) that belongs to men of cleansed and subdued souls. Those that are not righteous should not be counted among men even as grains without kennel are not counted among grain and as cockroaches are not counted among birds. The acts that one does, follow one even when one runs fast. Whatever acts one does, lie down with the doer who lays himself down. Indeed, the sins one does, sit when the doer sits, and run when he runs. The sins act when the doer

1 'Mokshadaisikam' is explained by the Commentator as 'Mokshahdeshataram.' K. P. Singha wrongly renders this word. This Section is called 'pavakadhyayanam,' meaning 'chitta-sodhakadhyayanam,' that is, the Lesson which, when read and mastered, is to lead to the cleansing of the heart.—T.

acts, and, in fact follow the doer like his shadow. Whatever the acts one does by whatever means and under whatever circumstances, are sure to be enjoyed and endured (in respect of their fruits) by the doer in his next life. From every side Time is always dragging all creatures, duly observing the rule in respect of the distance to which they are thrown and which is commensurate with their acts.[1] As flowers and fruits, without being urged, never suffer their proper time to pass away without making their appearance, even so the acts one has done in past life make their appearance at the proper time. Honour and dishonour, gain and loss, destruction and growth, are seen to set in. No one can resist them (when they come). None of them is enduring, for disappear it must after appearance. The sorrows one suffers is the result of one's acts. The happiness one enjoys flows from one's acts. From the time when one lies within the mother's womb one begins to enjoy and endure one's acts of a past life. Whatever acts good and bad one does in childhood, youth, or old age, one enjoys and endures their consequences in one's next life in similar ages. As the calf recognises its dam even when the latter may stand among thousands of her species, after the same manner the acts done by one in one's past life come to one in one's next life (without any mistake) although one may live among thousands of one's species. As a piece of dirty cloth is whitened by being washed in water, after the same manner, the righteous, cleansed by continuous exposure unto the fire of fasts and penances, at last attain to unending happiness. O thou of high intelligence, the desires and purposes of those whose sins have been washed off by long-continued penances well-performed, become crowned with fruition. The track of the righteous cannot be discerned even as that of birds in the sky or that of fishes in the water. There is no need of speaking ill of others ; nor of reciting the instances in which others have tripped. On the other hand, one should always do what is delightful, agreeable, and beneficial to one's own self.[2]' "

---

1 Time, as a personified agent, is throwing all creatures at unequal distances. Some are thrown near and some to a great distance. These distances are regulated by the nature of the acts done by the creatures thrown. Some are cast among animals, some among men. Throwing or hurling them thus, Time drags them again, the binding-cords being always in his hands.—T.

2 Both the Vernacular translators have misunderstood the first line of this verse although there is no difficulty in it. Apastamva says 'drishto dharma-vyatikrama ; Sahasancha purvesham.' What Bhishma says here is that one should not speak of those instances of 'Vyatikramah' and Sahasam.—T.

SECTION CCCXXIV

"Yudhishthira said,—'Tell me, O grandsire, how the high-souled Suka of austere penances took birth as the son of Vyasa, and how did he succeed in attaining to the highest success? Upon what woman did Vyasa, endued with wealth of asceticism, beget that son of his? We do not know who was Suka's mother, nor do we know anything of the birth of that high-souled ascetic. How was it that, when he was a mere boy, his mind became directed to the knowledge of the subtile (Brahma)? Indeed, in this world no second person can be seen in whom such predilections could be marked at so early an age. I desire to hear all this in detail, O thou of great intelligence. I am never satiated with hearing thy excellent and nectar-like words. Tell me, O grandsire, in their proper order, of the greatness, and the knowledge of Suka and of his union with the (Supreme) Soul!'

"Bhishma continued,—'The Rishis did not make merit depend upon years or decrepitude or wealth or friends. They said that he amongst them was great that studied the Vedas. All this that thou enquirest about has penances for its root. That penance, again, O son of Pandu, arises from the subjugation of the senses. Without doubt, one incurs fault by giving one's senses the reins. It is only by restraining them that one succeeds in earning success. The merit that attaches to a thousand Horse-sacrifices or a hundred Vajapeyas cannot come up to even a sixteenth portion of the merit that arises from Yoga. I shall, on the present occasion, recite to thee the circumstances of Suka's birth, the fruits he won of his penances, and the foremost end he achieved (by his acts), topics that are incapable of being understood by persons of uncleansed soul. Once on a time on the summit of Meru adorned with *Karnikara* flowers, Mahadeva sported, accompanied by the terrible spirits that were his associates. The daughter of the king of mountains, *viz*, the goddess Parvati, was also there. There at the close vicinity of that summit, the Island-born (Vyasa) underwent extraordinary austerities. O best of the Kurus, devoted to the practices of Yoga, the great ascetic withdrawing himself by Yoga into his own Soul, and engaged in Dharana, practised many austerities for the sake of (obtaining) a son. The prayer he addressed to the great God was,—O puissant one, let me have a son that will have the puissance of Fire and Earth and Water and Wind and Space. Engaged in the austerest of penances, the Island-born Rishi begged of that great God who is incapable of being approached by persons of uncleansed souls, (not by words but) by his Yoga-resolution. The puissant Vyasa remained there for a hundred years, subsisting on air alone, engaged in adoring Mahadeva of multifarious form, the lord of Uma. Thither all the regenerate Rishis and royal sages and the Regents of the world and the Sadhyas along with the Vasus, and the Adityas, the Rudras, and Surya and Chandramas, and the Maruts, and the Oceans, and the Rivers and the Aswins, the Deities, the Gandharvas, and Narada and Parvata and the Gandharva Viswavasu, and the Siddhas, and the Apsaras. There Mahadeva, called also by the name of Rudra, sat, decked with an excellent garland of Karnikara flowers, and blazed with efulgence like the Moon with his rays. In those delightful and celestial woods populous with deities and heavenly Rishis, the great Rishi remained, engaged in high Yoga-contemplation, from desire of obtaining a son. His strength suffered no diminution, nor did he feel any pain. At this the three worlds were much amazed. While the Rishi, possessed of immeasurable energy, sat in Yoga, his matted locks, in consequence of his energy, were seen to blaze like flames of fire. The illustrious Markandeya it was from whom I heard of this. He used always to recite to me the acts of the deities. It is for this that the matted locks of the high-souled and (Island-born) Krishna, thus emblazed by his energy on that occasion, seem to this day to be endued with the complexion of fire. Gratified with such penances and such devotion, O Bharata, of the Rishi, the great God resolved (to grant him his wish). The Three-eyed deity, smiling with pleasure, addressed him and said,—O Island-born one, thou shalt get a son like to what thou wishest! Possessed of greatness, he shall be as pure as Fire, as Wind, as Earth, as Water, and as Space! He shall be possessed of the consciousness of his being Brahma's self; his understanding and soul shall be devoted to Brahma, and he shall completely depend upon Brahma so as to be indentifiable with it!—' "

SECTION CCCXXV

"Bhishma said,—'The son of Satyavati having obtained this high boon from the great God, was one day employed in rubbing his sticks for making a fire. While thus engaged, the illustrious Rishi, O king, beheld the Apsara Ghritachi, who, in consequence of her energy, was then possessed of great beauty. Beholding the Apsara in those woods, the illustrious Rishi Vyasa, O Yudhishthira, became suddenly smitten with desire. The Apsara (Ghritachi), seeing the Rishi's heart troubled by desire, transformed herself into a she-parrot and came to that spot. Although he beheld the Apsara disguised in another form, the desire that had arisen in the Rishi's heart (without disappearing) spread itself over very part of his body. Summoning all his patience, the ascetic endeavour to suppress that desire. With all his effort, however, Vyasa did not succeed in controlling his agitated mind. In consequence of the inevitability of what was to happen, the Rishi's heart was attracted by Ghritachi's fair form. He set himself more earnestly to the task of making a fire for suppressing his emotion, but in spite of all his efforts his vital seed came out. That best of regenerate ones, however, O king, continued to rub his stick without feeling any scruples for what had happened. From the seed that fell, was born a son unto him, called Suka. In consequence of this circumstance attending his birth, he came to be called by name of Suka. Indeed, it was thus that great ascetic that foremost of Rishis and highest of Yogins, took birth from the two sticks (his father had for making fire). As in a sacrifice a blazing fire shed its effulgence all around when libations of clarified butter are poured upon it, after the same manner did Suka take his birth, blazing with effulgence in consequence of his own energy. Assuming the excellent form and complexion that were his sire, Suka, O son of Kuru, of cleansed Soul, shone like a smokeless fire. The foremost of rivers, *viz*, Ganga, O king, coming to the breast of Meru, in her own embodied form, bathed Suka (after his birth) with her waters. There fell from the welkin, O son of Kuru, an ascetic's stick and a dark deer-skin for the use, O monarch, of the high-souled Suka. The Gandharvas sang repeatedly and the diverse tribes of Apsaras danced; and celestial kettledrums of loud sound began to beat. The Gandharva Viswavasu, and Tumvuru and Narada, and those other Gandharvas called by the names of Haha, and Huhu, eulogised the birth of Suka. There the regents of the world with Sakra at their head came, as also the deities and the celestial and the regenerate Rishis. The Wind-god poured showers of celestial flowers upon the spot. The entire universe, mobile, and immobile, became, filled with joy. The high-souled Mahadeva of great effulgence, accompanied by the Goddess, and moved by affection, came there and soon after the birth of the Muni's son invested him with the sacred thread. Sakra, the chief of the gods, gave him, from affection, a celestial Kamandalu of excellent form, and some celestial robes. Swans and Satapatras and cranes by thousands, and many parrots and Chasas, O Bharata, wheeled over his head. Endued with great splendour and intelligence, Suka, having obtained his birth from the two sticks, continued to live there, engaged the while in the attentive observance of many vows and fasts. As soon as Suka was born, the Vedas with all their mysteries and all their abstracts, came for dwelling in him, O king, even as they dwell in his sire. For all that, Suka selected Vrihaspati, who was conversant with all the Vedas together with their branches and commentaries, for his preceptor, remembering the universal practice.[1] Having studied

1 Although the Vedas came to Suka of their own accord, yet he was

all the Vedas together will all their mysteries and abstracts, as also all the histories and the science of government, O puissant monarch, the great ascetic returned home, after giving his preceptor the tuition-fee. Adopting the vow of a Brahmacharin, he then commenced to practise the austerest penances concentrating all his attention thereon. In even his childhood, he bacame an object of respect with the gods and Rishis for his knowledge and penances. The mind of the great ascetic, O king, took no pleasure in the three modes of life with the domestic among them, keeping in view, as he did, the religion of Emancipation.' "

SECTION CCCXXVI

"Bhishma said,—'Thinking of Emancipation, Suka approached his sire and possessed as he was of humility and desirous of achieving his highest good, he saluted his great preceptor and said,—Thou art well versed in the religion of Emancipation. Do thou O illustrious one, discourse to me upon it, so that supreme tranquillity of mind, O puissant one, may be mine!—Hearing these words of his son, the great Rishi said unto him,—Do thou study, O son, the religion of Emancipation and all the diverse duties of life!—At the command of his sire, Suka, that foremost of all righteous men, mastered all the treatises on Yoga, O Bharata, as also the science promulgated by Kapila. When Vyasa beheld his son to be possessed of the resplendence of the Vedas, endued with the energy of Brahma, and fully conversant with the religion of Emancipation, he addressed him, saying,—Go thou to Janaka the ruler of Mithila. The king of Mithila will tell thee everything for thy Emancipation.—Bearing the command of his sire, O king, Suka proceeeded to Mithila for enquiring of its king about the truth of duties and the Refuge of Emancipation. Before he set out, his sire further told him,—Do thou go thither by that path which ordinary human beings take. Do not have recourse to thy Yoga-puissance for proceeding through the skies—At this Suka was not at all surprised (for he was humble by nature). He was further told that he should proceed thither with simplicity and not from desire of pleasure.—Along your way do not seek for friends and spouses, since friends and spouses are causes of attachment to the world. Although the ruler of Mithila is one in whose sacrifices we officiate, still thou shouldst not indulge in any feeling of superiority while living with him. Thou shouldst

in deference to the universal custom, obliged to formally acquire them from a preceptor.—T.

live under his direction and in obedience to him. Even he will dispel all thy doubts.[1] That king is well versed in all duties and well acquainted with the scriptures on Emancipation. He is one for whom I officiate in sacrifices. Thou shouldst, without any scruple, do what he bids.—Thus instructed, the righteous-souled Suka proceeded to Mithila on foot although he was able to traverse through the skies over the whole Earth with her seas. Crossing many hills and mountains, many rivers, many waters and lakes, and many woods and forests abounding with beasts of prey and other animals, crossing, the two *Varshas* of Meru and Hari successively and next the *Varsha* of Himavat, he came at last to the *Varsha* known by the name of Bharata. Having seen many countries inhabited by Chins and Huns, the great ascetic at last reached Aryavarta. In obedience to the commands of his sire and bearing them constantly in his mind, he gradually passed along his way on the Earth like a bird passing through the air. Passing through many delightful towns and populous cities, he saw diverse kinds of wealth without waiting to observe them. On his way he passed through many delightful gardens and planes and many sacred waters. Before much time had passed he reached the country of the Videhas that was protected by the virtuous and high-souled Janaka. There he beheld many populous villages, and many kinds of food and drink and viands and habitations of cowherds swelling with men and many herds of cattle. He beheld many fields abounding with paddy and barley and other grain, and many lakes and waters inhabited by swans and cranes and adorned with beautiful lotuses. Passing through the Videha country teeming with well-to-do people, he arrived at the delightful gardens of Mithila rich with many species of trees. Abounding with elephants and horses and cars, and peopled by men and women, he passed through them without waiting to observe any of the things that were presented to his eye. Bearing that burthen in his mind and ceaselessly dwelling upon it (*viz.*, the desire of mastering the religion of Emancipation), Suka of cheerful soul and taking delight in internal survey only, reached Mithila at last. Arrived at the gate, he sent word through the keepers. Endued with tranquillity of mind, devoted to contemplation and Yoga, he entered the city, having obtained permission. Proceeding along the principal street abounding with well-to-do men, he reached the king's palace and entered it without any scruples. The porters forbade him with rough words. Thereat, Suka, without any anger, stopped and waited. Neither

1 Vyasa was the priest or Ritwija of the house of Mithila and as such the kings of Mithila were his 'Yajyas' or 'Yajmanas.' The duty of a 'Yajamana' is to reverence every member of the priest's family. The sire, therefore, cautions the son that he should not, while living with the king of Mithila, assert his superiority over him in any respect.—T.

the sun nor the long distance he had walked had fatigued him in the least. Neither hunger, nor thirst, nor the exertion he had made, had weakened him. The heat of the Sun had not scorched or pained or distressed him in any degree. Among those porters there was one who felt compassion for him, beholding him staying there like the midday Sun in his effulgence. Worshipping him in due form and saluting him properly, with joined hands he led him to the first chamber of the palace. Seated there, Suka, O son, began to think of Emancipation only. Possessed of equable splendour he looked with an equal eye upon a shaded spot and one exposed to the Sun's rays. Very soon after, the king's minister, coming to that place with joined hands, led him to the second chamber of the palace. That chamber led to a spacious garden which formed a portion of the inner apartments of the palace. It looked like a second Chaitraratha. Beautiful pieces of water occurred here and there at regular intervals. Delightful trees, all of which were in their flowering season, stood in that garden. Bevies of damsels, of transcendent beauty, were in attendance. The minister led Suka from the second chamber to that delightful spot. Ordering those damsels to give the ascetic a seat, the minister left him there. Those well-dressed damsels were of beautiful features, possessed of excellent hips, young in years, clad in red robes of fine texture, and decked with many ornaments of burnished gold. They were well skilled in agreeable conversation and maddening revelry, and thorough mistresses of the arts of dancing and singing. Always opening their lips with smiles, they were equal to the very Apsaras in beauty. Well-skilled in all the acts of dalliance, competent to read the thoughts of men upon whom they wait, possessed of every accomplishment, fifty damsels, of a very superior order and of easy virtue, surrounded the ascetic. Presenting him with water for washing his feet, and worshipping him respectfully with the offer of the usual articles, they gratified him with exellent viands agreeable to the season. After he had eaten, those damsels then, one after another, singly led him through the grounds, showing him every object of interest, O Bharata. Sporting and laughing and singing, those damsels, conversant with the thoughts of all men, entertained that auspicious ascetic of noble soul. The pure-souled ascetic born in the fire-sticks, observant without scruples of any kind of his duties, having all his senses under complete control, and a thorough master of his wrath, was neither pleased nor angered at all this. Then those foremost of beautiful women gave him an excellent seat. Washing his feet and other limbs, Suka said his evening prayers, sat on that excellent seat, and began to think of the object for which he had come there. In the first part of the night, he devoted himself to Yoga. The puissant ascetic, passed the middle portion of the night in sleep. Very soon waking up from his slumber, he went through the necessary rites of cleansing his body, and though surrounded by those beautiful women, he once again devoted himself to Yoga. It was in this way, O Bharata, that the son of the Island-born Krishna passed the latter part of that day and the whole of that night in the palace of king Janaka.' "

SECTION CCCXXVII

"Bhishma said,—The next morning, king Janaka, O Bharata, accompanied by his minister and the whole household, came to Suka, placing his priest in the van. Bringing with him costly seats and diverse kinds of jewels and gems, and bearing the ingredients of the *Arghya* on his own head, the monarch approached the son of his reverend preceptor. The king, taking with his own hands, from the hands of his priest, that seat adorned with many gems, overlaid with an excellent sheet, beautiful in all its parts, and exceedingly costly, presented it with great reverence to his preceptor's son Suka. After the son of (the Island-born) Krishna had taken his seat on it, the king worshipped him according to prescribed rites. At first offering him water to wash his feet, he then presented him the *Arghya* and kine. The ascetic accepted that worship offered with due rites and *mantras*. That foremost of regenerate persons, having thus accepted the worship offered by the king, and taking the kine also that were presented to him, then saluted the monarch. Possessed of great energy, he next enquired after the king's welfare and prosperity. Indeed, O king, Suka embraced in his enquiry the welfare of the monarch's followers and officers also. Receiving Suka's permission, Janaka sat down with all his followers. Endued with a high soul and possessed of high birth, the monarch, with joined hands, sat down on the bare ground and enquired after the welfare and unabated prosperity of Vyasa's son. The monarch then asked his guest the object of his visit.

"Suka said,—Blessed be thou, my sire said unto me that his Yajamana, the ruler of the Videhas, known all over the world by the name of Janaka, is well versed in the religion of Emancipation. He commanded me to come to him without delay, if I had any doubts requiring solution in the matter of the religion of either Pravritti or Nivritti. He gave me to understand the king of Mithila would dispel all my doubts. I have, therefore, come hither, at the command of my sire, for the purpose of taking lessons from thee. It behoveth thee, O foremost of all righteous persons, to instruct me! What are the duties of a

Brahmana, and what is the essence of those duties that have Emancipation for their object. How also is Emancipation to be obtained? Is it obtainable by the aid of knowledge or by that of penances?—

" 'Janaka said,—Hear what the duties are of a Brahmana from the time of his birth. After his investiture, O son, with the sacred thread, he should devote his attention to the study of the Vedas. By practising penances and dutifully serving his preceptor and observing the duties of Brahmacharyya, O puissant one, he should pay off the debt he owes to the deities and the Pitris, and cast off all malice. Having studied the Vedas with close attention and subjugated his senses, and having given his preceptor the tuition fee, he should, with the permission of his preceptor, return home. Returning home, he should betake himself to the domestic mode of life and wedding a spouse confine himself to her, and live freeing himself from every kind of malice, and having established his domestic fire. Living in the domestic mode, he should procreate sons and grandsons. After that, he should retire to the forest, and continue to worship the same fires and entertain guests with cordial hospitality. Living righteously in the forest, he should at last establish his fire in his soul, and freed from all pairs of opposites, and casting off all attachments from the soul, he should pass his days in the mode called Sannyasa which is otherwise called the mode of Brahma.—

" 'Suka said,—If one succeeds in attaining to an understanding cleansed by study of the scriptures and to true conceptions of all things, and if the heart succeeds in freeing itself permanently from the effects of all pairs of opposites, is it still necessary for such a person to adopt, one after another, the three modes of life called Brahmacharyya, Garhastya, and Vanaprastha? This is what I ask thee. It behoveth thee to tell me. Indeed, O ruler of men, do tell me this according to the true import of the Vedas!—

" 'Janaka said,—Without the aid of an understanding cleansed by study of the scriptures and without that true conception of all things which is known by the name of Vijnana, the attainment of Emancipation is impossible. That cleansed understanding, again, it is said, is unattainable without one's connection with a preceptor. The preceptor is the helmsman, and knowledge is the boat (aided by whom and which one succeeds in crossing the ocean of the world). After having acquired that boat, one becomes crowned with success. Indeed, having crossed the ocean, one may abandon both. For preventing the destruction of all the worlds and for preventing the destruction of acts (upon which the worlds depend), the duties appertaining to the four modes of life were practised by the wise of old. By abandoning acts, good and bad, agreeably to this order of acts one succeeds, in course of many birth, in attaining to Emancipation.[1] That man who, through penances performed in course of many births, succeeds in obtaining a cleansed mind and understanding and soul, certainly becomes able to attain to Emancipation (in a new birth) in even the very first mode *viz.*, Brahmacharyya.[2] When, having attained to a cleansed understanding, Emancipation becomes his and in consequence thereof he becomes possessed of knowledge in respect of all visible things, what desirable object is there to attain by observing the three other modes of life?[3] One should always cast off faults born of the attributes of Rajas and Tamas. Adhering to the path of Sattwa, one should know Self by Self.[4] Beholding one's self in all creatures and all creatures in one's self, one should live (without being attached to anything) like aquatic animals living in water without being drenched by that element. He who succeeds in transcending all pairs of attributes and resisting their influence, succeeds in casting off all attachments, and attains to infinite felicity in the next world, going thither like a bird soaring into the sky from below. In this connection, there is a saying sung of old by king Yayati and borne in remembrance, O sire, by all persons conversant with the scriptures bearing upon Emancipation. The effulgent ray (*i.e.*, the Supreme Soul) exists in one's Soul and not anywhere else. It exists equally in all creatures. One can see it oneself if one's heart be devoted to Yoga. When a person lives in such a way that another is not inspired with fear at his sight, and when a person is not himself inspired with fear at the sight of others, when a person ceases to cherish desire and hate, he is then said to attain to Brahma. When a person ceases to entertain a sinful attitude towards all creatures in thought, word, and deed, he is then said to attain to Brahma.[5] By restraining the mind and the soul, by casting off malice that stupefies the mind, and by throwing off desire and stupefaction, one is said to attain to Brahma. When a person assumes an equality of attitude in respect of all objects of hearing and vision (and the operations of the other senses) as also in respect of all

---

1 It is certain that one must abandon all, acts before one can attain to Emancipation. But then acts should not be cast off all at once. It is according to this order that they should be abandoned, *i.e.*, in the order of the several modes.—T.

2 The 'karanas' are the inner faculties.—T.

3 *I.e.*, when Emancipation and omniscience have been attained in the very first mode of life, no further need exists for conforming to the three other modes of life.—T.

4 *i e*, behold the Supreme Soul by his own Soul.--T.

5 Instead of 'papakam' some texts read 'pavakam', meaning of the nature of fire.'—T.

living creatures, and transcends all pairs of opposites, he is then said to attain to Brahma. When person casts an equal eye upon praise and dispraise, gold and iron, happiness and misery, heat and cold, good and evil, the agreeable and the disagreeable, life and death, he is then said to attain to Brahma. One observing the duties of the mendicant orders should restrain one's senses and the mind even like a tortoise withdrawing its out-stretched limbs.[1] As a house enveloped in darkness is capable of being seen with the aid of a lighted lamp, after the same manner can the soul be seen with the aid of the lamp of the understanding. O foremost of intelligent persons, I see that all this knowledge that I am communicating to thee dwells in thee. Whatever else should be known by one desirous of learning the religion of Emancipation is already known to thee. O regenerate Rishi, I am convinced that through the grace of thy preceptor and through the instructions thou hast received, thou hast already transcended all objects of the senses.[2] O great ascetic, through the grace of that sire of thine, I have attained to omniscience, and hence I have succeeded in knowing thee. Thy knowledge is much greater than what thou thinkest thou hast. Thy perceptions also that result from intuition are much greater than what thou thinkest thou hast. Thy puissance also is much greater than thou art conscious of. Whether in consequence of thy tender age, or of the doubts thou hast not been able to dispel, or of the fear that is due to the unattainment of Emancipation, thou art not conscious of that knowledge due to intuition although it has arisen in thy mind. After one's doubts have been dispelled by persons like us, one succeeds in opening the knots of one's heart and then, by a righteous exertion one attains to and becomes conscious of that knowledge. As regards thyself, thou art one that hast already acquired knowledge. Thy intelligence is steady and tranquil. Thou art free from covetousness. For all that, O Brahmana, one never succeeds in attaining to Brahma, which is the highest object of acquisition, without exertion. Thou seest no distinction between happiness and misery. Thou art not covetous. Thou hast no longing for dancing and song. Thou hast no attachments. Thou hast no attachment to friends. Thou hast no fear in things that inspire fear. O blessed one, I see that thou castest an equal eye upon a lump of gold and a clod of earth. Myself and other persons possessed of wisdom, behold thee established in the highest and indestructible path of tranquillity. Thou

---

1 After 'manasa,' 'saha' is understood. It does not mean that the senses are to be restrained *by* the mind, but the words imply that the mind *and* the senses are to be restrained. K.P. Singha renders the line correctly. The Burdwan translator, as usual, is careless.—T.

2 K.P. Singha skips over this verse.—T.

stayest, O Brahmana, in those duties which obtain for the Brahmana that fruit which should be his and which is identical with the essence of the object represented by Emancipation. What else hast thou to ask me ?—' "

SECTION CCCXXVIII

"Bhishma said,—'Having heard these words of king Janaka, Suka of cleansed soul and settled conclusions began to stay in his Soul by his Soul, having of course seen Self by Self.[1] His object being accomplished, he became happy and tranquil, and without putting further questions to Janaka, he proceeded northwards to the mountains of Himavat with the speed of the wind and like the wind.[2] Those mountains abounded with diverse tribes of Apsaras and echoed with many lofty sounds. Teeming with thousands of Kinnaras and Bhringarajas[3] it was adorned, besides, with many Madgus and Khanjaritas and many Jivajivakas of variegated hue. And there were many peacocks also of gorgeous colours, uttering their shrill but melodious cries. Many bevies of swans also, and many flights of gladdened Kokilas too, adorned the place. The prince of birds, *viz.*, Garuda, dwelt on that summit constantly. The four Regents of the world, the deities, and diverse classes of *Rishis*, used always to come there from the desire of doing good to the world. It was there that the high-souled Vishnu had undergone the severest austerities for the object of obtaining a son. It was there that the celestial generalissimo named Kumara, in his younger days, disregarding the three worlds with all the celestial denizens, threw down his dart, piercing the Earth therewith. Throwing down his dart, Skanda, addressing the universe, said,—If there be any person that is superior to me in might, or that holds Brahmanas to be dearer, or that can compare with me in devotion to the Brahmanas and the Vedas, or that is possessed of energy like unto me, let him draw up this dart or at least shake it !—Hearing this challenge, the three worlds become filled with anxiety, and all creatures asked one another, saying,—Who will raise this dart ?—Bishnu beheld all the deities and Asuras and Rakshasas to be troubled in their senses and mind. He reflected upon what should

1 I.e., he turned his soul's gaze on his soul and withdrew himself from every worldly object.—T.

2 He no longer walked like ordinary men. Without trailing along the solid support of the Earth, he proceeded through the sky.—T.

3 Popularly, Bhimaraja, the Lanius Malabaricus.—T.

be the best to be done under the circumstances. Without being able to bear that challenge in respect of the hurling of the dart, he cast his eyes on Skanda, the son of the Fire-god. The pure-souled Vishnu caught hold of the blazing dart, with his left hand, and began to shake it. When the dart was being thus shaken by Vishnu possessed of great might, the whole Earth with her mountains, forests, and seas, shook with the dart. Although Vishnu was fully competent to raise the dart, still he contented himself with only shaking it. In this, the puissant lord only kept the honour of Skanda intact. Having shaken it himself, the divine Vishnu, addressing Prahlada, said,—Behold the might of Kumara! None else in the universe can raise this dart! Unable to bear this, Prahlada resolved to raise the dart. He seized it, but was unable to shake it at all. Uttering a loud cry, he fell down on the hill-top in a swoon. Indeed, the son of Hiranya-kasipu fell down on the Earth. Repairing towards the northern side of those grand mountains, Mahadeva, having the bull for his sign, had undergone the austerest penances. The asylum where Mahadeva had undergone those austerities is encompassed on all sides with a blazing fire. Unapproachable by persons of uncleansed souls, that mountain is known by the name of Aditya. There is a fiery girdle all around it, of the width of ten Yojanas, and it is incapable of being approached by Yakshas and Rakshasas and Danavas. The illustrious god of Fire, possessed of mighty energy, dwells there in person employed in removing all impediments from the side of Mahadeva of great wisdom who remained there for a thousand celestial years, all the while standing on one foot. Dwelling on the side of that foremost of mountains, Mahadeva of high vows (by his penances) scorched the deities greatly.[1] At the foot of those mountains, in a retired spot, Parasara's son of great ascetic merit, *viz.*, Vyasa, taught the Vedas unto his disciples. Those disciples were the highly blessed Sumantra, Vaisampayana, Jaimini of great wisdom, and Paila of great ascetic merit. Suka proceeded to that delightful asylum where his sire, the great ascetic Vyasa, was dwelling, surrounded by his disciples. Seated in his asylum, Vyasa beheld his son approach like a blazing fire of scattered flames, or resembling the sun himself in effulgence. As Suka approached, he did not seem to touch the trees or the rocks of the mountain. Completely dissociated from all objects of the senses, and engaged in Yoga, the high-souled ascetic came, resembling, in speed, a shaft let from a bow. Born on the fire-sticks, Suka, approaching, his sire, touched his feet. With

---

1 It is believed that a person, by performing austere penances, scorches the three worlds. It is in consequence of this effect of penances that the superior deities were always compelled by the Asuras and Danavas to grant them whatever boons they solicited.—T.

becoming formalities he then accosted the disciples of his sire. With great cheerfulness he then detailed to his father all the particulars of his conversation with king Janaka. Vyasa the son of Parasara, after the arrival of his puissant son, continued to dwell there on the Himavat engaged in teaching his disciples and his son. One day as he was seated, his disciples, all well-skilled in the Vedas, having their senses under control, and endued with tranquil souls, sat themselves around him. All of them had thoroughly mastered the Vedas with their branches. All of them were observant of penances. With joined hands they addressed their preceptor in the following words.

"The disciples said.—We have, through thy grace, been endued with great energy. Our fame also has spread. There is one favour that we humbly solicit thee to grant us.—Hearing these words of theirs, the regenerate Rishi answered them, saying,—Ye sons, tell me what that boon is which ye wish I should grant you!—Hearing this answer of their preceptor, the disciples became filled with joy. Once more bowing their heads low unto their preceptor and joining their hands, all of them in one voice said, O king, these excellent words:—If our preceptor has been pleased with us, then, O best of sages, we are sure to be crowned with success! We all solicit thee, O great Rishi, to grant us a boon. Be thou inclined to be graceful to us. Let no sixth disciple (besides us five) succeed in attaining to fame! We are four. Our preceptor's son forms the fifth. Let the Vedas shine in only us five! Even this is the boon that we solicit;—Hearing these words of his disciples, Vyasa, the son of Parasara, possessed of great intelligence, well conversant with the meaning of the Vedas, endued with a righteous soul, and always engaged in thinking of objects that confer benefits on a person in the world hereafter, said unto his disciples these righteous words fraught with great benefit:—The Vedas should always be given unto him who is a Brahmana, or unto him who is desirous of listening to Vedic instructions, by him who eagerly wishes to attain a residence in the region of Brahman! Do ye multiply. Let the Vedas spread (through your exertions). The Vedas should never be imparted unto one that has not formally become a disciple. Nor should they be given unto one who is not observant of good vows. Nor should they be given for dwelling in one that is of uncleansed soul. These should be known as the proper qualifications of persons that can be accepted as disciples (for the communication of Vedic knowledge). No science should be imparted unto one without a proper examination of one's character, as pure gold is tested by heat, cutting and rubbing, after the same manner disciples should be tested by their birth and accomplishments. Ye should never set your disciples to tasks to which they should not be set, or to tasks that are fraught with danger. One's knowledge is always commensurate with one's understanding and diligence in study. Let all disciples conquer all difficulties, and let all of them meet with auspicious success. Ye are competent to lecture on the scriptures unto persons of all the orders. Only ye should, while lecturing, address a Brahmana, placing him in the van. These are the rules in respect of the study of the Vedas. This again is regarded as a high task. The Vedas were created by the Self-born for the purpose of praising the deities therewith. That man who, through stupefaction of intellect, speaks ill of a Brahmana well-conversant with the Vedas, is certain to meet with humiliation in consequence of such evil-speaking. He who disregarding all righteous rules, solicits knowledge, and he who, disregarding the rules of righteousness, communicates knowledge, either of them falls off and instead of that affection which should prevail between preceptor and disciple, such, questioning and such communication are sure to produce distrust and suspicion. I have now told ye everything about the way in which the Vedas should be studied and taught. Ye should act in this way towards your disciples, bearing these instructions in your minds ;—' "

SECTION CCCXXIX

"Bhishma said,—'Hearing these words of their preceptor, Vyasa's disciples endued with energy, became filled with joy and embraced one another. Addressing one another, they said,—That which has been said by our illustrious preceptor in view of our future good, will live in our remembrance and we shall certainly act according to it.—Having said this unto one another with joyful hearts, the disciples of Vyasa, who were thorough masters of words, once more addressed their preceptor and said,—If it pleases thee, O puissant one, we wish to descend from this mountain to the Earth, O great ascetic, for the purpose of subdividing the Vedas !—Hearing these words of his disciples, the puissant son of Parasara replied unto them in these beneficial words that were fraught, besides, with righteousness and profit,—You may repair to the Earth or to the regions of the celestials, as ye like. You should always be heedful, for the Vedas are such that they are always liable to be misunderstood ![1]—Permitted by their preceptor of truthful speech, the disciples left him after circumambulating him and bowing their heads unto him. Descending upon the Earth they performed the Agnishtoma

1 The sense is that if the Vedas are not constantly studied, they are likely to be forgotten.—T.

and other sacrifices; and they began to officiate at the sacrifices of Brahmanas and Kshatriyas and Vaidyas. Happily passing their days in the domestic mode of life, they were treated by the Brahmanas with great respect. Possessed of great fame and prosperity, they were employed in teaching and officiating in sacrifices. After his disciples had gone away, Vyasa remained in his asylum, with only his son in his company. Passing his days in anxious thoughtfulness, the great Rishi, possessed of wisdom, kept silent, sitting in a retired corner of the asylum. At that time Narada of great ascetic merit came to that spot for seeing Vyasa, and addressing him, said these words of melodious sound.

" 'Narada said,—O regenerate Rishi of Vasishtha's race, why are Vedic sounds silent now? Why art thou sitting silent and alone engaged in meditation like one taken up with an engrossing thought? Alas, shorn of Vedic echoes, this mountain hath lost its beauty, even as the Moon shorn of splendour when assailed by Rahu or enveloped in dust.[1] Though inhabited by the celestial Rishis, yet shorn of Vedic sounds, the mountain no longer looks beautiful now but resembles a hamlet of Nishadas.[2] The Rishis, the deities, and the Gandharvas, too, no longer shine as before in consequence of being deprived of Vedic sound!—Hearing these words of Narada, the Island-born Krishna answered, saying,—O great Rishi, O thou art conversant with the declarations of the Vedas, all that thou hast said is agreeable to me and it truly behoves thee to say it unto me! Thou omniscient, thou hast seen everything. Thy curiosity also embraces all things within its sphere. All that has ever occurred in the three worlds is well known to thee. Do thou then, O regenerate Rishi, set thy commands on me. O, tell me what I am to do! Tell me, O regenerate Rishi, what should now be done by me. Separated from my disciples, my mind has become very cheerless now.

" 'Narada said,—The stain of the Vedas is the suspension of their recitation. The stain of the Brahmanas is their non-observance of vows. The Valhika race is the stain of the Earth. Curiosity is the stain of women. Do thou with thy intelligent son recite the Vedas, and do thou with the echoes of Vedic sounds dispel the fears arising from Rakshasas:—

"Bhishma continued.—'Hearing these words of Narada, Vyasa, the foremost of all persons conversant with duties and firmly devoted

1 'Upaplava' is Rahu or the ascending node. In many parts of Upper India, during the hot months in particular, large quantities of dust are raised by whirl winds in the afternoon or at evening called "Andi" the clouds of dust cover the moon for hours together.—T.

2 The lowest order of men, living by slaying animals.—T,

to Vedic recitation, became filled with joy and answered Narada, saying, —So be it —With his son Suka, he set himself to recite the Vedas in a loud sonorours voice, observing all the rules of orthœpy and, as it were, filling the three worlds with that sound. One day as sire and son, who were well conversant with all duties, were engaged in reciting the Vedas, a violent wind arose that seemed to be impelled by the gales that blow on the bosom of the ocean. Understanding from this circumstance that the hour was not suited to sacred recitation. Vyasa immediately bade his son to suspend the recitation. Suka, thus forbidden by his sire, became filled with curiosity. He asked his sire, saying,—O regenerate one, whence is this wind? It behoveth thee to tell me everything about the conduct of the Wind.—Hearing this question of Suka, Vyasa became filled with amazement. He answered Suka, by telling him that an omen which indicated that the recitation of the Vedas should be suspended.—Thou hast obtained spiritual vision. Thy mind too has, of itself, become cleansed of every impurity. Thou hast been freed from the attributes of Passion and Darkness. Thou stayest now in the attribute of Goodness. Thou beholdest now thy Soul with thy Soul even as one beholds one's own shadow in a mirror. Staying thyself on thy own Soul, do thou reflect on the Vedas. The path of the Supreme Soul is called Deva-yana (the path of the gods). The path that is made up of the attribute of Tamas is called Pitri-yana (the path of Pitris). These are the two paths in the world hereafter. By one, people go to heaven. By the other, people go to hell. The winds blow on the Earth's surface and in the welkin. There are seven courses in which they blow. Listen to me as I recount them one after another. The body is furnished with the senses. The senses are dominated over by the Sadhyas and many great beings of mighty strength. These gave birth to an invincible son named Samana. From Samana sprang a son called Udana. From Udana sprang Vyana. From Vyana arose Apana, and lastly from Apana sprung the wind called Prana. That invincible scorcher of all foes, *viz.*, Prana, became childless. I shall now recite to thee the different functions of those winds. The wind is the cause of the different functions of all living creatures, and because living creatures are enabled to live by it, therefore is the wind called Prana (or life). That wind which is the first in the above enumeration and which is known by the name of Pravaha (Samana) urges, along the first course, masses of clouds born of smoke and heat. Coursing through the welkin, and coming into contact with the water contained in the clouds, that wind displays itself in effulgence among the darts of lightning.[1] The second wind called Avaha blows with a loud noise. It is this wind that causes Soma and

1 This Verse in the Bengal texts, is a triplet. In the Bombay edition,

the other luminaries to rise and appear. Within the body (which is a microcosm of the universe) that wind is called Udana by the wise. That wind which sucks up water from the four oceans, and having sucked it up imparts it to the clouds in the welkin, and which, having imparted it to the clouds presents them to the deity of rain, is third in the enumeration and known by the name of Udvaha. That wind which supports the clouds and divided them into diverse portions, which melts them for pouring rain and once more solidifies them, which is perceived as the sound of the roaring clouds, which exists for the preservation of the world by itself assuming the form of the clouds, which bears the cars of all celestial beings along the sky, is known by the name of Samvaha. The fourth in the enumeration, it is endued with great strength so that it is capable of ending the very mountains. The fifth wind is fraught with great force and speed. It is dry and uproots and breaks down all trees. Existing with it, the clouds come to be called by the name of Valahaka. That wind causes calamitous phenomena of many kinds, and produces roaring sounds in the firmament. It is known by the name of Vivaha. The sixth wind bears all celestial waters in the firmament and prevents them from falling down. Sustaining the sacred waters of the celestial Ganga, that wind blows, preventing them from having a downward course. Obstructed by that wind from a distance, the Sun, which is really the source of a thousand rays, and which enlightens the world, appears as a luminous body of but one ray. Through the action of that wind, the Moon, after waning, wanes again till he displays his full disc. That wind is known, O foremost of ascetics, by the name Parivaha.[1] That wind which takes away the life of all living creatures when the proper hour comes, whose track is followed by Death and Surya's son Yama, which becomes the source of that immortality which is attained by Yogins of subtile sight who are always engaged in Yoga meditation, by whose aid the thousands of grandsons of Daksha, that lord of creatures, by his ten sons, succeeded in days of old in attaining to the ends of the universe, whose touch enables one to attain to Emancipation by freeing oneself from the obligation of returning to the world,—that wind is called by the name of Paravaha. The foremost of all winds, it is incapable of being resisted by anybody. Wonderful are

---

the third line is excluded from Verse 36. There is no inconvenience in this, only, it should be construed as referring to the wind called Samana or *Pravaha*.—T.

1 Some texts read 'Jayatamvarah.' If this be accepted, it should be an adjective of Parivaha, meaning the foremost of all in strength or energy. —T.

these winds all of whom are the sons of Diti. Capable of going everywhere and upholding all things, they blow all around thee without being attached to thee at any time. This, however, is exceedingly wonderful, *viz.*, that this foremost of mountains should thus be suddenly shaken by that wind which has begun to blow. This wind is the breath of Vishnu's nostrils. When urged forth with speed, it begins to blow with great force at which the whole universe becomes agitated. Hence, when the wind begins to blow with violence, persons conversant with the Vedas do not recite the Vedas. The Vedas are a form of wind. If uttered with force, the external wind becomes tortured.'—'

"Having said these words, the puissant son of Parasara bade his son (when the wind had ceased) to go on with his Vedic recitation. He then left that spot for plunging into the waters of the celestial Ganga.[1]' "

SECTION CCCXXX

"Bhishma said.—'After Vyasa had left the spot, Narada, traversing through the sky, came to Suka employed in studying the scriptures. The celestial Rishi came for the object of asking Suka the meaning of certain portions of the Vedas. Beholding the celestial Rishi Narada arrived at his retreat, Suka worshipped him by offering him the Arghya according to the rites laid down in the Vedas. Pleased with the honours bestowed upon him, Narada addressed Suka, saying,—Tell me, O foremost of righteous persons, by what means, O dear child, may I accomplish what is for thy highest good!—Hearing these words of Narada, Suka, said unto him, O Bharata, these words:—It behoveth thee to instruct me in respect of that which may be beneficial to me:—

" 'Narada said,—In days of yore the illustrious Sanatkumara had said these words unto certain Rishis of cleansed souls that had repaired to him for enquiring after the truth. There is no eye like that of knowledge. There is no penance like renunciation. Abstention from sinful acts, steady practice of righteousness, good conduct the due observance of all religious duties,—these constitute the highest good. Having obtained the status of humanity which is

1 The sacred river Ganga has it is said, three courses or streams. One flows on the surface of the Earth ; the second flows through the nether regions, and the third flows through heaven.—T,

fraught with sorrow, he that becomes attached to it, becomes stupefied : such a man never succeeds in emancipating himself from sorrow. Attachment (to things of the world) is an indication of sorrow. The understanding of person that is attached to worldly things becomes more and more enmeshed in the net of stupefaction. The man who becomes enmeshed in the net of stupefaction attains to sorrow, both here and hereafter. One should, by every means in one's power, restrain both desire and wrath if one seeks to achieve what is for one's good. Those two (*viz.*, desire and wrath) arise for only destroying one's good.[1] One should always protect one's penances from wrath, and one's prosperity from pride. One should always protect one s knowledge from honour and dishonour, and one's soul from error.[2] Compassion is the highest virtue. Forgiveness is the highest might. The knowledge of self is the highest knowledge. There is nothing higher than truth. It is always proper to speak the truth. It is better again to speak what is beneficial than to speak what is true. I hold that that is truth which is fraught with the greatest benefit in all creatures.[3] That man is said to be truly learned and truly possessed of wisdom who abandons every act, who never indulges in hope, who is completely dissociated from all worldly surroundings, and who has renounced everything that appertains to the world. That person who, without being attached thereto, enjoys all objects of sense with the aid of senses that are completely under his control, who is possessed of a tranquil soul, who is never moved by joy or sorrow, who is engaged in Yoga-meditation, who lives in companionship with the deities presiding over his senses and dissociated also from them, and who, though endued with a body, never regards himself as identifiable with it, becomes emancipated and very soon attains to that which is his highest good. One who never sees others, never touches

---

1 The first line runs into the second.—T.

2 Penances should be protected from wrath. By penances one attains to great power. The ascetic's puissance frequently equals that of Brahman himself. If, however, the ascetic indulges in wrath and curses one from wrath, his puissance becomes diminished. For this reason, forgiveness is said to be the highest virtue a Brahmana can practise. A Brahmana's might lay in forgiveness. Knowledge also should be protected from honour and dishonour, *i. e.* one sohuld never *receive* honour for his knowledge, that is, do anything for the object of achieving honour. Similarly, one should never do anything which may have the effect of dishonouring one's knowledge. These are some of the highest duties preached in scriptures.—T.

3 The saying 'Satyadapi hitam vadet' is frequently misunderstood. The scriptures do not say that truth should be sacrificed in view of what is beneficial. for such a view will militate with the saying that there is nothing higher than truth. The saying has reference to those exceptional instances where truth becomes a source of positive harm. The story of the Rishi who spoke the truth respecting the place where certain travellers lay concealed, when questioned by certain robbers who were for killing the travellers, is an instance to the point. The goldsmith s son who died with a falsehood on his lips for allowing his lawful prince to escape from the hands of his pursuers did a meritorious act of loyalty. Then, again, the germ of the utilitarian theory may be detected in the second line of this Verse.—T.

others, never talks with others, soon, O ascetic, attains to what is for one's highest good. One should not injure any creature. On the other hand, one should conduct oneself in perfect friendliness towards all. Having obtained the status of humanity, one should never behave inimically towards any being. A complete disregard for all (worldly) things, perfect contentment, abandonment of hope of every kind, and patience,—these constitute the highest good of one that has subjugated one's senses and acquired a knowledge of self. Casting off all attachments, O child, do thou subjugate all thy senses, and by that means attain to felicity both here and hereafter. They that are free from cupidity have never to suffer any sorrow. One should, therefore, cast off all cupidity from one's soul. By casting off cupidity, O amiable and blessed one, thou shalt be able to free thyself from sorrow and pain. One who wishes to conquer that which is unconquerable should live devoting oneself to penances, to self-restraint, to taciturnity, to a subjugation of the soul. Such a person should live in the midst of attachments without being attached to them.[1] That Brahmana who lives in the midst of attachments without being attached to them and who always lives in seclusion, very soon attains to the highest felicity. That man who lives in happiness by himself in the midst of creatures who are seen to take delight in leading lives of sexual union, should be known to be a person whose thirst has been slaked by knowledge. It is well known that that man whose thirst has been slaked by knowledge has never to indulge in grief. One attains to the status of the deities by means of good acts; to the status of humanity by means of acts that are good and bad; while by acts that are purely wicked, one helplessly falls down among the lower animals. Always assailed by sorrow and decrepitude and death, a living creature is being cooked in this world (in the cauldron of Time). Dost thou not know it? Thou frequently regardest that to be beneficial which is really injurious; that to be certain which is really uncertain; and that to be desirable and good which is undesirable and not good. Alas, why dost thou not awake to a correct apprehension of these? Like a silkworm that ensconces itself in its own cocoon, thou art continually ensconcing thyself in a cocoon made of thy own innumerable acts born of stupefaction and error. Alas, why dost thou not awake to a correct apprehension of thy situation? No need of attaching thyself to things of this world. Attachment to worldly objects is productive of evil. The silk-worm that weaves a cocoon round itself is at last destroyed by its own act. Those persons that become attached to sons and spouses and relatives meet with destruction at last, even as wild elephants sunk in the mire of a lake are gradually weakened till overtaken by

1 'To conquer the unconquerable' means to attain to Brahma.—T.

Death. Behold, all creatures that suffer themselves to be dragged by the net of affection become subject to great grief even as fishes on land, dragged thereto by means of large nets! Relatives, sons, spouses, the body itself, and all one's possessions stored with care, are unsubstantial and prove of no service in the next world. Only acts, good and bad, that one does, follow one to the other world. When it is certain that thou shalt have to go helplessly to the other world, leaving behind thee all these things alas, why dost thou then suffer thyself to be attached to such unsubstantial things of no value, without attending to that which constitutes thy real and durable wealth? The path which thou shalt have to travel through is without resting places of any kind (in which to take rest). There is no support along that way which one may catch for upholding oneself. The country through which it passes is unknown and undiscovered. It is, again, enveloped in thick darkness. Alas, how shalt thou proceed along that way without equipping thyself with the necessary expenses? When thou shalt go along that road, nobody will follow thee behind. Only thy acts, good and bad, will follow behind thee when thou shalt depart from this world for the next. One seeks one's object of objects by means of learning, acts, purity (both external and internal), and great knowledge. When that foremost of objects is attained, one becomes freed (from rebirth). The desire that one feels for living in the midst of human habitations is like a binding cord. They that are of good acts succeed in tearing that bond and freeing themselves. Only men of wicked deeds do not succeed in breaking them. The river of life (or the world) is terrible. Personal beauty or form constitutes its banks. The mind is the speed of its current. Touch forms its island. Taste constitutes its current. Scent is its mire. Sound is its waters. That particular part of it which leads towards heaven is attended with great difficulties. Body is the boat by which one must cross that river. Forgiveness is the oar by which it is to be propelled. Truth is the ballast that is to steady that boat. The practice of righteousness is the string that is to be attached to the mast for dragging that boat along difficult waters. Charity or gift constitutes the wind that urges the sails of that boat. Endued with swift speed, it is with that boat that one must cross the river of life. Cast off both virtue and vice, and truth and falsehood. Having cast off truth and falsehood, do thou cast off that by which these are to be cast off. By casting off all purpose, do thou cast off virtue; do thou cast off sin also by casting off all desire. With the aid of the understanding, do thou cast off truth and falsehood; and, at last, do thou cast off the understanding itself by knowledge of the highest topic (*viz.*, the supreme Soul). Do thou cast off this body having bones for its pillars; sinews for its binding strings and cords; flesh and blood for its outer plaster; the skin for its outer case; full of urine and faeces and, therefore, emitting a foul smell; exposed to the assaults of decrepitude and sorrow; forming the seat of disease and weakened by pain; possessed of the attribute of Rajas in predominance: not permanent or durable, and which serves as the (temporary) habitation of the indwelling creature. This entire universe of matter, and that which is called Mahat or Buddhi, are made up of the (five), great elements. That which is called Mahat is due to the action of the Supreme. The five senses, the three attributes of Tamas, Sattwa, and Rajas,—these (together with those which have been mentioned before) constitute a tale of seventeen. These seventeen, which are known by the name of the Unmanifest, with all those that are called Manifest, *viz.*, the five objects of the five senses, (that is to say, form, taste, sound, touch, and scent), with Consciousness and the Understanding, from the well-known tale of four and twenty. When endued with these four and twenty possessions, one comes to be called by the name of Jiva (or Puman). He who knows the aggregate of three (viz., Religion, Wealth, and Pleasure), as also happiness and sorrow and life and death, truly and in all their details, is said to know growth and decay. Whatever objects exist of knowledge, should be known gradually, one after another. All objects that are apprehended by the senses are called Manifest. Whatever objects transcend the senses[1] and are apprehended by means only of their indications are said to be Unmanifest. By restraining the senses, one wins great gratification, even like a thirsty and parched traveller at a delicious shower of rain. Having subjugated the senses one beholds one's soul spread out for embracing all objects, and all objects in one's soul. Having its roots in knowledge, the puissance is never lost of the man who (thus) beholds the Supreme in his soul,—of the man, that is to say, who always beholds all creatures in all conditions (in his own soul).[1] He who by the aid of knowledge, transcends all kinds of pain born of error and stupefaction, never catches any evil by coming into contact with all creatures.[2] Such a man, his understanding being fully displayed, never finds fault with the course of conduct that prevails in the world. One conversant with Emancipation says that the Supreme Soul is without beginning and without end; that it takes birth as all creatures; that it resides (as a

1 In the Srutis, 'Paravara is an equivalent for the Supreme Soul. The correct reading is 'nasyati' at the and of the first line, and not pasyati as in some of the Bengal texts. Adhering to 'pasyati (which gives no meaning), the Burdwan translator gives a ridiculous and unmeaning version of this Verse. K P. Singha, of course adopts the correct reading.—T.

2 This Verse is not at all difficult. The sense is that the man who transcends all attachments never comes to grief if brought into union with other creatures. The Burdwan translator gives a thoroughly unmeaning version of this couplet—T.

witness) in the Jiva-soul; that it is inactive, and without form. Only that man who meets with grief in consequence of his own misdeeds, slays numerous creatures for the purpose of warding off that grief. In consequence of such sacrifices, the performers have to attain to rebirths and have necessarily to perform innumerable acts on every side. Such a man, blinded by error, and regarding that to be felicity which is really a source of grief, is continually rendered unhappy even like a sick person that eats food that is improper. Such a man is pressed and grinded by his acts like any substance that is churned. Bound by his acts, he obtains rebirth, the order of his life being determined by the nature of his acts. Suffering many kinds of torture, he travels in a repeated round of rebirths even like a wheel that turns ceaselessly. Thou, however, hast cut through all thy bonds. Thou, abstainest from all acts! Possessed of omniscience and the master of all things, let success be thine, and do thou become freed from all existent objects. Through subjugation of their senses and the power of their penances, many persons (in days of yore), having destroyed the bonds of action, attained to high success and uninterrupted felicity.—' "

SECTION CCCXXXI

" 'Narada said,—By listening to such scriptures as are blessed, as bring about tranquillity, as dispel grief, and as are productive of happiness, one attains to (a pure) understanding, and having attained to it obtains to high felicity. A thousand causes of sorrow, a hundred causes of fear, from day to day, afflict one that is destitute of understanding, but not one that is possessed of wisdom and learning. Do thou, therefore, listen to some old narratives as I recite them to you, for the object of dispelling thy griefs. If one can subjugate one's understanding, one is sure to attain to happiness. By association of what is undesirable and dissociation from what is agreeable, only men of little intelligence, become subject to mental sorrow of every kind. When things have become past, one should not grieve, thinking of their merits. He that thinks of such past thinks with affection can never emancipate himself. One should always seek

1 The object of this Verse is to show that men of knowledge do not perform sacrifices, in which, as a matter of course, a large number of creatures is slain. Men wedded to the religion of Pravriti perform sacrifices. Coming into the world in consequence of past acts, they seek happiness (by repairing to heaven) along the way of sacrifices and religious rites. A large number of creatures is slain, for besides the victims ostensibly offered, an infinite number of smaller and minuter creatures is killed in the sacrificial fires and in course of the other preparations that are made in sacrifices.—T.

to find out the faults of those things to which one begins to become attached. One should always regard such things to be fraught with much evil. By doing so, one should soon free oneself therefrom. The man who grieves for what is past fails to acquire either wealth or religious merit or fame. That which exists no longer cannot be obtained. When such things pass away, they do not return (however keen the regret one may indulge in for their sake). Creatures sometimes acquire and sometimes lose worldly object. No man in this world can be grieved by all the events that fall upon him. Dead or lost, he who grieves for what is past, only gets sorrow for sorrow. Instead of one sorrow, he gets two.[1] Those men who, beholding the course of life and death in the world with the aid of their intelligence, do not shed tears, are said to behold properly. Such persons have never to shed tears, (at anything that may happen). When any such calamity comes, productive of either physical or mental grief, as is incapable of being warded off by even one's best efforts, one should cease to reflect on it with sorrow. This is the medicine for sorrow, *viz.*, not to think of it. By thinking of it, one can never dispel it ; on the other hand, by thinking upon sorrow, one only enhances it. Mental griefs should be killed by wisdom ; while physical grief should be dispelled by medicines. This is the power of knowledge. One should not, in such matters, behave like men of little understandings. Youth, beauty, life, stored wealth, health, association with those that are loved,—these all are exceedingly transitory. One possessed of wisdom should never covet them. One should not lament individually for a sorrowful occurrence that concerns an entire community. Instead of indulgence in it when grief comes, one should seek to avert it and apply a remedy as soon as one sees the opportunity for doing it. There is no doubt that in this life the measure of misery is such greater than that of happiness. There is no doubt in this that all men show attachment for objects of the senses and that death is regarded as disagreeable. That man who casts off both joy and sorrow, is said to attain to Brahma. When such a man departs from this world, men of wisdom never indulge in any sorrow on his account. In spending wealth there is pain. In protecting it there is pain. In acquiring it there is pain. Hence, when one's wealth meets with destruction, one should not indulge in any sorrow for it. Men of little understanding, attaining to different grades of wealth, fail to win contentment and at last perish in misery. Men of wisdom, however, are always contented. All combinations are destined to end in dissolution.

1 Sorrow increases by indulgence.—T.

All things that are high are destined to fall down and become low. Union is sure to end in disunion, and life is certain to end in death. Thirst is unquenchable. Contentment is the highest happiness. Hence, persons of wisdom regard contentment to be the most precious wealth. One's allotted period of life is running continually. It stops not in its course for even a single moment. When one's body itself is not durable, what other thing is there (in this world) that one should reckon as durable? Those persons who, reflecting on the nature of all creatures and concluding that it is beyond the grasp of the mind, turn their attention to the highest path, and, setting out, achieve a fair progress in it, have not to indulge in sorrow.[1] Like a tiger seizing and running away with its prey, Death seizes and runs away with the man that is employed in such (unprofitable) occupation and that is still unsatiated with objects of desire and enjoyment. One should always seek to emancipate oneself from sorrow. One should seek to dispel sorrow by beginning one's operations with cheerfulness, that is, without indulging in sorrow the while, having freed oneself from a particular sorrow, one should act in such a way as to keep sorrow at a distance by abstaining from all faults of conduct.[2] The rich and the poor alike find nothing in sound and touch and form and scent and taste, after the immediate enjoyment thereof.[3] Before union, creatures are never subject to sorrow. Hence, one that has not fallen off from one's original nature, never indulges in sorrow when that union comes to an end.[4] One should restrain one's sexual appetite and the stomach with the aid of patience. One should protect one's hands and feet with the aid of the eye. One's eyes and ears and the other senses should be protected by the mind. One's mind and speech should be ruled with the aid of wisdom. Casting off love and affection for persons that are known as well as for those that

1 This is a very doubtful Verse. The commentator is silent. I follow the meaning as it lies on the surface. The object of the Verse seems to be this: there are men that are employed in reflecting upon the nature of things: these should know that such occupation is useless, for truly the nature of things is beyond the grasp of the mind. The greatest philosopher is ignorant of all the virtues of a blade of grass, the purpose for which it exists, the changes that it undergoes every instant of time and from day to day. Those men, however, who have such unprofitable occupation for walking along the highest path (the path, that is, which leads to Brahma) free themselves from grief.—T.

2 I am not sure that I have understood this Verse correctly.—T.

3 What is intended to be said is that the gratification of the senses leaves nothing behind. The pleasure lasts as long as the contact continues of the objects with the senses. The Burdwan translator, not suspecting that the word used is 'adhana,' gives a ridiculous version.—T.

4 What is said here is this: a man has spouses and children, or wealth, &c.: there was no sorrow when these were not: with his union with these his sorrow commences. Hence, when these things disappear, an intelligent man should not indulge in any sorrow. Bonds or attachments are always productive of grief. When bonds are severd or destroyed, there ought to be no grief.—T.

are unknown, one should conduct oneself with humility. Such a person is said to be possessed of wisdom, and such a one surely finds happiness. That man who is pleased with his own Soul[1] who is devoted to Yoga, who depends upon nothing out of self, who is without cupidity, and who conducts himself without the assistance of anything but his self, succeeds in attaining to felicity.—' "

SECTION CCCXXXII

" 'Narada said,—When the vicissitudes of happiness and sorrow appear or disappear, the transitions are incapable of being prevented by either wisdom or policy or exertion. Without allowing oneself to fall away from one's true nature, one should strive one's best for protecting one's own Self. He who betakes himself to such care and exertion, has never to languish. Regarding Self as something dear, one should always seek to rescue oneself from decrepitude, death, and disease. Mental and physical diseases afflict the body, like keen-pointed shafts shot from the bow by a strong bowman. The body of a person that is tortured by thirst, that is agitated by agony, that is perfectly helpless, and that is desirous of prolonging his life, is dragged towards destruction.[2] Days and nights are ceaselessly running bearing away in their current the periods of life of all human beings. Like currents of rivers, these flow ceaselessly without ever turning back.[3] The ceaseless succession of the lighted and the dark fortnights is wasting all mortal creatures without stopping for even a moment in this work. Rising and setting day after day, the Sun, who is himself undecaying, is continually cooking the joys and sorrows of all men. The nights are ceaselessly going away, taking with them the good and bad incidents that befall man, that depend on destiny, and that are unexpected by him. If the fruits of man's acts were not dependent on other circumstances, then one would obtain whatever object one would desire. Even men of restrained senses, of cleverness, and of intelligence, if destitute of acts, never succeed in earning any fruits.[4] Others, though destitute of intelligence and unendued with accomplishments of any kind, and who are really the lowest of men, are seen, even when

1 *I.e.*, whose pleasures do not depend upon external objects such as spouses and children, &c.—T.

2 'Vidhitsabhih' is 'pipasabhih.' It comes from 'dhe' meaning 'drinking'.—T.

3 Vyasa lived in northern India and was evidently unacquainted with the tides that appear in the Bengal rivers.—T.

4 The object of this Verse is to show the utility and necessity of acts. Without acting no one, however clever, can earn any fruit. Both the Vernacular translators give ridiculous versions of this plain aphorism.—T.

they do not long after success, to be crowned with the fruition of all their desires.[1] Some one else, who is always ready to do acts of injury to all creatures, and who is engaged in deceiving all the world, is seen to wallow in happiness. Some one that sits idly, obtains great prosperity; while another, by exerting earnestly, is seen to miss desirable fruits almost within his reach.[2] Do thou ascribe it as one of the faults of man! The vital seed, originating in one's nature from sight of one person, goes to another person. When imparted to the womb, it sometimes produces an embryo and sometimes fails. When sexual congress fails, it resembles a mango tree that puts forth a great many flowers without, however, producing a single fruit.[3] As regards some men who are desirous of having offspring and who, for the fruition of their object, strive heartily (by worshipping diverse deities), they fail to procreate an embryo in the womb. Some person again, who fears the birth of an embryo as one fears a snake of virulent poison, finds a long-lived son born unto him and who seems to be his own self come back to the stages through which he has passed. Many persons with ardent longing for offspring and cheerless on that account, after sacrificing to many deities and undergoing severe austerities, at last beget children, duly borne for ten long months (in the wombs of their spouses), that prove to be veritable wretches of their race. Others, who have been obtained through virtue of such blessed rites and observances, at once obtain wealth and grain and diverse other sources of enjoyment earned and stored by their sires. In an act of congress, when two persons of opposite sexes come into contact with one another, the embryo takes birth in the womb, like a calamity afflicting the mother. Very soon after the suspension of the vital breaths, other physical forms possess that embodied creature whose gross body has been destroyed but whose acts have all been performed with that gross body made of flesh and phlegm.[4] Upon the dissolution of the body, another body, which is as much destructible as the one that is destroyed, is kept ready for the burnt

1 'Asi' is used in the sense of 'akansha.'—T.

2 'Naprapyamadhigacbchati' is 'na aprayam &.'—T.

3 I do not quite understand in what the fault lies that is referred to here. Perhaps the sense is this. In Hindu Philosophy, the vital seed is said to be generated by the sight of a desirable woman. When sexual congress takes place with one whose sight has not originated the vital seed but with another it fails to be productive. Whoever indulges in such intercourse is to blame.-T

4 'Parasarirani' has 'prapnuvanti' understood after it 'Chinnavijam' means 'whose seed has broken,' that is the creature whose gross body has met with destruction. The gross body is called the 'Vijam' or seed of (heaven and hell). The sense of the Verse is that every one, after death, attains to a new body. A creature can never exist without the bonds of body being attached to him. Of course, the case is otherwise with persons who succeed in achieving their Emancipation by the destruction of all acts. The Burdwan translator, following the Commentator faithfully, renders this Verse correctly. K. P. Singha skips over it entirely.—T.

and destroyed creature (to migrate into) even as one boat goes to another for transferring to itself the passengers of the other.[1] In consequence of an act of congress, a drop of the vital seed, that is inanimate, is cast into the womb. I ask thee, through whose or what care is the embryo kept alive? That part of the body into which the food that is eaten goes and where it is digested, is the place where the embryo resides, but it is not digested there. In the womb, amid urine and fæces, one's sojourn is regulated by Nature. In the matter of residence therein or escape therefrom, the born creature is not a free agent. In fact, in these respects, he is perfectly helpless. Some embryos fall from the womb (in an undeveloped state). Some come out alive (and continue to live). While as regards some, they meet with destruction in the womb, after being quickened with life, in consequence of some other bodies being ready for them (through the nature of their acts)[2]. That man who, in an act of sexual congress, injects the vital fluid, obtains from it a son or daughter. The offspring thus obtained, when the time comes, takes part in a similar act of congress. When the allotted period of a person's life is at its close, the five primal elements of his body attain to the seventh and the ninth stages and then cease to be. The person, however, undergoes no change.[3] Without doubt, when persons are afflicted by diseases as little animals assailed by hunters, they then lose the power of rising up and moving about. If when men are afflicted by diseases, they wish to spend even vast wealth, physicians with their best efforts fail to alleviate their pain. Even physicians, that are well-skilled and well-up in their scriptures and well-equipt with excellent medicines, are themselves afflicted by disease like animals assailed by hunters. Even if men drink many astringents and diverse kinds of medicated *ghee*, they are seen to be broken by decrepitude like trees by strong elephants. When animals and birds and beasts of prey and poor men are afflicted by ailments, who treats them with medicines? Indeed, these are not

---

1 This is a not a difficult Verse. Then, again, the Commentator explains it carefully. K.P. Singha gives a ridiculous version. The Burdwan translator is correct. 'Nirddagdham' and 'vinasyantam' imply the dying or dead Jivar 'paradeham chalachalam abitam bhavati' means 'another body, as much subject to destruction, is kept ready.'—T.

2 I expand this Verse a little for bringing out its meaning. What is said here is that some coma out of the womb alive; some die there before being quickened with life, the reason being that their acts of past lives bring for them other bodies even at that stage.—T.

3 This Verse is certainly a 'crux.' The Commentator, I think, displays considerable ingenuity in explaining it. The order of the words is 'Gatayushah tasya sahajatasya pancha saptamim navamim dasam prapnuvanti; tatah na bhavanti; sa na.' The ten stages of a person's life are (1) residence within the womb, (2) birth, (3) infancy, up to 5 years, (4) childhood, up to 12 years, (5) 'Pauganda,' up to 16 years, (6) youth, up to 48 years, (7) old age, (8) decrepitude, (9) suspension of breath, (10) destruction of body.—T.

seen to be ill. Like larger animals assailing smaller ones, ailments are seen to afflict even terrible kings of fierce energy and invincible prowess. All men, reft of the power of even uttering cries indicate of pain, and overwhelmed by error and grief, are seen to be borne away along the fierce current into which they have been thrown. Embodied creatures, even when seeking to conquer nature, are unable to conquer it with the aid of wealth, of sovereign power, or of the austerest penances.[1] If all attempts men make were crowned with success, then men would never be subject to decrepitude, would never come upon anything disagreeable, and lastly would be crowned with fruition in respect of all their wishes. All men wish to attain to gradual superiority of position. To gratify this wish they strive to the best of their power. The result, however, does not agree with wish.[2] Even men that are perfectly heedful, that are honest, and brave and endued with prowess, are seen to pay their adorations to men intoxicated with the pride of affluence and with even alcoholic stimulants.[3] Some men are seen whose calamities disappear before even these are marked or noticed by them. Others there are who are seen to possess no wealth but who are free from misery of every kind. A great disparity is observable in respect of the fruits that wait upon conjunctions of acts. Some are seen to bear vehicles on their shoulders, while some are seen to ride on those vehicles. All men are desirous of affluence and prosperity. A few only have cars (and elephants and steeds) dragged (or walking) in their processions. Some there are that fail to have a single spouse when their first-wedded ones are dead ; while others have hundreds of spouses to call their own. Misery and happiness are the two things that exist side by side. Men have either misery or happiness. Behold, this is a subject of wonder ! Do not, however, suffer thyself to be stupefied by error at such a sight ! Cast off both righteousness and sin ! Cast off also truth and falsehood ! Having cast off both truth and falsehood, do thou then cast off that with whose aid thou shalt cast off the former ! O best of Rishis, I have now told thee that which is a great misery ! With the aid of such instructions, the deities (who were all human beings) succeeded in leaving the Earth for becoming the denizens of heaven !—

1 'Niyuktah' means employed. I take it to imply 'employed in the task of conquering Nature.' It may also mean, 'set to their usual tasks by the influence of past acts.' Nature here means, of course the grand laws to which human existence is subject, viz., the law of birth, of death, of disease and decrepitude, &c.—T.

2 'Uparyupari' implies gradual superiority. If one becomes wealthy, one desires to be a councillor ; if a councillor, one wishes to be prime minister ; and so on. The sense of the Verse is that man's desire to rise is unsatiable.—T.

3 The reading I prefer is 'asathah' and not sathah. If the latter reading be kept, it would mean of both descriptions are seen to pay court to the wicked.—T.

"'Hearing these words of Narada, Suka, endued with great intelligence and possessed of tranquillity of mind, reflected upon the drift of the instructions be received, but could not arrive at any certainty of conclusion. He understood that one suffers great misery in consequence of the accession of children and spouses ; that one has to undergo great labour for the acquisition of science and Vedic lore. He, therefore, asked himself, saying,—What is that situation which is eternal and which is free from misery of every kind but in which there is great prosperity?—Reflecting for a moment upon the course ordained for him to run through, Suka, who was well acquainted with the beginning and the end of all duties, resolved to attain to the highest end that is fraught with the greatest felicity. He questioned himself, saying,—How shall I, tearing all attachments and becoming perfectly free, attain to that excellent end? How, indeed, shall I attain to that excellent situation whence there is no return into the ocean of diverse kinds of birth! I desire to obtain that condition of existence whence there is no return! Casting off all kinds of attachments, arrived at certainty by reflection with the aid of the mind, I shall attain to that end! I shall attain to that situation in which thy Soul will have tranquillity, and when I shall be able to dwell for eternity without being subject to decrepitude or change. It is, however, certain that that high end cannot be attained without the aid of Yoga. One that has attained to the state of perfect knowledge and enlightenment never receives an accession of low attachments through acts.[1] I shall, therefore, have recourse to Yoga, and casting off this body which is my present residence, I shall transform myself into a wind and enter that mass of effulgence which is represented by the sin.[2] When Jiva enters that mas of effulgence, he no longer suffers like Shoma who, with the gods, upon the exhaustion of merit, falls down on the Earth and having once more acquired sufficient merit returns to heaven.[3] The Moon is

---

1 'Avavandhab' is low attachments, implying those that appertain to the body. In fact, the acquisition of the body itself is such an attachment. What is said here is that Jiva who has become enlightened becomes freed from the obligation of rebirth or contact with body once more.—T.

2 The mass of effulgence constituting the Sun is nothing else than Brahma. Brahma is pure effulgence. 'Savitri-mandala-madhyavartir-Narayanah' does not mean a deity with a physical form in the midst of the solar effulgence but incorporeal and universal Brahma. That effulgence is adored in the Gayatri.—T.

3 The Commentator takes 'Shomah' to mean 'Shomagath Jivah.' He does not explain the rest of the Verse. The grammatical construction presents no difficulty. If, 'Shomah' be taken in the sense in which the Commentator explains it, the meaning would be this. He who enters the solar effulgence has not to undergo any change, unlike 'Shomah' and the deities who have to undergo changes, for they fall down upon the exhaustion of their merit and re-ascend when they once more acquire merit. Both the vernacular translators have made a mess of the Verse. The fact is, there are two paths, 'archiradi-margah' and 'dhumadi-margah.' They who go by the former ,reach Brahma and have never to return. While they who go by the latter way, enjoy felicity for some time and then come back.—T.

always seen to wane and once more wax. Seeing this waning and waxing that go on repeatedly, I do not wish to have a form of existence in which there are such changes. The Sun warms all the worlds by means of his fierce rays. His disc never undergoes any diminution. Remaining unchanged, he drinks energy from all things. Hence, I desire to go into the Sun of blazing effulgence.[1] There I shall live, invincible by all, and in my inner soul freed from all fear, having cast off this body of mine in the solar region. With the great Rishis I shall enter the unbearable energy of the Sun. I declare unto all creatures, unto these trees, these elephants, these mountains, the Earth herself, the several points of the compass, the welkin, the deities, the Danavas, the Gandharvas, the Pisachas, the Uragas, and the Rakshasas, that I shall, verily, enter all creatures in the world.[2] Let all the gods with the Rishis behold the prowess of my Yoga today!—Having said these words, Suka, informed Narada of world wide celibrity of his intention. Obtaining Narada's permission, Suka then proceeded to where his sire was. Arrived at his presence, the great Muni, *viz.*, the high-souled and Island-born Krishna, Suka walked round him and addressed him the usual enquiries. Hearing of Suka's intention, the high-souled Rishi became highly pleased. Addressing him, the great Rishi said,—O son, O dear son, do thou stay here to-day so that I may behold thee for some time for gratifying my eyes;—Suka, however, was indifferent to that request. Freed from affection and all doubt, he began to think only of Emancipation, and set his heart on the journey. Leaving his sire, that foremost of Rishis then proceeded to the spacious breast of Kailasa which was inhabited by crowds of ascetics crowned with success.' "

SECTION CCCXXXIII

'Bhishma said,—Having ascended the summit of the mountain, O Bharata, the son of Vyasa sat down upon a level spot free from blades of grass and retired from the haunts of other creatures. Agreeably to the direction of the scriptures and to the ordinances laid down, that ascetic, conversant with the gradual order of the successive processes of Yoga, held his soul first in one place and then in another, commencing from his feet and proceeding through all the limbs. Then when the Sun had not risen long, Suka sat, with his face turned Eastwards, and

---

1 Here, the words Sun and Moon are indicative of the two different paths mentioned in the note immediately before.—T.

2 What Suka says here is that he would attain to universal Brahma and thus identify himself with all things.—T.

hands and feet drawn in, in an humble attitude. In that spot where the intelligent son of Vyasa sat prepared to address himself to Yoga, there were no flocks of birds, no sound, and no sight that was repulsive or terror-inspiring. He then beheld his own Soul freed from all attachments. Beholding that highest of all things, he laughed in joy.[1] He once more set himself prepared to Yoga for attaining to the path of Emancipation. Becoming the great master of Yoga, he transcended the element of space. He then circumambulated the celestial Rishi Narada, and represented unto that foremost of Rishis the fact of his having addressed himself to the highest Yoga.

" 'Suka said,—I have succeeded in beholding the path (of Emancipation), I have addrest myself to it. Blessed be thou, O thou of wealth of penances! I shall, through thy grace, O thou of great splendour, attain to an end that is highly desirable!"

"Bhishma said,—'Having received the permission of Narada, Suka the son of the Island-born Vyasa saluted the celestial Rishi and once more set himself to Yoga and entered the element of space. Ascending then from the breast of the Kailasa mountain, he soared into the sky. Capable of traversing through the welkin, the blessed Suka of fixed conclusion, then identified himself with the element of Wind. As that foremost of regenerate ones, possessed of effulgence like that of Garuda, was traversing through the skies with the speed of the wind or thought, all creatures cast their eyes upon him. Endued with the splendour of fire or the Sun, Suka then regarded the three worlds in their entirety as one homogenous Brahma, and proceeded along that path of great length. Indeed, all creatures, mobile and immobile, cast their eyes upon him as he proceeded with concentrated attention, and a tranquil and fearless soul. All creatures, agreeably to the ordinance and according to their power, worshipped him with reverence. The denizens of heaven rained showers of celestial flowers upon him. Beholding him, all the tribes of Apsaras and Gandharvas became filled with wonder. The Rishis also, that were crowned with success, became equally amazed. And they asked themselves,—who is this one that has attained to success by his penances? With gaze withdrawn from his own body but turned upwards he is filling us all with pleasure by his glances!—Of highly righteous soul and celebrated throughout the three worlds, Suka proceeded in silence, his face turned towards the East and gaze directed towards the Sun. As he proceeded, he seemed to fill the entire welkin with an all-pervading noise. Beholding him coming in that way, all the tribes of the Apsaras, struck with awe, O king, became filled with

---

1 Jahasa hasam' is an instance in Sanskrit of the cognate government of neuter Verbs.—T.

amazement. Headed by Panchachuda and others, they looked at Suka with eyes expanded by wonder. And they asked one another, saying, —What deity is this one that has attained to such a high end? Without doubt, he comes hither, freed from all attachments and emancipated from all desires!—Suka then proceeded to the Malaya mountains where Urvasi and Purvachitti used to dwell always. Both of them beholding the energy of the son of the great regenerate Rishi, became filled with wonder. And they said,—Wonderful is this concentration of attention (to Yoga) of a regenerate youth who was accustomed to the recitation and study of the Vedas! Soon will he traverse the entire welkin like the Moon. It was by dutiful service and humble ministrations towards his sire that he acquired this excellent understanding. He is firmly attached to his sire, possessed of austere penances, and is very much loved by his sire. Alas, why has he been dismissed by his inattentive father to proceed (thus) along a way whence there is no return?—Hearing these words of Urvasi, and attending to their import, Suka, that foremost of all persons conversant with duties, cast his eyes on all sides, and once more beheld the entire welkin, the whole Earth with her mountains and waters and forests, and also all the lakes and rivers. All the deities also of both sexes, joining their hands, paid reverence to the son of the Island born Rishi and gazed at him with wonder and respect. That foremost of all righteous men, Suka, addressing all of them, said these words,—If my sire follow me and repeatedly call after me by my name, do all of you together return him an answer for me. Moved by the affection all of you bear for me, do you accomplish this request of mine!—Hearing these words of Suka, all the points of the compass, all the forests, all the seas, all the rivers, and all the mountains, answered him from every side, saying,—We accept thy command, O regenerate one! It shall be as thou sayst! It is in this way that we answer the words spoken the Rishi!—

SECTION CCCXXXIV

"Bhishma said.—'Having spoken in this way (unto all things), the regenerate Rishi of austere penances, *viz.*, Suka, stayed on his success casting off the four kinds of faults. Casting off also the eight kinds of Tamas, he dismissed the five kinds of Rajas. Endued with great intelligence, he then cast off the attribute of Sattwa. All this seemed exceedingly wonderful. He then dwelt in that eternal station that is destitute of attributes, freed from every indication, that is, in *Brahma*, blazing like a smokeless fire. Meteors began to shoot. The points of the compass seemed to be ablaze. The Earth trembled. All those phenomena seemed exceedingly wonderful. The trees began to cast off their branches and the mountains their summits. Loud-reports (as of thunder) were heard that seemed to rive the Himavat mouutains. The Sun seemed at that moment to be shorn of splendour. Fire refused to blaze forth. The lakes and rivers and seas were all agitated. Vasava poured showers of rain of excellent taste and fragrance. A pure breeze began to blow, bearing excellent perfumes. Suka as he proceeded through the welkin, beheld two beautiful summits, one belonging to Himavat and another to Meru. These were in close contact with each other. One of them was made of gold and was, therefore yellow ; the other was white, being made of silver. Each of them. O Bharata, was a hundred Yojanas in height and of the same measure in breadth. Indeed, as Suka journeyed towards the north, he saw those two beautiful summits. With a fearless heart he dashed against those two summits that were united with each other. Unable to bear the force, the summits were suddenly rent in twain. The sight they thereupon presented, O monarch, was exceedingly wonderful to behold. Suka pierced through those summits, for they were unable to stop his onward course. At this a loud noise arose in heaven, made by the denizens thereof. The Gandharvas and the Rishis also and others that dwelt in that mountain being rent in twain and Suka passing through it. Indeed, O Bharata, a loud noise was heard everywhere at that moment, consisting of the words—Excellent, Excellent !—He was adored by the Gandharvas and the Rishis, by crowds of Yakshas and Rakshasas, and by all tribes of the Vidyadharas. The entire firmament became strewn with celestial flowers showered from heaven at that moment when Suka thus pierced through that impenetrable barrier, O monarch ! The righteous-souled Suka then beheld from a high region the celestial stream Mandakini of great beauty, running below through a region adorned by many flowering groves and woods. In these waters many beautiful Apsaras were sporting. Beholding Suka who was bodiless, those unclad aerial beings felt shame. Learning that Suka had undertaken his great journey, his sire Vyasa, filled with affection, followed him behind along the same aerial path. Meanwhile Suka, proceeding through that region of the firmament that is above the region of the wind displayed his Yoga-prowess and identified himself with Brahma.[1] Adopting the subtile path of high Yoga, Vyasa of austere penances, reached within the twinkling of the eye that spot whence Suka first undertook his journey. Proceeding along the same way, Vyasa beheld the mountain

1 The Rishis knew that the height of the atmosphere is not interminable—T

summit rent in twain and through which Suka has passed. Encountering the Island-born ascetic, the Rishis began to represent to him the achievements of his son. Vyasa, however, began to indulge in lamentations, loudly calling upon his son by name and causing the three worlds to resound with the noise he made. Meanwhile, the righteous-souled Suka, who had entered the elements, had become their soul and acquired omnipresence, answered his sire by uttering the monosyllable *Bho* in the form of an echo. At this, the entire universe of mobile and immobile creatures, uttering the monosyllable *Bho*, echoed the answer of Suka. From that time to this, when sounds are uttered in mountain-caves or on mountain-breasts, the latter, as if in answer to Suka still echo them (with the monosyllable *Bho*). Having cast off all the attributes of sound, etc., and showing his Yoga-prowess in the manner of his disappearance, Suka in this way attained to the highest station. Beholding that glory and puissance of his son of immeasurable energy, Vyasa sat down on the breast of the mountain and began to think of his son with grief. The Apsaras were sporting on the banks of the celestial stream Mandakini, seeing the Rishi seated there, became all agitated with grave shame and lost heart. Some of them, to hide their nudity, plunged into the stream, and some entered the groves hard by, and some quickly took up their clothes, at beholding the Rishi. (None of them had betrayed any signs of agitation at sight of his son). The Rishi, beholding these movements, understood that his son had been emancipated from all attachments, but that he himself was not freed therefrom. At this he became filled with both joy and shame. As Vyasa was seated there, the auspicious god Siva, armed with Pinaka, surrounded on all sides by many deities and Gandharvas and adored by all the great Rishis came thither. Consoling the Island born Rishi who was burning with grief on account of his son, Mahadeva said these words unto him.—Thou hadst formerly solicited from me a son possessed of the energy of Fire, of Water, of Wind, and of Space ! Procreated by thy penances, the son that was born unto thee was of that very kind. Proceeding from my grace, he was pure and full of Brahma-energy. He has attained to the highest end—an end which none can win that has not completely subjugated his senses, nor can be won by even any of the deities. Why then, O regenerate Rishi, dost thou grieve for that son ? As long as the hills will last, as long as the ocean will last, so long will the fame of thy son endure undiminished ! Through my grace, O great Rishi thou shalt behold in this world a shadowy form resembling thy son, moving by the side and never deserting thee for a single moment !—Thus favoured by the illustrious Rudra himself, O Bharata, the Rishi beheld a shadow of his son by his side. He returned from that place, filled with joy at this. I have now told thee, O chief of Bharata's race, everything regarding the birth and life of Suka about which thou hadst asked me. The celestial Rishi Narada and the great Yogin Vyasa had repeatedly told all this to me in days of yore when the subject was suggested to him in course of conversation. That person devoted to tranquillity hears this sacred history directly connected with the topic of Emancipation is certain to attain to the highest end.[1]"

SECTION CCCXXXV

"Yudhishthira said,—'If a man be a house-holder or a Brahmacharin, a forest-recluse or a mendicant, and if he desires to achieve success, what deity should he adore? How can he certainly acquire heaven and attain that which is of the highest benefit (*viz.*, Emancipation)? According to what ordinances should he perform the *homa* in honour of the gods and the *Pitris*? What is the region to which one goes when one becomes emancipated? What is the essence of Emancipation? What should one do so that one, having attained to heaven, would not have to fall down thence? Who is the deity of the deities? And who is the *Pitri* of the *Pitris*? Who is he that is superior to him, who is the deity of the deities and the *Pitri* of the *Pitris*? Tell me all this, O Grandsire!'

"Bhishma said,—O thou that art well acquainted with the art of questioning, this question that thou hast asked me, O sinless one, is one that touches a deep mystery. One cannot answer it with the aid of the science of argumentation, even if one were to strive for a hundred years. Without the grace of Narayana, O king, or an accession of high knowledge, this question of thine is incapable of being answered. Connected though this topic be with a deep mystery, I shall yet, O slayer of foes, expound it to thee![2] In this connection is cited the old history of the discourse between Narada and the Rishi Narayana. I heard it from my sire that in the Krita age, O monarch, during the epoch of the Self-born Manu, the eternal Narayana, the Soul of the universe, took birth as the son of Dharma in a quadruple form, *viz.*, as Nara, Narayana, Hari, and the Self-create Krishna.[3] Amongst them all,

---

1 In this Section, Bhishma recites to Yudhishthira the fact of Suka's departure from this world, and Vyasa's grief at that occurrence. He speaks of the fact as one that had been related to him in bygone times by both Narada and Vyasa himself. It is evident from this that the Suka who recited the Srimad Bhagavat to Parikshit, the grandson of Arjuna, could not possibly be the Suka who was Vyasa's son.—T.

2 What Bhishma says here is that without faith this subject is incapable of being understood.—T.

3 This is a triplet, The last word of the third line, *viz.*, 'Swayambhu-

Narayana and Nara underwent the severest austerities by repairing to the Himalayan retreat known by the name of Vadari, by riding on their golden cars. Each of those cars was furnished with eight wheels, and made up of the five primal elements, and looked exceedingly beautiful.[1] Those original regents of the world who had taken birth as the sons of Dharma, became exceedingly emaciated in person in consequence of the austerities they had undergone. Indeed, for those austerities and for their energy, the very deities were unable to look at them. Only that deity with whom they were propitiated could behold them. Without doubt, with his heart devoted to them, and impelled by a longing desire to behold them, Narada dropped down on Gandhamadana from a summit of the high mountains of Meru and wandered over all the world. Possessed of great speed, he at last repaired to that spot whereon was situate the retreat of Vadari. Impelled by curiosity he entered that retreat at the hour of Nara's and Narayana's, performing their daily rites. He said unto himself.—This is truly the retreat of that Being in whom are established all the worlds including the deities, the Asuras, the Gandharvas, the Kinnaras, and the great snakes! There was only one form of this great Being before. That form took birth in four shapes for the expansion of the race of Dharma which have been reared by that deity. How wonderful it is that Dharma has thus been honoured by these four great deities *viz.*, Nara, Narayana, and Hari and Krishna! In this spot Krishna and Hari dwelt formerly. The other two, however, *viz.*, Nara and Narayana, are now dwelling here engaged in penances for the object of enhancing their merit. These two are the highest refuge of the universe. What can be the nature of the daily rites these two perform? They are the sires of all creatures, and the illustrious deities of all beings. Endued with high intelligence, what is that deity whom these two worship? Who are those Pitris whom these two Pitris of all beings adore? —Thinking of this in his mind, and filled with devotion towards Narayana, Narada suddenly appeared before those two gods. After those two deities had finished their adoration to *their* deities and the *Rishis*, they looked at the celestial Rishi arrived at their retreat. The latter was honoured with those eternal rites that are ordained in the scriptures. Beholding that extraordinary conduct of the two original deities in themselves worshipping other deities and Pitris, the illustrious Rishi Narada

vah' refers to 'Krishnah,' but it has no special meaning. It is an adjective used more for the sake of measure than for anything else.—

1 The golden cars referred to here are the fleshly bodies of the two deities. The body is called the car because like the car, it is propelled by some force other than the Soul which owns it for a time, the Soul being inactive. It is regarded as golden because every one becomes attached to it as something very valuable. The eight wheels are Avidya and the rest.—

took his seat there, well pleased with the honours he had received. With a cheerful soul he cast his eyes then on Narayana, and bowing unto Mahadeva he said these words.

"Narada said,—In the Vedas and the Puranas, in the Angas and the subsidiary Angas thou art sung with reverence, thou art unborn and eternal. Thou art the Creator. Thou art the mother of the universe. Thou art the embodiment of Immortality and thou art the foremost of all things. The Past and the Future, indeed, the entire universe has been established on thee! The four modes of life, O lord, having the domestic for their first, ceaselessly sacrifice to thee that art of diverse forms. Thou art the father and the mother and the eternal preceptor of the universe. We know not who is that deity or that Pitri unto whom thou art sacrificing to-day!—

"The holy one said,—This topic is one about which nothing should be said. It is an ancient mystery. Thy devotion to me is very great. Hence, O regenerate one, I shall discourse to thee on it agreeably to the truth. That which is minute, which is inconceivable, unmanifest, immobile, durable, destitute of all connection with the senses and the objects of the senses, that which is dissotiated from the (five) elements —that is called the in-dwelling Soul of all existent creatures. That is known by the name of Kshetrajna. Transcending the three attributes of Sattwa, Rajas, and Tamas, that is regarded as Purusha in the scriptures. From Him hath followed the unmanifest, O foremost of regenerate ones, possessed of the three attributes of Sattwa, Rajas, and Tamas. Though really unmanifest, she is called indestructible Prakriti and dwell in all manifest forms. Know that She is the source whence we two have sprung. That all-pervading Soul, which is made up of all existent and non-existent things, is adored by us. Even He is what we worship in all those rites that we perform in honour of the deities and the Pitris. There is no higher deity or Pitri than He, O regenerate one. He should be known as our Soul. It is him that we worship. This course of duties followed by men has, O regenerate one, been promulgated by Him. It is His ordinance that we should duly perform all the rites laid down in respect of the deities and the Pitris. Brahman, Sthanu, Manu, Daksha, Bhrigu, Dharma, Yama, Marichi, Angiras, Atri, Pulastya, Pulaha, Kratu, Vasishtha, Parameshthi, Vivaswat, Shoma, he that has been called Karddama, Krodha, Avak, and Krita,—these one and twenty persons, called Prajapatis, were first born. All of them obeyed the eternal law of the Supreme God. Observing all the rites, in detail, that were ordained in honour of the deities and the Pitris, all those foremost of regenerate persons acquired all those objects which they sought. The incorporeal denizens of Heaven itself bow to that Supreme deity and through His grace they attain to those fruits and that end which He ordains for them. This is the settled conclusion of the scriptures that these persons freed from these seven and ten attributes, (*viz.*, the five senses of knowledge, the five senses of action, the five vital breaths, and mind and understanding), who have cast off all acts, and are divested of the five and ten elements which constitute the gross body, are said to be Emancipate. That which the Emancipate attain to as their ultimate end is called by the name of Kshetrajna. He is regarded (in the scriptures) as both possessed of and freed from all the attributes. He can be apprehended by Knowledge alone. We two have sprung from Him. Knowing him in that way, we adore that eternal Soul of all things. The Vedas and all the modes of life, though characterised by divergences of opinion, all worship Him with devotion. It is He who, speedily moved to grace, confers on them high ends fraught with felicity. Those persons in this world who, filled with His spirit, become fully and conclusively devoted to Him, attain to ends that are much higher, for they succeed in entering Him and becoming merged in his Self. I have now, O Narada, discoursed to thee on what is a high mystery moved by the love I bear to thee for thy devotion to me. Indeed, in consequence of that devotion which thou professest towards me, thou hast succeeded in listening to this my discourse !—' "

SECTION CCCXXXVI

"Bhishma said,—'Addressed by Narayana, that foremost of beings, in these words, Narada, the foremost of men, then said these words unto Narayana for the good of the world.

"Narada said,—Let that object be accomplished for which thou, O Self-born Being, hast taken birth in four forms in the house of Dharma ! I shall now repair (to the White Island) for beholding thy original nature. I always worship my seniors. I have never divulged the secrets of others. O lord of the universe, I have studied the Vedas with care. I have undergone austere penances. I have never spoken an untruth. As ordained in the scriptures, I have always protected the four that should be protected.[1] I have always behaved equally towards

1 *i.e.*, the hands, the feet, the stomach, and the organ of pleasure. The hands are said to be protected when they are restrained from the commission of all improper acts ; the feet are said to be duly protected when they are restrained from touching all improper places. The stomach is said to be protected when one never takes any kind of improper food, and when one abstains from all evil acts for appeasing one's hunger. And lastly, one is said to restrain the organ of pleasure when one abstains from all acts of improper congress.—T.

friends and foes. Wholly and conclusively devoted to Him, that first of deities, *viz.*, the Supreme Soul, I incessantly adore Him. Having cleansed my soul by these acts of special merit, why shall I not succeed in obtaining a sight of that Infinite Lord of the universe?—Hearing these words of Parameshthi's son, Narayana, that protector of the scriptures, dismissed him, saying,—Go, O Narada!—Before dismissing him, however, the great deity worshipped the celestial Rishi with those rites and ceremonies which have been laid down in the scriptures by himself. Narada also gave due honours to the ancient Rishi Narayana. After such honours had been mutually given and received, the son of Parameshthi departed from that spot. Endued with high Yoga-puissance, Narada suddenly soared into the firmament and reached the summit of the mountains of Meru. Proceeding to a retired spot on that summit, the great ascetic took rest for a short while. He then cast his eyes towards the north western direction and beheld an exceedingly wonderful sight. Towards the north, in the ocean of milk, there is a large island named the White Island. The learned say that its distance from the mountains of Meru is greater than two and thirty thousand Yojanas. The denizens of that realm have no senses. They live without taking food of any kind. Their eyes are winkless. They always emit excellent perfumes. Their complexions are white. They are cleansed from every sin. They blast the eyes of those sinners that look at them. Their bones and bodies are as hard as thunder. They regard honour and dishonour in the same light. They all look as if they are of celestial origin. Besides, all of them are endued, with auspicious marks and great strength. Their heads seem to be like umbrellas. Their voices are deep like that of the clouds. Each of them has four Mushkas.[1] The soles of their feet are marked by hundreds of lines. They have sixty teeth all of which are white (and large), and eight smaller ones. They have many tongues. With those tongues they seem to lick the very Sun whose face is turned towards every direction. Indeed, they seem to be capable of devouring that great deity from whom hath sprung the entire universe, the Vedas, the deities, and the Munis wedded to the attribute of tranquillity.'

"Yudhishthira said,—'O grandsire, thou hast said that those beings have no senses, that they do not eat anything for supporting their lives; that their eyes are winkless; and that they always emit excellent perfumes. I ask, how were they born? What also is the superior end to

1 The word 'Mushka' as ordinarily understood, implies the scrotum or testes. The Commentator Nilakantha supposes that it may stand for the shoulder-knot. He believes that the phrase implies that the people of this Island had each four arms.—T.

which they attain? O chief of Bharata's race, are the indications of those men that become emancipate the same as those by which the denizens of the White Island are distinguished? Do thou dispel my doubts! The curiosity I feel is very great. Thou art the repositary of all histories and discourses. As regards ourselves, we entirely depend on thee for knowledge and instruction!

"Bhishma continued,—'This narrative, O monarch, which I have heard from my sire, is extensive. I shall now recite it to thee. Indeed, it is regarded as the essence of all narratives. There was, in times past, a king on Earth of the name of Uparichara. He was known to be the friend of Indra, the chief of the celestials. He was devoted to Narayana known also by the name of Hari. He was observant of all the duties laid down in the scriptures. Ever devoted to his sire, he was always heedful and ready for action. He won the sovereignty of the world in consequence of a boon he had obtained from Narayana. Following the *Sattwata* ritual that had been declared in days of yore by Surya himself, king Uparichara used to worship the God of gods (Narayana), and when his worship was over, he used to adore (with what remained) the grandsire of the universe.[1] After worshipping the Grandsires (Pitris), he worshipped the Brahmanas. He then divided the offerings among those that were dependent on him. With what remained after serving those, the king satisfied his own hunger. Devoted to truth, the monarch abstained from doing any injury to any creature. With his whole soul, the king was devoted to that God of gods, *viz.*, Janarddana, who is without beginning and middle and end, who is the Creator of the universe, and who is without deterioration of any kind. Beholding the devotion to Narayana of that slayer of foes, the divine chief of the celestials himself shared with him his own seat and bed. His kingdom and wealth and spouses and animals were all regarded by him as obtained from Narayana. He, therefore, offered all his possessions to that great deity.[2] Adopting the *Sattwata* ritual, king Uparichara, with concentrated soul, used to discharge all his sacrificial acts and observances, both optional and obligatory. In the palace of that illustrious king, many foremost Brahmanas, well conversant with the *Pancharatra* ritual, used to eat before all others the food offered to the god Narayana. As long as that slayer of foes continued to rule his kingdom righteously, no untruth

---

1 The 'Sattwata' ritual is explained by the Commentator to mean the 'Pancharatra' ritual. 'Tachcheshena' implies with what remained after Vishnu's worship was over.—T.

2 *i.e.*, dedicated his possessions to the service of Narayana, and held them as the great God's custodian. In other words, he never regarded his wealth as his own, but was always ready to devote it to all good and pious purposes.—T.

ever escaped his lips and no evil thought ever entered his mind. With his limbs he never committed even the slightest sin. The seven celebrated Rishis, *viz.*, Marichi, Atri, Angiras, Pulastya, Pulaha, Kratu, and Vasishtha of great energy, who came to be known by the name of Chitra-sikhandins, uniting together on the breast of that foremost of mountains, viz., Meru, promulgated an excellent treatise on duties and observances that was consistent with the four Vedas. The contents of that treatise were uttered by seven mouths, and constituted the best compendium of human duties and observances. Known, as already stated, by the name of Chitra-sikhandins, those seven Rishis constitute the seven (Prakriti) elements (of Mahat, Ahankara, &c.) and the Self-born Manu, who is the eighth in the enumeration, constituted original Prakriti. These eight uphold the universe, and it was these eight that promulgated the treatise adverted to. With their senses and minds under complete control, and ever devoted to Yoga, these eight ascetics, with concentrated souls, are fully conversant with the Past, the Present and the Future, and are devoted to the religion of Truth.—This is good —this is Brahma,—this is highly beneficial,—reflecting in their minds in this way, those Rishis created the worlds, and the science of morality and duty that governs those worlds. In that treatise the authors discoursed on Religion and Wealth and Pleasure, and subsequently on Emancipation also. They also laid down in it the various restrictions and limitations intended for the Earth as also for Heaven. They composed that treatise after having worshipped with penances the puissant and illustrious Narayana called also Hari, for a thousand celestial years, in company with many other Rishis. Gratified with their penances and worship, Narayana commanded the goddess of speech, viz. Saraswati, to enter into the person of those Rishis. The goddess, for the good of the worlds, did what she was ordered. In consequence of the entrance of the goddess of speech into their persons, those Rishis, well conversant with penances, succeeded in composing that foremost of treatises in respect of vocables, import, and reason.[1] Having composed that treatise sanctified with the syllable *Om*, the Rishis first of all read it to Narayana who became highly pleased with what he heard. That foremost of all Beings then addressed those Rishis in an incorporeal voice and said,—Excellent is this treatise that ye have composed consisting of a hundred thousand verses. The duties and observances of all the worlds will flow from this your work! In complete accordance with the four Vedas, viz., the Yajushes, the Samans, and the Atharvans of Angiras, this treatise of

1 *I.e.*, the treatise those Rishis composed was the foremost of its kind in respect of choice and harmony of vocables, of import or sense and of reasons with which every assertion was fortified.—T.

yours will be an authority in all the worlds in respect of both Pravritti and Nivritti.[1] Agreeably to the authority of the scriptures I have created Brahman from the attribute of Grace, Rudra from my Wrath, and yourselves, Ye Brahmanas, as representing the Prakriti-elements (of Mahat, Ahankara, &c.), Surya, and Chandramas, Wind, and Earth, and Water and Fire, all the stars and planets and constellations, all else that is called by the name of creatures, and utterers of Brahma (or the Vedas), they all live and act in their respective spheres and are all respected as authorities. Even this treatise that ye have composed shall be regarded by all persons in the same light, viz., as a work of the highest authority. This is my command. Guided by this treatise, the Self-born Manu himself will declare to the world its course of duties and observances. When Usanas and Vrihaspati will arise, they also will promulgate their respective treatises on morality and religion, guided by and quoting from this your treatise.[2] After the publication of his treatise by the Self-born Manu and of that by Usanas, and after the publication of the treatise also by Vrihaspati, this science composed by you will be acquired by king Vasu (otherwise known by the name of Uparichara). Indeed ye foremost of regenerate ones, that king will acquire this knowledge of this work from Vrihaspati. That King, filled with all good thoughts, will become deeply devoted to me. Guided by this treatise, he will accomplish all his religious acts and observances. Verily, this treatise composed by you will be the foremost of all treatises on morality and religion. Possessed of the excellence, this treatise is fraught with instructions for acquiring both Wealth and Religious merit, and is full of mysteries. In consequence of the promulgation of this treatise of yours, ye will be progenitors of an extensive race. King Uparichara also will become endued with greatness and prosperity. Upon the death, however, of that king, this eternal treatise will disappear from the world. I tell you all this.—Having said these words unto all those Rishis, the invisible Narayana left them and proceeded to some place that was not known to them. Then those sires of the world, those Rishis that bestowed their thoughts on the ends pursued by the world, duly promulgated that treatise which is the eternal origin of all duties

---

1 There are two religions, *viz*, that of Pravritti, implying act and observances, and that of Nivritti, implying a complete abstention from all acts and observances. The last is also called the religion of Emancipation. —T.

2 Whether any work on morality and religion was ever actually composed by the seven Rishis or not, no such work, it is certain, is in existence now. Besides this mention of the work in the Mahabharata, no reference to it has been made anywhere else. As to 'Sukra-niti' it is extant, Vrihaspati's 'niti-sastram' is defunct. It is probable, however, that before 'Sukra-niti', there was an anterior work, brief if not exhaustive on the same subjects.—T.

and observances. Subsequently, when Vrihaspati was born in Angiras's race in the first or the Krita age, those seven Rishis charged him with the task of promulgating their treatise which was consistent with the Upanishads and the several branches of the Vedas. They themselves who were upholders of the universe and the first promulgators of duties and religious observances, then proceeded to the place they chose, resolved to devote themselves to penances.' "

SECTION CCCXXXVII

"Bhishma said,—'Then, upon the expiration of the great Kalpa, when the celestial Purohita Vrihaspati was born in the race of Angiras, all the deities became very happy. The words *Vrihat*, *Brahma*, and *Mahat* all bear the same sense.[1] The celestial Purohita, O king came to be called Vrihaspati because he was endued with all these attributes. King Uparichara, otherwise called Vasu, became a disciple of Vrihaspati and soon became the foremost of his disciples. Admitted as such, he began to study at the feet of his preceptor that science which was composed by the seven Rishis who were (otherwise) known by the name of Chitrasikhandins. With soul cleansed from all sorts of evil by sacrifices and other religious rites, he ruled the Earth like Indra ruling the Heaven. That illustrious king performed a great Horse-sacrifice in which his preceptor Vrihaspati became the *Hota*. The sons of Prajapati (Brahman) themselves, *viz.*, Ekata, Dwita, and Trita, became the *Sadasyas* in that sacrifice.[2] There were others also who became Sadasyas in that sacrifice, viz., Dhanusha, Raivya, Arvavasu, Parvavasu, the Rishi Medhatithi, the great Rishi Tandya, the blessed Rishi Santi, otherwise called Vedasiras, the foremost of Rishis, viz., Kapila, who was the father of Salihotra, the first Kalpa, Tittiri the elder brother of Vaisampayana, Kanwa, and Devahotra, in all forming sixteen. In that great sacrifice, O monarch, all the requisite articles were collected. No animals were slain in it. The king had ordained it so. He was full of compassion. Of pure and liberal mind, he had cast off all desires, and was well-conversant with

1 'Paryyaya' literally means a list. The fact is, in all Sanskrit lexicons words expressive of the same meanings occur together. These lists are known by the name of 'Paryyaya.' A more definite idea of the meaning of this word may be had by the English reader when he remembers that in a lexicon like Rogett's *Thesaurus*, groups are given of words expressive of the same signification. Such groups are called 'Paryyayas.'—T.

2 *The Hotri* has to pour libations on the sacrificial fire, reciting *mantras* the while. 'Sadasyas' are persons that watch the sacrifice, *i.e.*, take care that the ordinances of the scriptures are duly complied with. They are, what is called, 'Vidhidarsinas.—T.

all rites. The requisites of that sacrifice all consisted of the products of the wilderness. The ancient God of gods (viz., Hari), became highly gratified with the king on account of that sacrifice. Incapable of being seen by any one else, the great God showed himself to his worshipper. Accepting by taking its scent, the share offered to him he himself took up the *Puradasa*.[1] The great God took up the offerings without being seen by any one. At this, Vrihaspati became angry. Taking up the ladle he hurled it with violence at the sky, and began to shed tears in wrath. Addressing king Uparichara he said,—Here, I place this as Narayana's share of the sacrificial offerings. Without doubt, he shall take it before my eyes.—'

"Yudhishthira said,—'In the great sacrifice of Uparichara, all the deities appeared in their respective forms for taking their shares of the sacrificial offerings and were seen by all. Why is it that the puissant Hari only acted otherwise by invisibly taking his share ?'

"Bhishma continued,—'When Vrihaspati gave way to wrath, the great king Vasu and all his Sadasyas sought to pacify the great Rishi. With cool heads, all of them addressed Vrihaspati, saying,—It behoveth thee not to give way to anger. In this Krita age, this anger to which thou hast given way, should not be the characteristic of any one. The great deity for whom the share of the sacrificial offerings was designed by thee, is himself free from anger. He is incapable of being seen either by ourselves or by thee, O Vrihaspati! Only he can see Him to whom He becomes gracious.—Then the Rishis Ekata, Dwita, and Trita, who were well conversant with the science of morality and duties compiled by the seven Rishis, addressed that conclave and began the following narration.—We are the sons of Brahman, begotten by a fiat of his will (and not in the ordinary way). Once on a time we repaired to the north for obtaining what is for our highest good. Having undergone penances for thousands of years and acquired great ascetic merit, we again stood on only one foot like fixed stakes of wood. The country where we underwent the austerest of penances, lies to the north of the mountains of Meru and on the shores of the Ocean of Milk. The object we had in mind was how to behold the divine Narayana in his own form. Upon the completion of our penances and after we had performed the final ablutions, an incorporeal voice was heard by us, O puissant Vrihaspati, at once deep as that of the clouds and exceedingly sweet and filling the heart with joy. The voice said,—Ye Brahmanas, well have ye performed these penances with cheerful souls. Devoted

---

1 Clarified butter offered in sacrifices, with cakes of powdered barley steeped in it.—T.

unto Narayana, ye seek to know how ye may succeed in beholding that god of great puissance! On the northern shores of the Ocean of Milk there is an island of great splendour called by the name of White Island. The men that inhabit that island have complexions as white as the rays of the Moon and that are devoted to Narayana. Worshippers of that foremost of all Beings, they are devoted to Him with their whole souls. They all enter that eternal and illustrious deity of a thousand rays.[1] They are divested of senses. They do not subsist on any kind of food. Their eyes are winkless. Their bodies always emit a fragrance. Indeed, the denizens of White Island believe and worship only one God. Go thither, ye ascetics, for there I have revealed myself!—All of us, hearing these incorporeal words, proceeded by the way indicated to the country described. Eagerly desirous of beholding Him and our hearts full of Him, we arrived at last at that large island called White Island. Arrived there, we could see nothing. Indeed, our vision was blinded by the energy of the great deity and accordingly we could not see Him.[2] At this, the idea, due to the grace of the great God Himself, arose in our minds that one that had not undergone sufficient penances could not speedily behold Narayana. Under the influence of this idea we once more set ourselves to the practice of some severe austerities, suited to the time and place, for a hundred years. Upon the completion of our vows, we beheld a number of men of auspicious features. All of them were white and looked like the Moon (in colour) and possessed of every mark of blessedness. Their hands were always joined in prayer. The faces of some were turned towards the North and of some towards the East. They were engaged in silently thinking on Brahma.[3] The Yapa performed by those high-souled persons was a *mental yapa* (and did not

1 Professor Weber supposes that in this narrative of the three Rishis Ekata, Dwita, and Trita, the poet is giving a description of either Italy or some island in the Menditerranean, and of a Christian worship that certain Hindu pilgrims might have witnessed. Indeed, a writer in the *Calcutta Review* has gone so far as to say that from what follows, the conjecture would not be a bold one that the whole passage refers to the impression made on certain Hindu pilgrims upon witnessing the celebration of the Eucharist according to the ordinances of the Roman Catholic Church. The Hon'ble K. P. Telang supposes that the whole passage is based on the poets imagination. 'Ekantabhavepagatah' is taken by some to mean "worshippers of the divine Unity." I do not think that such a rendering would be correct —T.

2 The Bombay reading is 'tadapratihato abhavat.' This seems to be better than the Bengal reading 'tato-apratihata &c.' If the Bengal reading be adhered to, 'apratihatah should be taken in the sense of 'nasti pratihato-yasmat.' The meaning, of course, would remain the same —T.

3 'Yapa' means the silent recitation of certain sacred *mantras* or of the name of some deity. In the case of the inhabitants of White Island, the silent recitation was no recitation of *mantras* or words, but was a meditation on incorporeal Brahma. The next Verse makes this clear.—T.

consist of the actual recitation of any *mantras* in words). In consequence of their hearts having been entirely set upon Him, Hari became highly pleased with them. The effulgence that was emitted by each of those men resembled, O foremost of ascetics, the splendours which Surya assumes when the time comes for the dissolution of the universe. Indeed, we thought that Island was the home of all Energy. All the inhabitants were perfectly equal in energy. There was no superiority or inferiority there among them.[1] We then suddenly beheld once more a light arise, that seemed to be the concentrated effulgence of a thousand Suns, O Vrihaspati. The inhabitants, assembling together, ran towards that light, with hands joined in reverential attitude, full of joy, and uttering the one word *Namas* (we bow thee!) We then heard a very loud noise uttered by all of them together. It seemed that those men were employed in offering a sacrifice to the great God. As regards ourselves, we were suddenly deprived of our senses by his Energy. Deprived of vision and strength and all the senses, we could not see or feel anything.[2] We only heard a loud volume of sound uttered by the assembled inhabitants. It said,—Victory to thee, O thou of eyes like lotus-petals! Salutations to thee, O Creator of the universe! Salutations to thee, O Hrishikesa, O foremost of Beings, O thou that art the First-born! Even this was the sound we heard, uttered distinctly and agreeably to the rules of orthoepy.[3] Meanwhile, a breeze, fragrant and pure, blew, bearing perfumes of celestial flowers, and of certain herbs and plants that were of use on the occasion. Those men, endued with great devotion, possessed of hearts full of reverence, conversant with the ordinances laid down in the *Pancharatra*, were then worshipping the great deity with mind, word, and deed.[4] Without doubt, Hari appeared in that place whence the sound we heard arose. As regards ourselves, stupefied by His illusion, we could not see Him. After the breeze had ceased and the sacrifice had been over, our hearts became agitated with anxiety, O

---

1 This would seem to show that it was the Roman Republic which the pilgrims saw —T.

2 Professor Weber thinks that this has reference to the absence of idols or images. The pilgrims saw no deities there such as they had in their own temples.—T.

3 Professor Weber wrongly renders the words 'Purvaja' and 'sikshaksharaiamanwitah.' The first word does not, as he renders it, imply, 'eldest son of God,' but simply 'first-born.' It is seen in almost every hymn in the Mahabharata to the Supreme Deity. It is synonymous with 'Adipurusha.' Then 'siksha &c.' does not, as he thinks, mean 'accompanied by *teaching*,' but it is the science of Orthoepy and is one of the Angas (limbs) of the Vedas. The Vedas were always chanted melodiously; the science of Orthoepy was cultivated by the Rishis with great care.—T.

4 The 'Pancha-kala,' or 'Pancha-ratra,' or 'Sattwatas vidhi,' means certain ordinances laid down by Narada and other Rishis in respect of the worship of Narayana.—T.

foremost one of Angira's race. As we stood among those thousands of men all whom were of pure descent, no one honoured us with a glance or nod. Those ascetics, all of whom were cheerful and filled with devotion and who were all practising the Brahma-frame of mind, did not show any kind of feeling for us.[1] We had been exceedingly tired. Our penances had emaciated us. At that time, an incorporeal Being addressed us from the sky and said unto us these words—These white men, who are divested of all outer senses, are competent to behold (Narayana). Only those foremost of regenerate persons whom these white men honoured with their glances, become competent to behold the great God.[2] Go hence, ye Munis, to the place whence ye have come. That great Deity is incapable of being ever seen by one that is destitute of devotion. Incapable of being seen in consequence of his dazzling effulgence, that illustrious Deity can be beheld by only those persons that in course of long ages succeed in devoting themselves wholly and solely to Him. Ye foremost of regenerate one, ye have a great duty to perform. After the expiration of this the Krita age, when the Treta age comes in course of the Vivaswat cycle, a great calamity will overtake the worlds. Ye Munis, ye shall then have to become the allies of the deities (for dispelling that calamity).—Having heard these wonderful words that were sweet as nectar, we soon got back to the place we desired, through the grace of that great Deity. When with the aid of even such austere penances and of offerings devoutly given in sacrifices, we failed to have a sight of the great Deity, how, indeed, can you expect to behold Him so easily? Narayana is a Great Being. He is the Creator of the universe. He is adored in sacrifices with offerings of clarified butter and other food dedicated with the aid of Vedic *mantras*. He has no beginning and no end. He is Unmanifest. Both the Deities and the Danavas worship Him.—Induced by these words spoken by Ekata and approved by his companions, viz., Dwita and Trita, and solicited also by the other Sadasyas, the high-minded Vrihaspati brought that sacrifice to a completion after duly offering the accustomed adorations to the Deities. King Uparichara also, having completed his great sacrifice, began to rule his subjects righteously. At last, casting off his body, he ascended to heaven. After some time, through the curse of the Brahmanas, he fell down from those regions of felicity and sank deep into the bowels of the Earth. King Vasu, O tiger among monarchs, was always devoted to the true religion. Although sunk

1 The sense is this ; as all of them were practising that frame of mind which resembles Brahma, they did not regard us, *i.e.*, neither honoured nor dishonoured us.—T.

2 Both the vernacular translators have erred in rendering this simple Verse.—T.

deep into the bowels of the Earth, his devotion to virtue did not abate. Ever devoted to Narayana, and ever reciting sacred *mantras* having Narayana for their deity, he once more ascended to heaven through Narayana's grace. Ascending from the bowels of the Earth, king Vasu in consequence of the very highest end that he attained, proceeded to a spot that is even higher than the region of Brahman himself.[1] "

SECTION CCCXXXVIII

"Yudhishthira said,—'When the great king Vasu was so wholly devoted to Narayana, for what reason then did he fall down from heaven and why again had he to sink beneath the surface of the Earth?"

"Bhishma said,—'In this connection is cited an old narrative, O Bharata, of a discourse between the Rishis and the gods. The gods, once on a time, addressing many foremost of Brahmanas, said unto them that sacrifices should be performed by offering up *Ajas* as victims. By the word *Aja* should be understood the goat and no other animal.'

"The *Rishis* said,—The Vedic *Sruti* declares that in sacrifices the offerings should consist of (vegetable) seeds. Seeds are called *Ajas*. It behoveth you not to slay goats. Ye deities, that cannot be the religion of good and righteous people in which slaughter of animals is laid down. This, again, is the Krita age. How can animals be slaughtered in this epoch of righteousness?—'

"Bhishma continued,—While this discourse was going between the Rishis and the deities, that foremost of kings, *viz.*, Vasu, was seen to come that way. Endued with great prosperity, the king was coming through the welkin, accompanied by his troops and vehicles and animals. Beholding king Vasu coming to that spot through the skies, the Brahmanas addressing the deities, said,—This one will remove our doubts. He performs sacrifices. He is liberal in making gifts. He always seeks the good of all creatures. How, indeed, will the great Vasu speak otherwise. —Having thus spoken unto each other, the deities and the Rishis quickly approached king Vasu and questioned him, saying,—O king, with what should one perform sacrifices? Should one sacrifice with the goat or with herbs and plants? Do thou dispel this doubt of ours. We

1 The construction seems to be this: 'Parangatimanuprapta iti Brahmanah samanantaram naishthikam sthanam &c.,' It does not mean, as K. P. Singha puts it, that he proceeded to Brahman's region, nor, as the Burdwan translator puts it, that having gone to Brahman's region he attained to the highest end. The sense, on the other hand, is that as his was the very highest end, he, therefore, ascended to a spot that is higher than Brahman's region. The simple meaning is that king Uparichara attained to identification with Brahma.--T.

constitute thee our judge in this matter.—Thus addressed by them, Vasu joined his hands in humility and said unto them.—Tell me truly, ye foremost of Brahmanas, what opinion is entertained by you in this matter ?—

" 'The *Rishis* said,—The opinion entertained by us, O king, is that sacrifices should be performed with grain. The deities, however, maintain that sacrifices should be performed with animals. Do thou judge between us and tell us which of these opinions is correct.—'

"Bhishma continued,—'Learning what the opinion was that was entertained by the deities, Vasu, moved by partiality for them, said that sacrifices should be performed with animals. At this answer, all the Rishis, endued with the splendour of the Sun, became very angry. Addressing Vasu who was seated on his car and who had (wrongly) taken up the side of the deities, they said unto him,—Since thou hast (wrongly) taken up the side of the deities, do thou fall down from heaven. From this day, O monarch, thou shalt lose the power of journeying through the sky. Through our curse, thou shalt sink deep below the surface of the Earth.—After the Rishis had said these words, king Uparichara immediately fell down, O monarch, and went down a hole in the Earth. At the command, however, of Narayana, Vasu's memory did not leave him. To the good fortune of Vasu, the deities, pained at the curse denounced on him by the Brahmanas, began to think anxiously as to how that curse might be neutralised. They said,—This high-souled king hath been cursed for our sake. We, denizens of heaven, should unite together for doing what is good to him in return for that which he has done to us.—Having quickly settled this in their minds with the aid of reflection, the deities proceeded to the spot where king Uparichara was. Arrived, at his presence, they addressed him, saying,—Thou art devoted to the great God of the Brahmanas (viz., Narayana). That great Lord of both the deities and the Asuras, gratified with thee, will rescue thee from the curse that has been denounced upon thee. It is proper, however, that the high-souled Brahmanas should be honoured. Verily, O best of kings, their penances should fructify.[1] Indeed, thou hast already fallen down from the sky on the Earth. We desire, however, O best of kings, to show thee a favour in one respect. As long as thou, O sinless one, shalt dwell in this hole, so long shalt thou receive (due sustenance, through our boon) ! Those streaks of clarified butter which Brahmanas with concentrated minds pour in sacrifices in accompaniment with sacred *mantras*, and which are called by the name of *Vasudhara*, shall be thine, through our care for thee ! Indeed weakness

---

1 *i.e.*, when they have cursed thee, their curse should fructify. Thou shouldst not do anything that may have the effect of nullifying that curse. —T.

or distress shall not touch thee.[1] While dwelling, O king of kings, in the hole of the Earth, neither hunger nor thirst shall afflict thee for thou shalt drink those streaks of clarified butter called *Vasudhara*. Thy energy also shall continue unabated. In consequence also of this our boon that we grant thee, the God of gods, *viz*, Narayana, will be gratified with thee, and He will bear thee hence to the region of Brahman !—Having granted these boons unto the king, the denizens of heaven, as also all those Rishis possessed of wealth of penances, returned each to his respective place. Then Vasu, O Bharata, began to adore the Creator of the universe and to recite in silence those sacred *mantras* that had come out of Narayana's mouth in days of yore.[2] Although dwelling in a pit of the Earth, the king still worshipped Hari, the Lord of all the deities, in the well-known five sacrifices that are performed five times every day, O slayer of foes! In consequence of these adorations, Narayana, otherwise called Hari, became highly pleased with him who thus showed himself to be entirely devoted to Him, by wholly relying upon Him as his sole refuge, and who had completely subjugated his senses. The illustrious Vishnu, that giver of boons, then addressing Garuda of great speed, that foremost of birds, who waited upon Him as his servant, said these desirable words :—O foremost of birds, O thou that art highly blessed, listen to what I say ! There is a great king of the name of Vasu who is of righteous soul and rigid vows. Through the wrath of the Brahmanas, he has fallen into a pit of the Earth. The Brahmanas have been sufficiently honoured (for their curse has fructified). Do thou go to that king now. At my command, O Garuda, go to that foremost of kings, viz., Uparichara, who is now dwelling in a hole of the Earth and incapable of any longer sailing through the sky, and bring him up without delay into the welkin. Hearing these words of Vishnu, Garuda, spreading his wings and rushing with the speed of the wind, entered that hole in the Earth in which king Vasu was living. Suddenly taking the king up, the son of Vinata soared into the sky and there released the king from his beaks. At that moment, king Uparichara once more acquired his celestial form and re-entered the region of Brahman. It was in this way, O son of Kunti, that great king first fell down through the curse of the Brahma-

1 To this day, in many religious rites, these streaks of *ghee* are poured with *mantras* recited the while. They are called *Vasudhara* and are poured along the surface of a wall. First, a waving line of red is drawn horizontally on the wall. Then seven spots are made under that line. Then with the sacrificial ladle, Ghee is poured from each of the spots in such a way that a thick streak is poured along the wall. The length of those streaks is generally 3 to 4 feet and their breadth about half an inch—

2 The *mantras* recited by Vasu were Vedic mantras,—T.

nas for a fault of speech, and once more ascended to heaven at the command of the great God (Vishnu). Only the puissant Lord Hari, that foremost of all Beings, was devoutly worshipped by him. It was for this devout worship that the king succeeded very soon in escaping from the curse denounced upon him by the Brahmanas and in regaining the felicitous regions of Brahman.

"Bhishma continued,—'I have thus told thee everything respecting the origin of the spiritual sons of Brahman. Listen to me with undivided attention, for I shall now narrate to thee how the celestial Rishi Narada proceeded in days of yore to White Island.'"

SECTION CCCXXXIX

"Bhishma said,—'Arrived at the spacious realm called White Island, the illustrious Rishi beheld those same white men possessed of lunar splendour (of whom I have already spoken to thee). Worshipped by them, the Rishi worshipped them in return by bending his head and reverencing them in his mind.[1] Desirous of beholding Narayana, he began to reside there, attentively engaged in the silent recitation of *mantras*, sacred to him, and observant of vows of the most difficult kind. With concentrated mind, the regenerate Rishi, with arms upraised, stood in Yoga, and then sang the following hymn unto the Lord of the universe, Him, viz., who is at once the soul of attributes and divested of all attributes.

"Narada said,—Salutations to thee, O God of gods, O thou that art freed from all acts! Thou art he who is divested of all attributes, who is the Witness of all the worlds, who is called Kshetrajna, who is the foremost of all Beings, who is Infinite, who is called Purusha, who is the great Purusha, who is the foremost of all Purushas, who is the soul of the three attributes, who is called the Foremost, who is Amrita (nectar), who is called Immortal, who is called Ananta (Sesha), who is Space,[2] who is without beginning, who is both Manifest and Unmanifest as existent and not-existent things, who is said to have his home in Truth,[3] who is the first of gods (Narayana), who is the giver of wealth (or of the fruits of acts), identified with Daksha and other Lords of the

---

1 The Burdwan translator, as also K. P. Singha, both err in translating the first line of this Verse. It does *not* mean that Narada worshipped them with a bend of his head and that they in return worshipped him mentally. —T.

2 In the sense of His being unmodified, even as space is an entity that cannot be modified in any way.—T.

3 *i e*, as the commentator expands, who is displayed without any modification, all else being modifications of Thyself.—T.

Creation, who is the Aswattha and other big trees, who is the four-headed Brahman, who is the Lord of all created Beings, who is the Lord of Speech,[1] who is the Lord of the universe (or Indra), who is the all-pervading Soul, who is the Sun, who is the breath called Prana, who is the Lord of the waters (viz., Varuna), who is identifiable with the Emperor or the King, who is identifiable with the Regents of the several points of the compass, who is the refuge of the universe when it is dissolved in the final destruction,[2] who is Undisplayed (unrevealed), who is the giver of the Vedas unto Brahman, who is identifiable with the sacrifices and Vedic studies achieved by Brahmanas with the aid of their bodies, who is identifiable with the four principal orders of the deities, who is every one of those four orders, who is possessed of effulgence, who is possessed of great effulgence, who is he unto whom the seven largest offerings in sacrifices are presented with the Gayatri and other sacred *mantras*, who is Yama, who is Chitragupta and the other attendants of Yama, who is called the wife of Yama, who is that order of the deities called Tushita, who is that other order called Mahatushita, who is the universal grinder (Death), who is desire and all diseases that have been created for aiding the advent of Death, who is health and freedom from disease, who is subject to desire and passions, who is free from the influence of desire and passions, who is Infinite as exhibited in species and forms, who is he that is chastised, who is he that is the chastiser, who is all the lesser sacrifices (like Agnihotra and others), who is all the larger sacrifices (like those called Brahma, &c.), who is all the Ritwijas, who is the origin of all sacrifices (viz., the Vedas), who is fire, who is the very heart of all sacrifices (viz., the *mantras* and hymns uttered in them), who is he that is hymned in sacrifices, who takes those shares of the sacrificial offerings that are presented to him, who is the embodiment of the five sacrifices, who is the maker of the five sections or divisions of time (viz., day, night, month, season and year), who is incapable of being understood except by those scriptures that are called *Pancharatra*, who never shrinks from anything, who is unvanquished, who is only Mind (without a physical frame), who is known only by name, who is the Lord of Brahman himself, who was completed all the vows and observances mentioned in the Vedas,[3] who is the *Hansa* (bearer of the triple stick), who is the Parama-hansa

1 *i.e.*, from whom speech has flowed, or who is Vrihaspati the celestial priest, so famous for his learning and intelligence.—T.

2 *i.e.*, the original home of the universe. The idea is that when the universal dissolution comes, all things take refuge in thee. I follow the Commentator in all the interpretations he gives.—T.

3 *i.e.*, who has performed the 'avabhrita', or final bath upon the completion of all vows and observances and sacrifices.—T.

(divested of stick), who is the foremost of all sacrifices, who is Sankhya-yoga, who is the embodiment of the Sankhya philosophy, who dwells in all Jivas, who lives in every heart, who resides in every sense, who floats on the ocean-water, who lives in the Vedas, who lies on the lotus (the image of the egg whence the universe has sprung), who is the Lord of the universe, and whose troops go everywhere for protecting his worshippers. Thou takest birth as all creatures. Thou art the origin of the universe (of all creatures). Thy mouth is fire. Thou art that fire which courses through the waters of the ocean, issuing out all the while from an Equine head. Thou art the sanctified butter that is poured into the sacrificial fire. Thou art the car-driver (fire or heat that impels the body and causes it to live and grow). Thou art *Vashat*. Thou art the syllable Om. Thou art Penances. Thou art Mind. Thou art Chandramas. Thou sanctifiest the sacrificial butter. Thou art the Sun. Thou art the Dikgajas (Elephants) that are sanctioned in the four cardinal points of the compass. Thou illuminest the cardinal points of the compass. Thou illuminest the subsidiary points also. Thou art the Equine head. Thou art the first three mantras of the Rig Veda. Thou art the protector of the several orders of men (viz., Brahmanas, Kshatriyas, Vaisyas, and Sudras). Thou art the five fires (beginning with Garhapatya). Thou art He who has thrice ignited the sacrificial fire called *Nachi*.[1] Thou art the refuge of the six limbs (viz., the Vedas).[2] Thou art the foremost of those Brahmanas that are employed in singing the Samans in sacrifices and other religious rites. Thou art Pragjyotish, and thou art he who sings the first Saman.[3] Thou art the observer of those vows that depend upon the Vedas and that are observed by singers of Samanas. Thou art the embodiment of the Upanishad, called by the name of Atharvasiras. Thou art he who is the topic of the five foremost of scriptures (viz., those that appertain to the worship of Surya, of Sakti, of Ganesa, of Siva, and of Vishnu). Thou art called the preceptor that subsists only on the froth of water. Thou art a Valikhilya.[4] Thou art the embodiment of him who has not fallen away from Yoga. Thou art the embodiment of correctness of judgment of reasoning. Thou art the beginning of the Yugas, thou art the middle of the Yugas

---

1 *i.e.*, thou hast performed sacrifices.—T.

2 The Vedas have six limbs or divisions.—T.

3 Pragjyotish is the name of a particular Saman. The Rich beginning with 'Murddhanam &c,' when sung, comes to be called by the name of 'jeshtha Saman.' What is said here, therefore, is that thou art both the foremost of Samanas and he that sings that Saman.—T.

4 In the Bombay text, the reading for 'Vainagarbha' is 'Vaikhanasa' which means a class or sect of ascetics.—T.

and thou art their end. Thou art Akhandala (Indra). Thou art the two Rishis Prachina-garbha and Kausika. Thou art Purusthuta, thou art Puruhuta, thou art the artificer of the universe. Thou hast the universe for thy form. Thy motions are infinite. Thy bodies are infinite; thou art without end and without beginning, and without middle. Thy middle is unmanifest. Thy end is unmanifest. Thou hast vows for thy abode. Thou residest in the ocean. Thou hast thy home in Fame, in Penances, in Self-restraint, in Prosperity, in Knowledge, in grand Achievements, and in Everything belonging to the universe. Thou art Vasudeva. Thou art the grantor of every wish. Thou art Hanuman that bore Rama on his shoulders. Thou art the great Horse-sacrifice. Thou takest thy share of offerings made in great sacrfiices.[1] Thou art the grantor of boons, of happiness, of wealth. Thou art devoted to Hari. Thou art Restraint of the senses. Thou art vows and observances. Thou art mortifications, thou art severe mortifications, thou art very severe mortifications.[2] Thou art he who observes vows and religious and other pious rites. Thou art freed from all errors. Thou art a Brahmacharin. Thou tookest birth in the womb of Prisni. Thou art he from whom have flowed all Vedic rites and acts. Thou art unborn. Thou pervadest all things. Thy eyes are on all things. Thou must not be apprehended by the senses. Thou art not subject to deterioration. Thou art possessed of great puissance. Thy body is inconceivably vast. Thou art holy, thou art beyond the ken of logic or argument. Thou art unknowable. Thou art the foremost of Causes. Thou art the Creator of all creatures and thou art their destroyer. Thou art the possessor of vast powers of illusion. Thou art called Chittrasikhandin. Thou art the giver of boons. Thou art the taker of thy share of the sacrificial offerings. Thou hast obtained the merit of all sacrifices. Thou art he who has been freed from all doubts. Thou art omnipresent. Thou art of the from of a Brahmana. Thou art fond of Brahmanas. Thou hast the universe for thy form. Thy form is very vast. Thou art the greatest friend. Thou art kind to all thy worshippers. Thou art the great deity of the Brahmanas. I am thy devoted disciple. I am desirous of beholding thee. Salutations to thee that art of the form of Emancipation;—' "

---

1 The commentator explains that by 'Mahayajna'—great sacrifice—is meant 'Yoga.' The Jiva-Soul is like the libation poured in the sacrifice, for by Yoga the Jiva-Soul is annihilated and merged into the Supreme Soul. —T.

2 In treatises on the *Smriti*, the indications of these three kinds or degrees of modifications are given.—T.

SECTION CCCXL

"Bhishma said.—'Thus hymned with names that were not known to others, the Divine Narayana having the universe for his form showed himself to the ascetic Narada. His form was somewhat purer than the moon and differed from the moon in some respects. He somewhat resembled a blazing fire in complexion. The puissant Lord was somewhat of the form of Vishti.[1] He resembled in some respects the feathers of the parrot, and in some a mass of pure crystal. He resembled in some respects a hill of antimony and in some a mass of pure gold. His complexion somewhat resembled the coral when first formed, and was somewhat white. In some respects that complexion resembled the hue of gold and in some that of the *lapis lazulus.* In some respects it resembled the hue of the blue *lapis lazulus* and in some that of sapphire. In some respects it resembled the hue of the peacock's neck, and in some that of a string of pearls. Bearing these diverse kinds of hues on his person, the eternal Deity appeared before Narada. He had a thousand eyes and was possessed of great beauty. He had a hundred heads and a hundred feet. He had a thousand stomachs and a thousand arms. He seemed to be still inconceivable to the mind. With one of his mouths he uttered the syllable *Om* and then the *Gayatri* following Om. With mind under complete control, the great Deity, called by the names of Hari and Narayana, by his other mouths, multitudinous in number, uttered many *mantras* from the four Vedas which are known by the name of *Aranyaka.* The Lord of all the deities, the great God who is adored in sacrifices, held in his hands a sacrificial altar, a *Kamandalu,* few white gems, a pair of sandal, a bundle of *Kusa* blades, a deer-skin, a toothstick, and a little blazing fire.[2] With cheerful soul, that foremost of regenerate persons, viz., Narada of restraining speech, bowed unto the great God and adored Him. Unto him whose head was still bent low in veneration, the first of all the deities, who is free from deterioration, said the following words.

" 'The Holy one said,—The great Rishis, Ekata, Dwita, and Trita, came to this realm from desire of obtaining a sight of me. They, however, were unable to have the fruition of their wishes. Nor can any one have a sight of me save those persons that are devoted to me with their

---

1 By this word is meant a particular conjunction of heavenly bodies. This conjunction is represented as having a peculiar form.—T.

2 The word 'Upanaha' used here in the dual number, has puzzled many persons. It is difficult to conceive why the great God should appear with a pair of shoes in one of his hands. Probably, the 'Upanaha,' in ancient times, was a wooden sandal, and what the poet means to say is that Narayana, appeared with all the requisites of a Brahmacharin on his person.—T,

whole hearts. As regards thee, thou art verily the foremost of all persons devoted to me with all their souls. These are my bodies, the best ones that I assume. These were born, O regenerate one, in the house of Dharma. Do thou worship them always, and do thou perform those rites that are laid down in the ordinances with respect to that worship. O Brahmana, do thou ask of me the boons thou desirest. I am gratified with thee to-day, and I appear unto thee now in my universal form as freed from decay and deterioration.—

"'Narada said,—Since, O holy one, I have today succeeded in obtaining a sight of thee, I regard that I have won without any delay the fruits of my penances, O God, of my self-restraint, and of all the vows and observances that I have gone through. This, indeed, is the highest boon thou hast granted me for thou hast shown thyself to me today, O Eternal Lord. Thou, O holy one, hast the universe for thy eye. Thou art the Lion. Thy form is identifiable with everything. Possessed of puissance, thou, O Lord, art vast and infinite.

"Bhishma continued,—'Having thus shown Himself unto Narada, the son of Parameshthi, the great God addressed that ascetic and said, —Go hence, O Narada, and do not delay! These worshippers of mine, possessed of lunar complexions, are divested of all senses and do not subsist upon any kind of food. They are, again, all Emancipate; with minds wholly concentrated upon Me, people should think of Me. Such worshippers will never meet with any impediments. These men are all crowned with ascetic success and are highly blessed. In ancient times they became entirely devoted to me. They have been freed from the attributes of Rajas and Tamas. Without doubt, they are competent to enter me and become merged into my Self.—He that cannot be seen with the eye, touched with the sense of touch, smelt with the sense of scent, and that is beyond the ken of the sense of taste. He whom the three attributes of Sattwa, Rajas, and Tamas do not touch, who pervades all things and is the one Witness of the universe, and who is described as the Soul of the entire universe; He who is not destroyed upon the destruction of the bodies of all created things, who is unborn and unchangeable and eternal, who is freed from all attributes, who is indivisible and entire; He who transcends the twice twelve topics of enquiry and is regarded the Twentyfifth, who is called by the name of Purusha, who is inactive, and who is said to be apprehended by Knowledge alone, He into whom the foremost of regenerate persons enter and become emancipate, He who is the eternal Supreme Soul and is known by the name of Vasudeva. Behold, O Narada, the greatness and puissance of that God. He is never touched by acts good or bad. Sattwa, Rajas and Tamas, are said to be the three (original) attributes. These dwell and act in the bodies of all creatures. The Jiva-soul, called

Kshetrajna, enjoys and endorse the action of these three attributes. He, however, transcends them and they cannot touch Him. Freed from these attributes, He is again their enjoyer and endorser. Having created them Himself, He is above them all. O celestial Rishi, the Earth, which is the refuge of the universe, disappears[1] (when the hour for universal dissolution comes) into water, Water disappears into Light, and Light into Wind, Wind disappears into Space, and Space into Mind. Mind is a great creature, and it disappears into Unmanifest Prakriti. Unmanifest Prakriti, O Brahmana, disappears into inactive Purusha. There is nothing higher than Purusha which is Eternal. There is nothing among mobile and immobile things in the universe that is immutable, except Vasudeva, the eternal Purusha. Endued with great puissance, Vasudeva is the Soul of all creatures. Earth, Wind, Space, Water, and Light forming the fifth, are primal elements of great puissance. Mingling together they form what is called the body. Possessed of subtile prowess and invisible to all eyes, O Brahmana, the puissant Vasudeva then enter that combination of the five primal elements, called body. Such entrance is called his birth, and taking birth, He causes the body to move about and act. Without a combination of the five primal elements, no body can ever be formed. Without, again, the entrance of Jiva into the body, the mind dwelling within it cannot cause it to move and act. He that enters the body is possessed of great puissance and is called Jiva. He is known also by other names, viz., Sesha and Sankarshana. He that takes his rise, from that Sankarshana, by his own acts, Sanatkumara, and in whom all creatures merge when the universal dissolution comes, is the Mind of all creatures and is called by the name of Praddyumna. From Him (*i.e.*, Praddyumna), arises He who is the Creator, and who is both Cause and Effect. From this last, everything, viz., the mobile and immobile universe, takes its rise. This one is called Aniruddha. He is otherwise called Isana, and He is manifest in all acts.[2] That illustrious one, viz., Vasudeva, who is called Kshetrajna, and who is freed from attributes, should, O king of kings, be known as the puissant Sankarshana, when he takes birth as

---

1 *i.e.*, merges into—T.

2 This cosmogony is agreeable to the Vaishnava scriptures. Above all, without beginning is Vasudeva. From Vasudeva is Sankarshana. From Sankarshana is Praddyumna. From Praddyumna is Aniruddha. Some persons find in this quadruple creation the distinct trace of the Christian Trinity. It is very difficult, however, to say which doctrine, the Hindu or the Christian, is the original and which is derived from which.—T.

Jiva.[1] From Sankarshana arises Praddyumna who is called 'He that is born as Mind.' From Praddyumna is He who is Aniruddha. He is Consciousness, He is Iswara (Supreme Lord). It is from me that the entire mobile and immobile universe springs. It is from me, O Narada, that the indestructible and destructible, the existent and the non-existent, flow. They that are devoted to me enter into me and become emancipate. I am known as Purusha. Without acts, I am the Twenty-fifth. Transcending attributes, I am entire and indivisible. I am above all pairs of opposite attributes and freed from all attachments. This, O Narada, thou wilt fail to understand. Thou beholdest me as endued with a form. In a moment, if the wish arises, I can dissolve this form. I am the Supreme Lord and the Preceptor of the universe. That which thou beholdest of me, O Narada, is only an illusion of mine. I now seem to be endued with the attributes of all created things. Thou art not competent to know me. I have disclosed to thee duly my quadruple form. I am, O Narada, the Doer, I am Cause, and I am Effect. I am the sum-total of all living creatures. All living creatures have their refuge in me. Let not the thought be thine that thou hast seen the Kshetrajna. I pervade all things, O Brahmana, and am the *Jiva-Soul* of all creatures. When the bodies of all creatures, however, are destroyed, I am not destroyed. Those highly blessed men who, having won ascetic success, become wholly devoted to me, become freed from the attributes of both Rajas and Tamas and succeed, on that account, in entering me, O great ascetic. He who is called Hiranyagarbha, who is the beginning of the world, who has four faces, who cannot be understood with the aid of the *Nirukta*, who is otherwise called Brahman, who is an eternal deity, is employed in attending to many of my concerns. The deity Rudra, born of my wrath, is sprung from my forehead. Behold, the eleven Rudras are swelling (with might) on the right side of my body. The twelve Adityas are on the left side of my body. Behold, the eight Vasus, those foremost of deities, are in my front, and see, Nasatya and Dasra, those two celestial physicians (Aswini Kumars), are in my rear. Behold also in my body all the Prajapatis and behold the seven Rishis also. Behold also the Vedas, and all the Sacrifices numbering by hundreds, the Amrita (nectar), and all the (medicinal) herbs and plants, and Penances, and vows and observances of diverse kinds. Behold also in me the eight attributes indicative of puissance, viz., those particularly called the attributes o Lordship, all dwelling together in my body in their united and embodied form. Behold also Sree and Lakshmi, and Kirti, and the Earth with her hump as also the goddess, Saraswati,

1 The reader is requested to mark the address 'king of kings.' This is evidently a slip of the pen. The whole speech is that of Narayana and Narada is the listener.—T.

that mother of the Vedas, dwelling in me. Behold, O Narada, Dhruva, that foremost of luminaries ranging the firmament, as also all the Oceans those receptacles of water, and lakes, and, rivers, dwelling in me. Behold also, O best of men, the four foremost ones amongst the Pitris in their embodied forms, as also, the three attributes (of Sattwa, Rajas, and Tamas) which are formless dwelling in me. The acts done in honour of the Pitris are superior (in point of merit) to those done in honour of the deities. I am the *Pitri* of both the deities and the Pitris, and am existing from the beginning (that is, from a time when they were not). Becoming the Equine-head I rove through the Western and the Northern ocean and drink sacrificial libations duly poured with *mantras* and solid sacrificial food offered with reverence and devotion. In days of yore I created Brahman who himself adored me in sacrifices. Gratified with him on that account I granted him many excellent boons. I said unto him that in the beginning of the Kalpa he would be born unto me as my son, and the sovereignty of all the worlds would vest on him, coupled with diverse names being bestowed on diverse objects in consequence of the starting of Ahankara into existence.[1] I also told him that none would ever violate the limits and boundaries he would assign (for the observance of creatures) and, further, that he would be the giver of boons unto persons that would (in sacrifices and by proper acts) solicit him for them. I further assured him that he would be an object of adoration with all the deities and Asuras, all the Rishis and Pitris, and the diverse creatures forming the creation. I also gave him to understand that I would always manifest myself for accomplishing the business of the deities and that for that matter I would suffer myself to be commanded by him even as a son by his sire.[2] Granting these and other highly agreeable boons unto Brahman of immeasurable energy in consequence of my being gratified with him I (once more) adopted the

---

1 The Commentator is silent. The sense seems to be that as Brahman is to be the son of Narayana in the beginning of a Kalpa when there is no other existent object mobile or immobile, the same Brahman is to be vested with dominion over all things which he would himself create through *Ahankara.* Of course, as long as Brahman is without 'Ahankara' so long there can be no Creation, *i.e.*, no subjects mobile and immobile, to be known by different names.—T.

2 'Nityada' is 'always.' Some persons believe that Narayana has to manifest himself always for achieving the business of the deities. This Earth is not the only world where such manifestations needed. As to the object of the manifestations considerable difference of opinion prevails. In the Gita, the great deity himself explains that that object is to rescue the good and destroy the wicked. Others hold that this is only a secondary object, the primary one being to gladden the hearts of the devout by affording them opportunities of worshipping him and applauding his acts, and to indulge in new joys by serving his own worshippers.—T.

course dictated by Nivritti. The highest Nivritti is identical with the annihilation of all duties and acts. Hence, by adopting Nivritti one should conduct oneself in complete felicity. Learned preceptors, with settled convictions deduced from the truths of the Sankhya philosophy, have spoken of me as Kapila endued with the puissance of Knowledge, dwelling within the effulgence of Surya, and concentrated in Yoga.[1] In Chcchandas (Vedas) I have been repeatedly hymned as the illustrious Hiranyagarbha. In the Yoga scriptures, O Brahmana, I have been spoken of as one who takes a delight in Yoga. I am eternal. Assuming a form that is manifest, I dwell, at present, in the heavens. At the end of a thousand Yugas I shall once more withdraw the universe into myself. Having withdrawn all creatures, mobile and immobile into myself, I shall exist all alone with knowledge only for my companion. After the lapse of ages I shall again create the universe, with the aid of that knowledge. That which is my fourth form creates the indestructible Sesha. That Sesha is called by the name of Sankarshana. Sankarshana creates Praddyumna. From Praddyumna I take birth myself as Aniruddha. I create (myself) repeatedly. From Aniruddha springs Brahman. The latter takes birth from Aniruddha's navel. From Brahman spring all creatures mobile and immobile. Know that Creation springs in this way repeatedly at the beginning of every Kalpa. Creation and destruction succeed each other even as sunrise and sunset in this world. Then, again, as Time, endued with immeasurable energy, forcibly brings back the Sun after his disappearance, after the same manner I shall, assuming the form of boar and putting forth my strength, bring back the Earth with her belt of seas to her own position for the good of all creatures when she becomes submerged in water. I shall then slay the son of Diti, named Hiranyaksha, filled with pride of strength.[2] Assuming the form then of a Man-lion (Nrisingha), I shall, for benefitting the deities, slay Hiranyakasipu the son of Diti, who will be a great destroyer of sacrifices. Unto Virochana (the son of Prahlada) will be born a mighty son of the name of Vali. That great Asura will be unslayable in the whole universe consisting of deities, Asuras and Rakshasas. He will hurl Sakra from the sovereignty of the universe. When after routing the Lord of Sachi, that Asura will take unto himself the sovereignty of the three worlds, I shall take birth in Aditi's womb,

---

1 This is a reference to the well-known description of Narayana as 'Savitrimandala-madhyavartih &c.' It is not the visible Sun whose disc is meant, but that pure fountain of effulgence which is inconceivable for its dazzling brightness that is implied.—T.

2 The tense used in the original is future. What is meant, however, is that the great deity does these acts at the beginning of every Kalpa when he recreates the Earth. All cycles or Kalpas are similar in respect of the incidents that occur in them.—T.

by Kasyapa, as the twelfth Aditya. I shall (taking the sovereignty of the three worlds from Vali) restore it to Indra of immeasurable splendour, and replace the deities, O Narada, in their respective stations. As regards Vali, that foremost of Danavas, who is to be unslayable by all the deities, I shall cause him to dwell in the nether regions. In the Treta age I shall take birth as Rama in the race of Bhrigu, and exterminate the Kshatriyas who will become proud of their strength and possessions. Towards the close of Treta and the beginning of Dwapara, I shall take birth as Rama, the son of Dasaratha in Iskshaku's royal line. At that time, the two Rishis, *viz.*, the two sons of Prajapati, called by the names of Ekata and Dwita, will in consequence of the injury done by them unto their brother Trita, have to take birth as apes, losing the beauty of the human form. Those apes that shall take birth in the race of Ekata and Dwita, shall become endued with great strength and mighty energy and will equal Sakra himself in prowess. All those apes, O regenerate one, will become my allies for accomplishing the business of the deities. I shall then slay the terrible lord of the Rakshasas, that wretch of Pulastya's race, viz., the fierce Ravana, that thorn of all the worlds, together with all his children and followers. Towards the close of the Dwapara and the beginning of Kali ages, I shall again appear in the world taking birth in the city of Mathura for the purpose of slaying Kansa. There, after slaying innumerable Danavas that will be as thorns in the side of the deities, I shall take up my residence in Kusasthali at the city of Dwaraka. While residing in that city I shall slay the Asura Naraka, the son of the Earth,—him, that is, who will do an injury to Aditi, as also some other Danavas of the names of Muru and Pitha. Slaying also another foremost of Danavas, viz., the lord of Pragjyotisha, I shall transplant his delightful city furnished with diverse kinds of wealth into Dwaraka. I shall then subjugate the two gods worshipped of all the deities, viz., Maheswara and Mahasena, who will become fond of the Danava Vana and do him diverse good offices and who will exert themselves vigorously for that worshipper of theirs.[1] Vanquishing next the son of the Danava Vali, viz., Vana, who will be endued with a thousand arms, I shall next destroy all the inhabitants of the Danava city called Saubha.[2] I shall next, O foremost of Brahmanas, compass the death of Kalayavana, a Danava who will be endued with great might

1 Maheswara is Mahadeva or Siva, Mahasena is Kartikeya, the generalissimo of the celestial forces.—T.

2 Vana, the son of Vali, was a devout worshipper of Mahadeva. Vana's daughter Usha fell in love with Krishna's grandson Aniruddha. Aniruddha was imprisoned by Vana. It was to rescue Aniruddha that Krishna fought with Vana, after having vanquished both Mahadeva and Kartikeya. The thousand and one arms of Vana, less two, were lopped off by Krishna. The episode of the love of Aniruddha and Usha is a very beautiful one.—T.

in consequence of his being equipt with the energy of Gargya.[1] A proud Asura will appear as a king at Girivraja, of the name of Jarasandha, who will quarrel with all the other kings of the world. His death will be compassed by me through some one else guided by my intelligence. I shall next slay Sisupala in the sacrifice of king Yudhishthira, the son of Dharma, which sacrifice all the kings of the world will bring tribute. In some of these feats, only Arjuna, the son of Vasava, will become my assistant. I shall establish Yudhishthira with all his brothers in his ancestral kingdom. People will call me and Arjuna as Narayana and Nara, when, endued with puissance, we two, exerting our strength, shall consume a large number of Kshatriyas, for doing good to the world. Having lightened the burthen of the Earth according to our pleasure, I shall absorb all the principal Sattwatas as also Dwaraka, my favourite city, into my own self, recollecting my all-embracing Knowledge. Endued with four forms, I shall, in this way, achieve many feats of great prowess, and attain at last to those regions of felicity created by me and honoured by all the Brahmanas. Appearing in the forms of a swan, a tortoise, a fish, O foremost of regenerate ones, I shall then display myself as a boar, then as a Man-lion (Nrisingha), then as a dwarf, then as Rama of Bhrigu's race, then as Rama, the son of Dasaratha, then as Krishna the scion of the Sattwata race, and lastly as Kalki. When the auditions in the Vedas disappeared from the world, I brought them back. The Vedas with the auditions in them, were re-created by me in the Krita age. They have once more disappeared or may only be partially heard here and there in the Puranas. Many of my best appearances also in the world have become events of the past. Having achieved the good of the worlds in those forms in which I appeared, they have re-entered into my own Prakriti. Brahman (the Creator) himself never obtained a sight of me in this form of mine, which thou, O Narada, hast seen today in consequence of thy entire devotion to me. I have now said everything, O Brahmana,—unto thee that art devoted to me wholly, I have disclosed to thee my ancient appearances and future ones also, O Best of men, together with all their mysteries.

---

1 Saubha was the name of a flying city of the Danavas. Krishna felled this city into the ocean, having killed all its Danava inhabitants. As to Kala-yavana, his death was brought about by Krishna under the following circusmstances. Pursued by the Danava, Krishna took refuge in a mountain-cave in which a king of the Satya Yuga was lying asleep. Entering the cave, Krishna stood at the head of the sleeping king. The Danava, entering the cave after Krishna, found the sleeping king and awaked him. As soon as the king looked at the Danava, the latter was consumed into ashes, for the gods had given a boon to the king that he who would awake him would be consumed by a glance of his.—T.

"Bhishma continued,—The holy and illustrious deity, of universal and immutable form, having said these words unto Narada, disappeared there and then. Narada also, endued with great energy, having obtained the high favour that he had solicited, then proceeded with great speed to the retreat called Vadari, for beholding Nara and Narayana. This great Upanishad, perfectly consistent with the four Vedas, in harmony with Sankya-yoga, and called by him by the name of the Pancharatra scriptures, and recited by Narayana himself with his own mouth, was repeated by Narada in the presence of many hearers in the abode of Brahman (his sire) in exactly the same way in which Narayana (while that great god had showed himself unto him) had recited it, and in which he had heard it from his own lips.

"Yudhishthira said,—'Was not Brahman, the Creator of all things, acquainted with this wonderful narrative of the glory of Narayana endued with intelligence that he heard it from the lips of Narada? Is the illustrious Grandsire of all the worlds any way different from or inferior to the great Narayana? How then is it that he was unacquainted with the puissance of Narayana of immeasurable energy?'

"Bhishma continued,—'Hundreds and thousands of great-Kalpas, hundreds and thousands of Creations and Dissolutions, O king of kings, have been over and have become incidents of the past.[1] In the beginning of every cycle of Creation, Brahman, endued with great puissance and who creates all things, is remembered (by Narayana). Brahman knows well, O king, that Narayana, that foremost of all gods is very much superior to him. He knows that Narayana is the Supreme Soul, that He is the Supreme Lord, that He is the Creator of Brahman himself. It was only unto that conclave of Rishis, crowned with ascetic success, that came to the abode of Brahman, that Narada recited his narrative which is a very ancient one, and which is perfectly consistent with the Vedas. The deity Surya, having heard that narrative from those Rishis crowned with ascetic success,[2] repeated it to the six and sixty thousands

1 The idea of Eternity without any conceivable beginning and conceivable end was so thoroughly realised by the Hindu sages that the chiefdom of Heaven itself was to them the concern of a moment. Nothing less than unchangeable felicity for all time was the object they pursued. All other things and states being mutable, and only Brahman being immutable, what they sought was an identification with Brahma. Such identification with the Supreme Soul was the Emancipation they sought. No other religion has ever been able to preach such a high ideal. The Hindu's concern is with Eternity. He regards his existence here as having the duration of but the millionth part of a moment. How to prevent re-birth and attain to an identification with the Supreme Soul is the object of his pursuit.—T.

2 K.P. Singha has completely misunderstood the sense of Verse 113. Bhishma does not certainly mean that Brahman was unacquainted with the narrative. What Bhishma says is that it was not to Brahman, but to

of Rishis, O king, of cleansed souls, that follow in his train. And Surya, the deity that imparts heat unto all worlds, repeated that narrative unto those Beings also, of cleansed souls, that have been created (by Brahman) for always journeying in the van of Surya.[1] The high-souled Rishis that follow in Surya's train, O son, repeated that excellent narrative unto the deities assembled on the breast of Meru. That best of ascetics, viz., the regenerate Asita, then having heard the narrative from the deities, repeated it unto the Pitris, O king of kings. I heard it from my sire Santanu, O son, who recited it to me formerly. Myself having heard it from my sire, I have repeated it to thee, O Bharata. Deities and Munis, who have heard this excellent old narrative, which is a *Purana*—all adore the Supreme Soul. This narrative, belonging to the Rishis and thus handed down from one to another, should not, O king, be communicated by thee to any one that is not a worshipper of Vasudeva. This narrative, O king, is really the essence of the hundreds of other narratives that thou hast heard from me. In days of yore, O monarch, the deities and the Asuras, uniting together, churned the Ocean and raised the Amrita. After the same manner, the Brahmanas, uniting together in days of yore, churned all the scriptures and raised this narrative which resembles nectar. He who frequently reads this narrative, and he who frequently listents to it, with concentrated attention, in a retired spot, and filled with devotion, succeeds in becoming a denizen, possessed of lunar complexion, of the spacious island known by the name of White Island. Without doubt, such a man succeeds in entering into Narayana of a thousand rays. A sick person, by listening to this narrative from the beginning, becomes freed from his illness. The man that simply desires to read or listen to this narrative obtains the fruition of all his wishes. The devoted worshipper, by reading or listening to it, attains to the high end that is reserved for devoted worshippers. Thou a so, O monarch, shouldst always adore and worship that foremost of all Beings. He is the father and the mother of all creatures, and He is an object of reverence with the entire universe. Let the illustrious and Eternal God of the Brahmanas, viz., Janarddana of high intelligence, be gratified with thee, O Yudhishthira of mighty arms!' "

---

the Siddhas assembled in Brahman's abode, that Narada recited his narrative.—T.

1 K.P. Singha misunderstands Verses 115 and 116 completely. The fact is, Surya recited the narrative unto those that precede and those that follow him in his journey through the firmament. K.P. Singha confounds the two classes of persons together. The Burdwan translator, as usual, makes nonsense of Verse 116. The correct reading (as given in the Bombay text) is 'lokan,' the grammatical construction being 'lokan tapatah suryasya &c.' The Burdwan translator makes Surya repeat the narrative "to the worlds created and placed before Surya.'—T.

Vaisampayana continued,—"Having listened to this best of narratives, O Janamejaya, king Yudhishthira the just and all his brothers became devoted to Narayana. And all of them, O Bharata, betaking themselves to the practice of silently meditating upon Narayana (from that day), uttered these words for His glorification, viz., 'Victory to that holy and illustrious Being!' He, again, who is our best of preceptors, viz., the Island-born Krishna, devoted to penances, sung, uttering the word *Narayana*, that high *mantra* which is worthy of being recited in silence. Sojourning through the welkin to the Ocean of Milk which is always the abode of nectar, and worshipping the great God there, he came back to his own hermitage.

"Bhishma continued,—'I have now repeated to thee the narrative that was recited by Narada (unto the conclave of Rishis assembled in the abode of Brahman). That narrative has descended from one person to another from very ancient times. I heard it from my sire who formerly repeated it to me.' "

Suta continued,—I have now told you all that Vaisampayana recited to Janamejaya. Having listened to Vaisampayana's narration, king Janamejaya properly discharged all his duties according to the ordinances laid down in the scriptures. Ye have all undergone very severe penances and observed many high and excellent vows. Residing in this sacred forest that is known by the name of Naimisha, ye are foremost of all persons conversant with the Vedas. Ye foremost of regenetate ones, ye all have come to this great sacrifice of Saunaka. Do ye all adore and worship that Eternal and Supreme Lord of the universe in excellent sacrifices, properly pouring libations of clarified butter into the fire with the aid of *mantras* and dedicating the same unto Narayana. As regards myself, I heard this excellent narrative that has descended from generation to generation, from my sire who recited it to me in former times.

SECTION CCCXLI

Saunka said,—How is that illustrious god, viz., the puissant Narayana, who is fully conversant with the Vedas and their branches, at once the doer and the enjoyer of sacrifices? Endued with forgiveness, he has adopted, again, the religion of Nivritti (abstention). Indeed, it is that holy and puissant one who has himself ordained the duties of Nivritti. Why then has he made many of the deities the takers of shares in sacrifices which, of course, are all due to the disposition of Pravritti? Why has he again created some with a contrary disposition, for they follow the ordinances of the religion of abstention? Do thou O Suta, dispel this doubt of ours. This doubt seems to be eternal and is connected with a great mystery. Thou hast heard all discourses on Narayana, discourses that are consistent with the (other) scriptures.[1]

Suti said,—O excellent Saunaka, I shall recite to thee what Vaisampayana, the disciple of the intelligent Vyasa, said when questioned on these very topics by king Janamejaya. Having heard the discourse on the glory of Narayana who is the Soul of all embodied creatures, Janamejaya, endued with great intelligence and wisdom, questioned Vaisampayana on these very subjects.

Janamejaya said,—"The whole world of Beings, with Brahma, the deities, the Asuras and human beings, are seen to be deeply attached to actions which have been said to be productive of prosperity. Emancipation has, O regenerate one, been said by thee to be the highest felicity and to consist of the cessation of existence. They who, being divested of both merit and demerit, become emancipate, succeed, we hear, in entering the great God of a thousand rays. It seems to be, O Brahmana, that the eternal religion of Emancipation is exceedingly difficult of observance. Turning away from it, all the deities have become enjoyers of the libations of clarified butter poured with *mantras* on sacrificial fires and other offerings presented to them by the same or similar means. Then, again, Brahman, and Rudra, the puissant Sakra the slayer of Vala, Surya, Chandramas (the Lord of the stars), the Wind-god, the Deity of fire, the Deity of the Waters, Infinite Space (as a living Being), the Universe too (as a conscious agent), and the rest of the denizens of heaven,—they, it seems, are ignorant of the way of securing annihilation of conscious existence, that is capable of being brought about by self-realisation.[2] Hence, perhaps, they have not betaken themselves to the path that is certain, indestructible, and immutable. Hence perhaps, turning away from that path they have adopted the religion of Pravritti which leads to conscious existence that is measured by time. This, indeed, is one great fault that attaches to those that are wedded to actions, for all their rewards are terminable. This doubt, O regenerate one, is planted in my heart like a dagger. Remove it out by reciting to me

---

1 The drift of Saunaka's queries seems to be this; the religion of Pravritti is opposed to that of Nivritti. How is it that both have been created by the same Narayana? How is it that he has made some with dispositions to follow the one, and others with dispositions to follow the other?—T.

2 'Atmanah parinirmitam pralayam' means that destruction or cessation of existences which is brought about by self-realisation. What the king says here is,—If the religion of Nivritti be so superior in consequence of its superior end, why is it that the deities who are all superior to us did not pursue it? Were they ignorant of the method by which Emancipation is attainable? Were they ignorant of the means by which to win cessation of existence? K. P. Singha renders the Verse correctly. The Burdwan translator misunderstands it although he repeats the exact words of the second foot of the second line.—T.

some discourses of old on this topic. Great is my curiosity to listen to thee. For what reason, O regenerate one, have the deities been said to be takers of their respective shares of sacrificial offerings presented to them with the aid of *mantras* in sacrifices of diverse kinds? Why again are the denizens of heaven adored in sacrifices? And, O best of regenerate persons, to whom do they, that take their shares of offerings in sacrifices performed to their honour, themselves make offerings when they perform great sacrifices?"

Vaisampayana said,—"The question thou has asked me, O ruler of men, relates to a deep mystery. No man that has not undergone penances, and that is not acquainted with the Puranas, can speedily answer it. I shall, however, answer thee by reciting to thee what my preceptor the Island-born Krishna, otherwise called Vyasa, the great Rishi who has classified the Vedas, had said unto us on a former occasion when questioned by us. Sumanta, and Jaimini, and Paila of firm vows, and myself numbering the fourth, and Suka forming the fifth, were disciples of the illustrious Vyasa. We, numbering five in all, endued with self-restraint and purity of observances, had completely subjugated wrath and controlled our senses. Our preceptor used to teach us the Vedas, having the Mahabbharata for their fifth. Once on a time, while we were engaged in studying the Vedas on the breast of that foremost of mountains, *viz.*, the delightful Meru, inhabited by Siddhas and Charanas, this very doubt arose in our minds that has been expressed by thee today. We, therefore, questioned our preceptor about it. I heard the answer that our preceptor made. I shall now recite that answer to thee, O Bharata. Hearing these words that were addressed to him by his disciples, that dispeller of all kinds of darkness represented by ignorance, *viz.*, the blessed Vyasa, the son of Parasara, said these words:—I have undergone very severe, in fact, the austerest of penances. Ye best of men, I am fully conversant with the Past, the Present, and the Future. In consequence of those penances of mine and of the restraint under which I kept my senses while I dwelt on the shores of the Ocean of milk, Narayana became gratified with me. As the result of the great God's gratification, this omniscience with respect to the Past, the Present, and the Future, that was desired by me, arose in my mind. Listen now to me as I discourse to you, in due order, on this great doubt that has disturbed your minds. I have, with the eye of knowledge, beheld all that occurred in the beginning of the Kalpa. He whom both the Sankhyas and those conversant with Yoga call by the name of Paramatma (the Supreme Soul) comes to be regarded as Mahapurusha (the Great Purusha) in consequence of his own acts. From Him springs forth Abyakta (the Unmanifest), whom the learned call Pradhana. From the puissant Unmanifest sprang, for the creation of all the worlds, the Manifest (Baktya). He is called Aniruddha. That Aniruddha is known among all creatures by the name of the Mahat Atma. It is that Aniruddha who, becoming manifest, created the Grandsire Brahman. Aniruddha is known by another name, *viz.*, Ahankara (consciousness) and is endued with every kind of energy. Earth, Wind, Space, Water, and Light numbering the fifth,—these are the five Mahabhutas (elements) that have sprung from Ahankara. Having created the Mahabhutas (five in number), he then created their attributes.[1] Combining the Mahabhutas, he then created diverse embodied Beings. Listen to me as I recount them to you. Marichi, Angiras, Atri, Pulastya, Pulaha, Kratu, the high-souled Vasishtha, and the Self-born Manu,—these should be known as the eight Prakritis. Upon these rest all the worlds. Then the Grandsire of all the worlds, *viz.*, Brahman, created, for the fulfilment of all creatures, the Vedas with all their branches, as also the Sacrifices with their limbs. From these eight Prakritis have sprung this vast universe. Then sprang Rudra from the principle of wrath. Starting into life, he created ten others that were like him. These eleven Rudras are called by name of Vikara-Purushas. The Rudras, the (eight) Prakritis, and the several celestial Rishis, having started into life, approached Brahman with the object of upholding the universe and its operations. Addressing the Grandsire, they said,—We have been created, O holy one, by thee, O thou of great puissance. Tell each of us, O Grandsire, the respective juridisction we shall be vested with. What particular jurisdictions have been created by thee for supervising the different affairs? We, each, should be endued with what kind of consciousness and shall take charge of which of these? Do thou ordain also unto each of us the measure of strength that we are to have for discharging the duties of our respective jurisdictions.'—Thus addressed by them, the great god replied unto them in the following way.

" 'Brahman said,—You have done well, ye deities, in speaking to me of this matter. Blessed be you all! I was thinking of this very subject that has engaged your attention. How should the three worlds be upheld and kept agoing? How should your strength and mine be utilized towards that end? Let all of us, leaving this place, repair to that unmanifest and foremost of Beings who is the witness of the world, for seeking his protection. He will tell us what is for our good.—After this, those deities and Rishis, with Brahman, proceeded to the northern shores of the Ocean of milk, desirous of doing good to the three worlds. Arrived there, they began to practise those austere penances that are declared by Brahman in the Vedas. Those austerest of penances are known by the name of Mahaniyama (the foremost vows and obser-

---

1 That is, the attributes of vision to Light, taste to Water, sound to Space, touch to Wind, and smell to Earth.—T.

vances). They stood there with mind fixed, immovable as posts of wood, and with eyes upturned and arms raised upwards. For a thousand celestial years they were engaged in those severe penances. At the conclusion of that period they heard these sweet words in harmony with the Vedas and their branches.

" 'The blessed and holy one said,—Ye deities and Rishis possessed of wealth of asceticism, with Brahman in your company, after according you all welcome, I say unto you these words. I know what is in your hearts. Verily, the thoughts that engage you are for the good of the three worlds. I shall increase your energy and strength investing the same with Pravritti (prediliction for acts). Ye gods, well have you undergone these penances from desire of adoring me. Ye foremost of Beings, enjoy now the excellent fruits of austerities which ye have gone through. This Brahman is the Lord of all the worlds. Endued with puissance, he is the Grandsire of all creatures. Ye also are foremost of deities. Do ye all, with concentrated minds perform sacrifices for my glory. In the sacrifices which you will perform, do ye always give me a portion of the sacrificial offerings. I shall then, ye lords of creation, assign to each of you your respective jurisdictions and ordain what will be for your good !—' "

Vaisampayana continued,—"Hearing these words of that God of gods, all those deities and great Rishis and Brahman became filled with such delight that the hair on their bodies stood on its end. They forthwith made arrangements for a sacrifice in honour of Vishnu according to the ordinances laid down in the Vedas. In that sacrifice, Brahman himself dedicated a portion of the offerings to Vishnu. The deities and the celestial Rishis also, after the manner of Brahman, dedicated similar portions each unto the great God. The portions, thus offered with great reverence unto Vishnu, were, in respect of both the measure and the quality of the articles used, according to the ordinances laid down for the Krita age. The deities and the Rishis and Brahman, in that sacrifice, adored the great God as one endued with the complexion of the Sun, as the foremost of Beings, situate beyond the reach of Tamas, vast, pervading all things, the Supreme Lord of all, the giver of boons, and possessed of puissance. Thus adored by them, the boon-giving and great God, invisible and bodiless, addressed those assembled celestials from heaven and said unto them :—"The offerings dedicated by you in this sacrifice have all reached me. I am gratified with all of you. I shall bestow rewards on you that will however, be fraught with ends whence there will be return.[1] This shall be your distinctive feature, ye gods,

1 'Avritti lakshanam' means that the reward to be bestowed shall not be Emancipation whence there is no return, but such reward (as the felicity of heaven) whence there will be a return for each of the receivers.—T.

from this day, in consequence of my grace and kindness for you. Performing sacrifices in every Yuga, with large presents, ye will become enjoyers of fruits born of Pravritti. Ye gods, those men also that will perform sacrifices according to the ordinances of the Vedas, will give unto all of you shares of their sacrificial offerings. In the Veda-sutras I make him the receiver (in such sacrifices) of a share similar to that which he has himself offered one in this sacrifice. Created to look after those affairs that appertain to your respective jurisdictions, do ye uphold the worlds according to the measures of your strength as dependent on the shares you receive on those sacrifices. Indeed, drawing strength from those rites and observances that will be current in the several worlds, taking their rise from the fruits of Pravritti, do ye continue to uphold the affairs of those worlds.[1] Strengthened by the sacrifices that will be performed by men, ye will strengthen me. These are the thoughts that I entertain for you all. It is for this purpose that I have created the Vedas and sacrifices and plants and herbs. Duly served with these by human beings on Earth, the deities will be gratified. Ye foremost of deities, 'till the end of this Kalpa, I have ordained your creation, making your constitution depend upon the consequence of the religion of Pravritti. Ye foremost of Beings, do ye then, as regards your respective jurisdictions, engage yourselves in seeking the good of the three worlds. Marichi, Angiras, Atri,, Pulastya, Pulaha, Kratu, and Vasishtha,—these seven Rishis have been created by a fiat of the will. These will become the formost of persons conversant with the vedas. In fact, they will become the preceptors of the Vedas. They will be wedded to the religion of Pravritti, for they have been intented to devote themselves to the act of procreating offspring. This is the eternal path that I disclose of creatures engaged in acts and observances. The puissant Lord who is charged with the creation of all the worlds is called Aniruddha, Sana, Sanatsujata, Sanaka, Sanandana, Sanatkumara, Kapila, and Sanatana numbering the seventh,—these seven Rishis are known as the spiritual sons of Brahman. Their knowledge comes to them of itself (without being dependant on study or exertion). These seven are wedded to the religion of Nivritti. They are the formost of all persons conversant with Yoga. They are possessed also of deep knowledge of the Sankhya philosophy. They are preceptors of the scriptures on duty and it is they that introduce the duties of the religion of Nivritti and cause them to flow in the worlds. From Unmanifest (Prakriti) has flowed Consciousness and the three great attributes (of Sattwa, Rajas, and Tamas). Transcending

1 'Taking their rise from the fruits of Pravritti' implies 'having their origin in their desire for such fruits as appertain to the religion of Pravritti or acts.'—T.

Prakriti is he called Kshetrajna. That Kshetrajna is myself. The path of those that are wedded to Karma emerging out of Ahankara is fraught with return. One cannot, by that path, reach the spot whence there is no return. Different creatures have been created with different ends. Some are intended for the path of Pravritti and some for that of Nivritti. According to the path that a creature follows is the reward that he enjoys. This Brahman is the master of all the worlds. Endued with puissance it is he that creates the universe.[1] He is your mother and father, and he is your grandfather. At my command, he will be the giver of boons unto all creatures. His son Rudra, who has sprung from his brow at his command, will, endued with puissance, uphold all created beings. Go ye to your respective jurisdictions, and seek, according to the ordinances, the good of the worlds. Let all the scriptural acts flow in all the worlds. Let there be no delay in this. Ye foremost of celestials, do ye ordain the acts of all creatures and the ends that they are to attain therefor. Do ye appoint also the limits of the periods for which all creatures are to live. This present epoch that has been set to run is the foremost of all epochs and should be known by the name of Krita. In this Yuga living creatures should not be slain in the sacrifices that may be performed. It should be as I ordain and let it not be otherwise. In this age, ye celestials, Righteousness will flourish in its entirety.[2] After this age will come the epoch called Treta. The Vedas, in that Yuga, will lose one quarter. Only three of them will exist. In the sacrifice that will be performed in that age, animals, after dedication with the aid of sacred *mantras*, will be slain. As regards Righteousness again, it will lose one quarter; only three quarters thereof will flourish. On the expiration of the Treta will come the mixed Yuga known by the name of Dwapara. In that Yuga, Righteousness will lose two quarters and only two quarters thereof will flourish. Upon the expiration of Dwapara the Yuga that will set in will be called Kali yuga which will come under the influence of Tisya constellation. Righteousness will lose full three quarters. Only a quarter thereof will exist in all places.

" 'When the great God said these words, the deities and the celestial Rishis addressed him and said,—If only a fourth part of Righteousness is to exist in that age in every place, tell us O holy one, whither shall we then go and what shall we do !—

---

1 What is stated here is that creature following the path of Pravritti cannot hope to reach the spot whence there is no return. It is by the path of Nivritti that spot is capable of being reached. The path of Pravritti is always fraught with return. One may become, by walking along that path the very chief of the celestials, but that status is not eternal. Since the beginning (if a beginning can be conceived), millions and millions of Indras have arisen and fallen down.—T.

2 Literally, 'with their four quarters entire.'—T.

"'The blessed and holy one said,—Ye foremost of celestials, ye should, in that age, repair to such places where the Vedas and sacrifices and Penances and Truth and Self-restraint, accompanied by duties fraught with compassion for all creatures, will still continue to flourish. Sin will never be able to touch you at all!—,

"Vyasa continued,—'Thus commanded by the great God, the deities with all the Rishis bowed their heads unto him and then proceeded to the places they desired. After the Rishis and denizens of heaven had left that place, Brahman remained there, desirous of beholding the great Deity emanant in the form of Aniruddha. The formost of deities then manifested himself to Brahmana, having assumed a form that had a vast equine head. Bearing a bowl (Kamandula) and the triple stick, he manifested himself before Brahman, reciting the while the Vedas with all their branches. Beholding the great Deity of immeasurable energy in that form crowned with an equine head, the puissant Brahman, the Creator of all the worlds, moved by the desire of doing good to his Creation, worshipped that boon-giving Lord with a bend of his head, and stood before him with hands joined in reverence. The great Deity embraced Brahman and then told him these words.

"'The holy one said,—Do thou, O Brahman, duly think of the courses of acts which creatures are to follow. Thou art the great ordainer of all created Beings. Thou art the Master and the lord of the universe. Placing this burthen on thee I shall soon be free from anxiety. At such times, however, when it will be difficult for thee to accomplish the purposes of the deities I shall then appear in incarnate forms according to my self-knowledge. Having said these words, that grand form with the equine head disappeared then and there. Having received his command, Brahman too proceeded quickly to his own region. It is for this, O blessed one, that the eternal Deity, with the lotus in his navel, became the acceptor of the first share offered in sacrifices and hence it is that He came to be called as the eternal upholder of all Sacrifices. He himself adopted the religion of Nivritti, the end after which those creatures strive that are desirous of indestructible fruits. He ordained at the same time the religion of Pravritri for others, with the view to giving variety to the universe. He is the beginning, He is the middle, and He is the end of all created Beings. He is their Creator and He is their one object of meditation. He is the actor and He is the act. Having withdrawn the universe into Himself at the end of the Yuga, He goes to sleep, and awakeing at the commencement of another Yuga, He once more creates the universe. Do you all bow unto that illustrious one who is possessed of high soul and who transcends the three attributes, who is unborn, whose form is the universe, and who is the abode or refuge of all the denizens of heaven,

Do you bow unto Him who is the Supreme Lord of all creatures, who is the Lord of the Rudras, who is the Lord of the Adityas, and of the Vasus as well. Do you bow unto Him who is the Lord of the Aswins, and the Lord of the Maruts, who is the Lord of all the Sacrifices ordained in the Vedas, and the Lord of the Vedangas. Bow unto Him who always resides in the Ocean, and who is called Hari, and whose hair is like the blades of the Munja grass. Bow unto Him who is Peace and Tranquility, and who imparts the religion of Moksha unto all creatures. Bow unto Him who is the Lord of Penances, of all kinds of energy, and of Fame, who is ever the Lord of Speech and the Lord of all the Rivers also. Bow unto Him who is called Kaparddin (Rudra), who is the Great Boar, who is the Unicorn, and who is possessed of great intelligence : who is the Sun, who assumed the well-known form with the equine head; and who is always displayed in a fourfold form. Bow unto Him who is unrevealed, who is capable of being apprehended by knowledge only, who is both indestructible and destructible. The supreme Deity, who is immutable, pervadeth all things. He is the Supreme Lord who can be known with the aid of the eye of knowledge alone. It was thus that, aided by the eye of Knowledge, I beheld in days of yore that foremost of deities. Asked by you, I have told you everything in detail, ye disciples, and do you act according to my words and dutyfully serve the Supreme Lord called Hari. Do you hymn His praises in Vedic words and adore and worship Him also according to due rites !' "

Vaisampayana continued,—"It was thus that the arranger of the Vedas, endued with great intelligence, discoursed to us, questioned by us on that occasion. His son, the highly righteous Suka, and all his disciples (*viz.*, ourselves) listened to him whiie he delivered that discourse. Our preceptor, with ourselves, O king, then adored the great Deity with Richs extracted from the four Vedas. I have thus told thee everything about what thou hadst asked me. It was thus, O king, that our Island-born preceptor discoursed to us. He who, having uttered the words—I bow unto the holy Lord,—frequently listens, with concentrated attention, to this discourse or reads or recites it to others, becomes endued with intelligence and health, and possessed of beauty and strength. If ill, he becomes freed from that illness, bound, freed from his bonds. The man who cherishes desires obtains (be this) the fruition of all his desires, and easily attains to a long life also. A Brahmana, by doing this, becomes conversant with all the Vedas, and a Kshatriya becomes crowned with success. A Vaisya, by doing it, makes considerable profits, and a Sudra attains to great felicity. A sonless man obtains a son. A maiden obtains a desirable husband. A woman that has conceived brings forth a son. A barren woman conceives and attains to wealth of sons and grandsons. He who recites this discourse on the way succeeds in passing happily and without impediments of any kind along his way. In fact, one attains to whatever objects one cherishes, if one reads or recites this narrative. Hearing these words of the great Rishi, fraught with certainty of conclusion, and embodying a recital of the attributes of that high-souled one who is the foremost of all beings, hearing this narrative of the great conclave of Rishis and other denizens of heaven,—men who are devoted to the Supreme Deity derive great happiness.' "

SECTION CCCXLII

Janamejaya said,—"O holy one, it behoveth thee to tell me the significance of those diverse names uttering which the great Rishi Vyasa with his disciples hymned the praises of the illustrious slayer of Madhu. I am desirous of hearing those names of Hari, that Supreme Lord of all creatures. Indeed, by listening to those names, I shall be sanctified and cleansed even like the bright autumnal moon!"

Vaisampayana said,—"Listen, O king, to what the significances are of the diverse names, due to attributes and acts, of Hari as the puissant Hari himself of cheerful soul explained them to Phalguna. That slayer of hostile heroes, *viz.*, Phalguna, had at one time asked Kesava, enquiring after the imports of the some of the names by which the high-souled Kesava is adored.

"Arjuna said,—'O holy one, O Supreme ordainer of the Past and the Future, O Creator of all Beings, O immutable one, O Refuge of all the worlds, O Lord of the universe, O dispeller of the fears of all persons, I desire to hear from thee in detail, O Kesava, the significance of all those names of thine, O God, which have been mentioned by the great Rishis in the Vedas and the Puranas in conqseuence of diverse acts of thine. None else than thee, O Lord, is competent to explain the significations of those names.'

"The holy one said,—'In the Rigveda, in the Yajurveda, in the Atharvans and the Samans, in the Puranas and the Upanishads, as also in the treatises on Astrology, O Arjuna, in the Sankhya scriptures, in the Yoga scriptures, and in the treatises also on the Science of Life, many are the names that have been mentioned by the great Rishis. Some of those names are derivable from my attributes and some of them relate to my acts. Do thou hear, with concentrated attention, O sinless one, what the import is of each of those names (in particular) that have reference to my acts. I shall recite them to you. It is said that in days of yore you were half my body. Salutations unto Him of great glory,

Him, *viz.*, that is the Supreme Soul of all embodied creatures.[1] Salutations unto Narayana, unto Him that is identifiable with the universe, unto Him that transcends the three (primal) attributes (of Sattwa, Rajas, and Tamas), unto Him that is, again, the Soul of those attributes. From His grace hath arisen Brahman and from His wrath hath arisen Rudra. He is the source whence have sprung all mobile and immobile creatures. O foremost of all persons endued with Sattwa, the attribute of Sattwa consists of the eight and ten qualities.[2] That attribute is Supreme Nature having for her soul the Sky and Earth and succeeding by her creative forces in upholding the universe. That Nature is identical with the fruit of all acts (in the form of the diverse regions of felicity to which creatures attain through their acts). She is also the pure Chit. She is immortal, and invincible, and is called the Soul of the universe. From her flows all the modifications of both Creation and Destruction. (She is identical with my Prakriti or Nature). Divested of sex, She or He is the penances that people undergo. He is both the sacrifice that is performed and the sacrificer that performs the sacrifice. He is the ancient and the infinite Purusha. He is otherwise called Aniruddha and is the source of the Creation and the Destruction of the universe. When Brahma's night wore off, through the grace of that Being of immeasurable energy, a lotus made its appearance first, O thou of eyes like lotus petals. Within that lotus was born Brahma, springing from Aniruddha's grace. Towards the evening of Brahma's day, Aniruddha became filled with wrath, and as a consequence of this, there sprang from his forehead a son called Rudra vested with the power of destroying everything (when the hour for destruction comes). These two, *viz.*, Brahma and Rudra, are the foremost of all the deities, having sprung respectively from the Propitiousness and the Wrath (of Aniruddha). Acting according to Aniruddha's direction, these two deities create and destroy. Although capable of granting boons unto all creatures, they are, however, in the matter of the concerns to which they attend (viz., Creation and Destruction), merely instruments in the hands of Aniruddha. (It is Aniruddha that does everything, making Brahma and Rudra the visible agents in respect of the universe). Rudra is otherwise called Kaparddin. He has matted locks on his head, and sometimes displays a head that is bald. He loves to dwell in the midst of crematoriums which constitute his home. He is an observer of the austerest vows. He is Yogin of mighty puissance and energy. He is the destroyer of Daksha's sacrifice and the tearer of Bhaga's eyes. O son of Pandu,

---

1 This salutation of Krishna unto the Supreme Soul is very characteristic. He salutes himself by saluting the Supreme Soul.—T.

2 Sattwa is the attribute of righteousness. It is said to consist of eight and ten qualities. The Commentator mentions them all.—T.

Rudra should be known to have always Narayana for his Soul. If that deity of deities, viz., Maheswara, be worshipped, then O Partha, is the puissant Narayana also worshipped. I am the Soul, O son of Pandu, of all the worlds, of all the universe. Rudra, again, is my Soul. It is for this that I always adore him. If I do not adore the auspicious and boon-giving Isana nobody would then adore my own self. The ordinances I set are followed by all the worlds. Those ordinances should always be adored, and it is, therefore, that I adore them. He who knows Rudra knows myself, and he who knows myself knows Rudra. He who follows Rudra follows me. Rudra is Narayana. Both are one ; and one is displayed in two different forms. Rudra and Narayana, forming one person, pervade all displayed things and cause them to act. No one else than Rudra is competent to grant me a boon, O son of Pandu. Having settled this in my mind, I adored in days of yore the ancient and puissant Rudra, for obtaining the boon of a son. In adoring Rudra thus I adored my own self. Vishnu never bows his head unto any deity except his own self. It is for this reason that I adore Rudra, (Rudra being, as I have already told thee, my own self). All the deities, including Brahma and Indra and the deities and the great Rishis, adore Narayana, that foremost of deities, otherwise called by the name of Hari. Vishnu is the foremost of all Beings past, present, or future, and as such should always be adored and worshipped with reverence. Do thou bow thy head unto Vishnu. Do thou bow thy head unto Him who gives protection to all. Do thou bow, O son of Kunti, unto that great boon-giving deity, that foremost of deities, who eats the offerings made unto him in sacrifices. I have heard that there are four kinds of worshippers, viz., those who are eager for a religious life, those who are enquirers, those who strive to comprehend what they learn and those who are wise. Among them all, they that are devoted to realising the self and do not adore any other deity, are the foremost. I am the end they seek, and though engaged in acts, they never seek the fruits thereof. The three remaining classes of my worshippers are those that are desirous of the fruits of their acts. They attain to regions of great felicity, but then they have to fall down therefrom upon the exhaustion of their merits. Those amongst my worshippers, therefore, that are fully awakened (and, as such, that know that all happiness is terminable except what is attainable by persons that become identified with me) obtain what is foremost (and invaluable).[1] Those that are awakened and whose conduct displays such enlightenment, may be engaged in adoring Brahman or Mahadeva or the other deities that occur in heaven but they succeed at least in attaining to myself. I have thus told thee,

---

1 *i.e.*, Emancipation or complete identification with the Supreme Soul. —T.

O Partha, what the distinctions are between my worshippers. Thyself, O son of Kunti, and myself are known as Nara and Narayana. Both of us have assumed human bodies only for the purpose of lightening the burthen of the Earth. I am fully cognisant of self-knowledge. I know who I am and whence I am, O Bharata. I know the religion of Nivritti, and all that contributes to the prosperity of creatures. Eternal as I am, I am the one sole Refuge of all men. The waters have been called by the name of Nara, for they sprang from Him called Nara. And since the waters in former times, were my refuge, I am, therefore, called by the name of Narayana. Assuming the form of the Sun I cover the universe with my rays. And because I am the home of all creatures, therefore, am I called by the name of Vasudeva. I am the end of all creatures and their sire, O Bharata. I pervade the entire firmament on high and the Earth, O Partha, and my splendour transcends every other splendour. I am He, O Bharata, whom all ereatures wish to attain to at the time of death. And because I pervade all the universe, I have come to be called by the name of Vishnu. Desirous of attaining to success through restraint of their senses, people seek to attain to me who am heaven and Earth and the firmament between the two. For this am I called by the name of Damodara. The word Prisni includes food, the Vedas, water, and nectar. These four are always in my stomach. Hence am I called by the name of Prisnigarbha. The Rishis have said that once on a time when the Rishi Trita was thrown into a well by Ekata and Dwiti, the distressed Trita invoked me, saying,—O Prisnigarbha, do thou rescue the fallen Trita!—That foremost of Rishis, viz., Trita, the spiritual son of Brahma, having called on me thus, was rescued from the pit. The rays that emanate from the Sun who gives heat to the world, from the blazing fire, and from the Moon, constitute my hair. Hence do foremost of learned Brahmanas call me by the name of Kesava. The high-souled Utathya having impregnated his wife disappeared from her side through an illusion of the gods. The younger brother Vrihaspati then appeared before that high-souled one's wife. Unto that foremost of Rishis that had repaired thither from desire of congress, the child in the womb of Utathya's wife, O son of Kunti, whose body had already been formed of the five primal elements, said,—O giver of boons, I have already entered into this womb. It behoveth thee not to assail my mother.—Hearing these words of the unborn child, Vrihaspati, became filled with wrath and denounced a curse on him, saying,—Since thou obstructest me in this way when I have come hither from desire of the pleasures of congress, therefore shalt thou, by my curse, be visited by blindness, without doubt!—Through this curse of that foremost of Rishis, the child of Utathya was born blind, and blind he remained for a long time. It was for this reason that, that the Rishi, in days of yore, came to be known by the name of Dirghatamas. He, however, acquired the four Vedas with their eternal limbs and subsidiary parts. After that he frequently invoked me by this secret name of mine. Indeed, according to the ordinance as laid down, he repeatedly called upon me by the name of Kesava. Through the merit he acquired by uttering this name repeatedly, he became cured of his blindness and then came to be called by the name of Gotama. This name of mine, therefore, O Arjuna is productive of boons unto them that utter it among all the deities and the high-souled Rishis. The deity of Fire (Appetite) and Shoma (food) combining together, become transfused into one and the same substance. It is for this reason that the entire universe of mobile and immobile creatures is said to be pervaded by those two deities.[1] In the Puranas, Agni and Soma are spoken of as complementary to one another. The deities also are said to have Agni for their mouth. It is in consequence of these two beings endued with natures leading to the unification that they are said to be deserving of each other and upholders of the universe.' "

SECTION CCCXLIII

"Arjuna said,—'How did Agni and Shoma, in days of yore, attain to uniformity in respect of their original nature ? This doubt has arisen in my mind. Do thou dispel it, O slayer of Madhu !'

"The highly and holy one said,—'I shall recite to thee, O son of Pandu, an ancient story of incidents originating from my own energy. Do thou listen to it with rapt attention ! When four thousand Yugas according to the measure of the celestials elapse, the dissolution of the universe comes. The Manifest disappears into the Unmanifest. All creatures, mobile and immobile, meet with destruction. Light, Earth, Wind, all disappear. Darkness spreads over the universe which becomes one infinite expanse of water. When that infinite waste of water only exists like Brahma without second, it is neither day nor night. Neither aught nor naught exists ; neither manifest nor unmanifest. Then only undifferentiated Brahman existed. When such is the condition of the universe, the foremost of Beings, viz., springs from Tamas, the eternal and immutable Hari that is the combination of the attributes (of omni-

---

1 The object of this Verse, the Commentator says, is to explain the meaning of the word 'Hrishikesa.' Agni is the digestive fire, and Shoma is food. Uniting together, Agni and Shoma, therefore uphold the universe. In the form of digestive fire and food, Agni and Shoma are two gladdeners of the universe. They are called on this account 'Hrishi' (in the dual number). And since they are, as it were, the 'kesa' or hair of Narayana, therefore is he called 'Hrishikesa.' All these etymologies are very fanciful. Elsewhere the word 'Hrishikesa' is explained as the 'Isa' or lord of 'Hrishika or the senses.—T.

potence and the rest) belonging to Narayana, that is in-destructible and immortal, that is without senses, that is inconceivable and unborn, that is Truth's self fraught with compassion, that is endued with the form of existence which the rays of the gem called Chintamani have, that causes diverse kinds of inclinations to flow in diverse directions, that is divested of the principles of hostility and deterioration and mortality and decay, that is formless and all-pervading, and that is endued with the principle of universal Creation and of Eternity without beginning, middle, or end. There is authority for this assertion. The Sruti declares,—Day was not. Night was not. Aught was not. Naught was not. In the beginning there was only Tamas[1] in the form of the universe, and she is the night of Narayana of universal form. Even this is the meaning of the word Tamas. From that Purusha (called Hari), thus born of Tamas and having Brahman for his parent, started into existence the Being called Brahman. Brahman, desiring to create creatures, caused Agni and Shoma to spring from his own eyes. Afterwards when creatures came to be created, the created persons came out in their due order as Brahmanas and Kshatriyas. He who started into life as Shoma was none else than Brahma; and they that were born as Brahmanas were all Shoma in reality. He who started into Being as Kshatriyas were none else than Agni. The Brahmanas became endued with greater energy than the Kshatras. If you ask the reason why, the answer is that this superiority of the Brahmanas to the Kshatriyas is an attribute that is manifest to the whole world. It occurred as follows. The Brahmanas represent the eldest creation as regards men. None were created before, that was superior to the Brahmanas. He who offers food into the mouth of a Brahmana is regarded as pouring libations into a blazing fire (for gratifying the deities). I say that having ordained things in comprising this way, the creation of creatures was accomplished by Brahma. Having established all created Beings in their respective positions, he upholds the three worlds. There occurs a declaration to the same effect in the *Mantras* of the Srutis.—Thou, O Agni, art the Hotri in sacrifices, and the benefactor of the universe. Thou art the benefactor of the deities, of men, and of all the worlds.—There is (other) authority also for this.—Thou art, O Agni, the Hotri of the universe and of sacrifices. Thou art the source through which the deities and men do good to the universe.—Agni is truly the Hotri and the performer of sacrifices. Agni is again the Brahma of the sacrifice. No libations can be poured into sacrificial fire without uttering *mantras*;

---

1 'Sat' is existent or aught 'Asat' is naught or non-existent. Very generally, these two words are used to imply Effects and Causes, the former being gross or manifest, and the latter, subtile or unmanifest. 'Tamas' here does not mean one of the three primal attributes but primeval darkness. Comp Manu, 'asitidam tamobhutam &c'—T.

there can be no penances without a person to perform them ; the worship of the deities and men and the Rishis is accomplished by the libations poured with *mantras*. Hence, O Agni, thou hast been regarded as the Hotri in sacrifices.[1] Thou art, again, all the other *mantras* that have been declared in respect of the Homa rites of men. For the Brahmanas the duty is ordained of officiating for others in the sacrifices they perform. The two other orders, *viz*., Kshatras and Vaisyas, that are included within the regenerate or twice-born class, have not the same duty prescribed for them. Hence, Brahmanas are like Agni, who uphold sacrifices. The sacrifices (which the Brahmanas perform) strengthen the deities. Strengthened in this way, the deities fructify the Earth (and thereby support all living creatures). But the result that may be achieved by the foremost of sacrifices may as well be accomplished through the mouth of the Brahmanas. That learned person who offers food into the mouth of a Brahmana is said to pour libations into the sacred fire for gratifying the deities. In this way the Brahmanas have come to be regarded as Agni. They that are possessed of learning adore Agni. Agni, is again, Vishnu. Entering all creatures, he upholds their life-breaths. In this connection there is a verse sung by Sanatkumara. Brahman, in creating the universe, first created the Brahmanas. The Brahmanas become immortal by studying the Vedas, and repair to heaven through the aid of such study. The intelligence, speech, acts and observances, faith, and the penances of the Brahmanas uphold both the Earth and the heaven like slings of strings upholding bovine nectar.[2] There is no duty higher than Truth. There is no superior more worthy of reverence than the mother. There is none more efficient than the Brahmana for conferring felicity both here and hereafter. The inhabitants of those realms where Brahmanas have no certain means of support (from lands or other kinds of property assigned to them) become very miserable. There the oxen do not carry the people or draw the plough, nor do vehicles of any kind bear them. There milk kept in jars is never churned for yielding butter. On the other hand, the residents become divested of prosperity of every kind, and betake themselves to the ways of robbers (instead of being able to enjoy the blessings of peace).[3] In the Vedas, the Puranas, the histories, and other authorita-

---

1 I do not know whether I have understood correctly the last part of this sentence. I think what is stated is that by honouring Hari and Mantras, one honours the deities and men and the Rishis. By men, I think, dead men or the Pitris are referred to.—T.

2 The reading 'vagamritam' is an error. The correct reading is 'gavamritam.'.—T.

3 In former times kings and chiefs always used to assign rent-free lands to learned Brahmanas for their support. Those countries where Brahmanas had not such lands assigned to them, were, as it were, under a

tive writings, it is said that Brahmanas, who are the souls of all creatures, who are the creators of all things, and who are identifiable with all existent objects, sprang from the mouth of Narayana. Indeed, it is said that the Brahmanas first came at the time when the great boon-giving god had restrained his speech as a penance and the other orders have originated from the Brahmanas. The Brahmanas are distinguished above the deities and Asuras, since they were created by myself in my indescribable form as Brahma. As I have created the deities and the Asuras and the great Rishis so I have placed the Brahmanas in their respective situations and have to punish them occasionally. In consequence of his licentious assault on Ahalya, Indra was cursed by Gautama, her husband, through which Indra got a green beard on his face. Through that curse of Kausika Indra lost, also, his own testicles, which loss was afterwards (through the kindness of the other deities) made up by the substitution of the testicles of a ram. When in the sacrifice of king Sarjjati, the great Rishi Chyavana became desirous of making the twin Aswins sharers of the sacrificial offerings, Indra objected. Upon Chyavana insisting, Indra sought to hurl his thunderbolt at him. The Rishi paralysed Indra's arms. Incensed at the destruction of his sacrifice by Rudra, Daksha once more set himself to the practice of severe austerities and attaining to high puissance caused something like a third eye to appear on the forehead of Rudra for the destruction of Tripurasura.[1] When Rudra addressed himself for the destruction of the triple city belonging to the Asuras, the preceptor of the Asuras, viz., Usanas, provoked beyond endurance, tore a matted lock from his own head and hurled it at Rudra. From that matted lock of Usanas sprang many serpents. Those serpents began to bite Rudra, at which his throat became blue. During a byegone period, viz., that connected with the Self-born Manu,[2] it is said that Narayana had seized Rudra by the throat and hence did Rudra's throat become blue. On the occasion of churning the Ocean for raising the *amrita*, Vrihaspati of Angiras race sat on the shores of the Ocean for performing the rite of *Puruscharana*. When he took up a little water for the purpose of the initial *achamana*, the water seemed to him to be very muddy. At this Vrihaspati became

---

ban. What is said in this verse is that in such countries the blesssings of peace are wanting. The inhabitants are borne on vehicles drawn by oxen or steeds.—T.

1 In consequence of this third eye on Rudra's forehead, he came to be called by the name of 'Virupaksha' or the 'ugly or fierce-eyed.'—T.

2 A Manwantarah consists of about 72 'Chaturyugas.' i.e., 283 yugas according to the measurement of the celestials. The present yuga is called the Vaivaswat Manwantarah, i.e, the period connected with Manu the son of Vivaswat. At each Manwantarah a new Manu appears. The self-born Manu was a different person.—T.

angry and cursed the Ocean, saying,—Since thou continuest to be so dirty regardless of the fact of my having come to thee for touching thee, since thou hast not become clear and transparent, therefore from this day thou shalt be tainted with fishes and sharks and tortoises and other aquatic animals.—From that time, the waters of the ocean have become infested with diverse kinds of sea-animals and monsters. Viswarupa, the son of Tashtri, formerly became the priest of the deities. He was, on his mother's side, related to the Asuras, for his mother was the daughter of an Asura. While publicly offering unto the deities their shares of sacrificial offerings, he privately offered shares thereof unto the Asuras. The Asuras, with their chief Hiranyakasipu at their head, then repaired to their sister, the mother of Viswarupa, and solicited a boon from her, saying,—The son Viswarupa by Tashtri, otherwise called Trisiras, is now the priest of the deities. While he gives unto the deities their shares of sacrificial offerings publicly, he gives us our shares of the same privately. In consequence of this, the deities are being aggrandised, and we are being weakened. It behoveth thee, therefore, to prevail upon him that he may take up our cause.—Thus addressed by them, the mother of Viswarupa repaired to her son who was then staying in the Nandana woods (of Indra) and said unto him,—How is it, O son, that thou art engaged in aggrandising the cause of thy foes and weakening that of thy maternal uncles? It behoveth thee not to act in this way.—Viswarupa, thus solicited by his mother, thought that he should not disobey her words, and as the consequence of that reflection he went over to the side of Hiranyakasipu, after having paid proper respects to his mother. King Hiranyakasipu, upon the arrival of Trisiras, dismissed his old Hotri, viz., Vasishtha, the son of Brahma, and appointed Trisiras to that office. Incensed at this, Vasishtha cursed Hiranyakasipu, saying,—Since thou dismissest me and appointest another person as thy Hotri, this sacrifice of thine shall not be completed, and some Being the like of whom has not existed before will slay thee!—In consequence of this curse, Hiranyakasipu was slain by Vishnu in the form of a man-lion. Viswarupa, having adopted the side of his maternal relations, employed himself in severe austerities for aggrandsing them. Impelled by the desire of causing him to swerve from his vows, Indra despatched to him many beautiful Apsaras. Beholding those celestial nymphs of transendent beauty, the heart of Viswarupa became agitated. Within a very short time he became exceedingly attached to them. Understanding that he had become attached to them, the celestial nymphs said unto him one day,—We shall not tarry here any longer. In fact, we shall return to that place whence we came.—Unto them that said so, the son of Tashtri replied,—Where will you go? Stay with me. I shall do you good.—Hearing him say so, the Apsaras rejoined,—We are celestial nymphs called Apsaras. We chose in days of old the illustrious and boon-giving Indra of great puissance.—Viswarupa then said unto them.—This very day I shall so ordain that all the deities with Indra at their head shall cease to be.—Saying this, Trisiras began to recite mentally certain sacred Mantras of great efficacy. By virtue of those Mantras he began to increase in energy. With one of his mouths he began to drink all the Soma that Brahmanas engaged in Sacrifices poured on their sacred fires with due rites. With a second mouth he began to eat all food (that was offered in sacrifices). With his third mouth he began to drink up the energy of all the deities with Indra at their head. Beholding him swelling with energy in every part of his body that was strengthened by the Soma he was drinking, all the deities, then, with Indra in their company, proceeded to the Grandsire Brahma. Arrived at his presence, they addressed him and said,—All the Soma that is duly offered in the sacrifices performed everywhere is being drink by Viswarupa. We no longer obtain our shares. The Asuras are being aggrandised, while we are being weakened. It behoveth thee, therefore, to ordain what is for our good.—After the deities ceased, the Grandsire replied,—The great Rishi Dadhichi of Bhrigu's race is now engaged in performing severe austerities. Go, ye deities, unto him and solicit a boon from him. Do ye so arrange that he may cast off his body. With his bones let a new weapon be created called the Thunder-bolt.—Thus instructed by the Grandsire, the deities proceeded to that place where the holy Rishi Dadhichi was engaged in his austerities. The deities with Indra at their head addressed the sage, saying,—O holy one, your austerities, we hope, are being well performed and uninterrupted. —Unto them the sage Dadhichi said,—Welcome to all of you. Tell me what I should do for you. I shall certainly do what you will say.—They then told him,—It behoveth thee to cast off thy body for benefiting all the worlds.—Thus solicited, the sage Dadhichi, who was a great Yogin and who regarded happiness and misery in the same light, without being at all cheerless, concentrated his Soul by his Yoga power and cast off his body. When his Soul left its temporary tenement of clay, Dhatri, taking his bones, created an irresistible weapon called the Thunder-bolt. With the Thunder-bolt thus made with the bones of a Brahmana, which was impenetrable by other weapons and irresistible and pervaded by the energy of Vishnu, Indra struck Viswarupa the son of Tashtri. Having slain the son of Tashtri thus, Indra severed his head from the body. From the lifeless body, however, of Viswarupa, when it was pressed, the energy that was still residing in it gave birth to a mighty Asura of the name of Vritra. Vritra became the foe of Indra, but Indra slew him also with the Thunder-bolt. In consequence of the sin of Brahmanicide, being thus doubled Indra became overcome with a great fear and as the consequence thereof he had to abandon the sovereignty of heaven. He entered a cool lotus stalk that grew in the Manas lake. In consequence of the Yoga attribute of Anima, he became very minute and entered the fibres of that lotus stalk.[1] When the lord of the three worlds, the husband of Sachi, had thus disappeared from sight through fear of the sin of Brahmanicide, the universe became lordless. The attributes of Rajas and Tamas assailed the deities. The Mantras uttered by the great Rishis lost all efficacy. Rakshasas appeared everywhere. The Vedas were about to disappear. The inhabitants of all the worlds, being destitute of a king, lost their strength and began to fall an easy prey to Rakshasas and other evil Beings. Then the deities and the Rishis, uniting together, made Nahusha, the son of Ayusha, the king of the three worlds and duly crowned him as such. Nahusha had on his forehead full five-hundred luminaries of blazing effulgence, which had the virtue of despoiling every creature of energy. Thus equipt Nahusha continued to rule heaven. The three worlds were restored to their normal condition. The inhabitants of the universe once more became happy and cheerful. Nahusha then said,—Everything that Indra used to enjoy is before me. Only, his spouse Sachi is not by.—Having said this, Nahusha proceeded to where Sachi was and, addressing her, said,—O blessed lady, I have become the lord of the deities. Do thou accept me.—Unto him Sachi replied, saying,—Thou art, by nature, wedded to righteousness of behaviour. Thou belongest, again, to the race of Shoma. It behoveth thee not to assail another person's wife.—Nahusha, thus addressed by her, said,—The position of Indra is now being occupied by me. I deserve to enjoy the dominions and all the precious possessions of Indra. In desiring to enjoy thee there can be no sin. Thou wert Indra's and, therefore, should be mine.—Sachi then said unto him,—I am observing a vow that has not yet been completed. After performing the final ablutions I shall come to thee within a few days.—Extracting this promise from Indra's spouse, Nahusha left her presence. Meanwhile Sachi, afflicted with pain and grief, anxious to find her lord and assailed by her fear of Nahusha proceeded to Vrihaspati (the chief priest of the celestials). At the first sight Vrihaspati understood her to be struck with anxiety. He immediately had recourse to Yoga-meditation and learnt that she was intent upon doing what was necessary for restoring her husband to his true position. Vrihaspati then addressed her, saying,—Equipt with penances and the merit that will be thine in consequence of this vow that thou art observing, do thou invoke the boon-giving goddess Upasruti. Invoked by thee, she will appear and

1 By practising Yoga one acquires certain superhuman powers. These are called 'Yogaiswaryya.' They include Anima, by which one can become very minute ; Laghima, by which one can become very gross, &c.—T.

show thee where thy husband is dwelling.—While in the observance of that very austere vow, she invoked with the aid of proper Mantras the boon-giving goddess Upasruti. Invoked by Sachi, the goddess presented herself before her and said,—I am here at thy bidding. Invoked by thee I have come. What cherished wish of thine shall I accomplish ?—Bowing unto her with a bend of the head, Sachi said,—O blessed lady, it behoveth thee to show me where my husband is. Thou art Truth. Thou art Rita.—Thus addressed, the goddess Upasruti took her to the lake Manasa. Arrived there, she pointed out to Sachi her lord Indra residing within the fibres of a lotus stalk. Beholding his spouse pale and emaciated, Indra became exceedingly anxious. And the lord of heaven said unto himself,—Alas, great is the sorrow that has overtaken me. I have fallen off from the position that is mine. This my spouse, afflicted with grief on my account, finds out my lost self and comes to me here.—Having reflected in this strain, Indra addressed his dear spouse and said, —In what condition art thou now ? She answered him,—Nahusha invites me to make me his wife. I have obtained a respite from him, having fixed the time when I am to go to him.—Unto her Indra then said,—Go and say unto Nahusha that he should come to thee on a vehicle never used before, viz., one unto which some Rishis should be harnessed, and arriving at thine in that state he should wed thee. Indra has many kinds of vehicles that are all beautiful and charming. All these have borne thee. Nahusha, however, should come on such a vehicle that Indra himself had not possessd. Thus counselled by her lord, Sachi left that spot with a joyous heart. Indra also once more entered the fibres of that lotus-stalk. Beholding the Queen of Indra come back to heaven, Nahusha addressed her saying.—The time thou hadst fixed is over.—Unto him Sachi said what Indra had directed her to say. Harnessing a number of great Rishis unto the vehicle he rode, Nahusha set out from his place for coming to where Sachi was living. The foremost of Rishis, viz., Agastya, born within a jar, of the vital seed of Maitravaruna, beheld those foremost of Rishis insulted by Nahusha in that way. Him Nahusha struck with his foot. Unto him, Agastya said,—Wretch, as thou hast betaken thyself to a highly improper act, do thou fall down on the Earth. Be transformed into a snake and do thou continue to live in that form as long as the Earth and her hills continue.—As soon as these words were uttered by the great Rishi, Nahusha fell down from that vehicle. The three worlds once more became masterless. The deities and the Rishis then united together and proceeded to where Vishnu was and appealed to him for bringing about the restoration of Indra. Approaching him, they said,—O holy one, it behoveth thee to rescue Indra who is overwhelmed by the sin of Brahmanicide.—The boon-giving Vishnu replied unto them, saying,—Let

Sakra perform a Horse-sacrifice in honour of Vishnu. He will then be restored to his former position.—The deities and the Rishis began to search for Indra, but when they could not find him, they went to Sachi and said unto her,—O blessed lady, go unto Indra and bring him here. Requested by them, Sachi once more proceeded to the lake Manasa. Indra, rising from the lake, came to Vrihaspati. The celestial priest Vrihaspati then made arrangements for a great Horse-sacrifice, substituting a black antelope for a good steed every way fit to be offered up in sacrifice. Causing Indra, the lord of the Maruts, to ride upon that very steed (which was saved from slaughter) Vrihaspati led him to his own place. The lord of heaven was then adored with hymns by all the deities and the Rishis. He continued to rule in heaven, cleansed of the sin of Brahmanicide which was divided into four portions and ordained to reside in woman, fire, trees, and kine. It was thus that Indra, strenghthened by the energy of a Brahmana, succeeded in slaying his foe (and when, as the result of that act of his, he had been overpowered by sin, it was the energy of another Brahmana that rescued him). It was thus that Indra once more regained his position.

" 'In days of yore, while the great Rishi Bharadwaja was saying his prayers by the side of the celestial Ganga, one of the three feet of Vishnu, when he assumed his three-footed form, reached that spot[1]. Beholding that strange sight, Bharadwaja assailed Vishnu with a handful of water, upon which Vishnu's bosom received a mark (called Sreevatsa).[2] Cursed by that foremost of Rishis, viz., Bhrigu, Agni was obliged to become a devourer of all things. Once on a time, Aditi, the mother of the deities, cooked some food for her sons. She thought that, eating that food and strenghthened by it, the deities would succeed in slaying the Asuras. After the food had been cooked, Vudha (the presiding deity of the luminary known by that name), having completed the observance of an austere vow, presented himself before Aditi and said unto her,—Give me alms.—Aditi, though thus solicited for food gave him none, thinking that no one should eat of the food she had cooked, before her sons, the deities, had first taken it. Incensed at the conduct of Aditi who thus refused to give him alms, Vudha, who was Brahma's self through the

---

1 The river Ganga has three currents. One flows through heaven : one is visible on the Earth, and a third flows through the nether regions. Persons of the regenerate classes, when saying their morning, midday, or evening prayers, have to touch water often. What is meant, therefore, by 'Bharadwaja touching the water' is that Bharadwaja was saying his prayers. Vishnu assumed his three-footed form for beguiling Vali of the sovereignty of the universe. With one foot he covered the Earth, with another he covered the firmament. There was no space left for placing his third foot upon.—T.

2 The 'Sreevatsa' is a beautiful whirl on Vishnu's bosom.—T.

austere vow he had completed, cursed her, saying that as Aditi had refused him alms she would have a pain in her womb when Vivaswat, in his second birth in the womb of Aditi, would be born in the form of an egg. Aditi reminded Vivaswat at that time of the curse of Vudha, and it is for that reason that Vivaswat, the deity who is adorned in Sraddhas, coming out of the womb of Aditi, came to be called by the name of Martanda. The Prajapati Daksha became the father of sixty daughters. Amongst them, three and ten were bestowed by him upon Kasyapa; ten upon Dharma; ten upon Manu; and seven and twenty upon Shoma. Although all the seven and twenty that were called Nakshatras and bestowed upon Shoma were equal in respect of beauty and accomplishments, yet Shoma became more attached to one, viz., Rohini, than the rest. The rest of his spouses, filled with jealousy, leaving him, repaired to their sire and informed him of this conduct of their husband, saying,—O holy one, although all of us are equal in point of beauty, yet our husband Shoma is exclusively attached to our sister Rohini.—Incensed at this representation of his daughters, the celestial Rishi Daksha cursed Shoma, saying, that thenceforth the disease phthisis should assail his son-in-law and dwell in him. Through this curse of Daksha, phthisis assailed the puissant Shoma and entered into his body. Assailed by phthisis in this way, Shoma came to Daksha. The latter addressed him, saying,—I have cursed thee because of thy unequal behaviour towards thy wives. The Rishi then said unto Shoma,—Thou art being reduced by the disease phthisis that has assailed thee. There is a sacred water called Hiranyasarah in the Western ocean. Repairing to that sacred water, do thou bathe there.—Counselled by the Rishi, Shoma proceeded thither. Arrived at Hiranyasarah, Soma bathed in that sacred water. Performing his oblations, he cleansed himself from his sin. And because that sacred water was illumined (abhasita) by Shoma, therefore was it from that day called by the name of *Prabhasa*. In consequence, however, of the curse denounced upon him in days of old by Daksha, Shoma, to this day, begins to wane from the night of the full moon till his total disappearance on the night of the new moon whence he once more begins to wax till the night of full moon. The brightness also of the lunar disc from that time received a stain, for the body of Shoma, since then, has come to present certain dark spots. In fact, the splendid disc of the moon has, from that day, come to exhibit the mark of a hare. Once on a time, a Rishi of the name of Sthulasiras was engaged in practising very severe austerities on the northern breasts of the mountains of Meru. While engaged in those austerities, a pure breeze, charged with all kinds of delicious perfumes, began to blow there and fan his body. Scorched as his body was by the very severe austerities he was undergoing, and living as he did upon air alone to the exclusion of every kind of food, he became highly gratified in consequence of that delicious breeze which blew around him. While he was thus gratified with the delicious breeze that fanned him, the trees around him (moved by jealousy) put forth their flowers for making a display and extorting his praise. Displeased at this conduct of the trees because it was dictated by jealousy, the Rishi cursed them, saying,—Henceforth, ye shall not be able to put forth your flowers at all times.—In days of yore, for doing good to the world, Narayana took birth as the great Rishi Vadavamukha. While engaged in practising severe austerities on the breast of Meru, he summoned the Ocean to his presence. The Ocean, however, disobeyed his summons. Incensed at this, the Rishi, with the heat of his body, caused the waters of the Ocean to become as saltish in taste as the human sweat. The Rishi further said,—Thy waters shall henceforth cease to be drinkable. Only when the Equine-head, roving within thee, will drink thy waters, they will be as sweet as honey.—It is for this curse that the waters of the Ocean to this day are saltish to the taste and are drunk by no one else than the Equine-head.[1] The daughter, named Uma, of the Himavat mountains, was desired by Rudra in marriage. (After Himavat had promised the hand of Uma to Mahadeva, the great Rishi Bhrigu, approaching Himavat, addressed him, saying,—Give this daughter of thine unto me in marriage.—Himavat replied unto him, saying,—Rudra is the bridegroom already selected by me for my daughter.—Angry at this reply, Bhrigu said,—Since thou refugest my suit for the hand of thy daughter and insultest me thus, thou shalt no longer abound with jewels and gems.—To this day, in consequence of the Rishi's words, the mountains of Himavat have not any jewels and gems. Even such is the glory of the Brahmanas. It is through the favour of the Brahmanas that the Kshatriyas are able to possess the eternal and undeteriorating Earth as their wife and enjoy her. The power of the Brahmanas, again, is made up of Agni and Shoma. The universe is upheld by that power and, therefore, is upheld by Agni and Shoma united together. It is said that Surya and Chandramas are the eyes of Narayana. The rays of Surya constitute my eyes. Each of them, viz., the Sun and the Moon, invigorate and warm the universe respectively. And because of the Sun and

---

1 The Hindu scriptures mention that there is an Equine-head of vast proportions which roves through the seas. Blazing fires constantly issue from its mouth and these drink up the sea-water. It always makes a roaring noise. It is called Vadava-mukha. The fire issuing from it is called Vadavanala. The waters of the Ocean are like clarified butter. The Equine-head drinks them up as the sacrificial fire drinks the libations of clarified butter poured upon it. The origin of the Vadava fire is sometimes ascribed to the wrath of Urva, a Rishi of the race of Jamadagni. Hence it is sometimes called Aurvya-fire.—T.

the Moon thus warming and invigorating the universe, they have come to be regarded as the *Harsha* (joy) of the universe. It is in consequence of these acts of Agni and Shoma that uphold the universe that I have come to be called by the name of Hrishikesa, O son of Pandu. Indeed, I am the boon-giving Isana, the Creator of the universe.[1] Through virtue of the Mantras with which libations of clarified butter are poured on the sacred fire, I take and appropriate the (principal) share of the offerings made in sacrifices. My complexion also is of that foremost of gems called Harit. It is for these reasons that I am called by the name of Hari. I am the highest abode of all creatures and am regarded by persons conversant with the scriptures to be identical with Truth or Nectar. I am, for this reason, called by learned Brahmanas by the name of Ritadhama (abode of Truth or Nectar). When in days of yore the Earth became submerged in the waters and lost to the view, I found her out and raised her from the depths of the Ocean. For this reason the deities adore me by the name of Govinda. Sipivishta is another name of mine. The word Sipi indicates a person that has no hair on his body. He who pervades all things in the form of Sipi is known by the name of *Sipivishta.* The Rishi Yaksha, with tranquil soul, in many a sacrifice invoked me by the name Sipivishta. It is for this reason that I came to bear this secret name. Yaksha of great intelligence, having adored me by the name Sipivishta, succeeded in restoring the Niruktas which had disappeared from the surface of the Earth and sunk into nether regions. I was never born. I never take birth. Nor shall I ever be born. I am the Kshetrajna of all creatures. Hence am I called by the name of Aja (unborn).[2] I have never uttered anything base or anything that is obscene. The divine Saraswati who is Truth's self, who is the daughter of Brahma and is otherwise called by the name of Rita, represents my speech and always dwells in my tongue. The existent and the non-existent have been merged by me in my Soul. The Rishis dwelling in Pushkara, which is regarded as the abode of Brahman, called me by the name of Truth. I have never swerved from the attribute of Sattwa, and know that the attribute of Sattwa has flowed from me. In this birth also of mine, O Dhananjaya, my ancient attribute of Sattwa has not left me, so that in even this life, establishing myself on Sattwa, I set myself to acts without ever wishing for their fruits. Cleansed of all sins as I am through the attribute of Sattwa, which is

---

1 The etymology of the word 'Hrishikesa' is thus explained. Agni and Shoma are called by the name of 'Hrishi' in the dual number. He is called 'Hrishikesa' who has those two for his kesa or hair. Elsewhere, the word is explained as the 'Isa' or lord of 'Hrishika.'—T.

2 I am the Soul of all creatures, and, therefore, unborn, the Soul being Eternal, Unbeginning and Unending. Hence am I called the Unborn. —T.

my nature, I can be beheld by the aid of that knowledge only which arises from adoption of the attribute of Sattwa. I am reckoned also among those that are wedded to that attribute. For these reasons am I known by the name of Sattwata.[1] I till the Earth, assuming the form of a large plough-share of black iron. And because my complexion is black, therefore am I called by the name of Krishna. I have united the Earth with Water, Space with Mind, and Wind with Light. Therefore am I called Vaikuntha.[2] The cessation of separate conscious existence by indentification with Supreme Brahman is the highest attribute or condition for a living agent to attain. And since I have never swerved from that attribute or condition, I am, therefore, called by the name of Achyuta.[3] The Earth and the Firmament are known to extend in all directions. And because I uphold them both, therefore am I called by the name of Adhokshaja. Persons conversant with the Vedas and employed in interpreting the words used in those scriptures adore me in sacrifices by calling upon me by the same name. In days of yore, the great Rishis, while engaged in practising severe austerities, said,—No one else in the universe than the puissant Narayana, is capable of being called by the name of Adhokshaja. Clarified butter which sustains the lives of all creatures in the universe constitutes my effulgence. It is for this reason that Brahmanas conversant with the Vedas and possessed of concentrated souls call me by the name of Ghritarchis.[4] There are three well-known constituent elements of the body. They have their origin in action, and are called Bile, Phlegm, and Wind. The body is called a union of these three. All living creatures are upheld by these three, and when these three become weakened, living creatures also become weakened. It is for this reason that all persons conversant with the scriptures bearing on the science of Life call me by the name

1 The race in which Krishna took birth was known by the name of Sattwata. All these etymologies are, of course, exceedingly fanciful. Not that the etymologies do not correspond with the rules of Sanskrit Grammar, but that they are not accepted by lexicographers. The fact is that each root in Sanskrit has a variety of meanings.—T.

2 This Verse refers to 'Panchikarana.' The fact is, Earth, Water, Light, Wind and Space are the five primal elements. Each of these is divided into five portions and the portions so arrived at are then united or mingled together forming the different substances of the universe, the proportions in which they are mingled being unequal.—T.

3 'Achyuta' has been variously rendered into English. Its true sense is here explained. 'Unswerving' is the meaning. He who never swerves (from his highest nature or Brahma) is Achyuta. Hence, ordinarily, immutable or undeteriorating is the rendering that I have adopted.—T.

4 Clarified butter is the great sustainer of the universe, for the libations poured on the sacrificial fire uphold the deities, and the deities, thus upheld, pour rain which causes crops and other food to grow, upon which, of course, the universe of living creatures lives.—T.

of Tridhatu.[1] The holy Dharma is known among all creatures by the name of Vrisha, O Bharata. Hence it is that I am called the excellent Vrisha in the Vedic lexicon called Nighantuka. The word 'Kapi' signifies the foremost of boars, and Dharma is otherwise known by the name of Vrisha. It is for this reason that that lord of all creatures, viz., Kasyapa, the common sire of the deities and the Asuras, called me by the name Vrishakapi. The deities and the Asuras have never been able to ascertain my beginning, my middle, or my end. It is for this reason that I am sung as Anadi, Amadhya and Ananta. I am the Supreme Lord endued with puissance, and I am the eternal witness of the universe (beholding as I do its successive creations and destructions). I always hear words that are pure and holy, O Dhananjaya, and never hold anything that is sinful. Hence am I called by the name of Suchisravas. Assuming, in days of old, the form of a boar with a single tusk, O enhancer of the joys of others, I raised the submerged Earth from the bottom of the ocean. From this reason am I called by the name of Ekasringa. While I assumed the form of mighty boar for this purpose, I had three humps on my back. Indeed, in consequence of this peculiarity of my form at that time that I have come to be called by the name of Trikakud (three-humped). Those who are conversant with the science propounded by Kapila call the Supreme Soul by the name of Virincha. That Virincha is otherwise called the great Prajapati (or Brahman). Verily I am identical with Him, called Virincha, in consequence of my imparting animation to all living creatures, for I am the Creator of the universe. The preceptors of Sankhya philosophy, possessed of definite conclusions (regarding all topics), call me the eternal Kapila staying in the midst of the solar disc with but Knowledge for my companion.[2] On Earth I am known to be identical with Him who has been sung in the Vedic verses as the effulgent Hiranyagarbha and who is always worshipped by Yogins. I am regarded as the embodied form of the Rich Veda consisting of one and twenty thousand verses. Persons conversant with the Vedas also call me the embodiment of the Samans of a thousand branches. Even thus do learned Brahmans that are my devoted worshippers and that are very rare sing me in the Aranyakas.[3]

---

1 The constituent elements, called 'Dhatu,' of the body, are, of course Bile, Phlegm and Wind. They are due to actions because birth itself is due to actions. There can be no birth without a body, and no body without these three. Hence, these three have their origin in previous actions unexhausted by enjoyment or endurance.—T.

2 Narayana is said to always dwell in the midst of 'Savitri-mandala.' The solar disc represents eternal effulgence, or Milton's 'flaming mount' at which even the highest angels cannot gaze.—T.

3 Durlabha may also mean 'not easily attainable' : *i.e.*, they that are my devoted worshippers are as unattainable as I myself. People cannot readily obtain *their* grace as they cannot mine.—T.

In the Adhyaryus I am sung as the Yajur-Veda of six and fifty and eight and seven and thirty branches.[1] Learned Brahmans conversant with the Atharvans regard me as identical with the Atharvans consisting of five Kalpas and all the Krityas.[2] All the sub-divisions that exist of the different Vedas in respect of branches and all the verses that compose those branches, and all the vowels that occur in those verses, and all the rules in respect of pronunciation, know, O Dhananjaya, are my work. O Partha, he that rises (at the beginning of Creation from the Ocean of Milk at the earnest invocation of Brahmana and all the deities) and who gives diverse boons unto the diverse deities, is none else than myself. I am He who is the repository of the science of syllables and pronunciation that is treated of in the supplementary portions of the Vedas. Following the path pointed out by Vamadeva, the high-souled Rishi Panchala, through my grace, obtained from that eternal Being the rules in respect of the division of syllables and words (for reading the Vedas). Indeed, Galava, born in the Vabhravya race, having attained to high ascetic success and obtained a boon from Narayana, compiled the rules in respect of the division of syllables and words (for reading the Vedas). Indeed, Galava, born in the Vabhravya race, having attained to high ascetic success and obtained a boon from Narayana, compiled the rules in respect of the division of syllables and words, and those about emphasis and accent in utterance, and shone as the first scholar who became conversant with those two subjects. Kundrika and king Brahmadatta of great energy,[3] repeatedly thinking of the sorrow that attends birth and death, attained to that prosperity which is acquired by persons devoted to Yoga, in course of seven births, in consequence of my favour. In days of yore, O Partha, I was, for some reason, born as the son of Dharma, O chief of Kuru's race, and in consequence of such birth of mine I was celebrated under the name of Dharmaja. I took birth in two forms, *viz.*, as Nara and Narayana. Riding on the vehicle that helps towards the performance of scriptural and other duties, I practised, in those two forms, undying austerities on

1 The Yajur-Veda consists, according to this calculation, of one hundred and one branches.—T.

2 'The 'Krityas' are acts of incantation, performed with the aid of Atharvan Mantras. They are of great efficacy. Brahmanas conversant with the Atharvans are competent, with the aid of 'Krityas' to alter the laws of Nature and confound the very universe.—T.

3 'The path pointed out by Vama' is the path of Dhyana or contemplation. 'Vama is Mahadeva or Rudra.' Panchala is Galava of the Vabhravya race. The Burdwan translator makes a mess of these Verses. He represents Galava as belonging to the Kundarika race. The fact is, as the Commentator explains, that 'Kundarika' is a name derived from that of the Gotra or race' to which the person belonged. Panchala is the same person as Galava of the Vabhravya race.—T.

the breast of Gandhamadana.[1] At that time the great sacrifice of Daksha took place. Daksha, however, in that sacrifice of his, refused to give a share unto Rudra, O Bharata, of the sacrificial offerings. Urged by the sage Dadhichi, Rudra destroyed that sacrifice. He hurled a dart whose flames blazed up every moment. That dart, having consumed all the preparations of Daksha's sacrifice, came with great force towards us (Nara and Narayana) at the retreat of Vadari. With great violence that dart then fell upon the chest of Narayana. Assailed by the energy of that dart, the hair on the head of Narayana became green. In fact, in consequence of this change in the hue of my hair I came to be called by the name of Munjakesa.[2] Driven off by an exclamation of *Hun* which Narayana uttered, the dart, its energy being lost, returned to Sankara's hands. At this, Rudra became highly angry and as the result thereof he rushed towards the Rishis Nara and Narayana, endued with the puissance of severe austerities. Narayana then seized the rushing Rudra with his hand by the throat. Seized by Narayana, the lord of the universe, Rudra's throat changed colour and became dark. From that time Rudra came to be called by the name of Sitikantha. Meanwhile Nara, for the purpose of destroying Rudra, took up a blade of grass, and inspired it with Mantras. The blade of grass, thus inspired, was converted into a mighty battle-axe. Nara suddenly hurled that battle-axe at Rudra but it broke into pieces. In consequence of that weapon thus breaking into pieces, I came to be called by the name of Khandaparasu.[3]'

"Arjuna said,—In that battle capable of bringing about the destruction of the three worlds, who obtained the victory, O Janarddana, do thou tell me this !'

"The blessed and holy one said,—'When Rudra and Narayana became thus engaged in battle, all the universe became suddenly filled with anxiety. The deity of fire ceased to accept libations of even the purest clarified butter duly poured in sacrifices with the aid of Vedic Mantras. The Vedas no longer shone by inward light in the minds of the Rishis of cleansed souls. The attributes of Rajas and Tamas possessed the deities. The Earth trembled. The vault of the firmament

---

1 Elsewhere it is said that Narayana took birth in Dharma's house in four forms named Nara, Narayana, Krishna, and Hari. 'Dharmayanam samarudau' means 'riding on the Dharma-car,' i.e., endued with bodies with which to perform all the scriptural duties.—T.

2 'Munja' literally means green, or a grass of a particular kind.—T.

3 Nara and Narayana were the same person. Hence, Nara's weapon having been broken into pieces, Narayana came to be called by this name. Elsewhere it is explained that Mahadeva is called 'Khandaparasu' in consequence of his having parted with his 'parasu' (battle-axe) unto Rama of Bhrigu's race.—T.

seemed to divide in twain. All the luminaries became deprived of their splendour. The Creator, Brahman, himself fell from his seat. The Ocean itself became dry. The mountains of Himavat became riven. When such dire omens appeared everywhere, O son of Pandu, Brahma surrounded by all the deities and the high-souled Rishis, soon arrived at that spot where the battle was raging. The four-faced Brahma, capable of being understood with the aid of only the Niruktas, joined his hands and addressing Rudra, said,—Let good happen to the three worlds. Throw down thy weapons, O lord of the universe, from desire of benefiting the universe. That which is unmanifest, indestructible, immutable, supreme, the origin of the universe, uniform, and the supreme actor, that which transcends all pairs of opposites, and is inactive, has, choosing to be manifested, been pleased to assume this one blessed form, (for though double, the two but represent the same form). This Nara and Narayana (the displayed forms of Supreme Brahman) have taken birth in the race of Dharma. The foremost of all deities, these two are observers of the highest vows and endued with the severest penances. Through some reason best known to Him, I myself have sprung from the attribute of His Grace. Eternal as thou art, for thou hast ever existed since all the past creations, thou too hast sprung from His Wrath. With myself then, these deities, and all the great Rishis, do thou adore this displayed form of Brahma, and let peace be unto all the worlds without any delay.—Thus addressed by Brahma, Rudra forthwith cast off the fire of his wrath, and set himself to gratify the illstrious and puissant God Narayana.[1] Indeed, he soon placed himself at the disposal of the adorable boon-giving and puissant God Narayana. That boon-giving God Narayana, who hath his wrath and the senses under control, soon became gratified and reconciled with Rudra. Well-adored by the Rishis, by Brahma, and by all the deities, that great God, the Lord of the universe, otherwise called by the name of Hari, then addressed the illustrious Isana and said these words :—He that knows thee, knows me. He that follows thee, follows me. There is no difference between thee and me. Do thou never think otherwise. The mark made by thy lance on my chest will from this day assume the form of a beautiful whirl, and the mark of my hand on thy throat will also assume a beautiful shape in consequence of which thou shalt, from this day, be called by the name of Sreekantha.

"The blessed and holy one[2] continued.—'Having mutually caused such marks on each other's person, the two Rishis Nara and Narayana thus made friends with Rudra, and dismissing the deities, once more

1 He has been pleased to assume the forms of Rishis Nara and Narayana.—T.

2 *i.e.*, he that was speaking to Arjuna.—T.

set themselves to the practice of penances with a tranquil soul. I have thus told thee, O son of Pritha, how in that battle which took place in days of yore between Rudra and Narayana, the latter got the victory. I have also told thee the many secret names by which Narayana is called and what the significations are, O Bharata, of one of those names, which, as I have told thee, the Rishis have bestowed upon the great God. In this way, O son of Kunti, assuming diverse forms do I rove at will through the Earth, the region of Brahma himself, and that other high and eternal region of felicity called Goloka. Protected by me in the great battle, thou hast won a great victory. That Being whom, at the time of all thy battles, thou beheldest stalking in thy van, know, O son of Kunti, is no other than Rudra, that god of gods, otherwise called by the name of Kaparddin. He is otherwise known by the name of Kala,[1] and should be known as one that has sprung from my wrath. Those foes whom thou hast slain were all, in the first instance, slain by him.[2] Do thou bend thy head unto that god of gods, that lord of Uma, endued with immeasurable puissance. With concentrated soul, do thou bend thy head unto that illustrious Lord of the universe, that indestructible deity, otherwise called by the name of Hari. He is none else than that deity who, as I have repeatedly told thee, has sprung from my wrath. Thou hast, before this, heard, O Dhananjaya, of the puissance and energy that reside in him!' "

SECTION CCCXLIV

Saunaka said,—O Sauti, excellent is this narrative which thou hast recited. Verily, these ascetics, having heard it have all been filled with wonder. It is said, O Sauti, that a discourse that has Narayana for its topic, is more fruitful of merit than sojourns unto all the sacred retreats and ablutions performed in all the sacred waters on the Earth. Having listened to this discourse of thine that has Narayana for its topic, that is sacred and capable of cleansing one of every sin, all of us have certainly become holy. Adored of all the worlds, that illustrious and foremost of deities is incapable of being beheld by the deities with Brahma numbering among them and all the Rishis. That Narada was able to obtain a sight of the God Narayana, otherwise called Hari, was due, O son of Suta, to the special grace of that divine and puissant Lord.

---

1 'Kala is literally Time or Eternity.' It frequently means, however, death or destruction, or he that brings about death or destruction.—T.

2 The sense is that Arjuna was only the ostensible instrument.—T.

When, however, the celestial Rishi Narada had succeeded in obtaining a sight of the Supreme Lord of the universe, as residing in the form of Aniruddha, why did he again proceed so quickly (to the retreat of Vadari on the breast of Himavat) for beholding those two foremost of godly of Rishis, *viz.*, Nara and Narayana ? Do you, O Sauti, tell us the reason of such conduct on the part of Narada.

Sauti said,—During the continuance of his snake-sacrifice, Janamejaya, the royal son of Parikshit, availing himself of an interval in the sacrificial rites, and when all the learned Brahmanas were resting, O Saunaka, that king of kings, addressed the grand-father of his grand-father, viz., the Island-born Krishna, otherwise called Vyasa, that ocean of Vedic lore, that foremost of ascetics endued with puissance, and said these words.

Janamejaya said,—"After the celestial Rishi Narada had returned from White Island, reflecting, as he came, on the words spoken to him by the holy Narayana, what indeed, did the great ascetic next do ? Arrived at the retreat known by the name of Vadari on the breast of the Himvat mountains, and seeing the two Rishis Nara and Narayana who were engaged in severe austerities at that spot, how long did Narada dwell there and what were the topics of conversation between him and the two Rishis ? This discourse on Narayana, that is really an ocean of knowledge, has been raised by thy intelligent self by churning that vast history called Bharata which consists of a hundred thousand verses. As butter is raised from curds, sandal-wood from the mountains of Malaya, the Aranyakas from the Vedas, and nectar from all the medicinal herbs, after the same manner, O ocean of austerities, hath this discourse that is like nectar and that has Narayana for its object, been raised by thee, O Brahmana, from diverse histories and Puranas existing in the world. Narayana is the Supreme Lord. Illustrious and endued with great puissance, He is the soul of all creatures. Indeed, O foremost of regenerate ones, the energy of Narayana is irresistible. Into Narayana, at the end of the Kalpa, enter all the deities having Brahman for their foremost, all the Rishis with the Gandharvas, and all things mobile and immobile. I think, therefore, that there is nothing holier on earth or in heaven, and nothing higher, than Narayana. A sojourn unto all the sacred retreats on Earth, and ablutions performed in all the sacred waters, are not productive of as much merit as a discourse that has Narayana for its topic. Having listened from the beginning to this discourse on Hari, the lord of the universe, that destroys all sins, we feel that we have been cleansed of all our sins and sanctified entirely. Nothing wonderful was accomplished by my ancestor Dhananjaya whose was the victor in the great battle on Kurukshetra, for it should be remembered that he had Vasudeva for his ally. I think that, that person could have nothing unattainable in the three worlds, who had for his ally Vishnu himself, that great Lord of the universe. Exceedingly fortunate and commendable were those ancestors of mine, since they had Janarddana himself for looking after their temporal and spiritual prosperity. Adored of all the worlds, the holy Narayana is capable of being beheld with the aid of austerities alone. They, however, succeeded in beholding Narayana, adorned with the beautiful whirl on his chest. More fortunate than my ancestors was the celestial Rishi Narada, the son of Pramesthi. Indeed, I think that Narada, who transcends all destruction, was endued with an energy that was not little, for repairing to White-Island he had succeeded in beholding the person of Hari. Indeed, it is evident that the sight he had obtained of the Supreme Lord was due to only the grace of that Being. Fortunate was Narada inasmuch as he had succeeded in beholding Narayana as existing in the form of Aniruddha. Having beheld Narayana in that form, why did Narada hasten once more to the retreat of Vadari for the purpose of beholding Nara and Narayana? What was the reason, O ascetic, of this step taken by Narada? How long also did Narada the son of Pramesthi, after his return from White Island and arrival at Vadari and meeting with the two Rishis Nara and Narayana, live there, and what conversations had he with them? What did those two high-souled and foremost of Rishis say unto him? It behoveth thee to say all this unto me!' "

Vaisampayana said,[1]—"Salutations unto the holy Vyasa of immeasurable energy. Through his grace I shall recite this narrative having Narayana for its topic. Arrived at White Island, Narada beheld the immutable Hari. Leaving that spot he quickly proceeded, O king, to the mountains of Meru, bearing in his mind those weighty words that Paramatma (the Supreme Lord) had said unto him. Arrived at Meru he became filled with wonder at the thought, O king, of what he had achieved. And he said unto himself.—'How wonderful is it! The journey I have performed is a long one. Having proceeded to such a distance, I have come back safe and sound. From the mountains of Meru he then proceeded towards Gandhamadana. Traversing through the skies he quickly alighted upon that extensive retreat known by the name of Vadari. There he beheld those ancient deities, viz., those two foremost of Rishis, (called Nara and Narayana), engaged in the practice of penances, observing high vows, and devoted to the worship of their own selves. Both of those adorable persons bore on their chests the beautiful whirls called Sreevatsa, and both had matted locks on their

1 The questions of Janamejaya, it would seem, were addressed to Vyasa. All the editions, however, make Vaisampayana answer those questions.—T.

heads. And in consequence of the effulgence with which they illumined the world they seemed to transcend the very Sun in energy. The palms of each bore the mark called the swan's foot. The soles of their feet bore the mark of the discus. Their chests were very broad ; their arms reached down to their knees. Each of them had four 'Mushkas.'[1] Each of them had sixty teeth and four arms.[2] The voice of each was as deep as the roar of the clouds. Their faces were exceedingly handsome, their foreheads broad, their brows fair, their cheeks well-formed, and their noses aquiline. The heads of those two deities were large and round, resembling open umbrellas. Possessed of these marks, they were certainly very superior persons in appearance. Beholding them, Narada became filled with joy. He saluted them with reverence and was saluted by them in return. They received the celestial Rishi, saying 'Welcome,' and made the ordinary enquiries. Beholding those two foremost of Beings, Narada began to reflect within himself,—'These two foremost of Rishis seem to be very like, in appearance, unto those Rishis respected by all, whom I have seen in White-island.—Thinking in this way, he circumambulated them both and then sat down on the excellent seat made of Kusa grass that had been offered unto him. After this, those two Rishis that were the abode of penances, of famous achievements, and of energy,—and were endued with tranquility of heart and self-restraint, went through their morning rites. They then, with controlled hearts, worshipped Narada with water to wash his feet and the usual ingredients of the Arghya. Having finished their morning rites and the observances necessary for receiving their guest, they sat down on two seats made of wooden planks.[3] When those two Rishis took their seats, that place began to shine with peculiar beauty even as the sacrificial altar shines with beauty in consequence of the sacred fires when libations of clarified butter are poured upon them. Then Narayana, seeing Narada refreshed from fatigue and seated at his ease and well-pleased with the rites of hospitality he had received, addressed him, saying these words.

"Nara and Narayana said,—'Hast thou seen in White Island the

---

1 It is difficult to say what this word means. I think with the Commentator that it means shoulder joints.—T.

2 The Bengal reading is 'ashta-bhujau.' The Bombay reading 'ashta-daugshtrau' does not seem to be correct. By accepting the Bengal reading, the word 'mushka' becomes clear.—T.

3 'Avyagran' means 'with tranquil souls.' It is said that with most young men what occurs is that their hearts at first leave them when they see a respected guest arrived who is to be received with due honours. A little while after, they get back their hearts. In the Nara and Narayana, however, nothing of this kind happened when they saw Narada first, although Narada was one to whom their reverence was due.—T.

Paramatma (Supreme Soul), who is eternal and divine, and who is the high source whence we have sprung ?'

"Narada said.—'I have seen that beautiful Being who is immutable and who has the universe for his form. In Him dwell all the worlds, and all the deities with the Rishis. Even now I behold that immutable Being, in beholding you two. Those marks and indications that characterise Hari himself of undisplayed form, characterise you two that are endued with forms displayed before the senses.[1] Verily, I behold both of you by the side of that great God. Dismissed by the Supreme Soul, I have today come hither. In energy and fame and beauty, who else in the three worlds can equal Him than you two that have been born in the race of Dharma ? He has told me the entire course of duties having reference to Kshetrajna. He has also told me of all those incarnations which he will, in the future, have in this world. The inhabitants of White Island, whom I have seen, are all divested of the five senses that are owned by ordinary persons. All of them are of awakened souls, endued as they are with true knowledge. They are, again, entirely devoted to the foremost of Beings, *viz.*, the Supreme Lord of the universe. They are always engaged in worshipping that great Deity, and the latter always sports with them. The holy and Supreme Soul is always fond of those that are devoted to him. He is fond also of the regenerate ones. Always fond of those that are devoted to Him, He sports with those worshippers of His. Enjoyer of the universe, pervading everything, the illustrious Madhava is ever affectionate towards his worshippers. He is the Actor ; He is the Cause ; and He is the effect. He is endued with omnipotence and immeasurable splendour. He is the Cause whence all things spring. He is the embodiment of all the scriptural ordinances. He is the embodiment of all the topics. He is possessed of great fame. Uniting Himself with penances, He has illumined Himself with a splendour that is said to represent an energy that is higher than (what occurs in) White Island. Of soul cleansed by penances, He has ordained Peace and Tranquility in the three worlds. With such an auspicious understanding, he is engaged in the observance of a very superior vow which is the embodiment of holiness. That realm where he resides, engaged in the austerest penances, the Sun does not warms and the Moon does not shine. There the wind does not blow. Having constructed an altar measuring eight fingers' breadth, the illustrious Creator of the universe is practising penances there, standing on one foot, with arms upraised, and with face directed towards the East, reciting the Vedas with their branches, he is engaged in practising the severest austerities. Whatever libations of clarified butter

1 Nara and Narayana are the displayed forms of the undisplayed Hari.—T.

or meat are poured on the sacrificial fire according to the ordinances of Brahma, by the Rishis, by Pasupati himself, by the rest of the principal deities, by the Daityas, the Danavas, and the Rakshasas, all reach the feet of that great divinity. Whatever rites and religious acts are performed by persons whose souls are entirely devoted to him, are all received by that great Deity on his head. No one is dearer to him in the three worlds than those persons that are awakened and possessed of high souls. Dearer even than those persons is one that is entirely devoted to him. Dismissed by him who is the Supreme Soul, I am coming here. This is what the illustrious and holy Hari has himself said unto me. I shall henceforth reside with you two, devoted to Narayana in the form of Aniruddha.' "

SECTION CCCXLV

"Nara and Narayana said,—'Deserving art thou of the highest praise, and highly favoured hast thou been, since thou hast beheld the puissant Narayana himself (in the form of Aniruddha). None else, not even Brahma himself who was sprung from the primal lotus. has been able to behold him. That foremost of Purushas, endued with puissance and holiness, is of unmanifest origin and incapable of being seen. These words that we say unto thee are very true, O Narada. There exists no one in the universe that is dearer to him than one that adores him with devotion. It is for this, O best of regenerate ones, that he showed himself unto thee. No one can repair to that realm where the Supreme Soul is engaged in the observance of penances, except we two, O foremost of regenerate persons. In consequence of that spot being adorned by Him, its splendour resembles the effulgence of a thousand Suns collected together.[1] From that illustrious Being, O Brahmana, from Him who is the origin of the Creator of the universe, O foremost of all persons endued with forgiveness, springs the attribute of forgiveness which attaches to the Earth.[2] It is from that illustrious Being who seek the welfare of all beings, that *Rasa* (Taste) hath arisen. The attribute of Rasa attaches to the waters which are, again, liquid. It is from Him that Heat or Light having the attribute of form or vision has arisen. It attaches itself to the sun in consequence of which the Sun becomes able to shine and give heat. It is from that illustrious and foremost of Beings that Touch also has arisen. It is attached to the Wind, in consequence of which the Wind moves about in the world producing the

1 Cf. Milton's description of the mount of God. The highest angles are not competent to bear its effulgence, being obliged to cover their eyes with their wings in looking at it.—T.

2 'Prithivi' or Earth is said to be 'sarvamsaha.' 'As forgiving as the Earth' is a common form of expression in almost every Indian dialect.—T.

sensation of touch. It is from that puissant Lord of the entire universe that Sound has arisen. It attaches to Space, which, in consequence thereof, exists uncovered and unconfined. It is from that illustrious Being that Mind, which pervades all Beings, has arisen. It attaches to Chandramas, in consequence of which Chandramas comes to be invested with the attribute of displaying all the things. That spot where the divine Narayana, that partaker of the libations and other offerings made in sacrifices, resides with Knowledge alone for his companion, has in the Vedas, been called by the name of the productive cause of all things or *Sat*.[1] The path that is theirs, O foremost of regenerate persons, that are stainless and that are freed from both virtue and sin, is fraught with auspiciousness and felicity. Aditya, who is the dispeller of the darkness of all the worlds, is said to be the door (through which the Emancipate must pass). Entering Aditya, the bodies of such persons become consumed by his fire. They then become invisible for after that they cannot be seen by anybody at any time. Reduced into invisible atoms, they then enter (Narayana in manifested form and residing in the middle of the region covered by Aditya) into the form of Aniruddha. Losing all physical attributes and being altogether and transformed into Mind alone, they then enter into Pradyumna. Passing out of Pradyumna, those foremost of regenerate persons, including both those that are conversant with Sankhya philosophy and those that are devoted to the Supreme deity, then enter Sankarsana who is otherwise called Jiva. After this, divested of the three primal attributes of Sattwa, Rajas, and Tamas, those foremost of regenerate beings quickly enter the Paramatma (Supreme Soul) otherwise called Kshetrajna and which itself transcends the three primal attributes. Know that Vasudeva is He when called Kshetrajna. Verily shouldst thou know that, that Vasudeva is the abode or original refuge of all things in the universe. Only they whose minds are concentrated, who are observant of all kinds of restraint, whose senses are controlled, and who are devoted to One, succeed in entering Vasudeva. We two, O foremost of regenerate ones, have taken birth in the house of Dharma. Residing in this delightful and spacious retreat we are undergoing the austerest penances. We are thus engaged, O regenerate one, being moved by the desire of benefiting those manifestations of the Supreme Deity, dear to all the celestials, that will occur in the three worlds (for achieving diverse feats that are incapable of being achieved by any other Being).

1 By 'Sat' is meant all existent things The correlative word is 'Asat' or non-existent. Hence, aught and nought are the nearest approaches to these words. There are many secondary significations, however of these two words. 'Sat,' for example, indicates effects or all gross objects; and 'asat' indicates causes, &c.—T.

In accordance with such ordinances as are uncommon and as apply to us two only, O best of regenerate persons, we are duly observing all excellent and high vows fraught with the austerest penances. Thou, O celestial Rishi, endued with wealth of penances wert beheld by us in White Island when thou wert there. Having met with Narayana, thou hast made a particular resolution, which is known to us. In the three worlds consisting of mobile and immobile Beings, there is nothing that is unknown to us. Of good or evil that will occur or has occurred or is occuring, that God of gods, O great ascetic, has informed thee !' "

Vaisampayana continued,—"Having heard these words of Nara and Narayana both of whom were engaged in the practice of the austerest penances, the celestial Rishi Narada joined his hands in reverence and became entirely devoted to Narayana. He employed his time in mentally reciting, with due observances, innumerable sacred Mantras that are approved by Narayana. Worshipping the Supreme Deity Narayana, and adoring those two ancient Rishis also that had taken birth in the house of Dharma, the illustrious Rishi Narada, endued with great energy, continued to reside, thus employed, in that retreat, called Vadari, on the breast of Himavat, belonging to Nara and Narayana, for a thousand years as measured by the standard of the celestials.' "

SECTION CCCXLVI

Vaisampayana said,—"On one occasion, while residing in the retreat of Nara and Narayana, Narada the son of Pramesthi, having duly accomplished the rites and observances in honour of the deities, set himself to perform thereafter the rites in honour of the Pitris. Beholding him thus prepared, the eldest son of Dharma, *viz.*, the puissant Nara, addressed him, saying,—'Whom art thou worshipping, O foremost of regenerate persons, by these rites and observances in connection with the deities and the Pitris ? O foremost of all persons endued with intelligence, tell me this, agreeably to the scriptures. What is this that thou art doing ? What also are the fruits desired by thee of those rites thou hast addrest thyself in performing ?'

"Narada said,—"Thou saidst unto me on a former occasion that rites and observances in honour of the deities should be accomplished. Thou saidst that the rites in honour of the deities constitute the highest sacrifice and are equivalent to the worship of the eternal Supreme Soul. Instructed by that teaching, I always sacrifice in honour of the eternal and immutable Vishnu, through these rites that I perform in worshipping the deities. It is from that Supreme Deity that Brahma, the Grandsire of all the worlds, took his rise in days of yore. That Brahma, otherwise called Prameshthi, filled with cheerfulness, caused my sire (Daksha) to start into being. I was the son of Brahma, created before all others, by a fiat of his will (although I had to take birth afterwards as the son of Daksha through a curse of that Rishi). O righteous and illustrious one, I am performing these rites in honour of the Pitris for the sake of Narayana, and agreeable to those ordinances that have been laid down by himself. The illustrious Narayana is the father, mother, and grandfather (of all creatures). In all sacrifices performed in honour of the Pitris, it is that Lord of the universe who is adored and worshipped. On one occasion, the deities, who were sires, taught their children the Srutis. Having lost their knowledge of the Srutis, the sires had to acquire it again from those sons unto whom they had communicated it. In consequence of this incident, the sons, who had thus to communicate the Mantras unto their sires, acquired the status of sires (and the sire, for having obtained the Mantras from their sons, acquired the status of sons).[1] Without doubt, what the deities did on that occasion is well known to you two. Sons and sires (on that occasion) had thus to worship each other. Having first spread some blades of Kusa grass, the deities and the Pitris (who were their children) placed three *Pindas* thereon and in this way worshipped each other. I wish to know, however, the reason why the Pitris in days of yore acquired the name of *Pindas*.'

"Nara and Narayana said.—'The Earth, in days of yore, with her belt of seas, disappeared from the view. Govinda, assuming the form of a gigantic boar, raised her up (with his mighty tusk). Having replaced the Earth in her former position, that foremost of Purushas, his body smeared with water and mud, set himself to do what was necessary for the world and its denizens. When the Sun reached the meridian, and the hour, therefore, came for saying the morning prayers, the puissant Lord, suddenly shaking off three balls of mud from his tusk, placed them upon the Earth, O Narada, having previously spread thereon certain blades of grass. The puissant Vishnu dedicated those balls of mud unto his own self, according to the rites laid down in the eternal ordinance. Regarding the three balls of mud that the puissant Lord had shaken off from his tusks as Pindas, he then, with sesame seeds of oily kernel that arose from the heat of his own body, himself performed the rite of dedication, sitting with face turned towards the East. That foremost

---

1 The story is that once on a time the deities, on the eve of going out on a campaign against the Asuras, communicated the Vedas unto their children, Agnishatta and others. In consequence, however, of the length of time for which they were occupied on the field, they forgot their Vedas. Returning to heaven, they had actually to re-acquire them from their own children and disciples. The Scriptures declare that the preceptor is ever the sire, and the disciple is the son. Difference of age would not disturb the relationship. A youth of sixteen might thus be the father of an octogenarian. With Brahmanas, reverence is due to knowledge, not age.—T.

of deities then, impelled by the desire of establishing rules of conduct for the denizens of the three worlds, said these words :—

"Vrishakapi said,—I am the Creator of the worlds. I am resolved to create those that are to be called Pitris.—Saying these words, he began to think of those high ordinances that should regulate the rites to be gone through in honour of the Pitris. While thus engaged, he saw that the three balls of mud, shaken off his tusk, had fallen towards the South. He then said unto himself,—These balls, shaken off my tusk, have fallen on the Earth towards the southern direction of her surface. Led by this, I declare that these should be known henceforth by the name of Pitris. Let these three that are of no particular shape, and that are only round, come to be regarded as Pitris in the world. Even thus do I create the eternal Pitris. I am the father, the grand father, and the great grand-father, and I should be regarded as residing in these three Pindas. There is no one that is superior to me. Who is there whom I myself may worship or adore with rites ? Who, again, is my sire in the universe ? I myself am my grand-father. I am, indeed, the Grandsire and the Sire. I am the one cause (of all the universe).— Having said these words, that God of gods, Vrishakapi by name, offered those Pindas, O learned Brahmana, on the breast of the Varaha mountains, with elaborate rites. By those rites He worshipped His own self, and having finished the worship, disappeared there and then. Hence have the Pitris come to be called by the name of Pinda. Even this is the foundation of the designation. Agreeably to the words uttered by Vrishakapi on that occasion, the Pitris receive the worship offered by all. They who perform sacrifices in honour of and adore the Pitris, the deities, the preceptor or other reverend senior guests arrived at the house, kine, superior Brahmanas, the goddess Earth, and their mothers, in thought, word, and deed, are said to adore and sacrifice unto Vishnu himself. Pervading the bodies of all existent creatures, the illustrious Lord is the Soul of all things. Unmoved by happiness or misery, His attitude towards all is equal. Endued with greatness, and of great soul, Narayana has been said to be the soul of all things in the universe.' "

SECTION CCCXLVII

Vaisampayana said,—'Having heard these words of Nara and Narayana, the Rishi Narada became filled with devotion towards the Supreme Being. Indeed, with his whole soul he devoted himself to Narayana. Having resided for a full thousand years in the retreat of Nara and Narayana, having beheld the immutable Hari, and heard the exeellent discourse having Narayana for its topic, the celestial Rishi repaired to his own retreat on the breast of Himavat. Those foremost of ascetics viz., Nara and Narayana, however, continued to reside in their delightful retreat of Vadari, engaged in the practice of the severest austerities. Thou art born in the race of the Pandavas. Thou art of immeasurable energy. O perpetuator of the race of the Pandavas, having listened to this discourse on Narayana from the beginning, thou hast certainly been cleansed of all thy sins and thy soul has been sanctified. His is neither this world nor the world hereafter, O best of kings, who hates instead of loving and reverencing the immurable Hari. The ancestors of that person who hates Narayana, who is the foremost of deities, and is otherwise called Hari, sink into hell for eternity. O riger among men, Vishnu is the soul of all beings. How, then, can Vishnu be hated, for in hating him one would hate one's own self. He who is our preceptor, viz., the Rishi Vyasa, the son of Gandhavati, has himself recited this discourse unto us on the glory of Narayana, that glory which is the highest and which is immutable. I heard it from him and have recited it to thee exactly as I heard it, O sinless one. This cult, with its mysteries and its abstract of details, was obtained by Narada, O king, from that Lord of the universe, viz., Narayana himself. Even such are the particulars of this great cult. I have, before this, O foremost of kings, explained it to thee in the Hari-Gita, with a brief reference to its ordinances.[1] Know that the Island-born Krishna, otherwise called Vyasa, is Narayana on Earth. Who else than he, O tiger among kings, could compile such a treatise as the Mahabharata? Who else than that puissant Rishi could discourse upon the diverse kinds of duties and cults for the observance and adoption of men? Thou hast resolved upon performing a great sacrifice. Let that sacrifice of thine proceed as determined by thee. Having listened to the diverse kinds of duties and cults, let thy Horse-sacrifice go on."

Sauti continued,—That best of kings, having heard this great discourse, began all those rites that are laid down in the ordinance, for the completion of his great sacrifice. Questioned by thee, O Saunaka, I have duly recited to thee and all these Rishis that are denizens of the Naimisha forest, that great discourse having Narayana for its topic. Formerly Narada had recited it to my preceptor in the hearing of many Rishis and the sons of Pandu and in the presence of Krishna and Bhishma also.[2] The Supreme deity Narayana is the Lord of all the foremost of Rishis, and of the three worlds. He is the upholder of Earth herself of vast proportions. He is the receptacle of the Srutis and of

---

1 The 'Hari-Gita' is the 'Bhagavad-Gita.' It is sometimes called also 'Narayana-Gita.'—T.

2 It is not clear who is the 'Guru' referred to in this Verse. The Commentator thinks that it is Vribaspati, the preceptor of the celestials. The celestial preceptor never came to the Pandavas. It is probable that either Vyasa or Vaisampayana is meant.—T.

the attribute of humility. He is the great receptacle of all those ordinances that should be practised for attaining to tranquility of heart, as also of all those that go by the name of Yama. He is always accompanied by the foremost of regenerate persons. Let that great deity be thy refuge. Hari ever does what is agreeable and beneficial to the denizens of heaven. He is always the slayer of such Asuras (as become troublesome to the three worlds). He is the receptacle of penances. He is possessed of great fame. He is the slayer of the Daityas known by the name of Madhu and Kaitabha. He is the ordainer of the ends that are attained to by persons acquainted with and observant of scriptural and other duties. He dispels the fears of all persons. He takes the foremost of those offerings that are dedicated in sacrifices. He is thy refuge and protection. He is endued with attributes. He is freed from attributes. He is endued with a quadruple form. He shares the merits arising from the dedication of tanks and the observance of similar religious rites. Unvanquished and possessed of great might, it is He that always ordains the end approachable by the Soul alone, of Rishis of righteous deeds. He is the witness of the worlds. He is unborn. He is the one ancient Purusha. Endued with the complexion of the Sun, He is the Supreme Lord, and he is the refuge of all. Do all of you bow your heads unto Him since He who sprang from the waters (*viz.*, Narayana himself) bends his head unto Him.[1] He is the origin of the universe. He is that Being who is called Amrita. He is minute. He is the refuge upon whom all things depend. He is the one Being to whom the attribute of immutability attaches. The Sankhyas and Yogins, of restrained souls, hold Him who is eternal in their understandings.

SECTION CCCXLVIII

Janamejaya said,—'I have heard from thee the glory of the divine and Supreme Soul. I have heard also of the birth of the Supreme Deity in the house of Dharma, in the form of Nara and Narayana. I have also heard from thee the origin of the Pinda from the mighty Baraha (Boar) (which form the supreme Deity had assumed for raising by the submerged Earth). I have heard from thee about those deities and Rishis that were ordained for the religion of Pravritti and of those that were ordained for the religion of Nivritti. Thou hast also, O regenerate one, discoursed to us on other topics. Thou hast said also unto us of that vast form, with the Equine head, of Vishnu, that partaker of the libations and other offerings made in sacrifices,—the form, viz., that

1 In these Verses, it is to Vasudeva that the speaker is referring. 'The witness of the worlds' means that he has witnessed innumerable Creation and Destructions and will witness them through eternity.—T.

appeared in the great ocean on the North-East. That form was beheld by the illustrious Brahman, otherwise known by the name of Parameshthi. What, however, were the exact features, and what the energy, the like of which among all great objects, had never appeared before, of that form which Hari, the upholder of the universe, displayed on that occasion? What did Brahman do, O ascetic, after having seen that foremost of deities, him whose likeness had never been seen before, him who was of immeasurable energy, him who had the Equine head, and him who was Sacredness itself? O regenerate one, this doubt hath arisen in our mind about this ancient subject of knowledge. O thou of foremost intelligence, for what reason did the supreme Deity assume that form and display himself in it unto Brahman? Thou hast certainly sanctified us by discoursing unto us on these diverse sacred subjects![1]

Sauti said,—I shall recite to thee that ancient history, which is perfectly consistent with the Vedas, and which the illustrious Vaisampayana recited unto the son of Parikshit on the occasion of the great Snake-sacrifice. Having heard the account of the mighty form of Vishnu, equipt with the horse-head, the royal son of Parikshit too had entertained the same doubt and put the same questions to Vaisampayana.

Janamejaya said,—"Tell me, O best of men, for what reason did Hari appear in that mighty form equipt with a horse-head and which Brahma, the Creator, beheld on the shores of the great northern Ocean on the occasion referred to by yourself?

Vaisampayana said,—"All existent objects, O king, in this world, are the result of a combination of the five primal elements, a combination due to the intelligence of the Supreme Lord. The puissant Narayana, endued with infinity, is the Supreme Lord and Creator of the universe. He is the inner Soul of all things, and the giver of boons. Divested of attributes, he is again possessed of them. Listen now, O best of kings, to me as I narrate to thee how the Destruction is brought about of all things. At first, the element of Earth becomes merged in Water and nothing then is seen save one vast expanse of Water on all sides. Water then merges into Heat, and Heat into Wind. Wind then merges into Space, which in its turn, merges into Mind. Mind merges into the Manifest (otherwise called Consciousness or Ego). The Mani-

---

1 This speech is really that of Saunaka. Some incorrect texts represent it as the speech of Janamejaya. The following speech is that of Sauti, though the texts alluded to above make it that of Vaisampayana. It is true in this speech the vocative 'Brahman' occurs, but we may easily take it as a slip of the pen. K P. Singha makes the correction. The Burdwan translator, without perceiving the absurdity, adheres to the incorrect text.—T.

fest merges into the Unmanifest (or Prakriti). The Unmanifest (or Prakriti) merges into Purusha (Jivatman) and Purusha merges into the Supreme Soul (or Brahman). Then Darkness spreads over the face of the universe, and nothing can be perceived. From that primal Darkness arises Brahma (endued with the principle of Creation). Darkness is primeval and fraught with immortality. Brahma that arises from primeval Darkness develops (by its own potency) into the idea of the universe, and assumes the form of Purusha. Such Purusha is called Aniruddha. Divested of sex, it is called otherwise by the name of *Pradhana* (Supreme or Primary). That is also known by the name of Manifest, or the combination of the triple attribute, O best of kings. He exists with Knowledge alone for his companion. That illustrious and puissant Being is otherwise called by the name of Viswaksena or Hari. Yielding to Yoga-sleep, he lays himself down on the waters. He then thinks of the Creation of the Universe of diversified phenomena and fraught with immeasurable attributes. While engaged in thinking of Creation, he recollects his own high attributes. From this springs the four-faced Brahma representing the Consciousness of Aniruddha. The illustrious Brahma, otherwise called Hiranyagarbha, is the Grandsire of all the worlds. Endued with eyes like lotus petals, he takes birth within the Lotus that springs from (the navel of) Aniruddha. Seated on that Lotus, the illustrious, puissant, and eternal Brahma of wonderful aspect saw that the waters were on all sides. Adopting the attribute of Sattwa, Brahma, otherwise called Parameshthi, then commenced to create the universe. In the primeval Lotus that was endued with the effulgence of the Sun, two drops of water had been cast by Narayana that were fraught with great merit. The illustrious Narayana, without beginning and without end, and transcending destruction, cast his eyes on those two drops of water. One of those two drops of water, of very beautiful and bright form, looked like a drop of honey. From that drop sprang, at the command of Narayana, a Daitya of the name of Madhu made up of the attribute of Tamas (Dullness). The other drop of water within the Lotus was very hard. From it sprang the Daitya Kaitabha made up of the attribute of Rajas. Endued thus with the attributes of Tamas and Rajas, the two Daityas possessed of might and armed with maces, immediately after their birth, began to rove within that vast primeval Lotus. They beheld within it Brahma of immeasurable effulgence, engaged in creating the four Vedas, each endued with the most delightful form. Those two foremost of Asuras, possessed of bodies, beholding the four Vedas, suddenly seized them in the very sight of their Creator. The two mighty Danavas, having seized the eternal Vedas, quickly dived into the ocean of waters which they saw and proceeded to its bottom. Seeing the Vedas forcibly taken away from him, Brahma became filled with grief. Robbed of the Vedas in this way, Brahma then addressed the Supreme Lord in these words.

"Brahma said,—'The Vedas are my great eyes. The Vedas are my great strength. The Vedas are my great refuge. The Vedas are my high Brahman. All the Vedas, however, have been forcibly taken away from me by the two Danavas. Deprived of the Vedas, the worlds I have created have become enveloped in darkness. Without the Vedas (beside me), how shall I succeed in causing my excellent Creation to start into existence? Alas, great is the grief I suffer in consequence of the loss of the Vedas (through such agency). My heart is very much pained. It has become the abode of a great sorrow. Who is there that will rescue me from this ocean of grief in which I am sunk for the loss I have endured? Who is there that will bring me the Vedas I have lost? Who is there that will take compassion on me?—While Brahma was uttering these words, O best of kings, the resolution suddenly arose in his mind, O foremost of intelligent persons, for hymning the praises of Hari in these words. The puissant Brahma then, with hands joined in reverence, and seizing the feet of his progenitor, sang this highest of hymns in honour of Narayana.

"Brahma said,—'I bow to thee, O heart of Brahman. I bow to thee that hast been born before me. Thou art the origin of the universe. Thou art the foremost of all abodes. Thou, O puissant one, art the ocean of Yoga with all its branches. Thou art the Creator of both what is Manifest and what is Unmanifest. Thou treadest along the path whose auspiciousness is of inconceivable extent. Thou art the consumer of the universe. Thou art the Antaralock (Inner Soul) of all creatures. Thou art without any origin. Thou art the refuge of the universe. Thou art self-born, for origin thou hast none that is not thyself. As regards myself, I have sprung through thy Grace. From thee have I derived my birth. My first birth from thee, which is regarded sacred by all regenerate persons, was due to a fiat of thy Mind. My second birth in days of yore was from thy eyes. Through thy Grace, my third birth was from thy speech. My fourth birth, O puissant Lord, was from thy ears. My fifth birth, excellent in all respects, was from thy nose. O Lord, My sixth birth was, through thee, from an egg. This is my seventh birth. It has occurred, O Lord, within this Lotus, and it is meant to stimulate the intellect and desires of all the beings. At each Creation I take birth from thee as thy son, O thou that art divested of the three attributes. Indeed, O lotus-eyed one, I take birth as thy eldest son, made up of Sattwa the foremost of three attributes. Thou art endued with that nature which is Supreme. Thou springest from thyself. I have been created by thee. The Vedas are my eyes. Hence, I transcend Time itself. Those Vedas, which constitute my eyes, have been taken away from me. I have, therefore, become blind. Do Thou awake from this Yoga-sleep. Give me back my eyes. I am dear to thee and thou art dear to me. Thus praised by Brahma, the illustrious Purusha, with face turned towards every side, then shook off his slumber, resolved to recover the Vedas (from the Daityas that had forcibly snatched them away). Applying his Yoga-puissance, he assumed a second form. His body, equipt with an excellent nose, became as bright as the Moon. He assumed an equine head of great effulgence, which was the abode of the Vedas. The firmament, with all its luminaries and constellations, became the crown of his head. His locks of hair were long and flowing, and had the splendour of the rays of the Sun. The regions above and below became his two ears. The Earth became his forehead. The two rivers Ganga and Saraswati became his two hips. The two oceans became his two eyebrows. The Sun and the Moon became his two eyes. The twilight became his nose. The syllable Om became his memory and intelligence. The lightning became his tongue. The Soma-drinking Pitris became, it is said, his teeth. The two regions of felicity, *viz.*, Goloka and Brahmaloka, became his upper and lower lips. The terrible night that succeeds universal destruction, and that transcends the three attributes, became his neck. Having assumed this form endued with the equine head and having diverse things for its diverse limbs, the Lord of the universe disappeared then and there, and proceeded to the nether regions. Having reached those regions, he set himself to high Yoga. Adopting a voice regulated by the rules of the science called Siksha, he began to utter loudly Vedic Mantras. His pronounciation was distinct and reverberated through the air, and was sweet in every respect. The sound of his voice filled the nether region from end to end. Endued with the properties of all the elements, it was productive of great benefits. The two Asuras, making an appointment with the Vedas in respect of the time when they would come back to take them up again, threw them down in the nether region, and ran towards the spot whence those sounds appeared to come. Meanwhile, O king, the Supreme Lord with the equine head, otherwise called Hari, who was himself in the nether region, took up all the Vedas. Returning to where Brahma was staying, he gave the Vedas unto him. Having restored the Vedas unto Brahma, the Supreme Lord once more returned to his own nature. The Supreme Lord also established his form with the equine head in the North-Eastern region of the great ocean. Having (in this way) established him who was the abode of the Vedas, he once more became the equine-headed form that he was.[1] The

1 It is difficult to settle the reading of this Verse. The Bengal texts have 'alayah', the Bombay edition has 'alayam'. At any rate, Verse 58 seems to contradict the previous Verse. If after restoring the Vedas to

two Danavas Madhu and Kaitabha, not finding the person from whom those sounds proceeded, quickly came back to that spot. They cast their eyes arround but beheld that the spot on which they had thrown the Vedas was empty. Those two foremost of mighty Beings, adopting great speed of motion, rose from the nether region. Returning to where the primeval Lotus was that had given them birth, they saw the puissant Being, the original Creator, staying in the form of Aniruddha of fair complexion and endued with a splendour resembling that of the Moon. Of immeasurable prowess, he was under the influence of Yoga-sleep, his body stretched on the waters and occupying a space as vast as itself. Possessed of great effulgence and endued with the attribute of stainless Sattwa, the body of the Supreme Lord lay on the excellent hood of a snake that seemed to emit flames of fire for the resplendence attaching to it. Beholding the Lord thus lying, the two foremost of Danavas roared out a loud laugh. Endued with the attributes of Rajas and Tamas, they said,—'This is that Being of white complexion. He is now lying asleep. Without doubt, this one has brought the Vedas away from the nether region. Whose is he? Whose is he? Who is he? Why is he thus asleep on the hood of a snake?'—Uttering these words, the two Danavas awakened Hari from his Yoga-slumber. The foremost of Beings, (*viz.*, Narayana), thus awakened, understood that the two Danavas intended to have an encounter with him in battle. Beholding the two foremost of Asuras prepared to do battle with him, he also set his mind to gratify that desire of theirs. Thereupon an encounter took place between those two on one side and Narayana on the other. The Asuras Madhu and Kaitabha were embodiments of the attributes of Rajas and Tamas. Narayana slew them both for gratifying Brahma. He thence came to be called by the name of Madhusudana (slayer of Madhu). Having compassed the destruction of the two Asuras and restored the Vedas to Brahma, the Supreme Being dispelled the grief of Brahma. Aided then by Hari and assisted by the Vedas, Brahma created all the worlds with their mobile and immobile creatures. After this, Hari, granting unto the Grandsire intelligence of the foremost order relating to the Creation, disappeared there and then for going to the place he had come from. It was thus that Narayana, having assumed the form equipt with the horse-head, slew the two Danavas Madhu and Kaitabha (and disappeared from the sight of Brahma). Once more, however, he assumed the same form for the sake of causing the religion of Pravritti to flow in the universe.

"Thus did the blessed Hari assume in days of old that grand form

---

Brahma, Narayana returned to his own nature, where would his form be that had the horse-head?—T.

having the equine head. This, of all his forms, endued with puissance, is celebrated as the most ancient. That person who frequently listens or mentally recites this history of the assumption by Narayana of the form equipt with the equine head, will never forget his Vedic or other lore. Having adored with the austerest penances the illustrious deity with the equine head, the Rishi Panchala (otherwise known as Galava) acquired the science of *Krama* by proceeding along the path pointed out by the deity (Rudra).[1] I have thus recited to thee, O king the old story of Hayasiras, consistent with the Vedas about which thou hadst asked me. Whatever forms, the Supreme Deity desires to assume with a view to ordaining the various affairs of the universe, he assumes those forms immediately within himself by exercise of his own inherent powers. The Supreme Deity, endued with every prosperity, is the receptacle of the Vedas. He is the receptacle of Penances also. The puissant Hari is Yoga. He is the embodiment of the Sankhya philosophy. He is that Para Brahman of which we hear. Truth has Narayana for its refuge. Rita has Narayana for its soul. The religion of Nivritti, in which there is no return, has Narayana for its high abode. The other religion which has Pravritti for its basis, has equally Narayana for its soul. The foremost of all the attributes that belong to the element of Earth is scent. Scent has Narayana for its soul. The attributes of Water, O king, are called the Tastes (of the various kinds). These Tastes have Narayana for their soul. The foremost attribute of Light is form. Form also has Narayana for its soul. Touch, which is the attribute of Wind, is also said to have Narayana for its soul. Sound, which is an attribute of space, has like the others, Narayana for its soul. Mind also, which is the attribute of the unmanifest (Prakriti), has Narayana for its soul. Time which is computed by the motion of the celestial luminaries has similarly Narayana for its soul. The presiding deities of Fame, of Beauty, and of Prosperity have the same Supreme Deity for their soul. Both the Sankhya philosophy and Yoga have Narayana for their soul. The Supreme Being is the cause of all this, as Purusha. He is, again the cause of everything, as Pradhana (or Prakriti). He is Swabhaba (the basis on which all things rest). He is the doer or agent, and is the cause of that variety that is witnessed in the universe. He is the diverse kinds of energy that act in the universe. In these five ways he is that all-controlling invisible influence of which people speak. Those

---

1 Both the Vernacular translators give ridiculous Versions of this Verse. K. P. Singha takes Panchala to be a king and understands the Verse to mean that king Panchala got back his kingdom through the grace of Narayana. The Burdwan translator errors as usual, by taking *krama* to imply 'gati' or end. The fact is this Verse repeats what has been already said in Verses 100 to 102 of Section 343 *ante*. *Krama* means the science by whose aid the words used in the Vedas are separated from each other. —T.

employed in investigating the several topics of enquiry with the aid of such reasons as are of wide application, regard Hari to be indentical with the five reasons adverted to above and as the final refuge of all things. Indeed, the puissant Narayana, endued with the highest Yoga puissance, is the one topic (of enquiry). The thoughts of the denizen of all the worlds including Brahma and the high-souled Rishis, of those that are Sankhyas and Yogins, of those that are Yatis, and of those, generally, that are conversant with the Soul are fully known to Kesava, but none of these can know what his thoughts are. Whatever acts are performed in honour of the gods or the Pitris, whatever gifts are made, whatever penances are performed, have Vishnu for their refuge.—who is established upon his own supreme ordinances. He is named Vasudeva because of his being the abode of all creatures. He is immutable. He is Supreme. He is the foremost of Rishis. He is endued with the highest puissance. He is said to transcend the three attributes. As Time (which runs smoothly without any sign) assumes indications when it manifests itself in the form of successive seasons, even so He, though really divested of attributes (for manifesting Himself). Even they that are high-souled do not succeed in understanding his motions. Only those foremost of Rishis that have knowledge for their Souls, succeed in beholding in their hearts that Purusha who transcends all attributes."

SECTION CCCXLIX

Janamejaya said,—"The illustrious Hari becomes gracious unto them that are devoted to him with their whole souls. He accepts also all worship that is offered to Him agreeably to the ordinance. Of those persons that have burnt off their fuel,[1] and that are divested of both merit and demerit, that have attained the Knowledge as handed down from preceptor to preceptor—such persons always attain to that end which is called the fourth, viz., the essence of the Purushottama or Vasudeva,[2]—through the three others. Those persons, however, that are devoted to Narayana with their whole souls at once attain to the highest end.[3] Without doubt, the religion of devotion seems to be

1 'Those who have burnt of their fuel' means men that have freed themselves from desire. 'Param-paryyagati' means Knowledge as handed down from preceptor to preceptor.—T.

2 Vasudeva is called the Fourth because below Him is Sankarshana, Pradyumna, and Aniruddha.—T.

3 What is stated in these two Verses is the difference between the ends of those that rely on Knowledge, and those that are devoted to Narayana with their whole souls. The former attain to Vasudeva, it is true, but then they have to pass gradually through the three others one after another, viz., Aniruddha, Pradyumna, and Sankarshana. The latter, however, at once attain to Vasudeva. It is curious to note how the Burdwan translator, with the Commentary before him and from which he quotes, misunderstands the second Verse completely. K.P. Singha's Version also is not clear though not incorrect.—T.

superior (to that of Knowledge) and is very dear to Narayana. These, without going through the three successive stages (of Aniruddha, Pradyumna, and Sankarshana), at once attain to the immutable Hari. The end that is attained by Brahmanas, who, attending to due observances, study the Vedas with the Upanishads according to the rules laid down for regulating such study, and by those that adopt the religion of Yatis, is inferior, I think, to that attained by persons devoted to Hari with their whole souls. Who first promulgated this religion of Devotion? Was it some deity or some Rishi that declared it? What are the practices of those that are said to be devoted with their whole souls? When did those practices begin? I have doubts on these topics. Do thou remove those doubts. Great is my curiosity to hear thee explain the several points![1]

Vaisampayana said,—"When the diverse divisions of the Pandava and the Kuru armies were drawn up in array for the battle and when Arjuna became cheerless, the holy one himself explained the question of what is the end and what is not the end attained by persons of different characters. I have before this recited to thee the words of the holy one. The religion preached by the holy one on that occasion is difficult of comprehension. Men of uncleansed souls cannot apprehend it at all. Having created this religion in days of yore, viz., in the Krita age, in perfect consolance with the Samans, it is borne, O king, by the Supreme Lord, *viz.*, Narayana, himself. This very topic was raised by the highly blessed Partha to Narada (for the latters discourse) in the midst of the Rishis and in the presence of Krishna and Bhishma. My preceptor, *viz.*, the Island-born Krishna heard what Narada said. Receiving it from the celestial Rishis, O best of kings, my preceptor imparted it to me in exactly the same way in which he had obtained it from the celestial Rishi. I shall now recite it to thee, O monarch, in the same way as it has been received from Narada. Listen, therefore, to me. In that Kalpa when Brahma the Creator, O king, took his birth in the mind of Narayana and issued from the latter's mouth, Narayana himself performed, O Bharata, his Daiva and Paitra rites in accordance with this religion. Those Rishis that subsist upon the froth of water then obtained it from Narayana. From the froth-eating Rishis, this religion was obtained by those Rishis that go by the name of Vaikanasas. From the Vaikanasas, Shoma got it. Afterwards, it disappeared from the universe. After the second birth of Brahma, viz., when he sprang from

1 The word 'Ekantin' is explained by the Commentator to mean a 'nishkama worshipper, *i.e.*, one who adores the Supreme Deity without the expectation of any fruit whatever. There can be no error, however in rendering it as one devoted with his whole soul.' Such devotion verily implies 'nishkama' worship.—T.

the eyes of Narayana, O king, the Grandsire (that is Brahma) then received this religion from Shoma. Having received it thus, Brahma imparted this religion, which has Narayana for its soul, unto Rudra. In the Krita age of that ancient Kalpa, Rudra, devoted to Yoga, O monarch, communicated it to all those Rishis that are known by the name of Valikhilyas. Through the illusion of Narayana, it once more disappeared from the universe. In the third birth of Brahma, which was due to the speech of Narayana, this religion once more sprang up, O king, from Narayana himself. Then a Rishi of the name of Suparna obtained it from that foremost of Beings. The Rishi Suparna used to recite this excellent religion, this foremost of cults, three times during the day In consequence of this, it came to be called by the name of Trisauparna in the world. This religion has been referred to in the Rigveda. The duties it inculcates are exceedingly difficult of observance. From the Rishi Suparna, this eternal religion was obtained, O foremost of men, by the God of wind, that sustainer of the lives of all creatures in the universe. The God of wind communicated it unto such Rishis as subsist upon what remains of sacrificial offerings after feeding guests and othres. From those Rishis this excellent religion was obtained by the Great Ocean. It once more disappeared from the universe and became merged into Narayana. In the next birth of the high-souled Brahman when he sprang from the ear of Narayana, listen, O chief of men, to what happened in that Kalpa. The illustrious Narayana, otherwise called Hari, when he resolved upon Creation, thought of a Being who would be puissant enough to create the universe. While thinking of this, a Being sprang from his ears competent to create the universe. The Lord of all called him by the name of Brahma. Addressing Brahma, the Supreme Narayana said unto him,—Do thou, O son, create all kinds of creatures from thy mouth and feet. O thou of excellent vows, I shall do what will be beneficial for thee, for I shall impart to thee both energy and strength sufficient to render thee competent for this task. Do thou receive also from me this excellent religion known by the name of Sattwata. Aided by that religion do thou create the Krita age and ordain it duly. Thus addressed, Brahma bowed his head unto the illustrious Hari, the god of the gods and received from him that foremost of all cults with all its mysteries and its abstract of details, together with the Aranyakas,—*viz.*, that cult, which sprang from the mouth of Narayana. Narayana then instructed Brahma of immeasurable energy in that cult, and addressing him, said,—Thou art the creator of the duties that are to be observed in the respective Yugas. Having said this unto Brahma, Narayana disappeared and proceeded to that spot which is beyond the reach of Tamas, where the Unmanifest resides, and which is known by the men of acts without desire of fruits. After this, the boon-giving Brahma, the Grandsire of the worlds, created the different worlds with their mobile and immobile creatures. The age that first commenced was highly auspicious and came to be called by the name of Krita. In that age, the religion of Sattwa existed, pervading the entire universe.[1] With the aid of that primeval religion of righteousness, Brahma, the Creator of all the worlds, worshipped the Lord of all the deities, *viz.*, the puissant Narayana, otherwise called Hari. Then for the spread of that religion and desirous of benefiting the worlds, Brahman instructed that Manu who is known by the name of Swarochish in that cult. Swarochish-Manu, that Lord of all the worlds, that foremost of all persons endued with puissance, then cheerfully imparted the knowledge of that cult to his own son, O king, who was known by the name of Sankhapada. The son of Manu, viz., Sankhapada, communicated the knowledge of that to his own son Suvarnabha who was the Regent of the cardinal and subsidiary points of the compass. When, upon the expiration of the Krita Yuga, the Treta came, that cult once more disappeared from the world. In a subsequent birth of Brahman, O best of kings, viz., that which was derived from the nose of Narayana, O Bharata, the illustrious and puissant Narayana or Hari with eyes like lotus petals, himself sang this religion in the presence of Brahma. Then the son of Brahma, created by a fiat of his will, viz., Sanatkumara, studied this cult. From Sanatkumara, the Prajapati Virana, in the beginning of the Krita age, O tiger among Kurus, obtained this cult. Virana having studied it in this way, taught it to the ascetic Raivya. Raivya, in his turn, imparted it to his son of pure soul, good vows, and great intelligence, viz., Kukshi, that righteous Regent of the cardinal and subsidiary points of the compass. After this, that cult, born of the mouth of Narayana, once more disappeared from the world. In the next birth of Brahma, viz., that which he was derived from an egg which sprang from Hari, this cult once more issued from the mouth of Narayana. It was received by Brahma, O king, and practised duly in all its details by him. Brahma then communicated it, O monarch, to those Rishis that are known by the name of Varhishada. From the Varhishadas it was obtained by a Brahmana well-versed in the Sama-Veda, and known by the name of Jeshthya. And because he was well-versed with the Samans, therefore was he known also by the name of Jeshthya-Samavrata Hari.[2] From the Brahmana known by the name of Jeshthya, this cult was obtained by a king of the name of Avikampana. After this, that cult, derived from the puissant Hari, once more disappeared from the

1 i.e., all creatures were righteous and compassionate. Of evil, there was nothing in that age.—T.

2 One of the foremost of Samans is called by the name of Jeshthya. One conversant with the Jeshthya Saman would have this name.—T.

world. During the seventh birth of Brahma due to the lotus, O king, that sprang from the navel of Narayana, this cult was once more declared by Narayana himself, unto the Grandsire of pure soul, the Creator of all the worlds, in the beginning of this Kalpa. The Grandsire gave it in days of yore to Daksha (one of his sons created by a fiat of his will). Daksha, in his turn, imparted it to the eldest of all the sons of his daughters, O monarch, *viz.*, Aditya who is senior in age to Savitri. From Aditya, Vivaswat obtained it. In the beginning of the Treta Yuga, Vivaswat imparted the knowledge of this cult to Manu. Manu, for the protection and support of all the worlds, then gave it to his son Ikshaku.[1] Promulgated by Ikshaku, that cult over-spreads the whole world. When the universal destruction comes, it will once more return to Narayana and be merged in Him. The religion which is followed and practised by the Yatis, has, O best of kings, been narrated to thee before this in the Hari Gita, with all its ordinances in brief. The celestial Rishi Narada got it from that Lord of universe, viz., Narayana himself, O king, with all its mysteries and abstract of details. Thus, O monarch, this foremost of cults is primeval and eternal. Incapable of being comprehended with ease and exceedingly difficult of being practised, it is always upheld by persons wedded to the attribute of Sattwa. It is by means of acts that are well-performed and accomplished with a full knowledge of duties and in which there is nothing of injury to any creature,—that Hari the Supreme Lord becomes gratified. Some persons adore Narayana as possessed of only one form, viz., that of Aniruddha. Some adore Him as endued with two forms, viz., that of Aniruddha and Pradyumna. Some adore Him as having three forms, viz., Aniruddha, Pradyumna, and Sankarshana. A fourth class adore him as consisting of four forms, viz., Aniruddha, Pradyumna, Sankarshana, and Vasudeva. Hari is Himself the Kshetrajna (Soul). He is without parts (being ever full). He is the Jiva in all creatures, transcending the five primal elements. He is the Mind, O monarch, that directs and controls the five senses. Endued with the highest intelligence, He is the Ordainer of the universe, and the Creator thereof. He is both active and inactive. He is both Cause and the Effect. He is the one immutable Purusha, who sports as He likes, O king. Thus have I recited to thee the religion of desireless Devotees, O best of kings, incapable of being comprehended by persons of uncleansed souls but this I acquired through the grace of my preceptor. Persons are very rare, O king, that are devoted to Narayana with whole souls. If, O son of Kuru's race the world had been full of such persons, that are full of universal compassion, that are endued with knowledge of the soul, and that are always employed in

1 Ikshaku was the progenitor of the solar race of kings.—T.

doing good to others, then the Krita age would have set in. All men would have betaken themselves to the accomplishment of acts without desire of fruit. It was even in this way, O monarch, that, that foremost of regenerate persons, viz., the illustrious Vyasa, my preceptor, fully conversant with all duties, discoursed unto king Yudhishthira the just on this religion of Devotion, in the presence of many Rishis and in the hearing of Krishna and Bhishma. He had obtained it from the celestial Rishi Narada endued with wealth of penances. Those persons that are devoted to Narayana with their whole souls and are desireless succeed in attaining to the region of that highest of deities, identical with Brahma, pure in complexion, possessed of the effulgence of the moon and endued with immutability.

Janamejaya said,—"I see that those regenerate persons whose souls have been awakened practise diverse kinds of duties. Why is it that other Brahmanas instead of practising those duties betake themselves to the observance of other kinds of vows and rites?

Vaisampayana said,—"Three kinds of disposition, O monarch, have been created in respect of all embodied creatures, viz., that which relates to the attribute of Sattwa, that which relates to the attribute of Rajas, and lastly that which relates to the attribute of Tamas, O Bharata. As regards embodied creatures, O perpetuator of Kuru's race, that person is the foremost who is wedded to the attribute of Sattwa, for, O tiger among men, it is certain that he will attain to Emancipation. It is with the aid of this very attribute of Sattwa that one endued therewith succeeds in understanding the person that is conversant with Brahma. As regards Emancipation, it is entirely dependent upon Narayana. Hence it is that persons striving after Emancipation are regarded as made up of the attribute of Sattwa. By thinking of Purushottama the foremost of Beings, the man that is devoted with his whole soul to Narayana, acquires great wisdom. Those persons that are endued with wisdom, that have betaken themselves to the practices of Yatis and the religion of Emancipation,—those persons of quenched thirst, always find that Hari favours them with the fruition of their desire.[1] That man subject to birth (and death) upon whom Hari casts a kind eye should be known as endued with the attribute of Sattwa and devoted to the acquisition of Emancipation. The religion followed by a person that is devoted with his whole soul to Narayana is regarded as similar or equal in merit to the system of the Sankhyas. By adopting that religion one attains to the highest end and attains to Emancipation which has Narayana for its soul. That person upon whom Narayana looks with

1 This desire, of course, relates to the acquisition of Emancipation. 'Yoga-kshema' literally means the acquisition of what is desired and the protection of what has been acquired.—T.

compassion succeeds in becoming awakened.[1] No one, O king, can become awakened through his own wishes. That nature which partakes of both Rajas and Tamas is said to be mixed. Hari never casts a kind eye upon the person subject to birth (and death) that is endued with such a mixed nature and that has, on that account, the principle of Pravritti in him. Only Brahma, the Grandsire of the worlds, looks upon the person that is subject to birth and death because of his mind being overwhelmed with the two inferior attributes of Rajas and Tamas.[2] Without doubt, the deities and the Rishis are wedded to the attributes of Sattwa, O best of kings. But then they that are divested of that attribute in its subtile form are always regarded to be of mutable nature.[3]"

Janamejaya said,—"How can one that is fraught with the principle of change succeed in attaining to that Purushottama (the foremost of Purusha)? Do tell me all this, which is, no doubt, known to thee. Do thou discourse to me also of Pravritti in due order."

Vaisampayana said,—"That which is the twentyfifth (in the enumeration of topics as made in the Sankhya system) viz., when it becomes able to abstain entirely from acts, succeeds in attaining to the Purushottama which is exceedingly subtile, which is invested with the attribute of Sattwa (in its subtile form), and which is fraught with the essences symbolised by three letters of the alphabet (*viz.*, A, U, and M). The Sankhya system, the Aranyaka-Veda, and the Pancharatra scriptures, are all one and the same and form parts of one whole. Even this is the religion of those that are devoted with their whole souls to Narayana,—the religion that has Narayana for its essence.[4] As waves of the ocean, rising from the ocean, rush away from it only to return to it in the end, even so diverse kinds of knowledge, springing from Nara-

---

1 'Buddha' or 'Pratibuddha' literally implies 'awakened.' The sense, of course, is that such a person has succeeded in casting off all impurities and desires. He has, as it were, been awakened from the slumber of ignorance or darkness.—T.

2 Those that follow the religion of Pravritti acquire heaven, &c., through their merits. Merits, however, are exhaustible. They have, therefore, to fall down from heaven. The Creator Brahma casts his eye on men that follow Pravritti. The religion of Nivritti, however, leads to Emancipation. It is Narayana that looks upon men that betake to Nivritti.—T.

3 What is stated here is this: the deities and Rishis are certainly endued with Sattwa. But then that Sattwa is of a gross form. Hence, they cannot attain to Emancipation. It is only that Sattwa which is of subtile form that leads to Emancipation. The deities, without being able to attain to Emancipation, remain in a state that is mutable or fraught with change.—T.

4 That is, the practices which constitute the religion of the Ekantins are not really different for those laid down in the scriptures adverted to above.—T.

yana, return to Narayana in the end. I have thus explained to thee, O son of Kuru's race, what the religion of Sattwa is. If thou beest competent for it, O Bharata, do thou practise that religion duly. Even thus did the highly-blessed Narada explain to my preceptor,—the Island-born Krishna—the eternal and immutable course, called Ekanta, (ending in One) followed by the Whites[1] as also by the yellow-robed Yatis. Vyasa gratified with Dharma's son Yudhishthira, imparted this religion to king Yudhishthira the just who was possessed of great intelligence. Derived from my preceptor I have also communicated it to thee! O best of kings, this religion is for these reasons, exceedingly difficult of practice. Others, hearing it, become as much confounded as thou hast suffered thyself to be. It is Krishna who is the protector of the universe and its beguiler. It is He who is the destroyer and the cause, O monarch."

SECTION CCCL

Janamejaya said,—"The Sankhya system, the Panchratra scriptures, and the Aranyaka-Vedas,—these different systems of knowledge or religion,—O regenerate Rishi, are current in the world. Do all these systems preach the same course of duties, or are the courses of duties preached by them, O ascetic, different from one another? Questioned by me, do thou discourse to me on Pravritti in due order!"

Vaisampayana said,—"I bow unto that great Rishi who is the dispeller of darkness, and whom Satyavati bore to Parasara in the midst of an island, who is possessed of great knowledge and who is endued with great liberality of soul. The learned say that he is the origin of the Grandsire Brahma; that he is the sixth form of Narayana; that he is the foremost of Rishis; that he is endued with the puissance of Yoga; that as the only son of his parents he is an incarnate portion of Narayana; and that, born under extraordinary circumstances on an Island, he is the inexhaustible receptacle of the Vedas. In the Krita age, Narayana of great puissance and mighty energy, created him as his son. Verily, the high-souled Vyasa is unborn and ancient and is the inexhaustible receptacle of the Vedas!"

Janamejaya said,—"O best of regenerate persons, it was thou that saidst before this that the Rishi Vasishtha had a son of the name of Saktri and that Saktri had a son of the name of Parasara, and that Parasara begot a son named the Island-born Krishna endued with great

---

1 Who are the Whites referred to in this place? The Commentator explains that the word has reference to persons leading the domestic mode of life. Yatis wear robes that are coloured yellow or yellowish red. Householders, however, use cloth that is white. The word may also mean the inhabitants of White Island.—T.

ascetic merit. Thou tellest me again that Vyasa is the son of Narayana. I ask, was it in some former birth that Vyasa of immeasurable energy had sprung from Narayana ? O thou of great intelligence, do tell me of that birth of Vyasa which was due to Narayana !"

Vaisampayana said,—"Desirous of understanding the meaning of the Srutis, my preceptor, that ocean of penances, who is exceedingly devoted to the observance of all scriptural duties and the acquisition of knowledge, dwelt for some time in a particular region of the Himavat mountains. Endued with great intelligence, he became fatigued with his penances in consequence of the great strain on his energies occasioned by the composition of the Mahabharata. At that time, Sumanta and Jaimini and Paila of firm vows and myself numbering the fourth, and Suka his own son, attended on him. All of us, O king, in view of the fatigue our preceptor felt, waited dutifully upon him, engaged in doing all that was necessary for dispelling that fatigue of his. Surrounded by these disciples of his, Vyasa shone in beauty on the breast of the Himavat mountains like the Lord of all the ghostly beings, viz., Mahadeva, in the midst of those ghostly attendants of his. Having recapitulated the Vedas with all their branches as also the meanings of all the Verses in the Mahabharata, one day, with rapt attention, all of us approached our preceptor who, having controlled his senses, was at time rapt up in thought. Availing ourselves of an interval in the conversation, we asked that foremost of regenerate persons to expound to us the meanings of the Vedas and the Verses in the Mahabharata and narrate to us the incidents as well of his own birth from Narayana. Conversant as he was with all topics of enquiry, he at first discoursed to us on the interpretations of the Srutis and the Mahabharata, and then set himself to narrate to us the following incidents relating to his birth from Narayana.

"Vyasa said,—'Listen, ye disciples, to this foremost of narratives, to this best of histories that relates again to the birth of a Rishi. Appertaining to the Krita age, this narrative has become known to me through my penances, ye regenerate ones. On the occasion of the seventh creation, viz., that which was due to the primeval Lotus, Narayana, endued with the austerest penances, transcending both good and ill, and possessed of unrivalled splendour, at first created Brahma, from his navel. After Brahma had started into birth, Narayana addressed him, saying,—Thou hast sprung from my navel. Endued with puissance in respect of creation, do thou set thyself to create diverse kinds of creatures, rational and irrational. Thus addressed by the author of his being, Brahma with his mind penetrated by anxiety, felt the difficulty of his task and became unwilling to do what he was commenced to do. Bowing his head unto the boon-giving and illustrious Hari, the Lord of the universe, Brahma said these words unto him,—I bow to thee, O

Lord of the deities, but I ask what puissance have I to create diverse creatures ? I have no wisdom. Do thou ordain what should be ordained in view of this. Thus addressed by Brahma, the Lord of the universe, viz., Narayana, disappeared there and then from Brahma's sight. The Supreme Lord, the god of gods, the chief of those endowed with intelligence, then began to think. The Goddess of Intelligence forthwith made her appearance before the puissant Narayana. Himself transcending all Yoga, Narayana then, by dint of Yoga, applied the Goddess of Intelligence properly. The illustrious and puissant and immutable Hari, addressing the Goddess of Intelligence who was endued with activity and goodness and all the puissance of Yoga, said unto her these words :—For the accomplishment of the task of creating all the worlds do thou enter into Brahma. Commanded thus by the Supreme Lord, Intelligence forthwith entered Brahma. When Hari beheld that Brahma had become united with Intelligence, He once more addressed him, saying,—Do thou now create diverse kinds of creatures.—Replying unto Narayana by uttering the word 'Yes.' Brahma reverently accepted the command of his progenitor. Narayana then disappeared from Brahma's presence, and in a moment repaired to his own place, known by the name of Deva (Light or Effulgence). Returning to His own disposition (of Unmanifestness), Hari remained in that state of oneness. After the task of creation, however, had been accomplished by Brahma, another thought arose in the mind of Narayana. Indeed, he reflected in this strain :—Brahma, otherwise called Parameshthi, has created all these creatures, consisting of Daityas and Danavas and Gandharvas and Rakshasas. The helpless Earth has become burthened with the weight of creatures. Many among the Daityas and Danavas and Rakshasas on Earth will become endued with great strength. Possessed of penances, they will at diverse times succeed in acquiring many excellent boons. Swelling with pride and might in consequence of those boons that they will succeed in obtaining, they will oppress and afflict the deities and the Rishis possessed of ascetic might. It is, therefore, meet that I should now and then lighten the burthen of the Earth, by assuming diverse forms one after another as occasion would require. I shall achieve this task by chastising the wicked and upholding the righteous. (Thus looked after by me), the Earth, which is the embodiment of Truth, will succeed in bearing her load of creatures. Assuming the form of a mighty snake I myself have to uphold the Earth in empty space. Upheld by me thus, she will uphold the entire creation, mobile and immobile. Incarnated on the Earth, therefore, in different forms, I shall have to rescue her at such times from peril. Having reflected in this way, the illustrious slayer of Madhu created diverse forms in his mind in which to appear from time to time for accomplishing the task in view. Assuming the form of a Boar, of Man-lion, of a Dwarf, and of human beings, I shall quell or slay such enemies of the deities as will become wicked and ungovernable. After this, the original Creator of the universe once more uttered the syllable *Bho*, causing the atmosphere to resound with it. From this syllable of speech (Saraswati) arose a Rishi of the name Saraswat. The son, thus born of the Speech of Narayana, came to be, also called by the name of Apantara-tamas. Endued with great puissance, he was fully conversant with the past, the present, and the future. Firm in the observance of vows, he was truthful in speech.[1] Unto that Rishi who, after birth, had bowed his head unto Narayana, the latter, who was the original Creator of all the deities and possessed of a nature that was immutable, said those words:—Thou shouldst devote thy attention to the distribution of the Vedas, O foremost of all persons endued with intelligence.[2] Do thou, therefore, O ascetic, accomplish what I command thee.—In obedience to this command of the Supreme Lord from whose Speech the Rishi Apantaratamas sprang into existence, the latter, in the Kalpa named after the Self-born Manu, distributed and arranged the Vedas. For that act of the Rishi, the illustrious Hari became gratified with him, as also for his well-performed penances, his vows and observances, and his restraint of the senses or passions. Addressing him,—Narayana said,—At each Manwantara, O son, thou wilt act in this way with respect to the Vedas. Thou shalt, in consequence of this act of thine, be immutable, O regenerate one, and incapable of being transcended by any one. When the Kali age will set in, certain princes of Bharata's line, to be called by the name of Kauravas, will take their birth from thee. They will be celebrated over the Earth as high-souled princes ruling over powerful kingdoms. Born of thee, dissensions will break out among them ending in their destruction at one another's hands excepting yourself. O foremost of regenerate persons,[3] in that age also, endued with austere penances, thou wilt distribute the Vedas into diverse classes. Indeed, in that dark age, thy complexion will become dark. Thou shalt cause diverse kinds

---

1 The name 'Apantara-tamas' implies one whose darkness or ignorance has been dispelled.—T.

2 'Vedakhyane Srutih karyya,' literally, I think, means 'thou shouldst turn thy ears to the description of the Vedas,' implying that 'thou shouldst set thyself to a distribution or arrangement of the Vedic hymns and Mantras.'—T.

3 It is difficult to understand what is the precise meaning of the expression 'twamrite'. Literally' it means 'without thee'. Whether however, the speaker means that all the princes will meet with destruction except thee' or that they will be destroyed without thy being present among them, or that such destruction will overtake them without thyself being the cause of it, it is difficult to determine.—T.

of duties to flow and diverse kinds of knowledge also. Although endued with austere penances, yet thou shalt never be able to free thyself from desire and attachment to the world. Thy son, however, will be freed from every attachment like unto the Supreme Soul, through the grace of Madhava. It will not be otherwise. He whom learned Brahmanas call the mind-born son of the Grandsire, *viz.*, Vasishtha endued with great intelligence and like unto an ocean of penances, and whose splendour transcends that of the Sun himself, will be the progenitor of a race in which a great Rishi of the name of Parasara, possessed of mighty energy and prowess, will take his birth. That foremost of persons, that ocean of Vedas, that abode of penances, will become thy sire (when thou wilt take birth in the Kali age). Thou shalt take thy birth as the son of a maiden residing in the house of her sire, through an act of congress with the great Rishi Parasara. Doubts thou wilt have none with respect to the imports of things past, present, and future. Endued with penances and instructed by me, thou wilt behold the incidents of thousands and thousands of ages long past away. Thou wilt see through thousands and thousands of ages also in the future. Thou shalt, in that birth, behold me, O ascetic,—me that am without birth and death,—incarnated on Earth (as Krishna of Yadu's race), armed with the discus. All this will happen to thee, O ascetic, through the merit that will be thine in consequence of thy ceaseless devotion to me. These words of mine will never be otherwise. Thou shalt be one of the foremost of creatures. Great shall be thy fame. Surya's son Sani (Saturn) will, in a future Kalpa, take birth as the great Manu of that period. During that Manwantara, O son, thou shalt, in respect of merits, be superior to even the Manus of the several periods. Without doubt, thou shalt be so through my grace. Whatever exists in the world represents the result of my exertion. The thoughts of others may not correspond with their acts. As regards myself, however, I always ordain what I think, without the least impediment![1] Having said these words unto the Rishi Apantaratamas, otherwise called by the name of Saraswat, the Supreme Lord dismissed him, saying unto him,—Go. I am he that was born as Apantaratamas through the command of Hari. Once more have I taken birth as the celebrated Krishna-Dwaipayana, a delighter of the race of Vasishtha.[2] I have thus told you, my dear disciples, the circumstances, of my own former birth which was due to the grace of

---

1 'Anyo hanyam chintayati' seems to mean that the thoughts of others do not correspond with their act.—T.

2 It is scarcely necessary to remark that the word 'nandana' means both sons and delighter. The etymological meaning is, of course, delighter. The son or grandson is so called because of his being a source of delight to the sire or the grandsire with the other members of the family. In Verse 68, 'nandana' seems to be used in the sense of 'delighter',—T.

Narayana in so much that I was a very portion of Narayana himself. Ye foremost of intelligent persons, I underwent, in days of yore, the austerest penances, with the aid of the highest abstraction of the mind. Ye sons, moved by my great affection for yourselves that are devoted to me with reverence, I have told you everything relating to what you wished to know from me, viz., my first birth in days of remote antiquity and that other birth subsequent to it (viz., the present one)!"

Vaisampayana continued,—"I have thus narrated to thee, O monarch, the circumstances connected with the former birth of our revered preceptor, viz., Vyasa of unstained mind, as asked by thee. Listen to me once again. There are diverse kinds of cults, O royal sage, that go by diverse names such as Sankhya, Yoga, the Pancha-ratra, Vedas, and Pasupati. The promulgator of Sankhya cult is said to be the great Rishi Kapila. The primeval Hiranyagarbha, and none else, is the promulgator of the Yoga system. The Rishi Apantaratamas is said to be the preceptor of the Vedas, some call that Rishi by the name of Prachina-garbha. The cult known by the name of Pasupata was promulgated by the Lord of Uma, that master of all creatures, viz., the cheerful Siva, otherwise known by the name of Sreekantha, the son of Brahma. The illustrious Narayana is himself the promulgator of the cult, in its entirety, contained in the Pancharatra scriptures. In all these cults, O foremost of kings, it is seen that the puissant Narayana is the one sole object of exposition. According to the scriptures of these cults and the measure of knowledge they contain, Narayana is the one sole object of worship they inculcate. Those persons whose visions, O king, are blinded by darkness, fail to understand that Narayana is the Supreme Soul pervading the entire universe. Those persons of wisdom who are the authors of the scriptures say that Narayana, who is a Rishi, is the one object of reverent worship in the universe. I say that there is no other being like Him. The Supreme Deity, called by the name of Hari, resides in the hearts of those that have succeeded (with the aid of the scriptures and of inference) in dispelling all doubts. Madhava never resides in the hearts of those that are under the sway of doubts and that would dispute away everything with the aid of false dialectics. They that are conversant with the Pancharatra scriptures, that are duly observant of the duties laid down therein, and that are devoted to Narayana with their whole souls, succeed in entering into Narayana. The Sankhya and the Yoga systems are eternal. All the Vedas, again, O monarch, are eternal. The Rishis, in all these systems of cult, have declared that this universe existing from ancient times is Narayana's self. Thou shouldst know that whatever acts, good or bad, are laid down in the Vedas and occurance in heaven and Earth, between the sky and the waters, are all caused by and flow from that ancient Rishi Narayana.

SECTION CCCLI

Janamejaya said,—"O regenerate one, are there many Purushas or is there only one? Who, in the universe, is the foremost of Purushas? What, again, is said to be the source of all things?"

Vaisampayana said,—In the speculations of the Sankhya and the Yoga systems many Purushas have been spoken of, O jewel of Kuru's race. Those that follow these systems do not accept that there is but one Purusha in the universe.[1] In the same manner in which the many Purushas are said to have one origin in the Supreme Purusha, it may be said that this entire universe is identical with that one Purusha of superior attributes. I shall explain this now, after bowing to my preceptor Vyasa, that foremost of Rishis, who is conversant with the soul, endued with penances, self-restrained, and worthy of reverent worship. This speculation on Purusha, O king, occurs in all the Vedas. It is well known to be identical with Rita and Truth. The foremost of Rishis, viz., Vyasa, has thought upon it. Having occupied themselves with reflection on what is called Adhyatma, diverse Rishis, O king, having Kapila for their first, have declared their opinions on this topic both generally and particularly. Through the grace of Vyasa of immeasurable energy, I shall expound to thee what Vyasa has said in brief on this question of the Oneness of Purusha. In this connection is cited the old narrative of the discourse between Brahma, O king, and the Three-eyed Mahadeva. In the midst of the Ocean of milk, there is a very high mountain of great effulgence like that of gold, known, O monarch, by the name of Vaijayanta. Repairing thither all alone, from his own abode of great splendour and felicity, the illustrious deity Brahma used very often to pass his time, engaged in thinking on the course of Adhyatma. While the four-faced Brahma of great intelligence was seated there, his son Mahadeva, who had sprung from his forehead encountered him one day in course of his wanderings through the universe. In days of yore, the Three-eyed Siva endued with puissance and high Yoga, while proceeding along the sky, beheld Brahma seated on that mountain and, therefore, dropped down quickly on its top. With a cheerful heart he presented him before his progenitor and worshipped his feet. Beholding Mahadeva prostrated at his feet, Brahma took him up with his left hand. Having thus raised Mahadeva up, Brahma, that

---

1 The Commentator explains these Verse in this way. 'So far as ordinary purposes are concerned, both the Sankhyas and Yogins speak of many Purushas'. In reality, however, for purposes of the highest truth, there is but one Purusha. I do not see this limitation in the Verse itself. The fact is what the Commentator says is to be seen in the next Verse.—T.

puissant and one Lord of all creatures, then addressed his son, whom he met after a long time, in these words.

"The Grandsire said,—'Welcome art thou, O thou of mighty arms. By good luck I see thee after such a long time come to my presence. I hope, O son, that everything is right with thy penances and thy Vedic studies and recitations. Thou art always observant of the austerest penances. Hence I ask thee about the progress and well-being of those penances of thine!'

"Rudra said,—'O illustrious one, through thy grace, all is well with my penances and Vedic studies. It is all right, again, with the universe. I saw thy illustrious self a long while ago in thy own home of felicity and effulgence. I am coming thence to this mountain that is now the abode of thy feet.[1] Great is the curiosity excited in my mind by this withdrawal of thyself into such a lone spot from thy usual region of felicity and splendour. Great must the reason be, O Grandsire, for such an act on thy part. Thy own foremost abode is free from the pains of hunger and thirst, and inhabited by both deities and Asuras, by Rishis of immeasurable splendour, as also by Gandharvas and Apsaras. Abandoning such a spot of felicity, thou residest alone in this foremost of mountains. The cause of this cannot but be grave.

"Brahma said,—'This foremost of mountains, called Vaijayanta, is always my residence. Here, with concentrated mind, I meditate on the one universal Purusha of infinite proportions.'

"Rudra said,—'Self-born thou art. Many are the Purushas that have been created by thee. Others again, O Brahma, are being created by thee. The Infinite Purusha, however, of whom thou speakest, is one and single. Who is that foremost of Purushas, O Brahma, that is being meditated by thee ? Great is the curiosity I feel on this point. Do thou kindly dispel the doubt that has taken possession of my mind.

"Brahma said,—'O son, many are those Purushas of whom thou speakest. The one Purusha, however, of whom I am thinking, transcends all Purushas and is invisible. The many Purushas that exist in the universe have that one Purusha as their basis ; and since that one Purusha is said to be the source whence all the innumerable Purushas have sprung, hence all the latter, if they succeed in divesting themselves of attributes, become competent to enter into that one Purusha who is identified with the universe, who is supreme, who is the foremost of the foremost, who is eternal, and who is himself divested of and is above all attributes."

1 'The abode of thy feet' means *thy* abode. To this day, in mentioning persosns that are entitled to reverence, the Hindu speaks of them as the "feet of so and so"—T.

SECTION CCCLII

"Brahma said,—'Listen, O son, as to how that Purusha is indicated. He is eternal and immutable. He is undeteriorating and immeasurable. He pervades all things.'[1] O best of all creatures, that Purusha cannot be seen by thee, or me, or others. Those that are endued with the understanding and the senses but destitute of self-restraint and tranquility of soul cannot obtain a sight of him. The Supreme Purusha is said to be one that can be seen with the aid of knowledge alone. Though divested of body, He dwells in every body. Though dwelling, again, in bodies, He is never touched by the acts accomplished by those bodies. He is my Antaratma (inner soul). He is thy inner soul. He is the all-seeing Witness dwelling within all embodied creatures and engaged in marking their acts. No one can grasp or comprehend him at any time. The universe is the crown of his head. The universe is his arms. The universe is his feet. The universe is his eyes. The universe is his nose. Alone and single, he roves through all Kshetras (Bodies) unrestrained by any limitations on his will and as he likes. Kshetra is another name for body. And because he knows all Kshetras as also all good and bad deeds, therefore he, who is the soul of Yoga, is called by the name of Kshetrajna.[2] No one succeeds in perceiving how he enters into embodied creatures and how he goes out of them. Agreeably to the Sankhya mode, as also with the aid of Yoga and the due observance of the ordinances prescribed by it, I am engaged in thinking of the cause of that Purusha, but alas, I am unable to comprehend that cause, excellent as it is. I shall, however, according to the measure of my knowledge, discourse to thee upon that eternal Purusha and his Oneness and supreme greatness. The learned speak of him as the one Purusha. That one eternal Being deserves the appellation of Mahapurusha (the great supreme Purusha). Fire is an element, but it may be seen to blaze up in a thousand places under thousand different circumstances. The Sun is one and single, but his rays extend over the wide universe. Penances are of diverse kinds, but they have one common origin whence they have flowed. The Wind is one, but it blows in diverse forms in the

---

1 The Commentator explains the meanings of the words used in this Verse in this way: He is called 'Purusha, because of the attribute of fulness eternal, incause he has neither beginning nor end; immutable, because there is no change in him: undeteriorating, because he has no body that may be subject to decay; immeasurable, because the mind cannot conceive of him in his fulness.—T.

2 Acts are called seeds. Seeds produce tree. Acts lead to the attainment of bodies. For the production of bodies, therefore, acts operate like seeds,—T.

world. The great Ocean is the one parent of all the waters in the world seen under diverse circumstances. Divested of attributes, that one Purusha is the universe displayed in infinitude. Flowing from him, the infinite universe enters into that one Purusha again who transcends all attributes, when the time of its destruction comes. By casting off the consciousness of body and the senses, by casting off all acts good and bad, by casting off both truth and falsehood, one succeeds in divesting oneself of attributes. The person who realises that inconceivable Purusha and comprehends his subtile existence in the quadruple form of Aniruddha, Pradyumna, Sankarshana, and Vasudeva, and who, in consequence of such comprehension, attains to perfect tranquility of heart, succeeds in entering into and identifying himself with that one auspicious Purusha. Some persons possessed of learning speak of him as the supreme soul. Others regarded him as the one soul. A third class of learned men describe him as the soul.[1] The truth is that he who is the Supreme Soul is always divested of attributes. He is Narayana. He is the universal soul, and he is the one Purusha. He is never affected by the frutis of acts even as the leaf of the lotus is never drenched by the water one may throw upon it. The Karamta (acting Soul) is different. That Soul is sometimes engaged in acts and when it succeeds in casting off acts attains to Emancipation or identity with the Supreme Soul. The acting Soul is endued with the seven and ten possessions.[2] Thus it is said that there are innumerable kinds of Purushas in due order. In reality, however, there is but one Purusha. He is the abode of all the ordinances in respect of the universe. He is the highest object of knowledge. He is at once the knower and the object to be known. He is at once the thinker and the object of thought. He is the eater and the food that is eaten. He is the smeller and the scent that is smelled. He is at once he that touches and the object that is touched. He is the agent that sees and the object that is seen. He is the hearer and the object that is heard. He is the conceiver and the object that is conceived. He is possessed of attributes and is free from them. What has previously, O son, been named Pradhana, and is the mother of the Mahat tattwa is no other than the Effulgence of the Supreme Soul;

1 The sense seems to be this; in the Yoga system He is called the Supreme Soul, for Yogins affirm the existence of two souls, the Jivatman and the Supreme Soul, and assert the superiority of the latter over the former. The Sankhyas regard the Jiva-soul and the Supreme Soul to be one and the same. A third class of men think everything as Soul, there being no difference between the one Soul and the universe displayed in infinitude. —T.

2 The acting Soul is ensconced in the Linga-sarira with which it becomes now a human being, now a deity, now an animal, &c given and ten possessions are five pranas, mind, intelligence and ten organs of senses.—T.

because He it is who is eternal, without destruction and any end and ever immutable. He it is who creates the prime ordinance in respect of Dhatri himself. Learned Brahmanas call Him by the name of Aniruddha. Whatever acts, possessed of excellent merits and fraught, with blessings, flow in the world from the Vedas, have been caused by Him.[1] All the deities and all the Rishis, possessed of tranquil souls, occupying their places on the altar, dedicate to Him the first share of their sacrificial offerings.[2] I, that am Brahma, the primeval master of all creatures, have started into birth from Him, and thou hast taken thy birth from me. From me have flowed the universe with all its mobile and immobile creatures, and all the Vedas, O son, with their mysteries. Divided into four portions (viz., Aniruddha, Pradyumna, Sankarashana, and Vasudeva), He sports as He pleases. That illustrious and divine Lord is even such, awakened by His own knowledge. I have thus answered thee, O son, according to thy questions, and according to the way in which the matter is expounded in the Sankhya system and the Yoga philosophy."

SECTION CCCLIII

Sauti said,—After Vaisampayana had explained to king Janamejaya in this way the glory of Narayana, he began to discourse on another topic by reciting the question of Yudhishthira and the answer that Bhishma gave in the presence of all the Pandavas and the Rishis as also of Krishna himself. Indeed, Vaisampayana began by saying what follows.[3]

"Yudhishthira said,—'Thou hast, O grandsire discoursed to us on the duties appertaining to the religion of Emancipation. It behoveth thee now to tell us what the foremost duties are of persons belonging to the several modes of life!'[4]

Bhishma said,—'The duties ordained in respect of every mode of life are capable, if well performed, of leading to heaven and the high

---

1 'Dhaturadyam Vidhanam' is supposed by the Commentator to imply what is known as 'Mahat', i. e., the existence of Jiva before the consciousness of Ego arises.—T.

2 'Pragvansa' is a certain part of the altar. Both the Vernacular translators omit the word in their renderings,—T.

3 This portion does not occur in all the texts. I have thought fit to add it for explaining the connection. Most texts begin abruptly by saying—"Yudhishthira said, &c., &c.'—T.

4 The object of the question is to ascertain which is the foremost of all the modes of life. Although Renunciation has been described to be the best of all modes, still the duties of that mode are exceedingly difficult of practice. Hence, Yudhishthira wishes to know if the duties of any other mode can be regarded as superior.—T.

fruit of Truth. Duties which are as so many doors, to great sacrifices and gifts and none of the practices inculcated by them are futile in respect of consequence. One who adopts particular duties with steady and firm faith, praises these duties adopted by him to the exclusion of the rest, O chief of Bharata's race. This particular topic, however, on which thou wishest me to discourse was in days of yore the subject of conversation between the celestial Rishi Narada and the chief of the deities, viz., Indra. The great Rishi Narada, O king, revered by all the world is a siddha *i.e.*, his sadhana has met fulfilment. He wanders through all the worlds unobstructed by anything, like the all-pervading wind itself. Once upon a time he repaired to the abode of Indra. Duly honoured by the chief of the deities, he sat close to his host. Beholding him seated at his ease and free from fatigue, the lord of Sachi addressed him, saying,—O great Rishi, is there any thing wonderful that has been beheld by thee, O sinless one? O regenerate Rishi, crowned with ascetic success, thou rovest, moved by curiosity, through the universe of mobile and immobile objects, witnessing all things. O celestial Rishi, there is nothing in the universe that is unknown to thee. Do thou tell me, therefore, of any wonderful incident which thou mayst have seen or heard of or felt. Thus questioned, Narada, that foremost of speakers, O king, then commenced to recite unto the chief of the celestials the extensive history that follows. Listen now to me as I recite that story which Narada told before Indra. I shall narratte it in the same manner in which the celestial Rishi had narrated it, and for the same purpose that he had in view!' "

SECTION CCCLIV

"Bhishma said,—In an excellent town called by the name of Mahapadma which was situate on the southern side of the river Ganga, there lived, O, best of men, a Brahmana of concentrated soul. Born in the race of Atri, he was endued with amiability. All his doubts had been dispelled (by faith and contemplation) and he was well conversant with the path he was to follow. Ever observant of the religious duties, he had his anger under perfect control. Always contented, he was the complete master of his senses. Devoted to penances and study of the Vedas, he was honoured by all good men. He earned wealth by righteous means and his conduct in all things corresponded with the mode of life he led and the order to which he belonged. The family to which he belonged was large and celebrated. He had many kinsmen and relatives, and many children and spouses. His behaviour was always respectable and faultless. Observing that he had many children, the Brahmana betook himself to the accomplishment of religious acts on a large scale. His religious observances, O king, had reference to the customs of his own family.[1] The Brahmana reflected that three kinds of duties have been laid down for observances. There were first, the duties ordained in the Vedas in respect of the order in which he was born and the mode of life he was leading (*viz.*, a Brahmana in the observance of domesticity). There were secondly, the duties prescribed in the scriptures, *viz.*, those especially called the Dharmasastras. And, thirdly, there were those duties that eminent and revered men of former times have followed though not occuring either in the Vedas or the scriptures[2]. Which of these duties should I follow ? Which of them, again, followed by me, are likely to lead to my benefit ? Which, indeed, should be my refuge ?—Thoughts like these always troubled him. He could not solve his doubts. While troubled with such reflections, a Brahmana of concentrated soul and observant of a very superior religion, came to his house as a guest. The householder duly honoured his guest according to those ordinances of worship that are laid down in the scriptures. Beholding his guest refreshed and seated at ease, the host addressed him in the following words."

"The Brahmana said,—O sineless one, I have become exceedingly attached to thee in consequence of the sweetness of thy conversation. Thou hast become my friend. Listen to me, for I wish to say something unto thee. O foremost of Brahmanas, after making over the duties of a householder to my son, I wish to discharge the highest duties of man. What, O regenerate one, should be my path ? Relying upon the Jiva soul, I wish to achieve existence in the one (supreme) soul. Alas, bound up in the ties of attachment, I have not the heart to actually set myself to the accomplishment of that task.[3] And since the best portion of my

---

1 Family customs are always observed with great care. Even when inconsistent with the ordinances of the scriptures, such customs do not lose their binding force. Reprehensible as the sale of a daughter or sister is, the great king Salya, when he bestowed his sister Madri on Pandu, insisted upon taking a sum of money, alleging family custom not only as an excuse but as something that was obligetory. To this day, animals are slain in the sacrifices of many families which follow the Vaishnava faith, the justification being family custom—T.

2 The Vedas are, strictly speaking, not scriptures, for they are *heard* the scriptures being those ordinances that are written down. Of course, the Vedas have been reduced into writing, but for all that, they continue to be called the Srutis, as the Common Law of England, though reduced into writing, is still called the Unwritten Law.—T.

3 Some texts erroneously read 'sthitah' for 'sthitim'. 'Eka eva atmani sthitim kartum', literally rendered, is 'to achieve existence in the one soul. This means 'to realise the union of the Jiva-soul with the Supreme Soul.' 'Relying upon the Soul I shall try to exist in the one Soul,' in brief, means, I shall try to unite the Jiva with Supreme Soul. The difference between Kankhami' and 'Ichchhami' is well illustrated by the Commentator by

life has passed away in the observance of domesticity, I desire to devote the remnant of my life in earning the means of defraying the expenses of my journey in respect of the time to come. The desire has arisen in my mind of crossing the ocean of the world. Alas, whence shall I get the raft of religion (with which to accomplish my purposes)? Hearing that even the very deities are persecuted and made to endure the fruits of their acts, and beholding the rows of Yama's standards and flags floating over the heads of all creatures, my heart fails to derive pleasure from the diverse objects of pleasure with which it comes into contact. Beholding also that the Yatis depend for their sustenance upon alms obtained in course of their rounds of mendicancy, I have no respect for the religion of the Yatis as well. O my reverend guest, do thou, aided by that religion which is founded upon the basis of intelligence and reason, set me to the observance of a particular course of duties and observances![1]—'

"Bhishma continued,—'Endued with great wisdom, the guest, hearing this speech of his host which was consistent with righteousness, said these sweet words in a melodious voice.

"The guest said,—I myself also am confounded with respect to this topic. The same thought occupies my mind. I am unable to arrive at definite conclusions. Heaven has many doors. There are some that applaud Emancipation. Some regenerate persons praise the fruits attainable by the performance of sacrifices. Some there are that take refuge in the forest mode of life. Some, again, betake themselves to the domestic mode of life. Some rely upon the merits attainable by an observance of the duties of kings. Some rely upon the fruits of that culture which consists in restraining the soul. Some think that the merits resulting from a dutiful obedience to preceptors and seniors are efficacious. Some betake themselves to restraints imposed on speech. Some by waiting dutifully upon their mothers and fathers, have gone to heaven. Some have ascended to heaven by practising the duty of compassion, and some by practising Truth. Some rush to battle, and after laying down their lives, have attained to heaven. Some, again, attaining to success by practising the vow called Unccha, have betaken themselves to the path of heaven. Some have devoted themselves to

---

referring to the case of the man of weak stomach who craves for food of every kind but who does not wish to actually eat from fear of increasing his illness.—T.

1 'Sattwikani' implies the deities and others that are endued with the attribute of Sattwa. 'Samyujyamanani' refers to their births and deaths as deities and men in consequence of the fruits reaped of acts done. 'Niryyatyamanani' is distressed or afflicted (in consequence of such birth and deaths)'. The rows of Yama's standards and flags' refer to the diverse diseases that afflict all creatures.—T.

the study of the Vedas. Endued with auspiciousness and wedded to such study, these men, possessed of intelligence, with tranquil souls, and having their senses under complete control, attain to heaven. Others characterised by simplicity and truth, have been slain by men of wickedness. Endued with pure souls, such men of truth and simplicity, have become honoured denizens of heaven. In this world, it is seen, that men betake themselves to heaven, through a thousand doors of duty, all standing wide open. My understanding has been troubled by thy question, like a fleecy cloud before the wind.—' "

SECTION CCCLVI

" 'The guest continued.—For all that, O Brahmana, I shall endeavour to instruct thee duly. Listen to me as I recite to thee that which I have heard from my preceptor. In that place whence, in course of a former creation, the wheel of righteousness was set in motion, in that forest which is known by the name of Naimisha, and which is situate on the banks of the Gomati, there is a city called after the Nagas. There, in that region, all the deities, being assembled together, had in days of old performed a grand sacrifice. There the foremost of earthly kings, Mandhatri, vanquished Indra, the chief of the celestials. A mighty Naga, of righteous soul, dwells in the city that stands in that region. That great Naga is known by the name of Padmanabha or Padma. Walking in the triple path (of acts, knowledge, and adoration) he gratifies all creatures in thought, word, and deed. Reflecting upon all things wtih great care, he protects the righteous and chastises the wicked by adopting the quadruple policy of conciliation, provoking dissensions, making gifts or bribes, and using force. Repairing thither, thou shouldst put to him the questions thou wishest. He will show thee truly what the highest religion is. That Naga is always fond of guests, Endued with great intelligence, he is well conversant with the scriptures. He is possessed of all desireable virtues the like of which are not to be noticed in any other person. By disposition he is always observant of those duties which are performed with or in water.[1] He is devoted to the study of the Vedas. He is endued with penances and self-restraint. He has great wealth. He performs sacrifice, makes gifts, abstains from inflicting injury and practises forgiveness. His conduct in all respects is excellent. Truthful in speech and freed from malice, his behaviour, is good and his senses are under proper control. He eats after feeding all his guests and attendants. He is kind of speech. He has knowledge of what is beneficial and what is simple and right and

1 The Commentator explains that 'nityah-salilah' means 'pure as water.' I think this is not the sense of the word here.—T.

what is censurable. He takes stock of what he does and what he leaves undone. He never acts with hostility towards any one. He is always engaged in doing what is beneficial to all creatures. He belongs to a family that is as pure and stainless as the water of a lake in the midst of the Ganges.—' "

SECTION CCCLVII

" 'The host replied.—I have heard these words of thine, that are so consoling, with as much gratification as is felt by a person heavily loaded when that load is taken off his head or shoulders. The gratification that a traveller who has made a long journey on foot feels when he lies down on a bed, that which a person feels when he finds a seat after having stood for a long while for want of room, or that which is felt by a thirsty person when he finds a glass of cool water, or that which is felt by a hungry man when he finds savoury food set before him, or that which a guest feels when a dish of desirable food is placed before him at the proper time, or that which is felt by an old man when after long coveting he gets a son, or that which is experienced by one when meeting with a dear friend or relative about whom one had become exceedingly anxious, resembles that with which I have been filled in consequence of these words uttered by thee.[1] Like a person with upturned gaze I have heard what has fallen from thy lips and am reflecting upon their import. With these wise words of thine thou hast truly instructed me! Yes, I shall do what thou hast commanded me to do. Thou mayst go tomorrow at dawn, passing the night happily with me and dispelling thy fatigue by such rest. Behold, the rays of the divine Surya have been partially dimmed and the god of day is proceeding in his downward course!—"

"Bhishma continued.—'Hospitably waited upon by that Brahmana, the learned guest, O slayer of foes, passed that night in the company of his host. Indeed, both of them passed the night happily, conversing cheerfully with each other on the subject of the duties of the fourth mode of life, *viz.*, Sannyasa (Renunciation). So engrossing was the nature of their conversation that the night passed away as if it were day. When morning came, the guest was worshipped with due rites by the

1 It is desirable to note that the word 'atithi' which is rendered 'guest' here and elsewhere, means a person who enters without invitation the abode of a householder. Such an individual is adorable. All the deities reside in his person. He is supposed to favour the householder by giving him an opportunity of performing the rites of hospitality. Whatever the respect, however, that is paid to a guest, he cannot expect to be served with food till the householder, has done his best for serving him as sumptuously as his circumstances would permit....Hence, by the time the food is placed before him, the guest becomes very hungry.—S.

Brahmana whose heart had been eagerly set upon the accomplishment of what (according to the discourse of the guest) was regarded by him to be beneficial for himself. Having dismissed his guest, the righteous Brahmana, resolved to achieve his purpose, took leave of his kinsmen and relatives, and set out in due time for the abode of that foremost of Nagas, with heart steadily directed towards it.' "

SECTION CCCLVIII

"Bhisma said,—Proceeding by many delightfull forests and lakes and sacred waters, the Brahmana at last arrived at the retreat of a certain ascetic. Arrived there, he enquired of him, in proper words, about the Naga of whom he had heard from his guest, and instructed by him he pursued his journey. With a clear idea of the purpose of his journey, the Brahmana then reached the house of the Naga. Entering it duly, he proclaimed himself in proper words, saying,—Ho! who is there!' I am a Brahmana, come hither as a guest!—Hearing these words, the chaste wife of the Naga, possessed of great beauty and devoted to the observance of all duties, showed herself. Always attentive to the duties of hospitality, she worshipped the guest with due rites, and welcoming him, said,—What can I do for you?—

" 'The Brahmana said,—O lady, I am sufficiently honoured by thee with the sweet words thou hast said unto me. The fatigue of my journey has also been dispelled. I desire, O blessed lady, to see thy excellent lord. This is my high object. This is the one object of my desire. It is for this reason that I have come today to the residence of the Naga, thy husband.

" 'The wife of the Naga said,—Reverend sir, my husband has gone to drag the car of Surya for a month. O learned Brahmana, he will be back in fifteen days, and will, without doubt show himself unto thee. I have thus told thee the reason of my husband's absence from home. Be that as it may, what else is there that I can do for thee? Tell me this!—

" 'The Brahmana said,—O chaste lady, I have come hither with the object of seeing thy husband. O reverend dame, I shall dwell in the adjacent forest, waiting for his return. When thy husband comes back, do kindly tell him that I have arrived at this place impelled by the desire of seeing him. Thou shouldst also inform me of his return when that event occurs. O blessed lady, I shall, till then, reside on the banks of the Gomati, waiting for his return and living all the while upon frugal fare.—Having said this repeatedly unto the wife of the Naga, that foremost of Brahmanas proceeded to the banks of the Gomati for residing there till the time of the Naga's return.' "

SECTION CCCLIX

Bhishma continued,—'The Nagas of that city became exceedingly distressed when they saw that that Brahmana, devoted to the practice of penances, continued to reside in the forest, entirely abstaining all the while from food, in expectation of the arrival of the Naga chief. All the kinsmen and relatives of the great Naga, including his brother and children and wife, assembling together, repaired to the spot where the Brahmana was staying. Arrived on the banks of the Gomati, they beheld that regenerate person seated in a secluded spot, abstaining from food of every kind, observant the while of excellent vows, and engaged in silently reciting certain Mantras. Approaching the presence of the Brahmana and offering him due worship, the kinsmen and relatives of the great Naga said unto him these words fraught with candour :—O Brahmana, endued with wealth of asceticism, this is the sixth day of thy arrival here, but thou sayest no word about thy food, O regenerate one, thou art devoted to righteousness. Thou hast come to us. We two are here in attendance upon thee. It is absolutely necessary that we should do the duties of hospitality by thee. We are all relations of the Naga chief with whom thou hast business. Roots or fruits, leaves, or water, or rice or meat, O best of Brahmanas, it behoveth thee to take for thy food. In consequence of thy dwelling in this forest under such circumstances of total abstention from food, the whole community of Nagas, young and old, is being afflicted, since this thy fast implies negligence on our part to discharge the duties of hospitality. We have none amongst us that has been guilty of Brahmanicide. None of us has ever lost a son immediately after birth. No one has been born in our race that has eaten before serving the deities or guests or relatives arrived at his residence.

" 'The Brahmana said,—In consequence of these solicitations of you all, I may be regarded to have broken my fast. Eight days are wanting for the day to come when the chief of the Nagas will return.[1] If, on the expiry of the eighth night hence, the chief of the Nagas does not come back, I shall then break this fast by eating. Indeed, this vow of abstaining from all food that I am observing is in consequence of my regard for the Naga chief. You should not grieve for what I am doing. Do you all return to whence you came. This my vow is on his account. You should not do anything in consequence of which this my vow may be broken.—The assembled Nagas, thus addressed by the Brahmana, were dismissed by him, whereupon, O foremost of men, they returned to their respective residences.' "

---

1 Some of the Bengal texts have 'dwigunam for 'dwiruna,' 'Less than ten by two is the meaning.—T.

SECTION CCCLX

"Bhishma said,—Upon the expiry of the period of full fifteen days, the Naga chief (Padmanabha), having finished his task of dragging the car of Surya and obtained the latter's permission, came back to his own house. Beholding him come back, his spouse approached him quickly for washing his feet and dutifully discharging other tasks of a similar nature. Having gone through these tasks, she took her seat by his side. The Naga then, refreshed from fatigue, addressed his dutiful and chaste wife, saying,—I hope, my dear wife, that during my absence thou hast not been unmindful of worshipping the deities and guests agreeably to the instructions I gave thee, and according to the ordinances laid down in the scriptures. I hope, without yielding to that uncleansed understanding which is natural to persons of thy sex, thou hast, during my absence from home, been firm in the observance of the duties of hospitality. I trust that thou hast not transcended the barriers of duty and righteousness.

" 'The wife of the Naga said,—The duty of disciples is to wait with reverence upon their preceptor accomplishing his bidding ; that of Brahmanas is to study the Vedas and bear them in memory ; that of servants is to obey the commands of their masters ; that of the king is to protect his people by cherishing the good and chastising the wicked. It is said that the duties of a Kshatriya embrace the protection of all creatures from wrong and oppression. The duty of the Sudra is to serve with humility persons of the three regenerate orders, viz., Brahmanas, Kshatriyas and Vaisyas. The religion of the house-holder, O chief of the Nagas, consists in doing good to all creatures. Frugality of fare and observance of vow in due order, constitute merit (for persons of all classes) in consequence of the connection that exists between the senses and the duties of religion.[1]—Who am I? Whence have I come? What are others to me and what am I to others?—these are the thoughts to which the mind should ever be directed by him who leads that course of life which leads to Emancipation. Chastity and obedience to the husband constitute the highest duty of the wife. Through thy instruction, O chief of the Nagas, I have learnt this well. I, therefore, that am well conversant with my duty, and that have thee for my husband

1 This Verse seems to be unintelligible. I think the sense is this. Frugality of fare and observance of vows constitute merit for person of all classes. These imply the restraint of the senses, for if the senses be not restrained, no one can observe vows or practise frugality. There is a connection, thus between the duties of religion and the senses.—T.

—thee that art devoted to righteousness,—O, why shall I, swerving from the path of duty, tread along the path of disobedience and sin? During thy absence from home, the adorations to the deities have not fallen off in any respect. I have also, without the slightest negligence, attended to the duties of hospitality towards persons arrived as guests in thy abode. Fifteen days ago a Brahmana has come here. He has not disclosed his object to me. He desires to have an interview with thee. Dwelling the while on the banks of the Gomati he is anxiously expecting thy return. Of rigid vows, that Brahmana is sitting there, engaged in the recitation of the Vedas. O chief of the Nagas, I have made a promise to him to the effect that I would despath thee to him as soon as thou wouldst come back to thy abode. Hearing these words of mine, O best of Nagas, it behoveth thee to repair thither. O thou that hearest with thy eyes, it behoveth thee to grant unto that regenerate person the object that has brought him hither ![1]—' "

SECTION CCCLXI

"The Naga said,—O thou of sweet smiles, for whom hast thou taken that Brahmana? Is he really a human being or is he some deity that has come hither in the disguise of a Brahmana? O thou of great fame, who is there among human beings that would be desirous of seeing me or that would be competent for the purpose? Can a human being, desiring to see me, leave such a command with thee about despatching me to him for paying him a visit at the place where he is dwelling? Amongst the deities and Asuras and celestial Rishis, O amiable lady, the Nagas are endued with great energy. Possessed of great speed, they are endued again with excellent fragrance. They deserve to be worshipped. They are capable of granting boons. Indeed, we too deserve to be followed by other in our train. I tell thee, O lady, that we are incapable of being seen by human beings.[2]—

"The spouse of the Naga chief said,—Judging by his simplicity and canbour I know that that Brahmana is not any deity who subsists on air. O thou of great wrath, I also know this, *viz.*, that he reveres thee with all his heart. His heart is set upon the accomplishment of

1 'Darsana-sravas' means one who hears with the eye. The Nagas or snakes are believed to have no ears, but to use their eyes both for seeing and hearing. Who the Nagas of the Mahabharata or the Puranas were, it is difficult to determine. They seem to have been a superior order of beings, having their abode in the nether regions.—T

2 The meaning of 'annyayinah' is that we should be followed by others, *i., e.*, we deserve to walk at the head of others—T.

some object that depends upon thy aid. As the bird called Chataka, which is fond of rain, waits in earnest expectation of a shower (for slaking its thirst), even so is that Brahmana waiting in expectation of a meeting with thee.[1] Let no calamity betake him in consequence of his inability to obtain a sight of thee. No person born like thee in a respectable family can be regarded to remain respectable by neglecting a guest arrived at his house.[2] Casting off that wrath which is natural to thee, it behoveth thee to go and see that Brahmana. It behoveth thee not to suffer thyself to be consumed by disappointing that Brahmana. The king or the prince, by refusing to wipe the tears of persons that come to him from hopes of relief, incurs the sin of foeticide. By abstaining from speech one attains to wisdom. By practising gifts one acquires great fame. By adhering to truthfulness of speech, one acquires the gift of eloquence and comes to be honoured in heaven. By giving away land one attains to that high end which is ordained for Rishis leading the sacred mode of life. By earning wealth through righteous means, one succeeds in attaining to many desirable fruits. By doing in its entirety what is beneficial for oneself, one can avoid going to hell. This is what the righteous say.

"The Naga said,—I had no arrogance due to pride. In consequence, however, of my birth, the measure of my arrogance was considerable. Of wrath, which is born of desire, O blessed lady, I have none. It has all been consumed by the fire of thy excellent instructions. I do not behold, O blessed dame, any darkness that is thicker than wrath. In consequence, however, of the Naga having excess of wrath, they have become object of reproach with all persons.[3] By succumbing to the influence of wrath, the ten-headed Ravana of great prowess, became the rival of Sakra and was for that reason slain by Rama in battle. Hearing that the Rishi Rama of Bhrigu's race had entered the inner

---

1 The Indian bird Chataka has a natural hole on the upper part of its long neck in consequence of which it is seen to always sit with beaks upturned, so that the upper part of the neck keeps the hole covered. The Chataka is incapable of slaking its thirst in a lake or river, for it cannot bend its neck down. Rain water is what it must drink. Its cry is shrill and sharp but not without sweetness. 'Phate-e-ek-jal' is supposd to be the cry uttered by it. When the Chataka cries, the hearers expect rain. Eager expectation with respect to anything is always compared to the Chataka's expectation of rain water.—T

2 The Burdwan translator erroneously renders this Verse. The Commentator explains that 'hitwa' is equivalent to 'vina' and sums up the meaning of the first line in these words, viz, 'twaddarsanam vina asya kopi vighnomabhut.' In the second line, 'naprayupasate' is equal to 'paritajya na aste.'—T.

3 It is a pity that even such Verses have not been rendered correctly by the Burdwan translator. K. P. Singha gives the sense correctly, but the translation is not accurate.—T.

apartments of their palace for bringing away the calf of the Homa cow of their sire, the sons of Karttaviryya, yielding to wrath, took such entry as an insult to their royal house, and as the consequence thereof, they met with destruction at the hands of Rama. Indeed, Karttaviryya of great strength, resembling the Thousand-eyed Indra himself, in consequence of his having yielded to wrath, was slain in battle by Rama of Jamadagni's race. Verily, O amiable lady at thy words I have restrained my wrath, that foe of penances that destroyer of all that is beneficial for myself. I praise my own self greatly since, O large-eyed one, I am fortunate enough to own thee for my wife,—thee that art possessed of every virtue and that hast inexhaustible merits. I shall now proceed to that spot where the Brahmana is staying. I shall certainly address that Brahmana in proper words and he shall certainly go hence, his wishes being accomplished.—"

SECTION CCCLXII

"Bhishma said,—Having said these words unto his dear spouse, the chief of the Nagas proceeded to that place where the Brahmana was sitting in expectation of an interview with him. As he proceeded, he thought of the Brahmana and wandered as to what the business could be that had brought him to the Naga city. Arrived at his presence, O chief of men, that foremost of Nagas devoted by his nature to righteousness, addressed his guest in sweet words, saying,—O Brahmana do not yield to wrath. I address thee in peace. Do not be angry. After whom hast thou come hither? What is thy object? Coming to thee, I ask thee in affection, O regenerate one whom dost thou adore in this retired spot on the banks of the Gomati!

" 'The Brahmana said,—Know that my name is Dharmaranya, and that I have come hither for obtaining a sight of the Naga Padmanabha, O foremost of all regenerate persons. With him I have some business. I have heard that he is not at home and that, therefore, I am not now near his present quarters. Like a Chataka waiting in expectation of the clouds, I am waiting for him whom I regard as dear to me. For dispelling all evil from him and bringing about what is beneficial to him, I am engaged in reciting the Vedas till he comes and am in Yoga and passing my time happily—

"The Naga said,—Verily, thy conduct is exceedingly good. Pious thou art and devoted to the good of all righteous persons. O highly blessed Brahmana, every praise is due to thee. Thou beholdest the Naga with eyes of affection. I am that Naga, O learned Rishi, whom thou seekest. Do thou command me, as thou wishest, in respect of what is agreeable to thee and what I should do for thee. Having heard from my spouse that thou art here, I have approached this spot, O regenerate one, for beholding thee. When thou hast come hither, thou art certain to return hence with thy object fulfilled. It behoveth thee, O foremost of regenerate persons, to employ me to any task with all confidence. All of us have certainly been purchased by thee with thy merits,[1] since thou, disregarding what is for thy own good, hast employed thy time in seeking the good of ourselves.—

" 'The Brahmana said,—O highly blessed Naga, I have come hither, moved by the desire of obtaining a sight of thee. I have come here, ignorant as I am with all things, for asking thee about something. O Naga, relying on the Jiva-Soul, I desire to attain to the Supreme Soul which is the end of the Jiva-Soul. I am neither attached to, nor dissociated from, the world.[2] Thou shinest with the effulgence of thy own merits covered by pure fame,—with an effulgence that is as agreeable as that of the moon. O thou that livest on air alone, do thou first answer a question that I wish to put to thee. Afterwards I shall inform thee of the object that has brought me hither!' "

SECTION CCCLXIII

" 'The Brahmana said,—Thou goest away for dragging the one-wheeled car of Vivaswat according to thy turn. It behoveth thee to describe to me anything wonderful that thou mayst have noticed in those regions through which thou sojournest!—

" 'The Naga said,—The divine Surya is the refuge or home of innumerable wonders. All the creatures that inhabit the three worlds have flowed from Surya. Innumerable Munis, crowned with ascetic success, together with all the deities, reside in the rays of Surya like birds perching on the branches of trees. What, again, can be more wonderful than this that the mighty Wind, emanating from Surya, takes refuge in his rays and thence yawns over the universe? What can be more wonderful than this, O regenerate Rishi, that Surya, dividing the Wind into many portions from desire of doing good to all creatures, creates rain that falls in the rainy season? What can be more wonderful than this that the Supreme Soul, from within the solar disc, himself bathed in blazing effulgence, looketh upon the universe? What can be more wonderful than this that Surya has a dark ray which transforms itself into clouds charged with rain and pours showers of rain when the season comes? What can be more wonderful than this that

---

1 A form of expression meaning that 'we are your slaves'.—T

2 'Atmanam' is Brahma; 'atmasthah' is 'relying in the Soul', i, e, 'withdrawn from all worldly objects; 'atmanogatim' implies 'the end of the Jiva-soul', i., e, the Supreme Soul; the last is an adjective of atmanam.—T.

drinking up for eight months the rain he pours down, he pours it down once again in the rainy season? In certain rays of Surya, the Soul of the universe is said to reside. From Him is the seed of all things, and it is He that upholds the Earth with all her mobile and immobile creatures. What can be more wonderful, O Brahmana, than this, that the foremost of Purushas, eternal and mighty-armed, endued with exceeding effulgence, eternal, and without beginning and without end, resides in Surya? Listen however, to one thing I shall tell you now. It is the wonder of wonders. I have seen it in the clear sky, in consequence of my adjacence to Surya. In former times, one day at the hour of noon, while Surya was shining in all his glory and giving heat to everything we beheld a Being coming towards Surya, who seemed to shine with effulgence that was equal to that of Surya himself. Causing all the worlds to blaze up with his glory and filling them with his energy, he came, as I have already told thee, towards Surya, rending the firmament, as it were, for making his path through it. The rays that emanated from his body seemed to resemble the blazing effulgence of libations of clarified butter poured into the sacrificial fire. In consequence of his energy and splendour he could not be looked at. His form seemed to be indescribable. Indeed, he appeared to us to be like a second Surya. As soon as he came near, Surya extended his two hands (for giving him a respectful reception). For honouring Surya in return, he also extended his right-hand. The latter then, piercing through the firmament, entered into Surya's disc. Mingling then with Surya's energy, he seemed to be transformed into Surya's self. When the two energies thus met together, we were so confounded that we could not any longer distinguish which was which. Indeed, we could not make out who was Surya whom we bore on his car, and who was the Being that we had seen coming through the sky. Filled with confusion, we then addressed Surya, saying,—O illustrious one who is this Being that has mixed himself with thee and has been transformed into thy second self?—' "

SECTION CCCLXIV

"Surya said,—This Being is not the god of fire, he is not an Asura. Nor is he a Naga. He is a Brahmana who has attained to heaven in consequence of his having been crowned with success in the observance of the vow called Unccha.[1] This person had subsisted upon fruits and

1 It has been explained in the previous sections that the Unccha vow consists in subsisting on grains picked up from the fields after the corn has been reaped and taken away by the owners. It is a most difficult vow to observe. The merit attaching to it is' therefore, very great.—T.

roots and upon the fallen leaves of trees. He had sometimes subsisted upon water, and sometimes upon air alone, passing his days with concentrated soul. The deity Mahadeva had been gratified by him with constant recitation of the Samhitas. He had endeavoured to accomplish those acts that lead to heaven. Through the merits of those acts he hath now attained to heaven. Without wealth and without desire of any kind, he had observed the vow called Uncchа in the matter of his sustenance. This learned Brahmana, ye Nagas, had been devoted to the good of all creatures. Neither deities, nor Gandharvas, nor Asuras, nor Nagas, can be regarded as superior to those creatures that attain to this excellent end of coming into the solar disc ?—Even such, O regenerate one, was the wonderful incident that I beheld on that occasion. That Brahmana, who was crowned with success by the observance of the Uuccha vow and who thus obtained an end that persons crowned with ascetic success scquire, to this day, O regenerate one, goes round the Earth, staying in the disc of Surya !—' "

SECTION CCCLXV

" 'The Brahmana said,—Without doubt, this is very wonderful, O Naga, I have been highly gratified by listening to thee. By these words of thine that are fraught with subtile meaning, thou hast shown me the way I am to follow. Blessed be thou, I desire to depart hence O best of Nagas, thou shouldst recollect me now and then and enquire after me by sending thy servant.

" 'The Naga said,—The object that brought thee hither is still in thy breast, for thou hast not as yet disclosed it to me. Where then wilt thou go ? Tell me, O regenerate one, what should be done by me, and what that object is which brought thee hither. After the accomplishment of thy business, whatever it is, expressed or unexpressed in speech, thou mayst depart, O foremost of regenerate persons, saluting me and dismissed by me cheerfully, O thou of excellent vows. Thou hast conceived a friendship for me. O regenerate Rishi, it behoveth thee not to depart from this place after having only seen me, thyself sitting under the shade of this tree. Thou hast become dear to me and I have become dear to thee, without doubt. All the persons in this city are thine. What objection then is there, O sinless one, to pass some time in my house ?—

" 'The Brahmana said,—It is even so, O thou of great wisdom, O Naga that hast acquired a knowledge of the soul. It is very true that the deities are not superior to thee in any respect. He that is thyself, is verily myself, as he that is myself is truly thyself. Myself, thyself, and all other creatures, shall all have to enter into the Supreme Soul.

Doubt penetrated my mind, O chief of Nagas, in the matter of the best means for winning righteousness or merit. That doubt has been dispelled by thy discourse, for I have learnt the value of the Uncha vow. I shall hence follow that which is so very efficacious in the matter of beneficial consequences. That, O blessed one, has become my certain conclusion now, based on excellent reasons. I take thy leave. Blessings to thee. My object has been accomplished, O Naga.' "

"Bhishma said.—'Having saluted that foremost of Nagas in this way, the Brahmana (named Dharmaranya), firmly resolved to follow the Uncha mode of life, proceeded to the presence, O king, of Chyavana of Bhrigu's race, from desire of being formally instructed and initiated in that vow.[1] Chyavana performed the Samskara rites of the Brahmana and formally initiated him into the Uncha mode of life. The son of Bhrigu, O monarch, recited this history to king Janaka in his place. King Janaka, in his turn, narrated it to the celestial Rishi Narada of high soul. The celestial Rishi Narada too, of stainless acts, repairing on one occasion to the abode of Indra, the chief of the deities, gave to Indra this history upon being asked by him. The chief of the celestials, having obtained it thus from Narada, recited this blessed history to a conclave consisting of all the foremost Brahmanas, O monarch. On the occasion, again, of my dreadful encounter with Rama of Bhrigu's race (on the field of Kurukshetra), the celestial Vasus, O king, recited this history to me.[2] Asked by thee, O foremost of righteous men, I have recited this history that is excellent and sacred and fraught with great merit. Thou hadst asked me about that constitutes the highest duty, O king. This history is my answer to thy query. A brave man he was, O monarch, that betook himself to the practice of the Uncha vow in this way, without expectation of any fruit. Firmly resolved, that Brahmana, instructed, by the chief of Nagas in this way about his duty, betook himself to the practice of Yama and Niyama, and subsisting the while upon such food as was allowed by the Uncha vow, proceeded to another forest.' "

FINIS SANTI PARVA.

---

1 The formal initiation or 'diksha' is a ceremony of great importance. No sacrifice or vow, no religious rite, can be performed without the 'diksha'. The rite of 'diksha' is performed with the assistance of a preceptor or priest. In leaving the domestic mode for the like of a forest recluse, the 'diksha' is necessary. In following the Uncha vow, this rite is needed. Any religious act performed by one without having undergone the formal 'diksha', becomes sterile of results.—T.

2 Bhishma abducted, with the might of his single arms, the three daughters of the king of Kasi, *viz*, Amva, Amvika, and Amvalika. He wished to marry the princesses to his brother Vichitravirya. The eldest princess, having previously to her abduction selected king Salwa for her lord was let off. When, however, she presented herself before her lover, the latter refused to wed her. She, therefore, applied to Rama for wreaking vengeance on Bhishma whom she regarded as the author of her wrongs. Rama took up her cause and fought with Bhishma, but was obliged to acknowledge defeat at the hands of his antagonist who was his disciple in arms. For fuller particulars, '*vide Amvopakhyana Parvan* in Udyoga Parvan.—T.

ANUSASANA PARVA

SECTION I

(*Anusasanika Parva.*)

Having bowed down unto Narayana, and Nara the foremost of male beings, and unto the goddess Saraswati, must the word Jaya be uttered.

"Yudhishthira said,—O grandsire, tranquility of mind has been said to be subtile and of diverse forms. I have heard all thy discourses, but still tranquility of mind has not been mine. In this matter, various means of quieting the mind have been related (by thee), O sire, but how can peace of mind be secured from only a knowledge of the different kinds of tranquility, when I myself have been the instruments of bringing about all this ? Beholding thy body covered with arrows and festering with bad sores, I fail to find, O hero, any peace of mind, at the thought of the evils I have wrought. Beholding thy body, O most valiant of men, bathed in blood, like a hill overrun with water from its springs, I am languishing with grief even as the lotus in the rainy season. What can be more painful than this, that thou, O grandsire, hast been brought to this plight on my account by my people fighting against their foes on the battle-field ? Other princes also, with their sons and kinsmen, have met with destruction on my account. Alas, what can be more painful than this. Tell us, O prince, what destiny awaits us and the sons of Dhritarashtra, who, driven by fate and anger, have done this abhorrent act. O lord of men, I think the son of Dhritarashtra is fortunate in that he doth not behold thee in this state. But I, who am the cause of thy death as well as of that of our friends, am denied all peace of mind by beholding thee on the bare earth in this sorry condition. The wicked Duryodhana, the most infamous of his race, has, with all his troops and his brothers, perished in battle, in the observance of Kshatriya duties. That wicked-souled wight does not see thee lying on the ground. Verily, for this reason, I would deem death to be preferable to life. O hero that never swervest from virtue, had I with my brothers met with destruction ere this at the hands of our enemies on the battle-field, I would not have found thee in this pitiful plight, thus pierced with arrows. Surely, O prince, the Maker had created us to become perpetrators of evil deeds. O king, if thou wishest to do me good, do thou then instruct me in such a way that I may be cleansed of this sin in even another world.

"Bhishma replied,—'Why, O fortunate one, dost thou consider thy soul, which is dependent (on God and Destiny and Time) to be the cause of thy actions ? The manifestation of its inaction is subtle and imperceptible to the senses. In this connection is cited the ancient story of the conversation between Mrityu and Gautami with Kala and the Fowler and the serpent. There was, O son of Kunti, an old lady of the name of Gautami, who was possessed of great patience and tranquility of mind . One day she found her son dead in consequence of having been bitten by a serpent. An angry fowler, by name Arjunaka, bound the serpent with a string and brought it before Gautami. He then said to her,—This wretched serpent has been the cause of thy son's death, O blessed lady. Tell me quickly how this wretch is to be destroyed. Shall I throw it into the fire or shall I hack it into pieces ? This infamous destroyer of a child does not deserve to live longer.

'Gautami replied,—Do thou, O Arjunaka of little understanding, release this serpent. It doth not deserve death at thy hands. Who is so foolish as to disregard the inevitable lot that awaits him and burdening himself with such folly sink into sin ? Those that have made themselves light by the practice of virtuous deeds, manage to cross the sea of the world even as a ship crosses the ocean. But those that have made themselves heavy with sin sink into the bottom, even as an arrow thrown into the water. By killing this serpent, this my boy will not be restored to life, and by letting it live, no harm will be caused to thee. Who would go to the interminable regions of Death by slaying this living creature ?—

"The fowler said,—I know, O lady that knowest the difference between right and wrong, that the great are afflicted at the afflictions of all creatures. But these words which thou hast spoken are fraught with instruction for only a self-contained person (and not for one plunged in sorrow). Therefore, I must kill this serpent. Those who value peace of mind, assign everything to the course of Time as the cause, but practical men soon assuage their grief (by revenge). People through constant delusion, fear loss of beatitude (in the next world for acts like these). Therefore, O lady, assuage thy grief by having this serpent destroyed (by me).

'Gautami replied,—People like us are never afflicted by (such misfortune). Good men have their souls always intent on virtue. The death of the boy was predestined : therefore, I am unable to approve of the destruction of this serpent. Brahmanas do not harbour resentment, because resentment leads to pain. Do thou, O good man, forgive and release this serpent out of compassion.

'The fowler replied,—Let us earn great and inexhaustible merit hereafter by killing (this creature), even as a man acquires great merit, and confers it on his victim sacrificed as well, by sacrifice upon the altar. Merit is acquired by killing an enemy: by killing this despicable creature, thou shalt acquire great and true merit hereafter.—

'Gautami replied,—What good is there in tormenting and killing an enemy, and what good is won by not releasing an enemy in our power? Therefore, O thou of benign countenance, why should we not forgive this serpent and try to earn merit by releasing it?—

'The fowler replied,—A great number (of creatures) ought to be protected from (the wickedness of) this one, instead of this single creature being protected (in preference to many). Virtuous men abandon the vicious (to their doom): do thou, therefore, kill this wicked creature.—

'Gautami replied,—By killing this serpent, O fowler, my son will not be restored to life, nor do I see that any other end will be attained by its death: therefore, do thou, O fowler, release this living creature of a serpent.—

The fowler said,—By killing Vritra, Indra secured the best portion (of sacrificial offerings), and by destroying a sacrifice Mahadeva secured his share of sacrificial offerings: do thou, therefore, destroy this serpent immediately without any misgivings in thy mind!—

"Bhishma continued,—The high-souled Gautami, although repeatedly incited by the fowler for the destruction of the serpent did not bend her mind to that sinful act.' The serpent, painfully bound with the cord: sighing a little and maintaining its composure with great difficulty, then uttered these words slowly, in a human voice.

'The serpent said,—O foolish Arjunaka, what fault is there of mine? I have no will of my own, and am not independent. Mrityu sent me on this errand. By his direction have I bitten this child, and not out of any anger or choice on my part. Therefore, if there be any sin in this, O fowler, the sin is his.—

'The fowler said,—If thou hast done this evil, led thereto by another, the sin is thine also as thou art an instrument in the act. As in the making of an earthen vessel the potter's wheel and rod and other things are all regarded as causes, so art thou, O serpent, (cause in the production of this effect). He that is guilty deserves death at my hands. Thou, O serpent, art guilty. Indeed, thou confessest thyself so in this matter!—

'The serpent said,—As all these, viz., the potter's wheel, rod, and other things, are not independent causes, even so I am not an independent cause. Therefore, this is no fault of mine, as thou shouldst grant. Shouldst thou think otherwise, then these are to be considered as causes working in unison with one another. For thus working with one other, a doubt arises regarding their relation as cause and effect. Such being the case, it is no fault of mine, nor do I deserve death on this account, nor am I guilty of any sin. Or, if thou thinkest that there is sin (in even such causation), the sin lies in the aggregate of causes.—

'The fowler said,—If thou art neither the prime cause nor the agent in this matter, thou art still the cause of the death (of this child). Therefore, thou dost deserve death in my opinion. If, O serpent, thou thinkest that when an evil act is done, the doer is not implicated therein, then there can be no cause in this matter: but having done this, verily thou deservest death. What more dost thou think?—

'The serpent said,—Whether any cause exists or not,[1] no effect is produced without an (intermediate) act. Therefore, causation being of no moment in either case, my agency only as the cause (in this matter) ought to be considered in its proper bearings. If, O fowler, thou thinkest me to be the cause in truth, then the guilt of this act of killing a living being rests on the shoulders of another who incited me to this end.[2]

'The fowler said,—Not deserving of life, O foolish one, why dost thou bandy so many words, O wretch of a serpent? Thou deservest death at my hands. Thou hast done an atrocious act by killing this infant.

'The serpent said,—O fowler, as the officiating priests at a sacrifice do not acquire the merit of the act by offering oblations of clarified butter to the fire, even so should I be regarded with respect as to the result in this connection.—

"Bhishma continued,—'The serpent directed by Mrityu having said this. Mrityu himself appeared there and addressing the serpent spoke thus.

'Mrityu said,—Guided by Kala, I, O serpent, sent thee on this errand, and neither art thou nor am I the cause of this child's death. Even as the clouds are tossed hither and thither by the wind, I am like the clouds, O serpent, influenced by Kala. All attitudes appertaining to *Sattwa*, or *Rajas*, or *Tamas*,[3] are provoked by Kala, and operate in all creatures. All creatures, mobile and immobile, in heaven, or earth, are influenced by Kala. The whole universe, O serpent, is imbued with this same influence of Kala. All acts in this world and all abstentions, as also all their modifications, are said to be influenced by Kala, Surya,

---

1 The commentator explains this passage by the illustration that in the act of felling a tree the effect is produced by the intermediate act of raising the axe by some sentient agent, but that in the case of the burning of a forest, the fire is produced by the friction of the dry branches of trees without the intervention of any sentient agent.—T.

2 'Even as the wind indicates the dry twigs to ignite,' add the Commentator.—T.

3. For explanation of these terms *vide* foot note (in page 577 of Santi Parva, Sec, 102, *ante*—T.

Soma, Vishnu, Water, Wind, the deity of a hundred sacrificer, Fire, Sky, Earth, Mitra and Parjanya, Aditi, and the Vasus, Rivers and Oceans, all existent and non-existent objects, are created and destroyed by Kala. Knowing this, why dost thou, O serpent, consider me to be guilty ? If any fault attaches to me in this, thou also wouldst be to blame.—

'The serpent said,—I do not, O Mrityu, blame thee, nor do I absolve thee from all blame. I only aver that I am directed and influenced (in my actions) by thee. If any blame attaches to Kala, or, if it be not desirable to attach any blame to him, it is not for me to scan the fault. We heve no right to do so. As it is incumbent on me to absolve myself from this blame, so it is my duty to see that no blame attaches to Mrityu.—'

"Bhishma continued,—'Then the serpent, addressing Arjunaka, said.—'Thou hast listened to what Mrityu has said. Therefore, it is not proper for thee to torment me, who am guiltless, by tying me with this cord.—

'The fowler said,—I have listened to thee, O serpent, as well as to the words of Mrityu, but these, O serpent, do not absolve thee from all blame. Mrityu and thyself are the causes of the child's death. I consider both of you to be the cause and I do not call that to be the cause which is not truly so. Accursed be the wicked and vengeful Mrityu that causes affliction to the good. Thee too I shall kill that art sinful and engaged in sinful acts !—

'Mrityu said,—We both are not free agents, but are dependent on Kala, and ordained to do our appointed work. Thou shouldst not find fault with us if thou dost consider this matter thoroughly.

'The fowler said,—If ye both, O serpent and Mrityu, be dependent on Kala, I am curious to know how pleasure (arising from doing good) and anger (arising from doing evil) are caused.—

'Mrityu said,—Whatever is done is done under the influence of Kala. I have said it before, O fowler, that Kala is the cause of all and that for this reason we both, acting under the inspiration of Kala, do our appointed work and therefore, O fowler, we two do not deserve censure from thee in any way !—'

"Bhishma continued,—'Then Kala arrived at that scene of disputation on this point of morality, and spoke thus to the serpent and Mrityu and the fowler Arjunaka assembled together.—

'Kala said,—Neither Mrityu, nor this serpent, nor I, O fowler, am guilty of the death of any creature. We are merely the immediate exciting causes of the event. O Arjunaka, the *Karma* of this child formed the exciting cause of our action in this matter. There was no other cause by which this child came by its death. It was killed as a result of its own Karma. It has met with death as the result of its Karma in the past. Its Karma has been the cause of its destruction. We all are subject to the influence of our respective Karma. Karma is an aid to salvation even as sons are, and Karma also is an indicator of virtue and vice in man. We urge one another even as acts urge one another. As men make from a lump of clay whatever they wish to make, even so do men attain to various results determined by Karma. As light and shadow are related to each other, so are men related to Karma through their own actions. Therefore, neither art thou, nor am I, nor Mrityu, nor the serpent, nor this old Brahmana lady, is the cause of this child's death. He himself is the cause here.—Upon Kala, O king, expounding the matter in this way, Gautami, convinced in her mind that men suffer according to their actions, spoke thus to Arjunaka.

'Gautami said,—Neither Kala, nor Mrityu, nor the serpent, is the cause in this matter. This child has met with death as the result of its own Karma. I too so acted (in the past) that my son has died (as its consequence). Let now Kala and Mrityu retire from this place, and do thou too, O Arjunaka, release this serpent.—

"Bhishma continued,—'Then Kala and Mrityu and the serpent went back to their respective destinations, and Gautami became consoled in mind as also the fowler. Having heard all this, O king, do thou forego all grief, and attain to peace of mind. Men attain to heaven or hell as the result of their own Karma. This evil has neither been of thy own creation, nor of Duryodhana's. Know this that these lords of Earth have all been slain (in this war) as a result of acts of Kalas.

Vaisampayana said,—"Having heard all this, the powerful and virtuous Yudhishthira became consoled in mind, and again enquired as follows."

SECTION II

"Yudhishthira said,—'O grandsire, O wisest of men, O thou that art learned in all the scriptures, I have listened to this great story, O foremost of intelligent men. I am desirous of again hearing the recital of some history full of religious instruction, and it behoves thee to gratify me. O lord of Earth, tell me if any householder has ever succeeded in conquering Mrityu by the practice of virtue. Do thou recite this to me with all details!'

"Bhishma said,—'This ancient history is recited as an illustration of the subject of the conquest by a householder, over Mrityu, through the practice of virtue. The Prajapati Manu had a son, O king, of the name of the Ikshwaku. Of that king, illustrious as Surya, were born a hundred sons. His tenth son, O Bharata, was named Dasaswa, and this virtuous prince of infallible prowess became the king of Mahismati.

Dasaswa's son, O king, was a righteous prince whose mind was constantly devoted to the practice of truth and charity and devotion. He was known by the name of Madiraswa and ruled over the Earth as her lord. He was constantly devoted to the study of the Vedas as also of the science of arms. Madiraswa's son was the king named Dyutimat who possessed great good fortune and power and strength and energy. Dyutimat's son was the highly dovout and pious king who was famous in all the worlds under the name of Suvira. His soul was intent on religion and he possessed wealth like another Indra, the lord of the deities. Suvira too had a son who was invincible in battle, and who was the best of all warriors and known by the name of Sudurjaya. And Durjya too, possessed of a body like that of Indra, had a son who beamed with splendour like that of fire. He was the great monarch named Duryodhana who was one of the foremost of royal sages. Indra used to pour rain profusely in the kingdom of this monarch, who never fled from the battlefield and was possessed of valour like unto Indra himself. The cities and the kingdom of this king were filled with riches and gems and cattle and grain of various kinds. There was no miser in his kingdom nor any person afflicted with distress or poverty. Nor was there in his kingdom any person that was weak in body or afflicted with disease. This king was very clever, smooth in speech, without envy, a master of his passions, of a righteous soul, full of compassion, endued with prowess, and not given to boasting. He performed sacrifices, and was self-restrained and intelligent, devoted to Brahmanas and Truth. He never humiliated others, and was charitable, and learned in the Vedạs and the Vedanta. The celestial river Narmada, auspicious and sacred and of cool waters, in her own nature, O Bharata, courted him. He begot upon that river, a lotus eyed daughter, by name Sudarsana, who was, O king, endued with great beauty. No creature, O Yudhisthira, had ever been born before among womankind, that was, possessed of such beauty as that excellent damsel who was the daughter of Duryodhana. The god Agni himself courted the beautiful princess Sudarsana, and taking the shape of a Brahmana, O monarch, sought her hand from the king. The king was unwilling to give his daughter in marriage to the Brahmana who was poor and not of the same rank with himself. Thereupon Agni vanished from his great sacrifice. The king, grieved at heart, then addressed the Brahmanas, saying,—Of what sin have I, ye excellent Brahmanas, or you, been guilty, that Agni should disappear from this sacrifice, even as good done unto wicked men disappears from their estimation. Great, indeed, must that sin of ours be for which Agni has thus disappeared. Either must the sin be yours, or, must it be mine. Do you fully investigate the matter.—Then hearing the king's words, O foremost prince of Bharata's race, the Brahmanas, restraining speech, sought with concentrated faculties the protection of the god of fire. The divine carrier of oblations, resplendent as the autumnal Sun, appeared before them, enveloping his self in glorious refulgence. The high-souled Agni then addressed those excellent Brahmanas, saying,—I seek the daughter of Duryodhana for my own self.—At this all those Brahmanas were struck with wonder, and rising on the marrow, they related to the king what had been said by the fire-god. The wise monarch, hearing the words of those utterers of *Brahma*, was delighted at heart, and said,—Be it so.—The king craved a boon of the illustrious fire-god as the marriage dower,—Do thou, O Agni, deign to remain always with us here.—Be it so—said the divine Agni to that lord of Earth. For this reason Agni has always been present in the kingdom of Mahismati to this day, and was seen by Sahadeva in course of his conquering expedition to the south. Then the king gave his daughter, dressed in new garments and decked with jewels, to the high-souled deity, and Agni too accepted, according to Vedic rites, the princess Sudarsana as his bride, even as he accepts libations of clarified butter at sacrifices. Agni was well pleased with her appearance, her beauty, grace, character, and nobility of birth, and was minded to beget offspring upon her. And a son by Agni, of the name of Sudarsana, was soon born of her. Sudarsana also was, in appearance, as beautiful as the full moon, and even in his childhood he attained to a knowledge of the supreme and everlasting *Brahma*. There was also a king of the name of Oghavat, who was the grandfather of Nriga. He had a daughter of the name of Oghavati, and a son too of the name of Ogharatha born unto him. King Oghavat gave his daughter Oghavati, beautiful as a goddess, to the learned Sudarsana for wife. Sudarsana, O king, leading the life of a householder with Oghavati, used to dwell in Kurukshetra with her. This intelligent prince of blazing energy took the vow, O lord, of conquering Death by leading the life of even a householder. The son of Agni, O king, said to Oghavati,—Do thou never act contrary to (the wishes of) those that seek our hospitality. Thou shouldst make no scruple about the means by which guests are to be welcomed, even if thou have to offer thy own person. O beautiful one, this vow is always present in my mind, since for house-holders, there is no higher virtue than hospitality accorded to guests. Do thou always bear this in mind without ever doubting it, if my words be any authority with thee. O sinless and blessed one, if thou hast any faith in me, do thou never disregard a guest, whether I be at thy side or at a distance from thee! Unto him, with hands clasped and placed on her head, Oghavati replied, saying,—'I shall leave nothing undone of what thou commandest me.—Then Mrityu, O king, desiring to over-reach Sudarsana, began to watch him for finding out his *laches*. On a certain occasion, when the son of Agni went out to fetch firewood from the forest, a graceful Brahmana sought the hospitality of Oghavati with these words :—O beautiful lady, if thou hast any faith in the virtue of hospitality as prescribed for householders, then I would request thee to extend the rites of hospitality to me to-day.—The princess of great fame, thus addressed by that Brahmana, O king, welcomed him according to the rites prescribed in the Vedas. Having offered him a seat, and water to wash his feet, she enquired, saying.—What is thy business? What can I offer thee?—The Brahmana said unto her,—My business is with thy person, O blessed one. Do thou act accordingly without any hesitation in thy mind. If the duties prescribed for householders be acceptable to thee, do thou, O princess, gratify me by offering up thy person to me.—Though tempted by the princess with offers of diverse other things, the Brahmana, however, did not ask for any other gift than the offer of her own person. Seeing him resolved, that lady, remembering the directions which had before been given to her by her husband, but overcome with shame, said, to that excellent Brahmana,—Be it so.—Remembering the words of her husband who was desirous of acquiring the virtue of householders, she cheerfully approached the regenerate Rishi. Meanwhile, the son of Agni, having collected his firewood, returned to his home. Mrityu, with his fierce and inexorable nature, was constantly by his side, even as one attends upon one's devoted friend. When the son of Pavaka returned to his own hermitage, he called Oghavati by name, and (receiving no answer) repeatedly, exclaimed,—Whither art thou gone?—But the chaste lady, devoted to her husband, being then locked in the arms of that Brahmana, gave no reply to her husband. Indeed, that chaste woman, considering herself contaminated became speechless, overcome with shame. Sudarsana, addressing her again, exclaimed,—Where can my chaste wife be? Whither has she gone? Nothing can be of greater moment to me than this (her disappearance). Why does not that simple and truthful lady, devoted to her husband, alas, answer to my call today as she used to do before with sweet smiles?—Then that Brahmana, who was within the hut, thus replied to Sudarsana,—Do thou learn, O son of Pavaka, that a Brahmana guest has arrived, and though tempted by this thy wife with diverse other offers of welcome, I have, O best of Brahmanas, desired only her person, and this fair-faced lady is engaged in welcoming me with due rites. Thou art at liberty to do whatever thou thinkest to be suitable to this occasion.—Mrityu, armed with the iron club, pursued the Rishi at that moment, desirous of compassing the destruction of one that would, he thought, deviate from his promise. Sudarsana was struck with wonder, but casting off all jealousy and anger by look, word, deed, or thought, said,—Do thou enjoy thyself, O Brahmana. It is a great pleasure to me. A householder obtain the highest merit by honouring a guest. It is said by the learned that, as regards the householder, there is no higher merit than what results unto him from a guest departing from his house after having been duly honoured by him. My life, my wife, and whatever other worldly possessions I have, are all dedicated to the use of my guests. Even this is the vow that I have taken. As I have truly made this statement, by that truth, O Brahmana, I shall attain to the knowledge of Self. O foremost of virtuous men, the five elements, *viz.*, fire, air, earth, water, and sky, and the mind, the intellect and the Soul, and time and space and the ten organs of sense, are all present in the bodies of men, and always witness the good and evil deeds that men do. This truth has today been uttered by me, and let the gods bless me for it or destroy me if I have spoken falsely. At this, O Bharata, there arose in all directions, in repeated echoes, a voice, crying,—This is true, this is not false. Then that Brahmana came out of the hovel, and like the wind rising and encompassing both Earth and sky, and making the three worlds echo with Vedic sounds, and calling that virtuous man by name, and congratulating him, said,—O sinless one, I am Dharma ; All glory to thee. I came here, O truth-loving one, to try thee, and I am well pleased with thee by knowing thee to be virtuous. Thou hast subdued and conquered Mrityu who always has pursued thee, seeking thy *laches* ? O best of men, no one in the three worlds has the ability to insult, even with looks, this chaste lady devoted to her husband, far less to touch her person. She has been protected from defilement by thy virtue and by her own chastity. There can be nothing contrary to what this proud lady will say. This utterer of *Brahma*, endued with austere penances, shall, for the salvation of the world, be metamorphosed into a mighty river. And thou shalt attain to all the worlds in this thy body, and as truly as the science of Yoga is within her control, this highly blessed lady will follow thee with only half of her corporeal self, and with the other half will she be celebrated as the river Oghavati ! And thou shalt attain with her to all the worlds that acquired through penances. Those eternal and everlasting worlds from which none cometh back will be attained by thee even in this gross body of thine. Thou hast conquered Death, and attained to the highest of all felicities, and by thy own power (of mind), attaining to the speed of thought, thou hast risen above the power of the five elements ! By thus adhering to the duties of a householder, thou hast conquered thy passions, desires, and anger, and this princess, O prince of virtuous men has, by serving thee, conquered affliction, desire, illusion, enmity and lassitude of mind ! —

"Bhishma continued,—Then the glorious Vasava (the lord of the gods), riding in a fine chariot drawn by a thousand white horses, approached that Brahmana. Death and Soul, all the worlds, all the elements, intellect, mind, time, and space as also desire and wrath, were all conquered. Therefore, O best of men, do thou bear this in mind, that to a householder there is no higher divinity than the guest. It is said by the learned that the blessings of an honoured guest are more efficacious than the merit of a hundred sacrifices. Whenever a deserving guest seeks the hospitality of a householder and is not honoured by him, he takes away (with him) all the virtues of the latter giving him his sins (in return). I have now recited to thee, my son, this excellent story as to how Death was conquered of old by a householder. The recital of this excellent story confers glory, fame, and longevity (upon those that listen to it). The man that seeks worldly prosperity should consider it as efficacious in removing all evil. And, O Bharata, the learned man that daily recites this story of the life of Sudarsana attains to the regions of the blessed.' "

SECTION III

"Yudhishthira said,—'If, O prince, Brahmanahood be so difficult of attainment by the three classes (Kshatriyas, Vaisyas and Sudras), how then did the high-souled Viswamitra, O king, though a Kshatriya (by birth), attain to the status of a Brahmana? I desire to know this, O sire. Therefore, do thou truly relate this matter to me. That powerful man, O sire, by virtue of his austerities, destroyed in a moment the hundred sons of the high-souled Vasishtha. While under the influence of anger, he created numerous evil spirits and Rakshasas of mighty vigour and resembling the great destroyer Kala himself. The great and learned race of Kusika, numbering hundreds of regenerate sages and belauded by the Brahmanas, was founded in this world of men by him. Sunasepha of austere penances, the son of Richika, having been sought to be slain as an animal in the great sacrifice of Amvarisha, obtained his deliverance through Viswamitra. Harishchandra, having pleased the gods at a sacrifice, became a son of the wise Viswamitra. For not having honoured their eldest brother Devarat, whom Viswamitra got as a son from the gods, the other fifty brothers of his were cursed, and all of them became Chandalas. Trisanku, the son of Ikshwaku, through the curse of Vasistha became a Chandala, and when abandoned by his friends, and remaining suspended with his head downwards in the lower regions, was translated to heaven at the pleasure of Viswamitra. Viswamitra had a large river, by name Kausika, that was frequented by celestial Rishis. This sacred and auspicious stream was frequented by the gods and regenerate Rishis. For disturbing his devotions, the famous celestial nymph Rambha of fine bracelets, was cursed and metamorphosed into a rock. Through fear of Viswamitra the glorious Vasishtha, in olden times, binding himself with creepers, threw himself down into a river and again rose released from his bonds. In consequence of this, that large and sacred river became thenceforth celebrated by the name of Vipasa.[1] He prayed to the glorious and puissant Indra who was pleased with him and absolved him from a curse.[2] Remaining on the northern side of the firmament, he sheds his lustre from a position in the midst of the seven regenerate *Rishis*,[3] and Dhruva the son of Uttanpada[4]. These are his achievements as well as many others. O descendant of Kuru, as they were performed by a Kshatriya, my curiosity has been roused in this matter. Therefore, O foremost one of Bharata's race, do thou relate this matter to me truly. How without casting off his corporeal frame and taking another tenement of flesh could he become a Brahmana? Do thou, O sire, truly relate this matter to me as thou hast related to me the story of Matanga. Matanga was born as a Chandala,[5] and could not attain to Brahmanahood (with all his austerities) but how could this man attain to the status of a Brahmana?"

SECTION IV

"Bhishma said,—'Listen truly in detail, O son of Pritha, how in olden times Viswamitra attained to the status of a Brahamana Rishi. There was, O foremost of Bharata's descendants, in the race of Bharata, a king of the name of Ajamida, who performed many sacrifices and was the best of all virtuous men. His son was the great king named Jahnu. Ganga was the daughter of this high-minded prince. The farfamed and equally virtuous Sindhudwipa was the son of this prince. From Sindhudwipa sprung the great royal sage Valakaswa. His son was named Vallabha who was like a second Dharma in embodied form. His son again was Kusika who was refulgent with glory like unto the thousand-eyed Indra. Kusika,s son was the illustrious King Gadhi who,

1 Literally, the releaser from bonds—T.

2 Refers to the curse pronounced on Viswamitra by the son of Vasistha, when the former acted as the priest of Trisanku. The curse was that Viswhmitra would partake of canine flesh by officiating as the priest of one who himself was the partaker of such flesh. It is said that at a time of great scarcity, Viswamitra was obliged to resort to dog's flesh for food, and that as he was about to cook it, Indra pounced upon it and took it away.—T.

3 The constellation of the Great Bear.—T.

4 The Pole Star.—T.

5 Matanga was begotten upon a Brahmana woman by a Sudra father.—T.

being childless and desiring to have a son born unto him, repaired to the forest. Whilst living there, a daughter was born unto him. She was called Satyavati by name, and in beauty of appearance she had no equal on Earth. The illustrious son of Chyavana, celebrated by the name of Richika, of the race of Bhrigu, endued with austere penances, sought the hand of this lady. Gadhi, the destroyer of his enemies, thinking him to be poor, did not bestow her in marriage upon the high-souled Richika. But when the latter, thus dismissed, was going away, the excellent king, addressing him, said,—If thou givest me a marriage dower thou shalt have my daughter for thy wife.—

"'Richika said,—What dower, O king, shall I offer thee for the hand of thy daughter? Tell me truly, without feeling any hesitation in the matter.—Gadhi said,—O descendant of Bhrigu, do thou give me a thousand horses fleet as the wind, and possessing the hue of moon-beams, and each having one ear black.—

"Bhishma said,—'Then that mighty son of Chyavana who was the foremost of Bhrigu's race, besought the deity Varuna, the son of Aditi, who was the lord of all the waters.—O best of gods, I pray to thee to give me a thousand horses, all endued with the speed of the wind and with complexion as effulgent as the moon's, but each having one ear black. The god Varuna, the son of Aditi, said to that excellent scion of Bhrigu's race,—Be it so. Wheresoever thou shalt seek, the horses shall arise (in thy presence).—As soon as Richika thought of them, there arose from the waters of Ganga a thousand high-mettled horses, as lustrous in complexion as the moon. Not far from Kanyakuvja, the sacred bank of Ganga is still famous among men as Aswatirtha in consequence of the appearance of those horses at that place. Then Richika, that best of ascetics, pleased in mind, gave those thousand excellent horses unto Gadhi as the marriage-dower. King Gadhi, filled with wander and fearing to be cursed, gave his daughter, bedecked with jewels, unto that son of Bhrigu. That foremost of regenerate Rishis accepted her hand in marriage according to the prescribed rites. The princess too was well-pleased at finding herself the wife of that Brahmana. That foremost of regenerate Rishis, O Bharata, was well pleased with her conduct and expressed a wish to grant her boon. The princess, O excellent king, related this to her mother. The mother addressed the daughter that stood before her with down-cast eyes, saying,—It behoves thee, O my daughter, to secure a favour for me also from thy husband. That sage of austere penances is capable of granting a boon to me,—the boon, viz. of the birth of a son to me.— Then, O king, returning quickly to her husband Richika, the princess related to him all that had been desired by her mother. Richika said,— By my favour, O blessed one, she will soon give birth to a son possessed of every virtue. May thy request be fulfilled. Of thee too shall be born a mighty and glorious son who, endued with virtue, shall perpetuate my race. Truly do I say this unto thee! When you two shall bathe in your season, she shall embrace a pepul tree, and thou, O excellent lady, shalt likewise embrace a fig tree, and by so doing shall ye attain the object of your desire. O sweetly-smiling lady, both she and you shall have to partake of these two sacrificial offerings (*charu*)[1] consecrated with hymns, and then shall ye obtain sons (as desired).—At this, Satyavati, delighted at heart, told her mother all that had been said by Richika as also of the two balls of *charu*. Then the mother, addressing her daughter Satyavati, said:—O daughter, as I am deserving of greater consideration from thee than thy husband, do thou obey my words. The *charu*, duly consecrated with hymns, which thy husband has given to thee, do thou give unto me and thyself take the one that has been prescribed for me. O sweetly-smiling one of blameless character, if thou hast any respect for my word, let us change the trees respectively designed for us. Every one desires to possess an excellent and stainless being for his own son. The glorious Richika too must have acted from a similar motive in this matter, as will appear in the end. For this reason, O beautiful girl, my heart inclines towards thy *charu*, and thy tree, and thou too shouldst consider how to secure an excellent brother for thyself.—The mother and the daughter Satyavati having acted in this way, they both, O Yudhishthira, became big with child. And that great *Rishi*, the excellent descendant of Bhrigu, finding his wife quick with child, was pleased at heart, and addressing her, said,—O excellent lady, thou hast not done well in exchanging the *charu* as will soon become apparent. It is also clear that thou hast changed the trees. I had placed the entire accumulated energy of *Brahma* in thy *charu* and Kshatriya energy in the *charu* of thy mother. I had so ordered that thou wouldst give birth to a Brahmana whose virtues would be famous throughout the three worlds, and that she (thy mother) would give birth to an excellent Kshatriya. But now, O excellent lady, that thou hast reversed the order (of the *charu*) so, thy mother will give birth to an excellent Brahmana and thou too, O excellent lady, wilt give birth to a Kshatriya terrible in action. Thou hast not done well, O lady, by acting thus out of affection for thy mother.—Hearing this, O king the excellent lady Satyavati, struck with sorrow, fell upon the ground like a beautiful creeper cut in twain. Regaining her senses and bowing unto her lord

1. 'Charu' is properly an oblation of rice, barley, and pulse, boiled with butter and milk, for presentation to the gods in a sacrifice or ordinary worship.—T.

with head (bent), the daughter of Gadhi said to her husband, that foremost one of Bhrigu's race,—O regenerate *Rishi*, O thou that art foremost amongst those versed in *Brahma*, do thou take pity on me, thy wife, who is thus appeasing thee and so order that a Kshatriya son may not be born unto me. Let my grandson be such a one as will be famous for his terrible achievements, if it be thy desire, but not my son, O Brahmana. Do thou confer this fovour on me.—Be it so,—said that man of austere penances to his wife and then, O king, she gave birth to a blessed son named Jamadagni. The celebrated wife of Gadhi too gave birth to the regenerate *Rishi* Viswamitra versed in the knowledge of *Brahma*, by favour of that *Rishi*. The highly devout Viswamitra, though a Kshatriya, attained to the state of a Brahmana and became the founder of a race of Brahmanas. His sons became high-souled progenitors of many races of Brahmanas who were devoted to austere penances, learned in the Vedas, and founders, of many clans. The adorable Madhuchcchanda and the mighty Devrat, Akshina, Sakunta, Vabhru, Kalapatha, the celebrated Yajnavalkya, Sthula of high vows, Uluka, Mudgala, and the sage Saindhavayana, the illustrious Valgujangha and the great *Rishi* Galeva, Ruchi, the celebrated Vajra, as also Salankayana, Liladhya and Narada, the one known as Kurchamuka, and Vahuli, Mushala, as also Vakshogriva, Anghrika, Naikadrik, Silayupa, Sita, Suchi, Chakraka, Marrutantavya, Vataghna, Aswalayana, and Syamayana, Gargya, and Javali, as also Susruta, Karishi, Sangsrutya, and Para Paurava, and Tantu, the great sage Kapila, Tarakayana, Upagabana, Asurayani, Margama, Hiranyksha, Janghari, Bhavravayani, and Suti, Bibhuti, Suta, Surakrit, Arani, Nachika, Champeya, Ujjayana, Navatantu, Vakanakha, Sayanya, Yati, Ambhoruha, Amatsyasin, Srishin, Gardhavi, Urjjayoni, Rudapekahin, and the great *Rishi* Naradin,—these *Munis* were all sons of Viswamitra and were versed in the knowledge of *Brahma*. O king Yudhishthira, the highly austere and devout Viswamitra, although a Kshatriya (by descent), became a Brahmana for Richika having placed the energy of supreme *Brahma* (in the *charu*), O foremost prince of Bharata's race, I have now related to you, with all details, the story of the birth of Viswamitra who was possessed of the energy of the sun, the moon, and the fire-god. O best of kings, if thou hast any doubt with regard to any other matter, do thou let me know it, so that I may remove it.

SECTION V

"Yudhishthira said,—'O thou that knowest the truths of religion, I wish to hear of the merits of compassion, and of the characteristics of devout men. Do thou, O sire, describe them to me.'

"Bhishma said.—'In this connection, this ancient legend, the story of Vasava and the high-minded Suka, is cited as an illustration. In the territories of the king of Kasi, a fowler, having poisoned arrows with him went out of his village on a hunting excursion in search of antelopes. Desirous of obtaining meat, when in a big forest in pursuit of the chase, he discovered a drove of antelopes not far from him, and discharged his arrow at one of them. The arrow of that fowler of irresistible arms, discharged for the destruction of the antelope, missed its aim and pierced a mighty forest-tree. The tree, violently pierced with that arrow tipped with virulent poison, withered away, shedding its leaves and fruits. The tree having thus withered a parrot that had lived in a hollow of its trunk all his life, did not leave his nest out of affection for the lord of the forest. Motionless and without food silent and sorrowful, that grateful and virtuous parrot also withered away with the tree. The conqueror of Paka (Indra) was struck with wonder upon finding that high-souled, and generous-hearted bird thus uninfluenced by misery or happiness and possessing extraordinary resolution. Then the thought arose in Sakra's mind,—How could this bird come to possess humane and generous feelings which are impossible in one belonging to the world of lower animals? Perchance, there is nothing wonderful in the matter, for all creatures are seen to evince kindly and generous feelings towards others.—Assuming then the shape of a Brahmana, Sakra descended on the Earth and addressing the bird, said, —O Suka, O best of birds, the grand-daughter (Suki) of Daksha has become blessed (by having thee as her offspring). I ask thee, for what reason dost thou not leave this withered tree?—Thus questioned, the Suka bowed unto him and thus replied:—Welcome to thee O chief of the gods, I have recognised thee by the merit of my austere penances—Well-done, well-done!—exclaimed the thousand-eyed deity. Then the latter praised him in his mind, saying,—O, how wonderful is the knowledge which he possesses.—Although the destroyer of Vala knew that parrot to be of a highly virtuous character and meritorious in action, he still enquired of him about the reason of his affection for the tree. This tree is withered and it is without leaves and fruits and is unfit to be the refuge of birds. Why dost thou then cling to it? This forest, too, is vast and in this wilderness there are numerous other fine trees whose hollows are covered with leaves and which thou canst choose freely and to thy heart's content. O patient one exercising due discrimination in thy wisdom, do thou forsake this old tree that is dead and useless and shorn of all its leaves and no longer capable of any good.—

"Bhishma said.—'The virtuous Suka, hearing these words of Sakra, heaved a deep sigh and sorrowfully replied unto him, saying—O consort of Sachi, and chief of the gods, the ordinances of the deities are always to be obeyed. Do thou listen to the reason of the matter in regard to which thou hast questioned me. Here, within this tree, was I born, and here in this tree have I acquired all the good traits of my character, and here in this tree was I protected in my infancy from the assaults of my enemies. O sinless one, why art thou, in thy kindness, tampering with the principle of my conduct in life ? I am compassionate, and devoutly intent on virtue, and steadfast in conduct. Kindliness of feeling is the great test of virtue amongst the good, and this same compassionate and humane feeling is the source of perennial felicity to the virtuous. All the gods question thee to remove their doubts in religion, and for this reason, O lord, thou hast been placed in sovereignty over them all. It behoves thee not, O thousand-eyed one, to advise me now to abandon this tree for ever. When it was capable of good, it supported my life. How can I forsake it now?—The virtuous destroyer of Paka, pleased with these well-meant words of the parrot, thus said to him :—I am gratified with thy humane and compassionate disposition. Do thou ask a boon of me.—At this, the compassionate parrot craved this boon of him, saying,—Let this tree revive.—Knowing the great attachment of the parrot to that tree and his high character, Indra, well-pleased, caused the tree to be quickly sprinkled over with nectar. Then that tree became replenished and attained to exquisite grandeur through the penances of the parrot, and the latter too, O great king, at the close of his life, obtained the companionship of Sakra by virtue of that act of compassion. Thus, O lord of men, by communion and companionship with the pious, people attain all the objects of their desire even as the tree die through its companionship with the parrot.' "

SECTION VI

"Yudhishthira said,—Tell me, O learned sire that art versed in all the scriptures, of Exertion and Destiny which is the most powerful ?

"Bhishma said,—'This ancient story of the conversation of Vasishtha and Brahma, O Yudhishthira, is an illustration in point. In olden times the adorable Vasishtha enquired of Brahma as to which among these two, *viz.*, the Karma of a creature acquired in this life, or that acquired in previous lives (and called Destiny), is the more potent in shaping his life. Then, O king, the great god Brahma, who had sprung from the primeval lotus, answered him in these exquisite and well-reasoned words, full of meaning.

"Brahma said,—Nothing comes into existence without seed. Without seed, fruits do not grow. From seeds spring other seeds. Hence are fruits known to be generated from seeds. Good or bad as the seed is that the husbandman soweth in his field, good or bad are the fruits that he reaps. As, unsown with seed, the soil, though tilled, becomes fruitless, so, without individual Exertion, Destiny is of no avail. One's own acts are like the soil, and Destiny (or the sum of one's acts in previous births) is compared to the seed. From the union of the soil and the seed doth the harvest grow. It is observed every day in the world that the doer reaps the fruit of his good and evil deeds; that happiness results from good deeds, and pain from evil ones; that acts, when done, always fructify; and that, if not done, no fruit arises. A man of (good) acts acquires merits with good fortune, while an idler falls away from his estate, and reaps evil like the infusion of alkaline matter injected into a wound. By devoted application, one acquires beauty, fortune, and riches of various kind. Everything can be secured by Exertion: but nothing can be gained through Destiny alone, by a man that is wanting in personal Exertion. Even so does one attain to heaven, and all the objects of enjoyment, as also the fulfilment of one's heart's desires, by well-directed individual Exertion. All the luminous bodies in the firmament, all the deities, the *Nagas*, and the *Rakshasas*, as also the Sun and the Moon and the Winds, have attained to their high status by evolution from man's status, through dint of their own action. Riches, friends, prosperity descending from generation to generation, as also the graces of life, are difficult of attainment by those that are wanting in Exertion. The Brahmana attains to prosperity by holy living, the Kshatriya by prowess, the Vaisya by manly exertion, and the Sudra by service. Riches and other objects of enjoyment do not follow the stingy, nor the impotent, nor the idler. Nor are these ever attained by the man that is not active or manly or devoted to the exercise of religious austerities. Even he, the adorable Vishnu, who created the three worlds with the *Daityas* and all the gods, even He is engaged in austere penances in the bosom of the deep. If one's *Karma* bore no fruit, then all actions would become fruitless, and relying on Destiny men would become idlers. He who, without pursuing the human modes of action, follows Destiny only, acts in vain, like unto the woman that has an impotent husband. In this world the apprehension that accrues from performance of good or evil actions is not so great if Destiny be unfavourable as one's apprehension of the same in the other world if Exertion be wanting while here.[1] Man's powers, if properly exerted, only follow his Destiny,

1 The meaning seems to be that if Destiny be unfavourable, there need not be much fear with respect to this world. But if one be wanting in Exertion, great must his fear be with respect to the next world, for happiness can never be obtained in the next world unless one *acts* righteously while here.—T.

but Destiny alone is incapable of conferring any good where Exertion is wanting. When it is seen that even in the celestial regions, the position of the deities themselves is unstable, how would the deities maintain their own position or that of others without proper *Karma*? The deities do not always approve of the good deeds of others in this world, for, apprehending their own overthrow, they try to thwart the acts of others. There is a constant rivalry between the deities and the Rishis, and if they all have to go through their *Karma*, still it can never be averted that there is no such thing as Destiny, for it is the latter that initiates all *Karma*. How does *Karma* originate, if Destiny from the prime spring of human action? (The answer is) that by this means, an accretion of many virtues is made even in the celestial regions. One's own self is one's friend and one's enemy too, as also the witness of one's good and evil deeds. Good and evil manifest themselves through *Karma*. Good and evil acts do not give adequate results. Righteousness is the refuge of the gods, and by righteousness is everything attained. Destiny thwarts not the man that has attained to virtue and righteousness.

In olden times, Yayati, falling from his high estate in heaven, descended on the Earth but was again restored to the celestial regions by the good deeds of his virtuous grandsons. The royal sage Pururavas, celebrated as the descendant of Ila, attained to heaven through the intercession of the Brahmanas. Saudasa, the king of Kosala, though dignified by the performance of *Aswamedha* and other sacrifices, obtained the status of a man-eating *Rakshasa*, through the curse of a great *Rishi*. Aswatthaman and Rama, though both warriors and sons of *Munis*, failed to attain to heaven by reason of their own actions in this world. Vasu, though he performed a hundred sacrifices like a second Vasava, was sent to the nethermost regions, for making a single false statements. Vali, the son of Virochana, righteoulsy bound by his promise, was consigned to the regions under the Earth, by the prowess of Vishnu. Was not Janamejaya, who followed the foot-prints of Sakra, checked and put down by the gods for killing a Brahmana woman. Was not the regenerate *Rishi* Vaisampayana too, who slew a Brahmana in ignorance, and was polluted by the slaughter of a child, put down by the gods? In olden times the royal sage Nriga became transmuted into a lizard. He had made gifts of kine unto the Brahmanas at his great sacrifice, but this availed him not. The royal sage Dhundhumara was overwhelmed with decrepitude even while engaged in performing his sacrifices, and foregoing all the merits thereof, he fell asleep at Girivraja. The Pandavas too regained their lost kingdom, of which they had been deprived by the powerful sons of Dhritarashtra, not through the intercession of the fates, but by recourse to their own valour. Do the *Munis* of rigid vows, and devoted to the practice of austere penances, denounce their curses with the aid of any supernatural power or by the exercise of their own puissance attained by individual acts? All the good which is attained with difficulty in this world if possessed by the wicked, is soon lost to them. Destiny does not help the man that is steeped in spiritual ignorance and avarice. Even as a fire of small proportions, when fanned by the wind, becomes of mighty power, so does Destiny, when joined with individual Exertion, increase greatly (in potentiality). As with the diminution of oil in the lamp its light is extinguished so does the influence of Destiny's lost if one's acts stop. Having obtained vast wealth, and women and all the enjoyments of this world, the man, without action is unable to enjoy them long, but the high-souled man, who is even diligent, is able to find riches buried deep in the Earth and watched over by the fates. The good man who is prodigal (in religious charities and sacrifices) is sought by the gods for his good conduct, the celestial world being better than the world of men, but the house of the miser though abounding in wealth is looked upon by the gods as the house of dead. The man that does not exert himself is never contented in this world nor can Destiny alter the course of a man that has gone wrong. So there is no authority inherent in Destiny. As the pupil follows one's own individual preception, so the Destiny follows Exertion. The affairs in which one's own Exertion is put forth, there only Destiny shows its hand. O best of *Munis*, I have thus described all the merits of individual Exertion, after having always known them in their true significance with the aid of my yogic insight. By the influence of Destiny, and by putting forth individual Exertion, do men attain to heaven. The combined aid of Destiny and Exertion, becomes efficacious.' "

SECTION VII

"Yudhishthira said,—'O the best of Bharata's race and the foremost of great men, I wish to know what the fruits are of good deed. Do thou enlighten me on thts point.'

"Bhishma said,—'I shall tell thee what thou hast asked. Do thou, O Yudhishthira, listen to this which constitutes the secret knowledge of the *Rishis*. Listen to me as I explain what the ends, long coveted, are which are attained by men after death. Whatever actions are performed by particular corporeal beings, the fruits thereof are reaped by the doers while endued with similar corporeal bodies; for example, the fruits of actions done with mind are enjoyed at the time of dreams, and those of actions performed physically are enjoyed in the working state physically. In whatever states creatures perform good or evil deeds, they reap the fruits thereof in similar states of succeeding lives.

No act done with the aid of the five organs of sensual perception, is ever lost. The five sensual organs and the immortal soul which is the sixth, remain its witnesses. One should devote one's eye to the service of the guest and should devote one's heart on the same; one should utter words that are agreeable; one should also follow and worship (one's guest). This is called Panchadakshin Sacrifice, (the sacrifice with five gifts). He who offers good food to the unknown and weary travellers, fatigued by a long journey, attains to great merit. Those that use the sacrificial platform as their only bed obtain commodious mansions and beds (in subsequent births). Those that wear only rags and barks of trees for dress, obtain good apparel and ornaments in next birth. One possessed of penances and having his soul on Yoga, get vehicles and riding animals (as the fruit of their renunciation in this life). The monarch that lies down by the side of the sacrifical fire, attains to vigour and valour. The man who renounces the enjoyment of all delicacies, attains to prosperity, and he that abstains from animal food, obtains children and cattle. He who lies down with his head downwards, or who lives in water, or who lives secluded and alone in the practice of Brahmacharya, attains to all the desired ends. He who offers shelter to a guest and welcomes him with water to wash his feet as also with food, light and bed, attains to the merits of the sacrifice with the five gifts. He who lays himself down on a warrior's bed on the battle-field in the posture of a warrior, goes to those eternal regions where all the object of desire are fulfilled. A man, O king, attains to riches that makes charitable gifts. One secures obedience to one's command by the vow of silence, all the enjoyments of life by practice of austerities, long life by *Brahmacharya*, and beauty, prosperity and freedom from disease by abstaining from injury to other. Sovereignty falls to the lot of those that subsist on fruits and roots only. Residence in heaven is atained by those that live on only leaves of trees. A man, O king, is said to obtain happiness, by abstention from food. By confining one's diet to herbs alone, one becomes possessed of cows. By living on grass one attains to the celestial regions. By foregoing all intercourse with one's wife and making ablutions three times during the day and by inhaling the air only for purposes of subsistence, one obtains the merit of a sacrifice. Heaven is attained by the practice of truth, nobility of birth by sacrifices. The Brahmana of pure practices that subsists on water only, and performs the Agnihotra ceaselessly, and recites the Gayatri, obtains a kingdom. By abstaining food or by regulating it, one attains to residence in heaven. O king, by abstaining from all but the prescribed diet while engaged in sacrifices, and by making pilgrimage for twelve years, one attains to a place better than the abodes reserved for heroes. By reading all the Vedas, one is instantly liberated from misery, and by practising virtue in thought, one attains to the heavenly regions. That man who is able to renounce that intense yearning of the heart for happiness and material enjoyments,—a yearning that is difficult of conquest by the foolish ,and that doth not abate with the abatement of bodily vigour and that clings like a fatal disease unto him,—is able to secure happiness. As the young calf is able to recognise its dam from among a thousand cows, so does the previous acts of a man pursue him (in all his different transformations). As the flowers and fruits of a tree, unurged by visible influences, never miss their proper season, so does Karma done in a previous existence bring about its fruits in proper time. With age, man's hair grows gray ; his teeth become loose ; his eyes and ears too become dim in action ; but the only thing that does not abate is his desire for enjoyments. Prajapati is pleased with those acts that please one's father, and the Earth is pleased with those acts that please one's mother, and Brahma is adored with those acts that please one's preceptor. Virtue is honoured by him who honours these three. The acts of those that despise these three do not avail them.'

Vaisampayana said,—"The princes of Kuru's race became filled with wonder upon listening to this speech of Bhishma. All of them became pleased in mind and overpowered with joy. As Mantras applied with a desire to win victory, or the performance of the *Shoma* sacrifice made without proper gifts, or oblations poured on the fire without proper hymns, become useless and lead to evil consequences, even so sin and evil results flow from falsehood in speech. O prince, I have thus related to thee this doctrine of the fruition of good and evil acts, as narrated by the *Rishis* of old. What else dost thou wish to hear ?"

SECTION VIII

"Yudhishthira said,—'Who are deserving of worship ? Who are they unto whom one may bow ? Who are they, O Bharata, unto whom thou wouldst bend thy head ? Who, again, are they whom thou likest ? Tell me all this, O prince. What is that upon which thy mind dwells when affliction overwhelms thee ? Do thou discourse to me on what is beneficial here, that is, in this region of human beings, as also hereafter.[1]

"Bhishma said.—I like those regenerate persons whose highest wealth is Brahman, whose heaven consists in their knowledge of the soul, and whose penances are constituted by their diligent study of the Vedas. My heart yearns after those in whose race persons, young and old diligently bear the ancestral burthens without languishing under

1 The Commentator explains that 'hitam tad vada' are understood in the last line—T.

them. Brahmanas well-trained in several branches of knowledge, self-controlled, mild-speeched, conversant with the scriptures, well-behaved, possessed of the knowledge of Brahman and righteous in conduct, discourse in respectable assemblies like flights of swans.[1] Auspicious, agreeable, excellent, and well-pronounced are the words, O Yudhishthira, which they utter with a voice as deep as that of the clouds. Fraught with happiness both temporal and spiritual, such words are uttered by them in the courts of monarchs, themselves being received with honour and attention and served with reverence by those rulers of men. Indeed, my heart yearns after them who listen to the words uttered in assemblies or the courts of kings by persons endued with knowledge and all desirable attributes, and are respected by others. My heart, O monarch, always yearns after them who, for the gratification of Brahmanas, O Yudhishthira, give unto them, with devotion, food that is well-cooked and clean and wholesome. It is easy to fight in battle, but not so to make a gift without pride or vanity. In this world, O Yudhishthira, there are brave men and heroes by hundreds. While counting them, he that is a hero in gifts should be regarded as superior, O amiable one, if I had been even a vulgar Brahmana, I would have regarded myself as very great, not to speak of one born in a good Brahmana family endued with righteousness of conduct, and devoted to penances and learning. There is no one, O son of Pandu, in this world that is dearer to me than thou, O chief of Bharata's race, but dearer to me than thou are the Brahmanas. And since, O best of the Kurus, the Brahmanas are very much dearer to me than thou, it is by that truth that I hope to go to all those regions of felicity which have been acquired by my sire Santanu. Neither my sire, nor my sire's sire, nor any one else connected with me by blood, is dearer to me than the Brahmanas. I do not expect any fruit, small or great, from my worship of the Brahmanas (for I worship them as deities because they are deserving of such worship).[2] In consequence of what I have done to the Brahmanas in thought, word, and deed, I do not feel any pain now (even though I am lying on a bed of arrows). People used to call me as one devoted to the Brahmanas. This style of address always pleased me highly. To do good to the Brahmanas is the most sacred of all sacred acts. I behold many regions of beautitude waiting for me that have

---

1 The Commentator explains that the allusion here is to the adage that swans in drinking milk mixed with water always drink the milk leaving out the water. Learned Brahmanas are like swans for in discoursing upon even the topics of the world they select what is good and instructive but reject what is evil and sinful, or, as the Commentator puts it, they know the difference between what is soul and what is not soul—T.

2 'Vrijinam' is explained by the Commentator as 'Sankatam, phalasa iti yavat &c.'—T.

reverentially walked behind the Brahmanas. Very soon shall I repair to those regions for everlasting time, O son. In this world, O Yudhishthira, the duties of women have reference to and depend upon their husbands. To a woman, verily, the husband is the deity and he is the highest end after which she should strive. As the husband is to the wife, even so are the Brahmanas unto Kshatriyas. If there be a Kshatriya of full hundred years of age and a good Brahmana child of only ten years, the latter should be regarded as a father and the former as a son, for among the two, verily, the Brahmana is superior. A woman in the absence of her husband, takes his younger brother for her lord; even so the Earth, not having obtained the Brahmana, made the Kshatriya her lord. The Brahmanas should be protected like sons and worshipped like sires or preceptors. Indeed, O best of the Kurus, they should be waited upon with reverence even as people wait with reverence upon their sacrificial or Homa fires. The Brahmanas are endued with simplicity and righteousness. They are devoted to truth. They are always engaged in the good of every creature. Yet when angry they are like snakes of virulent poison. They should, for these reasons, be always waited upon and served with reverence and humility. One should, O Yudhishtira, always fear these two, viz. Energy and Penances. Both these should be avoided or kept at a distance. The effects of both are speedy. There is this superiority, however, of Penances, viz., that Brahmanas endued with Penances, O monarch, can, if angry, slay the object of their wrath (regardless of the measure of Energy with which that object may be endued). Energy and Penances, each of the largest measure, become neutralised if applied against a Brahmana that has conquered wrath. If the two,—that is, Energy and Penances,—be set against each other, then destruction would overtake both but not destruction without a remnant, for while Energy, applied against Penances, is sure to be destroyed without leaving a remnant. Penances applied against Energy cannot be destroyed completely.[1] As the herdsman, stick in hand, protects the herd, even so should the Kshatriya always pretects the Vedas and the Brahmanas. Indeed, the Kshatriya should protect all righteous Brahmanas even as a sire protects his sons. He should always have his eye upon the house of the Brahmanas for seeing that their means of subsistence may not be wanting.'

---

1 *i.e.*, one should keep oneself aloof from both Energy and Penances, for both these can consume, if troubled or interfered with. By 'Energy' is meant both physical and mental force. It belongs to the Kshatriya as Penances belong to the Brahmana.—T.

SECTION IX

"Yudhisthira said,—O grandsire, O thou of great splendour, what do those men become who, through stupefaction of intellect, do not make gifts unto Brahmanas after having promised to make those gifts? O thou that art the foremost of all righteous persons, do tell me what the duties are in this respect. Indeed, what becomes the end of those wicked wights that do not give after having promised to give.

"Bhishma said,—The person that, after having promised, does not give, be it little or much, has the mortification to see his hopes (in every direction) become fruitless like the hopes of a eunuch in respect of progeny. Whatever good acts such a person does between the day of his birth and that of his death, O Bharata, whatever libations he pours on the sacrificial fire, whatever gifts he makes, O chief of Bharata's race, and whatever penances he performs all become fruitless. They that are conversant with the scriptures declare this as their opinion, arriving at it, O chief of the Bharatas, with the aid of a well-ordered understanding. Persons conversant with the scriptures are also of opinion that such a man may be cleansed by giving away a thousand horses with ears of a dark hue. In this connection is cited the old narrative of the discourse between a jackal and an ape. While both were human beings, O scorcher of foes, they were intimate friends. After death one of them became a jackal and the other an ape. Beholding the jackal one day eating an animal carcase in the midst of a crematorium, the ape, remembering his own and his friend's former birth as human beings, addressed him, saying,—Verily, what terrible sin didst thou perpetrate in thy former birth in consequence of which thou art obliged in this birth to feed in a crematorium upon such repulsive fare as the putrid carcase of an animal?—Thus addressed, the jackal replied unto the ape, saying,—Having promised to give unto a Brahmana I did not make him the gift. It is for that sin, O ape, that I have fallen into this wretched order of existence. It is for that reason that, when hungry, I am obliged to eat such food.—'

"Bhishma continued,—The jackal then, O best of men, addressed the ape and said,—What sin didst thou commit for which thou hast become an ape?

"The ape said,—In my former life I used to appropriate the fruits belonging to Brahmanas. Hence have I become an ape. Hence it is clear that one possessed of intelligence and learning should never appropriate what belongs to Brahmanas. Verily, as one should abstain from this, one should avoid also all disputes with Brahmanas. Having promised, one should certainly make the promised gift unto them.—

"Bhishma continued,—'I heard this, O king, from my preceptor while he was engaged in discoursing upon the subject of Brahmanas. I heard this from that righteous person when he recited the old and sacred declaration on this topic. I heard this from Krishna also, O king, while he was engaged in discoursing, O son of Pandu, upon Brahmanas.[1] The property of a Brahmana should never be appropriated. They should always be let alone. Poor, or miserly, or young in years, they should never be disregarded. The Brahmanas have always taught me this. Having promised to make them a gift, the gift should be made. A superior Brahmana should never be disappointed in the matter of his expectations. A Brahmana, O king, in whom an expectation has been raised, has, O king, been said to be like a blazing fire.[2] That man upon whom a Brahmana with raised expectations casts his eye, is sure, O monarch, to be consumed even as a heap of straw is capable of being consumed by a blazing fire.[3] When the Brahmana, gratified (with honours and gifts) by the king addresses the king in delightful and affectionate words, he becomes, O Bharata, a source of great benefit to the king, for he continues to live in the kingdom like a physician combating against diverse ills of the body.[4] Such a Brahmana is sure to maintain by his puissance and good wishes, the sons and grandsons and animals and relatives and ministers and other officers and the city and the provinces of the king.[5] Even such is the energy, so great, of the Brahmana like unto that of the thousand-rayed Surya himself, on the Earth. Therefore, O Yudhishthira, if one wishes to attain to a respectable or happy order of being in one's next birth, one should, having passed the promise to a Brahmana, certainly keep it by actually making the gift to him. By making gifts to a Brahmana one is sure to attain to the highest heaven. Verily, the making of gifts is the highest of acts that one can achieve. By the gifts one makes to a Brahmana, the deities and the pitris are supported. Hence one possessed of knowledge should ever make gifts unto the Brahmanas. O chief of the Bharatas, the Brahmana is regarded as the highest object unto whom gifts should be made. At no time should a Brahmana be received without being properly worshipped."

---

1 The Commentator thinks that by Krishna, the Island-born Krishna or Vyasa is meant.--T.

2 The sense is that such a Brahmana, if his expectation be not gratified, is competent to consume the person that has falsely raised that expectation.—T.

3 'Akshyayyam' is fire, because it is fire that eats the food offered to the Pitris and makes it inexhaustible.—T.

4 The sense is that as a physician cures diverse ailments of the body, after the same manner, a gratified Brahmana cures diverse faults of the kingdom in which he continues to live honoured and gratified by the king.-T.

5 'Santirishta' is the 'rishti' or benefits caused by 'santi.' The Commentator cites *Medini* for explaining that 'rishti' is 'kshema.'—T.

SECTION X

"Yudhisthira said,—'I wish to know, O royal sage, whether any fault is incurred by one who from interested or disinterested friendship imparts instructions unto a person belonging to a low order of birth!' O grandsire, I desire to hear this, expounded to me in detail. The course of duty is exceedingly subtile. Men are often seen to be stupefied in respect of that course.'

"Bhishma said,—In this connection, O king, I shall recite to thee, in due order, what I heard certain Rishis say in days of yore. Instruction should not be imparted unto one that belongs to a low or mean caste. It is said that the preceptor who imparts instruction to such a person incurs great fault. Listen to me, O chief of Bharata's race, as I recite to thee, O Yudhishthira, this instance that occurred in days of old, O monarch, of the evil consequences of the imparting of instruction unto a low-born person fallen into distress. The incident which I shall relate occurred in the asylum of certain regenerate sages that stood on the auspicious breast of Himavat. There, on the breast of that prince of mountains, was a sacred asylum adorned with trees of diverse kinds. Overgrown also with diverse species of creepers and plants, it was the resort of many animals and birds. Inhabited by Siddhas and Charanas also, it was exceedingly delightful in consequence of the woods that flowered there at every season. Many were the Brahmacharins that dwelt there, and many belonging to the forest mode of life. Many also were the Brahmanas that took up their residence there, that were highly blessed and that resembled the sun or the fire in energy and effulgence. Ascetics of diverse kinds, observant of various restraints and vows, as also others, O chief of the Bharatas, that had undergone *Diksha* and were frugal in fare and possessed of cleansed souls, took up their residence there. Large numbers of Valakhilyas and many that were observant of the vow of Sanyasa also, used to dwell there. The asylum, in consequence of all this, resounded with the chanting of the Vedas and the sacred Mantras uttered by its inhabitants. Once upon a time a Sudra endued with compassion for all creatures, ventured to come into that asylum. Arrived at that retreat, he was duly honoured by all the ascetics. Beholding those ascetics of diverse classes that were endued with great energy, that resembled the deities (in purity and power), and that were observing diverse kinds of *Diksha*, O Bharata, the Sudra became highly pleased at heart. Beholding everything, O chief of Bharata's race, the Sudra felt inclined to devote himself to the practice of penances. Touching the feet of the Kulapati (the head man of the group), O Bharata, he addressed him saying.[1]—Through thy grace, O foremost of regenerate persons, I desire, to learn (and practise) the duties of religion. It behoveth thee, O illustrious one, to discourse to me on those duties ahd introduce me (by performing the rites of initiation) into a life of Renunciation. I am certainly inferior in colour, O illustrious one, for I am by caste a Sudra, O best of men. I desire to wait upon and serve you here. Be gratified with me that humbly seek thy shelter.—

"The Kulapati said,—It is impossible that a Sudra should live here adopting the marks specially intended for those practising lives of Renunciation. If it pleases thee, thou mayest stay here, engaged in waiting upon and serving us. Without doubt, by such service thou shalt attain to many regions of high felicity.—

"Bhishma continued,—'Thus addressed by the ascetic, the Sudra began to reflect in his mind, O king, saying,—How should I now act? Great is my reverence for those religious duties that lead to merit. Let this, however, be settled, that I shall do what would be for my benefit.'[2] Proceeding to a spot that was distant from that asylum, he made a hut of the twigs and leaves of trees.—Erecting also a sacrificial platform, and making a little space for his sleep, and some platforms for the use of the deities, he began, O chief of the Bharatas, to lead a life regulated by rigid observances and vows and to practise penances, abstaining entirely from speech all the while. He began to perform ablutions thrice a day, observe other vows (in respect of food and sleep), make sacrifices to the deities, pour libations on the sacrificial fire, and adore and worship the deities in this way. Restraining all carnal desires, living abstemiously upon fruits and roots, controlling all his senses, he daily welcomed and entertained all that came to his retreat as guests, offering them herbs and fruits that grew plentifully around. In this way he passed a very long time in that hermitage of his.[3] One day an ascetic came to that Sudra's retreat for the purpose of making his acquaintance. The Sudra welcomed and worshipped the Rishi with due rites, and gratified him highly. Endued with great energy, and possessed of a righteous soul, that Rishi of rigid vows conversed with his host on many agreeable subjects and informed him of the place whence he had

---

1 'Tapasye' is 'Tapah karishye.' There being no indirect narration in Sanskrit, such forms cannot be helped. A Kulapati is an ascetic that owns ten thousand ascetics for his disciples, Kanwa, the foster-father of Sakuntala, was a Kulapati.—

2 *i.e.* renouncing service which is the duty ordained for person of his order, he desired to betake himself to universal Renunciation or Sanyasa, without, however, the *lingam* or marks of that vow.—T.

3 'Sankalpa-niyamopetah' means 'Sankalpasya nigraha, of 'chitra-vritti nirodha'; 'tena upetah.'—T.

come. In this way, O chief of the Bharatas, that Rishi, O best of men, came into the asylum of the Sudra times out of number for the object of seeing him. On one of these occasions, the Sudra, O king, addressing the Rishi said,—I desire to perform the rites that are ordained for the Pitris. Do thou instruct me kindly in this matter.—Very well,—the Brahmana said in reply unto him, O monarch. The Sudra then, purifying himself by a bath, brought water for the Rishi to wash his feet, and he also brought some Kusa grass, and wild herbs and fruits, and a sacred seat, and the seat called Vrishi. The Vrishi, however, was placed by the Sudra towards the south, with his head turned to the west. Beholding, this and knowing that it was against the ordinance, the Rishi addressed the Sudra, saying,—Place the Vrishi with its head turned towards the East, and having purified thyself, do thou sit with thy face turned towards the north—The Sudra did everything as the Rishi directed. Possessed of great intelligence, and observant of righteousness, the Sudra received every direction, about the Sraddha, as laid down in the ordinance, from that Rishi endued with penances regarding the manner of spreading the Kusa grass, and placing the Arghyas, and as regards the rites to be observed in the matter of the libations to be poured and the food to be offered. After the rites in honour of the Pitris had been accomplished, the Rishi, was dismissed by the Sudra, whereupon he returned to his own abode.[1] After a long time, the whole of which he passed in the practice of such penances and vows, the Sudra ascetic met with his death in those woods. In consequence of the merit he acquired by those practices, the Sudra in his next life, took birth in the family of a great king, and in course of time became possessed of great splendour. The regenerate Rishi also, when the time came, paid his debt in Nature. In his next life, O chief of Bharata's race, he took birth in the family of a priest. It was in this way that those two, *viz*, that Sudra who had passed a life of penances and that regenerate Rishi who had in kindness given the former some instructions in the matter of the rites performed in honour of the Pitris, became reborn, the one as scion of a royal race and the other as the member of a priestly family. Both of them began to grow and both acquired great knowledge in the usual branches of study. The Brahmana became well versed in the Vedas as also in the

1 No Brahmana, the scriptures declare, should ever assist a Sudra in the performance of his religious or Pitri rites. Those Brahmanas that violate this injunction fall away from their superior position. They are condemned as 'Sudra-yajins.' Here the Rishi, by only giving directions to the Sudra as to how the Pitri rites were to be performed, became a 'Sudra-yajin. There are many families to this day whose status has been lowered in consequence of such or similar acts of indiscretion on the part of their ancestors.—T.

Atharvans.[1] In the matter, again of all sacrifices ordained in the Sutras, of that Vedanga which deals with religious rites and observances, astrology and astronomy the reborn Rishi attained great excellence. In the Sankhya philosophy too he began to take great delight. Meanwhile, the reborn Sudra who had become a prince, when his father, the king died, performed his last rites ; and after he had purified himself by accomplishing all the obsequial ceremonies, he was installed by the subjects of his father as their king on his paternal throne. But soon after his own installation as king, he installed the reborn Rishi as his priest. Indeed, having made the Brahmana his priest, the king began to pass his days in great happiness. He ruled his kingdom righteously and protected and cherished all his subjects. Everyday, however, the king on the occasion of receiving benedictions from his priest as also of the performance of religious and other sacred rites, smiled or laughed at him loudly. In this way, O monarch, the reborn Sudra who had become a king, laughed at sight of his priest on numberless occasions.[2] The priest, marking that the king always smiled or laughed whenever he happened to cast his eyes on him, became angry. On one occasion he met the king in a place where there was nobody else. He pleased the king by agreeable discourse. Taking advantage of that moment, O chief of Bharata's race, the priest addressed the king, saying,—O thou of great splendour, I pray thee to grant me a single boon.—

"The king said,—O best of regenerate persons, I am ready to grant thee a hundred of boons, what dost thou say then of one only ? From the affection I bear thee and the reverence in which I hold thee, there is nothing that I cannot give thee.—

"The priest said,—I desire to have only one boon, O king, thou hast been pleased with me. Swear that thou wouldst tell me the truth instead of any untruth.—

"Bhishma continued,—Thus addressed by the priest, O Yudhishthira, the king said unto him—So be it. If what thou wouldst ask me be known to me, I shall certainly tell thee truly. If on the other hand, the matter be unknown to me, I shall not say anything.—

"The priest said,—Every day, on occasions of obtaining my benedictions, when, again, I am engaged in the performance of religious rites

1 'Atharva Veda Veda cha' implies that the Atharvans were not generally included under the term 'Veda' by which the first three Vedas only were meant.—

2 'Punyaha-vachana' is a peculiar rite. The priest or some other Brahmana is invited. Gifts are then made to him, and he utters benedictions in return upon the giver. Yudhishthira used to invite every day a large number of Brahmanas and make them very valuable presents for obtaining their benedictions.—T.

on thy behalf, on occasions also of the *Homa* and other rites of propitiation, why is it that thou laughest upon beholding me? Seeing thee laugh at me on all occasions, my mind shrinks with shame. I have caused thee to swear, O king, that thou wouldst answer me truly. It does not behove thee to say what is untrue. There must be some grave reason for thy behaviour. Thy laughter cannot be causeless. Great is my curiosity to know the reason. Do thou speak truly unto me.—

" 'The king said,—When thou hast addressed me in this strain, O regenerate one, I am bound to enlighten thee, even if the matter be one that should not be divulged in thy hearing. I must tell thee the truth. Do thou listen to me with close attention, O regenerate one. Listen to me, O foremost of twice-born persons, as I disclose to thee what happened (to us) in our former births. I remember that birth. Do thou listen to me with concentrated mind. In my former life I was a Sudra employed in the practice of severe penances. Thou, O best of regenerate persons, wert a Rishi of austere penances. O sinless one, gratified with me, and impelled by the desire of doing me good, thou, O Brahmana, wert pleased to give me certain instructions in the rites I performed (on one occasion) in honour of my Pitris. The instructions thou gavest me were in respect of the manner of spreading the Vrishi and the Kusa blades and of offering libations and meat and other food to the manes, O foremost of ascetics. In consequence of this transgression of thine thou hast taken birth as a priest, and I have taken birth as a king, O foremost of Brahmanas. Behold the vicissitudes that Time brings about. Thou hast reaped this fruit in consequence of thy having instructed me (in my former birth). It is for this reason, O Brahmana, that I smile at sight of thee, O foremost of regenerate persons. I do not certainly laugh at thee from desire of disregarding thee. Thou art my preceptor.[1] At this change of condition I am really very sorry. My heart burns at the thought. I remember our former births, hence do I laugh at sight of thee. Thy austere penances were all destoyed by the instructions thou gavest me. Relinquishing thy present office of priest, do thou endeavour to regain a superior birth. Do thou exert so that thou mayst not obtain in thy next life a birth meaner than thy present one. Take as much wealth as thou wishest, O learned Brahmana, and cleanse thy soul, O best of men.—

"Bhishma continued,—'Dismissed by the king (from the office of priest), the Brahmana made many gifts, unto persons of his own order, of wealth and land and villages. He observed many rigid and severe vows as laid down by the foremost of Brahmanas. He sojourned to many

1 Or rather, superior. 'Guru' is used to denote any senior as well as preceptor.—T.

sacred waters and made many gifts unto Brahmanas in those places. Making gifts of kine unto persons of the regenerate order; his soul became cleansed and he succeeded in acquiring a knowledge of it. Repairing to that very asylum whither he had lived in his former birth, he practised very severe penances. As the consequence of all this, O foremost of kings, that Brahmana succeeded in attaining to the highest success. He became an object of veneration with all the ascetics that dwelt in that asylum. In this way, O best of monarchs, that regenerate Rishi fell into great distress. Unto Sudras, therefore, the Brahmanas should never give instructions. Hence, O king, the Brahmana should avoid imparting [instructions (to such as are low-born), for it was by imparting instruction to a low-born person a Brahmana came to grief. O best of kings, the Brahmana should never desire to obtain instruction from, or impart instruction to, a person that belongs to the lowest order. Brahmanas and Kshatriyas and Vaisyas, the three orders, are regarded as twice-born. By imparting instruction unto these, a Brahmana does not incur any fault. They, therefore, that are good, should never discourse on any subject, for imparting any instruction, before persons of the inferior order. The course of morality is exceedingly subtile and incapable of being comprehended by persons of uncleansed souls. It is for this reason that ascetics adopt the vow of silence, and being respected by all, pass through Diksha (initiation) without indulging in speech.[1] For fear of saying what is incorrect or what may offend, ascetics often forego speech itself. Even men that are righteous and possessed of every accomplishment, and endued with truth and simplicity of behaviour, have been known to incur great fault in consequence of words spoken improperly. Instruction should never be imparted on anything unto any person. If in consequence of the instructions imparted, the instructed commit any sin, that sin, attaches to the Brahmana who imparted the instruction. The man of wisdom, therefore, that desires to earn merit, should always act with wisdom. That instruction which is imparted in barter for money always pollutes the instructor.[2] Solicited by others, one should say only what is correct after settling it with the aid of reflection. One should impart instruction in such a way that one may, by imparting it, earn meric. I have thus told thee everything respecting the subject of instructions. Very often persons become plunged into great afflictions in consequence of imparting instructions. Hence it is meet that one should abstain from giving instruction unto others.' "

---

1 The 'Diksha' is that rite which one passes through by way of preparation for those sacrifices and vows that one seeks to perform.—

2 'Satyanrite' is equivalent to trade or barter.—T,

SECTION XI

Yudhishthira said,—Tell me, O grandsire, in what kind of man or woman, O chief of the Bharatas, does the goddess of prosperity always reside ?'

"Bhishma said.—'I shall, in this connection, narrate to thee what occurred and what I have heard. Once on a time, beholding the goddess of prosperity blazing with beauty and endued with the complexion of the lotus, the princess Rukmini the mother of Pradyumna that bore the device of the *Makara* on his banner, filled with curiosity, asked this question in the presence of Devaki's son.—Who are those beings by whose side thou stayest and whom thou favoures ? Who again, are those whom thou dost not bless with favour. O thou that art dear unto Him that is the lord of all creatures, tell me this truly, O thou that art equal to a great Rishi in penances and puissance. Thus addressed by the princess, the goddess of prosperity, with a face as beautiful as the moon, and moved by grace, in the presence of him who has Gadura on his banner, said these words in reply that were sweet and charming.

" 'Sree said,—O blessed lady, I always reside with him that is eloquent, active, attentive to business, free from wrath, given to the worship of the deities, endued with gratitude, has his passions under complete control, and is high-minded in every thing. I never reside with one that is inattentive to business, that is an unbeliever, that causes an intermixture of races in consequence of his lustfulness, that is ungrateful, that is of impure practices, that uses harsh and cruel words, that is a thief, that cherishes malice towards his preceptors and other seniors, those persons that are endued with little energy, strength, life, and honour, that are distressed at every trifle, and that always indulge in wrath. I never reside with these that think in one strain and act in a different one.[1] I never reside also with him who never desires any acquisition for himself, of him who is so blinded as to rest content with the lot in which he finds himself without any exertion or with those that are contented with small acquisitions. I reside with those that are observant of the duties of their own order, or those that are conversant with the duties of righteousness, or those that are devoted to the service of the aged or those that have their passions under control, or those that are endued with cleansed souls, or those that observe the virtue of forgiveness, or those that are able and prompt in action, or with such women as are forgiving and self-restrained. I reside with those women also that are devoted to truth and sincerity and that worship the deities.

1 'Sanguptamanoratheshu' is explained by the Commentator as persons who conceal their real sentiments by acting differently from what they think flowers. The reference is to hypocrites.—T.

I do not reside with those women also that do not attend to household furniture and provisions scattered all around the house, and that always utter words contrary to the wishes of their husbands. I always avoid those women that are fond of the houses of other people and that have no modesty. On the other hand, I reside with those women that are devoted to their husbands, that are blessed in behaviour, and that are always decked in ornaments and attired in good robes. I always reside with those women that are truthful in speech, that are of handsome and agreeable features, that are blessed and that are endued with all accomplishments. I always avoid such women as are sinful and unclean or impure, as always lick the corners of their mouths, as have no patience or fortitude, and as are fond of dispute and quarreling, as are given to much sleep, and as always lie down. I always reside in conveyances and the animals that drag them, in maidens, in ornaments and good vestments, in sacrifices, in clouds charged with rain, in full-blown lotuses, and in those stars that bespangle the autumnal firmament. I reside in elephants, in the cow pen, in good seats, and in lakes adorned with full-blown lotuses. I live also in such rivers as babble sweetly in their course, melodious with the music of cranes, having banks adorned with rows of diverse trees, and resorted to by Brahmanas and ascetics and others crowned with success. I always reside in those rivers also that have deep and large volumes of rolling waters rendered turbid by lions and elephants plunging into them for bathing or slaking their thirst. I reside also in infuriate elephants, in bovine bulls, in kings, on the throne and good men. I always reside in that house in which the inmate pours libation on the sacrificial fire and worships kine, Brahmanas and the deities. I reside in that house where at the proper time offerings are made unto the deities, in course of worship.[1] I always reside in such Brahmanas as are devoted to the study of the Vedas, in Kshatriyas devoted to the observance of righteousness, in Vaisyas devoted to cultivation, and the Sudras devoted to the (menial) service of the three upper classess. I reside, with a heart firm and unchangeable, in Narayana, in my embodied self. In Him is righteousnes in its perfection and full measure, devotion to the Brahmanas, and the quality of agreeableness. Can I not say, O lady that I do not reside in my embodied form, (in any of these places that I have mentioned, except Narayana)? That person in whom I reside in spirit increases in righteousness and fame and wealth and objects of desire.—

---

1 'Vali' (sing. of 'valayah') means anything offered or dedicated to the deities. The sense of the second line is that the goddess of prosperity resides in that house in which flowers are offered to the deities instead of animal life.

SECTION XII

"Yudhishthira said,—'It behoveth, O king to tell me truly which of the two *viz.*, man or woman derives the greater pleasure from an act of union with each other. Kindly resolve my doubt in this respect.'

"Bhishma said,—'In this connection is cited this old narrative of the discourse between Bhangaswana and Sakra as a precedent illustrating the question. In days of yore there lived a king of the name of Bhangaswana. He was exceedingly righteous and was known as a royal sage. He was, however, childless, O chief of man, and therefore performed a sacrifice from desire of obtaining an issue. The sacrifice which that mighty monarch performed was the *Agnishtuta*. In consequence of the fact that the deity of fire is alone adored in that sacrifice, this is always disliked by Indra. Yet it is the sacrifice that is desired by men when for the purpose of obtaining an issue they seek to cleanse themselves of their sins.[1] The highly blessed chief of the celestials, *viz.* Indra, learning that the monarch was desirous of performing the *Agnishtuta*, began from that moment to look for the *laches* of that royal sage of well-restrained soul (for if he could succeed in finding some *laches*, he could then punish his disregarder). Notwithstanding all his vigilance, however, O king, Indra failed to detect any *laches*, on the part of the high-souled monarch. Some time after, one day, the king went on a hunting expedition. Saying unto himself—This, indeed, is an opportunity,—Indra stupefied the monarrch. The king proceeded alone on his horse, confounded because of the chief of the celestials having stupefied his senses. Afflicted with hunger and thirst, the king's confusion was so great that he could not ascertain the points of the compass. Indeed, afflicted with thirst, he began to wonder hither and thither. He then beheld a lake that was exceedingly beautiful and was full of transparent water. Alighting from his steed, and plunging into the lake, he caused his animal to drink. Tying his horse then, whose thirst had been slaked, to a tree, the king plunged into the lake again for performing his ablutions. To his amazement he found that he was changed, by virtue of the waters, into a woman. Beholding himself thus transformed in respect of sex itself, the king became overpowered with shame. With his senses and mind completely agitated, he began to reflect with his whole heart in this strain:—Alas, how shall I ride my steed? How shall I return to my capital? In consequence of the *Agnishtuta* sacrifice I have got a hundred sons all endued with

---

1 The belief is that a man remains childless in consequence of his sins. If these sins can be washed away, he may be sure to obtain children.—T.

great might, and all children of my own loins. Alas, thus transformed, what shall I say unto them? What shall I say unto my spouses, my relatives and well-wishers, and my subjects of the city and the provinces? Rishis conversant with the truths of duty and religion and other matters say that mildness and softness and liability to extreme agitation are the attributes of women, and that activity, hardness, and energy are the attributes of men. Alas, my manliness has disappeared. For what reason has femininity come over me? In consequence of this transformation of sex, how shall I succeed in mounting my horse again? —Having indulged in these sad thoughts, the monarch, with great exertion, mounted his steed and came back to his capital, transformed though he had been into woman. His sons and spouses and servants, and his subjects of the city and the provinces, beholding that extraordinary transformation, became exceedingly amazed. Then that royal sage, that foremost of eloquent men, addressing them all, said,—I had gone out on a hunting expedition, accompanied by a large force. Losing all knowledge of the points of the compass, I entered a thick and terrible forest, impelled by the fates. In that terrible forest, I became afflicated with thirst and lost my senses. I then beheld a beautiful lake abounding with fowl of every description. Plunging into that stream for performing my ablutions, I was transformed into a woman!—Summoning then his spouses and counsellers, and all his sons by their names, that best of monarchs transformed into a woman said unto them these words:—Do ye enjoy this kingdom in happiness. As regards myself, I shall repair to the woods, ye sons.—Having said so unto his children, the monarch proceeded to the forest. Arrived there, she came upon an asylum inhabited by an ascetic. By that ascetic the transformed monarch gave birth to a century of sons. Taking all those children of hers, she repaired to where her former children were, and addressing the latter, said,—Ye are the children of my loins while I was a man. These are my children brought forth by me in this state of transformation. Ye sons, do ye all enjoy my kingdom together, like brothers born of the same parents.—At this command of their parent, all the brothers, uniting together, began to enjoy the kingdom as their joint property. Beholding those children of the king all jointly enjoying the kingdom as brothers born of the same parents, the chief of the celestials, filled with wrath, began to reflect,—By transforming this royal sage into a woman I have, it seems, done him good instead of an injury.—Saying this, the chief of the celestials *viz.*, Indra of a hundred sacrifices, assuming the form of a Brahmana, repaired to the capital of the king and meeting all the children succeeded in disuniting the princes. He said unto them —Brothers never remain at peace even when they happen to be the children of the same father. The sons of the sage Kasyapa, *viz.*, the deities and the Asuras, quarrelled with each other on account of the sovereignty of the three worlds. As regards ye princes, ye are the children of the royal sage Bhangaswana. These others are the children of an ascetic. The deities and the Asuras are children of even one common sire, (and yet the latter quarrelled with each other. How much more, therefore, should *you* quarrel with each other)? This kingdom that is your paternal property is being enjoyed by these children of an ascetic. With these words, Indra succeeded in causing a breach between them, so that they were very soon engaged in battle and slew each other. Hearing this, king Bhangaswana, who was living as an ascetic woman, burnt with grief and poured forth her lamentations. The lord of the celestials *viz.* Indra, assuming the guise of a Brahmana, came to that spot where the ascetic lady was, living and meeting her, said,—O thou that art possessed of a beautiful face, with what grief dost thou burn so that thou art pouring forth thy lamentaions?—Beholding the Brahmana the lady told him in a piteous voice,—Two hundred sons of mine O regenerate one, have been slain by Time. I was formerly a king, O learned Brahmana and in that state had a hundred sons. These were begotten by me after my own form, O best of regenerate persons. On one occasion I went on a hunting expedition. Stupefied, I wandered amidst a thick forest. Beholding at last a lake, I plunged into it. Rising, O foremost of Brahmanas, I found that I had become a woman. Returning to my capital I installed my sons in the sovereignty of my dominions and then departed for the forest. Transformed into a woman, I bore a hundred sons to my husband who is a high souled ascetic. All of them were born in the ascetic's retreat. I took them to the capital. My children, through the influence of Time, quarrelled with each other, O twice-born one. Thus afflicted by Destiny, I am indulging in grief,—Indra addressed him in these harsh words.—In former days, O lady, thou gavest me great pain, for thou didst perform a sacrifice that is disliked by Indra. Indeed, though I was present, thou didst not invoke me with honours. I am that Indra, O thou of wicked understanding. It is I with whom thou hast purposely sought hostilities. Beholding Indra, the royal sage fell at his feet, touching them with his head, and said,—Be gratified with me, O foremost of deities. The sacrifice of which thou speakest was performed from desire of offspring (and not from any wish to hurt thee). It behoveth thee therefore, to grant me thy pardon.—Indra, seeing the transformed monarch prostrate himself thus unto him, became gratified with him and desired to give him a boon. Which of your sons, O king, dost thou wish, should revive, those that were brought forth by thee transformed into a woman, or those that were begotten by thee in thy condition as a person of the male sex ?—The ascetic lady, joining her hands, answered Indra, saying,—O Vasava, let those sons of mine come to life that were borne by me as a woman.—Filled with wonder at this reply, Indra once more asked the lady.—Why dost thou entertain less affection for those children of thine that were begotten by thee in thy form of a person of the male sex? Why is it that thou bearest greater affection for those children that were borne by thee in thy transformed state ? I wish to hear the reason of this difference in respect of thy affection. It behoveth thee to tell me everything.—

" 'The lady said,—The affection that is entertained by a woman is much greater than that which is entertained by a man. Hence, it is, O Sakra, that I wish those children to come back to life that were borne by me as a woman.—'

"Bhishma continued,—Thus addressed, Indra became highly pleased and said unto her,—O lady that art so truthful, let all thy children come back into life. Do thou take another boon, O foremost of kings, —in fact, whatever boon thou likest. O thou of excellent vows, do thou take from me whatever status thou choosest, that of woman or of man.—

" 'The lady said,—I desire to remain a woman, O Sakra. In fact, I do not wish to be restored to the status of manhood, O Vasava.—Hearing this answer, Indra once more asked her, saying,—Why is it, O puissant one, that abandoning the status of manhood thou wishest that of womanhood ?—Questioned thus, that foremost of monarchs transformed into a woman answered,—In acts of congress, the pleasure that women enjoy is always much greater than what is enjoyed by men. It is for this reason, O Sakra, that I desire to continue a woman; O foremost of the deities, truly do I say unto thee that I derive greater pleasure in my present status of womanhood. I am quite content with this status of womanhood that I now have. Do thou leave me now, O lord of heaven.—Hearing these words of hers, the lord of the celestials answered,—So be it,—and bidding her farewell, proceeded to heaven. Thus, O monarch, it is known that woman derives much greater pleasure than men under the cricumstances thou hast asked.

SECTION XIII

"Yudhishthira said,—'What should a man do in order to pass pleasantly through this and the other world. How, indeed, should one conduct oneself ? What practices should one adopt with this end in view ?'

"Bhishma said,—'One should avoid the three acts that are done with the body, the four that are done with speech, the three that are done with the mind, and the ten paths of action. The three acts that are done with the body and should be wholly avoided are the destruction of the lives of other creatures, theft or appropriation of what belongs to other persons, and the enjoyment of other people's wives. The four acts that are done with speech, O king, and that should never be indulged in or even thought of, are evil conversation, harsh words, publishing other people's faults, and falsehood. Coveting the possessions of others, doing injury to others, and disbelief in the ordinances of the Vedas, are the three acts done with the mind which should always be avoided.[1] Hence, one should never do any evil act in word, body, or mind. By doing good and evil acts, one is sure to enjoy or endure the just consequences thereof. Nothing can be more certain than this.' "

SECTION XIV

Yudhishthira said,—'O son of the River Ganga, thou hast heard all the names of Maheswara, the Lord of the universe. Do thou tell us, O grandsire, all the names that are applied, O puissant one, unto Him who is called Isa and Sambhu. Do thou tell us all those names that are applied unto Him who is called Vabhru or vast, Him that has the universe for his form, Him that is the illustrious preceptor of all the deities and the Asuras, that is called Swayambhu (self-creating) and that is the cause of the origin and dissolution of the universe. Do thou tell us also of the puissance Mahadeva.

"Bhishma said,—'I am quite incompetent to recite the virtues of Mahadeva of highest intelligence. He pervades all things in the universe and yet is not seen anywhere. He is the creator of universal self and the Pragna (knowing) self and he is their master. All the deities, from Brahman to the Pisachas, adore and worship him. He transcends both Prakriti and Purusha. It is of Him that Rishis, conversant with Yoga and possessing a knowledge of the tattwas, think and reflect. He is indestructible and Supreme *Brahma*. He is both existent and nonexistent. Agitating both Prakriti and Purusha by means of His energy, He created therefrom the universal lord of creatures, viz., Brahma. Who is there that is competent to tell the virtues of that god of gods, that is endued with supreme Intelligence? Man is

1 I give, in the affirmative form of speech, the three mental acts that are directed to be avoided. In the original, these are given in the negative form. Absence of coveting the possessions of others is the act that is directed to be followed. So compassion for all creatures is prescribed; and, lastly, the belief is directed to be entertained that acts have fruits, for the Vedas declare as such. He that does not believe that acts have fruits disbelieve the very Vedas which of course, is a sinful act.—T.

subject to conception (in the mother's womb), birth, decrepitude, and death. Being such, what man like me is competent to understand Bhava? Only Narayana, O son, that bearer of the discus and the mace, can comprehend Mahadeva. He is with deterioration. He is the foremost of all beings in attributes. He is Vishnu, because of his pervading the universe. He is irresistible. Endued with spiritual vision, He is possessed of supreme Energy. He sees all things with the eye of Yoga. It is in consequence of the devotion of the high-souled Krishna to the illustrious Rudra whom he gratified, O Bharata, in the retreat of Vadari, by penances, that he has succeeded in pervading the entire universe. O king of kings, it is through Maheswara of celestial vision that Vasudeva has obtained the attribute of universal agreeableness,—an agreeableness that is much greater than what is possessed by all articles included under the name of wealth.[1] For a full thousand years this Madhava underwent the austerest penances and at last suceeded in gratifying the illustrious and boon giving Siva, that Master of all the mobile and the immobile universe. In every new Yuga has Krishna (by such penances) gratified Mahadeva. In every Yuga has Mahadeva been gratified with the great devotion of the high-souled Krishna. How great is the puissance of the high-souled Mahadeva,—that original cause of the universe,—has been seen with his own eyes by Hari who himself transcends all deterioration, on the occasion of his penances in the retreat of Vadari undergone for obtaining a son.[2] I do not, O Bharata, behold any one that is superior to Mahadeva. To expound the names of that god of gods fully and without creating the desire of hearing more only Krishna is competent. This mighty-armed one of Yadu's race is alone competent to tell the attributes of the illustrious Siva. Verily, O king, only he is able to discourse on the puissance, in its entirety of the Supreme deity?

Vaisampayana continued,—"Having said these words, the illustrious Bhishma, the grandsire of the Kurus, addressing Vasudeva, said the following words, dealing with the subject of the greatness of Bhava, O monarch.

---

1 The sense is this: wealth is always agreeable to all persons but Vasudeva is more agreeable than wealth. This attribute of being more agreeable than wealth itself,—that is being agreeable to all the universe,—is due to the favour of Mahadeva. The Commentator explains it in an esoteric sense, coming to the conclusion that 'arthat priyataratwancha' means 'the attribute of becoming the Soul of all things in the universe.—T.

2 The allusion is to Krishna's penances for gratifying Mahadeva in order to obtain a son. The son so obtained,—that is, as a boon from Mahadeva, was Pradyumna begotten by Krishna upon Rukmini, his favourite spouse.—T.

"Bhishma said,—'Thou art the Master of all the deities and the Asuras. Thou art illustrious. Thou art Vishnu in consequence of thy pervading the whole universe. It behoveth thee to discourse on those subjects connected with Siva of universal form about which Yudhishthira has asked me. In days of yore, the Rishi Tandin, sprung from Brahma, recited in Brahma's region and before Brahma himself the thousand names of Mahadeva. Do thou recite those names before this conclave so that these Rishis endued with wealth of asceticism, observant of high vows, possessed of self-restraint, and numbering the Island-born Krishna among them, may hear thee. Do thou discourse on the high blessedness of Him who is immutable, who is always cheerful and happy, who is Hotri, who is the universal Protector, who is Creator of the universe, and who is called Mundin and Kaparddin.[1]

"Vasudeva said,—'The very deities with Indra, and the Grandsire Brahma numbering among them, and the great Rishis also, are incompetent to understand the course of Mahadeva's acts truly and in all their details. Even He is the end which all righteous people attain. The very Adityas, who are endued with subtile sight, are unable to behold his abode. How then can one that is merely a man succeed in comprehending Him ?[2] I shall, therefore, truly recite to you some only of the attributes of that illustrious slayer of Asuras, who is regarded as the Lord of all sacrifices and vows."

Vaisampayana continued,—"Having said these words, the illustrious Vasudeva began his discourse on the attributes of the high-souled Mahadeva endued with the highest intelligence, after having purified himself by touching water.

"Vasudeva said,—'Hear, ye foremost of Brahmana's and thou Yudhishthira also, O sire, and hear thou too, O Ganga's son, the names that are applied unto Kaparddin. Hear ye, how in former days, I obtained a sight, so difficult to obtain, (of that great god), for the sake of Samva. Verily, in those days was the illustrious deity seen by me in consequence of Yoga-abstraction.[3] After twelve years had expired

---

1 It is not necessary to explain these names here. They have been fully explained in previous portions and will be explained later on in this very chapter.—T.

2 Such Verses are explained by the esoteric school in a different way. "Bhavanam" is taken as standing for 'Hardakasam,' i.e., the firmament of the heart; 'adityas' stand for the senses. The meaning then becomes,—'How can one that is merely a man comprehend Sambhu whom the senses cannot comprehend, for Sambhu dwells in the firmament of the heart and cannot be seen but by the internal vision that Yoga supplies.' Some texts read 'nidhanamadim meaning end and beginning.'—T.

3 It is said that for obtaining a worthy son, Krishna underwent the austerest of penances on the breast of Himavat, with a view to gratifying

from the time when Pradyumna, the son of Rukmini, who is endued with great intelligence, slew the Asura Samvara in days of yore, my spouse Jamvavati addressed me. Indeed, beholding Pradyumna and Charudeshna and other sons born of Rukmini, Jamvavati, desirous of a son, said these words unto me, O Yudhishthira,—Grant me, O thou of unfading glory, a son endued with heroism, the foremost of mighty men, possessed of the most agreeable features, sinless in conduct, and like unto thyself. And O, let there be no delay on thy part in granting this prayer of mine. There is nothing in the three worlds that is unattainable by thee. O perpetuator of Yadu's race, thou canst create other worlds if only thou wishest it. Observing a vow for twelve years and purifying thyself, thou hadst adored the Lord of all creatures (*viz.*, Mahadeva) and then begot upon Rukmini the sons that she has obtained from thee, viz., Charudeshna and Sucharu and Charuvesa and Yasodhana and Charusravas and Charuyasas and Pradyumna and Sambhu. O slayer of Madhu, do thou grant to me a son like unto those of great powers whom thou hast begotten upon Rukmini ?—Thus addressed by the princess, I replied unto her of slender waist,—Let me have thy permission (to leave thee for some time), O queen. I shall certainly obey thy behest. She answered me, saying,—Go, and may success and prosperity always attend thee. Let Brahman and Siva and Kasyapa, the Rivers, those deities that preside over the mind, the soil, all deciduous herbs, those Chhandas (Rhymes) that are regarded as bearers of the libations poured in sacrifices, the Rishis, Earth, the Oceans, the sacrificial presents, those syllables that are uttered for completing the cadences of Samans, the Rikshas, the Pitris, the Planets, the spouses of the deities, the celestial maidens, the celestial mothers, the great cycles, kine, Chandramas, Savitri Agni, Savitri, the knowledge of the Vedas, the seasons, the year, small and big divisions of time, *e.g.*, the Kshanas, the Labas, the Muhurtas, the Nimeshas, and the Yugas in succession, protect thee, O Yadava, and keep thee in happiness, wherever thou mayst stay. Let no danger overtake thee on thy way, and let no heedlessness be thine, O sinless one.—Thus blessed by her, I took her leave, bidding fare-well unto the daughter of the prince of apes. Repairing then into the presence of that foremost of men, viz., my father, of my mother, of the king, and of Ahuka, I informed them of what the daughter of the prince of the Vidyadharas, in great affliction, had said unto me. Bidding them farewell with a sorrowful heart, I then repaired to Gada and to Rama of great might.

---

the god Mahadeva. The son obtained as a boon from Mahadeva was Samva, as would appear from this and the succeeding Verses. Elsewhere, however, it is stated that the son so obtained was Pradyumna begotten upon Rukmini. The inconsistency would disappear if we suppose that Krishna adored Mahadeva twice for obtaining sons.—T.

These two cheerfully addressed me, saying,—Let thy penances increase without any obstruction.—Having obtained the permission of all of them, I thought of Gadura. He immediately came to me and bore me to Himavat (at my bidding). Arrived at Himavat, I dismissed him. There on that foremost of mountains, I beheld many wonderful sights. I saw an excellent, wonderful, and agreeable retreat for the practice of penances. That delightful retreat was owned by the high-souled Upamanyu who was a descendant of Vyaghrapada. That retreat is applauded and reverenced by the deities and the Gandharvas, and seemed to be covered with Vedic beauty. It was adorned with Dhavas and Kakubhas and Kadamvas and cocas, with Kuruvakas and Ketakas and Jamvus and Patalas, with banians and Varunakas and Vatsanabhas and Vilwas, with Saralas and Kapitthas and Piyalas and Salas and palmyras with Vadaris and Kundas and Punnagas and Asokas and Amras and Kovidaras and Champakas and Panasas, and with diverse other trees endued with fruits and flowers. And that retreat was also decked with the straight stems of the *Musa Supienta*.[1] Truly, that asylum was adorned with diverse other kinds of trees and with diverse kinds of fruits forming the food of diverse kinds of birds. Heaps of ashes (of sacrifical fires) were thrown in proper places all around, which added to the beauty of the scene. It abounded with Rurus and apes and tigers and lions and leopards, with deer of diverse species and peacocks, and with cats and snakes. Indeed, large numbers of other animals also were seen there, as also buffaloes and bears. Delicious breezes constantly blew bearing the melodious strains of celestial nymphs. The babblings of mountain rivullets and springs, the sweet notes of winged choristers, the gruntings of elephants, the delicious strains of Kinnaras, and the auspicious voice of ascetics singing the Samans, O hero, and diverse other kinds of music. rendered that retreat extremely charming. The very imagination cannot conceive another retreat as delightful as the one I beheld. There were also large houses in that asylum, intended for

---

1 Dhava is *Anogeissus latifolia*. Wall, sin, *Conocarpus latifolia Roxb* Kakubha is otherwise called Arjuna which is identified with *Terminalia Arjuna*, syn. *Pentaptera Arjuna*. Kadamva is *Nauclea cadamba*, *Roxb.* Kuruveka is *Barleria cristata*, *Linn.* Ketaka is *Pandanus odoratissimus*, *Linn.* Jamvu is *Eugenia Jambolana* Patala is *Stereospermum suaveolens*. syn. *Bignonia suaveolens*, *Roxb.* Varunaka is *Cratæa*, *religiosa*, syn. *Capparis trifoliata*, *Roxb.* Vatasanabha is *Aconitum ferox*, Wall. Vilwa is *Ægle Marmelos*. Sarala is *Pinus longifolia*, *Roxb.* Kapittha is *Feronia Elephantum*. Piyala is *Buchanania latifolia*. Sala is *Shorea robusta*. Vadari is *Zisyphus jujuba*. Kunda is *Balanites Roxburghii*, Punnaga is *Callophyllum inophyllum*. Asoka is *Saraca*. *Indica*, *Linn*, syn *Jonesia Asoka*. *Roxb.* Amra is *Mangifera Indica*. Kovidara is *Bauhinia*, *accuminata Linn.* Champaka is *Michelia Champaka*, *Linn.* Panasa is *Artocarpus integrifolia*, *Linn.*—T.

keeping the sacred fire, and covered all over with flowering creepers. It was adorned with the river Ganga of clear and sacred water. Indeed, the daughter of Jahnu always remained there. It was decked also with many ascetics who were the foremost of all righteous persons, who were endued with high souls, and who resembled fire itself in energy.[1] Some of those ascetics subsisted upon air and some upon water, some were devoted to Japa or the silent recitation of sacred Mantras, and some were engaged in cleansing their souls by practising the virtues of compassion while some amongst them were Yogins devoted to the abstraction of Yoga-meditation. Some amongst them subsisted upon smoke only, and some subsisted upon fire, and some upon milk. Thus was that retreat adorned with many foremost of regenerate persons. And some there were amongst them that had taken the vow of eating and drinking like kine,—that is, by giving up the use of the hands at once. And some used only two pieces of stone for husking their grain, and some used their teeth only for that purpose. And some subsisted by drinking only the rays of the moon, and some by drinking only froth. And some had betaken themselves to the vow of living like deer.[2] And some there were that lived upon the fruits of the Ficus religiosa, and some that used to lie upon water. And some dressed themselves in rags and some in animal skins and some in barks of trees. Indeed, I beheld diverse ascetics of the foremost order observing these and other painful vows. I desired then to enter that asylum. Verily, that asylum was honoured and adored by the deities and all high-souled beings, by Siva and others, O Bharata, and by all creatures of righteous acts. Thus addressed, it stood in all its beauty on the breast of Himavat, like the lunar disc in the firmament. The mongoose sported there with the snake, and the tiger with the deer, like friends, forgetting their natural enmity, in consequence of the energy of those ascetics of blazing penances and for their proximity to these high-souled ones. In that foremost of asylums, which was delightful to all creatures, inhabited by many foremost of Brahmanas fully conversant with the Vedas and their branches, and by many high-souled Rishis celebrated for the difficult vows they observed, I saw, as soon as I entered, a puissant Rishi with matted locks on head and dressed in rags, who seemed to blaze forth like fire with his penances and energy. Waited upon by his disciples and possessed of tranquil soul, that foremost of Brahmanas was young

---

1 Ganga is represented as the daughter of Rishi Jahnu, and hence is she known by the name of Jahnavi. What is meant by Jahnavi having been always represent there is that the goddess always stayed there in spirit, desirous of conferring merit upon those that would reverence her.—T

2 *i.e.*, never searching for food but taking what they saw, and never using their hands also.—T.

in aspect. His name was Upamanyu. Unto me who bowed unto him with a nod of the head, he said,—Welcome art thou, O thou of eyes like lotus petals. Today, by this visit of thine, we see that our penances have borne fruit. Thou art worthy of our adoration, but thou adorest us still. Thou art worthy of being seen, but thou desirest to see me.—Joining my hands I addressed him the usual enquiries respecting the well-being of the animals and birds that resided in his asylum, of the progress of his righteousness, and of his disciples. The illustrious Upamanyu then addressed me in words that were exceedingly sweet and delightful,—Thou shalt, O Krishna, obtain without doubt a son like unto thyself. Betaking thyself to severe penances, do thou gratify Isana, the Lord of all creatures. That divine Master, O Adhokshaja, sporteth here with his spouse by his side. O Janarddana, it was here that the deities with all the Rishis, in days of yore, gratified that foremost of deities by their penances and Brahmacharyya and truth and self-restraint, and succeeded in obtaining the fruition of many high desires. That illustrious god is verily the vast receptacle of all energies and penances. Projecting into existence and withdrawing once more unto himself all things fraught with good and evil, that inconceivable Deity whom thou seekest, O destroyer of foes, lives here with his spouse. He who took his birth as the Danava named Hiranykashipu, whose strength was so great that he could shake the very mountains of Meru, succeeded in obtaining from Mahadeva the puissance belonging to all the deities and enjoyed it for ten millions of years. He who was the foremost of all his sons and who was celebrated by the name of Mandara, succeeded, through the boon he had obtained from Mahadeva, in fighting Sakra for a million of years. The terrible discus of Vishnu and the thunderbolt of Indra were both unable to make the slightest impression, O Kesava, in days of yore, upon the body of that great cause of universal affliction.[1] The discus which thou bearest, O sinless one, was given unto thee by Mahadeva after he had slain a Daitya that was proud of his strength and used to live within the waters. That discus, blazing with energy and like unto fire, was created by the great god having for his device the bull. Wonderful and irresistible in energy it was given unto thee by that illustrious god. In consequence of its blazing energy it was incapable of being gazed at by any person save Siva the wielder of Pinaka. It was for this reason that Bhava (Siva) bestowed upon it the name of Sudarsana. From that time the name Sudarsana came to be current in all the worlds. Even the weapon, O Kesava, failed to make the slightest impression on the body of Hiranyakashipu's son

---

1 'Graha' is literally a planet; here, Mandara who is likened to an evil planet in consequence of the mischief he did unto all.—T.

Mandara, that appeared like an evil planet in the three worlds. Hundreds of Chakras like thine and thunderbolts like that of Sakra, could not inflict a scratch on the body of that evil planet endued with great might, who had obtained a boon from Mahadeva. Afflicted by the mighty Mandara, the deities fought hard against him and his associates, all of whom had obtained boons from Mahadeva. Gratified with another Danava named Vidyutprabha, Mahadeva granted to him the sovereignty of the three worlds. That Danava remained the sovereign of the three worlds for a hundred thousand years. And Mahadeva said unto him,—Thou shalt become one of my attendants.—Indeed, the puissant Lord further bestowed upon him the boon of a hundred millions of children. The Master without birth, of all creatures further gave the Danava the region known by the name of Kusadwipa for his kingdom. Another great Asura, of the name of Satamukha, was created by Brahma. For a hundred years he poured on the sacrificial fire (as offerings unto Mahadeva) the flesh of his own body. Gratified with such penances, Sankara said unto him,—What can I do for thee ?—Satamukha replied unto him, saying,—O thou that art most wonderful, let me have the power of creating new creatures and animals. Give also unto me, O foremost of all deities, eternal power.—The puissant lord, thus addressed by him, said unto him,—So be it.—The Self-born Brahma, concentrating his mind in Yoga, in days of yore, made a sacrifice for three hundred years, with the object of obtaining children. Mahadeva granted him a thousand sons possessed of qualifications commensurate with the merits of the sacrifice. Without doubt, thou knowest, O Krishna, the lord of Yoga, him that is, who is sung by the deities. The Rishi known by the name of Yajnavalkya is exceedingly virtuous. By adoring Mahadeva he has acquired great fame. The great ascetic who is Parasara's son, *viz*, Vyasa, of soul set on Yoga, has obtained great celebrity by adoring Sankara. The Valikhilyas were on a former occasion disregarded by Maghavat. Filled with wrath at this, they gratified the illustrious Rudra. That lord of the universe, that foremost one of all the deities, thus gratified by the Valikhilyas, said unto them,—Ye shall succeed by your penances in creating a bird that will rob Indra of the *Amrita*. Through the wrath of Mahadeva on a former occasion, all the waters disappeared. The deities gratified him by performing a sacrifice called Saptakapala, and caused, through his grace, other waters to flow into the worlds. Verily, when the three-eyed deity became gratified, water once more appeared in the world. The

1 'Yoga' in Verse 84 is explained by the Commentator as meaning the power of creation. 'Chandra-Surya-parjanya-prithivyadi-sristi-samarthyam'. Similarly, by 'Saswatam Valam' is meant that power which arises from Brahmavidya—T.

wife of Atri, who was conversant with the Vedas, abandoned her husband in a huff and said.—I shall no longer live in subjection to that ascetic.—Having said these words, she sought the protection of Mahadeva. Through fear of her lord, Atri, passed three hundred years, abstaining from all food. And all this time she slept on wooden clubs for the purpose of gratifying Bhava. The great deity then appeared unto her and then smilingly addressed her, saying—Thou shalt obtain a son. And thou shalt get that son without the need of a husband, simply through the grace of Rudra. Without doubt that son, born in the race of his father, shall become celebrated for his worth, and assume a name after thee. The illustrious Vikarna also, O slayer of Madhu, full of devotion to Mahadeva, gratified him with severe penances and obtained high and happy success. Sakalya, too, of restrained soul, adored Bhava in a mental sacrifice that he performed for nine hundred years, O Kesava. Gratified with him the illustrious deity said unto him,—Thou shalt become a great author. O son, inexhaustible shall thy fame be in the three worlds. Thy race also shall never come to an end and shall be adorned by many great Rishis that shall take birth in it. Thy son will become the foremost of Brahmanas and will make the Sutras of thy work. There was a celebrated Rishi of the name of Savarni in the Krita age. Here, in this asylum, he underwent severe penances for six thousand years. The illustrious Rudra said,—I am gratified with thee, O sinless one! Without being subject to decrepitude or death, thou shalt become an author celebrated through all the worlds!—In days of yore, Sakra, also, in Baranasi, filled with devotion, O Janarddana, adored Mahadeva who has empty space alone for his garments and who is smeared with ashes as an agreeable unguent. Having adored Mahadeva thus, he obtained the sovereignty of the celestials. Narada also, in days of yore, adored the great Bhava with devotion of heart. Gratified with him, Mahadeva, that preceptor of the celestial preceptor, said these words.—No one shall be thy equal in energy and penances. Thou shalt always attend upon me with thy songs and instrumental music. Hear also, O Madhava, how in former times I succeeded in obtaining a sight of that god of gods, that Master of all creatures, O lord. Hear also in detail for what object, O thou of great puissance, I invoked with restrained senses and mind that illustrious deity endued with supreme energy. I shall, O sinless one, tell thee with full details all that I succeeded in obtaining from that god of gods, viz., Maheswara. In ancient times, viz., Krita age, O son, there was a Rishi of great fame, named Vyaghrapada. He was celebrated for his knowledge and mastery over the Vedas and their branches. I was born as the son of that Rishi and Dhaumya took birth as my younger brother. On a certain occasion, O Madhava, accompanied by Dhaumya, I came upon the asylum of certain Rishis of cleansed souls. There I beheld a cow, that was being milked. I saw the milk and it appeared to me to resemble Amrita itself in taste. I then came home, and impelled by childishness, I addressed my mother and said,—Give me some food prepared with milk.—There was no milk in the house, and accordingly my mother was much grieved at my asking for it. My mother took a piece of (rice) cake and boiled it in water, O Madhava. The water became whitened and my mother placed it before us saying that it was milk and bade us drink it. I had before that drunk milk on one occasion, for my father had, at the time of a sacrifice, taken me to the residence of some of our great kinsmen. A celestial cow, who delights the deities, was being milked on that occasion. Drinking her milk that resembled Amrita in taste, I knew what the virtues are of milk. I therefore, at once understood the origin of the substance that my mother offered me, telling me that it was milk. Verily, the taste of that cake, O son, did not afford me any pleasure whatever. Impelled by childishness I then addressed mother, saying,—This O mother, that thou hast given me is not any preparation of milk.—Filled with grief and sorrow at this, and embracing me from parental affection and smelling my head, O Madhava, she said unto me,—Whence, O child, can ascetics of cleansed souls obtain food prepared with milk? Such men always reside in the forest and subsist upon bulbs and roots and fruits. Whence shall we who live by the banks of rivers that are the resort of the Valikhilyas, we who have mountains and forest, for our home,—whence, indeed, O child, shall we obtain milk? We, O dear child, live (sometimes) on air and sometimes on water. We dwell in asylums in the midst of forests and woods. We habitually abstain from all kinds of food that are taken by persons living in villages and towns. We are accustomed to only such food as is supplied by the produce of the wilderness. There cannot be any milk, O child, in the wilderness where there are no offspring of Surabhi.[1] Dwelling on the banks of rivers or in caves or on mountain-breasts, or in *tirthas* and other places of the kind, we pass our time in the practice of penances and the recitation of sacred Mantras, Siva being our highest refuge. Without gratifying the boon-giving Sthanu of unfading glory, —him, that is, who has three eyes,—whence, O child, can one obtain food prepared with milk and good robes and other objects of enjoyment in the world? Do thou devote thyself, O dear son, to Sankara with thy whole soul. Through his grace, O child, thou art sure to obtain all such objects as administer to the indulgence of all thy wishes.—Hearing these words of my mother, O slayer of foes, that day, I

1 'Surabhi' is the celestial cow, the original progenetrix of all kine in heaven and on Earth.—T.

joined my hands in reverence and bowing unto her, said,—O mother, who is this Mahadeva? In what manner can one gratify him? Where does that god reside? How may he be seen? With what does he become pleased? What also is the form of Sarva? How may one succeed in obtaining a knowledge of him? If gratified, will he, O mother, show himself unto me?—After I had said these words, O Krishna, to my mother, she, filled with parental affection, smelt my head, O Govinda, her eyes covered with tears the while. Gently patting my body, O slayer of Madhu, my mother, adopting a tone of great humility, addressed me in the following words, O best of the deities.—

"—My mother said,—Mahadeva is exceedingly difficult to be known by persons of uncleansed souls. These men are incapable of bearing him in their hearts or comprehending him at all. They can not retain him in their minds. They cannot seize him, nor can they obtain a sight of him. Men of wisdom aver that his forms are many. Many, again, are the places in which he resides. Many are the forms of his Grace. Who is there that can understand in their details the acts, which are all excellent, of Isa, or of all the forms that he has assumed in days of yore? Who can relate how Sarva sports and how he becomes gratified? Maheswara of universal form resides in the hearts of all creatures. While Munis discoursed on the auspicious and excellent acts of Isana, I have heard from them how, impelled by compassion towards his worshippers, he grants them a sight of his person. For the purpose of showing a favour unto the Brahmanas, the denizens of heaven have recited for their information the diverse forms that were assumed by Mahadeva in days of yore. Thou hast asked me about these. I shall recite them to thee, O son—

"—My mother continued,—Bhava assumes the forms of Brahama and Vishnu and the chief of the celestials of the Rudras, the Adityas, and the Aswins; and of those deities that are called Viswadevas. He assumes the forms also of men and women, of Pretas and Pisachas, of Kiratas and Savaras, and of all aquatic animals. That illustrious deity assumes the forms of also those Savaras that dwell in the woods and forests. He assumes the forms of tortoises and fishes and conches. He it is that assumes the forms of those coral sprouts that are used as ornaments by men. He assumes also the forms of Yakshas, Rakshasas and Snakes, of Daityas and Danavas. Indeed, the illustrious god assumes the forms of all creatures too that live in holes. He assumes the forms of tigers and lions and deer, of wolves and bears and birds, of owls and of jackals as well. He it is that assumes the forms of swans and crows and peacocks, of chameleons and lizards and storks. He it is that assumes the forms of cranes and vultures and Chakravakas. Verily, he it is that assumes the forms of Chasas and of mountains also.

O son, it is Mahadeva that assumes the forms of kine and elephants and horses and camels and asses. He assumes also the forms of goats and leopards and diverse other varieties of animals. It is Bhava who assumes the forms of diverse kinds of birds of beautiful plumage. It is Mahadeva who bears the forms of persons with sticks and those with umbrellas and those with calabashes among Brahmanas.[1] He sometimes becomes six-faced and sometimes becomes multifaced. He sometimes assumes forms having three eyes and forms having many heads. And he sometimes assumes forms having many millions of legs and forms having innumerable stomachs and faces and forms endued with innumerable arms and innumerable sides. He sometimes appears surrounded by innumerable spirits and ghosts. He it is that assumes the forms of Rishis and Gandharvas, and of Siddhas and Charanas. He sometimes assumes a form that is rendered white with the ashes he smears on it and is adorned with a half-moon on the forehead. Adored with diverse hymns uttered with diverse kinds of voice and worshipped with diverse Mantras fraught with encomiums, he, that is sometimes called Sarva, is the Destroyer of all creatures in the universe, and it is upon him, again, that all creatures rest as on their common foundation. Mahadeva is the soul of all creatures. He pervades all things. He is the speaker of all discourses (on duties and rituals). He resides everywhere and should be known as dwelling in the hearts of all creatures in the universe. He knows the desire cherished by every one of his worshippers. He becomes acquainted with the object in which one pays him adorations. Do thou then, if it pleases thee, seek the protection of that chief of the deities. He sometimes rejoices, and sometimes yields to wrath, and sometimes utters the syllable Hum with a very loud noise. He sometimes arms himself with the discus, sometimes with the trident, sometimes with the mace, sometimes with the heavy mullets, sometimes with the scimitar, and sometimes with the battle axe. He it is that assumes the form of Sesha who sustains the world on his head. He has snakes for his belt, and his ears are adorned with ear-rings made of snakes. Snakes form also the sacred thread he wears. An elephant skin forms his upper garment.[2] He sometimes laughs and sometimes sings and sometimes dances most beautifully. Surrounded by innumerable spirits and ghosts, he sometimes plays on musical instruments.

---

1 A Sanyasin is one that bears the stick as the badge of the mode of life he has adopted. 'Chatrin' is the king. 'Kundin' is one with the calabash. The meaning is that it is Mahadeva who becomes the Sanyasin or the mendicant on the one hand and the monarch on the other.—T.

2 Every person belonging to the three superior orders bears the *Upavita* or sacred thread as his badge. The deities also, including Mahadeva, bear the Upavita. Mahadeva's Upavita is made of living snakes.—T.

Diverse, again are the instruments upon which he plays, and sweet the sounds they yield. He sometimes wanders (over crematoria), sometimes yawns, sometimes cries, and sometimes causes others to cry. He sometimes assumes the guise of one that is mad, and sometimes of one that is intoxicated, and he sometimes utters words that are exceedingly sweet. Endued with appalling fierceness, he sometimes laughs loudly, frightening all creatures with his eyes. He sometimes sleeps and sometimes remains awake and sometimes yawns as he pleases. He sometimes recites sacred Mantras and sometimes becomes the deity of those Mantras which are recited. He sometimes performs penances and sometimes becomes the deity for whose adoration those penances are undergone. He sometimes makes gifts and sometimes receives those gifts; sometimes disposes himself in Yoga and sometimes becomes the object of the Yoga contemplation of others. He may be seen on the sacrificial platform or in the sacrificial stake; in the midst of the cow-pen or in the fire. He may not again be seen there. He may be seen as a boy or as an old man. He sports with the daughters and the spouses of the Rishis. His hair is long and stands erect. He is perfectly naked, for he has the horizon for his garments. He is endued with terrible eyes. He is fair, he is darkish, he is dark, he is pale, he is of the colour of smoke, and he is red. He is possessed of eyes that are large and terrible. He has empty space for his covering and he it is that covers all things. Who is there that can truly understand the limits of Mahadeva who is formless, who is one and indivisible, who conjures of illusions, who is of the cause of all actions and destructive operations in the universe, who assumes the form of Hiranyagarbha, and who is without beginning and without end, and who is without birth.[1] He lives in the heart (of every creature). He is the *prana*, he is the mind, and he is the Jiva (that is invested in the material case). He is the soul of Yoga, and it is that is called Yoga. He is the Yoga-contemplation into which Yogins enter.[2] He is the Supreme Soul. Indeed Maheswara, the purity in essence, is capable of being comprehended not by the senses but through only the Soul seizing his existence. He plays on diverse musical instruments. He is a vocalist. He has a hundred thousand eyes, he has one mouth, he has two mouths, he has three mouths, and he has many

---

1 'Arupa' is formless, or as the Commentator explains, 'nishkala,' *i.e.*, without parts, being indivisible. 'Arupa' is of the form of multifarious acts or operations or effects in the universe. 'Adyarupa' is 'Hiranyagarbha.'—T.

2 The Commentator explains that by saying that Maheswara is in the heart, &c., what is stated is that he is the several cases of which Jiva is made up while in his unemancipate state, *viz.*, the Annamaya kosha, the pranamaya kosha, the Manomaya kosha, and the Vijnanmaya kosha. What is meant by 'Yogatman' is that he is the Soul or essence of Yoga of the 'Chidachidgranthi,' *i.e.*, the Anandamaya kosha. By 'Yogasanjnita' is meant that he is Yoga or the 'Twam padarthah.'—T.

mouths. Devoting thyself to him, setting thy heart upon him, depending upon him, and accepting him as thy one refuse, do thou, O son, adore Mahadeva and then mayst thou obtain the fruition of all thy wishes. Hearing those words of my mother, O slayer of foes, from that day my devotion was directed to Mahadeva, having nothing else for its object. I then applied myself to the practice of the austerest penances for gratifying Sankara. For one thousand years I stood on my left toe. After that I passed one thousand years, subsisting only upon fruits. The next one thousand years I passed, subsisting upon the fallen leaves of trees. The next thousand years I passed, subsisting upon water only. After that I passed seven hundred years, subsisting on air alone. In this way I adored Mahadeva for a full thousand years of the celestials. After this, the puissant Mahadeva, the Master of all the universe, became gratified with me. Desirous of ascertaining whether I was solely devoted to him and him alone, he appeared before me in the form of Sakra surrounded by all the deities. As the celebrated Sakra, he had a thousand eyes on his person and was armed with the thunder bolt. And he rode on an elephant whose complexion was of the purest white, with eyes red, ears folded, the temporal juice trickling down his cheeks, with trunk contracted, terrible to look at, and endued with four tasks. Indeed, riding on such an elephant, the illustrious chief of the deities seemed to blaze forth with his energy. With a beautiful crown on his head and adorned with garlands round his neck and bracelets round his arms, he approached the spot where I was. A white umbrella was held over his head. And he was waited upon by many Apsaras, and many Gandharvas sang his praise. Addressing me, he said,—O foremost of regenerate persons, I have been gratified with thee. Beg of me whatever boon thou desirest,—Hearing these words of Sakra I did not become glad. Verily, O Krishna, I answerd the chief of the celestials in these words.—I do not desire any boon at thy hands, or from the hands of any other deity. O amiable deity, I tell thee truly, that it is Mahadeva only from whom I have boons to ask. True, true it is, O Sakra, true are these words that I say unto thee. No other words are at all agreeable to me save those which relate to Maheswara. At the command of Pashupati, that Lord of all creatures, I am ready to become a worm or a tree with many branches. If not obtained through the grace represented by Mahadeva's boons, the very sovereignty of the three worlds would not be acceptable to me. Let me be born among the very Chandalas but let me still be devoted to the feet of Hara. Without, again, being devoted to that Lord of all creatures, I would not like to have birth in the palace of Indra himself. If a person be wanting in devotion to that Lord of the universe,—that Master of the deities and the Asuras,—his misery will not end even if from want of food he has to subsist upon only air and water.[1] What is the need of other discourses that are even fraught with other kinds of morality and righteousness, unto those persons who do not like to live even a moment without thinking of feet of Mahadeva ? When the unrighteous or sinful Kali Yuga comes, one should never pass a moment without devoting his heart upon Mahadeva. One that has drunk the Amrita constituted by the devotion to Hara, one becomes freed from the fear of the world. One that has not obtained the grace of Mahadeva can never succeed to devote oneself to Mahadeva for a single day or for half a day or for a Muhurta or for a Kshana or for a Lava (very small unit time). At the command of Mahadeva I shall cheerfully become a worm or an insect, but I have no relish for even the sovereignty of the three worlds, if bestowed by thee, O Sakra. At the word of Hara I would become even a dog. In fact, that would accord with my highest wish. If not given by Maheswara, I would not have the sovereignty of the very deities. I do not wish to have this dominion of the Heavens. I do not wish to have the sovereignty of the celestials. I do not wish to have the region of Brahma. Indeed, I do not wish to have that cessation of individual existence which is called Emancipation and which involves a complete identification with Brahma. But I want to become the slave of Hara. As long as that Lord of all creatures, the illustrious Mahesa, with crown on his head and body possessed of the pure white complexion of the lunar disc, does not become gratified with me, so long shall I cheerfully bear all those afflictions, due to a hundred repetitions of decrepitude, death and birth, that befall to the lot of embodied beings. What person in the universe can obtain tranquility without gratifying Rudra that is freed from decripitude and death, that is endued with the effulgence of the Sun, the Moon, or the fire, that is the root or original cause of everything real and unreal in the three worlds, and that exists as one and indivisible entity ? If in consequence of my faults, rebirths be mine, I shall, in those new births, devote myself solely to Bhava.

" '—Indra said,—What reason canst thou assign for the existence of a Supreme Being or for His being the cause of all causes ?

" '—Upamanyu said—I solicit boons from that great Deity named Siva whom utterers of Brahma has described as existent and non-existent, manifest and unmanifest, eternal or immutable, one and many. I solicit boons from Him who is without beginning and middle and end, who is Knowledge and Puissance, who is inconceivable and who is the

---

1 The meaning seems to be this; the man that is not devoted to Mahadeva is sure to be subjected to misery. His distress will know no bounds. To think that such a man has reached the lowest depth of misery only when from want of food he has to live upon water or air would not be correct.—T.

Supreme Soul. I solicit boons from Him whence comes all Puissance, who has not been produced by any one, who is immutable, and who, though himself unsprung from any seed, is the seed of all things in the universe. I solicit boons from Him who is blazing Effulgence, (beyond Darkness) who is the essence of all penances, who transcends all faculties of which we are possessed and which we may devote for the purpose of comprehending him, and by knowing whom every one becomes freed from grief or sorrow. I worship him, O Purandara, who is conversant with the creation of all elements and thethought of all living creatures, and who is the original cause of the existence or creation of all creatures, who is omnipresent, and who has the puissance to give everything.[1] I solicit boons from Him who cannot be comprehended by argument, who represents the object of the Sankhya and the Yoga systems of philosophy, and who transcends all things, and whom all persons conversant with the topics of enquiry worship and adore.[2] I solicit boons from Him, O Maghavat, who is the soul of Maghavat himself, who is said to be the God of the gods, and who is the Master of all creatures. I solicit boons from Him who it is that first created Brahma, that creator of all the worlds, having filled Space (with His energy) and evoked into existence the primeval egg.[3] Who else than that Supreme Lord could be the creator of Fire, Water, Wind, Earth, Space, Mind, and that which is called Mahat? Tell me, O Sarkra, who else than Siva could create Mind, Understanding, Consciousness or Ego, the Tanmatras, and the senses? Who is there higher than Siva?[4] The wise say that the Grandsire Brahma is the creator of this universe. Brahma, however, acquired his high puissance and prosperity by adoring and gratifying Mahadeva, that God of gods. That high puissance (consisting of all the three attributes of creation, protection, and destruction), which dwells in that illustrious Being who is endowed with the quality of being one, who created Brahma, Vishnu, and Rudra, was derived from Mahadeva. Tell me who is there that is superior to the Supreme Lord?[5] Who else

---

1 'Bhuta-bhavana-Bhavajnam' is one acquainted with both the 'bhavana' and the 'bhava' of all 'bhutas,' *i e*, all the living creatures.—T.

2 Without the Srutis, He cannot be comprehended, for he is above all dialectics or arguments. The object which the Sankhya system has in view, flows from Him, and the object also which the Yogins have in view has its origin in Him.—T.

3 Mahadeva, has spoken of as Brahma, first filled Space with his energy. Space forming, as it were, the material with which everything else was created. Having filled Space as it were with creative energy, he created the primeval egg and placed Brahman or the Grandsire of the universe within it.—T

4 'Tanmatras' are the subtile elements, those which we perceive being gross ones —T.

5 Here Mahadeva is represented as Supreme Brahman. ence, Hthe

than that God of gods is competent to unite the sons of Diti with lordship and puissance, judging by the sovereignty and the power of oppessing conferred upon the foremost of the Daityas and the Danavas ?[1] The different points of the horizon, Time, the Sun, all fiery entities, planets, wind, water, and the stars and constellations,—these, know thou, are from Mahadeva. Tell us who is higher than the Supreme Lord ? Who else is there, except Mahadeva, in the matter of the creation of Sacrifice and the destruction of Tripura ? Who else except Mahadeva the grinder of the foes, has offered lordship to the principal ?[2] What need, O Purandara, of many well-sounding statemets fraught with spacious sophisms, when I behold thee of a thousand eyes, O best of the deities, —thee that art worshipred by Siddhas and Gandharvas and the deities and the Rishis ? O best of the Kusikas, all this is due to the grace of that God of gods *viz.*. Mahadeva. Know, O Kesava, that this all, consisting of animate and inanimate existences with heaven and other unseen entities, which occur in this worlds, and which has the all-pervading Lord for their soul, has flowed from Maheswara and has been created.(by him) for enjoyment by Jiva.[3] In the worlds that are known by the names of Bhu, Bhuva, Swah, and Maha, in the midst of the mountains of Lokaloka, in the islands, in the monntains of Meru, in all things that yield happiness, and in the hearts of all creatures, O illustrious Maghavat, resides Mahadeva, as persons conversant with all the topics of enquiry say. If, O Sakra, the Devas (deities) and the Asuras could see any other puissant form than Bhava's, would not both of them, especially the former, when opposed and afflicated by the latter, have sought the protection of that form ? In all hostile encounters of the deities, the Yakshas, the Uragas and the Rakshasas, that terminating in mutual destruction, it is Bhava that gives unto those that meet with destruction, puissance commensurate with their respective locations as dependent upon their acts. Tell me, who else than Maheswara is there for bestowing boons upon, and once more chastising the Andhaka and Sukra

Being that created Brahma, Vishnu, and Rudra, derived his power to create from Mahadeva. Thus Mahadeva is Unmanifest Brahma —T.

1 'Sampadayitum' is aisaryyena samyojayitum.' The difficulty lies in the first line ; the ablative is to be taken as 'yabartha or lyablope.'—T.

2 This is an instance of crux ; 'adhipati' is a verb of incomplete predication, implying 'etya' or encountering.—T.

3 Here the compassion of Mahadeva is shown. The Commentator explains that 'eshu' refers to 'these words' ; 'chatanachetanani' would include all animate and inanimate existences. The word 'adi' following implies 'heaven and all unseen entities. 'Avyaktamuktakesa' is a periphrasis for 'jiva' ; avyaktam aspashtam yathasyattatha muktah bhanti tirobitam nitya-muktatwama sya' is the explanation offered. This is, no doubt correct. The sense then is that all this has flowed from Maheswara and exists for being enjoyed by Jiva.—T.

and Dundubhi and Maharshi and many foremost of Yakshas, Indra and Vala and Rakshasas and the Nivatakavachas? Was not the vital seed of Mahadeva, that Master of both the deities and the Asuras, poured as a libation upon the fire? From that seed sprung a mountain of gold. Who else is their whose seed can be said to be possessed of such virtue.[1] Who else in this world is praised as having the horizon only for his garments? Who else can be said to be a Brahmacharin with his vital seed drawn up? Who else is their that has half his body occupied by his dear spouse?[2] Who else is there that has been able to subjugate Kama, the god of desire? Tell me, O Indra, what other Being possesses that high region of supreme felicity that is applauded by by all the deities? Who else has the crematorium as his sporting ground? Who else is there that is so praised for his dancing? Whose puissance and worship remain immutable? Who else is there that sports with spirits and ghosts? Tell me, O deity, who else has associate that are possessed of strength like his own and that are, therefore, proud of that strength or puissance?[3] Who else is their whose status is applauded as unchangable and worshipped with reverence by the three worlds? Who else there that pours rain, gives heat, and blazes forth in Energy? From whom else do we derive our wealth of herbs? Who else upholds all kinds of wealth? Who else sports as much as he pleases in the three worlds of mobile and immobile things? O Indra, know Maheswara to be the original Cause (of everything). He is adored by Yogins, by Rishis, by the Gandharvas, and by the Siddhas, with the aid of knowledge, (of ascetic) success, and of the rites laid down in the scriptural ordinances.[4] He is adored by both the deities and the Asuras with the aid of sacrifices by acts and the affliction of the ritual laid down in the scriptures. The fruits of action can never touch him for he transcends them all. Being such, I call him the original cause of everything.[5] He

---

1 The allusion is thus explained by the Commentator; once upon a time the seed of Mahadeva fell upon a blazing fire. The deity of fire removed it, unable to consume it. The seed, however, thus removed became converted into a mountain of gold. 'Haimagiri' is not Himavat or the mountains of Himalayas as the Burdwan translation wrongly renders it.—T.

2 'Ardhe sthita kanta' refers to the transformation of Mahadeva into a form half of which was male and half female, the male half being the half of his own usual form, and the female half the form of his dear spouse Uma or Parvati. This transformation is known by the name of 'Haragauri.'—T.

3 The associates of Mahadeva are called 'Gana.' 'Deva' is in the vocative case. The Burdwan translator wrongly takes 'deva-ganah' as a compound word and makes a mess of the meaning.—T.

4 The Bombay reading is 'Vihitam karanam param.' The Commentator adopts it, and explains it as 'vihitam, ajnatam sat jnapitam; param karanam avyaktasyapi karanam.' The Bengal reading, however, is not faulty.—T.

5 The Bengal reading 'karmayoga' is vicious. The Bombay text reads 'karmayajna' which, of course, is correct. By 'karmayajna' is meant that

is both gross and subtile. He is without compare. He cannot be conceived by the senses. He is endued with attributes and he is divested of them. He is the lord of attributes, for they are under his control. Even such is the place that is Maheswara's. He is the cause of the maintenance and the creation (of the universe). He is the cause of the universe and the cause also of its destruction. He is the Past, the Present, and the Future. He is the parent of all things. Verily, He is the cause of every thing. He is that which is mutable, He is the unmanifest, He is Knowledge ; He is ignorance ; He is every act, He is every omission ; He is righteousness ; and He is unrighteousness. Him, O Sakra, do I call the cause of everything. Behold, O Indra, in the image of Mahadeva the indications of both the sexes. That god of gods, *viz.*, Rudra, that cause of both creation and destruction, displays in his form the indications of both the sexes as the one cause of the creation of the universe. My mother formerly told me that he is the cause of the universe and the one cause of everything. There is no one that is higher than Isa, O Sakra. If it pleases thee, do thou throw thyself on his kindness and protection. Thou hast visible evidence, O chief of the celestials, of the fact that the universe has sprung from the union of the sexes (as represented by Mahadeva). The universe, thou knowest, is the sum of what is vested with attributes and what else is divested of attributes and has for its immediate cause the seeds of Brahma and others. Brahma and Indra and Hutasana and Vishnu and all the other deities, along with the Daityas and the Asuras, crowned with the fruition of a thousand desires, always say that there is none that is higher than Mahadeva.[1] Impelled by desire, I solicit, with restrained mind, that god known to all the mobile and immobile universe,—him, that is, who has been spoken of as the best and highest of all the gods, and who is auspiciousness itself, for obtaining without delay that highest of all acquisitions, *viz.*, Emancipation. What necessity is their of other reasons (for establishing what I believe) ? The supreme Mahadeva is the cause of all causes. We have never heard that the deities have, at any time, adored the sign of any other god than Mahadeva. If Maheswara be not accepted,

---

sacrifice which is performed with the aid of actual offerings of flowers and herbs and animals and libations of ghee, meat, &c., These are opposed to mental sacrifices or 'manasa yajna.' It is curious to see that the Burdwan translator adheres to the vicious reading and misunderstands the meaning. Mahadeva transcends the fruits of action, *i.e.*, he has no body unto which happiness and misery may attach.—T.

1 The Bombay reading 'savikara-nirguna-ganam' is correct. Then Bengal reading having 'gunam' (and not 'ganam') at the last word of this compound, is vicious. The Burdwan translator adheres to the vicious reading and wrongly renders the compound. K. P. Singha skips over it. Of course, 'ganam' means sum or total. 'Rectodbhavam' is *arsha* for 'Retasodbhavam.—T.

tell me, if thou hast ever heard of it, who eles is there whose sign has been worshipped or is being worshipped by all the deities? He whose sign is always worshipped by Brahma, by Vishnu, by thee, O Indra, with all the other deities, is verily the foremost of all adorable deities. Brahma has for his sign the lotus, Vishnu has for his the discus. Indra has for his sign the thunder-bolt. But the creatures of the world do not bear any of the sings that distinguish these deities. On the other hand, all creatures bear the signs that mark Mahadeva and his spouse. Hence, all creatures must be regarded as belonging to Maheswara. All creatures of the feminine sex, have sprung from Uma's nature as their cause, and hence it is they bear the mark of famininity that distinguishes Uma; while all creatures that are masculine, having sprung from Siva, bear the masculine mark that distinguishes Siva. That person who says that there is, in the three worlds with their mobile and immobile creatures, any other cause than the Supreme Lord, and that which is not marked with the mark of either Mahadeva or his spouse should be regarded as very wretched and should not be counted among the creatures of the universe. Every being with the mark of the masculine sex should be known to be of Isana, while every being with the mark of the feminine sex should be known to be of Uma. This universe of mobile and immobile creatures is pervaded by two kinds of forms (*viz.*, male and female). It is from Mahadeva that I wish to obtain boons. Failing in this, O Kausika, I would rather prefer dissolution itself. Go or remain, O Sakra, as thou, O slayer of Vala, desirest. I wish to have boons or curses from Mahadeva. No other deity shall I ever acknowledge, nor would I have from any other deity the fruition of all my wishes.—Having said these words unto the chief of the celestials, I became overwhelmed with grief at the thought of Mahadeva not having been gratified with me not withstanding my severe austerities. Within the twinkling of an eye, however, I saw the celestial elephant I had beheld before me transformed into a bull as white as a swan, or the Jasminum pubescens, or a stalk of the lotus or silver, or the ocean of milk. Of huge body, the hair of its tail was black and the hue of its eyes was tawny like that of honey. Its horns were hard as adamant and had the colour of gold. With their very sharp ends, whose hue was a mild red, the bull seemed to tear the Earth. The animal was adorned all over with ornaments made of the purest gold. Its face and hoofs and nose and ears were exceedingly beautiful and its waist too exceedingly well-formed. Its flanks were possessed of great beauty and its neck was very thick. Its whole form was exceedingly agreeable and beautiful to look at. Its hump shone with great beauty and seemed to occupy the whole of its shoulder-joint. And it looked like the summit of a mountain of snow or like a cliff of white clouds in the sky. Upon the back of that animal I beheld seated the illustrious Mahadeva with his spouse Uma. Verily, Mahadeva shone like the lord of stars while he is at his full. The fire born of his energy resembled in effulgence the lighting that flashes amid clouds. Verily, it seemed as if a thousand suns rose there, filling every side with a dazzling splendour. That energy of the Supreme Lord looked like the Samvartaka fire which destroys all creatures at the end of the Yuga. Overspread with that energy, the horizon became such that I could see nothing on any side. Filled with anxiety I once more thought what it could mean. That energy, however, did not pervade every side for any length of time, for soon, through the illusion of that god of gods, the horizon became clear. I then beheld the illustrious Sthanu or Maheswara seated on the back of his bull, of blessed and agreeable appearance and looking like a smokeless fire. And the great god was accompanied by Parvati of faultless features. Indeed, I beheld the blue-throated and high-souled Sthanu, unattached to everything, that receptacle of all kinds of force, endued with eight and ten arms and adorned with all kinds of ornaments. Clad in white vestments, he wore white garlands, and had white unguents smeared upon his limbs. The colour of his banner, irresistible in the universe, was white. The sacred thread round his person was also white. He was surrounded with associates, all possessed with prowess equal to his own, who were singing or dancing or playing on diverse kinds of musical instruments. A crescent moon, of pale hue, formed his crown, and placed on his forehead it looked like the moon that rises in the autumnal firmament. He seemed to dazzle with splendour, in consequence of his three eyes that looked like three suns. The garland of the purest white, that was on his body, shone like a wreath of lotuses, of the purest white, adorned with jewels and gems. I also beheld, O Govinda, the weapons in their embodied forms and fraught with every kind of energy, that belong to Bhava of immeasurable prowess. The high-souled deity held a bow whose hues resembled those of the rainbow. That bow is celebrated under the name of the Pinaka and is in reality a mighty snake. Indeed, that snake of seven heads and vast body, of sharp fangs and virulent poison, of large neck and the masculine sex, was twined round with the cord that served as its bowstring. And there was a shaft whose splendour looked like that of the sun or of the fire that appears at the end of the Yuga. Verily, that shaft was the excellent Pasupata that mighty and terrible weapon, which is without a second, indescribable for its power, and capable of striking every creature with fear. Of vast proportions, it seemed to constantly vomit sparks of fire. Possessed of one foot, of large teeth, and a thousand heads and thousand stomachs, it has a thousand arms, a thousand tongues, and a thousand eyes. Indeed, it seemed to continually vomit fire. O thou of mighty arms, that weapon is superior to the Brahma, the Narayana, the Aindra the Agneya, and the Varuna weapons. Verily, it is capable of neutralising every other weapon in the universe. It was with that weapon that the illustrious Mahadeva had in days of yore, burnt and consumed in a moment the triple city of the Asuras. With the greatest ease, O Govinda, Mahadeva, using that single arrow, achieved that feat. That weapon, shot by Mahadeva's arms, can, without doubt, consume in half the time taken up by a twinkling of the eyes the entire universe with all its mobile and immobile creatures. In the universe there is no being including even Brahma and Vishnu and the deities, that are incapable of being slain by that weapon. O sire, I saw that excellent, wonderful and incomparable weapon in the hand of Mahadeva. There is another mysterious and very powerful weapon which is equal or perhaps, superior to the Pasupata weapon. I beheld that also. It is celebrated in all the worlds as the Sula of the Sula-armed Mahadeva. Hurled by the illustrious deity, that weapon is competent to rive the entire Earth or dry up the waters of the ocean or annihilate the entire universe. In days of yore, Yuvanaswa's son, king Mandhatri, that conqueror of the three worlds, possessed of imperial sway and endued with abundant energy, was, with all his troops, destroyed by means of that weapon. Endued with great might and great energy and resembling Sakra himself in prowess, that king, O Govinda, was slain by the Rakshasa Lavana with the aid of this Sula which he had got from Siva. The Sula has a very keen point. Exceedingly terrible, it is capable of causing everybody's hair stand on its end. I saw it in the hand of Mahadeva, as if roaring with rage, having contracted its forehead into three wrinkles. It resembled, O Krishna, a smokeless fire or the sun that rises at the end of the Yuga. The handle of that Sula, was made of a mighty snake. It is really indescribable. It looked like the universal Destroyer himself armed with his noose. I saw this weapon, O Govinda, in the hand of Mahadeva. I beheld also another weapon, *viz.*, that sharp-edged battle-axe which, in days of yore, was given unto Rama by the gratified Mahadeva for enabling him to exterminate the Kshatriyas. It was with shis weapon that Rama (of Bhrigu's race) slew in dreadful battle the great Karttaviryya who was the ruler of all the world. It was with that weapon that Jamadagni's son, O Govinda, was able to exterminate the Kshatriyas for one and twenty times. Of blazing edge and exceedingly terrible, that axe was hanging on the shoulder, adorned with a snake, of Mahadeva. Indeed, it shone on Mahadeva's person like the flame of a blazing fire. I beheld innumerable other celestial weapons with Mahadeva of great intelligence. I have, however named only a few, O sinless one, in consequence of their principal character. On the left side of the great god stood the Grandsire Brahma seated on an excellent car unto which were attached swans endued with the speed of the mind. On the same side could be seen Narayana also, seated on the son of Vinata, and bearing the conch, the discus, and the mace. Close to the goddess Uma was Skanda seated on his peacock, bearing his fatal dart and bells, and looking like another Agni. In the front of Mahadeva I beheld Nandi standing armed with his Sula and looking like a second Sankara (for prowess and energy). The Munis headed by the Self-born Manu and Rishis having Bhrigu for their first, and the deities with Sakra at their head, all came there. All the tribes of spirits and ghosts, and the celestial Mothers, stood surrounding Mahadeva and saluting him with reverence. The deities were engaged in singing the praises of Mahadeva by uttering diverse hymns. The Grandsire Brahma uttering a Rathantara, praised Mahadeva. Narayana also, uttering the Jyestha Saman, sang the praises of Bhava. Sakra also did the same with the aid of those foremost of Vedic Mantras, *Viz.*, the Sata-Rudriam. Verily, Brahma and Narayana and Sakra,—those three high-souled deities,—shone there like three sacrificial fires. In their midst shone the illustrious God like the sun in the midst of his corona, emerged from autumnal clouds. I beheld myriads of suns and moons also in the sky, O Kesava. I then praised the illustrious Lord of everything, the supreme Master of the universe.

"'Upamanyu continued,—I said,—Salutations to thee, O illustrious one, O thou that constituest the refuge of all things, O thou that art called Mahadeva! Salutations to thee that assumest the form of Sakra, that art Sakra, and that disguisest thyself in the form and vestments of Sakra. Salutations to thee that art armed with the thunder, to thee that art tawny, and thee that art always armed with the Pinaka. Salutations to thee that always bearest the conch and the Sula. Salutations to thee that art clad in black, to thee that art of dark and curly hair, to thee that hast a dark deer-skin for thy upper garment, to thee that presidest over the eighth lunation of the dark fortnight. Salutations to thee that art of white complexion, to thee that art called white, to thee that art clad in white robes, to thee that hast limbs smeared with white ashes, to thee that art ever engaged in white deeds. Salutations to thee that art red of colour, to thee that art clad in red vestments, to thee that ownest a red banner with red flags, to thee that wearest red garlands and usest red unguents. Salutations to thee that art brown in complexion, to thee that art clad in brown vestments, to thee, that hast a brown banner with brown flags, to thee that wearest brown garlands and usest brown unguents. Salutations to thee that hast the umbrella of royalty held over thy head, to thee that wearest the foremost of crowns. Salutations unto thee that art adorned with half a garland and half an armlet, to thee that art decked with one ring for one year, to thee that art endued with the speed of the mind, to thee that art endued with great effulgence. Salutations to thee that art the foremost of deities, to thee that art the foremost of ascetics, to thee that art the foremost of celestials. Salutations to thee that wearest half a wreath of lotuses, to thee that hast many lotuses on thy body. Salutations to thee that hast half thy body smeared with sandal paste, to thee that hast half thy body decked with garlands of flowers and smeared with fragrant unguents.[1] Salutations to thee that art of the complexion of the Sun, to thee that art like the Sun, to thee whose face is like the Sun, to thee that hast eyes each of which is like the Sun. Salutations to thee that art Soma, to thee that art as mild as Soma, to thee that bearest the lunar disc, to thee that art of lunar aspect, to thee that art the foremost of all creatures, to thee that art adorned with a set of the most beautiful teeth. Salutations to thee that art of a dark complexion, to thee that art of a fair complexion, to thee that hast a form half of which is yellow and half white, to thee that hast a body half of which is male and half female, to thee that art both male and female. Salutations to thee that ownest a bull for thy vehicle, to thee that proceedest riding on the foremost of elephants, to thee that art obtained with difficulty, to thee that art capable of going to places unapproachable by others. Salutations to thee whose praises are sung by the Ganas, to thee that art devoted to the diverse Ganas, to thee that followest the track that is trod by the Ganas, to thee that art always devoted to the Ganas as to a vow. Salutations to thee that art of the complexion of white clouds, to thee that hast the splendour of the evening clouds, to thee that art incapable of being described by names, to thee that art of thy own form (having nothing else in the universe with which it can be compared). Salutations to thee that wearest a beautiful garland of red colour, to thee that art clad in robes of red colour. Salutations to thee that hast the crown of the head decked with gems, to thee that art adorned with a half-moon, to thee that wearest many beautiful gems in thy diadem, to thee that hast eight flowers on thy head. Salutations to thee that hast a fiery mouth and fiery eyes, to thee that hast eyes possessing the effulgence of a thousand moons, to thee that art of the form of fire, to thee that art beautiful and agreeable, to thee that art inconceivable and mysterious. Salutations to thee that rangest through the firmament, to thee that lovest and residest in lands affording pasture to kine, to thee that walkest on the Earth, to thee that art the Earth, to thee that art infinite, to thee that art excee-

1 Mahadeva's body is half male and half female. The male half has garlands of bones, the female half garlands of flowers. The male half has everything that is rejected by others ; the female half has all things that are coveted by others. This particular form of Mahadeva is called "Hara-Gauri."—T.

dingly auspicious. Salutations to thee that art unclad (or has the horizon alone for thy vestments), to thee that makest a happy home of every place where thou mayst happen to be for the moment. Salutations to thee that hast the universe for thy home, to thee that hast both Knowledge and Felicity for thy Soul. Salutations to thee that always wearest a diadem, to thee that wearest a large armlet, to thee that hast a snake for the garland round thy neck, to thee that wearest many beautiful ornaments on thy person. Salutations to thee that hast the Sun, the Moon, and Agni for thy three eyes, to thee that art possessed of a thousand eyes, to thee that art both male and female, to thee that art divested of sex, to thee that art a Sankhya, to thee that art a Yogin. Salutations to thee that art of the grace of those deities who are worshipped in sacrifices, to thee that art the Athravans, to thee that art the alleviator of all kinds of disease and pain, to thee that art the dispeller of every sorrow. Salutations to thee that roarest aș deep as the clouds, to thee that puttest forth diverse kinds of illusions, to thee that presidest over the soil and over the seed that is sown in it, to thee that art the Creator of everything. Salutations to thee that art the Lord of all the celestials, to thee that art the Master of the universe, to thee that art endued with the speed of the wind, to thee that art of the form of the wind. Salutations to thee that wearest a garland of gold, to thee that sportest on hills and mountains,[1] to thee that art adorned by all who are enemies of the gods, to thee that art possessed of fierce speed and energy. Salutations to thee that torest away one of the heads of the Grandsire Brahman, to thee that hast slain the Asura named Mahisha, to thee that assumest three forms, to thee that bearest every form. Salutations to thee that art the destroyer of the triple city of the Asuras, to thee that art the destroyer of (Daksha's) sacrifice, to thee that art the destroyer of the body of Kama (the deity of Desire), to thee that wieldest the rod of destruction. Salutations to thee that art Skanda, to thee that art Visakha, to thee that art the rod of the Brahmana, to thee that art Bhava, to thee that art Sarva, to thee that art of universal form. Salutations to thee that art Isana, to thee that art the destroyer of Bhaga, to thee that art the slayer of Andhaka, to thee that art the universe, to thee that art possessed of illusion, to thee that art both conceivable and inconceivable.[2] Thou art the one end of all creatures, thou art the foremost, thou art the heart of everything. Thou art the Brahman of all the deities, thou art the Nilardhita

1 'Girimala' is explained by the Commentator as one that sports on hills and mountains.—T.

2 All the texts have 'Bhavaghnaya.' The correct reading, however, seems to be 'Bhagaghnaya,' especially as the reference to Andhaka occurs immediately after.—T.

Red and Blue of the Rudras. Thou art the Soul of the creatures, thou art He who is called Purusha in the Sankhya philosophy, thou art the Rishabha among all things sacred, thou art that which is called auspicious by Yogins and which, according to them, is without parts (being indivisible). Amongst those that are observant of the different modes of life, thou art the House-holder, thou art the great Lord amongst the lords of the universe. Thou art Kuvera among all the Yakshas, and thou art Vishnu amongst all the sacrifices.[1] Thou art Meru amongst mountains, thou art the Moon among all luminaries of the firmament, thou art Vasishtha amongst Rishis, thou art Surya among the planets. Thou art the lion among all wild animals, and among all domoestic animals, thou art the bull that is worshipped by all people. Among the Adityas thou art Vishnu (Upendra), among the Vasu thou art Pavaka, among birds thou art the son of Vinata (Garuda), and among snakes thou art Ananta (Sesha). Among the Vedas thou art the Samans, among the Yojushes thou art the Sata-Rudriyam, among Yogins thou art Sanatkumara, and among Sankhyas thou art Kapila. Among the Maruts thou art Sakra, a mong the Pitris thou art Devarat, among all the regions (for the residence of created beings) thou art the region of Brahman, and amongst all the ends that creatures attain to, thou art Moksha or Emancipation. Thou art the Ocean of milk among all oceans, among all rocky eminences thou art Himavat, among all the orders thou art the Brahmana, and among all learned Brahmanas thou art he that has undergone and is observant of the Diksha. Thou art the Sun among all things in the world, thou art the destroyer called Kala. Thou art whatever else possessed of superior energy or eminence that exists in the universe. Thou art possessed of supreme puissance. Even this is what represents my certain conclusion. Salutations to thee, O puissant and illustrious one, O thou that art kind to all thy worshippers. Salutations to thee, O lord of Yogins. I bow to thee, O original cause of the universe. Be thou gratified with me that am thy worshipper, that am very miserable and helpless, O Eternal Lord, do thou become the refuge of this adorer of thine that is very weak and miserable. O Supreme Lord, it behoveth thee to pardon all those transgressions of which I have been guilty, taking compassion upon me on the ground of my being thy devoted worshipper. I was stupefied by thee, O Lord of all the deities, in consequence of the disguise in which thou showest thyself to me. O Maheswara, I did not give thee the Arghya or water to wash thy feet.[2] Having hymned the praises of Isana in this way, I offered him, with great devotion, water to

---

1 'Vishnu' means here the foremost of sacrifices.—T.

2 These articles must be offered to a visitor, whether he stands in need of them or not.—T.

wash his feet and the ingredients of the Arghya, and then, with joined hands, I resigned myself to him, being prepared to do whatever he would bid. Then, O sire, an auspicious shower of flowers fell upon my head, possessed of celestial fragrance and bedewed with cold water. The celestial musicians began to play on their kettle-drums. A delicious breeze, fragrant and agreeable, began to blow and fill me with pleasure. Then Mahadeva accompanied by his spouse, and having the bull for his sign, having been gratified with me, addressed the celestials assembled there in these words, filling me with great joy,—Behold, ye deities, the devotion of the high-souled Upamanyu. Verily, steady and great is that devotion, and entirely immutable, for it exists unalterably.—Thus addressed by the great God armed with the Sula, the deities, O Krishna, having bowed down unto him and joined their hands in reverence, said these words,—O illustrious one, O God of the gods, O master of the universe, O Lord of all, let this best of regenerate persons obtain from thee the fruition of all his desires.—Thus addressed by all the deities, with the Grandsire Brahma among them, Sarva, otherwise called Isa and Sankara, said these words, as if smiling unto me.

"'The illustrious Sankara said,—O dear Upamanyu, I am gratified with thee. Behold me, O foremost of Munis, O learned Rishi, thou art firmly devoted to me and well hast thou been tested by me. I have been very highly pleased with thee in consequence of this thy devotion to Siva. I shall, therefore, give thee today the fruition of whatever desires thou mayst have in thy heart.—Thus addressed by Mahadeva of great wisdom, tears of joy came into my eyes and my hair stood on its end (through emotion). Kneeling down unto him and bowing unto him repeatedly, I then, with a voice that was choked with delight, said unto him,—O illustrious god, it seems to me that I was hitherto dead and that it is only today that I have taken my birth, and that my birth hath today borne fruit, since I am staying now in the presence of Him who is the Master of both the deities and the Asuras! Who else is more praiseworthy than I, since I am beholding with these eyes of mine, Him of immeasurable prowess whom the very deities are unable to behold without first paying hearty worship? That which they that are possessed of learning and wisdom say is the highest of all topics, which is Eternal, which is distinguished from all else, which is unborn, which is Knowledge, which is indestructible, is identical with thee, O puissant and illustrious one, thee that art the beginning of all the topics, thee that art indestructible and changeless, thee that art conversant with the ordinances which govern all the topics, thee that art the foremost of Purushas, thee that art the highest of the high. Thou art he that hadst created from thy right side the Grandsire Brahman, the Creator of all things. Thou art he that hadst created from thy left side Vishnu for protecting the Creation. Thou art that puissant Lord who didst create Rudra when the end of the Yuga came and when the Creation was once more to be dissolved. That Rudra who sprang from thee destroyed the Creation with all its mobile and immobile beings, assuming the form of Kala of great energy, of the cloud Samvartaka (charged with water which myriads of oceans are not capacious enough to bear), and of the all-consuming fire. Verily, when the period comes for the dissolution of the universe, that Rudra stands, ready to swallow up the universe. Thou art that Mahadeva who is the original Creator of the universe with all its mobile and immobile entities. Thou art he who, at the end of the Kalpa, stands, withdrawing all things into thyself. Thou art he that pervadest all things, that art the Soul of all things, thou art the Creator of the Creator of all entities. Incapable of being seen by even any of the deities, thou art he that exists, pervading all entities. If, O lord, thou hast been gratified with me and if thou wouldst grant me boons, let this be the boon, O Lord of all the deities, that my devotion to thee may remain unchanged. O best of the deities, let me, through thy grace, have knowledge of the Present, the Past, and the Future. I shall also, with all my kinsmen and friends, always eat food mixed with milk. And let thy illustrious self be for ever present at our retreat.—Thus addressed by me, the illustrious Maheswara endued with supreme energy, that Master of all mobile and immobile, viz., Siva, worshipped of all the universe, then said unto me these words :—

" 'The illustrious Deity said,—Be thou free from every misery and pain, and be thou above decrepitude and death. Be thou possessed of fame, be thou endued with great energy, and let spiritual knowledge be thine. Thou shalt, through my grace, be always sought for by the Rishis. Be thy behaviour good and righteous, be every desirable attribute thine, be thou possessed of universal knowledge, and be thou of agreeable appearance. Let undecaying youth be thine, and let thy energy be like that of fire. Wherever, again, thou mayst desire the presence of the ocean of milk that is so agreeable to thee, there shall that ocean appear before thee, (ready for being utilised by thee and thy friends for purposes of thy food). Do thou, with thy friends, always obtain food prepared with milk, with the celestial nectar besides being mixed with it.[1] After the expiration of a Kalpa thou shalt then obtain my compainonship. Thy family and race and kinsmen shall be exhaustless. O foremost of regenerate ones, thy devotion to me shall be eternal. And, O best of Brahmanas, I shall always accord my presence to thy asylum. Live, O son, whithersoever thou likest, and let no anxiety be thine. Thought

1 All the texts read 'Kshirodasagarasohaiva.' The correct reading is 'Kshirodasagarasyaiva.' The nominative may be construed with the previous line, but the genetive would be better.--T.

of by thee. I shall, O learned Brahmana, grant thee a sight of myself again.—Having said these words, and granted me these boons, the illustrious Isana, endued with the effulgence of millions of Suns, disappeared there and then. It was even thus, O Krishna, that I beheld, with the aid of austere penances, that God of gods. I also obtained all that was said by the great Deity endued with supreme intelligence. Behold, O Krishna, before thy eyes, these Siddhas residing here and these Rishis and Vidyadharas and Yakshas and Gandharvas and Apsaras. Behold these trees and creepers and plants yielding all sorts of flowers and fruits. Behold them bearing the flowers of every season, with beautiful leaves, and shedding a sweet fragrance all around. O thou of mighty arms, all these are endued with a celestial nature through the grace of that god of gods, that supreme Lord, that high-souled Deity.—'

"Vasudeva continued,—'Hearing these words of his and beholding, as it were, with my own eyes all that he had related to me, I became filled with wonder. I then addressed the great ascetic Upamanyu and said unto him,—Deserving of great praise art thou, O foremost of learned Brahmanas, for what righteous man is there other than thou whose retreat enjoys the distinction of being honoured with the presence of that God of gods? Will the puissant Siva, will the great Sankara, O chief of ascetics, grant me also a sight of his person and show me favour?—

" '—Upamanyu said,—Without doubt, O thou of eyes like lotus petals, thou wilt obtain a sight of Mahadeva very soon, even as, O sinless one, I succeeded in obtaining a sight of him. O thou of immeasurable prowess, I see with my spiritual eyes that thou wilt, in the sixth month from this, succeed in obtaining a sight of Mahadeva, O best of all persons. Thou, O foremost of the Yadus, wilt obtain from Maheswara and his spouse, four and twenty boons. I tell thee what is true. Through the grace of that Deity endued with supreme wisdom, the Past, the Future and the Present are known to me. The great Hara has favoured these Rishis numbering by thousands and others as numerous. Why will not the puissant Deity show favour to thee, O Madhava? The meeting of the gods is always commendable with one like thee, with one that is devoted to the Brahmanas, with one that is full of compassion and that is full of faith. I shall give thee certain Mantras. Recite them continuously. By this thou art certain to behold Sankara.—

"The blessed Vishnu continued,—'I then said unto him,—O regenerate one, through thy grace, O great ascetic, I shall behold the lord of the deities, that grinder of multitudes of Diti's sons. Eight days, O Bharata, passed there like an hour, of all us being thus occupied with talk on Mahadeva. On the eighth day, I underwent the Diksha (initiation) according to due rites, at the hands of that Brahmana and received the staff from his hands. I underwent the prescribed shave. I took up a quantity of Kusa blades in my hand. I wore rags for my vestments. I rubbed my person with ghee. I encircled a cord of Munja grass round my loins. For one month I lived on fruits. The second month I subisted upon water. The third, the fourth and the fifth months I passed, living upon air alone. I stood all the while, supporting myself upon one foot and with my arms also raised upwards, and foregoing sleep all the while. I then beheld, O Bharata, in the firmament an effulgence that seemed to be as dazzling as that of a thousand Suns combined together. Towards the centre of that effulgence, O son of Pandu, I saw a cloud looking like a mass of blue hills, adorned with rows of cranes, embellished with many a grand rainbow, with flashes of lightning and the thunder-fire looking like eyes set on it.[1] Within that cloud was the puissant Mahadeva, himself of dazzling splendour, accompanied by his spouse Uma. Verily, the great Deity seemed to shine with his penances, energy, beauty, effulgence, and his dear spouse by his side. The puissant Maheswara, with his spouse by his side, shone in the midst of that cloud. The appearance seemed to be like that of the Sun in the midst of racking clouds with the Moon by his side. The hair on my body, O son of Kunti, stood on its end, and my eyes expanded with wonder upon beholding Hara, the refuge of all the deities and the dispeller of all their griefs. Mahadeva was adorned with a diadem on his head. He was armed with his Sula. He was clad in a tiger skin, had matted locks on his head, and bore the staff (of the Sanyasin) in one of his hands. He was armed, besides with his Pinaka and the thunder-bolt. His teeth was sharp-pointed. He was decked with an excellent bracelet for the upper arm. His sacred thread was constituted by a snake. He wore an excellent garland of diversified colours on his bosom, that hung down to his toes. Verily, I beheld him like the exceedingly bright moon of an autumnal evening. Surrounded by diverse clans of spirits and ghosts, he looked like the autumnal Sun difficult of being gazed at for its dazzling brightness. Eleven hundred Rudras stood around that Deity of restrained soul and white deeds, then seated upon his bull. All of them were employed in hymning his praises. The Adityas, the Vasus, the Sadhyas, the Viswadevas, and the twin Aswins praised that Lord of the universe by uttering the hymns occurring in the scriptures. The puissant Indra and his brother Upendra, the two sons of Aditi, and the Grandsire Brahma, all uttered, in the presence of Bhava, the Rathantara Saman. Innumerable masters of Yoga, all the regenerate Rishis with their children, all the

---

1 The Commentator does not explain what is meant by, Vidyunmalagavakshakam. The word 'go' means the Thunder fire. Very probably, what is implied is that flashes of lightning and the Thunder-fire looked like eyes set upon that cloud. 'Go' may also mean 'jyoti' or effulgence.—T.

celestial Rishis, the goddess Earth, the Sky (between Earth and Heaven), the Constellations, the Planets, the months, the Fortnights, the Seasons, Night, the Years, the Kshanas, the Muhurtas, the Nimeshas, the Yugas one after another, all the celestial Sciences and branches of knowledge, and all beings conversant with Truth, were seen bowing down unto that Supreme Preceptor, that great Father, that giver (or origin) of Yoga. Sanatkumara, the Vedas, the Histories, Marichi, Angiras, Atri, Pulastya, Pulaha, Kratu, the seven Manus, Soma, the Atharvans, and Vrihaspati, Bhrigu, Daksha, Kasyapa, Vasishtha, Kasya, the Schandas, Diksha, the Sacrifices, Dakshina, the Sacrificial Fires, the Havis (clarified butter) poured in sacrifices, and all the requisites of the sacrifices, were beheld by me, O Yudhishthira, standing there in their embodied forms. All the guardians of the worlds, all the Rivers, all the snakes, the mountains, the celestial Mothers, all the spouses and daughters of the celestials, thousands upon thousands and millions of ascetics, were seen to bow down to that puissant Lord who is the soul of tranquility. The Mountains, the Oceans, and the Points of the compass also did the same, the Gandharvas and the Apsaras highly skilled in music, in celestial strains, sang and hymned the praises of Bhava who is full of wonder. The Vidyadharas, the Danavas, the Guhyakas, the Rakshasas, and all created beings, mobile and immobile, adorned, in thought, word and deed, that puissant Lord. Before me, that Lord of all the gods, viz., Sarva, appeared, seated in all his glory. Seeing that Isana had showed himself to me by being seated in glory before my eyes, the whole universe, with the Grandsire and Sakra, looked at me. I, however, had not the power to look at Mahadeva. The great Deity then addressed me saying,—Behold, O Krishna, and speak to me. Thou hast adored me hundreds and thousands of times. There is no one in the three worlds that is dearer to me than thou.—After I had bowed unto him, his spouse, viz., the goddess Uma, became gratified with me. I then addressed in these words the great God whose praises are hymned by all the deities with the Grandsire Brahma at their head.'

"The blessed Vishnu said,—'I saluted Mahadeva, saying,—Salutations to thee, O thou that art the eternal origin of all things. The Rishis say that thou art the Lord of the Vedas. The righteous say that thou art Penance, thou art Sattwa, thou art Rajas, thou art Tamas, and thou art Truth. Thou art Brahman, thou art Rudra, thou art Varuna, thou art Agni, thou art Manu, thou art Bhava, thou art Dhatri, thou art Tashtri, thou art Vidhatri, thou art the puissant Master of all things, and thou art everywhere. All beings, mobile and immobile, have sprung from thee. This triple world with all its mobile and immobile entities, has been created by thee. The Rishis say that thou art superior to the senses, the mind, the vital breaths, the seven sacrificial fires, all others that have their refuge in the all-pervading Soul, and all the deities that are adored and worthy of adoration. Thou, O illustrious one, art the Vedas, the Sacrifices, Soma, Dakshina, Pavaka, Havi, and all other requisites of sacrifice. The merit obtained by sacrifices, gifts made to others, the study of the Vedas, vows, regulations in respect of restraint, Modesty, Fame, Prosperity, Splendour, Contentment, and Success, all exist for leading to thee.[1] Desire, Wrath, Fear, Cupidity, Pride, Stupefaction, and Malice, Pains and Diseases, are, O illustrious one, thy children. Thou art all acts that creatures do, thou art the joy and sorrow that flow from those acts, thou art the absence of joy and sorrow, thou art that Ignorance which is the indestructible seed of Desire, thou art the high origin of Mind, thou art Puissance, and thou art Eternity.[2] Thou art the Unmanifest, thou art Pavana, thou art inconceivable, thou art the thousand-rayed Sun, thou art the effulgent Chit, thou art the first of all the topics, and thou art the refuge of life.[3] The use of words like Mahat, Soul, Understanding, Brahman, Universe, Sambhu, and Self-born and other words occuring in succession (in the Vedas), show that thy nature has been judged (by persons conversant with the Vedas) as identical with Mahat and Soul. Verily, regarding thee as all this, the learned Brahmanas win over that ignorance which lies at the root of the world. Thou residest in the heart of all creatures, and thou art adored by the Rishis as Kshetrajna. Thy arms and feet extend to every place, and thy eyes, head, and face are everywhere. Thou hearest everywhere in the universe, and thou stayest, prevading all things. Of all acts that are performed in the Nimeshas and other divisions of time that spring in consequence of the puissance of the Sun, thou art the fruit.[4] Thou art the original effulgence (of the supreme Chit). Thou art Purusha, and thou residest in the hearts of all things. Thou art the various Yogic attributes of success, *viz.*, Subtility and Grossness and Fruition and Supremacy and Effulgence and Immuta-

---

1 'Tadarpani' is explained by the Commentator as 'Twatsarupasya-prapika.'—T.

2 'Kriti' is 'Kriya,' *i.e.*, all acts that creatures do. 'Vikara' is the fruits of 'kriya.' *i.e.*, joy or sorrow that creatures enjoy or endure. The Bengal texts read 'pralaya.' The Bombay reading is 'pranaya.' The latter is also the reading that the Commentator notices, but when he explains it to mean 'tadabhavah,' *i.e.*, the absence of joy and sorrow, I think, through the scribe's mistake, the 'I' has been changed into the palatal 'n.' 'Prabhavah' is explained as 'aiswaryya.' 'Saswata' is eternal *i.e.*, transcending the influence of acts.—T.

3 Thou art the 'adi' of the 'ganas.' By 'ganas' is meant 'ganayante sankhyayante iti ganah, *i.e.*, tattwah.'—T.

4 The Commentator explains this by saying that thou art the heavenly felicity which creatures earn by means of their righteous acts. Acts, again are performed in course of Time whose divisions are caused by the Sun.—T.

bility.[1] Understanding and inteligence and all the worlds rest upon thee. They that are devoted to meditation, that are always engaged in Yoga, that are devoted to or firm in Truth and that have subjugated their passions, seek thee and rest on thee.[2] They that know thee for one that is Immutable, or one that resides in all hearts, or one that is endued with supreme puissance, or one that is the ancient Purusha, or one that is pure Knowledge, or one that is the effulgent Chit, or one that is the highest refuge of all persons endued with intelligence, are certainly persons of great intelligence. Verily, such persons stay, transcending intelligence.[3] By understanding the seven subtile entities (*viz.*, Mahat, Ego, and the five subtile primal elements called Tanmatras), by comprehending thy six attributes (of Omniscience, Contentment of Fullness, Knowledge without beginning, Independence, Puissance that is not at fault at any time and that is infinite), and being conversant with Yoga that is freed from every false notion, the man of knowledge succeeds in entering into thy great self.—After I had said these words, O Partha, unto Bhava, that dispeller of grief and pain, the universe, both mobile and immobile, sent up a leonine shout (expressive of their approval of the correctness of my words). The innumerable Brahmanas there present, the deities and the Asuras, the Nagas, the Pisachas, the Pitris, the birds, diverse Rakshasas, diverse classes of ghosts and spirits, and all the great Rishis, then bowed down unto that great Deity. There then fell upon my head showers of celestial flowers possessed of great fragrance, and delicious winds blew on the spot. The puissant Sankara then, devoted to the good of the universe, looked at the goddess Uma and the lord of the celestials and myself also, and thus spoke unto me:—We know, O Krishna, that thou, O slayer of foes, art filled with the greatest devotion towards us. Do what is for thy good. My love and affection for thee is very great. Do thou ask for eight boons. I shall verily give them unto thee, O Krishna, O best of all persons, tell me what they are, O chief of the Yadavas. Name what thou wishest. However difficult of attainment they be, thou shalt have them still.[4]—

---

1 It has been explained in previous Sections that by success in Yoga one may make oneself as subtile as possible or as gross as possible. One may also attain to the fruition of all desires, extending to the very creation of worlds upon worlds peopled with all kinds of creatures. That Yogins do not create is due to their respect for the Grandsire and their wish not to disturb the ordinary course of things.—T.

2 'Satyasandhah' is the Bengal reading. The Bombay reading is 'satyasatwah,' meaning, as the Commentator explains, 'satya-sankalpah.—T.

3 'Vigraham' is explained by the Commentator as 'visishthanubhanubhava-rupam' or 'nishkalam jnaptimatram.'—T.

4 In Verse 369 *ante* Upamanyu says that Krishna is to receive from Mahadeva sixteen and eight boons. The Commentator, stretching the words

SECTION XV

"The blessed Krishna said,—Bowing my head with great joy unto that mass of energy and effulgence, I said these words unto the great Deity, with a heart filled with gladness,—Firmness in virtue, the slaughter of foes in battle, the highest fame, the greatest might; devotion to Yoga, thy adjacence, and hundreds upon hundreds of children,—these are the boons I solicit of thee,—So be it —said Sankara, repeating the words I had uttered. After this, the mother of the universe, the upholdress of all things, who cleanses all things, *viz.*, the spouse of Sarva, that vast receptacle of penances said with a restrained soul these words unto me :—The puissant Mahadeva has granted thee, O sinless one, a son who shall be named Samva. Do thou take from me also eight boons which thou choosest. I shall certainly grant them to thee.—Bowing unto her with a bend of my head, I said unto her, O son of Pandu,—I solicit from thee non-anger against the Brahmanas, grace of my father, a hundred sons, the highest enjoyments, love for my family, the grace of my mother, the attainment of tranquility and peace, and cleverness in every act !—

"Uma said,—It shall be even so, O thou that art possessed of prowess and puissance equal to that of a celestial. I never say what is untrue. Thou shalt have sixteen thousand wives. Thy love for them and theirs also for thee shall be unlimited. From all thy kinsmen also, thou shalt receive the highest affection. Thy body too shall be most beautiful. Seven thousand guests will daily feed at thy palace :—

"Vasudeva continued,—'Having thus granted me boons, both the god and the goddess, O Bharata, disappeared there and then with their Ganas, O elder brother of Bhima. All those wonderful facts I related fully, O best of kings, to that Brahmana of great energy *viz.* Upamanyu (from whom I had obtained the Diksha before adoring Mahadeva). Bowing down unto the great God, Upamanyu said these words to me.—

"Upamanyu said,—There is no deity like Sarva. There is no end or refuge like Sarva. There is none that can give so many or such high boons. There is none that equal him in battle.

---

has tried to explain them as signifying a total of eight, and eight *i.e*, eight are to be obtained from Mahadeva, and eight from his divine spouse Uma. The language, however, is such that this meaning cannot be put upon it without doing violence to it.—T.

SECTION XVI

"Upamanyu said,—There was in the Krita age, O sire, a Rishi celebrated under the name of Tandi. With great devotion of heart he adored, with the aid of Yoga-meditation, the great God for ten thousand years. Listen to me as I tell thee fruit or reward he reaped of such extraordinary devotion. He succeeded in beholding Mahadeva and praised him by uttering some hymns. Thinking, with the aid of his penances, of Him who is the supreme Soul and who is immutable and undeteriorating, Tandi became filled with wonder, and said these words,—I seek the protection of Him whom the Sankhyas describe and the Yogins think of as the Supreme, the Foremost, the Purusha, the pervader of all things, and the Master of all existent objects, of him who, the learned say, is the cause of both the creation and the destruction of the universe ; of him who is superior to all the celestials, the Asuras, and the Munis, of him who has nothing higher, who is unborn, who is the Lord of all things, who has neither beginning nor end, and who is endued with supreme puissance, who is possessed of the highest felicity, and who is effulgent and sinless.—After he had said these words, Tandi beheld before him that ocean of penances, that great Deity who is immutable and undeteriorating, who is without compare, who is inconceivable, who is eternal, and who is without any change, who is indivisible, who is whole, who is Brahma, who transcends all attributes, and who is endued with attributes, who is the highest delight of Yogins, who is without deterioration, who is called Emancipation, who is the refuge of the Mind, of Indra, of Agni, of the god of wind, of the entire universe, and of the Grandsire Brahma ; who is incapable of being conceived by the Mind, who is without mutation of any kind, who is pure, who is capable of being apprehended by understanding only and who is immaterial as the Mind ; who is difficult of comprehension, who is incapable of being measured, who is difficult of being attained by persons of uncleansed souls, who is the origin of the universe, and who transcends both the universe and the attribute of darkness ; who is ancient, who is Purusha, who is possessed of effulgence, and who is higher than the highest. The Rishi Tandin, desirous of beholding Him who making himself endued with life-breaths, resides in what results from it *viz.*, Jiva, in the form of that effulgence which is called the Mind, passed many years in the practice of the severest austerities, and having succeeded in beholding Him as the reward of those penances, he praised the great God in the following terms.

" '—Tandi said,—Thou art the holiest of holies[1] and the refuge of all, O foremost of all beings endued with intelligence. Thou art the fiercest energy of all kinds of energy. Thou art the austerest penance of all penances. Thou, O puissant one, art the liberal giver of blessings. Thou art the supreme Truth. Salutations to thee, O thou of a thousand rays, and, O refuge of all felicity. Thou art the giver of that Nirvana which, O puissant one, Yatis, standing in fear of birth and death, strive for so hard. The Grandsire Brahma, he of a hundred sacrifices, (*viz.*, Indra) Vishnu, the Viswadevas, the great Rishis, are incapable of comprehending thee and thy real nature. How then can persons like ourselves hope to comprehend thee? From thee flows everything. Upon thee rests everything. Thou art called Kala, thou art called Purusha, thou art called Brahma. Celestial Rishis conversant with the Puranas say that thou hast three bodies *viz.*, those pertaining to Kalas, those pertaining to Purusha and those pertaining to Brahma or the three forms namely Brahman, Vishnu and Rudra. Thou art Adhi-Purusha, (occupying the physical frame from head to foot) thou art Adhyatma, thou art Adhibhuta, and Adhi-Daivata, thou art Adhi-loka, Adhi-Vijnanam and Adhi-Yajna.[2] Men of wisdom, when they succeed in knowing thee that residest in themselves and that art incapable of being known by the very gods, become freed from all bonds and pass into a state of existence that transcends all sorrow.[3] They that do not wish to know thee, O thou of great puissance, have to undergo innumerable births and deaths. Thou art the door of heaven and of Emancipation. Thou art he that projectest all beings into existence and withdrawest them again into thyself. Thow art the great giver. Thou art heaven, thou art Emancipation, thou art desire (the seed of action). Thou art wrath that inspires creatures. Thou art Sattwa, thou art Rajas, thou art Tamas, thou art the nether regions, and thou art the upper regions. Thou art the Grandsire Brahma, thou art Bhava, thou art Vishnu, thou art Skanda, thou art Indra, thou art Savitri, thou art Yama, thou art Varuna, Soma, thou art Dhatri, thou art Manu, thou art Vidhatri and thou art Kuvera, the Lord of treasures. Thou

---

1 The Commentator explains this as 'thou art the cleanser of all cleansing entities, *i.e.*, it is in consequence of thee, Ganga and the others have received the power of cleansing other things and creatures.—T.

2 Adhyatma : that occupies the inner body. Adhibhuta : elements, prana eyes, ears, etc ; Adhidaivata : sun, moon, etc that control over the bhutas. Adhiloka—one occupying the lokas ; Adhivijnana—one occupying the plane of consciousness ; Adhiyajna—one conducting the sacrifices residing in the heart of the jivas.—T.

3 *i e.*, they attain to Emancipation when they behold thee in the firmament of their own hearts, or succeed in identifying their own souls with thee.—T.

art Earth, thou art Wind, thou art Water, thou art Agni, thou art Space, thou art Speech, thou art the Understanding, thou art Steadiness, thou art Intelligence, thou art the acts that creatures do, thou art Truth, thou art Falsehood, thou art existent and thou art non-existent. Thou art the senses, thou art that which transcends Prakriti, thou art immutable. Thou art superior to the universe of existent objects, thou art superior to the universe of non-existent objects, thou art capable of being conceived, thou art incapable of being conceived. That which is supreme Brahman, that which is the highest entity, that which is the end of both the Sankhyas and the Yogins, is, without doubt, identical with thee. Verily, rewarded have I been today by thee in consequence of thy granting me a sight of thy form. I have attained the end which the righteous alone attain to. I have been rewarded with that end which is solicited by persons whose understandings have been cleansed by Knowledge. Alas, so long I was steeped in Ignorance ; for this long period I was a senseless fool, since I had no knowledge of thee that art the Supreme Deity, thee that art the only eternal Entity as can be only known by all persons endued with wisdom. In course of innumerable lives have I at last succeeded in acquiring that Devotion towards thee in consequence of which thou hast shown thyself to me; O thou that art ever inclined to extend thy grace to those that are devoted to thee. He that succeeds in knowing thee is enable to enjoy immortality. Thou art that which is ever a mystery with the gods, the Asuras, and the ascetics. Brahman is concealed in the cave of the heart. The very ascetics are unable to behold or know Him.[1] Thou art that puissant deity who is the doer of everything and whose face is turned towards every direction. Thou art the Soul of all things, thou seest all things, thou pervadest all things, and thou knowest all things. Thou makest a body for thyself, and bearest that body. Thou art an embodied Being. Thou enjoyest a body, and thou art the refuge of all embodied creatures. Thou art the creator of the life-breaths, thou possessest the life-breaths, thou art one that is endued with life-breaths, thou art the giver of the life-breaths, and thou art the refuge of all beings endued with life-breaths. Thou art that Adhyatma which is the refuge of all righteous persons that are devoted to Yoga-meditation and conversant with the Soul and that are solicitous of avoiding rebirth. Verily, thou art that Supreme Lord who is identical with that refuge. Thou art the giver unto all creatures of whatever ends become theirs, fraught with happiness or misery. Thou art he that ordains all created beings to birth and death. Thou art the puissant Lord who grants success to Rishis crowned with success in respect of the fruition of their wishes. Having created all the

1 The 'guha' or cave in which Brahmans is concealed is the heart of every living creature.—T.

worlds beginning with Bhu, together with all the denizens of heaven, that upholdest and cherishest them all, distributing thyself into thy well-known forms numbering Eight.[1] From thee flows everything. Upon thee rests all things. All things, again, disappear in thee. Thou art the sole object that is Eternal. Thou art that region of Truth which is sought by the righteous and regarded by them as the highest. Thou art that cessation of individual existence which Yogins seek. Thou art that Oneness which is sought by persons conversant with the Soul. Brahma and the Siddhas expounding the mantras have concealed thee in a cave for preventing the deities and Asuras and human beings from beholding thee.[2] Although thou residest in the heart, yet thou concealed. Hence, stupefied by thee, deities and Asuras and human beings are all unable to understand thee, O Bhava, truly and in all thy details. Unto those persons that succeed in attaining to thee after having cleansed themselves by devotion, thou showest thyself of thy own accord, O thou that residest in all hearts.[3] By knowing thee one can avoid both death and rebirth. Thou art the highest object of knowledge. By knowing thee no higher object remains for one to know. Thou art the greatest object of acquisition. The person that is truly wise, by acquiring thee, thinks that there is no higher object to acquire. By attaining to thee that art exceedingly subtile and that art the highest object of acquisition, the man of wisdom becomes immortal and immutable. The followers of the Sankhya system, well conversant with their own philosophy and possessing a knowledge of the attributes (of Sattwa, Rajas and Tamas) and of those called the topics of enquiry,—those learned men who transcend the destructible by attaining to a knowledge of the subtile or indestructible—succeed, by knowing thee, in freeing themselves from all bonds. Persons conversant with the Vedas regard thee as the one object of knowledge, which has been expounded in the Vedantas. These men, devoted to the regulation of the breaths, always meditate on thee and at last enter into thee as their highest end. Riding on the car

---

1 The worlds or regions commonly enumerated are Bhu, Bhuva, Swa, Maha, Jana, Tapa, and Satya. The eight well-known forms of Mahadeva are Water, Fire, Hotri, Sun, Moon, Space, Earth and Wind. In his form of water he is called Bhava; in that of fire, he is called Rudra; in that of Hotri he is called Pasupati; in that of the Sun, he is called Isana, in that of the Moon, he is called Mahadeva; in that of Space, he is called Bhima; in that of Earth, he is called Sarva: and in that of wind, he is called Ugra. Compare the benediction in Kalidasa's *Sakuntalah.*—T.

2 The cave in which Mahadeva has been concealed in the cave of the Scriptures: probably, difficult texts.—T.

3 The sense is that these persons have not to make any extraordinary efforts for beholding thee. Their devotion is sufficient to induce thee to show thyself unto them.—T.

made of Om, those men enter into Maheswara. Of that which is called the Devayana (the path of the deities) thou art the door called Aditya. Thou art again, the door, called Chandramas, of that which is called the Pitriyana (the path of the Pitris.)[1] Thou art Kashtha, thou art the points of the horizon, thou art the year, and thou art the Yugas. Thine is the sovereignty of the heavens, thine is the sovereignty of the Earth, thou art the Northern and the Southern declensions. The Grandsire Brahma in days of yore uttered thy praises, O thou that art called Nilarohita (blue and red), by reciting diverse hymns and urged thee to create living creatures. Brahmanas conversant with Richs praise thee by uttering Richs, regarding thee as unattached to all things and as divested of all forms. Adhyaryus, in sacrifices, pour libations, uttering Yajushes the while, in honour of thee that art the sole object of knowledge, according to the three well-known ways.[2] Persons of cleansed understandings, that are conversant with Samans, sing thee with the aid of Samans. Those regenerate persons, again, that are conversant with the Atharvans, hymn thee as Rita, as Truth, as the Highest, and as Brahma. Thou art the highest cause, whence Sacrifice has flowed. Thou art the Lord, and thou art Supreme. The night and day are thy sense of hearing and sense of sight. The fortnights and months are thy head and arms. The seasons are thy energy, penances are thy patience, and the year is thy anus, thighs and feet. Thou art Mrityu, thou art Yama, thou art Hutasana, thou art Kala, thou art endued with speed in respect of destruction, thou art the original cause of Time, and thou art eternal Time. Thou art Chandramas and Aditya, with all the stars and planets and the atmosphere that fills space. Thou art the pole-star, thou art constellation called the seven Rishis, thou art the seven regions beginning with Bhu. Thou art Pradhana and Mahat, thou art Unmanifest, and thou art this world. Thou art the universe beginning with Brahman and ending with the lowest forms of vegetation. Thou art the beginning or original cause of all creatures. Thou art the eight Prakritis.[3] Thou art, again, above the eight Prakritis. Everything that exists, represents a portion of thy divine Self. Thou art that supreme Felicity which is also Eternal. Thou art the end which is attained to by all things. Thou art that highest existence which is sought for by the Righteous. Thou art that state which is freed from every anxiety. Thou art eternal

---

1 Deva-yana' and 'Pitri-yana' are the two courses or paths by which the departed have to attain to their ends. Those going by the former reach the Sun; while those that go by the latter reach the Moon.—T.

2 The first is that which is according to the rites inculcated in the Srutis; second is according to the procedure laid down in the Smritis; and the third is the way or manner constituted by Dhyana or meditation.—T.

3 Vide *Sankhya karika*. With original Prakriti, the seven beginning with Mahat and Ahankara and numbering the five *Tanmatras*.—T.

Brahman. Thou art that highest state which constitutes the meditation of persons learned in the scriptures and the Vedangas. Thou art the highest Kashtha, thou art the highest Kala. Thou art the highest Success, and thou art the highest Refuge. Thou art the highest Tranquility. Thou art the highest cessation of Existence. By attaining to thee, Yogins think that they attain to the highest success that is open to them. Thou art Contentment, thou art Success, thou art the Sruti, and thou art the Smriti. Thou art that Refuge of the Soul after which Yogins strive, and thou art that indestructible Prapti which men of Knowledge pursue. Thou art, without doubt, that End which those presons have in view that are habitutated to sacrifices and that pour sacrificial libations, impelled by specific desires, and that make large presents on such occassions. Thou art that high End which is sought for by persons that waste and scorch their bodies with severe penances with ceaseless recitations, with those rigid vows and fasts that appertain to their tranquil lives, and with other means of self-affliction. O Eternal one, thou art that End which is theirs that are unattached to all things and that have relinquished all acts. Thou, O Eternal one, art that End which is theirs that are desirous of achieving Emancipation from rebirth, that live in dissociation from all enjoyments, and that desire the annihilation of the Prakriti elements. Thou art that high End, O illustrious one, which is indescribable, which is strainless, which is the immutable one, and which is theirs that are devoted to knowledge and science. These are the five Ends that have been declared in the Vedas and the Scriptures and the Puranas. It is through thy grace that persons attain to those Ends, or, if they fail to attain to them, it is through thy grace being denied to them.—It was thus Tandi, who was a vast heap of penances, praised Isana. And he sang also that high Brahman which in ancient days was sung by the Creator himself (in honour of Mahadeva).

" 'Upamanyu continued,—Thus praised by that utterer of Brahma, *viz.*, Tandi, Mahadeva that illustrious and puissant Deity, who was accompanied by his spouse Uma, said these words. Tandi had further said,—Neither Brahma, nor Indra, nor Vishnu, nor the Viswedevas, nor the great Rishis, know thee.—Gratified at this, 'Siva said the following words.

" 'The holy one said,—Thou shalt be indestructible and eternal. Thou shalt be freed from all sorrow. Great fame shall be thine. Thou shalt be endued with energy. Spiritual knowledge shall be thine. All the Rishis shall seek thee, and thy son, through my grace, shall become the author of *Sutras*, O foremost of regenerate persons. What wishes of thine shall I grant today ? Tell me, O son, what those objects are which thou desirest.—At this, Tandi joined his hands and said—O Lord, let my devotion to thee be steady.—

"'Upamanyu continued,—Having given unto Tandi these boons and having received the adorations of both the deities and the Rishis, the great Deity disappeared there and then. When the illustrious deity, O lord of the Yadavas, thus, disappeared with all his followers, the Rishi came to my asylum and said unto me all that had happened to him. Do thou hear, O foremost of men, all those celebrated names (of Mahadeva) that Tandi said unto me for thy spiritual success. The Grandsire had at one time recited ten thousand names that apply to Mahadeva. In the scriptures, a thousand names occur of that illustrious deity. These names are not known to all. O thou that transcendest destruction, in days of yore, the Grandsire Brahma uttered these names for adoring the high-souled Deity. Having acquired them through the grace of the Grandsire, Tandi communicated them to me!'[1]—

SECTION XVII

"Vasudeva said,—Concentrating his mind, O Yudhishthira, the regenerate Rishi Upamanyu, with hands joined together in reverence uttered this abstract of names (applying to Mahadeva), commencing from the beginning.

"Upamanyu said,—I shall adore that great Deity who deserves the adorations of all creatures, by uttering those names that are celebrated over all the worlds,—names some of which were uttered by the Grandsire Brahma, some by the Rishis, and some of which occur in the Vedas and the Vedangas. Those names have been applied (unto the great Deity) by persons that are eminent. Those names of him that are, again, true and fraught with success and are capable of accomplishing all the purposes which the utterer may have in view, have been applied unto Mahadeva by Tandi after calling them from the Vedic lore with the aid of his devotion. Indeed, with those names that have been uttered by many well-known persons of righteousness and by ascetics conversant with all the spiritual principles, I shall adore him who is the foremost, who is the first, who leads to heaven, who is ready to confer benefits upon all creatures, and who is auspicious. Those names have been heard everywhere in the universe, having spread from the region of Brahma (where they were originally invented). All of them are fraught with the element of Truth. With those names

1 Both the Vernacular translators render the last Verse most erroneously. K. P. Singha skips over every difficulty. In the Anusasana, this characteristic of his is more marked than in the Santi. The Burdwan translators very rarely skip over a Verse, but they are very generally in the wrong. Nilakantha explains that 'Devesah' is Brahma. The meaning, therefore, is that Tandi said unto me those secret names which Brahma had applied unto the high-souled one or Mahadeva. The Bengal reading 'Devesa,' in the vocative, is incorrect.—T.

I shall adore him who is Supreme Brahman, who has been declared (unto the universe) by the Vedas, and who is Eternal. I shall now tell thee, O chief of Yadu's race those names. Do thou hear them with rapt attention. Thou art a devoted worshipper of the Supreme Deity. Do thou worship the illustrious Bhava, distinguishing him above all the deities. And because thou art devoted to him, I shall therefore, recite those names in thy hearing. Mahadeva is Eternal Brahman. Persons endued with Yoga ; Yoga's achievements are unable to know in even a hundred years, the glory and puissance of the great Deity in their entirety. Verily, the beginning, middle or end of Mahadeva cannot be apprehended by the very deities. Indeed, when the case is such, who is there O Madhava, that can recite the attributes of Mahadeva in their entirety ? For all that, I shall through the grace of that illustrious and supreme Deity of perfect wisdom, extended to me for my devotion to him, recite his attributes as embodied in an abstract of few words and letters. The Supreme Lord is incapable of being adored by any one if he does not grant his permission to the adorer. As regards myself, it is only when I become fortunate enough to receive his permission that I succeed in adoring him. I shall indicate only a few names of that great Deity who is without birth and without destruction, who is the original cause of the universe, who is endued with the highest Soul, and whose origin is unmanifest. Hear, O Krishna, a few names, that were uttered by Brahma himself, of that giver of boons, that adroable deity, that puissant one who has the universe for his form, and who is possessed of supreme wisdom. These names that I shall recite are extracted from the ten thousand names that the great Grandsire had uttered in days of yore, as ghee is extracted from curds. As gold represents the essence of rocky mountains, as honey represents the essence of flowers, as Manda represents the extract from ghee, even so have these names been extracted from and represent the essence of those ten thousand names that were uttered by Grandsire Brahma. This abstract of names is capable of cleansing every sin, however heinous. It possesses the same merit that is attached to the four Vedas. It should be comprehended with attention by spiritual aspirants and engraved on the memory. These names fraught with auspiciousness, leading to advancement, destructive of Rakshasas,[1] and great cleansers should be imparted to only him that is devoted to the great Lord, to him that has faith, to him that believes. Unto him that has no faith, him that is an unbeliever, him that has not subjugated his soul, it should never be communicated. That creature, O Krishna, who cherishes malice towards the illustrious Mahadeva who is the original cause of everything, who is the Supreme Soul, and who is

---

1 *i.e.*, if recited, it destroys all fear of Rakshasas, for these either fly away at its sound or are even killed.—T.

the great Lord, has certainly to go to hell with all his ancestors before and all his children after him. This abstract of names that I shall recite to thee is looked upon as Yoga.[1] This is looked upon as the highest object of meditation. This is that which one should constantly recite as *Japya.* This is equivalent to Knowledge. This is the highest Mystery. If one, even during his last moments, recites it or hears it recited unto him, one succeeds in attaining to the highest end. This is holy. This is auspicious, this is fraught with every kind of benefit. This is the best of all things. Brahma, the Grandsire of all the universe, having in days of old composed it, assigned to it the foremost place among all excellent hymns. From that time, this hymn to the greatness and glory of the highsouled Mahadeva, which is held in the highest esteem by all the deities, has come to be regarded as the king of all hymns. This king of all hymns was first conveyed from the region of Brahman to heaven, the region of the celestials. Tandi then obtained it from heaven. Hence is it known as the hymn composed by Tandi. From heaven Tandi brought it down on Earth. It is the most auspicious of all auspicious things, and is capable of cleansing the heart from all sins however heinous. O thou of mighty arms, I shall recite to thee that best of all hymns. This hymns relates to him who is the Veda of the Vedas, and the most ancient of all ancient objects, to him who is the energy of all energies, and the penance of all penances ; to him who is the most tranquil of all creatures endued with tranquility, and who is the splendour of all splendours; to him who is looked upon as the most restrained of all creatures that are restrained, and him who is the intelligence of all creatures endued with intelligence ; to him who is looked upon as the deity of all deities, and the Rishi of all Rishis ; to him who is regarded as the sacrifice of all sacrifices and the most auspicious of all things fraught with auspiciousness ; to him who is the Rudra of all Rudras and the effulgence of all things endued with effulgence ; to him who is the Yogin of all Yogins, and the cause of all causes ; to him from whom all the worlds start into existence, and unto whom all the worlds return when they cease to exist; to him who is the Soul of all existent creatures, and who is called Hara of immeasurable energy. Hear me recite those thousand and eight names of the great Sarva. Hearing those names, O foremost of all men, thou shalt be crowned with fruition in respect of all thy wishes,—Om ! thou art Immobile, thou art Fixed, thou art Puissant, thou art Terrible, thou art Foremost, thou art boon-giving, and thou art Superior.[2] Thou art the Soul of all creatures, thou

---

1 *i.e.*, it has the merit that is attached to either Meditation or Yoga.

2 Both 'Sthira' and 'Sthanu' imply immutability or freedom from change.—T.

art celebrated over all creatures, thou art all things, thou art the Creator of all, and thou art Bhava.[1] Thou art the bearer of matted locks on thy head. Thou wearest animal skins for thy vestments. Thou wearest a crest of matted hair on thy head like the peacock. Thou art he who has the whole universe for thy limbs.[2] Thou art the Creator of all things. Thou art Hara in consequence of thy being the destroyer of all things. Thou art he that has eyes resembling those of the gazelle. Thou art the destroyer of all creatures. Thou art the supreme enjoyer of all things. Thou art that Pravritti whence all actions flow. Thou art that Nivirtti or abstention from acts. Thou art observant of fasts and vows, thou art Eternal, thou art Unchangeable. Thou art he that residest in crematoria, thou art the possessor of the six well-known attributes of Lordship and the rest, thou residest in the heart of every creature, thou art he that enjoys all things with the senses, thou art the grinder of all sinful creatures.[3] Thou art he that deserves the salutations of all, thou art of great feats, thou art he that has penances for his wealth, thou createst all the elements at thy will, thou concealest thy real nature by putting on the guise of a lunatic. Thou art the Master of all the worlds and of all living creatures. Thou art of immeasurable form, thou art of vast body, thou art of the form of Righteousness, thou art of great fame, thou art of high Soul, thou art the Soul of all creatures, thou hast the universe for thy form.[4] Thou art of vast jaws (for thou swallowest the universe when the time comes for the dissolution of all things.) Thou art the protector of all the lokas (the worlds). Thou art the soul residing in the inner heart and as such devoid of *ahamkara* originating from ignorance[5] and is one and undivided ; Thou art *anandam* (gladness). Thou art he whose car is borne by

---

1 The Commentator explains that 'Bhava' is here used in the sense of that from which all things flow and into which all things merge when the universal dissolution comes. Or, it may imply, mere existence, without reference, that is, to any attribute by which it is capable of being described or comprehended.—T.

2 *i.e.*, 'Virat' or vast or Infinite.—T.

3 The task of rendering these names is exceedingly difficult. In the original, many of these names are such that they are capable of more than one interpretation. The Commentator often suggests more than one meaning. Each name would require a separate note for explaining all its bearings. 'Niyata' is literally one who is observant of fasts and vows and who has restrained his senses. Hence it means an ascetic. Mahadeva is an ascetic. 'Smasana' is either a crematorium, the place where dead creatures lie down, or, it may mean Varanasi, the sacred city of Siva, where creatures dying have not to take rebirth. Siva is both a resident of crematoria and of Varanasi.—T.

4 Or, the universe is displayed in thee.—T.

5 Probably, what is said here is that Mahadeva is the Pratyag Soul free from Ignorance.—T.

mules. Thou art he that protects Jiva from the thunderbolt of rebirth. Thou art adorable. Thou art obtained by purity and self-restraint and vows. Thou art again the refuge of all kinds of vows and observances including purity and self-restraint.[1] Thou art the celestial artificer that is conversant with every art. Thou art Self-create (for no one has created thee). Thou art the beginning of all creatures and things. Thou art Hiranyagarbha, the Creator of all things. Thou art inexhaustible puissance and felicity.[2] Thou hast a hundred eyes, thou hast eyes of vast power. Thou art Soma.[3] Thou art he that causest all righteous creatures to assume shapes of glory for shining in the firmament. Thou art Chandramas, thou art Surya, thou art the planet Saturn, thou art the descending node (of the moon), thou art the ascending node, thou art Mangala (Mars), and thou art Vrihaspati (Jupiter) and Sukra (Venus), thou art Vudha (Mercury) thou art the worshipper of Atri's wife, thou art he who shot his shaft in wrath at Sacrifice when Sacrifice fled away from him in the form of a deer. Thou art sinless.[4] Thou art possessed of penances that have conferred upon thee the power of creating the universe. Thou art possessed of penances that have rendered thee capable of destroying the universe. Thou art high minded (in consequence of thy great liberality towards thy devotees). Thou fulfillest the wishes of all who resign themselves to thee. Thou art the maker of the year (for it is thou who settest the wheel of Time revolving, by assuming the form of the sun and the

---

1 By 'Niyama' is meant purity both internal and external, contentedness. with whatever is got, penances, Vedic studies, meditation on the Deity, &c —T.

2 'Nidhi' implies the largest number that can be named in Arithmetical notation. Hence, it implies, as the Commentator correctly explains, the possessor of inexhaustible felicity and gladness.—T.

3 'Sahasraksha' is either Indra or possessor of innumerable eyes in consequence of Mahadeva's being identical with the universe. 'Visalaksha' is one whose eyes are of vast power, because the Past and the Future are seen by them even as the Present. 'Soma' implies either the Moon or the juice of the Soma, *i.e.* the libations poured in the sacrificial fire. All righteous persons, again, become luminaries in the firmament. It is Mahadeva that makes them so, *i.e.*, he is the giver of glorious forms to those that deserve them.—T.

4 Many of these names require comments to be intelligible. 'Ketu' is no plant but Hindu astronomers name the descending node of the Moon by that name. Hence Rahu is the ascending node of the Moon. 'Graha' is that which seizes ; 'Grahapati is Mangala, so called for its malevolence. 'Varah' is Vrihaspati or Jupiter, who is the counterself of Sukra or Venus. In Hindu mythology, Sukra is a male person, the preceptor of the Daityas and Asuras. 'Atri' is Vudha or Mercury, represented as the sons of Atri. 'Atryabnamaskarta' is Durvasas who was the son of Atri's wife, got by the lady through a boon of Mahadeva. Daksha's Sacrifice sought to fly away from Siva, but the latter pursued it and shot his arrow at it for destroying it downright.—T.

planets). Thou art Mantra (in the form of Pranava and other sacred words and syllables). Thou art the authority for all acts (in the form of the Vedas and the scriptures). Thou art the highest Penance. Thou art devoted to Yoga. Thou art he who merges himself in Brahman (by Yoga-abstraction). Thou art the great seed (being the cause of causes). Thou art the displayer of what is unmanifest in the manifest form in which the universe exists. Thou art possessed of infinite might. Thou art he whose seed is gold.[1] Thou art omniscient, (being as thou art all things and the great knower). Thou art the cause of all things. Thou art he that has the seed of action (*viz.*, Ignorance and desire) for the means of sojourning from this world to the other and the other to this.[2] Thou hast ten arms. Thou hast winkless eyes (for thou seest at all times). Thou hast a blue throat (in consequence of thy bearing in thy throat the poison that arose upon churning the ocean and which, if not so borne, was capable of destroying the universe). Thou art the Lord of Uma. Thou art the origin of all the infinite forms that occur in the universe. Thou art he whose superiority is due to thyself. Thou art a hero in might (in consequence of thy having achieved such grand feats as the quick destruction of the triple city of the Asuras). Thou art inert matter (which cannot move unless co-existing with the Soul). Thou art all the tattwas (subjects of enquiry as counted by the Sankhyas). Thou art the ordainer and ruler of the tattwas. Thou art the chief of those beings that wait upon thee and are called Ganas.[3] Thou coverest infinite space.[4] Thou art Kama, the God of Desire. Thou art conversant with Mantras (in the sense of knowledge being thy penance).[5] Thou

---

1 'Suvarna-retas' is explained by the Commentator as follows : 'At first he created water and then cast his seed into it. That seed became a golden egg.' It may also mean that Mahadeva is Agni or the deity of fire, for gold represents the seed of Agni.—T.

2 The sense is this : Jiva carries that seed of acts, *i.e.*, Ignorance and Desire, with him. In consequence of this seed, Jiva travels from one world into another ceaselessly. This seed, therefore, is the conveyance or the means of locomotion of Jiva. Mahadeva is Jiva. The Soul is called the rider, and the body is the car that bears the Soul on it.—T.

3 'Ganapati' is Ganesa, the eldest son of Mahadeva. The Ganas are mighty beings that wait upon Mahadeva. This make up the first hundred names. The Commentator takes 'Avala' and 'Gana' together.—T.

4 'Digvasas' means nude. The Puranas say that for stupefying the wives of certain ascetics, Mahadeva became nude on one occasion. The real meaning, however, is that he is capable of covering and does actually cover even infinite space. In the sense of nude, the word means one that has empty space for his cover or vestments.—T.

5 The meaning is that with thee Knowledge is penance instead of actual physical austerities being so. This is only another way of saying that thou hast 'Jnanamayam Tapah.'—T.

art the highest Mantra (for thou art that philosophy which consists in the ascertainment of the nature and attributes of the soul and its differences from the Non-soul). Thou art the cause of the universe (since all that exists has sprung from thy Soul). Thou art universal destroyer (for all that ceases to exist becomes merged unto thee who art as the unmanifest Brahman). Thou bearest in one of thy hands the calabash, and in another thou holdest the bow ; in another hand thou bearest shafts and in another thou bearest a skull. Thou bearest the thunderbolt. Thou art armed with the hundred-killer.[1] Thou art armed with the sword. Thou wieldest the battle-axe. Thou art armed with the Sula (trident). Thou art adorable. Thou hast the sacrificial ladle in one of thy hands. Thou art of beautiful form. Thou art endued with abundant energy. Thou givest in the most liberal measure all that tends to adorn thos e that are devoted to thee. Thou wearest a turban on thy head. Thou art of beautiful face. Thou art he who swells with splendour and puissance. Thou art he that is humble and modest. Thou art exceedingly tall. Thou art he who has the senses for thy rays.[2] Thou art the greatest of preceptors. Thou art Supreme Brahman being a state of pure felicitous existence).[3] Thou art he that took the shape of a jackal (for consoling the Brahmana who, when insulted by a wealthy Vaisya, had resolved to commit suicide). Thou art he whose object are all crowned with fruition, of themselves and without waiting for the puissance derivable from penances). Thou art one who bears a bald head (as the sign of the mendicant order). Thou art one who does good to all creatures. Thou art unborn. Thou hast innumerable forms. Thou bearest all kinds of fragrance on thy person. The matted locks on thy head had sucked up the river Ganga when it first fell from heaven (although they again gave out the waters at the earnest solicitations of king Bhagiratha). Thou art the giver of sovereignty and lordship.[4] Thou art a Brahmacharin without having ever fallen away from

---

1 'Sataghni' a killer of hundred ; Wilson thinks it was a kind of rocket.—T.

2 'Harikesa' means one having the senses for one's rays, *i.e.*, one who displays all objects before the soul through the doors of the senses. The meaning is that Mahadeva is he through whose puissance the mind succeeds in acquiring knowledge through the senses.—T.

3 'Krisha' is explained by the Commentator thus. 'Krish' is a word signifying 'Bhu' or Existence. The letter *n* (the palatal one) signifies 'nirvriti.' Hence Krishna is 'ananda-sanmatra.'—T.

4 'Kaparddin' is thus explained by the Commentator 'Kam Jalam pivati iti kapah.' So called because of the incident noted in the text, for the matted locks of Mahadeva had sucked up the river Ganga when it first fell from heaven. Then 'Rit' means sovereignty or lordship. 'Riddah' is one that gives sovereignty. Combining the two, the compound 'Kaparddin' is formed.—T.

the rigid vow of continence. Thou art distinguished for thy sexual continence. Thou always liest on thy back. Thou hast thy abode in Puissance.[1] Thou hast three matted locks on thy head. Thou art he that is clad in rags. Thou art Rudra (in consequence of thy fierceness). Thou art the celestial generalissimo, and thou art all pervading. Thou art he that moves about during the day. Thou art he that moves about in the night.[2] Thou art of fierce wrath. Thou art possessed of dazzling effulgence (born of Vedic study and penances). Thou art the slayer of the mighty Asura who had come in the form of an infuriate elephant for destroying thy sacred city of Varanasi. Thou art the slayer of such Daityas as become the oppressors of the universe. Thou art Kala or Time which is the universal destroyer. Thou art the supreme ordainer of the universe. Thou art a mine of all excellent accomplishments. Thou art of the form of the lion and the tiger. Thou art he that is clad in the skin of an elephant. Thou art the Yogin who deceives Time by transcending its irresistible influence. Thou art the original sound.[3] Thou art the fruition of all desires. Thou art he that is adored in four ways.[4] Thou art a night-wanderer (like Vetala and others). Thou art he that wanders in the company of spirits. Thou art he that wanders in the company of ghostly beings. Thou art the Supreme Lord of even Indra and the other celestials. Thou art he that hast multiplied himself infinitely in the form of all existent and non-existent things. Thou art the upholder of both Mahat and all the innumerable combinations of the five primal elements. Thou art the primeval Ignorance or Tamas that is known by the name of Rahu. Thou art without measure and hence infinite. Thou art the supreme End that is attained by the Emancipate. Thou art fond of dancing. Thou art he that is always engaged in dancing. Thou art he that causes others to dance. Thou art the friend of the universe. Thou art he whose aspect is calm and mild. Thou art endued with penances puissant enough to create and destroy the universe. Thou art he who binds all creatures with the bonds of thy illusion. Thou art he that transcends destruction. Thou art he who dwells on the mount Kailasa. Thou transcendest all bonds and art

1 'Nabbah' means space which implies puissance. That 'Nabbah' is the 'sthala' or abode of Mahadeva. The Bengal texts which read 'Nabhastala' are vicious.—T.

2 The deities are said to move about during the day, while the Asuras and Rakshasas during the night. What is said, therefore, here is that thou art the deities and thou art their foes of the Daityas and others.—T.

3 Sound, only when manifested, becomes perceptible. When unmanifest and lying in the womb of eternal space, it is believed to have an existence. Unmanifest Brahman is frequently represented as 'anahatah savdah' or unstruck sound.—T.

4 These four ways are, as enumerated by Commentator, Visva Taijasa, Prajna Sivadhyana.—T.

unattached in respect of all things, like Space. Thou art possessed of a thousand arms. Thou art victory. Thou art that perseverance which is the cause of success or victory. Thou art without idleness or procrastination that interferes with persevering activity. Thou art dauntless. Thou art fear. Thou art he who put a stop to Vali's sacrifice.[1] Thou fulfillest the desires of all thy devotees. Thou art the destroyer of Daksha's sacrifice. Thou art amiable. Thou art slightly amiable. Thou art exceedingly fierce and robbest all creatures of their energy. Thou art the slayer of the Asura Vala. Thou art always cheerful. Thou art of the form of wealth which is coveted by all. Thou hast never been vanquished.[2] There is none more adorable than thou. Thou art he who utters deep roars (in the form of Ocean). Thou art that which is so deep that no one can measure it (because thou art of the form of space). Thou art he whose puissance and the might of whose companions and of the bull have never been measured by anybody. Thou art the tree of the world (whose roots extend upwards and branches hang downwards). Thou art the banian.[3] Thou art he that sleeps on a banian leaf when the universe, after dissolution, becomes one infinite expanse of waters. Thou art he that shows compassion to all worshippers, assuming, as thou listest, the form of Hari or Hara or Ganesa or Arka or Agni or Wind, etc. Thou art possessed of teeth that are exceedingly sharp (since thou art competent to chew innumerable worlds even as one munches nuts and swallows them speedily). Thou art of vast dimensions in respect of thy forms. Thou art possessed of a mouth that is vast enough to swallow the universe at once. Thou art he whose troops are adored everywhere.[4] Thou art he who dispelled all the fears of the deities when the prince of elephants had to be captured. Thou art the seed of the universe. Thou art he who has for his vehicle the same bull that forms again the device on his banner in battle. Thou hast Agni for thy soul. Thou art Surya who has green steeds yoked unto his car. Thou art the friend of Jiva. Thou art he that is conversant with the proper time for the accom-

1 It may also mean that thou art he called Buddha who preached against all sacrifices.—T.

2 The Commentator explains that Mahadeva's defeat at the hands of Krishna in the city of Vana was due to Mahadeva's kindness for Krishna, even as Krishna broke his own vow of never taking up arms in the battle of Kurukshetra, for honouring his worshipper Bhishma who had vowed that he would compel Krishna to take up arms.—T.

3 The sense is this : when the universal destruction comes and all becomes a mighty expanse of water, there appears a banian tree under whose shade the immortal Rishi Markandeya sees a boy who is Mahavishnu.—T.

4 It may also mean that thou art he at whose approach all the Daitya troops fled in all directions.—T.

plishment of all religious acts. Thou art he unto whom Vishnu paid his adorations (for obtaining his celebrated discus). Thou art the sacrifice being in the form of Vishnu. Thou art the ocean. Thou art the Barabanala Mare's head that ranges within the ocean, ceaselessly vomitting fire and drinking the saline waters as if they were sacrificial butter. Thou art Wind, the friend of Agni. Thou art of tranquil soul like the ocean when at rest and unstirred by the mildest breeze. Thou art Agni that drinks the libations of clarified butter poured in sacrifices with the aid of Mantras. Thou art he whom it is difficult to approach. Thou art he whose effulgence spreads over the infinite universe. Thou art ever skilful in battle. Thou art well conversant with the time when one should engage in battle so that victory may be achieved. Thou art that science which treats of the motions of heavenly bodies.[1] Thou art of the form of success or victory. Thou art he whose body is Time (for thy body is never subject to destruction). Thou art a house-holder for thou wearest a tuft of hair on thy head. Thou art a Sanyasin for thy head is bald. Thou wearest matted locks on thy head (being, as thou art, a Vanaprastha).[2] Thou art distinguished for thy fiery rays (for the effulgent path by which the righteous proceed is identical with thee). Thou art he that appears in the firmament in the heart encased in the body of every creature.[3] Thou art he who enters into the cranium (brain) of every creature. Thou bearest the wrinkles of age. Thou bearest the bamboo flute. Thou hast also the tabour. Thou bearest the musical instrument called Tali. Thou hast the wooden vessel used for husking grain. Thou art he who covers that illusion which covers Yama.[4] Thou art an astrologer inasmuch as thy understanding is always directed towards the motion of the wheel of time which is made up of the luminaries in the firmament. Thou art Jiva whose understanding is directed to things that are the result of the attributes of Sattwa, Rajas, and Tamas. Thou art that in which all things merge when dissolution overtakes them. Thou art stable and fixed, there being nothing in thee that is subject

---

1 *i.e.*, thou art Time itself. This is the implication.—T.

2 By these three names what is indicated is that Mahadeva is a house-holder, a Sanyasin, and a forest-recluse. House-holders bear a tuft of hair on their heads, Sanyasins have bald heads, while forest-recluses or Vanaprasthis have matted locks.—T.

3 The sense is that Brahman is felt by every one in the firmament of his own heart. Mahadeva, as identical with Brahman is displayed in the heart that is within the physical case. Hence, he may be said to take birth or appear in his effulgence within every one's body.—T.

4 'Kalakatankatah' is explained by the Commentator as follows:—'Kala' is 'Yama.' He is covered over with the illusion of the Supreme Deity. This all covering illusion, again, has the Supreme Deity for its cover. Thou art that Supreme Deity.—T.

to change or mutation of any kind. Thou art the Lord of all creatures. Thy arms extend all over the vast universe. Thou art displayed in innumerable forms that are but fractions of thyself. Thou pervadest all things.[1] Thou art he that has no mouth (for thou enjoyest not the objects of thy own creation). Thou art he who frees thy creatures from the bonds of the world. Thou art easily attainable.[2] Thou art he that manifested himself with a golden mail.[3] Thou art he that appears in the phallic emblem. Thou art he that wanders in the forests in quest of fowls and animals. Thou art he that wanders over the Earth. Thou art he that is omnipresent. Thou art the blare that is produced by all the trumpets blown in the three worlds. Thou art he that has all creatures for his relatives.[4] Thou art of the form of a snake (for thou art identical with the mighty Naga named Sesha). Thou art he that lives in mountain caves (like Jaigishavya) or any other Yogin. Thou art identical with Guha (the celestial generalissimo). Thou wearest garlands of flowers. Thou art he who enjoys the happiness that springs from the possession of worldly objects.[5] Thou art he from whom all creatures have derived their three states of birth, existence, and destruction. Thou art he that upholds all things that exist or occur in the three stages of time, *viz.*, the Past, the Present, and the Future. Thou art he that frees creatures from the effects of all acts belonging to previous lives as well as those accomplished in the present life and from all the bonds due to Ignorance and Desire. Thou art he who is the binder of Asura chiefs. Thou art he who is the slayer of foes in battle.[6] Thou art that which is attainable by knowledge alone. Thou art Durvasas. Thou art he who is waited upon and adored by all the righteous. Thou art he who causes the fall of even Brahma and the others. Thou art he that gives unto all creatures the just share of joy and grief that each deserves according to his own acts. Thou art he that is incomparable. Thou art well conversant with the shares that are given and appropriated in

---

1 'Vibhaga' and 'Sarvaga,' the Commentator explains, are used for indicating that thou art the universe as 'Vyashti and Samashti.'—T.

2 Some editions read 'susaranah,' meaning thou art he who well protects the universe.—T.

3 The golden mail being the illusion of the Supreme Deity in consequence of which the universe has become displayed.—T.

4 Thou art Pasupati ; 'atodyah pratodanarhah pasavah yasya iti.'—T.

5 The Commentator explains that 'Tarangavit,' which is literally 'conversant with waves' means one that is acquainted with the joys or pleasures that arise from the possession or enjoyment of worldly things, for such joys may truly be likened to waves which appear and disappear on the bosom of the sea or ocean of Eternity.—T.

6 The Commentator explains that the binder of Asura chiefs refers to the Supreme Deity's form of Vishnu in which he had bound Vali, the chief of the Asuras. The plural form has reference to successive Kalpas.'—T.

sacrifices.[1] Thou residest in every place. Thou wanderest everywhere. Thou art he that has mean vestments.[2] Thou art Vasava. Thou art immortal. Thou art identical with the Himavat mountains. Thou art the maker of pure gold. Thou art without acts. Thou upholdest in thyself the fruits of all acts. Thou art the foremost of all creatures that are regarded as upholders.[3] Thou art he that has bloody eyes. Thou art he that has eyes whose vision extends over the infinite universe. Thou art he that has a car whose wheels are ever victorious. Thou art he that is possessed of vast learning. Thou art he that accepts thy devotees for thy servants. Thou art he that restrains and subjugates thy senses. Thou art he that acts. Thou wearest clothes whose warp and woof are made of snakes. Thou art Supreme. Thou art he who is the lowest of the celestials.[4] Thou art he that is well-grown. Thou ownest the musical instrument called Kahala. Thou art the giver of every wish. Thou art the embodiment of grace in all the three stages of Time, viz., the Past, the Present, and the Future. Thou art possessed of might that is always well spent. Thou art he who had assumed the form of Valarama (the elder brother of Krishna). Thou art the foremost of all coveted things, being Emancipation or the highest of all ends to which creatures attain. Thou art the giver of all things. Thy face is turned towards all directions, Thou art he from whom diverse creatures have sprung even as all forms have sprung from space or are modifications of that primal element. Thou art he who falls into the pit called body.[5] Thou art he that is helpless (for, falling into the pit constituted by the body, thou canst not transcend the sorrow that is thy portion). Thou residest in the firmament of the heart. Thou art exceedingly fierce in form. Thou art the Deity called Ansu. Thou art the companion of Ansu and art called Aditya. Thou art possessed of innumerable rays. Thou art endued with dazzling effulgence. Thou hast the speed of the Wind.[6] Thou art possessed of speed that is greater than that of the

---

1 The sense is that thou art he that is well conversant with the ritual of sacrifices.—T.

2 Or, it may mean that thou art he that has no vestments, for no vestments can cover thy vast limbs.—T.

3 Those that uphold others are, for example, the elephants that stand at the different points of the compass, the snake Sesha, &c. What is said here is that thou art the best of all these or all such beings.—T.

4 The sense is that thou art Vishnu who is the foremost of the celestials and thou art Agni who is the lowest of the celestials; *i.e.*, thou art all the celestials.—T.

5 The body is as it were a pit into which the soul falls, determined by Desire and Ignorance.—T.

6 'Vasu,' the Commentator explains, indicates the Wind, for it means that which establishes all things into itself.—T.

Wind. Thou art possessed of the speed of the mind. Thou art Nishachara as thou enjoyest all things, being invested with Ignorance.[1] Thou dwellest in every body. Thou dwellest with Prosperity as thy companion. Thou art he that imparts knowledge and instruction. Thou art he who imparts instruction in utter silence. Thou art he that observes the vow of taciturnity (for thou instructest in silence). Thou art he who passes out of the body, looking at the soul.[2] Thou art he that is well adored. Thou art the giver of thousands (since the lord of all the treasures derived those treasures of his from thee). Thou art the prince of birds, (being Garuda the son of Vinata and Kasyapa). Thou art the friend that renders aid. Thou art possessed of exceeding effulgence (for thy splendour is like that of a million suns risen together). Thou art the Master of all created beings. Thou art he who provokes the appetites. Thou art the deity of Desire. Thou art of the form of lovely women that are coveted by all. Thou art the tree of the world. Thou art the Lord of Treasures. Thou art the giver of fame. Thou art the Deity that distributes unto all creatures the fruits (in the form of joys and griefs) of their acts. Thou art thyself those fruits which thou distributest. Thou art the most ancient (having existed from a time when there was no other existent thing). Thou art competent to cover with a single footstep of thine all the three worlds. Thou art Vamana (the dwarf) who deceived the Asura chief Vali (and depriving him of his sovereignty restored it unto Indra). Thou art the Yogin crowned with success (like Sanatkumara and others). Thou art a great Rishi (like Vasishtha and others). Thou art one whose objects are always crowned with success (like Rishava or Dattatreya). Thou art a Sanyasin (like Yajnavalkya and others). Thou art he that is adorned with the marks of the mendicant order. Thou art he that is without such marks.[3] Thou art he that transcends the usages of the mendicant order. Thou art he that assures all creatures from every sort of fear. Thou art without any passions thyself (so that glory and humiliation are alike to thee). Thou art he that is called the celestial generalissimo. Thou art that Visakha who took his rise from the body of the celestial generalissimo when Indra hurled his thunder-bolt at him. Thou art conversant with the sixty tattwas or heads of enquiry in the universe. Thou art the Lord of the senses (for these achieve their respective functions guided by thee). Thou art he that is armed with the thunder-bolt (and that

1 'Nisacharah' is one acting through 'nisa,' or 'Avidya,' *i.e.*, one who enjoys all objects, implying Jiva invested with Ignorance.—T.

2 The Soul can view the Soul or itself, if it can transcend the body with the aid of Yoga.—T.

3 The Commentator explains that the first word means that thou art 'Hansa' and that the second word means thou art 'Paramahansa.'—T.

rives the mountains). Thou art infinite. Thou art the stupefier of Daitya ranks in the field of battle. Thou art he that moves his car in circles among his own ranks and that makes similar circles among the ranks of his foes and who comes back safe and sound after devastating them. Thou art he that is conversant with the lowest depth of the world's ocean (in consequence of thy knowledge of Brahman). Thou art he called Madhu (who has founded the race in which Krishna has taken his birth). Thou hast eyes whose colour resembles that of honey. Thou art he that has taken birth after Vrihaspati.[1] Thou art he that does the acts which Adhyaryus have to do in sacrifices. Thou art he who is always adored by persons whatever their modes of life. Thou art devoted to Brahman. Thou wanderest amongst the habitations of men in the world (in consequence of thy being a mendicant). Thou art he that pervadest all beings. Thou art he that is conversant with truth. Thou knowest and guidest every heart. Thou art he that overspreads the whole universe. Thou art he that collects or stores the good and bad acts of all creatures in order to award them the fruits thereof. Thou art he that lives during even the night that follows the universal dissolution. Thou art the protector wielding the bow called Pinaka. Thou residest in even the Daityas that are the marks at which shootest thy arrows. Thou art the author of prosperity. Thou art the mighty ape Hanuman that aided Vishnu in the incarnation of Rama in his expedition against Ravana. Thou art the lord of those Ganas that are thy associates. Thou art each member of those diverse Ganas. Thou art he that gladdens all creatures. Thou art the enhancer of the joys of all.[2] Thou takest away the sovereignty and prosperity of even such high beings as Indra and others. Thou art the universal slayer in the form of Death. Thou art he that resides in the four and sixty *Kalas*. Thou art very great. Thou art the Grandsire (being the sire of the great sire of all). Thou art the supreme phallic emblem that is adored by both deities and Asuras. Thou art of agreeable and beautiful features. Thou art he who presides over the variety of evidences and tendencies for action and non-action. Thou art the lord of vision. Thou art the Lord of Yoga (in consequence of thy withdrawing all the senses into the heart and combining them together in that place). Thou art he that upholds the Krita and the other ages (by causing them to run ceaselessly). Thou art the Lord of seeds (in consequence of thy being the giver of the fruits of all acts good and bad). Thou art the original

---

1 'Varhaspatya' is a word that is applied to a priest. The deities first got their priest for assisting them at their sacrifices. Human beings then got theirs. Those born after Vrihaspati are Vrihaspatyas.—T.

2 This word 'Nandivardhanah' may also mean he that withdraws or takes away the joys previously conferred.—T.

cause of such seeds. Thou actest in the ways that have been pointed out in the scriptures beginning with those that treat of the Soul. Thou art he in whom reside might and the other attributes. Thou art the Mahabharata and other histories of the kind. Thou art the treatises called Mimansa. Thou art Gautama (the founder of the science of dialectics). Thou art the author of the great treatise on Grammar that has been named after the Moon. Thou art he who chastises his foes. Thou art he whom none can chastise. Thou art he who is sincere in respect of all his religious acts and observances. Thou art he that becomes obedient to those that are devoted to thee. Thou art he that is capable of reducing others to subjection. Thou art he who foments quarrels among the deities and the Asuras. Thou art he who has created the four and ten worlds (beginning with Bhu). Thou art the protector and cherisher of all Beings commencing from Brahma and ending with the lowest forms of vegetable life (like grass and straw). Thou art the Creator of even the five original elements. Thou art he that never enjoys anything (for thou art always unattached). Thou art free from deterioration. Thou art the highest form of felicity. Thou art a deity proud of his might. Thou art Sakra. Thou art the chastisement that is spoken of in treatises on morality and is inflicted on offenders. Thou art of the form of that tyranny which prevails over the world. Thou art of pure Soul. Thou art stainless, (being above faults of every kind). Thou art worthy of adoration. Thou art the world that appears and disappears ceaselessly. Thou art he whose grace is of the largest measure. Thou art he that has good dreams. Thou art a mirror in which the universe is reflected. Thou art he that has subjugated all internal and external foes. Thou art the maker of the Vedas. Thou art the maker of those declarations that are contained in the Tantras and the Puranas and that are embodied in language that is human.[1] Thou art possessed of great learning. Thou art the grinder of foes in battle. Thou art he that resides in the awful clouds that appear at the time of the universal dissolution. Thou art most terrible (in consequence of the dissolution of the universe that thou bringest about). Thou art he who succeeds in bringing all persons and all things into thy subjection. Thou art the great Destroyer. Thou art he that has fire for his energy. Thou art he whose energy is mightier than fire. Thou art the Yugafire that consumes all things. Thou art he that is capable of being gratified by means of sacrificial libations. Thou art water and other liquids that are poured in sacrifices with the aid of Mantras. Thou art in the form of the Deity of Righteousness, the distributor of the fruits that attach to acts good and bad. Thou art the giver of felicity. Thou

---

1 The language of the Veda is divine. That of the scriptures is human.—T.

art always endued with effulgence. Thou art of the form of fire. Thou art of the complexion of the emerald. (Thou art always present in the phallic emblem.) Thou art the source of blessedness. Thou art incapable of being baffled by anything in the prosecution of your objects. Thou art the giver of blessings. Thou art of the form of blessedness. Thou art he unto whom is given a share of sacrificial offerings. Thou art he who distributes unto each his share of that is offered in sacrifices. Thou art endued with great speed. Thou art he that is dissociated from all things. Thou art he that is possessed of the mightiest limb. Thou art he that is employed in the act of generation. Thou art of a dark complexion, (being of the form of Vishnu). Thou art of a white complexion (being of the form of Samva, the son of Krishna). Thou art the senses of all embodied creatures. Thou art possessed of vast feet. Thou hast vast hands. Thou art of vast body. Thou art endued with wide-extending fame. Thou hast a vast head.[1] Thou art of vast measurements. Thou art of vast vision. Thou art the home of the darkness of ignorance. Thou art the Destroyer of the Destroyer. Thou art possessed of vast ears. Thou hast vast lips. Thou art he that has vast cheeks. Thou hast a vast nose. Thou art of a vast throat. Thou hast a vast neck. Thou art he that tears the bond of body.[2] Thou hast a vast chest. Thou hast a vast bosom. Thou art the inner soul which resides in all creatures. Thou hast a deer on thy lap. Thou art he from whom innumerable worlds hang down like fruits hanging down from a tree. Thou art he who stretches his lips at the time of the universal dissolution for swallowing the universe. Thou art the ocean of milk. Thou hast vast teeth. Thou hast vast jaws. Thou hast a vast bristle.[3] Thou hast hair of infinite length. Thou hast a vast stomach. Thou hast matted locks of vast length. Thou art ever cheerful. Thou art of the form of grace. Thou art of the form of belief. Thou art he that has mountains for his bow (or weapons in battle). Thou art he that is full of affection to all creatures like a parent towards his offspring. Thou art he that has no affection. Thou art unvanquished. Thou art exceedingly devoted to (Yoga) contemplation.[4] Thou art of the form of the tree of the world.[5] Thou art he that is indicated by the tree of

1 Literally, crown of the head.—T.

2 *i.e.*, that succeeds in effecting his Emancipation.—T.

3 'Mahanakha' refers to the incarnation of Narasingha or the Man-lion assumed for slaying the Daitya Hiranyakasipu, the father of Prahlada. 'Maharoman' has reference to the form of the mighty or vast Boar that the Supreme Deity assumed for raising the submerged Earth on his tusks.—T.

4 'Mahamuni' may mean either one that is very 'mananasilah' or one that is exceedingly taciturn.—T.

5 How the world has been likened to a tree has been explained in the Moksha sections of the Santi Parvan.—T.

the world.[1] Thou art never satiated when eating (because of thy being of the form of fire, for of all elements, fire is never satiated with the quantity offered it for consumption). Thou art he that has the Wind for thy vehicle for going from place to place (in consequence of thy identity with fire). Thou art he that rangest over hills and little eminences. Thou art he that has his residence on the mountains of Meru. Thou art the chief of the celestials. Thou hast the Atharvans for thy head. Thou hast the Samans for thy mouth. Thou hast the thousand Richs for thy immeasurable eyes. Thou hast the Yajushes for thy feet and hands.[2] Thou art the Upanishads. Thou art the entire body of rituals (occurring in the scriptures). Thou art all that is mobile. Thou art he whose solicitations are never unfulfilled. Thou art he who is always inclined to grace. Thou art he that is of beautiful form. Thou art of the form of the good that one does to another. Thou art that which is dear. Thou art he that always advances towards thy devotees (in proportion as these advance for meeting thee). Thou art gold and other precious metals that are held dear by all. Thy effulgence is like that of burnished gold. Thou art the navel (of the universe). Thou art he that makes the fruits of sacrifices grow (for the benefit of those that perform sacrifices to thy glory). Thou art of the form of that faith and devotion which the righteous have in respect of sacrifices. Thou art the artificer of the universe. Thou art all that is immobile (in the form of mountains and other inert objects). Thou art the two and ten stages of life through which a person passes.[3] Thou art he that causes fright (by assuming the intermediate states between the ten enumerated). Thou art the beginning of all things. Thou art he that unites Jiva with Supreme Brahman through Yoga. Thou art identifiable with that Yoga which causes such a union between Jiva and Supreme Brahman. Thou art unmanifest (being the deepest stupefaction). Thou art the presiding deity of the fourth age (in consequence of thy identity with lust and wrath and cupidity and other evil passions that flow from that deity).[4]

---

1 This is explained in the sense of no one being able to enquire after Brahman unless he has a body, however subtile, with the necessary senses and understanding. It may also mean that the tree of the world furnishes evidence of the existence of the Supreme Deity.—T.

2 Both the Vernacular translators have rendered many of these names most carelessly. The Burdwan translator takes 'Yaju' as one name and 'Padabhuja' as another. This is very absurd.—T.

3 These are the ten previously enumerated, beginning with residence in the mother's womb and ending with death as the tenth, with heaven the eleventh and Emancipation the twelfth.—T.

4 It should be remembered that Kali which is either the age of sinfulness or the presiding deity of that age and, therefore, a malevolent one, is highly propitious to Emancipation. The world being generally sinful, those who succeed in living righteously in this age or under the sway of this malevolent deity, very quickly attain to heaven if heaven be their object, or Emancipation if they strive for Emancipation.—T.

Thou art eternal Time (because of thy being of the form of that ceaseless succession of birth and death that goes on in the universe). Thou art of the form of the Tortoise.[1] Thou art worshipped by the Destroyer himself. Thou livest in the midst of associates. Thou admittest thy devotees as members of thy Gana. Thou hast Brahma himself for the driver of thy car. Thou sleepest on ashes.[2] Thou protectest the universe with ashes.[3] Thou art he whose body is made of ashes.[4] Thou art the tree that grants the fruition of all wishes. Thou art of the form of those that constitute thy Gana. Thou art the protector of the four and ten regions. Thou transcendest all the regions. Thou art full, (there being no deficiency). Thou art adored by all creatures. Thou art white (being pure and stainless). Thou art he that has his body, speech and mind perfectly stainless. Thou art he who has attained to that purity of existence which is called Emancipation. Thou art he who is incapable of being stained by impurity of any kind. Thou art he who has been attained to by the great preceptors of old. Thou residest in the form of Righteousness or duly in the four modes of life. Thou art that Righteousness which is of the form of rites and sacrifices. Thou art of the form of that skill which is possessed by the celestial artificer of the universe. Thou art he who is adored as the primeval form of the universe. Thou art of vast arms. Thy lips are of a coppery hue. Thou art of the form of the vast waters that are contained in the Ocean. Thou art exceedingly stable and fixed (being of the form of mountains and hills). Thou art Kapila. Thou art brown. Thou art all the hues whose mixture produces white. Thou art the period of life. Thou art ancient. Thou art recent. Thou art a Gandharva. Thou art the mother of the celestials in the form of Aditi (or the mother of all things, in the form of Earth). Thou art Garuda, the prince of birds, born of Vinata by Kasyapa, otherwise called Tarkshya. Thou art capable of being comprehended with ease. Thou art of excellent and agreeable speech. Thou

1 Implying that thou assumest the form of the constellation called the Great Bear, and moving onward in space causest the lapse of Time. This constellation, in Hindu astronomy, is known by the name of 'Sisumara' because of its resemblance with the form of a tortoise.—T.

2 The word 'bhashma,' meaning ashes, literally signifies anything that dispels, tears off all bonds, and cures every disease. Ashes are used by Sanyasins for rubbing their bodies as a mark of their having consumed every sin and cut off every bond and freed themselves from all diseases—T.

3 Mahadeva gave a quantity of ashes to his devotees for protecting them from sin.—T.

4 *Vide* the story of Mankanaka. The Rishi of that name, beholding vegetable juice issuing from his body, began to dance in joy. The whole universe, overpowered by a sympathetic influence, began to dance with him. At this, for protecting the universe, Mahadeva showed himself to Mankanaka and, pressing his fingers, brought out a quantity of ashes, thus showing that his body was made of ashes.—T.

art he that is armed with the battle-axe. Thou art he that is desirous of victory. Thou art he that assists others in the accomplishment of their designs.[1] Thou art an excellent friend.[2] Thou art he that bears a Vina made of two hollow gourds. Thou art of terrible wrath (which thou displayest at the time of the universal dissolution). Thou ownest for thy offspring, beings higher than men and deities (*viz*. Brahma and Vihsnu). Thou art of the form of that Vishnu who floats on the waters after the universal dissolution. Thou devourest all things with great ferocity. Thou art he that procreates offspring. Thou art family and race, continuing from generation to generation. Thou art the blare that a bamboo flute gives out. Thou art faultless. Thou art he every limb of whose body is beautiful. Thou art full of illusion. Thou dost good to others without expecting any return. Thou art Wind. Thou art Fire. Thou art the bonds of the worlds which bind Jiva. Thou art the creator of those bonds. Thou art the tearer of such bonds. Thou art he that dwells with even the Daityas (who are the foes of all sacrifices). Thou dwellest with those that are the foes of all acts (and that have abandoned all acts). Thou art of large teeth, and thou art of mighty weapons. Thou art he that has been greatly censured. Thou art he that stupefied the Rishis dwelling in the Daruka forest. Thou art he that did good unto even thy detractors, viz., those Rishis residing in the Daruka forest. Thou art he who dispels all fears and who dispelling all the fears of those Rishis gave them Emancipation. Thou art he that has no wealth (in consequence of his inability to procure even his necessary wearing apparel). Thou art the lord of the celestials. Thou art the greatest of the gods (in consequence of thy being adored by even Indra and others that are regarded as the highest of the celestials). Thou art an object of adoration with even Vishnu. Thou art the slayer of those that are the foes of the deities. Thou art he that resides (in the form of the snake Sesha) in the nethermost region.[3] Thou art invisible but capable of being comprehended, even as the wind which though invisible is perceived by every body. Thou art he whose knowledge extends to the roots of everything and unto whom all things, even in their inner nature, are known. Thou art the object that is enjoyed by him that enjoys it. Thou art he among the eleven Rudras who is called Ajaikapat. Thou art the sovereign of the entire universe. Thou art of the form of all Jivas in the universe (in consequence of thy being covered by the

---

1 'Anukari' literally means an accessory. In the form of Vishnu or Krishna, the Supreme Deity addrest himself to aid Arjuna in slaying Bhishma.—T.

2 As Krishna the friend of Arjuna.—T.

3 In the Pauranik myth, the Earth is described as being supported in empty space by a mighty snake called Sesha. Mahadeva is that sesha, otherwise called Ananta.—T.

three well-known attibutes of Sattwa, Rajas, and Tamas). Thou art he that is not subject to those three attributes. Thou art he that transcends all attributes and is a state of pure existence which is incapable of being described with the aid of any adjective that language can yield. Thou art the prince of physicians called Dhanwantari. Thou art a comet (in consequence of the calamities that flow from thee unto the sinful). Thou art the celestial generalissimo called Skanda. Thou art the king of the Yakshas, called Kuvera, who is thy inseparable associate and who is the Lord of all treasures in the world. Thou art Dhatri. Thou art Sakra. Thou art Vishnu. Thou art Mitra. Thou art Tashtri (the celestial artificer). Thou art the Pole star. Thou art he that upholds all things. Thou art he called Prabhava amongst the Vasus. Thou art the wind which is capable of going everywhere, (being the Sutra-atma that connects all things in the universe with a thread). Thou art Aryaman. Thou art Savitri. Thou art Ravi. Thou art that ancient king of great celebrity known by the name of Ushangu. Thou art he who protects all creatures in diverse ways. Thou art Mandhatri (because of thy competence to gratify all creatures). Thou art he from whom all creatures start into life. Thou art he who exists in diverse form. Thou art he who causes the diverse hues to exist in the universe. Thou art he who upholds all desires and all attributes (because of these flowing from thee). Thou art he who has the lotus on thy navel.[1] Thou art he within whose womb are innumerable mighty creatures. Thou art of face as beautiful as the moon. Thou art wind. Thou art fire. Thou art possessed of exceeding might. Thou art endued with tranquility of soul. Thou art old. Thou art he that is known with the aid of Righteousness.[2] Thou art Lakshmi. Thou art the maker of the field of those actions (by which persons adore the supreme Deity). Thou art he who lives in the field of action. Thou art the soul of the field of action. Thou art the medicine or provoker of the attributes of sovereignty and the others.[3] All things lie in thee (for, as the Srutis declare, all things become one in thee, thyself being of the nature of that unconsciousness which exhibits itself in dreamless slumber). Thou art the lord of all creatures endued with life-breaths. Thou art the god of the gods.

---

1 *i.e.*, Mahavishnu, from whose navel arose the primeval lotus within which was born Brahma.—T.

2 The Bombay text has a misprint. It reads 'Punya-chanchu' for 'Punya-chunchu.' In printing the Commentary also, the well-known grammatical Sutra 'vrittanschanchu &c.' The Burdwan translator repeats the misprint in his rendering K. P. Singha avoids it.—T.

3 The world 'Kurukshetra' or its abbreviation 'Kuru' means the field or department of action. It means also the actual field, so called, on which king Kuru performed his penances, and which is so sacred that its very dust cleanses a person of all sins.—T.

Thou art he who is attached to felicity. Thou art Sat (in the form of cause). Thou art Asat (in the form of effect). Thou art he who possesses the best of all things. Thou art he who resides on the mountains of Kailasa. Thou art he who repairs to the mountains of Himavat. Thou washest away all things beside thee like a mighty current washing away trees and other objects standing on its banks. Thou art the maker of Pushkara and other large lakes and pieces of natural water. Thou art possessed of knowledge of infinite kinds. Thou art the giver of infinite blessings. Thou art a merchant (who conveys the goods of this country to that country and brings the goods of that country to this for the convenience of human beings). Thou art a carpenter. Thou art the tree (of the world that supplies the timber for thy axe). Thou art the tree called Vakula (*Mimusops Elengi, Linn*). Thou art the sandal-wood tree (*Santalum album, Linn*). Thou art the tree called Chcchada (*Alstonia Scholaris*, syn. *Echitis Scholaris, Roxb*). Thou art he whose neck is very strong. Thou art he whose shoulder-joint is vast. Thou art not restless (but endued with steadiness in all thy acts and in respect of all thy faculties). Thou art the principal herbs and plants with their produce (in the form of rice and wheat and the other varieties of grain). Thou art he that grants success upon others in respect of the objects upon which they bestow their heart. Thou art all the correct conclusions in respect of both the Vedas and Grammar.[1] Thou art he who utters leonine roars. Thou art endued with leonine fangs. Thou ridest on the back of a lion for performing thy journeys. Thou ownest a car that is drawn by a lion. Thou art he called the truth of truth.[2] Thou art he whose dish or plate is constituted by the Destroyer of the universe.[3] Thou art always engaged in seeking the good of the worlds. Thou art he who rescues all creatures from distress (and leads them to the felicity of Emancipation). Thou art the bird called Saranga. Thou art a new (Young) swan. Thou art he who is displayed in beauty in consequence of the crest thou bearest on thy head (like the cock or the peacock). Thou art he who protects the place where assemblies of the wise sit for dispensing justice. Thou art the abode of all creatures. Thou art the cherisher of all creatures. Thou art Day and Night (which are the constituent elements of Eternity). Thou art he that is without fault and therefore, never censured. Thou art the upholder of all creatures. Thou art the refuge of all creatures. Thou art without birth. Thou

1 The Commentator explains that 'Siddharthah' means 'Siddhantah,' and that the following compound is its adjective.—T.

2 Literally, the Soul of real existence.—T.

3 People eat off plates of silver or gold or of other metals. Mahadeva has for his plate Kala or destroyer of the universe. Both the Vernacular translators have erred in rendering this word. K. P. Singha takes the compound as really consisting of two names, etc.—T.

art existent. Thou art ever fruitful. Thou art endued with Dharana and Dhyana and Samadhi. Thou art the steed Uchchaisravas. Thou art the giver of food. Thou art he who upholds the life-breaths of living creatures. Thou art endued with patience. Thou art possessed of intellingence. Thou art endued with exertion and cleverness. Thou art honoured by all. Thou art the giver of the fruits of Righteousness and sin. Thou art the cherisher of the senses (for the senses succeed in performing their respective functions in consequence of thee that presidest over them). Thou art the lord of all the luminaries. Thou art all collections of objects. Thou art he whose vestments are made of cowhides. Thou art he who dispels the grief of his devotees. Thou hast a golden arm. Thou art he who protects the bodies of Yogins who seek to enter their own selves. Thou art he who has reduced to nothingness all his foes.[1] Thou art he the measure of whose gladness is very great. Thou art he who achieved victory over the deity of desire that is irresistible. Thou art he who has subjugated his senses. Thou art the note called Gandahara in the musical octave. Thou art he who has an excellent and beautiful home (in consequence of its being placed upon the delightful mountains of Kailasa). Thou art he who is ever attached to penances. Thou art of the form of cheerfulness and contentment. Thou art he called vast or infinite.[2] Thou art he in whose honour the foremost of hymns has been composed. Thou art he whose dancing is characterised by vast strides and large leaps. Thou art he who is adored with reverence by the diverse tribes of Apsaras. Thou art he who owns a vast standard (bearing the device of the bull). Thou art the mountain of Meru. Thou art he who roves among all the summits of that great mountain. Thou art so mobile that it is very difficult to seize thee. Thou art capable of being explained by preceptors to disciples, although thou art incapable of being described in words. Thou art of the form of that instruction which preceptors impart to disciples. Thou art he that can perceive all agreeable scents simultaneously or at the same instant of time. Thou art of the form of the porched gates of cities and palaces. Thou art of the form of the moats and ditches that surround fortified towns and give the victory to the besieged garrison. Thou art the Wind. Thou art of the form of fortified cities and towns encompassed by walls and moats. Thou art the prince of all winged creatures, (being, as thou art, of the

1 The sense is that Mahadeva is the foremost of 'Sadhakas' or worshippers engaged in acquiring a particular object, for he has emaciated or reduced to nothingness all his foes in the form of all passions good and evil. 'Prakarshena tanukritah arayah kamadayo yena sah.'—T.

2 'Narah' is thus explained by the Commentator.—T.

form of Garuda). Thou art he who multiplies the creation by union with the opposite sexes. Thou art the first of all in respect of virtues and knowledge. Thou art superior to even him who is the first of all in virtues and knowledge. Thou transcendest all the virtue and knowledge. Thou art eternal and immutable as also dependent on thyself. Thou art the master and protector of the deities and Asuras. Thou art the master and protector of all creatures. Thou art he who wears a coat of mail. Thou art he whose arms are competent to grind all foes. Thou art an object of adoration with even him who is called Suparvan in heaven.[1] Thou art he who grants the power of bearing or upholding all things.[2] Thou art thyself capable of bearing all things. Thou art fixed and steady (without being at all unstable). Thou art white or pure (being, as thou art, without any stain or blot). Thou bearest the trident that is competent to destroy (all things).[3] Thou art the grantor of bodies or physical forms unto those that constantly revolve in the universe of birth and death. Thou art more valuable than wealth. Thou art the conduct or way or the righteous (in the form of goodness and courtesy). Thou art he who had torn the head of Brahma after due deliberation (and not impelled by mere wrath). Thou art he who is marked with all those auspicious marks that are spoken of in the sciences of palmistry and phrenology and other branches of knowledge treating of the physical frame as the indicator of mental peculiarities. Thou art that wooden bar which is called the Aksha of a car and, therefore, art thou he who is attached to the car represented by the body. Thou art attached to all things (in consequence of thy pervading all things as their soul). Thou art endued with very great might, being as thou art a hero of heroes. Thou art the Veda. Thou art the Smritis, the Itihasas, the Puranas, and other scriptures. Thou art the illustrious deity of every sacred shrine. Thou art he who has the Earth for his car. Thou art the inert elements that enter into the composition of every creature. Thou art he who imparts life into every combination of those inert element. Thou art the Pranava and other sacred Mantras that instil life into dead matter. Thou art he that casts tranquil glances. Thou art exceedingly harsh (in consequence of thy being the destroyer of all things). Thou art he in whom are innumerable precious attributes

---

1 The Commentator explains that he who is called Suparvan in heaven is otherwise called Mahan.--T.

2 'Sarva-sahana-samarthya pradah' as the Commentator explains. Hence, it means that Mahadeva is he who makes creatures competent to bear all things, *i.e.*, all griefs and all joys, as also the influence all physical objects that is quietly borne without life being destroyed.—T.

3 The etymology of 'Hara' is thus explained by the Commentator; 'Hanti iti ha sulah ; tam rati or adatte.' This is very fanciful.—T.

and possessions. Thou hast a body that is red. Thou art he who has all the vast oceans as so many ponds filled for thy drinking.[1] Thou art the root of the tree of the world. Thou art exceedingly beautiful and shinest with surpassing grandeur. Thou art of the form of ambrosia or nectar. Thou art both cause and effect. Thou art an ocean of penances (being as thou art a great Yogin). Thou art he that desirous of ascending to the highest state of existence. Thou art he that has already attained to that state. Thou art he who is distinguished for the purity of his conduct and acts and observances. Thou art he who is possessed of great fame (in consequence of the Righteousness of his behaviour). Thou art the ornament of armies (being as thou art of the form of prowess and courage). Thou art he who is adorned with celestial ornaments. Thou art Yoga. Thou art he from whom flow eternal time measured by Yugas and Kalpas. Thou art he who conveys all creatures from place.[2] Thou art of the form of Righteousness and sin and their intermixture (such as are displayed in the successive Yugas). Thou art great and formless. Thou art he who slew the mighty Asura that had approached against the sacred city of Varanasi in the form of an infuriate elephant of vast proportions. Thou art of the form of death. Thou givest to all creatures such fruition of their wishes as accords with their merits. Thou art approachable. Thou art conversant with all things that are beyond the ken of the senses. Thou art conversant with the Tattwas (and therefore, thoroughly fixed). Thou art he who incessantly shines in beauty. Thou wearest garlands that stretch down from thy neck to the feet. Thou art that Hara who has the Moon for his beautiful eye. Thou art the salt ocean of vast expanse. Thou art the first three Yugas (*viz.*, Krita, Treta, and Dwapara). Thou art he whose appearance is always fraught with advantage to others. Thou art he who has three eyes (in the form of the scriptures, the preceptor, and meditation). Thou art he whose forms are exceedingly subtile (being as thou art the subtile forms of the primal elements). Thou art he whose ears are bored for wearing jewelled Kundalas. Thou art the bearer of matted locks. Thou art the point (in the alphabet) which indicates the nasal sound. Thou art the two dots *i. e.*, Visarga (in the Sanskrit alphabet which indicate the sound of the aspirated *H*). Thou art possessed of an excellent face. Thou art the shaft that is shot by the warrior for encompassing the destruction of his foe. Thou art all

---

1 The sense is this: a 'nipana' is a shallow pond or ditch where cattle drink. The very oceans are the 'nipanas' of Mahadeva.—T.

2 The Commentator thinks that this has reference to the incarnation of 'Trivikrama,' *i.e*, the dwarf suddenly expanding his form till with two steps he covered Heaven and Earth and demanded space for his third step. —T.

the weapons that are used by warriors. Thou art endued with patience capable of bearing all things. Thou art he whose knowledge has arisen from the cessation of all physical and mental functions.[1] Thou art he who has become displayed as Truth in consequence of the cessation of all other faculties. Thou art that note which, arising from the region called Gandhara, is exceedingly sweet to the ear. Thou art he who is armed with the mighty bow (called Pinaka). Thou art he who is the understanding and the desires that exist in all creatures, besides being the supreme upholder of all beings. Thou art he from whom all acts flow. Thou art that wind which rises at the time of the universal dissolution and which is capable of churning the entire universe even as the staff in the hands of the dairy-maid churns the milk in the milkpot. Thou art he that is full. Thou art he that sees all things. Thou art the sound that arises from slapping one palm against another. Thou art he the palm of whose hand serves as the dish or plate whence to take his food. Thou art he who is possessed of an adamantine body. Thou art exceedingly great. Thou art of the form of an umbrella. Thou art he who has an excellent umbrella. Thou art well-known to be identical with all creatures. Thou art he who having put forth three feet covered all the universe with two and wanted space for the remaining one. Thou art he whose head is bald. Thou art he whose form is exceedingly ugly and fierce. Thou art he who has undergone infinite modifications and become all things in the universe. Thou art he who bears the well-known badge of Sanyasa, *viz.*, the stick. Thou art he who has a Kunda. Thou art he who is incapable of being attained to by means of acts. Thou art he who is identical with the green-eyed king of beasts (viz., the lion). Thou art of the form of all the points of the compass. Thou art he who is armed with the thunder. Thou art he who has a hundred tongues. Thou art he who has a thousand feet and thousand heads.[2] Thou art the lord and chief of the celestials. Thou art he that is made up of all the gods. Thou art the great Master or preceptor. Thou art he who has a thousand arms. Thou art he who is competent to obtain the fruition of every wish. Thou art he whose protection is sought by every one. Thou art he who is the creator of all the worlds. Thou art he who is the great cleanser of all from every kind of sin, in the form of shrines and sacred waters. Thou art he who has three high Mantras.[3] Thou art the youngest son of Aditi and Kasyapa, (being in the form of the dwarf who is otherwise known by the name of Upendra and who beguiled the Asura Vali of his lordship

---

1 *i.e.*, thou art possessed of Yoga-knowledge.—T.

2 The two together form one name.—T.

3 These are Vija, Sakti, and Kilakani. A 'kakud' is a hump or elevated place in the body.—T.

of the three worlds and restored it to the chief of the celestials). Thou art both black and twany (being of the form which is known as Hari-Hara) Thou art the maker of the Brahmana's rod.[1] Thou art armed with the hundred-killer, the noose, and the dart. Thou art he that took his birth within the primeval lotus. Thou art he who is endued with a vast womb. Thou art he who has the Vedas in his womb. Thou art he who takes his rise from that infinite waste of waters which succeeds the dissolution of the universe. Thou art he who is endued with rays of effulgent light. Thou art the creator of the Vedas. Thou art he who studies the Vedas. Thou art he who is conversant with the meaning of the Vedas. Thou art devoted to Brahman. Thou art the refuge of all persons devoted to Brahman. Thou art of infinite forms. Thou art the bearer of innumerable bodies. Thou art endued with irresistible prowess.[2] Thou art the soul or nature that transcends the three universal attributes (of Sattwa, Rajas, and Tamas). Thou art the lord of all Jivas. Thou art endued with the speed of the wind. Thou art possessed of the fleetness of the mind. Thou art always smeared with sandal-paste. Thou art the end of the stock of the primeval lotus.[3] Thou art he who brought the celestial cow Surabhi down from a superior station to an inferior one by denouncing a curse upon her.[4] Thou art that Brahma who was unable to see thy end. Thou art adorned with a large wreath of Karnikara flowers. Thou art adorned with a diadem of blue gems. Thou art the wielder of the bow called Pinaka. Thou art the master of that knowledge which treats of Brahman.[5] Thou art he who has subjugated his senses by the aid of thy knowledge of

---

1 The thin bamboo rod in the hand of the Brahmana is mightier than the thunderbolt of Indra. The thunder scorches all existing objects upon which it falls. The Brahmana's rod (which symbolizes the Brahmana's might in the form of his curse) blasts even unborn generations. The might of the rod is derived from Mahadeva.—T.

2 'Sayambhuvah Tigmatejah' is one name. The Commentator explains that Brahman could not look at Mahadeva ; hence this reference to his prowess.—T.

3 Brahma, after his birth within the primeval lotus, became desirous of seeing the end of the stalk of that lotus. He went on and on, without succeeding to find what he sought. The meaning of the word, therefore, by implication is that Mahadeva is infinite.—T.

4 Once Brahma asked Suravi to bear evidence before Vishnu to the statement that Brahma has seen the foremost part of Siva. Suravi having given false evidence out of fear for Brahma was cursed by Siva that her offspring will eat unholy substances.

5 'Uma' is another name for 'Brahmavidya.'—T.

Brahman. Thou art he who bearest Ganga on thy head.[1] Thou art the husband of Uma, the daughter of Himavat. Thou art mighty (in consequence of thy having assumed the form of the vast Boar for raising the submerged Earth). Thou art he who protects the universe by assuming diverse incarnations. Thou art worthy of adoration. Thou art that primeval Being with the equine head who recited the Vedas with a thundering voice. Thou art he whose grace is very great. Thou art the great subjugator. Thou art he who has slain all his foes (in the form of passions). Thou art both white and tawny (being as thou art half male and half female).[2] Thou art possessed of a body whose complexion is like that of gold.[3] Thou art he that is of the form of pure joy, (being, as thou art, above the five sheathes which the Jiva consists of, viz., the Anna-maya, the Prana-maya, the Mona-maya, the Vijnana-maya, and the Ananda-maya ones). Thou art of a restrained soul. Thou art the foundation upon which rests that Ignorance which is called Pradhana and which, consisting of the three attributes of Sattwa, Rajas, and Tamas is the cause whence the universe has sprung. Thou art he whose faces are turned to every direction.[4] Thou art he who has three eyes (in the forms of the Sun, the Moon, and Fire). Thou art he who is superior to all creatures (in consequence of thy righteousness whose measure is the greatest). Thou art the soul of all mobile beings. Thou art of the form of the subtile soul (which is incapable of being perceived). Thou art the giver of immortality in the form of Emancipation as the fruit of all acts of righteousness achieved by creatures without the desire of fruits.[5] Thou art the preceptor of even those that are the gods of the gods. Thou art Vasu, the son of Aditi. Thou art he who is endued with innumerable rays of light, who brings forth the universe, and who is of the form of that Soma which is drunk in sacrifices. Thou art Vyasa, the author of the Puranas and other sacred histories. Thou art the creations of Vyasa's brain (because of thy being identical with the Puranas and other sacred histories) both abridged

1 Falling from the celestial regions, the river Ganga was held by Mahadeva on his head, among his matted locks. At the earnest solicitations of King Bhagiratha he gave her out so that flowing along the surface of the Earth she met the ocean, first passing over the spot where the ashes of Bhagiratha's ancestors, the sixty thousand sons of king Sagara of the solar race, lay.—T.

2 This form is called Hara-Gauri, as explained before.—T.

3 Some texts read 'Pritatma,' implying 'one of contented soul.' The reading noticed by the Commentator is 'Pitatma,' meaning 'gold-complexioned.' The Burdwan translator takes 'Pritatma' as one name. This is not correct.—T.

4 Mahadeva is represented as possessed of five heads, four on four sides and one above.—T.

5 'Amritogovrisherwarah' is one name.—T.

and unabridged. Thou art the sum total of Jivas. Thou art the Season. Thou art the Year. Thou art the Month. Thou art the Fortnight. Thou art those sacred Days that end or conclude these periods. Thou art the Kalas. Thou art the Kashthas. Thou art the Lavas. Thou art the Matras. Thou art the Muhurtas and Days and Nights. Thou art the Kshanas.[1] Thou art the soil upon which the tree of the universe stands. Thou art the seed of all creatures (being of the form of that Unmanifest Chaitanya (consciousness) endued with Maya or illusion whence all creatures spring). Thou art Mahattatwa. Thou art the sprout of Jiva, (being of the form of Consciousness which springs up after Mahattawa). Thou art Sat or Effect. Thou art Asat or Cause. Thou art Manifest (being seizable by the senses). Thou art the Father. Thou art the Mother. Thou art the Grandfather. Thou art the door to Heaven (because of thy identity with Penances). Thou art the door of the generation of all creatures (because of thy identity with desire). Thou art the door of Emancipation (because of thy identity with the absence of Desire which alone can lead to the merging into Brahman). Thou art those acts of righteousness which lead to the felicity of heaven. Thou art Nirvana (or that cessation of individual or separate existence which is Emancipation). Thou art the gladdener (who gives all kinds of joy to every creature). Thou art that region of Truth (to which they that are foremost in righteousness attain). Thou art superior to even that region of Truth which is attainable by the righteous). Thou art he who is the creator of both the deities and the Asuras. Thou art he who is the refuge of both the deities and the Asuras. Thou art the preceptor of both the deities and the Asuras (being as thou art of the form of both Vrihaspati and Sukra). Thou art he who is ever victorious. Thou art he who is ever worshipped by the deities and the Asuras. Thou art he who guides the deities and the Asuras even as the Mahamatra guides the elephant. Thou art the refuge of all the deities and the Asuras. Thou art he who is the chief of both the deities and the Asuras (being as thou art of the form of both Indra and Virochana). Thou art he who is the leader in battle of both the deities and the Asuras (being as thou art of the form of Kartikeya and Kesi, the leaders of the celestial and the Daitya armies). Thou art he who transcends the senses and shines by himself. Thou art of the form of the celestial Rishis like Narada and others. Thou art the grantor of boons unto the deities and Asuras (in the form of Brahman and Rudra). Thou art he who rules the hearts of the deities and the Asuras. Thou art he into whom the universe enters (when it is dissolved). Thou art the refuge of even him who is the ruler of the hearts of both the deities

1 These are names for different portions of time.—T.

and the Asuras. Thou art he whose body is made up of all the deities.[1] Thou art he who has no Being superior to thee of whom to think. Thou art he who is the inner soul of the deities. Thou art he who has sprung from his own self. Thou art of the form of immobile things. Thou art he who covers the three worlds with three steps of his. Thou art possessed of great learning. Thou art stainless. Thou art he who is freed from the quality of Rajas. Thou art he who transcends destruction. Thou art he in whose honour hymns should be sung. Thou art the master of the irresistible elephant represented by Time. Thou art of the form of that lord of Tigers who is worshipped in the country of the Kalingas.[2] Thou art he who is called the lion among the deities (in consequence of the pre-eminence of thy prowess). Thou art he who is the foremost of men. Thou art endued with great wisdom. Thou art he who first takes a share of the offerings in sacrifices. Thou art imperceptible. Thou art the sum-total of all the deities. Thou art he in whom penances predominate. Thou art always in excellent Yoga. Thou art auspicious. Thou art armed with the thunder-bolt. Thou art the source whence the weapons called Prasas have taken their origin. Thou art he whom thy devotees attain to in diverse ways. Thou art Guha (the celestial generalissimo). Thou art the supreme limit of felicity.[3] Thou art identical with thy creation. Thou art he who rescues thy creatures from death (by granting them Emancipation). Thou art the cleanser of all including Brahma himself. Thou art of the form of bulls and other horned animals. Thou art he who is fond of mountain summits. Thou art the planet Saturn. Thou art Kuvera, the chief of the Yakshas. Thou art complete faultlessness. Thou art he who inspires gladness. Thou art all the celestials united together. Thou art the cessation of all things. Thou art all the duties that appertain to all the modes of life. Thou art he who has an eye on his forehead. Thou art he who sports with the universe as his marble ball. Thou art of the form of deer. Thou art endued with the energy that is of the form of knowledge and penance. Thou art the lord of all immobile things (in the form of Himavat and Meru). Thou art he who has subjugated his senses by various regulations and vows. Thou art he whose objects have all been fulfilled. Thou art identical with Emancipation. Thou art different from him whom we worship. Thou hast truth for thy penances. Thou art of a pure heart. Thou art he who presides over all vows and fasts (in consequence of thy

---

1 The Srutis declare that Fire is his head, the Sun and the Moon are his eyes, &c.—T.

2 Mahadeva has an image in the country of the Kalingas that is called Vyaghreswara.—T.

3 'Kantah' is thus explained. 'Kasya Sukhasya antah sima.'—T.

being the giver of their fruits). Thou art the highest (being of the form of Turiya). Thou art Brahman. Thou art the highest refuge of the devotees. Thou art he who transcends all bonds (being Emancipate). Thou art freed from the *linga* body. Thou art endued with every kind of prosperity. Thou art he who enhances the prosperity of thy devotees. Thou art that which is incessantly undergoing changes.

"'I have thus, O Krishna, hymned the praises of the illustrious Deity by reciting his names in the order of their importance. Who is there that can hymn the praises of the lord of the universe, that great Lord of all who deserves our adorations and worship and reverence, whom the very gods with Brahma at their head are unable to praise and whom the Rishis also fail to sing ? Aided, however, by my devotion to him, and having received his permission, I have praised that Lord of sacrifices, that Deity of supreme puissance, that foremost of all creatures endued with intelligence. By praising with these names that enhance one's auspiciousness of the great lord of blessedness, a worshipper of devoted soul and pure heart succeeds in attaining to his own self. These names constitute a hymn that furnishes the best means of attaining to Brahman. With the aid of this hymn one is sure to succeed in attaining to Emancipation. Rishis and the deities all praise the highest deity by uttering this hymn. Hymned by persons of restrained soul Mahadeva becomes gratified with those that hymn his praises so. The illustrious deity is always full of compassion towards his devotees. Endued with omnipotence, he it is that gives Emancipation to those that worship him. So also, they among men that are foremost, that are possessed of faith and devotion hear and recite for others and utter with reverence, the praises of that highest and eternal Lord *viz.* Isana, in all their successive lives and adore him in thought, word, and deed, and adoring him thus at all times, *viz.* when they are lying or seated or walking or awake or opening the eyelids or shutting them, and thinking of him repeatedly, become objects of reverence with all their fellowmen and derive great gratification and exceeding joy. When a creature becomes cleansed of all his sins in course of millions of births in diverse orders of being, it is then that devotion springs up in his heart for Mahadeva. It is through good luck alone that undivided devotion to Bhava who is the original cause (of the universe) fully springs up in the heart of one that is conversant with every mode of worshipping that great Deity.[1] Such stainless and pure devotion to Rudra, that has singleness of purpose and that is simply irresistible in its course, is seldom to be found among even the deities, and never among men. It

1 "Undivided, *i.e.*, having nothing else for its object, 'Sarva-bhavatah' is 'bhagyat.' The sense is that unless one becomes conversant with all the modes of worshipping Bhava, *i.e.*, in thought, word and deed, and unless one has special good luck, one cannot have such devotion to Bhava.—T.

is through the grace of Rudra that such devotion arises in the hearts of human beings. In consequence of such devotion, men, identifying themselves wholly with Mahadeva, succeed in attaining to the highest success. The illustrious Deity who is always inclined to extend his grace towards them that seek him with humility, and throw themselves with their whole soul upon him rescues them from the world. Except the great Deity who frees creatures from rebirth, all other gods constantly nullify the penances of men, for men have no other source of puissance that is as great as these.[1] It was even thus Tandi of tranquil soul, resembling Indra himself in splendour, praised the illustrious Lord of all existent and non-existent things,—that great Deity clad in animal skins. Indeed, Brahma had sung this hymn in the presence of Sankara. Thou art a Brahmana (being conversant with Brahman and devoted to those that are conversant with Brahman). Thou shalt, therefore, comprehend it well. This is cleansing, and washes away all sins. This confers Yoga and Emancipation and heaven and contentment. He who recites this hymn with undivided devotion to Sankara succeeds in attaining to that high end which is theirs that are devoted to the doctrines of the Sankhya philosophy. That worshipper who recites this hymn daily for one year with singleness of devotion succeeds in obtaining the end that he desires. This hymn is a great mystery. It formerly resided in the breast of Brahma the Creator. Brahma imparted it unto Sakra. Sakra imparted unto Mrityu. Mrityu imparted it unto the Rudras. From the Rudras Tandi got it. Indeed Tandi acquired it in the region of Brahman as the reward of his severe austerities. Tandi communicated it to Sukra, and Sukra of Bhrigu's race communicated it to Gautama. Gautama in his turn, O descendant of Madhu, communicated it to Vaivaswata-Manu. Manu communicated it unto Narayana of great intelligence, numbered among the Sadhyas and held exceedingly dear by him. The illustrious Narayana, numbered among the Sadhyas and possessed of glory that knows no diminution, communicated it to Yama. Vaivaswat Yama communicated it to Nachiketa. Nachiketa, O thou of Vrishni's race, communicated to Markandeya. From Markandeya, O Janarddana, I obtained it as the reward of my vows and fasts. To thee, O slayer of foes, I communicate that hymn unheard by others. This hymn leads to heaven. It dispels disease and bestows long life. This is worthy of the highest praise, and is consistent with the Vedas.

"Krishna continued,—'That person, O Partha, who recites this hymn with a pure heart observing the vow of Brahmacharyya, and with

---

1 There are numerous instances of the gods having become alarmed at the penances of men and done their best to nullify those penances by despatching celestial nymphs for attracting them of carnal pleasures.—T.

his senses under control, regularly for one whole year, succeeds in obtaining the fruits of a horse-sacrifice. Danavas and Yakshas and Rakshasas and Pisachas and Yatudhanas and Guhyakas and snakes can do no injury to him.' "

SECTION XVIII

Vaisampayana said,—After Vasudeva had ceased to speak, the great Yogin, *viz.* the Island-born Krishna, addressed Yudhisthira, saying,—'O son, do thou recite this hymn consisting of the thousand and eight names of Mahadeva, and let Maheswara be gratified with thee. In former days, O son, I was engaged in the practice of severe austerities on the breast of the mountains of Meru from desire of obtaining a son. It is this very hymn that was recited by me. As the reward of this, I obtained the fruition of all my wishes, O son of Pandu. Thou wilt also, by reciting this same hymn, obtain from Sarva the fruition of all thy wishes.—After this, Kapila, the Rishi who promulgated the doctrines that go by the name of Sankhya, and who is honoured by the gods themselves, said,—I adore Bhava with great devotion for many lives together. The illustrious Deity at last became gratified with me and gave me knowledge that is capable of aiding the acquirer in getting over rebirth.—After this, the Rishi named Charusirsha, that dear friend of Sakra and known otherwise under the name of Alamvana's son and who is filled with compassion, said,—I, in former days, repaired to the mountains of Gokarna and sat myself to practise severe penances for a hundred years. As the reward of those penances, I obtained from Sarva, O son of king Pandu, a hundred sons, all of whom were born without the intervention of woman, of well-restrained soul, conversant with righteousness, possessed of great splendour, free from disease and sorrow, and endued with lives extending over a hundred thousand years—Then the illustrious Valmiki, addressing Yudhishithira, said,—Once upon a time, in course of a dialectical disputation, certain ascetics that were possessors of the *homa* fire denounced me as one guilty of Brahmanicide. As soon as they had denounced me as such, the sin of Brahmanicide, O Bharata, possessed me. I then, for cleansing myself, sought the protection of the sinless Isana who is irresistible in energy. I become cleansed of all my sins. That dispeller of all sorrows, *viz.*, the destroyer of the triple city of the Asuras, said unto me,—Thy fame shall be great in the world—Then Jamadagni's son, that foremost of all righteous persons, shining like the Sun with blazing splendour in the midst of that conclave of Rishis, said unto the son of Kunti these words;—I was afflicted with the sin, O eldest son of Pandu, of Brahmanicide for having slain my brothers who were all learned Brahmanas. For purifying myself, I sought the protection, O king, of Mahadeva. I hymned the praises of the great Deity by reciting his names. At this, Bhava became gratified with me and gave me a battle-axe and many other celestial weapons. And he said unto me,—Thou shalt be freed from sin and thou shalt be invincible in battle ; Death himself shall not succeed in overcoming thee for thou shalt be freed from disease.— Even thus did the illustrious and crested Deity of auspicious form said unto me. Through the grace of that Deity of supreme intelligence I obtained all that He had said. Then Viswamitra said,—I was formerly a Kshatriya. I paid my adorations to Bhava with the desire of becoming a Brahmana. Through the grace of that great Deity I succeeded in obtaining the high status of a Brahmana that is so difficult to obtain. —Then the Rishi Asita-Devala, addressing the royal son of Pandu, said, —In former days, O son of Kunti, through the curse of Sakra, all my merit due to the acts of righteousness I had performed, was destroyed. The puissant Mahadeva it was who kindly gave me back that merit together with great fame and a long life.—The illustrious Rishi Gritsamada, the dear friend of Sakra, who resembled the celestial preceptor Vrihaspati himself in splendour, addressing Yudhishthira of Ajamidha's race said,—The inconceivable Sakra had, in days of yore, performed a sacrifice extending over a thousand years. While that sacrifice was going on, I was engaged by Sakra in reciting the Samans. Varishtha, the son of that Manu who sprung from the eyes of Brahma, came to that sacrifice and addressing me, said.—O foremost of regenerate persons, the Rathantara is not being recited properly by thee. O best of Brahmanas, cease to earn demerit by reading so faultily, and with the aid of thy understanding do thou read the Samans correctly. O thou of wicked understanding, why dost thou perpetrate such sin that is destructive of sacrifice.—Having said these words, the Rishi Varishtha, who was very wrathful, gave way to that passion and addressing me once more, said,—Be thou an animal divested of intelligence, subject to grief, ever filled with fear, and a denizen of trackless forests destitute of both wind and water and abandoned by other animals. Do thou thus pass ten thousand years with ten and eight hundred years in addition. That forest in which thou shalt have to pass this period will be destitute of all holy trees and will, besides, be the haunt of Rurus and lions. Verily, thou shalt have to become a cruel deer plunged in excess of grief.—As soon as he had said these words, O son of Pritha, I immediately became transformed into a deer. I then sought the protection of Maheswara. The great Deity said unto me,—Thou shalt be freed from disease of every kind, and besides immortality shall be thine. Grief shall never afflict thee. Thy friendship with Indra shall remain unchanged, and let the sacrifices of both Indra and thyself increase. The illustrious and puissant Mahadeva favours all creatures in this way. He is always the great dispenser and ordainer in the matter of the happiness and sorrow of all living creatures. That illustrious Deity is incapable of being comprehended in thought, word, or deed. O son, O thou that art the best of warriors (through the grace of Mahadeva), there is none that is equal to me in learning.—After this, Vasudeva, that foremost of all intelligent men, once more said,—Mahadeva of golden eyes was gratified by me with my penances. Gratified with me, O Yudhishthira, the illustrious Deity said unto me,—Thou shalt, O Krishna, through my grace, become dearer to all persons than wealth which is coveted by all. Thou shalt be invincible in battle. Thy energy shall be equal to that of Fire. Thousands of other boons Mahadeva gave unto me on that occasion. In a former incarnation I adored Mahadeva on the Manimantha mountain for millions of years. Gratified with me, the illustrious Deity said unto me these words :—Blessed be thou, do thou solicit boons as thou wishest. Bowing unto him with a bend of my head, I said these words.—If the puissant Mahadeva has been gratified with me, then let my devotion to him be unchanged, O Isana ! Even this is the boon that I solicit.—The great God said unto me,—Be it so—and disappeared there and then.

"Jaigishavya said,—O Yudhishthira, formerly in the city of Varanasi, the puissant Mahadeva searching me out, conferred upon me the eight attributes of sovereignty.

"Garga said,—'O son of Pandu, gratified with me in consequence of mental sacrifice which I had performed, the great God bestowed upon me, on the banks of the sacred stream Saraswati, that wonderful science, *viz.*, the knowledge of Time with its four and sixty branches. He also, bestowed upon me, a thousand sons, all possessed of equal merit and fully conversant with the Vedas. Through his grace, their periods of life as also that of mine have become extended to ten millions of years."

"Parasara said,—'In former times I gratified Sarva, O king. I then cherished the desire of obtaining a son that would be possessed of great ascetic merit, endued with superior energy, and addressed to high Yoga, that would earn world-wide fame, arrange the Vedas, and become the home of prosperity, that would be devoted to the Vedas and the Brahmanas and be distinguished for compassion. Even such a son was desired by me from Maheswara. Knowing that this was the wish of my heart, that foremost of Deities said unto me.—Through the fruition of that object of thine which thou wishest to obtain from me, thou shalt have a son of the name of Krishna. In that creation which shall be known after the name of Savarni-Manu, that son of thine shall be reckoned among the seven Rishis. He shall arrange the Vedas, and be the propagator of Kuru's race. He shall, besides, be the author of the ancient histories and do good to the universe. Endued with severe penances, he shall, again, be the dear friend of Sakra. Freed from diseases of every kind, that son of thine, O Parasara, shall besides, be immortal.—Having said these words, the great Deity disappeared there and then. Even such is the good, O Yudhishthira, that I have obtained from that indestructible and immutable God, endued with the highest penances and supreme energy.'

"Mandavya said,—'In former times though not a thief and yet wrongly suspected of theft, I was impaled (under the orders of a king). I then adored the illustrious Mahadeva who said unto me,—Thou shalt soon be freed from impalement and live for millions of years. The pangs due to impalement shall not be thine. Thou shalt also be freed from every kind of affliction and disease. And since, O ascetic, this body of thine hath sprung from the fourth foot of Dharma, (*viz.*, Truth). Thou shalt be unrivalled on Earth. Do thou make thy life fruitful. Thou shalt, without any obstruction, be able to bathe in all the sacred waters of the Earth. And after the dissolution of thy body, I shall, O learned Brahmana, ordain that thou shall enjoy the pure felicity of heaven for unending Time.—Having said these words unto me, the adorable Deity having the bull for his vehicle, *viz.*, Maheswara of unrivalled splendour and clad in animal skin, O king, disappeared there and then with all his associates.'

"Galava said,—'Formerly I studied at the feet of my preceptor Viswamitra. Obtaining his permission I set out for home with the object of seeing my father. My mother (having become a widow), was filled with sorrow and weeping bitterly, said unto me,—Alas, thy father will never see his son who, adorned with Vedic knowledge, has been permitted by his preceptor to come home and who, possessed of all the graces of youth, is endued with self-restraint.—Hearing these words of my mother, I became filled with despair in respect of again beholding my sire. I then paid my adoration with a rapt soul to Maheswara who, gratified with me, showed himself to me and said, —Thy sire, thy mother, and thyself, O son, shall all be freed from death. Go quickly and enter thy abode; thou shall behold thy sire there.—Having obtained the permission of the illustrious Deity, I then repaired to my home, O Yudhishthira, and beheld my father, O son, coming out after having finished his daily sacrifice. And he came out, bearing in his hands a quantity of Homa-fuel and Kusa grass and some fallen fruits. And he seemed to have already taken his daily food, for he had washed himself properly. Throwing down those things from his hand, my father, with eyes bathed in tears (of joy), raised me, for I had prostrated myself at his feet. Embracing me he smelt my head, O son of Pandu, and said,—By good luck, O son, art thou seen by me.

Thou hast come back, having acquired knowledge from the preceptor.

"Vaisampayana continued,—'Hearing these marvellous and most wonderful feats of the illustrious Mahadeva recited by the ascetics, the son of Pandu became amazed. Then Krishna, that foremost of all intelligent persons, spoke once more unto Yudhishthira, that ocean of righteousness, like Vishnu speaking unto Puruhuta.'

"Vasudeva said,—'Upamanyu, who seemed to blaze with effulgence like the Sun, said unto me,—Those sinful men that are stained with unrighteous deeds, do not succeed in attaining to Isana. Their dispositions being stained by the attributes of Rajas and Tamas, they can never approach the Supreme Deity. It is only those regenerate persons who are of cleansed souls that succeed in attaining to the Supreme Deity. Even if a person lives in the enjoyment of every pleasure and luxury, yet if he be devoted to the Supreme Deity, he comes to be regarded as the equal of forest recluses of cleansed souls. If Rudra be gratified with a person, he can confer upon him the status of either Brahma or of Kesava or of Sakra with all the deities under him, or the sovereignty of the three worlds. Those men, O sire, who worship Bhava even mentally, succeed in freeing themselves from all sins and attain to a residence in heaven with all the gods. A person who raises houses to the ground and destroys tanks and lakes indeed, who devastates the whole universe, does not become stained with sin, if he adores and worships the illustrious Deity of three eyes. A person that is destitute of every auspicious indication and that is stained by every sin, has all his sins destroyed by meditating upon Siva. Even worm and insects and birds, O Kesava, that devote themselves to Mahadeva, are enable to rove in perfect fearlessness. Even this is my settled conviction that those men who devote themselves to Mahadeva become certainly emancipated from rebirth. After this, Krishna again addressed Yudhisthira the son of Dharma in the following words.

"Vishnu said,—O Great King, 'Aditya, Chandra, Wind, Fire, Heaven, Earth, the Vasus, the Viswedevas, Dhatri, Aryyaman, Sukra, Vrihaspati, the Rudras, the Saddhyas, Varuna, Brahma, Sakra, Maruts, the Upanishads that deal with knowledge of Brahman, Truth, the Vedas, the Sacrifices, Sacrificial Presents, Brahmanas reciting the Vedas, Soma, Sacrificer, the shares of the deities in sacrificial offerings or clarified butter poured in sacrifices, Raksha, Diksha, all kinds of restraints in the form of vows and fasts and rigid observances, Swaha, Vashat, the Brahmanas, the celestial cow, the foremost acts of righteousness, the wheel of Time, Strength, Fame, Self-restraint, the Steadiness of all persons endued with intelligence, all acts of goodness and the reverse, the seven Rishis, Understanding of the foremost order, all kinds of excellent touch, the success of all (religious) acts, the diverse tribes of the deities, those beings that drink heat, those that are drinkers of Soma, Clouds, Suyamas, Rishitas, all creatures having Mantras for their bodies, Abhasuras, those beings that live upon scents only, those that live upon vision only, those that restrain their speech, those that restrain their minds, those that are pure, those that are capable of assuming diverse forms through Yoga-puissance, those deities that live on touch (as their food), those deities that subsist on vision and those that subsist upon the butter poured in sacrifices, those beings that are competent to create by fiats of their will the objects they require, they that are regarded as the foremost ones among the deities, and all the other deities, O descendant of Ajamila, the Suparnas, the Gandharvas, the Pisachas, the Danavas, Yakshas, the Charanas, the snakes, all that is gross and all that is exceedingly subtile, all that is soft and all that is not subtile, all sorrows and all joys, all sorrows that come after joy and all joy that comes after sorrow, the Sankhya philosophy, Yoga, and that which transcends objects which are regarded as foremost and very superior,—all adorable things, all the deities, and all the protectors of the universe who entering into the physical forces sustain and uphold this ancient creation of that illustrious Deity,—have sprung from that Creator of all creatures. All this that I have mentioned is grosser than that which the wise think of with the aid of Penances. Indeed, that subtile Brahma is the cause of life. I bow my head in reverence to it. Let that immutable and indestructible Master, always adored by us, grant us desirable boons. That person who, subjugating his senses and purifying himself, recites this hymn, without interruption in respect of his vow, for one month, succeeds in obtaining the merit that is attached to a Horse-sacrifice. By reciting this hymn the Brahmana succeeds in acquiring all the Vedas ; the Kshatriya becomes crowned with victory, O son of Pritha ; the Vaisya becomes successful in obtaining wealth and cleverness ; and the Sudra, in winning happiness here and a good end hereafter. Persons of great fame, by reciting this prince of hymns that is competent to cleanse every sin and that is highly sacred and purifying, set their hearts on Rudra. A man by reciting this prince of hymns succeeds in living in heaven for as many years as there are pores in his body."

SECTION XIX

"Yudhishthira said,—I ask, O chief of Bharata's race, what is the origin of the saying, about discharging all duties jointly at the time of a person's taking the hand of his spouse in marriage? Is that saying in respect of discharging all duties together, due only to what is laid down by the great Rishis in days of yore, or does it refer to the duty of begetting offspring from religious motives, or has it reference to only the carnal pleasure that is expected from such union? The doubt that fills my mind in this respect is very great. What is spoken of as joint duties by the sages is in my consideration incorrect. That which is called in this world the union for practising all duties together ceases with death and is not to be seen to subsist hereafter. This union for practising all duties together leads to heaven. But heaven, O grandsire, is attained to by persons that are dead. Of a married couple it is seen that only one dies at a time. Where does the other then remain? Do tell me this. Men attain to diverse kinds of fruits by practising diverse kinds of duties. The occupations again, to which men betake themselves are of diverse kinds. Diverse, again, are the hells to which they go in consequence of such diversity of duties and acts. Women, in particular, the Rishis have said, are false in behaviour. When human beings are such, and when women in particular have been declared in the ordinances to be false, how, O sire, can there be a union between the sexes for purposes of practising all duties together? In the very Vedas one may read that women are false. The word 'Duty', as used in the Vedas, seems to have been coined in the first instance for general application (so that it is applied to practices that have no merit in them). Hence the application of that word to the rites of marriage is, instead of being correct, only a form of speech forcibly applied where application it has none.[1] The subject seems to me to be inexplicable although I reflect upon it incessantly. O grandsire, O thou of great wisdom, it behoveth thee to expound this to me in detail, clearly and according to what has been laid down in the Sruti. In fact, do thou explain to me what is characteristics are, and the way in which it has come to pass![2]

1 I expand this Verse a little for bringing out the sense clearly.—T.

2 The subject propounded by Yudhishthira is this: marriage is always spoken of as a union of the sexes for practising all religious duties together. The king asks, how can this be. Marriage, as seems to him, is a union sought for pleasure. If it be said that the two individuals married together are married for practising religious duties jointly, such practice is suspended by death. Persons act differently and attain to different ends. There is, therefore, no prospect of a reunion after death. When, again, one of them dies, the joint practice of duties can no longer take place. The other objections, urged by Yudhishthira, to the theory of marriage being a union of the sexes for only practising religious duties jointly, are plain.—T.

"Bhishma said,—'In this connection is cited the old narrative of the discourse between Ashtavakra and the lady known by the name of Disa. In days of yore Ashtavakra of severe penances, desirous of marriage, begged the high-souled Rishi Vadanya of his daughter. The name by which the damsel was known was Suprabha. In beauty she was unrivalled on Earth. In virtues, dignity, conduct, and manners, she was superior to all girls. By a glance alone that girl of beautiful eyes had robbed him of his heart even as a delightful grove in spring, adorned with flowers, robs the spectator of his heart. The Rishi addressed Ashtavakra and said,—Yes, I shall bestow my daughter on thee. Listen, however, to me. Make a journey to the sacred North. Thou wilt see many things there ![1]

" 'Ashtavakra said,—It behoveth thee to tell me what I shall see in that region. Indeed, I am ready to execute whatever command may be laid upon me by thee.

" 'Vadanya said,—Passing over the dominions of the lord of Treasures thou will cross the Himavat mountains. Thou wilt then behold the plateau on which Rudra resides. It is inhabited by Siddhas and Charanas. It abounds with the associates of Mahadeva, frolicsome and fond of dance and possessed of diverse forms. It is peopled with also many Pisachas, O master, of diverse forms and all daubed with fragrant powders of diverse hues, and dancing with joyous hearts in accompaniment with instruments of different kinds made of brass. Surrounded by these who move with electric rapidity in the mazes of the dance or refrain at times altogether from forward or backward or transverse motion of every kind, Mahadeva dwells there. That delightful spot on the mountains, we have heard, is the favourite abode of the great Deity. It is said that that great god as also his associates are always present there. It was there that the goddess Uma practised the severest austerities for the sake of (obtaining for her lord) the three-eyed Deity. Hence, it is said, that spot is much liked by both Mahadeva and Uma. In days of yore there, on the heights of the Mahaparswa, which are situate to the north of the mountains sacred to Mahadeva, the sessions, and the last Night, and many deities, and many human beings also (of the foremost order), in there embodied forms, had adored Mahadeva.[2] Thou shalt cross that region also in thy northward journey. Thou will then see a beautiful and charming forest blue of hue and resembling a mass of clouds. There, in that forest, thou wilt behold a beautiful female ascetic looking like Sree herself. Venerable

1 The sense is that if after returning from thy journey to that region thou claimest thy bride, thou mayst obtain her from me. Thy journey will be a sort of trial or test to which I mean to put thee.—T.

2 'Kala-ratri' is the Night that precedes the universal dissolution.—T.

in age and highly blessed, she is in the observance of the Diksha. Beholding her there thou shouldst duly worship her with reverence. Returning to this place after having beheld her, thou wilt take the hand of my daughter in marriage. If thou wanteth to make this agreement, proceed then on thy journey and do what I command thee.

"Ashtavakra said,—So be it. I shall do thy bidding. Verily, I shall proceed to that region which thou speakest of, O thou of righteous soul. On thy side, let thy words, accord with truth.

"Bhishma continued,—"The illustrious Ashtavakra set out on his journey. He proceeded more and more towards the north and at last reached the Himavat mountains peopled by Siddhas and Charanas.[1] Arrived at the Himavat mountains, that foremost of Brahmanas then came upon the sacred river Vahuda whose waters produce great merit. He bathed in one of the delightful *Tirthas* of that river, which was free from mud, and gratified the deities with oblations of water. His ablutions being over, he spread a quantity of Kusa grass and laid himself down upon it for resting awhile at his ease.[2] Passing the night in this way, the Brahmana rose with the day. He once more performed his ablutions in the sacred waters of the Vahuda and then ignited his *homa* fire and worshipped it with the aid of many foremost of Vedic mantras.[3] He then worshipped with due rites both Rudra and his spouse Uma, and rested for some more time by the side of that lake in the course of the Vahuda whose shores he had reached. Refreshed by such rest, he set out from that region and then proceeded towards Kailasa. He then beheld a gate of gold that seemed to blaze with beauty. He saw also the Mandakini and the Nalini of the high-souled Kuvera, the Lord of Treasures.[4] Beholding the Rishi arrived there, all the Rakshasas having Manibhadra for their head, who were engaged in protecting that lake abounding with beautiful lotuses, came out in a body for welcoming and honouring the illustrious traveller. The Rishi worshipped in return those Rakshasas of terrible prowess and asked them to report, without delay, his arrival unto the Lord of Treasures. Requested by him to do this, those Rakshasas, O king, said unto him,—King Vaisravana, without waiting for the new news from us, is coming of his own accord

1 The Commentator thinks that 'uttaram &c' means the *Sacred* north. —T.

2 'Tirtha' means here a Ghat, *i.e.*, an easy descent from the bank for access to the water.—T.

3 'Pradhanatah' is explained by the Commentator to mean 'with foremost of Vedic mantras.'—T.

4 'Mandakini' is that part of the river Ganga which flows through Kailasa ; while Nalini is a celebrated lake owned by the king of the Yakshas, so called because of the lotuses which occur there in plenty.—T.

to thy presence. The illustrious Lord of Treasures is well acquainted with the object of this thy journey. Behold him,—that blessed Master.—who blazes with his own energy. Then king Vaisravana, approaching the faultless Ashtavakra, duly enquired about his welfare. The usual enquiries of politeness being over, the Lord of Treasures then addressed the regenerate Rishi, saying,—Welcome art thou here. Do tell me what it is thou seekest at my hands. Inform me of it. I shall, O regenerate one, accomplish what ever thou mayst bid me to accomplish. Do thou enter my abode as pleases thee, O foremost of Brahmanas. Duly entertained by me, and after thy business is accomplished, thou mayst go without any obstacles being placed in thy way. —Having said these words, Kuvera took the hand of that foremost of Brahmanas and led him into his palace. He offered him his own seat as also water to wash his feet and the Arghya made of the usual ingredients. After the two had taken their seats, the Yakshas of Kuvera headed by Manibhadra, and many Gandharvas and Kinnaras, also sat down before them. After all of them had taken their seats, the Lord of Treasures said these words,—Understanding what thy pleasure is, the diverse tribes of Apsaras will commence their dance. It is meet that I should entertain thee with hospitality and that thou shouldst be served with proper ministrations. Thus addressed, the ascetic Ashtavakra said, in a sweet voice—Let the dance proceed. Then Urvata and Misrakesi, and Rambha and Urvasi, and Alumvusha and Ghritachi, and Chitra and Chitrangada and Ruchi, and Manohara and Sukesi and Sumukhi and Hasini and Prabha, and Vidyuta, and Prasami and Danta and Vidyota and Rati,—these and many other beautiful Apsaras began to dance. The Gandharvas played on diverse kinds of musical instruments. After such excellent music and dance had commenced, the Rishi Ashtavakra of severe penances unconsciously passed a full celestial year there in the abode of king Vaisravana.[1] Then king Vaisravana said unto the Rishi,—O learned Brahmana, behold, a little more then a year has passed away since thy arrival here. This music and dance, especially known by the name of Gandharva, is a stealer of the heart (and of time.) Do thou act as thou wishes or let this go on if that be thy pleasure. Thou art my guest and, therefore, worthy of adoration. This is my house. Givest thou thy commands. We are all bound to thee. The illustrious Ashtavakra, thus addressed by king Vaisravana, replied unto him, with a pleased heart, saying,—I have been duly honoured by thee. I desire now, O Lord of Treasures, to go hence. Indeed, I am highly pleased. All this befits thee, O Lord of Treasures. Through thy grace, O

1 'Divya' is excellent Gandharva, meaning music and dance.—T.

enjoyed by us. There is no pleasure more agreeable to women (than that which is derivable from the companionship of a person of the other sex). Verily, congress with a person of the opposite sex is the most delicious fruit of joy that we can reap. When urged by the god of desire, women become very capricious. At such times they do not feel any pain, even if they walk over a desert of burning sand :—

" 'Ashtavakra said,—O blessed lady, I never approach one that is another's spouse. One's congress with another man's wife is condemned by persons conversant with the scriptures on morality. I am an utter stranger to enjoyments of every kind. O blessed lady, know that I have become desirous of wedlock for obtaining offspring. I swear by truth itself. Through the aid of offspring righteously obtained, I shall proceed to those regions of felicity which cannot be attained without such aid. O good lady, know what is cosistent with morality, and knowing it, desist from thy efforts.—

" 'The lady said,—The very deities of wind and fire and water, or the other celestials, O regenerate one, are not so agreeable to women as the deity of desire. Verily, women are exeedingly fond of sexual congress. Among a thousand women, or, perhaps, among hundreds of thousands, sometimes only one may be found that is devoted to her husband. When under the influence of desire, they care not for family or father or mother or brother or husband or sons or husband's brother, (but pursue the way that desire points out). Verily, in pursuit of what they consider happiness, they destroy the family (to which they belong by birth or marriage) even as many queenly rivers eat away the banks that contain them. The Creator himself had said this, quickly marking the faults of women.[1]—

"Bhishma continued,—"The Rishi, bent upon finding out the faults of women, then addressed that lady, saying,—Cease to speak to me in this strain. Yearning springs from liking. Tell me what (else) I am to do.[2]—That lady then said in return,—O illustrious one, thou shalt see according to time and place (as do whether I have anything agreeable in me). Do thou only live here (for some time), O highly blessed one, and I shall regard myself amply rewarded.—Thus addressed by her, the regenerate Rishi, O Yudhishthira, expressed his resolution to comply with her request, saying,—Verily, I shall dwell

---

1 A woman is said to destroy a family by staining it with her unchastity.—T.

2 Both the Vernacular translators have totally misunderstood the second line 'Asyatam' is explained by the Commentator as 'tushnim sthiyatam. Ruchitabchchchandah' means 'chchhandah' or yearning arises from 'ruchi' or like. What the Rishi says is 'Asyet I do not yearn after thy company, for I do not like thee.' Of course, if, after staying with thee for some time, I begin to like thee, I may then feel a yearning for thee !—T.

with thee in this place as long as I can venture to do so.—The Rishi then, beholding that lady afflicted with decrepitude, began to reflect earnestly on the matter. He seemed to be even tortured by his thoughts. The eyes of that foremost of Brahmanas failed to derive any delight from those parts of that lady's person whereupon they were cast. On the other hand, his glances seemed to be dispelled by the ugliness of those particular limbs.—This lady is certainly the goddess of this palace. Has she been made ugly through some curse. It is not proper that I should hastily ascertain the cause of this.— Reflecting upon this in the secrecy of his heart, and curious to know the reason, the Rishi passed the rest of that day in an anxious state. The lady then addressed him, saying,—O illustrious one, behold the aspect of the Sun reddened by the evening clouds. What service shall I do unto thee.—The Rishi addressed her, saying,—'Fetch water for my ablutions. Having bathed, I shall say my evening prayers, restraining my tongue and the senses.—

SECTION XX

"Bhishma said,—Thus commanded, the lady said,—Be it so.—She then brought oil (for rubbing the Rishi's body therewith) and a piece of cloth for his wear during the ablutions. Permitted by the ascetic, she rubbed every part of his body with the fragrant oil she had brought for him. Gently was the Rishi rubbed, and when the process of rubbing was over, he proceeded to the room set apart for the performance of ablutions. There he sat upon a new and excellent seat of great splendour.[1] After the Rishi had taken his seat upon it, the old lady began to wash his person with her own soft hands whose touch was exceedingly agreeable. One after another in due order, the lady rendered the most agreeable services to the Rishi in the matter of his ablutions. Between the lukewarm water with which he was washed, and the soft hands that were employed in washing him, the Rishi of rigid vows failed to understand that the whole night had passed away in the process. Rising from the bath the Rishi became highly surprised. He saw the Sun risen above the horizon on the East. He was amazed at this and asked himself,—Was it really so or was it an error of the understanding?—The Rishi then duly worshipped the god of a thousand rays. This done, he asked the lady as to what he should do. The old lady prepared some food for the Rishi that was as delicious to the taste as Amrita itself. In consequence of the delicious character of that food the Rishi could not take much. In taking that little, however,

1 Utsaditah' is explained by the Commentator to mean "chalitah." Here, however, I think it does not mean so.—T.

the day passed away and evening came. The old lady then asked the Rishi to go to bed and sleep. An excellent bed was assigned to the Rishi and another was occupied by herself. The Rishi and the old lady occupied different beds at first but when it was midnight, the lady left her own bed for coming to that of the Rishi.

" 'Ashtavakra said,—O blessed lady, my mind turns away from sexual congress with one who is the spouse of another. Leave my bed, O good lady. Blessed be thou, do thou desist from this of thy own accord.[1]—

"Bhishma continued,—Thus dissuaded by that Brahmana with the aid of his self-restraint, the lady answered him, saying,—I am my own mistress. In accepting me thou wilt incur no sin.—

" 'Ashtavakra said,—Women can never be their own mistresses. This is the opinion of the Creator himself, *viz.*, that a women never deserves to be independent.—

"The lady said,—O learned Brahmana, I am tortured by desire. Mark my devotion to thee. Thou incurrest sin by refusing to accost me lovingly.—

"Ashtavakra said,—Diverse faults drag away the man that acts as he likes. As regards myself, I am able to control my inclinations by self-restraint. O good lady, do thou return to thy own bed.—

" 'The lady said,—I bow to thee, bending my head. It behoves thee to show me thy grace. O sinless one, I prostrate myself before thee, do thou become my refuge. If indeed, thou seest such sin in congress with one that is not thy spouse, I yield myself unto thee. Do thou, O regenerate one, accept my hand in marriage. Thou wilt incur no sin. I tell thee truly. Know that I am my own mistress. If there be any sin in this, let it be mine alone. My heart is devoted to thee. I am my own mistress. Do thou accept me.—

" 'Ashtavakra said,—How is it, O good lady, that thou art thy own mistress. Tell me the reason of this. There is not a single woman in the three worlds that deserves to be regarded as the mistress of her own self. The father protects her while she is a maiden. The husband protects her while she is in youth. Sons protect her when she is aged. Women can never be independent as long as they live !—

" 'The lady said,—I have, since my maidenhood, adopted the vow of Brahmacharyya. Do not doubt it. I am still a maid. Do thou make me thy wife. O Brahmana, do not kill this devotion of mine to thee.—

" 'Ashtavakra said,—As thou art inclined to me, so am I inclined to thee. There is this question, however, that should be settled. Is it

---

1 The last words may also mean—'Go to thy own bed and rest by thyself !'—T.

true that by yielding to my inclinations I shall not be regarded as acting in opposition to what the Rishi (Vadanya) wishes. This is very wonderful. Will this lead to what is beneficial ? Here is a maiden adorned with excellent ornaments and robes. She is exceedingly beautiful. Why did decrepitude cover her beauty so long ? At present she looks like a beautiful maiden. There is no knowing what form she may take hereafter.[1] I shall never swerve from that restraint which I have over desire and the other passions or from contentment with what I have already got. Such swerving does not seem to be good. I shall keep myself united with truth ![2]

SECTION XXI

"Yudhishthira said,—Tell me why had that lady no fear of Ashtavakra's curse although Ashtavakra was endued with great energy ? How also did Ashtavakra succeed in coming back from that place ?

"Bhishma said,—Ashtavakra asked her, saying,—How dost thou succeed in altering thy form so ? Thou shouldst not say anything that is untrue. I wish to know this. Speakest thou truly before a Brahmana.—

"The lady said,—O best of Brahmana, wherever thou mayst reside in heaven or on Earth, this desire of union between the sexes is to be observed. O thou of infallible prowess, listen, with concentrated attention, to this all. This trial was devised by me, O sinless one, for testing thee aright. O thou of infallible prowess, thou hast subjugated all the worlds for not foregoing your previous resolution. Know that I am the embodiment of the Northern point of the compass. Thou hast seen the lightness of the female character. Even women that are aged are tortured by the desire of sexual union. The Grandsire himself and all the deities with Indra have been pleased with thee. The object for which thy illustrious self has come here (is known to me). O foremost of regenerate persons, thou hast been despatched hither by the Rishi Vadanya—the father of thy bride—in order that I may instruct thee. Agreeably to the wishes of that Rishi I have already instructed thee. Thou wilt return home in safety. Thy journey back will not be toilsome. Thou wilt obtain for wife the girl thou hast chosen. She

---

1 The Commentator takes the wards 'kimivcttaram bhavet' to imply 'what will be better for me ? Shall I adhere to Vadanya's daughter or shall I take this girl ? I think this is rather far-fetched.—T.

2 By 'Sakti' is implied 'kamadidamanasamarthyam' and by 'dhriti purvapraptasya atyagah.' The last half of the last line of Verse 25 is rendered erroneously by both the Vernacular translators. Adhering to the Commentator's explanation, they add their own interpretation which is different. This sort of junble is very peculiar.—T.

will bear thee a son. Through desire I had solicited thee. Thou madest me the very best answer. The desire for sexual union is incapable of being transcended in the three worlds. Go back to thy quarters, having achieved such merit. What else is there that thou wishest to hear from me? I shall discourse on it, O Ashtavakra, in accordance with the truth. I was gratified by the Rishi Vadanya in the first instance for thy sake, O regenerate ascetic. For the sake of honouring him, I have said all this to thee.

"Bhishma continued,—'Hearing these words of hers, the regenerate Ashtavakra joined his hands in a reverential attitude. He then solicited the lady for her permission to go back. Obtaining the permission he came back to his own asylum. Resting himself for sometime at home and obtaining the permission of his kinsmen and friends, he then in a proper way, proceeded, O delighter of the Kurus, to the Brahmana Vadanya. Welcomed with the usual enquiries by Vadanya, the Rishi Ashtavakra, with a well-pleased heart, narrated all that he had seen (in course of his sojourn to the North). He said,—Commanded by thee I proceeded to the mountains of Gandhamadana. In the regions lying to the north of these mountains I beheld a very superior goddess. I was received by her with courtesy. She named you in my hearing and also instructed me in various matters. Having listened to her I have come back, O lord. Unto him that said so, the learned Vadanya said,—Take my daughter's hand according to due rites and under the proper constellations. Thou art the fittest bridegroom I can select for the girl.

"Bhishma continued,—'Ashtavakra said,—So be it and took the hand of the girl. Indeed, the highly righteous Rishi, having espoused the girl, became filled with joy. Having taken as his wife that beautiful damsel, the Rishi continued to dwell in his own asylum, freed from (mental) fever of every kind.

SECTION XXII

"Yudhishthira said,—'Whom do the eternal Brahmanas strictly observing religious rites call a proper object of gifts? Is a Brahmana that bears the symbols of the order of life he follows to be regarded as such or is one who does not bear such indications is to be so regarded?[1]

---

1 'Linga' means signs or indications. A 'Lingin' is one that bears signs and indications. 'Brahmanam' (in both places) means one conversant with Brahman. The first, that is, 'Lingin' implies either a Brahmacharin or a Sanyasin that always bears the marks of his order. An 'Alingin' is one that is divested of such marks. Yudhishthira's question is, who, amongst these, should be considered worthy of gifts?—T.

"Bhishma said,—O monarch, it has been said that gifts should be made unto a Brahmana that adheres to the duties of his own order, whether, he bears the indications of a Bramachari or not, for both are faultless, *viz.*, he that bears such indications and he that is divested of them.

"Yudhisthira said,—'What fault does an uncleansed person incur, if he makes gifts of sacrificial butter or food with great devotion unto persons of the regenerate order ?'

"Bhishma said,—'Even one that is most destitute of self-restraint becomes, without doubt, cleansed by devotion. Such a man, O thou of great splendour, becomes cleansed in respect of every act (and not with reference to gift alone).'

"Yudhishthira said,—'It has been said that a Brahmana that is sought to be employed in an act having reference to the deities, should never be examined. The learned, however, say that with respect to such acts as have reference to the Pitris, the Brahmana that is sought to be employed, should be examined (in the matter of both his conduct and competence).

"Bhishma said,—'As regards acts that have reference to the deities, these fructify not in consequence of the Brahmana that is employed in doing the rites but through the grace of the deities themselves. Without doubt, those persons that perform sacrifice obtain the merit attached to those acts, through the grace of the deities.[1] The Brahmanas, O chief of the Bharatas, are always devoted of Brahman. The Rishi Markandeya, one of the greatest Rishis endued with intelligence in all the worlds, said this in days of yore.—

"Yudhishthira said,—'Why, O grandsire, are their five *viz.*, he that is a stranger, he that is endued with learning (connected with the duties of his order), he that is connected by marriage, he that is endued with penances, and he that adheres to the performance of sacrifices, regarded as proper persons ?[2]

"Bhishma said,—The first three, *viz.*, strangers, relatives, and ascetics, when possessed of these attributes, *viz.*, purity of birth, devotion to religious acts, learning, compassion, modesty, sincerity, and truthfulness, are regarded as proper persons. The other two, *viz.*, men of learning and those devoted to sacrifices, when endued with five of these attributes, *viz.*, purity of birth, compassion, modesty, sincerity, truth-

1 The sense is that with respect to acts having reference to only the Pitris the conduct and competence of Brahmanas should be examined.—T.

2 The Commentator explains that five persons are mentioned in the question of Yudhishthira. K. P. Singha omits one. The Burdwan translator repeats the words of the original without any explanation. I take 'sammandhi' to mean relatives by marriage. To this day, in all India, people make gifts or presents unto sons-in-law, &c.—T.

fulness, are also regarded as proper persons. Listen now to me, O son of Pritha, as I recite to thee the opinions of these four persons of mighty energy, *viz.*, the goddess Earth, the Rishi Kasyapa, Agni (the deity of fire) and the ascetic Markandeya.

'The Earth said,—As a clod of mud, when thrown into the great ocean quickly dissolves away, evey so every kind of sin disappears in the three high attributes *viz.*, officiation at sacrifices, teaching and receiving of gifts.[1]—

"Kasyapa said,—the Vedas with their six branches, the Sankhya philosophy, the Puranas, and high birth, these fail to rescue a regenerate person if he falls away from good conduct.[2]—

"'Agni said,—That Brahmana who, engaged in study and regarding himself learned, seeks with the aid of his learning to destroy the reputation of others, falls away from righteousness, and comes to be regarded as dissociated from truth. Verily regions of felicity hereinafter are never attained to by such a person of destructive genius.—

"Markandeya said,—If a thousand Horse-sacrifices and Truth were weighed in the balance, I do not know whether the former would weigh even half as heavy as the latter.—

"Bhishma continued,—'Having spoken these words, those four persons, each of whom is endued with immeasurable energy, *viz.*, the goddess Earth, Kasyapa, Agni, and Bhrigu's son armed with weapons, quickly went away.

"Yudhishthira said,—If Brahmanas observant of the vow of Brahmacharyya in this world solicit the offerings one makes (unto one's deceased ancestors in Sraddhas) I ask, can the Sraddha be regarded well-performed, if the performer actually makes over those offerings unto such Brahmanas.'

"Bhishma said.—'If, having practised the vow of Brahmacharyya for the prescribed period (of twelve years) and acquired proficiency in the Vedas and their branches, a Brahmana himself solicits the offering made in Sraddhas and eats the same, he is regarded to fall away from his vow. The Sraddha, however, is not regarded as stained in any way.

"Yudhishthira said,—'The wise have said that duty of righteousness has many ends and numerous doors. Tell me, O grandsire, what however are the settled conclusions in this matter.[3]

---

1 The sense is that no sin can touch a Brahmana who observes these three acts. These three acts are efficacious in washing away all sins. The Commentator points out that by this the attributes of Birth and knowledge are referred to.—T.

2 By good conduct is implied modesty and candour.—T.

3 'Anekantam' is explained by the Commentator as 'Anekaphalakaram,' *i.e.*, of diverse kinds of fruits. The fruits attainable by a correct discharge of duties are of diverse kinds, because the objects of those duties, called 'Patras' are of various kinds.—T.

Bhishma said,—'Abstention from injury to others, truthfulness, the absence of wrath (forgiveness), compassion, self-restraint, and sincerity or candour, O monarch, are the indications of Righteousness. There are persons who wander over the earth, praising righteousness but without practising what they preach and engaged all the while in sin. O king, He who gives unto such persons gold or gems or steeds, has to sink in hell and to subsist there for ten years, eating the while the fæces of such persons as live upon the flesh of dead kine and buffalos, of men called Pukkasas, of others that live in the outskirts of cities and villages, and of men that publish, under the influence of wrath and folly, the acts and the omissions of others.[1] Those foolish men who do give unto a Brahmana observant of the vow of Brahmacharyya the offerings made in Sraddhas (unto one's deceased ancestors), have to go, O monarch into regions of great misery.'

"Yudhishthira said,—'Tell me, O grandsire, what is superior to Brahmacharyya? What is the highest indication of virtue? What is the highest kind of purity?

"Bhishma said,—'I tell thee, O son, that abstention from honey and meat is even superior to Brahmacharyya. Righteousness consists in keeping within boundaries or in self-restraint, the best indication of Righteousness is Renunciation (which is also the highest kind of purity).'[2]

"Yudhishthira said,—In what time should one practise Righteousness? In what time should wealth be sought? In what time should pleasure be enjoyed? O grandsire, do tell me this.'

"Bhishma said,—One should earn wealth in the first part of one's life. Then should one earn Righteousness, and then enjoy pleasure. One should not, however, attach oneself to any of these. One should regard the Brahmanas, worship one's preceptor and seniors, show

---

1 Verse 22 contains 4 substantives in the genetive plural. All those are connected with 'vishtham' in the previous Verse. The Commentator points out this clearly. Those living in the outskirts of towns and villages are tanners and other low castes. They who publish the acts and omissions of others are regarded as very vile persons, equivalent to such low caste men mentioned above. It is difficult to differ from the commentator, but it seems that genetives in the Verse as are used for datives, in which case the meaning would be that they who give unto such persons shall also sink into hell." The Burdwan translator gives a ridiculous version of Verse 22. —T.

2 The Bengal reading 'Brahmacharyya' is better than the Bombay reading of that word in the accusative. Bhishma apparently gives two answers. These however involve three. By 'maryyada' is meant boundaries or limits. The duties of men have known bounds. To transgress those bounds would be to transgress duty. The highest indication of Righteousness is 'samah' or absence of desire for all worldly objects; hence Renunciation.—T.

compassion for all creatures, be of mild disposition and agreeable speech. To utter falsehood in a court of justice, to behave deceitfully towards the king, to act falsely towards preceptors and seniors, are regarded as equivalent (in heinousness) to Brahmanicide. One should never do an act of violence to the king's person. Nor should one ever strike a cow. Both these offences are equivalent to the sin of fœticide. One should never abandon one's (*homa*) fire. One should also never cast off one's study of the Vedas. One should never assail a Brahmana by words or acts. All these offences are equivalent to Brahmanicide.

"Yudhishthira said,—'What kind of Brahmanas should be regarded as good? By making presents unto (what kind of) Brahmanas one may aquire great merit? What kind of Brahmanas are they whom one should feed? Tell me all this, O grandsire!

"Bhishma said,—'Those Brahmanas that are freed from wrath, that are devoted to acts of righteousness, that are firm in Truth, and that practise self-restraint are regarded as good. By making gifts unto them one acquires great merit. One wins great merit by making presents unto such Brahmanas as are free from pride, capable of bearing everything, firm in the pursuit of their objects, endued with mastery over their senses, devoted to the good of all creatures, and disposed to be friendly towards all. One earns great merit by making gifts unto such Brahmanas as are free from cupidity, as are pure of heart and conduct, possessed of learning and modesty, truthful in speech and observant of their own duties as laid down in the scriptures. The Rishis have declared that Brahmana to be a deserving object of gifts who studies the four Vedas with all their branches and is devoted to the six well-known duties (laid down in the scriptures). One acquires great merit by making gifts unto Brahmanas possessed of such qualifications. The man who makes gifts unto a deserving Brahmana multiplies his merit a thousand fold. A single righteous Brahmana possessed of wisdom and Vedic lore, observant of the duties laid down in the scriptures, distinguished by purity of behaviour, is competent to rescue a whole race.[1] One should make gifts of kine and horses and wealth and food and other kinds of articles unto a Brahmana that is possessed of such qualifications. By making such gifts unto such persons one earns great happiness in the next world. As I have already told thee even one such Brahmana is fully competent to rescue the entire race to which the giver belongs. What need I say, therefore, O dear son, of the merit of making gifts unto many Brahmanas of such qualifications? In making gifts, therefore one should always select the object to whom the gifts are to be made. Hearing of a Brahmana possessed of proper qualifications and

1 *i.e.*, by making gifts unto even a single such Brahmana, one rescues all the ancestors and descendants of one's race.—T.

regarded with respect by all good people, one should invite him even if he resides at a distance and welcome him when he arrives and one should worship him by all means in his power.' "

SECTION XXIII

"Yudhishthira said,—'I desire thee, O grandsire, to tell me what the ordinances are that have been laid down by the acts touching the deities and the (deceased) ancestors on occasions of Sraddhas.'

"Bhishma said,—Having purified oneself (by baths and other purificatory acts) and then going through the well-known auspicious rites, one should carefully do all acts relating to the deities in the fore-noon, and all acts relating to the *Pitris* in the afternoon. What is given to men should be given in the midday with affection and regard. That gift which is made untimely is appropriated by Rakshasas.[1] Gifts of articles that have been leapt over by any one, or been licked or sucked, that are not given peacefully, that have been seen by women that are impure in consequence of their season having come, do not produce any merit. Such gifts are regarded as the portion belonging to the Rakshasas. Gifts of articles that have been proclaimed before many people or from which a portion has been eaten by a Sudra, or that have been seen or licked by a dog, form portions of Rakshasas. Food which is mixed with hair or in which there are worms, or which has been stained with spittle or saliva or which has been gazed at by a dog or into which tear-drops have fallen or which has been trodden upon should be known as forming the portion of Rakshasas. Food that has been eaten by a person incompetent to utter the syllable Om, or that has been eaten by a person bearing arms, O Bharata, or that has been eaten by a wicked person, should be known to form the portion of Rakshasas.[2] The food that is eaten by a person from which a portion has already been eaten by another, or which is eaten without a part thereof having been offered to deities and guests and children, is appropriated by Rakshasas. Such stained food, if offered to the deities and *Pitris* is never accepted by them but is appropriated by Rakshasas. The food offered by the three regenerate classes in Sraddhas,

1 One makes gifts unto the deities, the *Pitris*, and unto human beings. There is a time for each kind of gift. If made untimely, the gift, instead of producing any merit, becomes entirely futile, if not sinful. Untimely gifts are appropriated by Rakshasas. Even food that is taken untimely, does not strengthen the body but goes to nourish the Rakshasas and other evil beings.—T.

2 *i.e.*, any food, a portion of which has been eaten by any of these persons, is unworthy of being given away. If given, it is appropriated by Rakshasas. One incompetent to utter Om is, of course, a Sudra.—T.

in which Mantras are either not uttered or uttered incorrectly and in which the ordinances laid down in the scriptures are not complied with, if distributed to guests and other people, is appropriated by Rakshasas. The food that is distributed to guests without having been previously dedicated to the deities or the Pitris with the aid of libation on the sacred fire, which has been stained in consequence of a portion thereof having been eaten by a person that is wicked or of irreligious behaviour, should be known to form the portion of Rakshasas.

" 'I have told thee what the portions are of the Rakshasas. Listen now to me as I lay down the rules for ascertaining who the Brahmana is that is deserving of gift.[1] All Brahmanas that have been outcasted (on account of the commission of heinous sins), as also Brahmanas that are idiots and out of mind, do not deserve to be invited to Sraddhas in which offerings are made to either the deities or the *Pitris*. That Brahmana who is afflicted with leucoderma, or he that is destitute of virility, or he that has got leprosy, or he that has got phthisis or he that is labouring under epilepsy (with delusions of the sensorium), or he that is blind, should not, O king, be invited.[2] Those Brahmanas that practise the calling of physicians, those that receive regular pay for worshipping the images of deities established by the rich, or live upon the service of the deities, those that are observant of vows from pride or other false motives, and those that sell Soma, do not deserve to be invited. Those Brahmanas that are, by profession, vocalists, or dancers or players or instrumental musicians, or reciters of sacred books, or warriors and athletes, do not, O king, deserve to be invited. Those Brahmanas who pour libations on the sacred fire for Sudras, or who are preceptors of Sudras, or who are servants of Sudra masters, do not deserve to be invited. That Brahmana who is paid for his services as preceptor, or who attends as pupil upon the lectures of some preceptor because of some allowance that is granted to him, does not deserve to be invited, for both of them are regarded as sellers of Vedic lore. That Brahmana who has been once induced to accept the gift of food in a Sraddha at the very outset, as also he who has married a Sudra wife, even if possessed of every kind of knowledge do not deserve to be invited.[3] Those Brahmanas that are destitute of their domestic fire,

1 The speaker, by first mentioning who are unworthy, means to point out those that are worthy.—T.

2 'Apasmara' is a peculiar kind of epilepsy in which the victim always thinks that he is pursued by some monster who is before his eyes. When epilepsy is accompanied by some delusion of the sensorium, it comes to be called by Hindu physicians as 'Apasmara.'—T.

3 An 'Agrani' or 'Agradani' is that Brahmana unto whom the food and other offerings to the Preta in the first Sraddha are given away. Such a person is regarded as fallen.—T.

and they that attend upon corpses, they that are thieves, and they that have otherwise fallen away do not, O king, deserve to be invited.[1] Those Brahmanas whose antecedents are not known or are vile, and they that are Purtika-putras, do not, O king, deserve to be invited on occasions of Sraddhas.[2] That Brahmana who gives loans of money, or he who subsists upon the interest of the loans given by him, or he who lives by the sale of living creatures, dose not deserve, O king, to be invited. Persons who have been subjugated by their wives, or they who live by becoming the paramours of unchaste women, or they who abstain from their morning and evening paryers no not deserve, O king, to be invited to Sraddhas.

"'Listen now to me as I mention who the Brahmana is that has been ordained for acts done in honour of the deities and the Pitris. Indeed, I shall tell thee what those merits are in consequence of which one may become a giver or a recipient of gifts in Sraddhas (notwithstanding the faults mentioned above).[3] Those Brahmanas that are observant of the rites and ceremonies laid down in the scriptures, or they that are possessed of merit, or they that are conversant with the Gayatri, or they that are observant of the ordinary duties of Brahmanas, even if they happen to betake themselves to agriculture for a living, are capable, O king, of being invited to Sraddhas. If a Brahmana happens to be well-born, he deserves to be invited to Sraddhas notwithstanding his profession of arms for fighting the battle of others.[4] That Brahmana, however, O son, who happens to betake himself to trade for a living should be discarded (even if possessed of merit). The Brahmana who pours libations every day on the sacred fire, or who resides in a fixed habitation, who is not a thief and who does the duties of hospitality to guests arrived at his house, deserves, O king, to be invited to Sraddhas. The Brahmana, O chief of Bharata's race, who recites the Savitri morning, noon, and night, or who subsists upon eleemosynary charity, who is observant of the rites and ceremonies laid down in the scriptures for persons of his order, deserves, O king, to be invited to Sraddhas.[5] That

---

1 When corpses are taken to crematoria, certain rites have to be performed upon them before they can be consumed. Those Brahmanas that assist at the performance of those rites are regarded as fallen.—T.

2 Sometimes the father of a daughter bestows her upon a bridegroom under the contract that the son born of that daughter by her husband should be the son of the daughter's father. Such a son, who is dissociated from the race of his own father, is called a Putrika-putra.—T.

3 'Anugraham' is that merit in consequence of which faults become neutralised and the stained person may come to be regarded as deserving.—T.

4 As Drona, Aswatthaman, Kripa, Rama and others.—T.

5 'Uditastamita' means one who having earned wealth spends it all in

Brahmana who having earned wealth in the morning becomes poor in the afternoon, or who poor in the morning becomes wealthy in the evening or who is destitute of malice, or is stained by a minor fault, deserves, O king, to be invited to Sraddhas. That Brahmana who is destitute of pride or sin, who is not given to dry disputation, or who subsists upon alms obtained in his rounds of mendicancy from house to house deserves, O king, to be invited to sacrifices. One who is not observant of vows, or who is addicted to falsehood (in both speech and conduct), who is a thief, or who subsists by the sale of living creatures or by trade in general, becomes worthy of invitation to Sraddhas, O king, if he happens to offer all to the deities first and subsequently drink Soma. That man who having acquired wealth by foul or cruel means subsequently spends it in adoring the deities and discharging the duties of hospitality, becomes worthy, O king, of being invited to Sraddhas. The wealth that one has acquired by the sale of Vedic lore, or which has been earned by a women, or which has been gained by meanness (such as giving false evidence in a court of law), should never be given to Brahmanas or spent in making offerings to the Pitris. That Brahmana, O chief of Bharata's race, who upon the completion of a Sraddha that is performed with his aid, refuses to utter the words '*astu swadha*', incurs the sin of swearing falsely in a suit for land.[1] The time for performing Sraddha, O Yudhishthira, is that when one obtains a good Brahmana and curds and ghee and the sacred day of the new moon, and the meat of wild animals such as deer and others.[2] Upon the completion of a Sraddha performed by a Brahmana the word Swadha should be uttered. If performed by a Kshatriya the words that should be uttered are—*Let thy Pitris be gratified.*—Upon the completion of a Sraddha performed by a Vaisya, O Bharata, the words that should be uttered are—Let everything become inexhaustible.—Similarly, upon the conclusion of a Sraddha performed by a Sudra, the word that should be uttered is *Swasti*,—In respect of a Brahmana, the declaration regarding *Punyaham* should be accompanied with the utterance of the syllable Om. In the case of a Kshatriya, such declaration should be

---

gifts. 'Astamitodita' is one who though poor at first succeed in earning wealth afterwards ; *i.e.*, one who having become rich, keeps that wealth for spending it on good purposes.—T.

1 Upon the completion of a Sraddha, the Brahmana who is officiating at it should utter the words *yukta* which means well-applied. Certain other words such as *Swadha*, &c., have to be uttered. The meaning is that the Brahmana who assists the performer of the Sraddha by reciting the Mantras should, upon completion, say unto the performer that the Sraddha is well-performed. As the custom is, these words are still uttered by every Branmana officiating at Sraddhas.—T.

2 K. P. Singha wrongly renders the word 'somakshayah' as equivalent to 'somarasab.—T.

without the utterance of syllable Om. In the rites performed by a Vaisya, the words that should be uttered, instead of beings the syllable Om, are,—Let the deities be gratified.'[1]—Listen now to me as I tell thee the rites that should be performed, one after another, conformably to the ordinances, (in respect of all the orders). All the rites that go by the name of *Jatakarma*, O Bharata, are indispensable in the case of all the three orders (that are regenerate). All these rites, O Yudhishthira, in the case of both Brahmanas and Kshatriyas as also in that of Vaisyas are to be performed with the aid of mantras. The girdle of a Brahmana should be made of Munja grass. That for one belonging to the royal order should be a bowstring. The Vaisya's girdle should be made of the Valwaji grass. Even this is what has been laid down in the scriptures. Listen now to me as I expound to thee what constitutes the merits and faults of both givers and recipients of gifts. A Brahmana becomes guilty of a dereliction of duty by uttering a falsehood. Such an act on his part is sinful. A Kshatriya incurs four times and a Vaisya eight times the sin that a Brahmana incurs by uttering a falsehood. A Brahmana should not eat elsewhere, having been previously invited by a Brahmana. By eating at the house of the person whose invitation has been posterior in point of time, he becomes inferior and even incurs the sin that attaches to the slaughter of an animal on occasions other than those of sacrifices.[2] So also, if he eats elsewhere after having been invited by a person of the royal order or a Vaisya, he falls away from his position and incurs half the sin that attaches to the slaughter of an animal on occasions other than those of sacrifices. That Brahmana, O king, who eats on occasions of such rites as are performed in honour of the deities or the Pitris by Brahmanas and Kshatriyas and Vaisyas, without having performed his ablutions, incurs the sin of uttering an untruth for a cow. That Brahmana, O king, who eats on occasions of similar rites performed by persons belonging to the three higher orders, at a time when he is impure in consequence either of a birth or a death among his cognates, through temptation, knowing well that he is impure incurs the same sin.[3] He who lives upon wealth obtained under false

---

1 Upon the conclusion of a Sraddha or other rites, the Brahmana who officiates at it, addresses certain other Brahmanas that are invited on the occasion and says,—Do you say *Punyaham*—The Brahmana addressed say, —Om, let it be *Punyaham* !—By 'Punyaham' is meant 'sacred day.'—T.

2 The fact is, the slaughter of animals in a sacrifice leads to no sin but if slaughtered for nothing (*i.e.*, for purposes of food only), such slaughter leads to sin.—T.

3 One is said to become impure when a birth or a death occurs among one's cognates of near degree. The period of impurity varies from one day to ten days in case of Brahmanas. Other periods have been prescribed for the other orders. During the period of impurity one cannot perform one's daily acts of worship, *&c.*—T.

pretences like that of sojourns to sacred places or who solicits the giver for wealth pretending that he would spend it in religious acts, incurs, O monarch, the sin of uttering a falsehood.[1] That person, belonging to any of the three higher orders, O Yudhishthira, who at Sraddhas and on other occasions distributes food with the aid of Mantras, unto such Brahmanas as do not study the Vedas and as are not observant of vows, or as have not purified their conduct, certainly incurs sin.'

"Yudhishthira said,—'I desire, O grandsire, to know by giving unto whom the things dedicated to the deities and the Pitris, one may earn the amplest rewards.'

"Bhishma said,—'Do thou, O Yudhishthira, feed those Brahmanas whose spouses reverently wait for the remnants of the dishes of their husbands like tillers of the soil waiting in reverence for timely showers of rain. One earn great merit by making gifts unto those Brahmanas that are always observant of pure conduct, O king, that are emaciaed through abstention from all luxuries and even full meals, that are devoted to the observances of such vows as lead to the emaciation of the body, and that approach givers with the desire of obtaining gifts. By making gifts unto such Brahmanas as regard conduct in ths light of food, as regard conduct in the light of spouses and children, as regard conduct in the light of strength, as regard conduct in the light of their refuge for crossing this world and attaining to felicity in the next, and as solicit wealth only when wealth is absolutely needed, one earns great merit. By making gifts unto those persons, O Yudhishthira, that having lost everything through thieves or oppressors, approach the giver, one acquires great merit.[2] By making gifts unto such Brahmanas as solicit food from the hands of even a poor person of their order who has just got something from others, one earns great merit. By making gifts unto such Brahmanas as have lost their all in times of universal distress and as have been deprived of their spouses on such occasions, and as come to givers with solicitations for alms, one acquires great merit. By making gifts unto such Brahmanas as are observant of vows, and as place themselves voluntarily under painful rules and regulations, as are respectful in their conduct to the declaration laid down in the Vedas, and as come to solicit wealth for spending it upon the rites necessary to complete their vows and other observances, one earns great merit. By making

1 In this country, to this day, there are many persons that go about begging, stating that they desire to go to Benaras or other places of the kind. Sometimes alms are sought on the ground of enabling the seeker to invest his son with the sacred thread or perform his father's Sraddha, &c. The Rishi declares such practices to be sinful.—T.

2 Literally 'that are afraid of thieves and others.' The sense, of course, is 'that have suffered at the hands of thieves and others and are still trembling with fear.'—T.

gifts unto such Brahmanas as live at a great distance from the practices that are observed by the sinful and the wicked, as are destitute of strength for want of adequate support, and as are very poor in earthly possessions, one earns great merit. By making gifts unto such Brahmanas as have been robbed of all their possessions by powerful men but as are perfectly innocent, and as desire to fill their stomachs any how without, that is, any scruples respecting the quality of the food they take, one earns great merit. By making gifts unto such Brahmanas as beg on behalf of others that are observant of penances and devoted to them and as are satisfied with even small gifts, one earns great merit. Thou hast now, O bull of Bharata's race, heard what the declarations are of the scriptures in respect of the acquisition of great merit by the making of gifts. Listen now to me as I expound what those acts are that lead to hell or heaven. They, O Yudhishthira, that speak an untruth on occasions other than those when such untruth is needed for serving the purpose of the preceptor or for giving the assurance of safety to a person in fear of his life, sink into hell.[1] They who ravish other people's spouses, or have sexual congress with them, or assist at such acts of delinquency, sink in hell. They who rob others of their wealth or destroy the wealth and possessions of other people, or proclaim the faults of other people, sink in hell. They who destroy the containers of such pieces of water as are used by cattle for quenching thirst, as injure such buildings as are used for purposes of public meetings, as break down bridges and causeways, and as pull down houses used for purposes of habitation, have to sink to hell. They who beguile and cheat helpless women, or girls, or aged dames, or such women as have been frightened, have to sink to hell. They who destroy the means of other people's living, they who exterminate the habitations of other people, they who rob others of their spouses, they who sow dissensions among friends, and they who destroy the hopes of other people, sink into hell. They who proclaim the faults of others, they who break down bridges or causeways, they who live by following vocations laid down for other people, and they who are ungrateful to friends for services received, have to sink in hell. They who have no faith in the Vedas and show no reverence for them, they who break the vows made by themselves or oblige others to break them, and they who fall away from their status through sin,

1 The two exceptions have been much animadverted upon by unthinking persons. I have shown that according to the code of morality, that is in vogue among people whose Christianity and civilisation are unquestionable, a lie may sometimes be honourable. However casuists may argue, the world is agreed that a lie for saving life and even property under certain circumstances, and for screening the honour of a confiding woman, is not inexcusable. The goldsmith's son who died with a lie on his lips for saving the Prince Chevalier did a meritorious act. The owner also who hides his property from robbers, cannot be regarded as acting dishonourably.—T.

sink in hell. They who betake themselves to improper conduct, they who take exhorbitant rates of interest, and they who make unduly large profits on sales, have to sink in hell. They who are given to gambling, they who indulge in wicked acts without any scruple, and they who are given to slaughter of living creatures, have to sink in hell. They who cause the dismissal by masters of servants that are hoping for rewards or are expectant of definite need or are in the enjoyment of wages or salaries or are waiting for returns in respect of valuable services already rendered, have to sink in hell. They who themselves eat without offering portions thereof unto their spouse or their sacred fires or their servants or their guests, and they who abstain from performing the rites laid down in the scriptures for honouring the Pitris and deities, have to sink in hell. They who sell the Vedas, they who find fault with the Vedas, and they who reduce the Vedas into writing, have all to sink in hell.[1] They who are out of the pale of the four well-known modes of life, they who betake themselves to practices interdicted by the Srutis and the scriptures, and they who live by betaking themselves to acts that are wicked or sinful or that do not belong to their order of birth, have to sink in hell. They who live by selling hair, they who subsist by selling poisons, and they who live by selling milk, have to sink in hell. They who put obstacles in the path of Brahmanas and kine and maidens, O Yudhishthira, have to sink in hell. They who sell weapons, they who forge weapons, they who make shafts, and they who make bows, have to sink in hell. They who obstruct paths and roads with stones and thorns and holes have to sink in hell. They who abandon and cast off preceptors and servants and loyal followers without any offence, O chief of Bharata's race, have to sink in hell. They who set bullocks to work before the animals attain to sufficient age, they who bore the noses of bullocks and other animals for controlling them the better while employed in work, and they who keep animals always tethered, have to sink in hell. Those kings that do not protect their subjects while forcibly taking from them a sixth share of the produce of their fields, and they who, though able and possessed of resources, abstain from making gifts, have to sink in hell. They who abandon and cast off persons that are endued with forgiveness and self-restraint and wisdom, or those with whom they have associated for many years, when these are no longer of service to them, have to sink in hell. Those men who themselves eat without giving portions of the food to children and aged men and servants, have to sink in hell.

---

1 By 'selling the Vedas' is meant the charging of fees for teaching them. As regards the Vedas, the injunction in the scriptures is to commit them to memory and impart them from mouth to mouth. Hence to reduce them into writing was regarded as a transgression.—T.

"'All these men enumerated above have to go to hell. Listen now to me, O bull of Bharata's race, as I tell thee who those men are that ascend to heaven. The man who transgresses against a Brahmana by impeding the performances of all such acts in which the deities are adored, becomes afflicted with the loss of all his children and animals. (They who do not transgress against Brahmanas by obstructing their religious acts ascend to heaven). Those men, O Yudhishthira, who follow the duties as laid down in the scriptures for them and practise the virtues of charity and self-restraint and truthfulness, ascend to heaven. Those men who having acquired knowledge by rendering obedient services to their preceptors and observing austere penances, become reluctant to accept gifts, succeed in ascending to heaven. Those men through whom other people are relieved and rescued from fear and sin and the impediments that lie in the way of what they wish to accomplish and poverty and the afflictions of disease, succeed in ascending to heaven. Those men who are endued with a forgiving disposition, who are possessed of patience, who are prompt in performing all righteous acts, and who are of auspicious conduct, succeed in ascending to heaven. Those men who abstain from honey and meat, who abstain from sexual congress with the spouses of other people, and who abstain from wines and spirituous liquors, succeed in ascending to heaven. Those men that help in the establishment of retreats for ascetics, who become founders of families, O Bharata, who open up new countries for purposes of habitation, and lay out towns and cities succeed in ascending to heaven. Those men who give away cloths and ornaments, as also food and drink, and who help in marrying others, succeed in ascending to heaven.[1] Those men that have abstained from all kinds of injury or harm to all creatures, who are capable of enduring everything, and who have made themselves the refuge of all creatures, succeed in ascending to heaven. Those men who wait with humility upon their fathers and mothers, who have subjugated their senses, and who are affectionate towards their brothers, succeed in ascending to heaven. Those men that subjugate their senses notwithstanding the fact of their being rich in worldly goods and strong in might and in the enjoyment of youth, succeed in ascending to heaven. Those men that are kind towards even those that offend against them, that are mild of disposition, that have an affection for all who are of mild behaviour, and that contribute to the happiness of others by rendering them every kind of service in humility, succeed in ascending to heaven. Those men that

1 In this country to this day, the act of marrying a helpless person with a good girl by paying all the expenses of the marriage, is regarded as an act of righteousness. Of course, the man that is so married is also given sufficient property for enabling him to maintain himself and his wife.—T.

protect thousands of people, that make gifts unto thousands of people, and that rescue thousands of people from distress, succeed in ascending to heaven. Those men who make gifts of gold and of kine, O chief of Bharata's race, as also those of conveyances and animals, succeed in ascending to heaven. Those men who make gifts of such articles as are needed in marriages, as also those of serving men and maids, and cloths and robes, succeed in ascending to heaven.[1] Those men who make public pleasure-houses and gardens and wells, resting houses and buildings for public meetings and tanks for enabling cattle and men to quench their thirst, and fields for cultivation, O Bharata, succeed in ascending to heaven.[2] Those men who make gifts of houses and fields and populated villages unto persons that solicit them, succeed in ascending to heaven. Those men who having themselves manufactured juicy drinks of sweet taste and seeds and paddy or rice, make gifts of them unto others succeed in ascending to heaven. Those men who being born in families high or low beget hundreds of children and live long lives practising compassion and keeping wrath under complete subjection, succeed in ascending to heaven. I have thus expounded to thee, O Bharata, what the rites are in honour of the deities and the Pitris which are performed by people for the sake of the other world, what the ordinances are in respect of making gifts, and what the views are of the Rishis of former times in respect of both the articles of gift and the manner of giving them.' "

SECTION XXIV

"Yudhishthira said,—'O royal son of Bharata's race, it behoveth thee to answer this question of mine truly and in detail. What are those circumstances under which a person may become guilty of Brahmanicide without actually slaying a Brahmana !'

"Bhishma said,—'Formerly, O monarch, I had one day requested Vyasa to explain to me this very subject. I shall now narrate to thee what Vyasa told me on that occasion. Do thou listen to it with undivided attention. Repairing to the presence of Vyasa, I addressed him, saying,—Thou, O great ascetic, art the fourth in descent from Vasishtha. Do thou explain to me this. What are those circumstances under which one becomes guilty of Brahmanicide without actually slaying a Brahmana ?—Thus addressed by me, the son of Parasara's loins, O king, well-skilled in the science of morality, made me the following

1 Articles needed in marriages are, of course, girls and ornaments.—T.

2 'Vapra' has various meanings. I think, it means here a field. Large waste lands often require to be enclosed with ditches and causeways. Unless so reclaimed, they cannot be fit for cultivation.—T.

answer, at once excellent and fraught with certainty,—Thou shouldst know that man as guilty of Brahmanicide who having of his own will invited a Brahmana of righteous conduct to his house for giving him alms subsequently refuses to give anything to him on the pretence of there being nothing in the house. Thou shouldst, O Bharata, know that man as guilty of Brahmanicide who destroys the means of living of a Brahmana learned in the Vedas and all their branches, and who is freed from attachments to worldly creatures and goods. Thou shouldst, O king, know that man to be guilty of Brahmanicide, who causes obstructions in the way of thirsty kine while employed in quenching that thirst. Thou shouldst take that man as guilty of Brahmanicide who, without studying the Srutis that have flowed from preceptor to pupil for ages and ages together, finds fault with the Srutis or with those scriptures that have been composed by the Rishis. Thou shouldst know that man as guilty of Brahmanicide who does not bestow upon a suitable bride-groom his daughter possessed of beauty and other excellent accomplishments. Thou shouldst know that foolish and sinful person to be guilty of Brahmanicide who inflicts such grief upon Brahmanas as afflict the very core of their hearts. Thou shouldst know that man to be guilty of Brahmanicide who robs the blind, the lame, and idiots of their all. Thou shouldst know that man to be guilty of Brahmanicide who sets fire to the retreats of ascetics or to woods or to a village or a town.—' "

SECTION XXV

"Yudhishthira said,—'It has been said that sojourns to sacred waters is fraught with merit ; that ablutions in such waters is meritorious ; and that listening to the excellence of such waters is also meritorious. I desire to hear thee expatiate on this subject, O grandsire. It behoveth thee, O chief of Bharata's race, to mention to me the sacred waters that exist on this earth. I desire, O thou of great puissance, to hear thee discourse on this topic.

"Bhishma said,—'O thou of great splendour, the following enumeration of the sacred waters on the Earth was made by Angiras. Blessed be thou, it behoveth thee to listen to it for thou shalt then earn great merit. Once on a time, Gautama of rigid vows, approaching the great and learned Rishi Angiras endued with tranquility of soul, while he was dwelling in a forest, questioned him, saying,—O illustrious one, I have some doubts regarding the merits attaching to sacred waters and shrines. So I desire to hear thee .discourse on that topic. Do thou, therefore, O ascetic, discourse to me. What merits are earned by a person in respect of the next world, by bathing in the sacred waters on the Earth,

O thou of great wisdom? Do thou expound to me this truly and according to the ordinance.—

"Angiras said,—A person by bathing for seven days in succession in the Chandrabhaga or the Vitasta whose waters are always seen to dance in waves, observing a fast the while, is sure to become cleansed of all his sins and endued with the merit of an ascetic.[1] The very many rivers that flowing through Kasmira, fall into the great river called Sindhu (Indus). By bathing in these rivers one is sure to become endued with good character and to ascend to heaven after departing from this world. By bathing in Pushkara, and Prabhasa, and Naimisha, and the ocean, and Devika, and Indramarga, and Swarnavindu, one is sure to ascend to heaven being seated on a celestial car, and filled with transports of joy at the adorations of Apsara. By plunging in the waters of Hiranyavindu with a concentrated mind and reverencing that sacred stream, and bathing next at Kusesaya and Devandra, one becomes cleansed of all one's sins. Repairing to Indratoya in the vicinity of the mountains of Gandhamadana and next to Karatoya in the country called Kuranga, one should observe a fast for three days and then bathe in those sacred waters with a concentrated heart and pure body. By doing this, one is sure to acquire the merit of a Horse-sacrifice. Bathing in Gangadwara and Kusavarta and Vilwaka in the Nila mountains, as also in Kankhala, one is sure to become cleansed of all one's sins and then ascend to heaven. If one becomes a Brahmacharin and subdues one's wrath, devotes oneself to truth and practises compassion towards all creatures, and then bathes in the Jala parda (Lake of Waters), one is sure to acquire the merit of a Horse-sacrifice. That part where Bhagirati-Ganga flows in a northward direction is known as the union of heaven, earth, and the nether regions. Observing a fast for one month and bathing in that sacred Tirtha which is known to be acceptable to Maheswara, one becomes competent to behold the deities. One who gives oblations of water unto one's Pitris at Saptaganga and Triganga and Indramarga, obtains ambrosia for food, if one has still to undergo rebirth. The man who in a pure state of body and mind attends to his daily Agnihotra and observes a fast for one month and then bathes in Mahasrama, is sure to attain to success in one month. By bathing, after a fast of three days and purifying the mind of all evil passions, in the large lake of Bhrigu Kunda, one becomes cleansed of even the sin of Brahmanicide. By bathing in Kanyakupa and performing one's ablutions in Valaka, one acquires great fame among even the deities and shines in glory. Bathing in Devika and the lake known by the name of Sundarika as also

1 The river Chenab in the Punjab was known in former times by the name of Chandrabhaga. So the river Jhelum was known by the name of Vitasta.—T.

in the Tirtha called Aswini, one acquires, in one's next life, great beauty of form. By fasting for a fortnight and bathing in Mahaganga and Krittikangaraka, one becomes cleansed of all one's sins and ascends to heaven. Bathing in Vaimanika and Kinkinika, one acquires the power of repairing everywhere at will and becomes an object of great respect in the celestial region of the Apsaras.[1] If a person, subduing his wrath and observing the vow of Brahmacharyya for three days, bathes in the river Vipasa at the retreat called Kalika, he is sure to succeed in transcending the obligation of rebirth. Bathing in the asylum that is sacred to the Krittikas and offering oblations of water to the Pitris, and then gratifying Mahadeva, one becomes pure in body and mind and ascends to heaven. If one, observing a fast for three days with a purified body and mind, bathes in Mahapura, one becomes freed from the fear of all mobile and immobile animals as also of all animals having two feet. By bathing in the Devadaru forest and offering oblations of water to the Pitris and dwelling there for seven nights with a pure body and mind, one attains to the region of the deities on departing from this world. Bathing in the waterfalls at Sarastamva and Kusastambha and Dronasarmapada, one is sure to attain to the region of the Apsaras where one is waited upon with dutiful services by those superhuman beings. If one, observing a fast, bathes at Chitrakuta and Janasthana and the waters of Mandakini, one is sure to be united with prosperity that is royal.[2] By repairing to the retreat that is known by the name of Samya and residing there for a fortnight and bathing in the sacred water that exists there, one acquires the power of disappearing at will (and enjoy the happiness that has been ordained for the Gandharvas). Repairing to the tirtha known by the name of Kausiki and residing there with a pure heart and abstaining from all food and drink for three days, one acquires the power of dwelling (in one's next life) in the happy region of the Gandharvas. Bathing in the delightful tirtha that goes by the name of Gandhataraka and residing there for one month, abstaining all the while from food and drink, one acquires the power of disappearing at pleasure and, then in one and twenty days, of ascending to heaven. He that bathes in the lake known by the name of Matanga is sure to attain to success in one night. He that bathes in Analamva or in eternal Andhaka, or in Naimisha, or the tirtha called Swarga, and offers oblations of water to the Pitris, subduing his senses the while, acquires the Merit of a human sacrifice.[3] Bathing in Ganga

1 The sense is that one proceeds to the region of the Apsaras and becomes an object of respect there.—T.

2 *i.e.*, one acquires sovereignty.—T.

3 It is difficult to understand the connection of the second line of

hrada and the tirtha known by the name of Utpalavana and daily offering oblations of water there for a full month to the Pitris, one acquires the merit of a Horse-sacrifice. Bathing in the confluence of the Ganga and the Yamuna as also at the tirtha in the Kalanjara mountains and offering every day oblations of water to the Pitris for a full month, one acquires the merit that attaches to ten Horse-sacrifices. Bathing in the Shashthi lake one acquires merit much greater than what is attached to the gift of food. Ten thousand tirthas and thirty millions of other tirthas come to Prayaga (the confluence of Ganga and Yamuna), O chief of Bharata's race in the month of Magha. He who bathes in Prayaga, with a restrained soul and observing rigid vows the while, in the month of Magha, becomes cleansed of all his sins, O chief of Bharata's race, and attains to heaven. Bathing in the tirtha that is sacred to the Maruts, as also in that which is situate in the retreat of the Pitris, and also in that which is known by the name of Vaivaswata, one becomes cleansed of all one's sins and becomes as pure and sanctified as a tirtha. Repairing to Brahmasaras as also to the Bhagirathi and bathing there and offering oblations to the Pitris every day for a full month, abstaining from food all the while, one is sure to attain to the region of Soma. Bathing in Utpataka and then in Ashtavakra and offering oblations of water to the Pitris every day for twelve days in succession, abstaining the while from food, one acquires the merits of a Horse-sacrifice. Bathing in Asmaprishtha and Niravinda mountains and Kraunchapadi,—all three in Gaya—one becomes cleansed of the sin of Brahmanicide. A bath in the first place cleanses one of a single Brahmanicide ; a bath in the second cleanses one of two offences of that character ; and a bath in the third cleanses one of three such offences. Bathing in Kalavinga, one acquires a large quantity of water (for use in the next world). A man, by bathing in the city of Agni, acquires such merit as entitles him to live during his next birth in the city of Agni's daughter. Bathing in Visala in Karavirapura and offering oblations of water unto one's Pitris, and performing one's ablutions in Devahrada too, one becomes identified with Brahma and shines in glory as such. Bathing in Punaravarta-nanda as also Mahananda, a man of restrained senses and universal compassion repairs to the celestial gardens called Nandana of Indra and is waited upon there by Apsaras of diverse tribes. Bathing with concentrated soul in the tirtha that is called after the name of Urvasi and that is situate in the river Lohitya, on the day of full moon of the month of Kartika, one attains to the merits that attach to the sacrifice called Pundarika. Bathing in Ramahrada and offering obla-

Verse 31. It does not mean 'enters the eternal region called Andhaka that rests on nothing.' Human sacrifices were performed sometimes in former days,—T.

tions of water to the Pitris in the river Vipasa (Beas), and observing a fast for twelve days, one becomes cleansed of all sins. Bathing in the tirtha called Maha-hrada with a purified heart and after observing a fast for one month, one is sure to attain to the end which was the sage Jamadagni's. By exposing oneself to heat in the tirtha called Vindhya, a person devoted to truth and endued with compassion for all creatures should then betake himself to austere penances, actuated by humility. By so doing, he is sure to attain to ascetic success in course of a single month. Bathing in the Narmada as also in the tirtha known by the name of Surparaka, observing a fast for a full fortnight, one is sure to become in one's next birth a prince of the royal line. If one proceeds with restrained senses and a concentrated soul to the tirtha known under the name of Jamvumarga, one is sure to attain to success in course of a single day and night. By repairing to Chandalikasrama and bathing in the tirtha called Kokamukha, having subsisted for sometime on pot-herbs alone and worn rags for vestments, one is sure to obtain ten maidens of great beauty for one's spouses. One who lives by the side of the tirtha known by the name of Kanya-hrada has never to go to the regions of Yama. Such a person is sure to ascend to the regions of felicity that belong to the celestials. One who bathes with restrained senses on the day of the new moon in the tirtha known by the name of Prabhasa, is sure, O thou of mighty arms, of at once attaining to success and immortality. Bathing in the tirtha known by the name of Ujjanaka which occurs in the retreat of Arshtisena's son, and next in the tirtha that is situate in the retreat of Pinga, one is sure to be cleansed of all one's sins. Observing a fast for three days and bathing in the tirtha known as Kulya and reciting the sacred mantras that go by the name of Aghamarshana, one attains the merit of a house-sacrifice. Observing a fast for one night and bathing in Pindaraka, one becomes purified on the dawn of the next day and attains to the merit of an Agnishtoma sacrifice. One who repairs to Brahmasara which is adorned by the woods called Dharmaranya, becomes cleansed of all one's sins and attains to the merit of the Pundarika sacrifice. Bathing in the waters of the Mainaka mountain and saying one's morning and evening prayers there and living at the spot for a month, restraining desire, one attains to the merit of all the sacrifices. Setting out for Kalolaka and Nandikunda and Uttara-manasa, and reaching a spot that is hundred yojanas remote from any of them, one becomes cleansed of the sin of foeticide. One who succeeds in obtaining a sight of image of Nandiswara, becomes cleansed of all sins. Bathing in the tirtha called Swargamarga one is sure to proceed to the regions of Brahman. The celebrated Himavat is sacred. That prince of mountains is the father-in-law of Sankara. He is a mine of all jewels and gems and is the resort of the Siddhas and

Charanas. That regenerate person who is fully conversant with the Vedas and who, regarding this life to be exceedingly unstable, casts off his body on those mountains, abstaining from all food and drink in accordance with the rites laid down in the scriptures, after having adored the deities and bent his head in worship of the ascetics, is sure to attain to success and proceed to the eternal regions of Brahman. There is nothing unattainable to him who resides in a tirtha, restraining lust and subjugating warth, in consequence of such residence. For the purpose of repairing to *all* the tirthas in the world, one should mentally think of those amongst them that are almost inaccessible or sojourns to which are attended with insurmountable difficulties. Sojourns to tirthas is productive of the merits of sacrifices. They are competent to cleanse everybody of sin. Fraught with great excellence, they are capable of leading to heaven. The subject is truly a great mystery. The very deities should bathe in tirthas. To them also they are sin-cleansing. This discourse on tirthas should be imparted to Brahmanas, and to such honest or righteous persons as are bent upon achieving what is for their own good. It should also be recited in the hearing of one's well-wishers and friends and of one's obedient and devoted disciples. Angiras possessed of great ascetic merit, had imparted this discourse to Gautama. Angiras himself had obtained it from Kasyapa of great intelligence. The great Rishis regard this discourse as worthy of constant repetition. It is the foremost of all cleansing things. If one recites it regularly every day, one is sure to become cleansed of every sin and to proceed to heaven after the termination of this life. One who listens to this discourse recited in his hearing,—this discourse, *viz.*, of Angiras, that is regarded as a mystery,—is sure to attain in one's next life to be born in a good family and, what is more, one would become endued with the memory of one's previous existence.'

SECTION XXVI

"Vaisampayana said,—'Equal unto Vrihaspati in intelligence and Brahma himself in forgiveness, resembling Sakra in prowess and Surya in energy, Bhishma the son of Ganga, of infinite might, had been overthrown in battle by Arjuna. Accompanied by his brothers and many other people, king Yudhisthira asked him these questions. The old hero was lying on a bed that is coveted by heroes, in expectation of that auspicious time when he could take leave of the physical frame. Many great Rishis had come there for seeing that foremost one of Bharata's race. Amongst them were Atri and Vasishtha and Bhrigu and Pulastya and Pulaha and Kratu. There were also Angiras and Gotama and Agastya and Sumati of well-restrained soul, and Viswamitra and Sthulasiras and Samvarta and Pramati and Dama. There were also

Vrihaspati and Usanas, and Vyasa and Chyavana and Kasyapa and Dhruva, and Durvasas and Jamadagni and Markandeya and Galava, and Bharadwaja and Raibhya and Yavakrita and Trita. There were Sthulaksha and Savalaksha and Kanwa and Medhatithi and Krisa and Narada and Parvata and Sudhanwa and Ekata and Dwita. There were also Nitambhu and Bhuvana and Dhaumya and Satananda and Akritavrana and Rama, the son of Jamadagni and Kacha. All these high-souled and great Rishis came there for seeing Bhishma lying on his bed of arrows. Yudhishthira with his brothers duly worshipped those high-souled Rishis who had come there, one after another in proper order. Receiving that worship, those foremost of Rishis sat themselves down and began to converse with one another. Their conversation related to Bhishma, and was highly sweet and agreeable to all the senses. Hearing that talk of theirs having reference to himself, Bhishma became filled with delight and regarded himself to be already in heaven. Those Rishis then, having obtained the leave of Bhishma and of the Pandava princes, made themselves invisible, vanishing in the very sight of all the beholders. The Pandavas repeatedly bowed and offered their adorations to those highly blessed Rishis, even after they had made themselves invisible. They then with cheerful souls waited upon the son of Ganga, even as Brahmanas versed in Mantras wait with reverence upon the rising Sun. The Pandavas beheld that the points of the compass blazed forth with splendour in consequence of the energy of their penances, and became filled with wonder at the sight. Thinking of the high blessedness and puissance of those Rishis, the Pandava princes began to converse on the subject with their grandsire Bhishma."

Vaisampayana continued,—"The conversation being over, the righteous Yudhishthira, the son of Pandu, touched Bhishma's feet with his head and then resumed his questions relating to morality and righteousness.

"Yudhishthira said,—Which countries, which provinces, which retreats, which mountains, and which rivers, O grandsire, are the foremost in point of sanctity ?"

"Bhishma said,—'In this connection is cited the old narrative of a conversation between a Brahmana in the observance of the Sila and the Uncha vows, O Yudhishthira, and a Rishi crowned with ascetic success. Once on a time, a foremost person, having roamed over this entire earth adorned with mountains, arrived at last in the house of a foremost person leading the domestic mode of life in accordance with the Sila vow. The latter welcomed his guest with due rites. Received with such hospitality, the happy Rishi passed the night happily in the house of his host. The next morning the Brahmana in the observance of the Sila vow, having finished all his morning acts and rites and purified himself duly, very cheerfully approached his guest crowned with ascetic success. Meeting with each other and seated at their ease, the two began to converse on agreeable subjects connected with the Vedas and the Upanishads. Towards the conclusion of the discourse, the Brahmana in the observance of the Sila vow respectfully addressed the Rishi crowned with success. Endued with intelligence, he put this very question which thou, O Yudhishthira, hast put to me.

" 'The poor Brahmana said,—What countries, what provinces, what retreats, what mountains, and what rivers should be regarded as the foremost in point of sanctity? Do thou discourse to me on this.—

" 'The Rishi crowned with success said,—Those countries, those provinces, those retreats, and those mountains, should be regarded as the foremost in point of sanctity through which or by the side of which that foremost of all rivers, *viz.*, Bhagirathi flows. That end which a creature is capable of attaining by penances, by Brahmacharyya, by sacrifices, or by practising renunciation, one is sure to attain by only living by the side of the Bhagirathi and bathing in its sacred waters. Those creatures whose bodies have been sprinkled with the sacred waters of Bhagirathi or whose bones have been laid in the channel of that sacred stream, have not to fall away from heaven at any time.[1] Those men, O learned Brahmana, who use the waters of Bhagirathi in all their acts, surely ascend to heaven after departing from this world. Even those men who, having committed diverse kinds of sinful deeds in the first part of their lives, betake themselves in after years to a residing by the side of Ganga, succeed in attaining to a very superior end. Hundreds of sacrifices cannot produce that merit which men of restrained souls are capable of acquiring by bathing in the sacred waters of Ganga. A person is treated with respect and worshipped in heaven for as long a period as his bones lie in the channel of Ganga. Even as the Sun, when he rises at the dawn of day, blazes forth in splendour, having dispelled the gloom of night, after the same manner the person that has bathed in the waters of Ganga is seen to shine in splendour, cleansed of all his sins. Those countries and those points of the compass that are destitute of the sacred waters of Ganga are like nights without the moon or like trees without flowers. Verily, a world without Ganga is like the different orders and modes of life when they are destitute of righteousness or like sacrifices without Soma. Without doubt, countries and points of the compass that are without Ganga are like the firmament without the Sun, or the Earth without mountains, or the welkin without air. The entire body of creatures in the three worlds, if served with the auspicious waters of Ganga, derive a pleasure, the like of which they are incapable of deriving from any other source. He who drinks Ganga

1 'Nyastani' has 'Gangayam' understood after it.—T.

water that has been heated by the Sun's rays derives merit much greater than that which attaches to the vow of subsisting upon the wheat or grains of other corn picked up from cowdung. It cannot be said whether the two are equal or not, viz., he who performs a thousand Chandrayana rites for purifying his body and he who drinks the water of Ganga. It cannot be said whether the two are equal or not, viz., one who stands for a thousand years on one foot and one who lives for only a month by the side of Ganga. One who lives permanently by the side of Ganga is superior in merit to one who stays for ten thousand Yugas with head hanging downwards. As cotton, when it comes into contact with fire, is burnt off without a remnant, even so the sins of the person that has bathed in Ganga become consumed without a remnant. There is no end superior to Ganga for those creatures who with hearts afflicted by sorrow, seek to attain to ends that may dispel that sorrow of theirs. As snakes become deprived of their poison at the very sight of Garuda, even so one becomes cleansed of all one's sins at the very sight of the sacred stream of Ganga. They that are without good name and that are addicted to deeds of sinfulness, have Ganga for their fame, their protection, their means of rescue, their refuge or cover. Many wretches among men who become afflicted with diverse sins of a heinous nature, when they are about to sink into hell, are rescued by Ganga in the next world (if, notwithstanding their sins, they seek the aid of Ganga in their after-years). They, O foremost of intelligent men, who plunge every day in the sacred waters of Ganga, become the equals of great Munis and the very deities with Vasava at their head. Those wretches among men that are destitute of humility or modesty of behaviour and that are exceedingly sinful, become righteous and good, O Brahmana, by betaking themselves to the side of Ganga. As Amrita is to the deities, as Swadha is to the Pritis, as Sudha is to the Nagas, even so is Ganga water to human beings. As children afflicted with hunger solicit their mothers for food, after the same manner do people desirous of their highest good pay court to Ganga. As the region of the self-born Brahma is said to be the foremost of all places, even so is Ganga said to be foremost of all rivers for those that desire to bathe. As the Earth and the cow are said to be the chief sustenance of the deities and other celestials, even so is Ganga the chief sustenance of all living creatures.[1] As the deities support themselves upon the Amrita that occurs in the Sun and the Moon and that is offered in diverse sacrifices, even so do human beings support themselves upon Ganga water. One besmeared with the

1 The deities are supported by the offerings made in sacrifices. These offerings consist of the productions of the Earth and the butter produced by the cow. The deities, therefore, are said to be chiefly supported by the Earth and the cow. The Asuras, by afflicting the Earth and killing kine, used to weaken the deities.—T.

sand taken from the shores of Ganga regards oneself as a denizen of heaven, adorned with celestial unguents. He who bears on his head the mud taken from the banks of Ganga presents an effulgent aspect equal to that of Sun himself bent on dispelling the surrounding darkness. When that wind which is moistened with the particles of Ganga-water touches one's person, it cleanses him immediately of every sin. A person afflicted by calamities and about to sink under their weight, finds all his calamities dispelled by the joy which springs up in his heart at sight of that sacred stream. By the melody of the swans and Kokas and other acquatic fowls that play on her breast, Ganga challenges the very Gandharvas and by her high banks the very mountains on the Earth. Beholding her surface teeming with swans and diverse other aquatic fowls, and having banks adorned with pasture lands with kine grazing on them, Heaven herself loses her pride. The high happiness which one enjoys by a residence on the banks of Ganga, can never be his who is residing even in heaven. I have no doubt in this that the person who is afflicted with sins perpetrated in speech and thought and overt act, becomes cleansed at the very sight of Ganga. By beholding that sacred stream, touching it, and bathing in its waters, one rescues one's ancestors to the seventh generation, one's descendants to the seventh generation, as also other ancestors and descendants. By hearing of Ganga, by wishing to repair to that river, by drinking its waters, by touching its waters, and by bathing in them a person rescues both his paternal and maternal races. By seeing, touching, and drinking the waters of Ganga, or even by applauding Ganga, hundreds and thousands of sinful men became cleansed of all their sins. They who wish to make their birth, life and learning fruitful, should repair to Ganga and gratify the Pitris and the deities by offering them oblations of water. The merit that one earns by bathing in Ganga is such that the like of it is incapable of being earned through the acquisition of sons or wealth or the performance of meritorious acts. Those who, although possessed of the physical ability, do not seek to have a sight of the auspicious Ganga of sacred current, are, without doubt, to be likened to persons afflicted with congenital blindness or those that are dead or those that are destitute of the power of locomotion through palsy or lameness. What man is there that would not reverence this sacred stream that is adored by great Rishis conversant with the Present, the Past, and the Future, as also by the very deities with Indra at their head. What man is there that would not seek the protection of Ganga whose protection is sought for by forest recluses and house-holders, and by Yatis and Brahmacharins alike? The man of righteous conduct who, with rapt soul, thinks of Ganga at the time when his life-breaths are about to leave his body, succeeds in attaining to the highest end. That man who dwells by the side of Ganga up to the time of his death, adoring her with reverence, becomes freed from the fear of every kind of calamity, of sin, and of kings. When that highly sacred stream fell from the firmament, Maheswara held it on his head. It is that very stream which is adored in heaven.[1] The three regions, *viz.*, (Earth, Heaven, and the nether place called Patala) are adorned by the three courses of this sacred stream. The man who uses the waters of that stream becomes certainly crowned with success. As the solar ray is to the deities in heaven, as Chandramas is to the Pitris, as the king is to human beings, even such is Ganga unto all streams.[2] One who becomes bereaved of mother or father or sons or spouses or wealth does not feel that grief which becomes one's, when one becomes bereaved of Ganga. One does not obtain that joy through acts that lead to the region of Brahma, or through such sacrifices and rites that lead to heaven, or through children or wealth, which one obtains from a sight of Ganga.[3] The pleasures that men derive from a sight of Ganga is equal to what they derive from a sight of the full moon. That man becomes dear to Ganga who adores her with deep devotion, with mind wholly fixed upon her, with a reverence that refuses to take any other object within its sphere, with a feeling that there is nothing else to the universe worthy of similar adoration, and with a steadiness that knows no failing away. Creatures that live on Earth, in the welkin, or in Heaven,—indeed, even beings that are very superior,—should always bathe in Ganga. Verily, this is the foremost of all duties with those that are righteous. The fame of Ganga for sanctity has spread over the entire universe, since she bore all the sons of Sagara, who had been reduced to ashes, from here to Heaven.[4] Men who are washed by the bright, beautiful, high, and rapidly moving waves, raised by the wind, of Ganga, became cleansed of all their sins and resemble in splendour the Sun with his thousand rays. Those men of tranquil souls that have cast off their bodies in the waters of Ganga whose sanctity is as great as that of the butter and other liquids poured in sacrifices and which are capable of conferring merits equal to those of the greatest of sacrifices, have certainly attained to a station equal

---

1 The river Ganga has three courses. On Earth it is called Bhagirathi or Ganga ; in heaven it is called Mandakini ; and in the nether regions it is known by the name of Bhogabati.—T.

2 'Devesh' is lit. the lord of the deities ; but here it means the King or Emperor.—T.

3 'Aranyaih' is explained by the Commentator as implying courses of conduct leading to Brahmaloka.—T.

4 The story referred to is this : King Sagara of the Solar race had sixty thousand sons, all of whom were reduced to ashes by the curse of Kapila. Afterwards Bhagiratha, a prince of the same race, brought down Ganga from heaven for their redemption.—T.

to that of the very deities. Verily, Ganga, possessed of fame and vast extent and identical with the entire universe and reverenced by the deities with Indra at their head, the Munis and human beings, is competent to bestow the fruition of all their wishes upon them that are blind, them that are idiots, and them that are destitute of all things.[1] They that sought the refuge of Ganga, that protectress of all the universe, that flows in three streams, that is filled with water at once highly sacred and sweet as honey and productive of every kind of good, have succeeded in attaining to the beatitude of Heaven.[2] That mortal who dwells by the side of Ganga and beholds her every day, becomes cleansed by her sight and touch. Unto him the deities give every kind of happiness here and a high end hereafter. Ganga is regarded as competent to rescue every creature from sin and lead him to the felicity of Heaven. She is held to be identical with Prisni, the mother of Vishnu. She is identical with the Word or Speech. She is very remote, being incapable of easy attainment. She is the embodiment of auspiciousness and prosperity. She is capable of bestowing the six well-known attributes beginning with lordship or puissance. She is always inclined to extend her grace. She is the displayer of all things in the universe, and she is the high refuge of all creatures. Those who have sought her protection in this life have surely attained heaven. The fame of Ganga has spread all over the welkin, and Heaven, and Earth, and all the points, cardinal and subsidiary, of the compass. Mortal creatures, by using the waters of that foremost of streams, always become crowned with high success. That person who himself beholding Ganga, points her out to others, finds that Ganga rescues him from rebirth and confers Emancipation on him. Ganga held Guha, the generalissimo of the celestial forces, in her womb. She bears the most precious of all metals, *viz.*, gold, also in that womb of hers. They who bathe in her waters every day in the morning, succeed in obtaining the aggregate of three, viz., Righteousness, Wealth and Pleasure. Those waters are, again, equal in point of sanctity to the butter that is poured with Mantras on the sacrificial fire. Capable of cleansing one from every sin, she has descended from the celestial region, and her current is held in high esteem by every one. Ganga is the daughter of Himavat, the spouse of Hara, and the ornament of both Heaven and Earth. She is the bestower of everything auspicious, and is competent to confer the six well-known attributes beginning with lordship or puissance. Verily O king, Ganga is the one object of great

---

1 'Identical with the universe' because capable of conferring the fruition of every wish. 'Vrihati'—literally, large or vast, is explained by the Commentator as implying 'foremost' or superior.—T.

2 'Madhumatim' is explained as 'conferring the fruits of all good actions."

sanctity in the three worlds and confers merit upon all. Truly, O monarch, Ganga is Righteousness in liquefied form. She is energy also running in a liquid form over the Earth. She is endued with the splendour or puissance that belongs to the butter that is poured with Mantras on the sacrifical fire. She is always adorned with large waves as also with Brahmanas who may at all times be seen performing their ablutions in her waters. Falling from Heaven, she was held by Siva on his head. The very mother of the heavens, she has sprung from the highest mountain for running over the plains and conferring the most precious benefits on all creatures of the Earth. She is the highest cause of all things; she is perfectly stainless. She is as subtile as Brahma. She affords the best bed for the dying. She leads creatures very quickly to heaven. She bears away a large volume of water. She bestows great fame on all. She is the protectress of the universe.[1] She is identical with every form. She is very much coveted by persons crowned with success. Verily, Ganga is the path to Heaven of those that have bathed in her current.[2] The Brahmanas hold Ganga as equalling the Earth in forgiveness, and in the portection and upholding of those that live by her; further, as equalling Fire and Surya in energy and splendour; and, lastly, as always equalling Guha himself in the matter of showing favours unto the regenerate class.[3] Those men who, in this life, even mentally seek with their whole souls that sacred stream which is praised by the Rishis, which has issued out of the feet of Vishnu, which is very ancient, and which is exceedingly sacred, succeed in repairing to the regions of Brahman. Fully convinced that children and other possessions, as also regions possessed of every kind of felicity, are transitory or liable to destruction, men of subdued souls, who are desirous of attaining to that everlasting station which is identical with Brahma, always pay their adorations to Ganga with that reverence and love which are due from a son to mother. The men of cleansed soul who is desirous of achieving success should seek the protection of Ganga who is like a cow that yields Amrita instead of ordinary milk, who is prosperity's self, who is possessed of omniscience, who exists for the entire universe of creatures, who is the source of all kinds of food, who is the mother of all mountains, who is the refuge of all righteous persons, who is immeasurable in puissance and energy, and who charms the heart of Brahma himself. Having, with austere penances, gratified all the deities with the Supreme Lord (Vishnu), Bhagiratha brought Ganga

1 'Viswam avanti iti.' Here the absence of 'num' is 'arsha.'—T.

2 'Bhuvanasya' is 'swargasya.'—T.

3 The construction of this Verse is not difficult though the order of the words is a little involved. Both the Vernacular translators have misunderstood it completely.—T.

down on the Earth. Repairing unto her, men always succeed in freeing themselves from every kind of fear both here and hereafter. Observing with the aid of intelligence, I have mentioned to thee only a small part of the merits of Ganga. My power, however, is inadequate to speak of all the merits of the sacred river, or, indeed, to measure her puissance and sanctity. One may, by putting forth one's best powers, count the stones that occur in the mountains of Meru or measure the waters that occur in the ocean, but one cannot count all the merits which belong to the waters of Ganga. Hence, having listened to these particular merits of Ganga which I have uttered with great devotion, one should, in thought, word and deed, reverence them with faith and devotion. In consequence of thy having listened to those merits which I have recited, thou art sure to fill all the three regions with fame and attain to a measure of success that is very large and that is difficult of being attained to by any other person. Verily, thou shalt, soon after that, sport in joy many a region of great felicity created by Ganga herself for those that reverence her. Ganga always extends her grace unto those that are devoted to her with humbleness of heart. She unites those that are so devoted to her with every kind of happiness. I pray that the highly-blessed Ganga may always inspire thy heart and mine with such attributes as are fraught with righteousness'—

"Bhishma continued,—'The learned ascetic endued with high intelligence and great illumination, and crowned with success, having in this manner discoursed unto that poor Brahmana in the observance of the Sila vow, on the subjects of the infinite merits of Ganga, then ascended the firmament. The Brahmana in the observance of Sila vow, awakened by the words of that ascetic crowned with success, duly worshipped Ganga and attained to high success. Do thou also, O son of Kunti, seek Ganga with great devotion, for thou shalt then, as the reward thereof, attain to high and excellent success.

Vaisampayana continued—"Hearing this discourse from Bhishma that was fraught with the praise of Ganga, Yudhishthira with his brothers became filled with great delight. That person who recites or hears recited this sacred discourse fraught with the praise of Ganga, becomes cleansed of every sin."

SECTION XXVII

"Yudhishthira said,—'Thou O grandsire, art endued with wisdom and knowledge of the scriptures, with conduct and behaviour, with diverse kinds of excellent attributes, and also with years. Thou art distinguished above others by intelligence and wisdom and penances. I shall, therefore, O thou that art the foremost of all righteous men, desire to address enquiries to thee respecting Righteousness. There is not another man, O king, in all the worlds, who is worthier of being questioned on such subjects. O best of kings, how may one, if he happens to be a Kshatriya or a Vaisya or a Sudra, succeed in acquiring the status of a Brahmana? It behoveth thee to tell me the means. Is it by penances the most austere, or by religious acts, or by knowledge of the scriptures, that a person belonging to any of the three inferior orders succeeds in acquiring the status of a Brahmana? Do tell me this, O grandsire!"

"Bhishma said,—The status of a Brahmana, O Yudhishthira, is incapable of acquisition by a person belonging to any of the three other orders. That status is the highest with respect to all creatures. Travelling through innumerable orders of existence, by undergoing repeated births, one at last, in some birth, becomes born as a Brahmana. In this connection is cited an old history, O Yudhishthira, of a conversation between Matanga and a she-ass. Once on a time a Brahmana obtained a son who, though procreated by a person belonging to a different order, had, however, the rites of infancy and youth performed in pursuance of the ordinances laid down for Brahmanas. The child was called by the name of Matanga and was possessed of every accomplishment. His father, desiring to perform a sacrifice, ordered him, O scorcher of foes, to collect the articles required for the act. Having received the command of his father, he set out for the purpose, riding on a car of great speed, drawn by an ass. It so happened that the ass yoked unto that car was of tender years. Instead therefore, of obeying the reins, the animal bore away the car to the vicinity of its dam, viz., the she-ass that had brought it forth. Matanga, dissatisfied with this, began to strike repeatedly the animal with his goad on its nose. Beholding those marks of violence on her child's nose, the she-ass, full of affection for him, said,—Do not grieve, O child, for this treatment. A chandala it is that is driving thee. There is no severity in a Brahmana. The Brahmana is said to be the friend of all creatures. He is the teacher also of all creatures and their ruler. Can he chastise any creature so cruelly? This fellow, however, is of sinful deeds. He hath no compassion to show unto even a creature of such tender years as thou. He is simply proving the order of his birth by conducting himself in this way. The nature which he hath derived from his sire forbids the rise of those sentiments of pity and kindness that are natural to the Brahmana. Hearing these harsh words of the she-ass, Matanga quickly, came down from the car and addressing the she-ass, said,—Tell me, O blessed dame, by what fault is my mother stained? How dost thou know that I am a Chandala? Do thou answer me without delay. How, indeed, dost thou know that I am a Chandala? How has my status as a Brahmana been lost? O thou of great wisdom, tell me all this in detail, from beginning to end.

" 'The she-ass said,—Begotten thou wert, upon a Brahmana woman excited with desire, by a Sudra following the profession of a barber. Thou art, therefore, a Chandala by birth. The status of Brahmana thou hast not at all.—

"Brahmana continued,—'Thus addressed by the she-ass, Matanga retraced his way homewards. Seeing him return, his father said,—I had employed thee in the difficult task of gathering the requisites of my intended sacrifice. Why hast thou come back without having accomplished thy charge? Is it the case that all is not right with thee?—

" 'Matanga said,—How can he who belongs to no definite order of birth, or to an order that is very low be regarded as all right and happy? How, O father, can that person be happy whose mother is stained? O father, this she-ass, who seems to be more than a human being, tells me that I have been begotten upon a Brahmani woman by a Sudra. I shall, for this reason, undergo the severest penances.—Having said these words to his father, and firmly resolved upon what he had said he proceeded to the great forest and began to undergo the austerest of penances. Setting himself to the performance of those penances for the purpose of happily acquiring the status of a Brahmana, Matanga began to scorch the very deities by the severity of his asceticism. Unto him thus engaged in penances, the chief of the celestials, viz., Indra, appeared and said, —Why, O Matanga, dost thou pass thy time in such grief, abstaining from all kinds of human enjoyments? I shall give thee boons. Do thou name the boons thou desirest. Do not delay, but tell me what is in thy breast. Even if that be unattainable, I shall yet bestow it on thee.

" 'Matanga said,—'Desirous of attaining to the status of Brahmana I have begun to practise these penances. After having obtained it, I shall go home. Even this is the boon solicited by me.

"Bhishma continued,—'Hearing these words of his, Purandara said unto him.—The status of a Brahmana, O Matanga, which thou desirest to acquire is really unattainable by thee. It is true, thou desirest to acquire it, but then it is incapable of acquisition by persons begotten on uncleansed souls. O thou of foolish understanding, thou art sure to meet with destruction if thou persistest in this pursuit. Desist, therefore, from this vain endeavour without any delay. This object of thy desire, *viz.*, the status of a Brahmana, which is the foremost of everything, is incapable of being won by penances. Therefore, by coveting that foremost status, thou wilt incur sure destruction. One born as a Chandala can never attain to that status which is regarded as the most sacred among the deities and Asuras and human beings!' "—

SECTION XXVIII.

"Bhishma said,—'Thus addressed by Indra, Matanga of restrained vows and well regulated soul, (without hearkening to the counsels of the chief of the celestials), stood for a hundred years on one foot, O thou of unfading glory. Sakra of great fame once more appeared before him and addressing him, said,—The status of a Brahmana, O child, is unattainable. Although thou covetest it, it is impossible for thee to obtain it. O Matanga, by coveting that very high status thou art sure to be destroyed. Do not, O son, betray such rashness. This cannot be a righteous path for thee to follow. O thou of foolish understanding, it is impossible for thee to obtain it in this world. Verily, by coveting that which is unattainable, thou art sure to meet with destruction in no time. I am repeatedly forbidding thee. By striving, however, to attain that high status by the aid of thy penances, notwithstading my repeated admonition, thou art sure to meet with destruction. From the order of brute life one attains to the status of humanity. If born as human being, he is sure to take birth as a Pukkasa or a Chandala. Verily, one having taken birth in that sinful order of existence, *viz.*, Pukkasa, one, O Matanga, has to wander in it for a very long time. Passing a period of one thousand years in that order, one attains next to the status of a Sudra. In the Sudra order, again, one has to wander for a long time. After thirty thousand years one acquire the status of a Vaisya. There, in that order, one has to pass a very long period. After a time that is sixty times longer than what has been stated as the period of Sudra existence, one becomes a person of the fighting order. In the Kshatriya order one has to pass a very long time. After a time that is measured by multiplying the period last referred to by sixty, one becomes born as a fallen Brahmana. In this order one has to wander for a long period. After a time measured by multiplying the period last named by two hundred, one becomes born in the race of such a Brahmana as lives by the profession of arms. There, in that order, one has to wander for a long period. After a time measured by multiplying the period last named by three hundred, one takes birth in the race of a Brahmana that is given to the recitation of the Gayatri and other sacred Mantras. There, in that order, one has to wander for a long period. After a time measured by multiplying the period last named by four hundred, one takes birth in the race of such a Brahmana as is conversant with the entire Vedas and the scriptures. There, in that order, one has to wander for a very long period. While wandering in that status of existence, joy and grief, desire and averson, vanity and evil speech, seek to enter into him and make a wretch of him. If he succeeds in subjugating those foes, he then attains a high end. If, on the other hand, those enemies succeed in subjugating him, he falls down from that high status like a person falling down on the ground from the high top of a palmyra tree. Knowing this for certain, O Matanga, I say unto thee, do thou name some other boon, for the status of a Brahmana is incapable of being attained by thee (that hast been born as a Chandala) !—' "

SECTION XXIX.

"Bhishma said,—Thus advised by Indra, Matanga, observant of vows, refused to hear what he was bid. On the other hand, with regulated vows and cleansed soul, he practised austere penances by standing on one foot for a thousand years, and was deeply engaged in Yoga-meditation. After a thousand years had passed away, Sakra once more came to see him. Indeed, the slayer of Vala and Vritra said unto him the same words.

" 'Matanga said,—I have passed these thousand years, standing on one foot, in deep meditation, observing of the vow of Brahmacharyya. Why is it that I have not yet succeeded in acquiring the status of a Brahmana ?—

" 'Sakra said,—One born on a Chandala cannot, by any means acquire the status of a Brahamana. Do thou, therefore name some boon so that all this labour of thine may not prove fruitless.—Thus addressed by the chief of the celestials, Matanga became filled with grief. He repaired to Prayaga, and passed there a hundred years, standing all the while on his toes. In consequence of the observance of such Yoga which was extremely difficult to bear, he became very much emaciated and his arteries and veins became swollen and visible. He was reduced to only skin and bones. Indeed, it has been heard by us that the righteous-souled Matanga, while practising those austerities at Gaya, dropped down on the ground from sheer exhaustion. The lord and giver of boons, engaged in the good of all creatures, viz., Vasava beholding him falling down, quickly came to that spot and held him fast.

" 'Sakra said,—It seems, O Matanga, that the status of a Brahmana which thou seekest is ill-suited to thee. That status is incapable of being attained by thee. Verily, in thy case, it is surrounded by many dangers. A person by worshipping a Brahmana obtains happiness ; while, by abstaining from such worship, he obtains grief and misery. The Brahmana is, with respect to all creatures, the giver of what they prize or covet and the protector of what they already have. It is through the Brahmanas that the Pitris and the deities become gratified. The Brahmana, O Matanga, is said to be foremost of all created Beings. The Brahmana grants all objects that are desired and in the way they are desired.[1] Wandering through innumerable orders of Being and undergoing repeated rebirths, one succeeds in some subsequent birth in acquiring the status of a Brahmana. That status is really incapable of being obtained by persons of uncleansed souls. Do thou, therefore, give up the idea. Do thou name some other boon. The particular boon which thou seekest is incapable of being granted to thee.—

" 'Matanga said.—Afflicted as I am with grief, why, O Sakra, dost thou afflict me furher (with such speeches as these)? Thou art striking one that is already dead, by this behaviour. I do not pity thee for having acquired the status of a Brahmana thou now failest to retain it (for thou hast no compassion to show for one like me). O thou of a hundred sacrifices, the status of a Brahmana as thou sayest be really unattainable by any of the three other orders, yet, men that have succeeded in acquiring (through natural means) that high status do not adhere to it (for what sins do not even Brahmanas commit). Those who having acquired the status of a Brahmana that, like affluence, is so difficult to acquire, do not seek to keep it up (by practising the necessary duties), must be regarded to be the lowest of wretches in this world. Indeed, they are the most sinful of all creatures. Without doubt, the status of a Brahmana is exceedingly difficult to attain, and once being attained, it is difficult to maintain it. It is capable of dispelling every kind of grief. Alas, having attained to it, men do not always seek to keep it up (by practising righteousness and the other duties that attach to it). When even such persons are regarded as Brahmanas why is it that I, who am contented with my own self, who am above all couples of opposites, who am dissociated from all wordly objects, who am observant of the duty of compassion towards all creatures and of self-restraint of conduct, should not be regarded as deserving of that status.[2] How unfortunate I am, O Purandara, that through the fault of my mother I have been reduced to this condition, although I am not unrighteous in my behaviour? Without doubt, Destiny is incapable of being warded off or conquered by individual exertion, since, O lord, I am unable to acquire, notwithstanding these persistent efforts of mine, the object, upon the acquisition of which I have set my heart. When such is the case, O righteous one, it behoves thee to grant me

---

1 'Kurute' may mean also 'makes.' The sense is that the Brahmana grants to others whatever objects are desired by them. In his own case also, he creates those objects that he himself desires. His puissance is great and it is through his kindness that others get what they wish or seeks.—T.

2 'Ekaramah' is one who spots with one's own self, *i.e.*, who is not dependant on others for his joy or happiness; one who has understood the soul.—T.

some other boon if, indeed, I have become worthy of thy grace or if I have a little of merit.

"Bhishma continued,—'The slayer of Vala and Vritra then said unto him,—Do thou name the boon.—Thus urged by the great Indra, Matanga said the following words :—

"Matanga said,—Let me be possessed of the power of assuming any form at will, and journeying through the skies and let me enjoy whatever pleasures I may set my heart upon. And let me also have the willing adorations of both Brahmanas and Kshatriyas. I bow to thee by bending my head, O god. It behoveth thee to do that also by which my fame, O Purandara, may live for ever in the world.

" 'Sakra said,—Thou shalt be celebrated as the deity of a particular measure of verse and thou shalt obtain the worship of all women. Thy fame, O son, shall become unrivalled in the three worlds.'—Having granted him these boons, Vasava disappeared there and then. Matanga also, casting off his life-breaths, attained to a high place. Thou mayst thus see, O Bharata, that the status of a Brahmana is very high. That status is incapable of being acquired here (except in the natural way of birth) as said by the great Indra himself."

SECTION XXX

"Yudhishthira said,—'I have heard this great narrative, O perpetuator of Kuru's race. Thou, O foremost of eloquent men, hast said that the status of a Brahmana is exceedingly difficult of acquisition. It is heard, however, that in former times the status of a Brahmana had been acquired by Viswamitra. Thou, however, O best of men, tellest us that that status is incapable of being acquired. I have also heard that king Vitahavya in ancient times succeeded in obtaining the status of a Brahmana. I desire to hear, O puissant son of Ganga, the story of Vitahavya's promotion. By what acts did that best of kings succeed in acquiring the status of a Brahmana? Was it through some boon (obtained from some one of great puissance) or was it through the virtue of penances? It behoveth thee to tell me everything.

"Bhishma said,—'Hear, O monarch, how the royal sage Vitahavya of great celebrity succeeded in ancient times in acquiring the status of a Brahmana that is so difficult to attain and that is held in such high reverence by all the world. While the high-souled Manu in days of yore was employed in righteously ruling his subjects, he obtained a son of righteous soul who became celebrated under the name of Saryati. In Saryati's race, O monarch, two kings took their birth, *viz.*, Haihaya and Talajangha. Both of them were sons of Vatsa, O foremost of victorious kings. Haihaya, O monarch, had ten wives. Upon them he begot, O

Bharata, a century of sons all of whom were highly inclined to fighting. All of them resembled one another in features and prowess. All of them were endued with great strength and all of them were possessed of great skill in battle. They all studied the Vedas and the science of weapons thoroughly. In Kasi also, O monarch, there was a king who was the grandfather of Divodasa. The foremost of victorious men, he was known by the name of Haryyaswa. The sons of king Haihaya, O chief of men, (who was otherwise known by the name of Vitahavya) invaded the kingdom of Kasi and advancing to the country that lies between the rivers Ganga and Yamuna, fought a battle with king Haryyaswa and also slew him in it. Having slain king Haryyaswa in this way, the sons of Haihaya, those great car-warriors, fearlessly went back to their own delightful city in the country of the Vatsas. Meanwhile Haryyaswa's son Sudeva, who looked like a deity in splendour and who was a second god of righteonsness, was installed on the throne of Kasi as its ruler. The delighter of Kasi, that righteous-souled prince ruled his kingdom for sometime, when the hundred sons of Vitahavya once more invaded his dominions and defeated him in battle. Having vanquished king Sudeva thus, the victors returned to their own city. After that Divodasa, the son of Sudeva, became installed on the throne of Kasi as its ruler. Realising the prowess of those high-souled princes, *viz.*, the sons of Vitahavya, king Divodasa, endued with great energy, rebuilt and fortified the city of Baranasi at the command of Indra. The territories of Divodasa were full of Brahmanas and Kshatriyas, and abounded with Vaisyas and Sudras. And they teemed with articles and provisions of every kind, and were adorned with shops and marts swelling with prosperity. Those territories, O best of kings, stretched northwards from the banks of Ganga to the southern banks of Gomati, and resembled a second Amravati (the city of Indra). The Haihayas once again, O Bharata, attacked that tiger among kings, as he ruled his kingdom. The mighty king Divodasa endued with great splendour, issuing out of his capital, gave them battle. The engagement between the two parties proved so fierce as to resemble the encounter in days of old between the deities and the Asuras. King Divodasa fought the enemy for a thousand days at the end of which, having lost a large number of followers and animals, he became exceedingly distressed.[1] King Divodasa, O monarch, having lost his army and seeing his treasury exhausted, left his capital and fled away. Repairing to the delightful retreat of Bharadwaja endued with great wisdom, the king, O chastiser of foes joining his hands in reverence, sought the Rishi's protection. Beholding king Divodasa before him, the

1 'Dasatirdasa' is 'ten times hundred' or one thousand 'Dasati,' like 'Saptati,' 'navati,' &c. means ten times ten. Both the Vernacular translators have erred in rendering the word.—T.

eldest son of Vrihaspati, *viz.*, Bharadwaja of excellent conduct, who was the monarch's priest, said unto him,—What is the reason of thy coming here? Tell me everything, O king. I shall do that which is agreeable to thee, without any scruple.

" 'The king said,—O holy one, the sons of Vitahavya have slain all the children and men of my house. I only have escaped with life, totally discomfited by the foe. I seek thy protection. It behoveth thee, O holy one, to protect me with such affection as thou hast for a disciple. Those princes of sinful deeds have slaughtered my whole race, leaving myself only alive.

"Bhishma continued,—'Unto him who pleaded so piteously, Bharadwaja of great energy said,—Do not fear! Do not fear! O son of Sudeva, let thy fears be dispelled. I shall perform a sacrifice, O monarch, in order that thou mayst have a son through whom thou shalt be able to smite thousands upon thousands of Vitahavya's party.—After this, the Rishi performed a sacrifice with the object of bestowing a son on Divodasa. As the result thereof, unto Divodasa was born a son named Pratarddana. Immediately on his birth he grew up like a boy of full three and ten years and quickly mastered the entire Vedas and the whole of arms. Aided by his Yoga powers, Bharadwaja of great intelligence had entered into the prince. Indeed, collecting all the energy that occurs in the objects of the universe, Bharadwaja put them together in the body of prince Pratarddana. Put on shining mail on his person and armed with the bow, Pratarddana, his praises sung by bards and the celestial Rishis, shone resplendent like the risen star of day. Mounted on his car and with the scimitar tied to his belt, he shone like a blazing fire. With scimitar and shield and whirling his shield as he went, he proceeded to the presence of his sire. Beholding the prince, the son of Sudeva, *viz.*, king Divodasa, became filled with joy. Indeed, the old king thought the sons of his enemy Vitahavya as already slain. Divodasa then installed his son Pratarddana as Yuvaraja, and regarding himself crowned with success became exceedingly happy. After this, the old king commanded that chastiser of foes, *viz.*, prince Pratarddana to march against the sons of Vitahavya and slay them in battle. Endued with great powers, Pratarddana, that subjugator of hostile cities speedily crossed Ganga on his car and proceeded against the city of the Vitahavyas. Hearing the clatter produced by the wheels of his car, the sons of Vitahavya, riding on their own cars that looked like fortified citadels and that were capable of destroying hostile vehicles, issued out of their city. Issuing out of their capital, those tigers among men, *viz.*, the sons of Vitahavya, who were all skilful warriors cased in mail, rushed with uplifited weapons towards Pratarddana, covering him with showers of arrows. Encompassing him with innumerable cars, O Yudhisthira, the Vitahavyas poured upon Pratarddana showers of weapons of various kinds like clouds pouring torrents of rain on the breast of Himavat. Baffling their weapons with his own, prince Pratarddana endued with mighty energy slew them all with his shafts that resembled the lightning fire of Indra. Their heads struck off, O king, with hundreds and thousands of broad-headed arrows, the warriors of Vitahavya fell down with blood-dyed bodies like Kinsuka trees felled by woodmen with their axes on every side. After all his warriors and sons had fallen in battle, king Vitahavya fled away from his capital to the retreat of Bhrigu. Indeed, arrived there, the royal fugitive sought the protection of Bhrigu. The Rishi Bhrigu, O monarch, assured the defeated king of his protection. Pratarddana followed in the footsteps of Vitahavya. Arrived at the Rishi's retreat, the son of Divodasa said in a loud voice.—Ho, listen ye disciples of the high souled Bhrigu that may happen to be present, I wish to see the sage. Go and inform him of this. Recognising that it was Pratarddana who had come, the Rishi Bhrigu himself came out of his retreat and worshipped that best of kings according to due rites. Addressing him then, the Rishi said,—Tell me, O king, what is thy business. The king, at this, informed the Rishi of the reason of his presence.

"The king said,—King Vitahavya has come here, O Brahmana. Do thou give him up. His sons, O Brahmana, had destroyed my race. They had laid waste the territories and the wealth of the kingdom of Kasi. Hundred sons, however, of this king proud of his might, have all been slain by me. By slaying that king himself I shall today pay off the debt I owe to my father. Unto him that foremost of righteous men, viz., the Rishi Bhrigu, penetrated with compassion, replied by saying,—There is no Kshatriya in this retreat. They that are here are all Brahmanas. Hearing these words of Bhrigu that must accord he thought with truth, Pratarddana touched the Rishi's feet slowly and, filled with delight, said,—By this, O holy one, I am, without doubt, crowned with success, since this king becomes abandoned by the very order of his birth in consequence of my prowess. Give me thy permission, O Brahmana, to leave thee, and let me solicit thee to pray for my welfare. This king, O founder of the race that goes by the name, has been compelled to leave of the very community of his birth, in consequence of my might. Dismissed by the Rishi Bhrigu, king Pratarddana then departed from that retreat , having even as a snake vomits forth its real poison and repaired to the place he had come from. Meanwhile, king Vitahavya attained to the status of a Brahamana sage by virtue of the words only of Bhrigu. And he acquired also a complete mastery over all the Vedas through the same cause. Vitahavya had a son named Gritsamada who in beauty of person was a second Indra. Once on a time the Daityas afflicted him much, believing him to be none else than Indra. With regard to that high-souled Rishi, one foremost of Srutis in the Richs goes like this viz., He with whom Gritsamada stays, O Brahmana, is held in high respect by all Brahamanas. Endued with great intelligence, Gritsamada become a regenerate Rishi in the observance of Brahmacharyya. Gritsamada had a regenerate son of the name of Sutejas. Sutejas had a son of the name of Varchas, and the son of Varchas was known by the name of Vihavya. Vihavya had a son of his loins who was named Vitatya and Vitatya had a son of name Satya. Satya had a son of name Santa. Santa had a son, viz., the Rishi Sravas. Sravas begot a son named Tama. Tama begot a son named Prakasa, who was a very superior Brahmana. Prakasa had a son named Vagindra who was the foremost of all silent reciters of sacred Mantras. Vagindra begot a son named Pramati who was a complete master of all the Vedas and their branches. Pramati begot upon the Apsara Ghritachi a son who was named Ruru. Ruru begot a son upon his spouse Pramadvara. That son was the regenerate Rishi Sunaka. Sunaka begot a son who is named Saunaka. It was even thus, O foremost of monarchs, that king Vitahavya, though a Kshatriya by the order of his birth, obtained the status of a Brahmana, O chief of Kshatriyas, through the grace of Bhrigu. I have also told thee the genealogy of the race that sprung from Gristsamada. What else wouldst thou ask?

SECTION XXXI

"Yudhishthira said,—'What men, O chief of Bharata's race, are worthy of reverent homage in the three worlds? Tell me this in detail verily. I am never satiated with hearing thee discourse on these topics.

"Bhishma said,—In this connection is cited the old narrative of the discourse between Narada and Vasudeva. Beholding Narada on one occasion worshipping many foremost of Brahmanas with joined hands, Kesava addressed him saying,—Whom dost thou worship? Whom amongst these Brahmanas, O holy one dost thou worship with so great reverence? If it is a matter that I can heard of, I then wish to hear it. Do, O foremost of righteous men, tell me this![1]—

" 'Narada said,—Hear, O Govinda, as to who those are whom I am worshipping, O grinder of foes. Who else is there in this world that so much deserves to hear this? I worship the Brahmanas. O puissant one, who constantly worship Varuna and Vayu and Aditya and Parjanya

1 'Teshu (Brahmaneshu) Vahumanaprah (san) kan namsyasi'—this is the Grammar, as explained by the Commentator.—T.

and the deity of Fire, and Sthanu and Skanda and Lakshmi and Vishnu and the Brahmanas, and the lord of speech, and Chandramas, and the Waters and Earth and the goddess Saraswati, O tiger of Vrishni's race, I always worship those Brahmanas that are endued with penances, that are conversant with the Vedas, that are always devoted to Vedic study, and that are possessed of high worth. O puissant one, I bow down my head unto those persons who are freed from boastfulness, who discharge, with an empty stomach, the rites in honour of the deities, who are always contented with what they have and who are endued with forgiveness. I worship them, O Yadava, that are performers of sacrifices, that are of a forgiving disposition, and self restrained, that are masters of their own senses, that worship truth and righteousness, and that give away land and kine unto good Brahmanas.[1] I bow unto them, O Yadava, that are devoted to the observance of penances, that dwell in forests, that subsist upon fruits and roots, that never store anything for the morrow, and that are observant of all the acts and rites laid down in the scriptures. I bow unto them, O Yadava, that feed and cherish their servants, that are always hospitable to guests, and that eat only the remnants of what is offered to the deities. I worship them that have become irresistible by studying the Vedas, that are eloquent in discoursing on the scriptures, that are observant of the vow of Brahmacharyya, and that are always devoted to the duties of officiating at the sacrifices of others and of teaching disciples. I worship them that are endued with compassion towards all creatures, and that study the Vedas till noon (*i. e.* till their backs are heated by the sun). I bow unto them, O Yadava, that strive to obtain the grace of their preceptors, that labour in the acquisition of their Vedas, that are firm in the observance of vows, that wait, with dutiful obedience, upon their preceptors and seniors, and that are free from malice and envy. I bow unto them, O Yadava, that are observant of excellent vows, that practice taciturnity, that have knowledge of Brahman, that are firm in truth, that are givers of libations of clarified butter and oblations of meat. I bow to them, O Yadava, that subsist upon eleemosynary alms, that are emaciated for want of adequate food and drink, that have lived in the abodes of their preceptors, that are averse to and destitute of all enjoyments, and that are poor in the goods of this Earth. I bow unto them, O Yadava, that have no affection for things of this Earth, that have no quarrels to wage with others, that do not clothe themselves, that have no wants, that have become irresistible through the acquisition of the Vedas, that are eloquent in the exposition of righteousness, and that are utterers of Brahma. I bow unto them that are devoted to the practice of the duty

1 'Yajanti' with reference to 'truth' and 'righteousness' means 'worship,' and with reference to land and 'kine' means 'give away.'—T.

of compassion towards all creatures, that are firm in the observance of truth, that are self-restrained, and that are peaceful in their behaviour. I bow unto them, O Yadava, that are devoted to the worship of deities and guests, that are observant of the domestic mode of life, and that follow the practice of pigeons in the matter of their subsistence.[1] I always bow unto those persons whose aggregate of three exists, without being weakened, in all their acts, and who are observant of truth and righteous behaviour.[2] I bow unto them, O Kesava, that are conversant with Brahma, that are endued with knowledge of the Vedas, that are attentive to the aggregate of three, that are free from cupidity, and that are righteous in their behaviour. I bow unto them, O Madhava, that subsist upon water only, or upon air alone, or upon the remnants of the food that is offered to deities and guests, and that are observant of diverse kinds of excellent vows. I always worship them that have no spouses (in consequence of the vow of celebacy they observe), that have spouses and the domestic fire (in consequence of the domestic mode of life they lead), that are the refuge of the Vedas, and that are the refuge of all creatures in the universe (in consequence of the compassion they feel towards them). I always bow unto those Rishis, O Krishna, that are the creators of the universe, that are the elders of the universe, that are the eldest members of the race or the family, that are dispellers of the darkness of ignorance, and that are the best of all persons in the universe (for righteousness of behaviour and knowledge of the scriptures). For these reasons, do thou also, O scion of Vrishni's race, worship every day those regenerate persons of whom I speak. Deserving as they are of reverent worship, they will when worshipped, confer happiness on thee, O sinless one. Those persons of whom I speak are always givers of happiness in this world as well as in the next. Reverenced by all, they move about in this world, and if worshipped by thee are sure to grant thee happiness. They who are hospitable to all persons that come unto them as guests, and who are always devoted to Brahmanas and kine, as also to truth (in speech and behaviour), succeed in crossing all calamities and obstacles. They who are always devoted to peacefulness of behaviour, as also they who are freed from malice and envy, and they who are always attentive to the study of the Vedas, succeed in crossing all calamities and obstacles. They who bow unto all the deities (without showing a preference for any and thereby prov-

1 Pigeons pick up scattered grains and never store for the morrow. In the Sila and other vows, the picking up of scattered and cast off grains from the field after the crops have been taken away by the owners, is recommended as the means of filling the stomach.—T.

2 The 'aggregate of three' is Righteousness, Wealth, and Pleasure. Persons who, in all the acts they do, keep an eye upon these three, are said to have their aggregate of three existing in all their acts.—T.

ing their tolerance), they who betake themselves to one Veda as their refuge, they who are possessed of faith and are self-restrained, succeed in crossing all calamities and obstacles. They who worship the foremost of Brahmanas with reverence and are firm in the observance of excellent vows and practise the virtue of charity, succeed in crossing all calamities and obstacles. They who are engaged in the practice of penances, they who are always observant of the vow of celebacy, and they whose souls have been cleansed by penances, succeed in crossing all calamities and obstacles. They who are devoted to the worship of the deities and guests and dependants, as also of the Pitris, and they who eat the remnant of the food that is offered to deities, Pitris, guests and dependants, succeed in crossing all calamities and obstacles. They who, having ignited the domestic fire, duly keep it burning and worship it with reverence and they who have duly poured libations (to the deities) in Soma-sacrifices, succeed in crossing all calamities and obstacles. They who behave as they should towards their mothers and fathers and preceptors and other seniors even as thou, O tiger among the Vrishnis, dost behave, succeed in crossing all calamities and obstacles.—Having said these words, the celestial Rishi ceased speaking.—

"Bhishma continued—'For these reasons, do thou also, O son of Kunti, always worship with reverence the deities, the Pitris, the Brahmanas, and guests arrived at thy mansion and as the consequence of such conduct thou art sure to attain to a desirable end !' "

SECTION XXXII

"Yudhishthira said,—'O grandsire, O thou of great wisdom, O thou that art conversant with all branches of knowledge, I desire to hear thee discourse on topics connected with duty and Righteousness. Tell me truly, O chief of Bharata's race, what the merits are of those persons that grant protection to living creatures of the four orders when these pray for protection.

"Bhishma said,—'O Dharma's son of great wisdom and wide-spread fame, listen to this old history touching the great merit of granting protection to others when protection is humbly sought. Once on a time, a beautiful pigeon, pursued by a hawk, dropped down from the skies and sought the protection of the highly-blessed king Vrishadarbha. The pure-souled monarch, beholding the pigeon take refuge in his lap from fear, comforted him, saying,—Be comforted, O bird ; do no fear. Whence hast thou taken such great fright ? What hast thou done and where hast thou done it in consequence of which thou hast lost thy senses in fear and art more dead than alive ? Thy colour, O beautiful bird, is such as to resemble that which adorns a fresh-blown lotus of the blue variety. Thy eyes are of the hue of the pomegranate or the Asoka flower. Do not fear. I bid thee, be comforted. When thou hast sought refuge with me, know that no one will have the courage to even think of seizing thee,—thee that hast such a protector to take care of thy person. I shall for thy sake, give up today the very kingdom of the Kasi and, if need be, my life too. Be comforted, therefore, and let no fear be thine, O pigeon.

" 'The hawk said,—This bird has been ordained to be my food. It behoves thee not, O king, to protect him from me. I have outcoursed this bird and have got him. Verily, with great effort have I got at him at last. His flesh and blood and marrow and fat will be of great good to me. This bird will be the means of gratifying me greatly. Do not, O king, place thyself between him and me in this way. Fierce is the thirst that is afflicting me, and hunger is gnawing my bowels. Release the bird and cast him off. I am unable to bear the pains of hunger any longer. I pursued him as my prey. Behold, his body is bruised and torn by me with my wings and talons. Look, his breath has become very weak. It behoves thee not, O king, to protect him from me. In the exercise of that power which properly belongs to thee, thou art, indeed competent to interfere in protecting human beings when they are sought to be destroyed by human beings. Thou canst not, however, be admitted to have any power over a sky-ranging bird afflicted with thirst. Thy power may extend over thy enemies, thy servants, thy relatives, the disputes that take place between thy subjects. Indeed, it may extend over every part of thy dominions and over also thy own senses. Thy power, however, does not extend over the welkin. Displaying thy prowess over such foes as act against thy wishes, thou mayst establish thy rule over them. Thy rule, however, does not extend over the birds that range the sky. Indeed, if thou hast been desirous of earning merit (by protecting this pigeon), it is thy duty to look at me also (and do what is proper for enabling me to appease my hunger and save my life) !

"Bhishma continued,—'Hearing these words of the hawk, the royal sage became filled with wonder. Without disregarding these words of his, the king, desirous of attending to his comforts, replied unto him saying the following words.

" 'The king said,—Let a bovine bull or boar or deer or buffalo be dressed today for thy sake. Do thou appease thy hunger on such food today. Never to desert one that has sought my protection is my firm vow. Behold, O bird, this bird does not leave my lap !'—

" 'The hawk said,—I do not, O monarch, eat the flesh of the boar or the ox or of any of the diverse kinds of fowl. What need have I of food of this or that kind ? My concern is with that food which has been eternally ordained for beings of my order ? Hawks feed on pigeons,—

this is the eternal ordinance. O sinless, Usinara, if thou feelest such affection for this pigeon, do thou then give me flesh from thy own body, of weight equal to that of this pigeon.—

"'The king said,—Great is the favour thou showest me today by speaking to me in this strain. Yes, I shall do what thou biddest.— Having said this, that best of monarchs began to cut off his own flesh and weigh it in a balance against the pigeon. Meanwhile, in the inner apartments of the palace, the spouses of king, adorned with jewels and gems, hearing what was taking place, uttered exclamations of woe and came out, stricken with grief. In consequence of those cries of the ladies, as also of the ministers and servants, a noise deep as the roar of the clouds arose in the palace. The sky that had been very clear became enveloped with thick clouds on every side. The Earth began to tremble, as the consequence of that act of truth which the monarch did. The king began to cut off the flesh from his flanks from the arms, and from his thighs, and quickly fill one of the scales for weighing it against the pigeon. In spite of all that, the pigeon continued to weigh heavier. When at last the king became a skeleton of bones, without any flesh, and covered with blood, he desired to give up his whole body and, therefore, ascended the scale in which he had placed the flesh that he had previously cut off. At that time, the three worlds, with Indra at their head, came to that spot for beholding him. Celestial kettle-drums and diverse drums were struck and played upon by invisible beings belonging to the firmament. King Vishadarbha was bathed in a shower of nectar that was poured upon him. Garlands of celestial flowers, of delicious fragrance and touch, were also showered upon him copiously and repeatedly. The deities and Gandharvas and Apsaras in large bands began to sing and dance around him even as they sing and dance around the Grandsire Brahma. The king then ascended a celestial car that surpassed (in grandeur and beauty) a mansion made entirely of gold, that had arches made of gold and gems, and that was adorned with columns made of *lapis lazuli.* Through the merit of his act, the royal sage Sivi proceeded to eternal Heaven. Do thou also, O Yudhishthira, act in the same way towards those that seek thy protection. He who protects those that are devoted to him, those that are attached to him from love and affection, and those that depend upon him, and who has compassion for all creatures, succeeds in attaining to great felicity hereafter. That king who is of righteous behaviour and who is observant of honesty and integrity, succeeds by his acts of sincerity in acquiring every valuable reward. The royal sage Sivi of pure soul and endued with great wisdom and unbaffled prowess, that ruler of the kingdom of Kasi, became celebrated over the three worlds for his deeds of righteousness. Anybody who would protect in the same way a seeker for protection, would certainly attain (like Sivi himself) to the same happy end, O best of the Bharatas. He who recites this history of the royal sage Vrishadarbha is sure to become cleansed of every sin, and the person who hears this history recited by another is sure to attain to the same result.' '

SECTION XXXIII

"Yudhishthira said,—'Which act, O grandsire, is the foremost of all those that have been laid down for a king? What is that act by doing which a king succeeds in enjoying both this world and the next?

"Bhishma said,—'Even this, viz., the worship of the Brahmanas, is the foremost of all those acts, O Bharata, which have been laid down for a king duly installed on the throne, if, indeed, he is desirous of obtaining great happiness. Even this is what the foremost of all kings should do. Know this well, O chief of Bharata's race. The king should always worship with reverence all righteous Brahmanas possessed of Vedic lore[1] The king should, with bows and comforting speeches and gifts of all articles of enjoyment, worship all Brahmanas possessed of great learning who may dwell in his city or provinces. This is the foremost of all acts laid down for the king. Indeed, the king should always keep his eyes fixed on this. He should protect and cherish these, even as he protects his own self or his own children. The king should worship with greater reverence those amongst the Brahmanas that may be worthy of it (for their superior sanctity and learning). When such men are freed from all anxiety, the whole kingdom blazes forth in beauty. Such individuals are worthy of adoration. Unto such the king should bow his head. Verily, they should be honoured, even as one honours one's sires and grandsires. Upon them depends the course of conduct followed by men, even as the existence of all creatures depends upon Vasava. Of prowess incapable of being baffled and endued with great energy, such men, if enraged, are capable of consuming the entire kingdom to ashes by only fiat of their will, or by acts of incantation, or by other means (derived from the power of penance). I do not see anything that can destroy them. Their power seems to be uncontrolled, being capable of reaching to the farthest end of the universe. When angry, their glances fall upon men and things like a blazing flame of fire upon a forest. The most courageous men are struck with fear at their men. Their virtues and powers are extraordinary and immeasurable. Some amongst them are like wells and pits with mouths covered by grass and creepers, while others resemble the firmament cleared of

---

1 Some texts read 'vriddhan' for 'Ishtan.' If the former reading be adopted, the meaning would be that kings should worship all *aged* Brahmanas possessed of Vedic lore.—T.

clouds and darkness. Some amongst them are of fierce dispositions (like Durvasas and others of that stamp). Some are as mild and soft in disposition as cotton (like Gautama and others). Some amongst them are very cunning (like Agastya who devoured the Asura Vatapi, and Rishis of that class). Some amongst them are devoted to the practice of penances. Some amongst them are employed in agricultural pursuits (like the preceptor of Uddalaka). Some amongst them are engaged in the keep of kine (as Upamanyu while attending his preceptor). Some amongst them live upon eleemosynary alms. Some amongst them are even thieves (like Valmiki in his early years and Viswamitra during a famine). Some amongst them are fond of fomenting quarrels and disputes (like Narada). Some, again, amongst them are actors and dancers (like Bharata). Some amongst them are competent to achieve all feats, ordinary and extraordinary (like Agastya drinking up the entire ocean, as if it were a palmful of water). The Brahmanas, O chief of Bharata's race are of diverse aspects and behaviour. One should always utter the praises of the Brahmanas who are conversant with all duties, who are righteous of behaviour, who are devoted to diverse kinds of acts, and who are seen to derive their sustenance from diverse kinds of occupations.[1] The Brahmanas, O ruler of men, who are highly blessed, are elder in respect of their origin than the Pitris, the deities, human beings (belonging to the three other orders), the Snakes and the Rakshasas. These regenerate persons are incapable of being vanquished by the deities or the Pitris, or the Gandharvas or the Rakshasas, or the Asuras or the Pisachas. The Brahmanas are competent to make him a deity that is not a deity. They can, again, divest one that is a deity of his status as such. He becomes a king whom they wish to make a king. He, on the other hand, goes to the wall whom they do not love or like. I tell thee truly, O king, that those foolish persons, without doubt, meet with destruction who calumniate the Brahmanas and utter their dispraise. Skilled in praise and dispraise, and themselves the origin or cause of other people's fame and ignominy, the Brahmanas, O king, always become angry with those that seek to injure others. That man whom the Brahmanas praise succeeds in growing in prosperity. That man who is censured and is cast off by the Brahmanas soon meets with discomfiture. It is in consequence of the absence of Brahmanas from among them that the Sakas, the Yavanas, the Kamvojas and other Kshatriya tribes have become fallen and degraded into the status of Sudras. The Dravidas, the Kalingas, the Pulandas, the Usinaras, the

1 Though really conversant with all duties, and of righteous behaviour, the Brahmanas, nevertheless, for concealing their real natures or for protecting the world, are seen to be employed in diverse kinds of occupations.—T.

Kolisarpas, the Mahishakas and other Kshatriyas, have, in consequence of the absence of Brahmanas from among their midst, become degraded into Sudras. Defeat at their hands is preferable to victory over them, O foremost of victorious persons. One slaying all other living creatures in the world does not incur a sin so heinous as that of slaying a single Brahmana. The great Rishis have said that Brahmanicide is a heinous sin. One should never utter the dispraise or calumny of the Brahmanas. Where the dispraise of Brahmanas is uttered, one should sit with face hanging down or leave that spot (for avoiding both the utterer and his words). That man has not as yet been born in this world or will not take birth here, who has been or will be able to pass his life in happiness after quarrelling with the Brahmanas. One cannot seize the wind with one's hands. One cannot touch the moon with one's hand. One cannot support the Earth on one's arms. After the same manner, O king, one is not able to vanquish the Brahmanas in this world.' "

SECTION XXXIV

"Bhishma said,—'One should always offer the most reverent worship unto the Brahmanas. They have Soma for their king, and they it is who confer happiness and misery upon others. They, O king, should always be cherished and protected as one cherishes and protects one's own sires and grandsires, and should be adroed with bows and gifts of food and ornaments and other articles of enjoyment, as also with such things as they may desire. The peace and happiness of the kingdom flow from such respect shown to the Brahmanas even as the peace and happiness of all living creatures flow from Vasava, the chief of the celestials. Let Brahamanas of pure behaviour and Brahma-effulgence be born in a kingdom. Kshatriyas also that are splendid car-warriors and that are capable of scorching all foes, should be desired (amongst those that settle in a kingdom). This was said unto me by Narada. There is nothing higher, O king, than this, viz, the act of causing a Brahmana possessed of good birth, having a knowledge of morality and righteousness, and steadfast in the observance of excellent vows, to take up his residence in one's mansion. Such an act is productive of every kind of blessing. The sacrificial offerings given unto Brahmanas reach the very deities who accept them. Brahmanas are the sires of all creatures. There is nothing higher than a Brahmana. Aditya, Chandramas, Wind, Water, Earth, Sky and the points of the compass, all enter the body of the Brahmana and take what the Brahmana eats.[1] In that

1 The argument, therefore, is that anything given to the Brahmana to eat and that is eaten by him apparently, is really eaten by these deities. —T.

house where Brahmanas do not eat, the Pitris refuse to eat. The deities also never eat in the house of the wretch who hates the Brahmanas. When the Brahmanas are gratified, the Pitris also are gratified. There is no doubt in this. They that give away the sacrificial butter unto the Brahmanas become themselves gratified (in this and the other world). Such men never meet with destruction. Verily, they succeed in attaining to high ends. Those particular offerings in sacrifices with which one gratifies the Brahmanas go to gratify both the Pitris and the deities. The Brahmana is the cause of that sacrifice whence all created things have sprung. The Brahmana is acquainted with that from which this universe has sprung and unto which, when apparently destroyed, it returns. Indeed the Brahmana knows the path that leads to Heaven and the other path that leads to the opposite place. The Brahmana is conversant with what has happened and what will happen. The Brahmana is the foremost of all to-legged beings. The Brahmana, O chief of the Bharatas, is fully conversant with the duties that have been laid down for his order. Those persons that follow the Brahmanas are never vanquished. Departing from this world, they never meet with destruction. Indeed victory is always theirs. Those high-souled persons,—indeed, those persons that have subdued their souls,—who accept the words that fall from the lips of the Brahmanas, are never vanquished. Victory always becomes theirs.[1] The energy and might of those Kshatriyas who scorch everything with their energy and might become neutralised when they encounter the Brahmanas. The Bhrigus conquered the Talajanghas. The son of Angiras conquered the Nipas. Bharadwaja conquered the Vitahavyas as also the Ailas, O chief of Bharata's race. Although all these Kshatriyas were capable of using diverse kinds of arms, yet the Brahmanas named, owning only black deer skins for their emblems, succeeded in conquering them effectually. Bestowing the Earth upon the Brahmanas and illuminating both the worlds by the splendour of such a deed, one should accomplish acts through which one may succeed in attaining to the end of all things.[2] Like fire concealed within wood, everything that is said or heard or read in this world, lies ensconced in the Brahmana. In this connection is cited the old history of the conversation between Vasudeva and the Earth, O chief of Bharata's race!'

"Vasudeva said,—O mother of all creatures, O auspicious goddess, I desire to ask thee for a solution of this doubt of mine. By what act

---

1 'Bhutatmanah' is explained by the Commentator as 'Bhuta praptah-vasikritahatma yaih.'—T.

2 The second line of Verse 18 is a crux. The Commentator explains that 'prakshipya' means 'dattwa;' 'Kun' is the Earth. 'Van' is diptim ukrvan, ubhaya-loke iti seshah.' 'Paragaminam' is 'paralokahitam.'—T.

does a man leading the domestic mode of life succeed in cleansing all his sins ?

" 'The Earth said,—One should serve the Brahmanas. This conduct is cleansing and excellent. All the impurities are destroyed of that man who serves the Brahmanas with reverence. From this (conduct) arises prosperity. From this arises fame. From this springs forth intelligence or knowledge of the soul. A Kshatriya by this conduct, becomes a mighty car-warrior and a scorcher of foes and succeeds in acquiring great fame. Even this is what Narada said unto me, viz., that one should always revere a Brahmana that is well-born, of rigid vows and conversant with the scriptures, if one desires every kind of prosperity. That man really grows in prosperity who is applauded by the Brahmanas, who are higher than those that are regarded superior to all men high or low. That man who speaks ill of the Brahmanas soon meets with discomfiture, even as a clod of unbaked earth meets with destruction when cast into the sea. After the same manner, all acts that are hurtful to the Brahmanas are sure to bring about discomfiture and ruin. Behold the dark spots on the Moon and the salt waters of the ocean. The great Indra had at one time been marked all over with a thousand sex-marks. It was through the power of the Brahmanas that those marks became altered into as so many eyes. Behold, O Madhava how all those things took place. Desiring fame and prosperity and diverse regions of beautitude in the next world, a person of pure behaviour and soul should, O slayer of Madhu, live in obedience to the dictates of the Brahmanas.[1]—

"Bhishma continued,—'Hearing these words of the goddess Earth, the slayer of Madhu, O thou of Kuru's race, exclaimed,—Excellent, Excellent—and honoured the goddess in due form. Having heard this discourse between the goddess Earth and Madhava, do thou, O son of Pritha, always, with rapt soul, worship all superior Brahmanas. Doing this, thou shalt verily obtain what is highly beneficial for thee !"

SECTION XXXV

"Bhishma said,—'O blessed king, Brahmana, by birth alone, becomes an object of adoration with all creatures and are entitled, as guests, to eat the first portion of all cooked food.[2] From them flow all the great objects of life (viz., Righteousness and Wealth and Pleasure and Emancipation). They are the friends of all creatures in the universe.

---

1 The dark spots on the Moon were due to the curse of Daksha. The waters of the Ocean became saltish owing to the curse of a Rishi.—T.

2 The sense is that one becomes a Brahmana by birth alone, without the aid of those purificatory rites that have been laid down in the scriptures. When food is cooked, none else than a Brahmana is entitled in the first portion thereof.—T.

They are again the mouths of the deities (for food poured into their mouths is eaten by the deities) Worshipped with reverence, they wish us prosperity by uttering words fraught with auspiciousness. Disregarded by our foes, let them be enraged with these, and let them wish evil unto those detractors of theirs, uttering words fraught with severe curses. In this connection, persons conversant with ancient history repeat the following verses sung of old respecting how in ancient times the Creator, after having created the Brahmanas, ordained their duties.—A Brahmana should never do anything else than what has been ordained for him. Protected, they should protect others. By conducting themselves in this way, they are sure to attain to what is mightily advantageous for them. By doing those acts that are ordained for them, they are sure to obtain Brahma-prosperity. Ye shall become the exemplars of all creatures, and reins for restraining them. A Brahmana possessed of learning should never do that which is laid down for the Sudras. By doing such acts, a Brahmana loses merit.[1] By Vedic study he is sure to obtain prosperity and intelligence and energy and puissance competent to scorch all things, as also glory of the most exalted kind. By offering oblations of clarified butter unto the deities, the Brahmanas attain to high blessedness and become worthy of taking the precedence of even children in the matter of all kinds of cooked food, and endued with Brahma-prosperity.[2] Endued with faith that is fraught with compassion towards all creatures, and devoted to self-restraint and the study of the Vedas, ye shall attain to the fruition of all your wishes. Whatever things exist in the world of men, whatever things occur in the region of the deities, can all be achieved and acquired with the aid of penances and knowledge and the observance of vows and restraints. I have thus recited to thee, O sinless one, the verses that were sung by Brahma himself. Endued with supreme intelligence and wisdom, the Creator himself ordained this, through compassion for the Brahmanas. The puissance of those among them that are devoted to penances is equal to the might of kings. They are verily irrestible, fierce, possessed of the speed of lightning, and exceedingly quick in what they do. There are amongst them those that are possessed of the might of lions and those are posses-

1 The Commentator thinks that 'saudram karma' has especial reference to the service of others. Hence what is interdicted for the Brahmanas is the service of others.—T.

2 In this country to this day, when food is prepared in view of guests invited to a house, no portion of such food can be offered to any one before it is dedicated to the deities and placed before those for whom it is intended. An exception, however, is made for children. What is stated here is that a good Brahmana can take the precedence of even children in the matter of such food.—T.

sed of the might of tigers. Some of them are endued with the might of boars, some with that of the deer, and some with that of crocodiles. Some there are amongst them whose touch resembles that of snakes of virulent poison, and some whose bite resembles that of sharks. Some amongst them are capable of compassing by speeeh alone the destruction of those that are opposed to them ; and some are competent to destroy by a glance only of their eyes. Some, amongst them, as already said, are like snakes of virulent poison, and some of them are possessed of very mild dispositions. The dispositions, O Yudhisthira, of the Brahmanas, are of diverse kinds. The Mekalas, the Dravidas, the Lathas, the Paundras, the Konwasiras, the Saundikas, the Daradas, the Darvas, the Chauras, the Savaras, the Varvaras, the Kiratas, the Yavanas, and numerous other tribes of Kshatriyas, have become degraded into the status of Sudras through the wrath of Brahmanas. In consequence of having disregarded the Brahmanas, the Asuras have been obliged to take refuge in the depths of the ocean. Through the grace of the Brahmanas, the deities have become denizens of the happy regions of Heaven. The element of space or ether is incapable of being touched. The Himavat mountains are incapable of being moved from their site. The current of Ganga is incapable of being resisted by a dam. The Brahmanas are incapable of being subjugated. Kshatriyas are incapable of ruling the Earth without cultivating the good will of the Brahmanas. The Brahmanas are high-souled beings. They are the deities of the very deities. Do thou always worship them with gifts and obedient services : if, indeed, thou wishest to enjoy the sovereignty of the whole Earth with her belt of seas. The energy and might of Brahmanas, O sinless one, become abated in consequence of the acceptance of gift. Thou shouldst protect thy race, O king, from those Brahmanas that do not desire to accept gifts ![1]

1 What is stated here is that those Brahmanas that do not accept gifts are very superior. Their energy and might are great. Bhishma directs Yudhishthira to be always careful of how he would treat such superior Brahmanas. After 'rakshyam,' the words 'swakulam' are understood. The Burdwan translator misunderstands the second line of the Verse.—T.

Treasure of Books

Under One Roof

Demand Any Rare Book at

www.facsimilepublisher.com

Demand Any Rare Book at:

www.facsimilepublisher.com

if not available, give information,
our team will search and update you.

Promote Knowledge:

If you have any rare book
which is not available at
www.facsimilepublisher.com,
offer it to other readers so that others can also be
benefitted with your cooperation.
The book will be printed with your courtesy.

Print & Publish:

If you wish to get your book printed or published,
we have the service for you.

Customization on Demand:

We offer customization of books
as per the demand of the customer.

Published by

Facsimile Publisher
Ashok Vihar, Delhi-110052 (India)
Website: www.facsimilepublisher.com

Distributed by

Gyan Books Pvt. Ltd.
5, Ansari Road, Daryaganj, New Delhi-110002 (India)
E-mail: books@gyanbooks.com, Website: www.gyanbooks.com

9 789332 840881